The Juvenile Justice System

Law and Process

Joseph B. Sanborn, Jr.
University of Central Florida

Anthony W. Salerno
Rowan University, Emeritus

Foreword by
Donna Bishop
Northeastern University

Instructor's Manual/Testing Program and
Interactive Student Study Guide available.

Roxbury Publishing Company
Los Angeles, California

Library of Congress Cataloging-in-Publication Data

Sanborn, Joseph B.
The juvenile justice system: law and process / Joseph Sanborn, Anthony W. Salerno.
  p. cm.
Includes bibliographical references.
ISBN 1-891487-95-7
1. Juvenile justice, Administration of—United States. I. Salerno, Anthony W., 1929-2003. II. Title.

KF9779.S26 2005
345.73'08—dc21

2002067953
CIP

Publisher: Claude Teweles
Managing Editor: Dawn VanDercreek
Production Editor: Nina M. Hickey
Assistant Editor: Carla Max-Ryan
Copyeditor: Jackie Estrada
Proofreaders: Cheryl Adams and Christy Graunke
Typography: Pegasus Type, Inc.
Cover Design: Marnie Kenney

Printed on acid-free paper in the United States of America. This book meets the standards for recycling of the Environmental Protection Agency.

ISBN 1-891487-95-7

ROXBURY PUBLISHING COMPANY
P.O. Box 491044
Los Angeles, California 90049-9044
Voice: (310) 473-3312 • Fax: (310) 473-4490
E-mail: roxbury@roxbury.net
Website: www.roxbury.net

Dedication

To those who are still here to inspire me
wife and mom. . . .
And to those who are not here but continue to inspire me
dad, grandparents, Tony. . . .

Foreword

Donna M. Bishop, Professor
College of Criminal Justice
Northeastern University

As every student learns, in college if not before, facts never speak for themselves. Understanding comes in our discernment of fact patterns or trends and our interpretations of them. Carefully developed, evidence-based analyses and interpretations shape the way we think about events and encourage us to think about them more deeply. Especially in the social sciences, sound analysis and interpretation of patterns and events can also play an important role in shaping public policy.

This book presents an account of the American juvenile justice system from its beginnings to the present. It focuses especially on challenges (and there have been many) that the system has faced and analyzes the adaptations it has made to changing times and circumstances. It differs from and is written largely in reaction to an alternative and influential interpretation of the current state of juvenile justice. This account—which has been described as the new "master narrative" (Tanenhaus 2000)—has been most clearly presented by Barry Feld (1997, 1999) and others.

According to both accounts, the establishment of a separate justice system for juveniles reflected the triumph of reformers at the turn of the twentieth century who felt a mixture of compassion and fear for immigrant children growing up in impoverished and overcrowded urban areas. The juvenile court was intended both to shield young offenders from the potentially devastating consequences of being tried and punished by the criminal courts and to intervene in the lives of at-risk youth to rescue them from lives of crime. In place of criminal courts that were adversarial and punitive, juvenile courts would be informal and therapeutic. Judges were asked to assess youth's needs and had virtually unlimited authority in deciding how best to respond. The system rested on a naive trust in the wisdom and benevolence of judges and their support staff (e.g., probation officers, institutional wardens) to act in the best interests of youth in trouble. It also rested on a naive trust in the willingness of the public to view even serious adolescent offenders as children in need of care. Both of these expectations would later be seriously challenged.

Although little is known about how the juvenile justice system functioned prior to the 1960s, it apparently faced no major obstacles. From the late 1960s to the present, however, it weathered some major storms. How it fared, where it stands today, and what its prospects are for the future are all points of controversy.

Beginning in 1966, the U.S. Supreme Court intervened to protect children from abuses of power by a lower court whose interests had previously been thought to be identical to its own. In fact, children were being torn from their families based on little evidence of wrongdoing for the purpose of being "helped" in programs whose benevolent rhetoric did not match reality. The U.S. Supreme Court granted youth some (but not all) procedural protections (e.g., right to counsel, right to remain silent, requirement of proof beyond a reasonable doubt) in an effort to prevent erroneous convictions, but simultaneously encouraged renewed investment in the justice system's rehabilitative mission.

According to Feld's account, the provision of procedural protections shifted the focus of juvenile proceedings from the needs of the child to the commission of a crime (Feld 1997, 73) and set in motion a punitive shift that has gathered momentum ever since. In the 1980s and 1990s, rising rates of serious youth violence and sensationalist media coverage toppled the image of the juvenile offender as young and needy, and prompted demands for "get-tough" approaches that struck a responsive chord with legislators. Many changes were made. Every jurisdiction revised its juvenile codes to endorse punishment and community protection as legitimate objectives. Probation officers' social work functions were largely displaced by a focus on surveillance and accountability. More juvenile offenders were incarcerated, and more large institutions were built to house them. Nearly every state enacted laws that sent more juveniles to criminal courts for prosecution as adults. Feld concluded that "virtually all of the conceptual and operational differences in strategies of social control for youths and adults" were eliminated (Feld 1999, 3). Along with others, he has recommended abolition of the juvenile court (Feld 1997, 1999; see also Ainsworth 1991; Federle 1990).

Sanborn and Salerno have a different interpretation. Whether or not you are persuaded by their evidence and arguments, you will find this book a provocative counterbalance to Feld's offering. In their view, the juvenile justice system bears only a partial resemblance to its adult counterpart. They acknowledge some overlap between the two systems, then focus on what is unique—both negative and positive—about juvenile justice.

Their analysis is based on a painstaking and comprehensive examination of current statutory and case law in all 50 states, DC, and the federal jurisdiction as well as a review of the latest social science research. They call attention to many important and often neglected features of the juvenile system (e.g., the parent as a central player). Some of what is unique about the juvenile court is troubling. For example, they observe that the juvenile court continues to function as a training ground for inexperienced prosecutors, defense attorneys, and judges. It is also a good place for the inept to hide. Unfairness is also a major theme in this text. The authors do a nice job of linking unfairness to the unavoidable tensions involved in the juvenile system's attempt to wed due process, crime control, and social welfare objectives. They also make a good case for positive features of juvenile justice. Their review of juvenile codes is especially illuminating—especially in what it reveals about states' continuing commitment to the amelioration of young offenders—as is their coverage of dispositional options, advances in correctional programming ("best practices"), and the infusion of resources to support the implementation and evaluation of innovative prevention and treatment methodologies. In the end, they regard juvenile justice as a flawed but adaptive institution that has benefited from the infusion of constitutional protections and notions of accountability and, at the same time, remained faithful to the core principles on which it was founded. They see in it much that is worth preserving.

Sanborn and Salerno also tell us that to truly comprehend juvenile justice in this country, one must understand 52 separate systems. Too often, texts imply that juvenile justice in the United States has an overarching theory or rationale, commonality in intake procedures, similarity in detention practices, and so on. Most do not begin to grasp the variety and complexity of our juvenile justice systems. This book goes a long way toward filling that gap. It is unfortunate that we have little comprehensive data on many critical aspects of juvenile justice (e.g., rates of representation by counsel, availability and utilization of dispositional options, prevalence of alternative correctional programming). However, this text provides information on jurisdictional differences where it can (e.g., with respect to waiver of counsel, sentencing practices, the authority of the court to order parents into treatment, the role and rights of victims, postdispositional review). The authors also offer thoughtful discussions of the implications of these differences for offenders, justice officials, and the overall operation of the system.

Sanborn and Salerno have written a well-researched, thought-provoking, and highly readable account. Students will come away from this book with an uncommon understanding of both the uniqueness and complexity of juvenile justice philosophy, law, and practice. They will surely think more deeply about the "why" of "what is." It is hoped that they will also think beyond "what is" to "what might be" and be inspired to have a hand in improving a system that is still too often characterized by unfairness, "sloppy justice," and ambivalence toward young offenders. ✦

Preface

Putting This Textbook Into Context

Juvenile justice comprises a complex association of agencies that address youthful misbehavior and, in many locations, various family-related problems as well (such as adoption, paternity, custody, and neglect). This text focuses only on the misbehavior aspect that includes crimes (violations, misdemeanors, and felonies) and behaviors—often referred to as status offenses—that are illegal only for juveniles (e.g., truancy, incorrigibility). Greater emphasis is placed on how the juvenile justice system reacts to criminal incidents.

Some aspects of the operation of the juvenile justice system duplicate what transpires in the criminal justice system. Other aspects, however, are completely distinct or different. This book identifies where overlap occurs (such as the law of arrest, *Miranda* warnings, the exclusionary rule), but gives particular attention to those features that are unique to juvenile justice (such as school searches).

This text is being written at an interesting time. Virtually any news broadcast seems to include items about bomb threats at schools or violent acts committed by juveniles. A critically important twofold question faces society: Which system (juvenile or adult) should prosecute which juvenile offenders, and what should be the nature of the state's response to crimes committed by juveniles? Chapter 12 focuses exclusively and in depth on this critical aspect of prosecuting serious and chronic juvenile offenders in juvenile versus criminal court.

It is not the intent of this text to promote any particular agenda for how society should react to juvenile misbehavior. Instead, the objective is to familiarize the student with the intricacies of juvenile justice workings and their implications. Armed with that knowledge, students can decide what the juvenile justice system should require in the way of processing offenders and what the juvenile and criminal justice systems should be able to do to someone who has violated laws while a juvenile.

This book should not be perceived as either an apology for or a denunciation of juvenile courts. Rather, the intention is to portray, as honestly as possible, what we perceive to be significant fairness problems in juvenile courts and critical operational differences between them and criminal courts. We take this approach because it explains juvenile justice and because it is unwise and inappropriate today to think of juvenile courts as tribunals in which nothing important happens.

Rather than focus on any one state's juvenile justice system, this text attempts to explain juvenile law and procedure in all 50 states, the federal system, and Washington, D.C. To do so, we have relied heavily on the juvenile court statutes from each jurisdiction. Statutes are subject to misinterpretation (especially ours) and change, however, so we invite readers from throughout the country to inform us if corrections are needed.

Finally, students will notice three interrelated themes that recur throughout the text. The **first theme** concerns the unique nature of juvenile court processing. This processing frequently involves fairness problems that do not exist in criminal court. The **second theme** concerns the unequal way in which juvenile courts can respond to two youths facing the same charges after compiling similar court records. Unlike criminal courts, which are designed to seek equal punishment based on crime and record, juvenile courts are structured to pursue rehabilitation based on the treatment needs of the offender. The **third theme** involves the fact that most juvenile courts dispense *both* treatment *and* punishment. In fact, some juvenile courts have developed a two-tier system in order to provide these different responses to offenders. Related to this theme is the fact that juvenile courts vary significantly among themselves, from one state to another, and even from one county to another.

We have chosen to highlight these themes because of one pervasive misperception that seems to dominate juvenile justice literature: that punishment has *replaced* rehabilitation in the juvenile system and that juvenile courts and criminal courts are virtually identical in operation today. This misperception can, in turn, lead to the idea that being found guilty of crime in juvenile court is equivalent to being found guilty of crime in criminal court. The mission of this text is to put an end to that misperception.

Because we refer to state statutes frequently in the text, the following list of abbreviations for each state is presented to aid students:

AL = Alabama	ID = Idaho	MO = Missouri	PA = Pennsylvania
AK = Alaska	IL = Illinois	MT = Montana	RI = Rhode Island
AR = Arkansas	IN = Indiana	NE = Nebraska	SC = South Carolina
AZ = Arizona	IA = Iowa	NV = Nevada	SD = South Dakota
CA = California	KS = Kansas	NC = North Carolina	TN = Tennessee
CO = Colorado	KY = Kentucky	ND = North Dakota	TX = Texas
CT = Connecticut	LA = Louisiana	NH = New Hampshire	UT = Utah
DE = Delaware	ME = Maine	NJ = New Jersey	VT = Vermont
DC = District of Columbia	MD = Maryland	NM = New Mexico	VA = Virginia
FED = Federal Jurisdiction	MA = Massachusetts	NY = New York	WA = Washington
FL = Florida	MI = Michigan	OH = Ohio	WV = West Virginia
GA = Georgia	MN = Minnesota	OK = Oklahoma	WI = Wisconsin
HI = Hawaii	MS = Mississippi	OR = Oregon	WY = Wyoming

The text is divided into seven sections. The first section (Chapters 1–3) addresses the basic tenets and philosophy of the juvenile justice system, along with its history and legal nature. The second section (Chapters 4–6) focuses on the jurisdiction of the juvenile court and the nature and extent of juvenile misbehavior. Section III (Chapters 7–9) introduces the gatekeepers of the juvenile justice system, or those who usher the youth into court. Section IV (Chapters 10–12) covers the initial or preliminary stages of the juvenile court process, including the ever-important decision to transfer the youth to criminal court. The trial and sentencing phases of juvenile court and the often-ignored postdisposition hearings are the topics of Section V (Chapters 13–15). Section VI (Chapters 16–17) is dedicated to the community and institutional corrections aspects of juvenile justice, which includes the programs available for nondelinquent youths as well as for delinquents either on probation or institutionalized. Finally, Section VII (Chapter 18) attempts to forecast what the future holds for juvenile justice. ✦

Acknowledgments

First, I would like to thank each of the juvenile courts that have opened their doors to me during the past few decades while I finished my dissertation and conducted the research necessary for a deeper understanding of the juvenile courts: Philadelphia, Delaware, and Chester counties in Pennsylvania. Those juvenile court workers were not only hospitable and cooperative, they also tried to do right by the juveniles processed in their system. I would like to thank the graduate faculty at SUNY Albany—particularly the late Don Newman and Fred Cohen—for long ago providing me with the foundation I needed to comprehend and appreciate the juvenile and adult systems of justice, and the issues involving both. I would also like to extend my gratitude to a man important in my academic development—my most influential undergraduate professor, the late James McKenna from Villanova University.

Barry Law School, in Orlando, Florida, was kind enough to open its doors to me. The school allowed me to use their resources to conduct a 50-state review of juvenile court statutes, which eventually became the foundation for this text. The staff at the University of Central Florida came to my rescue, especially Barbara Rubright, Denise Glover, and Seresa Guild. Barbara's son, Butch, also provided his invaluable assistance. My colleague, Gene Paoline, continued to provide moral support throughout this endeavor and allowed his graduate assistant, Michelle Brown, to help me with the tedious chore of typing out the references. Other fellow workers—Bernie and Belinda McCarthy, Dave Fabianic, and Stephanie Myers—at UCF provided constant encouragement. I would like to thank my colleague, Donna Bishop, for writing the foreword to this text. It is rare that someone of her caliber is available for such an endeavor. Although she and I do not agree on all aspects of juvenile justice, there is no one in this field that I respect more in terms of integrity, insight, and concern for the plight of delinquent youth.

I would like to thank Bernie Krieg, the director of admissions at Glen Mills School, for an extensive tour of the facility. It is encouraging to see individuals committed to the improvement of erring youth, and institutions that are well equipped to accomplish that task. Thanks also to Ron Berry, the director of the Delaware County (PA) detention center, and Tom Pilson, the facility's coordinator of information systems. Ron and Tom let me visit and photograph the detention center. The tour reaffirmed my belief that juvenile justice tries to be and is different from the adult system; it truly cares for its population. I am grateful to Judge Field, the administrative judge of Philadelphia's Family Court, who was kind enough to allow me to photograph the inner sanctum of the juvenile court and its numerous courtrooms. It was a nice trip down memory lane.

Claude Teweles, the president of Roxbury Publishing Company, was more than understanding in allowing me to put this text together. Rather than putting out something quick and uninformative, Claude gave me the time and encouragement to assemble and integrate a vast amount of information that hopefully will comprise the most informative juvenile justice textbook to date. I also want to thank the very competent people at Roxbury Publishing Company who assisted in the production of this text—Nina Hickey, Carla Plucknett, Phong Ho, and Jackie Estrada. Thanks also to the many individuals who gave me third-eye insight into this text and who provided me with their valuable comments and suggestions: Gordon Bazemore, Venessa Garcia, Vincent Hoffman, William E. Kelly, Sesha Kethineni, Peter Kratcoski, Michael Leiber, Richard F. Mancuso, David L. Myers, Rebecca Petersen, Becky Tatum, and Tim Wadsworth.

Finally, I would like to thank my family and friends: my wife Andrea, who was forced to play the textbook widow, and numerous friends who were unable to get together with me very often. My one worry is that no one complained very much about my absence. The last acknowledgment goes to my friend and co-author, Tony Salerno. Much to my regret, he did not live long enough to witness this final product. My only hope is that he would be satisfied that we wrote a thorough text telling the story of juvenile justice. ✦

About the Authors

Joseph (Joe) B. Sanborn, Jr. was born in the suburbs of Philadelphia in 1951. He graduated from Villanova University in 1973 with a B.A. in Sociology, and earned both his M.A. (1974) and Ph.D. (1984) in criminal justice from the State University of New York at Albany. Joe's dissertation topic was plea negotiation in juvenile court. His data collection and research involved analyzing more than 10,000 juvenile court cases collected over 265 days (between 1979 and 1981) in the Philadelphia juvenile court. His is the only large-scale analysis of this important topic. Most of Joe's research has involved studying various facets of the juvenile court's operation in three different courts—urban, suburban, and rural. For this research he interviewed 100 juvenile court personnel for each topic he examined. For the last 10 years Joe has taught at the University of Central Florida in Orlando. His recent work focuses on legislation analysis and trying to understand where the country is headed in terms of juvenile justice.

Anthony (Tony) Salerno was born in the Bronx in 1929. Tony earned a football scholarship to the University of Delaware, from which he graduated with a B.S. in Physical Education in 1955. His graduation was delayed by two years of service in Korea (1951–1953). He attended college after his honorable discharge from the army, and earned an M.S. in Physical Education from the University of Illinois in 1956. In 1968 Tony earned an M.A. in Sociology from Rutgers University, and eventually earned A.B.D. status at the School of Criminal Justice. Tony enjoyed a rich and productive professional career. For a short while in 1968 he was the director of the Robert Brewer Halfway House in Edison, New Jersey. He was assistant superintendent at the Correction Center in Smyrna, Delaware, from 1971 to 1973. Between 1973 and 1975 Tony was the chief of the Bureau of Juvenile Corrections and served as the director of juvenile justice at the Ferris School in Delaware. Between 1976 and 1997 he was an assistant professor at Rowan University in New Jersey (formerly Glassboro State College), where he taught with Joe Sanborn for more than a decade. During this time he also taught as an adjunct professor at the University of Delaware. At the time of his premature death in February 2002, Tony had just completed the first drafts of his four chapters in this text. ✦

Contents

Dedication   iii

Foreword   iv
    by Donna Bishop

Preface vii
    Putting This Textbook Into Context   vii

Acknowledgments   x

About the Authors   xii

Section I: A History of Juvenile Justice in the United States

Chapter 1: Putting Juvenile Justice Into Context **2**
    Focus of Chapter 1   2
    Some Preliminary Distinctions.   2
    Models or Philosophies of Juvenile Justice   4
    Impact of the Rehabilitation Model   6
    The Varied Purposes of Juvenile Justice   7
    The Terminology Differentiation   10
    Summary: Key Ideas and Concepts   11
    Discussion Questions   12
    Endnotes   12

Chapter 2: Historical Development of Juvenile Justice **14**
    Focus of Chapter 2   14
    Quakers' Reform Efforts in the Nineteenth Century   14
        Poverty Leads to Crime and Social Problems   16
        Juveniles Need to Be Separated From Adults   16
        The State Is the Ultimate Parent   16

            Education Is the Absolute Cure.   17
    Houses of Refuge   17
            Legal Foundation for the Houses of Refuge.   18
    Reformatories and Separate Trial Dockets   20
    The Emergence of Juvenile Court   21
            The Legal Foundation of Juvenile Court   22
            The Reasons Juvenile Defendants Had No Rights in Juvenile Court   24
    The Juvenile Justice System, 1899–1967: An Overview   25
            The Law   26
            The Police   26
            The Court   26
            The Corrections   28
    Summary: Key Ideas and Concepts   29
    Discussion Questions   29
    Endnotes   30

Chapter 3: United States Supreme Court Intervention:
The Legal Framework of Juvenile Justice **31**
    Focus of Chapter 3   31
    The Need for Changes in Juvenile Court Procedures   31
    Establishing the Legal Framework of Juvenile Justice in *Kent v. United States* . .   32
    In re Gault and the Modification of Juvenile Court Procedure   35
            Establishing a Legal Framework in *Gault*.   37
            Putting *Gault* and the Legal Framework Into Context.   39
            The Legacy of *Gault*   40
    In re Winship and the Burden of Proof.   40
    McKeiver v. Pennsylvania and the Right to Jury Trial   42
    Breed v. Jones and Trial in Both Juvenile and Adult Court   43
    The Overall Result of the Legal Framework   45
    Summary: Key Ideas and Concepts   45
    Discussion Questions   46
    Endnotes   46

Section II: The Nature
of Juvenile Misbehavior

Chapter 4: Juvenile Court Jurisdiction. **50**
    Focus of Chapter 4   50
    Factors Influencing Jurisdiction   50
            Geography.   51
            Age   52
            Act   55
    Juvenile Delinquency   56

Status Offenses 57
    Separating Delinquents and Status Offenders. 57
    Special Titles. 59
    Title Confusion 60
    The Illegal Status Behaviors 61
Mandatory Exclusion 62
Summary: Key Ideas and Concepts 64
Discussion Questions 65
Endnotes 65

Chapter 5: Measuring Juvenile Crime 67
Focus of Chapter 5 67
Measuring Juvenile Delinquency. 68
Uniform Crime Reports 68
    Reported Crime 68
    Arrest Data and Juvenile Crime 70
    A Cautionary Note on Arrest Data 76
Victimization Surveys 77
Self-Report Surveys 78
    Criticism of SRS 79
    Validation of SRS 79
Cohort Studies 80
    Cohorts I and II 81
    The Violent Few 83
    Critique of Cohort Studies 84
Evaluating Measures of Juvenile Delinquency 85
Age and Delinquency 85
Gender and Delinquency 89
Race and Delinquency. 91
Social Class and Delinquency 92
Juveniles Preying on Juveniles: Juveniles as Victims 92
Summary: Key Ideas and Concepts 96
Discussion Questions 96

Chapter 6: Patterns of Juvenile Crime. 97
Focus of Chapter 6 97
Considering Patterns 97
Crime in the Schools 98
Gangs. 102
    Definition of Gangs 102
    A Brief History of Gangs in America 104
    Gang Migration 105
    The Extent of Gangs 105
    Gang Characteristics 107
    Gangs and Crime Estimates 109

       Gangs, Drugs, and Violence 112
       Girls in the Gang 113
   Juvenile Violent Crime. 113
       Guns 114
       Drugs (and Guns and Race) 115
   Serious Violent Juveniles (SVJ) 118
   Summary: Key Ideas and Concepts 119
   Discussion Questions 120
   Endnotes 120

Section III: The Gatekeepers of Juvenile Justice

Chapter 7: Policing Juveniles **124**
   Focus of Chapter 7 124
   Policing: The Underdeveloped Component 124
   Unique Police Service and Prevention Roles 125
   Juveniles' Attitudes Toward Police 127
   Community-Oriented Policing 127
   Curfew Laws 128
   Detecting Youth Misbehavior 128
   Field Investigations and Stops and Frisks 129
   The Decision Not to Arrest a Youth 130
   Grounds and Evidence for Arrest (Taking Into Custody) 132
   Factors That Can Affect the Decision to Arrest 134
       Factors Related to the Offense 134
       Factors Related to the Youth's Record or Status 135
       Factors Related to the Offender 135
       Factors Related to the Complainant 137
       Factors Related to the Location of the Offense 137
       Factors Related to the Parents or Home 138
       Factors Related to the Officer 138
       Factors Related to the Police Organization 139
       Factor Interaction 139
   Procedures Following Arrest. 142
   Search and Seizure and Interrogation 143
       Search and Seizure 143
       Interrogation 146
   Fingerprints and Photographs 150
   Other Identification Methods 151
   The Decision to Refer the Case to Juvenile Court. 152
   Summary: Key Ideas and Concepts 153

Discussion Questions 154
Endnotes 155

Chapter 8: The Juvenile Court Personnel 159

Focus of Chapter 8 159
A Unique Place to Work 159
The Prosecutor 160
The Defense Attorney 164
The Judge. 167
Referees and Masters 169
Probation Officers. 170
Parents and Victims 173
    The Parent. 173
    The Victim. 176
Personnel Overview 179
Summary: Key Ideas and Concepts 179
Discussion Questions 181
Endnotes 181

Chapter 9: The Intake Process 183

Focus of Chapter 9 183
Intake Objectives 183
POs as Intake Workers 184
The Uniqueness of Intake 184
Intake Options 186
Intake Decision Making 187
The Essence of Diversion 190
Being Put on Diversion 192
    Diversion Tasks 192
    The Length of Diversion 194
Failure, Successful Completion, and Impact of Diversion. 194
Modern Aspects of Diversion 196
Research on Who Is Diverted 196
The Formal Prosecution Option 199
The Numbers at Intake 201
    Delinquent Youth 201
    Status Offenders 203
Summary: Key Ideas and Concepts 206
Discussion Questions 207
Endnotes 207

Section IV: The Juvenile Court: The Preliminary Stages

Chapter 10: Detention **212**
  Focus of Chapter 10 212
  POs as the Gatekeepers to Detention 212
  Humane Detention 213
  The Detention Alternative Movement 214
  Detention Settings 215
  Juveniles in Jail 216
  Juveniles Eligible for Detention 219
      The Traditional Absence of Bail 219
      Detention Criteria 221
  Detention Research 227
  Risk (and Needs) Assessments 228
  Detention Hearing 228
  Constitutional Rights at the Detention Hearing 232
  The Need to Detain 234
  Release Conditions 235
  Addressing the Charges at Detention 236
  The Numbers at Detention 237
      Delinquent Youth 237
      Status Offenders 239
  Expedited Trial Date for Detention Cases 241
  Summary: Key Ideas and Concepts 242
  Discussion Questions 242
  Endnotes 243

Chapter 11: The Pretrial Stage **246**
  Focus of Chapter 11 246
  An Underdeveloped Stage 246
  Pleading 247
  Pretrial Issues 248
  Informal Resolutions 251
      Informal Agreements 252
      Consent Decrees 252
      The Nol Pros Bargain 254
  Plea Bargaining 256
      Unique Aspects of Juvenile Court Plea Bargaining 258
      Does Plea Bargaining Belong in Juvenile Court? 258
      Is Juvenile Court Less Dependent on Plea Bargaining? 258
      Are Juvenile Courts Just as Dependent on Plea Bargaining? . . 260

Incentives for Plea Bargaining in Juvenile Court 260
Is Plea Bargaining Less Problematic in Juvenile Court? 264
Nonnegotiated Guilty Pleas 265
The Pleading Guilty Process 267
Heading to Transfer or to an Adjudicatory Hearing. 271
Summary: Key Terms and Concepts 271
Discussion Questions 272
Endnotes 273

Chapter 12: Transfer to Adult Court **275**
Focus of Chapter 12 275
The Prospect of Self-Transfer 276
The What of Transfer 276
The Why of Transfer. 277
The When of Transfer 278
The How (or Types) of Transfer: Judicial and Prosecutorial. 278
The First Stage of Judicial Transfer: The Probable Cause Hearing 280
The Second Stage of Judicial Transfer: The Amenability Hearing 282
Factors Considered at the Amenability Hearing. 282
Weighing the Amenability Factors: Regular and Presumptive
Judicial Transfer 284
Prosecutorial Transfer 286
Current Standards in Judicial and Prosecutorial Transfer. 289
The Extent of Transfer to Adult Court 291
Research on Transfer to Adult Court 293
Reverse Transfer: Sending the Youth Back to Juvenile Court 294
Transfer to Juvenile Court's Second Tier 295
The Juvenile's Future in Criminal Court 297
Youthful Offender Sentencing in Criminal Court 300
Use of the Juvenile Court Record in Criminal Court Sentencing 302
Research on Adult Court Sentencing of Juveniles 306
Some Numbers on Youth Convicted and Sentenced in Criminal Court 306
Summary: Key Ideas and Concepts 309
Discussion Questions 310
Endnotes 311

Section V: Juvenile Court's Trial and Sentencing Stages

Chapter 13: The Adjudicatory Hearing **316**
Focus of Chapter 13 316

Prosecutorial Case Preparation 316
The Right to Counsel in Juvenile Court 319
Waiving the Right to Counsel 320
The Nature of Defense Representation in Juvenile Court 322
Defense Case Preparation 324
The Right to a Speedy Trial in Juvenile Court 325
Listing the Case for an Adjudicatory Hearing 327
Using Masters or Referees to Conduct the Adjudicatory Hearing 328
The Nature of Judicial Decision Makers in Juvenile Court 330
The Private Versus Public Adjudicatory Hearing 332
The Nature of the Adjudicatory Hearing 334
The Adjudicatory Hearing for Detained Youth 336
Some Unique Aspects of the Adjudicatory Hearing 336
The Numbers at Adjudication 338
        Delinquent Youth 338
        Status Offenders 340
Summary: Key Ideas and Concepts 341
Discussion Questions 342
Endnotes 343

Chapter 14: The Disposition Hearing **345**
Focus of Chapter 14 345
The Timing of Disposition 345
The Participants at Disposition 347
The Youth's Rights at Disposition 349
The Predisposition Report 350
        Use of Teams for the PDR 350
        Factors in the PDR 351
Situational Factors That Can Affect Disposition 356
The Pandora's Box of Dispositional Factors 358
Research Into Factors Affecting Disposition 359
        The Shortcomings of Research 359
        Research Findings 360
        The Dilemma of Factors Appropriate in Juvenile Court Dispositions . . . 360
Dispositional Options in Juvenile Court 362
        Deferring the Adjudication or Disposition 363
        No Disposition 363
The Probation Disposition 364
        The Length of Probation 364
        The Location of Probation 365
        The Conditions of Probation 365
Partial or Temporary Confinement 367
The Disposition Ladder 368

The Commitment Disposition 369
Differentiated Sentencing 373
    Extended Jurisdiction 374
    Particular Crimes and Offenders 374
    Enhanced and Consecutive Sentences 375
    Multiple Sentence Levels 375
    Combined Juvenile/Adult Sentence 377
    Juvenile or Adult Sentence 378
Mandatory and Minimum Sentences 379
    Mandatory Sentences 379
    Minimum Sentences 382
Sentencing the Parents 383
The Numbers at Disposition 383
    Delinquent Youth 383
    Status Offenders 386
Summary: Key Ideas and Concepts 388
Discussion Questions 390
Endnotes 390

Chapter 15: Postdisposition Hearings and Matters in Juvenile Court **395**
Focus of Chapter 15 395
The Right to Appeal 396
Postdispositional Hearings 397
    Review Hearings 398
    Modification Hearings 400
    Violation of Probation/Parole (VOP) Hearings 402
    Juvenile-Adult Court Reviews 404
The Nonconfidential Juvenile Court Record 405
    Tell the Public 405
    Tell the School 406
Sealing and Expunging Juvenile Court Records 407
Summary: Key Ideas and Concepts 408
Discussion Questions 409
Endnotes 409

Section VI: Community and Institutional Corrections in Juvenile Justice

Chapter 16: Prevention and Treatment in the Community **414**
Focus of Chapter 16 414
Community Corrections and Juvenile Justice 415

Juvenile Probation. 415
    The Complexity of Juvenile Probation 416
    What Is Probation? 417
    Supervising Clients. 418
    Classifying Clients 419
    Intensity of Supervision 421
    Needs Assessment 423
Diversion 423
    History of Diversion 424
    Net Widening 425
    Diversion Today 426
Teen Courts 426
Juvenile Drug Courts 427
Juveniles in Community Correctional Programs 429
Prevention Programs 430
    Macrolevel Prevention Programs 431
    OJJDP and Microlevel Prevention Programs 433
Schools 436
    Truancy 437
    DARE 438
    GREAT 439
The Family 440
Postadjudication Programs 441
    Behavior Modification 442
    Guided Group Interaction 442
Best Practices for Probation and Community Corrections 443
Restorative Justice 445
Juvenile Gun Courts. 447
Intensive Aftercare Program 448
The Numbers at Probation 449
    Delinquent Youth 449
    Status Offenders 450
Summary: Key Ideas and Concepts 450
Discussion Questions 451
Endnotes 452

Chapter 17: Juvenile Institutions **453**
Focus of Chapter 17. 453
Putting Juvenile Institutions Into Context 454
Juvenile Detention. 455
    Who Is in Detention? 456
    Detention Facilities 457
    History of Juvenile Detention. 459
    Conditions in Detention 460
    Rehabilitation in Detention 461

The Costs of Detention. 462
Administration of Detention 462
Custody Staff 463
Treatment Staff 463
Boot Camps. 464
Overview of Juvenile Incarceration. 465
Reception Centers 466
Long-Term Institutions. 467
Wilderness Programs/Camps/Ranches 468
Public Versus Private Facilities. 469
Juvenile Populations 470
History of Juvenile Institutions. 472
Hidden Juvenile Corrections. 475
Privatizing Juvenile Corrections 477
Institutional Program Models 478
The Behavioral Model 478
The Therapeutic Community. 480
Best Practices for Education and Rehabilitation in Juvenile Corrections 482
Disproportionate Minority Confinement 484
The Institutional Subculture. 485
Incarcerated Girls 486
The Right to Treatment 487
Basis for the Right to Treatment 489
The Case for Juveniles 489
The Status of RT Today 490
Protecting the Rights of Incarcerated Juveniles. 491
Conditions in Juvenile Corrections. 492
The Numbers at Juvenile Corrections 493
Delinquent Youth 494
Status Offenders 495
The Costs of Juvenile Corrections 495
Release From Incarceration 496
Summary: Key Ideas and Concepts 497
Discussion Questions 498
Endnotes 499

Section VII: Future Directions in Juvenile Justice

Chapter 18: The Future of Juvenile Court **502**
Focus of Chapter 18. 502
Putting the History of Juvenile Justice Into Context: The Three Major Themes . . 502

Putting the Future of Juvenile Court Into Context 505
Factors Affecting the Future. 506
Probable Developments 507
Concluding Remarks: Abolish or Retain Juvenile Court? 508
Summary: Key Ideas and Concepts 509
Discussion Questions 510

Appendixes **511**
Appendix A: Disproportionate Arrest Rates for Minority Youth 511
Appendix B: Disproportionate Minority Confinement. 511
Appendix C: Deadline for Filing Petitions When Youth Is in "Detention" 513
Appendix D: Jurisdictions With Time Limits for Detention Hearings 513
Appendix E: Jurisdictions With Expedited Trials in Detention Cases 515
Appendix F: Requirements in the Juvenile Court Guilty Plea Process 517
Appendix G: Judicial Transfer Provisions. 519
Appendix H: Prosecutorial Transfer Provisions 523
Appendix I: Statutorily Recognized Rights at the Adjudicatory Hearing. 526
Appendix J: Jurisdictions With Speedy Trial Provisions. 528
Appendix K: Jurisdictions With Open Adjudicatory Hearing Provisions 529
Appendix L: Jurisdictions With Deadlines for Disposition Hearings in
Juvenile Court. 531
Appendix M: Jurisdictions Identifying Factors to Be Included in the PDR. 533
Appendix N: Jurisdictions Identifying Characteristics of
Probation Dispositions. 534
Appendix O: Custody Rates for Juveniles in 1997, for Detention and
Residential Placement 535

Glossary **537**

Informative Websites **555**

References **557**

Subject Index **577**

Name Index. **583**

Case Index **587**

A History of Juvenile Justice in the United States

- Chapter 1: Putting Juvenile Justice Into Context
- Chapter 2: Historical Development of Juvenile Justice
- Chapter 3: United States Supreme Court Intervention

Focus of Section I

In Section I you will learn some of the fundamental differences between the juvenile justice and criminal justice systems. You will also be given a brief historical outline of the evolution of the juvenile system in the United States. The emphasis is on the way in which the unique legal foundation of juvenile court was originally established. Finally, you will see how the United States Supreme Court modified, to some extent, that legal foundation. Most importantly, you will discover how the Supreme Court decided to provide defendants with some rights in juvenile court, but not with so many rights that the juvenile court would have collapsed. ✦

Putting Juvenile Justice Into Context

Focus of Chapter 1

Chapter 1 compares the juvenile system to the criminal justice system, especially with respect to its components and philosophical underpinnings. The different languages used by the two systems are also detailed.

Key Terms

- advocate
- crime control model
- criminalization effect
- due process model
- get-tough movement
- guardian

- legal interests
- purpose clauses
- rehabilitation model
- status offense
- treatment interests

Some Preliminary Distinctions

The criminal justice system—the police, courts, and correctional facilities that deal with adult offenders (or with juvenile offenders who have been sent to that system)—is older than its juvenile counterpart. The roots of criminal justice (the first criminal courts) can be traced to the twelfth century. Juvenile justice, on the other hand, is a relatively new system with antecedents dating only to the early nineteenth century (see Chapter 2). Criminal justice is also "larger" than juvenile justice, at least with respect to the number of system components. That is, juvenile justice involves only courts and corrections.

Philadelphia's Juvenile Court: Juvenile court is the focal point of the juvenile justice system. Would the juvenile justice system survive if the juvenile court were abolished?

While "juvenile corrections" began to emerge in the 1820s, "juvenile courts" would not appear until 1899, and "juvenile police" per se have yet to materialize.

While as a system juvenile justice is smaller and younger than its adult counterpart, the extent of behavior over which it has jurisdiction or control is considerably larger than that of the criminal courts. Like criminal court, juvenile court has jurisdiction over criminal behavior, which for youth is typically referred to as *juvenile delinquency*. Uniquely, however, juvenile court usually has jurisdiction over behavior that is noncriminal and illegal for juveniles only. Examples of this illegal behavior include running away from home, truancy, and incorrigibility. These behaviors are known as status offenses because it is the juvenile or underage status of the individual that makes the behavior illegal. Finally, the juvenile courts in some states have jurisdiction over family-oriented matters and involve such situations as adoption, paternity, support, and dependency. Chapter 4 explores the jurisdiction of the juvenile court in depth. We will see in that chapter how the legal definition of a juvenile varies among states and how the maximum juvenile court age ranges from 15 to 17.

The inquiry in juvenile court also tends to be broader than that in criminal court. Criminal court focuses mostly on the current charge and the prior criminal history of the offender in deciding what punishment to mete out to those convicted there. Although collateral issues such as employment history, drug use, and family status can influence the sentence the offender receives, today the impact of these features tends to be fairly minimal in criminal court; on the other hand, items that are relevant to examination of the accused in juvenile court extend far beyond offense and record. They range from family stability and school record (and even to the youth's educability) to the neighborhood and resources of the community in which the youth lives.

Juvenile court also tends to operate in a much different context than its criminal counterpart. While the criminal court tends to be a public and open forum from which the media constantly report convictions and other occurrences, juvenile courts operate in virtual anonymity. It is rare for anyone not involved in a particular case, let alone the media, to be permitted access to juvenile court hearings. The nonpublic nature of juvenile court affects what can happen there compared to adult court. We will see examples throughout the text and especially in Chapter 13, which deals with the adjudicatory hearing or trial.

Other differences between the juvenile and criminal justice systems range from the laws that govern each system to the operation of the police, courts, and corrections within each system. At the same time, there are many important similarities between the juvenile and adult systems. Most of this text is dedicated to highlighting the differences while noting the similarities. This chapter attempts to explain fully only two of the major distinctions: the philosophies and purposes that direct juvenile and criminal justice, and the language used by both systems. An understanding of these differences should enable you to start putting juvenile justice in context.

Models or Philosophies of Juvenile Justice

What makes juvenile justice so unique—and perhaps so confusing—is that it was created along philosophical guidelines that differ significantly from those affecting criminal justice. This philosophical disparity has in turn resulted in serious differences in the powers and operations of the two systems, in the rights enjoyed by those processed by each system, and even in the language used throughout each process.

Historically, criminal justice has been guided mostly by a crime control (also called *punishment*) model or philosophy. This makes the creation of the juvenile justice system understandable, as it has been designed to answer to a rehabilitation (also called *treatment*) model or philosophy.[1] Individuals (or agencies) who endorse a crime control perspective believe that the primary purpose of the system is to punish offenders and to protect society from offenders. People in this group likely perceive:

- all those arrested as guilty and requiring punishment from the state;

- the handcuffing of police with constitutional controls as interference and counter-productive; and

- the extension of numerous rights to defendants while proving guilt as misspent resources (would you rather hire police and build prisons or retain lawyers for criminals?).

In other words, a crime control person would favor an efficient trial process (i.e., not too costly or cumbersome, but not overly incorrect either) that culminates in punishment proportionate to the crime and record of the accused. A crime control–oriented system is designed more to hurt and to deter offenders than to benefit them per se. It is influenced more by the wishes of the public for protection and revenge than by the needs of the offender for improvement.

Interestingly, rehabilitation-oriented people can agree with those from the crime control camp on many of its basic propositions. The two models seriously disagree, however, on both the purpose of the system and the nature of the intervention awaiting those found guilty. For the "rehab" group, the purpose of the system is to rehabilitate youths so as to prevent them from furthering their self-destruction. Those in this group likely perceive:

- all those arrested as sick or disabled and needing help or treatment from the state;

- the handcuffing of personnel with legal rules and controls as interference and counter-productive; and

- the extension of rights to the accused while proving guilt as misspent resources (would you rather hire therapists and build facilities to cure children or retain lawyers for them?).

A "rehab" person would also favor an efficient trial process that results in treatment that responds to a youth's problems. A rehabilitation-oriented system is designed more to benefit offenders and turn them around than to promote society's interests in self-defense. It is influenced by the need of the offender for improvement and not by the wishes of the public for protection and revenge.

Thus, the crime control and rehabilitation models result in different sentencing and correctional responses to offenders. The policing and courts components of systems influenced by these models could be identical, however. There would be maximum powers and efficiency enjoyed by the system (or state) and, accordingly, few rights bestowed on those processed by the system.

Although the two models agree with and parallel each other more than they diverge, whether one philosophy or the other rules has serious implications for the operation of a system, particularly in a democracy. For example, there is no ambiguity about the fact that the criminal justice system promotes punishment and that its mission primarily is to protect society and hurt offenders (perhaps even to kill them). The reality of this mission makes the relevance of yet another model—the due process model—only too clear. That is, since criminal justice openly attempts to punish or hurt offenders, they are entitled to protections (or due process safeguards) from the state's "assault."

Individuals with a due process orientation could favor either punishment or rehabilitation as the state's response to crime. Regardless of the outcome they select, due process people believe that the primary purpose of the system is to check the powers of the government and actually to protect the accused from the state. People in this group likely perceive:

- all those arrested as innocent or as not needing help until proved otherwise;

- the handcuffing of police and system personnel as essential to maintaining a free society; and

- the extension of rights to defendants while proving guilt or need as a vital resource in keeping the state in control (would you rather hire lawyers or risk the prospect of a police state?).

A due process person would favor a cumbersome trial process that culminates in a factually accurate and legally sufficient verdict or finding. A due process–oriented system is designed more to protect the accused than to enhance the state's interests in treatment or protection. It is directed by the need of the defendant for rights and safeguards as opposed to the wishes of society for the punishment or salvation of offenders.

Because of the punitive nature of the criminal justice system, due process becomes a relevant and limiting factor in the state's objective to punish criminals. In fact, crime control and due process square off at each other throughout the entire criminal justice system. The disagreements and battles are relatively easy to comprehend. For a whole variety of rights extended to an accused, due process people would tend to favor what crime control people would tend to oppose. In many situations, whether rights should apply (and how the system should function) would be a simple tug of war between the two models, resulting in a yes or no answer depending on the model that dominates. So, for example, while crime control people would oppose (and say no to) items like *Miranda* warnings and the exclusionary rule, due process individuals would support (and say yes to) *Miranda* warnings and the exclusionary rule.

Impact of the Rehabilitation Model

When rehabilitation controls a system, the appropriateness of and need for due process is not nearly as clear. The presence of the rehabilitation model in the juvenile justice system has contributed to youth receiving fewer procedural safeguards than comparably situated adult defendants. That is, in the situation where the state is purportedly trying to help or improve an offender, his or her need for protection from the state's protection becomes somewhat cloudy. In a similar manner, the mental health system operates without many of the facets of due process considered necessary in criminal court (such as the protection against self-incrimination and proof beyond a reasonable doubt).

Here is where the confusion of juvenile justice begins. As we will see in the next chapter, the juvenile justice system was founded on principles associated with the rehabilitation model. Accordingly, the system was granted extensive powers by the state, while the young offenders were extended few legal rights. At the same time, however, the similarity between rehabilitation and crime control makes it impossible to determine whether crime control is actually operating within juvenile justice while masquerading as rehabilitation.

Regardless of which model was truly in charge in juvenile justice, rehabilitation was identified and accepted as the very reason for its existence for about six decades or so. In the 1960s, however, the U.S. Supreme Court reacted to the immense powers wielded by juvenile court officials by granting juveniles a number of constitutional rights. This meant that the due process model was now supposed to operate in the system. Subsequently, crime control emerged as an openly legitimate element of juvenile justice. Once juveniles were given rights, they were eligible to be punished as well. What this means is that, unlike in the criminal justice system in which only crime control and due process vie for control, in juvenile justice rehabilitation joins the contest. This addition makes the juvenile system responsive to three philosophies, each potentially pulling the system in a different direction.

An illustration may make this conflict and confusion more apparent. Although crime control and due process people might disagree as to when the right to counsel applies and/or to the tactics counsel can use, they would agree on one vital aspect of this right: the role of defense counsel. Both models would identify the role as an advocate, or one who is supposed to perform damage control (i.e., get the best legal results possible) for the defendant. Certainly the crime control person might wish defense counsel less success in this endeavor than would a due process–minded individual. Nevertheless, neither philosophy would suggest that the defense attorney's job is to help the state convict the defendant (even a guilty one). Thus, regardless of who the accused is, defense counsel is expected to act as an advocate within the criminal justice system.

In juvenile justice, where rehabilitation has reigned and where the right to counsel has existed for more than 36 years, debate continues about the proper role for a defense attorney in that forum. To be sure, the advocate is the role adopted by many, and perhaps most, of the defense attorneys who practice today in juvenile court. This role presents a problem to the juvenile system, however. It posits the attorney as the enemy of both the system and the youth's treatment needs and interests, especially when a guilty or needy child is "wrongfully" acquitted. For example, should a defense attorney automatically file a motion to suppress evidence in every relevant case so as to "beat" the system and to let the youth "walk"? Some would view this outcome as contrary to the youth's treatment needs (possession of a pound of marijuana could suggest that the juvenile has a "problem" that requires a response from the system) and as undermining the very reason for juvenile court's existence. Moreover, if all defense attorneys were to act this way, there would seem to be little need for a separate and unique juvenile court. This type of business can be done quite well in criminal court.

On the other hand, if defense attorneys act as guardians instead of as advocates, they arguably are pursuing the youth's treatment interests. They can ensure the defendant receives some help and assistance from the system by not winning the case outright (perhaps by not filing a motion to suppress). At the same time, however, such lawyers are working against the clients' legal interests. It is never in one's legal benefit to be found guilty of a crime (or adjudicated delinquent). Some feel this behavior posits the defense attorney as an enemy of the youth and constitutes an ethical violation. It could also serve as grounds for finding that the attorney has rendered ineffective assistance of counsel in violation of the Sixth Amendment right to counsel.

Regardless of whether the defense attorney's role in juvenile court should be that of an advocate or a guardian (we will return to this topic in Chapter 8), the point is that the presence of the rehabilitation model—the purported desire of the system to help and to improve youth—complicates and confuses this otherwise fairly straightforward issue and many others as well.

The Varied Purposes of Juvenile Justice

Because the dominant philosophies of the juvenile and criminal justice systems differ (rehabilitation versus crime control), it makes sense that the purposes that are supposed to be served by each system would differ as well. Besides its obligation to see that justice is done (a due process concern), the criminal justice system advances a variety of objectives:

- Punish the offender.
- Hold offenders accountable.
- Protect society.
- Vindicate the victim and society.
- Deter this and other offenders.

Rehabilitating the offender has been a primary pursuit of criminal justice, especially since the 1960s and 1970s. Although rehabilitation-oriented programs remain a part of the corrections component of criminal justice, rehabilitation itself has never been identified as the reason for the existence of the criminal justice system.

Chapter 2 will disclose how rehabilitation became the cornerstone on which the juvenile justice system was constructed. Without the desires of the system's founders to pursue this particular goal, there would have been no need to remove youth from the criminal justice system. Almost all of the state legislatures that created juvenile courts inserted purpose clauses into the legislation that authorized these courts to operate. Because these courts were being specially created as alternatives to already existing criminal courts, legislatures needed to explain why juvenile courts were necessary. They also needed to specify what goals juvenile courts would pursue that could not be obtained in the courts already available. For the most part, the purpose clauses suggested the mission of juvenile courts to be one-dimensional. That mission was to promote the best interests of the child and the child's family. Terms like *punishment, accountability,* and *protection of society* were not present in the clauses. Those purposes belonged in the criminal justice system.

To make a long story short—and not to get too far ahead of the history presented in Chapters 2 and 3—current purpose clauses are no longer one-dimensional. Today, no juvenile courts are invited to disregard the welfare of the public and, instead, to focus solely on what advances the interests of the child and the child's family. Moreover, thanks to changes demanded by the U.S. Supreme Court (see Chapter 3), juvenile courts are now obliged to seek justice, and the purpose clauses reflect this command. These and other revisions in the purpose clauses suggest not only that the juvenile court's mission has changed, but that this mission, in part at least, is dangerously close to replicating what criminal courts are designed to achieve.

As we will see throughout the text, juvenile courts have adopted some provisions and practices that are similar or even identical to facets of criminal court operation. This merger between the systems has been termed the criminalization effect,[2] which means that juvenile court is becoming more and more like criminal court. To some extent, the reality of a criminalization effect is undeniable. Numerous elements of both crime control and due process currently exist in the juvenile justice system. In fact, the purpose clauses of most states contain one or more statements that are readily associated with criminal court objectives.[3]

Legislatures today in many states are instructing their juvenile courts to remember that certain crimes by youth indicate that the public needs to be protected from these offenders. In addition, legislatures have insisted that ensuring the safety of the community should be a primary concern of the court.[4] Similarly, the courts are being reminded that deterring, controlling, and reducing crime is a major aspect of juvenile court operation.[5] Some legislatures have gone so far as to direct juvenile courts to implement swift, certain, and appropriate sanctions and punishment[6] and to hold juveniles accountable and responsible for their actions.[7] These words supposedly are repugnant to traditional juvenile court philosophy. Finally, victims and parents have also received more attention recently in the purpose clauses (we will return to these aspects in Chapter 8). Several legislatures have identified the protection of victims' rights and the offender's payment of restitution to the victim as vital objectives of juvenile court.[8] Parents have been informed by several legislatures that they are going to be held accountable for their children's conduct and that they will be expected to compensate both the victim and the juvenile justice system.[9]

Some critics have interpreted these recent revisions in the purpose clauses as signaling the juvenile court's abandonment of rehabilitation and its transformation into a clone of criminal court—or complete criminalization (Feld 1990, 1991, 1993b). This argument holds that juvenile courts exist only to punish juveniles and are no longer committed to pursuing their best interests or rehabilitation. If accurate, these allegations would have serious implications. They would suggest that juvenile courts have no justification or reason to continue to operate as a separate and unique system, at least with respect to processing young criminals. However, this view represents a selective reading of the purpose clauses and a complete disregard for the vast majority of provisions still contained in the clauses.

Nearly every jurisdiction in the country has specifically identified in a purpose clause what the mission of juvenile court is. Only Arizona and the federal jurisdiction have failed to announce a particular purpose per se. Nevertheless, case law and various provisions of the juvenile court acting in both these jurisdictions hold that the proceedings are not criminal in nature and that the objective of the juvenile court is to rehabilitate youth. All 50 jurisdictions that have purpose clauses have maintained one or more provisions compatible with traditional juvenile justice philosophy and seriously distinguish juvenile from criminal court objectives. These rehabilitation-oriented and child-focused objectives can be divided into three interrelated groups, dealing with the nature of juvenile court reaction to youthful misbehavior:

- Family- or child-centered intervention
- Minimized intervention
- Ameliorated intervention

Being focused on the child and the family has been a major attribute of the juvenile

justice system from its beginning. Although the interests of the public have made serious inroads into juvenile court, the child and the family remain foremost in various ways in the purpose clauses in 34 states. Twenty-four states contend that the juvenile court's aim is to preserve or strengthen the child's family or the child's ties to the family.[10] Similarly, 10 states now mention the rehabilitation of the family (through offering court services) as a purpose of the system.[11] Finally, eight states simply note that juvenile court proceedings are intended to be in the best interests of the child.[12]

Closely related to its child and family focus is the juvenile system's historical commitment to minimize its intervention into the youth's life. Even more states (43) continue to insist on limited responses to juvenile crime from the juvenile court. The most common way in which this philosophy is expressed is that the child is to be removed from the home or family only as a last resort and only when necessary for the child's best interests or for the protection and safety of the community. Thirty states endorse this position.[13] Similar is another common statement that juvenile court should secure for each child—preferably in the child's own home—such care, guidance, and control as needed for the youth's and soci-

A juvenile police force is one part of the juvenile justice system that has never been developed. Should there be a special police force dealing exclusively with juveniles?

ety's best interests. Sixteen states announce this guideline,[14] 11 of which also talk of removal from the home as a last resort. Altogether, 35 states currently follow the traditional policy of encouraging juvenile courts to rehabilitate the youth at home. This policy also reinforces the child- and family-centered policies. Complementing both these sets of policies is a mandate in six states that those children who are removed from home be reunited with their families as soon as possible.[15]

Compatible with these measures are various provisions that specifically emphasize prevention and diversion from the system (13 states),[16] the least restrictive disposition (five states),[17] and the development and use of community-based alternatives in sentencing (nine states).[18] Many more jurisdictions have enacted similar provisions that affect sentencing in juvenile court but simply have not included them in their purpose clauses (see Chapter 14).

A final characteristic that demonstrates how purpose clauses have remained true to the primarily benevolent mission of juvenile justice is the tendency to demand ameliorated or modified interventions. Forty-four jurisdictions continue to identify this objective. In 19 jurisdictions, if a juvenile is removed from home, the system is under obligation to provide custody, care, and discipline as nearly equivalent as possible to that which should have been provided by the parents.[19] Eight states believe a purpose of juvenile court is to remove from children committing delinquent acts the taint of criminality and the consequences of criminal behavior.[20] Finally, 25 states instruct their juvenile courts generally to provide guidance, care, and protection.[21] Another nine use words such as *reform, rehabilitate, reeducate, reintegrate,* or *treat.*[22] Sixteen mention the pursuit of "wholesome mental, emotional, and physical development"[23] (seven of these states even add the word "moral"[24]). Another seven list competency development[25] (to which Maryland adds "character"), and four states seek the youth's personal and social growth.[26]

These unique mandates result in significant differences in the operation of juvenile court as compared to criminal court, as we will see throughout the remainder of the text. To be sure, recent times have witnessed an escalation in both the severity of youthful offending and the system's reaction to these crimes. In this respect, there has been a get-tough movement resulting in the juvenile system's having less tolerance for juvenile crime and, accordingly, in its issuing of harsher sanctions. As we have seen, legislatures have added provisions to the purpose clauses advocating punishment and protection of society. Other examples of the impact of the criminalization effect on juvenile court will be seen in many of the following chapters. In fact, some of these examples support the second theme of this text: that juvenile court represents two realities, one that rehabilitates and one that punishes. To suggest, however, that the juvenile justice system has completely abandoned its traditional rehabilitation mission, replicating the punitiveness with which the criminal justice system tends to respond to adult offenders, is a gross and dangerous exaggeration.

The Terminology Differentiation

A final preliminary distinction between the two systems needs to be noted. Although the operation of the juvenile justice system parallels that of the criminal justice system, the founders of juvenile justice created a new language to distinguish it from the older

Table 1.1 Language Differentials Between Juvenile and Criminal Justice Systems	
Criminal Justice	**Juvenile Justice**
Crime/criminal	Delinquency/delinquent
Arrest	Take into custody
Complaint/indictment/information	Petition
Jail	Detention/shelter care
Bail hearing	Detention hearing
Trial	Adjudicatory hearing
Conviction	Adjudication
Sentencing	Disposition hearing
Punishment	Rehabilitation
Incarceration	Commitment/placement
Prison	Industrial/training school
Parole	Aftercare

system. Moreover, this new language was meant to emphasize the therapeutic, noncriminal mission of the new system. Each new term has a corresponding word in the criminal justice system. The behaviors behind or functions of the terms are identical in both systems. For example, being taken into custody is the physical equivalent to being arrested. Nevertheless, the differences between the terms are real and not merely semantic. Despite the physical and psychic comparability of the terms, a world of legal difference lies between any two sets of words. Thus, youths taken into custody can legally claim that they have not been arrested. Similarly, one who is adjudicated "delinquent" has not been convicted of a crime. Table 1.1 illustrates the terminology used by both systems.

Despite the legal differences between the terms, we will use the words interchangeably throughout the text. So, occasionally, we will refer to juveniles being arrested, convicted, or sentenced, even though these actions occurred within the juvenile justice system. One interesting item that supports the contention that juvenile justice has experienced a "get-tough" development is that some states are using criminal justice terms, such as conviction and sentencing, to refer to events in juvenile court.

Summary: Key Ideas and Concepts

- Juvenile justice a smaller and younger system than criminal justice
- Juvenile court jurisdiction broader than that of criminal court
- The broader focus and inquiry of juvenile court
- The nonpublic nature of juvenile court
- Criminal court operating under the influence of a crime control model
- Juvenile court operating under the influence of a rehabilitation model
- The impact of rehabilitation on the due process model
- The presence of guardian defense attorneys in juvenile court
- Conflict between legal interests and treatment interests in juvenile court
- The significance of a criminalization effect for juvenile court

- Purpose clauses distinguishing juvenile from criminal court
- Juvenile courts continuing to be held answerable to a unique purpose
- Juvenile courts working with a different vocabulary from criminal courts

Discussion Questions

1. Discuss some of the preliminary ways in which juvenile courts differ from criminal courts.

2. How does the rehabilitation model make the juvenile justice system differ from the criminal justice system, which is dominated by the crime control model?

3. What impact does the rehabilitation model have on the rights of juvenile defendants?

4. Which should prevail in juvenile court, the treatment interests or legal interests of the youth?

5. Should juvenile court defense attorneys operate as advocates or as guardians in juvenile court, and what are the implications of these roles for the juvenile defendant and the juvenile court?

6. In what ways are the purposes commanded of juvenile court the same as and different than those demanded of criminal court?

7. What support is there so far for the third theme of the text—that there are two realities operating in juvenile court?

Endnotes

1. Herbert Packer (1968) is credited with developing the model idea in criminal justice. His original work described the battle between the crime control and due process models. Because he was examining the adult system, Packer did not formulate a rehabilitation model. However, its description here is extrapolated from Packer's work.
2. Professor Barry Feld (1990) from the University of Minnesota Law School originally developed the notion of the criminalization effect in juvenile court.
3. A good deal of the material in this text concerns the statutes from the 50 states, Washington, DC, and the federal jurisdiction. The senior author recently conducted an analysis of these statutes and continues to update this analysis periodically. The material will be presented in the text without citing this analysis each and every time.
4. These states are: AK, CA, CT, FL, HI, ID, IN, KS, MD, MN, MT, NE, NH, NJ, NY, NC, OK, OR, TX, UT, VT, VA, WV, WA, WI, WY.
5. These states are: AK, CO, CT, HI, ID, MN, MT, NE, NV, NM, OK, OR, TX, VA, WV, WI, WY.
6. These states are: AK, AR, CA, CO, CT, FL, HI, IN, ME, NJ, OR, TX, UT, WA, WY.
7. These states are: AL, AK, CA, CT, ID, IN, KS, MD, MN, MS, NH, NJ, NM, OK, OR, PA, TX, UT, VA, WA, WI, WY.
8. These states are: AK, CT, FL, ID, NM, OR, VA, WA, WI.
9. These states are: CA, FL, ID, IN, MD, TX, WY.
10. These states are: AL, AR, CA, CO, DE, FL, ID, IL, IN, KS, KY, LA, ME, MD, MT, NH, NJ, NM, OK, PA, RI, SC, UT, WV.
11. These states are: AL, AK, CT, ID, KY, MD, NE, NM, WA, WY.
12. These states are: AK, CO, DE, MO, NY, SD, UT, VA.

13. These states are: AL, AR, CA, CO, CT, DE, FL, IL, IN, KY, ME, MD, MT, NE, NH, NJ, NM, NC, ND, OH, OK, PA, RI, TN, TX, UT, VT, VA, WV, WY.
14. These states are: AL, AR, CO, DE, GA, IL, IA, LA, ME, MI, MS, NV, NJ, RI, UT, SC.
15. These states are: AL, CA, MN, NE, NC, SC.
16. These states are: AL, CT, FL, IN, KS, NV, NM, NC, OR, SC, VA, WV, WI.
17. These states are: AL, KY, SC, VA, WV.
18. These states are: AL, CT, FL, ID, KS, NM, NC, WA, WV.
19. These jurisdictions are: AR, CA, DC, FL, GA, IL, IA, LA, MD, MA, MI, MO, NV, NJ, RI, SC, TX, WV, WY.
20. These states are: NJ, NM, ND, OH, TN, TX, VT, WY.
21. These states are: AL, CA, CT, FL, GA, HI, MD, MO, MT, NE, NH, NJ, NM, NC, ND, OH, PA, SD, TN, TX, UT, VT, WA, WI, WY.
22. These states are: AR, FL, HI, IN, KY, OK, OR, UT, WV.
23. These states are: AR, FL, IL, MD, MT, NH, NJ, NM, ND, OH, PA, SC, TN, TX, VT, WY.
24. These states are: IL, NH, ND, SC, TX, VT, WY.
25. These states are: FL, ID, IL, MD, MT, PA, WI.
26. These states are: IL, MN, NE, OK. ✦

Historical Development of Juvenile Justice

Focus of Chapter 2

Chapter 2 traces the major developments of the early and late nineteenth century that served as important precedents for the eventual introduction of the juvenile justice system. The chapter emphasizes the critical legal foundation that was established during this period because of its contribution to the eventual operation of the juvenile court. The chapter then focuses on the informal way in which juvenile courts initially worked until the U.S. Supreme Court modified this informality in the 1960s.

Key Terms

- Chicago women or child savers
- defense of infancy
- House of Refuge
- Juvenile Court Act
- *mens rea*
- *parens patriae* doctrine
- Quakers
- *quid pro quo* exchange
- reformatories
- trial dockets
- writ of *habeas corpus*

Quakers' Reform Efforts in the Nineteenth Century

Laws have distinguished children from adults for centuries—in regard to both rights and responsibilities and liabilities for criminal behavior. Criminal law has always reflected concern about the ability of very young persons to form *mens rea* or the intent necessary to commit a crime. Without intent, an individual lacks sufficient culpability or responsibility to be convicted of a crime and to be punished for it.

Prior to the nineteenth century, institutions such as the courts and prisons did not distinguish between juveniles and adults, for the most part. Instead, children were routinely prosecuted for crimes in criminal court and, if incarcerated, were housed with adults in prisons. Similarly, youth who were too poor to survive in free society were institutionalized with similarly situated adults (including their parents) in poorhouses, almshouses, and workhouses.

The early 1800s marked the beginning of the development of institutions catering solely to youth. During this time period, the Quakers, the reformers responsible for introducing the penitentiary, launched a program designed to create the first juvenile-only institutions in the United States (apart from places like orphanages, of course). At this time American society, especially in the northeast, was experiencing rapid changes due mostly to three interrelated phenomena: immigration, industrialization, and urbanization. Populations in American cities were expanding dramatically as the United States transformed from an agrarian society to an urban one. The country's growing pains were considerable at this time. Some saw this period as a threat to the very survival of the country (Pickett 1969).

The Quakers, who were quite active in social reform, decided to attack and remedy this urban situation. At first they set their sights on the ills of poverty in general. Ultimately, they narrowed that focus to poor children (Pickett 1969). Their motives for getting involved in this particular social reform were probably mixed. On the one hand, they seem to have been genuinely concerned with the plight of the poor children and, in many ways, were engaged in a crusade (Mennel 1973). On the other hand, they seem to have been revolted by the influx of immigrants, who were mostly Irish Catholics. The Quakers perceived these individuals as constituting a genuine threat to the basic fabric of American society. Thus, in some respects the Quakers' reform efforts represented ethnic, class, and religious warfare (Fox 1970a; Platt 1972). Their writings betray some of their hostility toward the new city dwellers. New York was the focus of the following remarks:

> Every person that frequents the out-streets of this city must be forcibly struck with the ragged and uncleanly appearance, the vile language, and the idle and miserable habits of great numbers of children, most of whom are of an age suitable for schools, or for some useful employment. The parents of these children, are, in all probability, too poor, or too degenerate, to provide them with clothing fit for them to be seen in at School; and know not where to place them in order that they may find employment, or be better cared for. Accustomed, in many instances, to witness at home nothing in the way of example, but what is degrading; early taught to observe intemperance, and to hear obscene and profane language without disgust; obliged to beg, and even encouraged to acts of dishonesty, to satisfy the wants induced by the indolence of their parents—what can be expected, but that such children will, in due time, become responsible to the laws for crimes, which have thus, in a manner, been forced upon them? Can it be consistent with real justice, that delinquents of this character, should be consigned to the infamy and severity of punishments, which must inevitably tend to perfect the work of degradation, to sink them still deeper in corruption, to deprive them of their remaining sensibility to the shame of exposure,

and establish them in all hardihood of daring and desperate villainy? So is it possible that a Christian community can lend its sanction to such a process without any effort to rescue and save?[1]

Pivotal in the development of juvenile-only institutions were four beliefs held by the Quakers. Although all four were somewhat radical at that time, none are today. The Quakers touched on all four beliefs in the above quote.

Poverty Leads to Crime and Social Problems

Rather than innate evil or depravity, social conditions produced crime, according to the Quakers. If innate evil were the cause of crime, then offenders should be executed or banished, which is what England had practiced for centuries. Environmental or social causation, however, allowed for the development of institutions (such as prisons) through which the effects of these conditions could be neutralized and remedied. This belief was critical in two ways. First, it gave the Quakers an excuse to direct their reforms at a large audience of youth who were poor, deviant, ill-mannered, or immoral but who were projected to develop into criminal types unless helped by the Quakers. Second, it gave the Quakers a reason to remove these youth from the corrupting influences of urban streets and inadequate families and to build a special facility in which they could be reformed.

Juveniles Need to Be Separated From Adults

At this time, poor and criminal children were being housed with their adult counterparts. The Quakers viewed this situation as problematic because children would have only negative role models (including their parents) from whom to learn. The chance was too great for corruption to spread to these children, which would produce a never-ending cycle of poverty or crime. Thus, juveniles needed confinement in their own facilities apart from adults. Even staying at home would not achieve this needed separation. Implicit in this view was a belief that youth were less intractable than adults. Whereas it was probably too late to turn around poor or criminal adults, hope remained for children, the younger the better. It was also thought better to get a hold of youth before their misbehaviors became seriously criminal.

The State Is the Ultimate Parent

As representatives of the state, Quakers saw themselves as the ultimate parent for all troubled and troublesome children. Quakers believed that the biological parents were obviously not equipped to raise their children if the kids were found roaming the streets or were incarcerated in prisons or poorhouses. Thus, the state (via the Quakers) needed to act as a surrogate parent, replacing the natural parent in raising the child. This broad perspective enabled the Quakers to exercise authority over virtually any youth who had virtually any problem, rather than being restricted to addressing only criminal youth.

Education Is the Absolute Cure

Although the Quakers believed in discipline and punishment, they placed primary emphasis on educating errant youth. The education thought to be required encompassed the three R's, as well as religious and moral instruction, and the ever-important vocational training. Quakers thought this broad-based education would equip juveniles to emerge into adulthood with the proper attitudes, values, and skills needed to become law-abiding, self-sufficient individuals. These young people would be neither a drain on nor a threat to society. Placed in this framework, the Quakers' program appeared to be benevolent rather than punitive. The main motivation was to improve the institutionalized youth and to enhance their future prospects. In fact, this agenda represented the first attempt of what today is regarded as rehabilitation. At the same time, however, there was room within this regimen for serious discipline and corporal punishment. As in the boot camps of today, military drill was common (Mennel 1973). Nevertheless, the official absence of punitive intentions would affect the legal procedures required in placing youth in the Quakers' facilities. In addition, the rehabilitative design enabled the Quakers to insist that juveniles be incarcerated until the education process had been successfully completed rather than after a specific sentence in months or years had expired. This policy in turn provided the Quakers with considerable power in determining when and how youth would be released from their facilities.

Houses of Refuge

Armed with these beliefs, the Quakers ultimately secured authority from the New York legislature to open their first House of Refuge on January 1, 1825, in New York City. Comparable facilities opened in Boston and Philadelphia within three years, and by midcentury there were nearly a dozen, located primarily throughout the northeast and midwest where major urban centers had developed. Houses of Refuge were designed to house poor and vagrant types together with petty offenders. Quakers had targeted two youth groups. The first group included minor delinquents who would either be placed in jails with adult offenders or be ignored by the criminal justice system because their offenses were so trivial (Bernard 1992). The second group involved noncriminal youth who were at risk because of their circumstances. Without the intervention of the Quakers, these youth would be free to continue associating with corrupting influences (such as parents and other miscreants) and would likely evolve into adult criminals.

Glen Mills School: The Philadelphia House of Refuge was the third to open in the United States (1826). How necessary is it to have facilities that deal with juveniles exclusively?

Typically, major juvenile felons remained in criminal courts and prisons during this period (Bernard 1992).

Minor young criminals could be referred to Houses of Refuge before or after conviction in criminal court. Police or any reputable citizen could escort youth found "hanging out" or looking or acting slovenly to these facilities. The managers of the almshouses sent some poor kids there. Before long, parents routinely dumped unwanted or unruly children at the Houses. Most juveniles were incarcerated without trial. Doing so did not mark a radical departure from past practices of committing the poor to workhouses. However, criminal youth would have been provided a hearing in criminal court before being "put away" like adult offenders. Moreover, youth committed to Houses of Refuge for various types of conditions or behaviors—ranging from appearance to language to growing up improperly—had not been subject to institutionalization before this time. Thus, Houses of Refuge marked an important expansion in state control of children (and of parents, too) (Bernard 1992; Fox 1970a; Platt 1972).

Houses of Refuge were also intended to compensate for an anomaly in the application of the criminal law (Bernard 1992). The relative harshness of criminal penalties in some instances had led to dismissals and acquittals of charges against some youthful defendants. Thus, these juveniles escaped penalties and consequences for their behaviors. The Quakers believed this learning process to be counterproductive for these beginning criminals, much like it was to confine them with adults. They believed Houses of Refuge would serve as a compromise measure, discouraging the extension of dangerous and unnecessary leniency to young offenders.

Juveniles could be committed to Houses of Refuge until their majority or adulthood began.[2] The daily regimen included various types of academic and moral instruction and physical labor. Workshops were established on the premises, enabling many youth to perform contract labor without ever leaving the facility (Mennel 1973). Most of the youth aged out, escaped, or were apprenticed or indentured to trades people. The escapes led to the Houses becoming more security conscious and prisonlike. The apprenticeships led to youth being placed all around the country in various jobs. Some of these children were permanently separated from their families (Bernard 1992; Mennel 1973; Pisciotta 1982). Houses of Refuge fell out of favor and use within a little more than a couple of decades.

Legal Foundation for the Houses of Refuge

Although their success was limited and their tenure short lived, Houses of Refuge provided a critical foundation for the desirability of separating juveniles from adults. Even more important, however, are the legal doctrines and precedents established at this time. It was certainly an accomplishment for the Quakers to have secured the endorsement of their social program from the legislatures in several states. Nevertheless, their movement would have been for naught if the state appellate courts had not granted it judicial sanction. In 1839, the Pennsylvania Supreme Court became the first state appellate court to provide that vital approval in *Ex parte Crouse*.

Mary Crouse's mother had committed her daughter to the Philadelphia House of Refuge for incorrigibility (failing to obey her lawful commands). After failing to secure her release, Mary's father filed a writ of *habeas corpus*, objecting to Mary's incarceration without a jury trial. The purpose of the writ was to demand that the state justify the incarceration of the girl. In a single paragraph, the Pennsylvania court dismissed the father's complaint and endorsed every facet of the Quakers' social program:

> The House of Refuge is not a prison, but a school, where reformation, and not punishment, is the end. . . . The object of the charity is reformation, by training its inmates to industry; by imbuing their minds with principles of morality and religion; by furnishing them with means to earn a living; and above all by separating them from the corrupting influence of improper associates. To this end may not the natural parents, when unequal to the task, or unworthy of it, be superceded by the *parens patriae,* or common guardian of the community? It is to be remembered that the public has a paramount interest in the virtue and knowledge of its members, and that of strict right, the business of education belongs to it. That parents are ordinarily entrusted with it is because it can seldom be put into better hands; but where they are incompetent or corrupt, what is there to prevent the public from withdrawing their facilities, held, as they obviously are, at its sufferance? The right of parental control is a natural, but not an inalienable one. . . . As to the abridgment of indefeasible rights by confinement of the person, it is no more than what is borne, to a greater or less extent, in every school; and we know of no natural right to exemption from restraints which conduct to an infant's welfare. Nor is there a doubt of the propriety of their application in the particular instance. The infant has to be snatched from a course which must have ended in confirmed depravity; and not only is the restraint of her person lawful, but it would be an act of extreme cruelty to release her from it.[3]

Perhaps the most important feature of the *Crouse* decision was the Pennsylvania court's creation of legal doctrine that upheld the Quakers' program. Prior to this era, parents faced only two likely situations in which they would lose custody of their children: loss of liberty due to conviction of crime, or being apprenticed out of the household due to the family's inability to provide financial support. The types of juveniles targeted by the Quakers' program extended well beyond these parameters, however. The legislatures had agreed that the Quakers were better equipped than some natural parents to fulfill the parental role. Nevertheless, the legislatures had not cited any common law principle or constitutional authorization that would allow the Quakers to take parental responsibility from parents who had neither abused nor abandoned their children or become financially dependent on the state. The Pennsylvania Supreme Court supplied that critical principle or authorization.

The *parens patriae* (or "father of the country") doctrine originated in England in the fourteenth century. It dealt with the king's appointment of a representative to manage the estate of any child of nobility who had been orphaned. This financial arrangement helped prevent the exploitation of these children while preserving members of noble ranks who were instrumental to the protection and preservation of the monarchy (Cogan 1970; Rendleman 1971). The doctrine had absolutely nothing to do with either stripping children from their families or incarcerating poor, obnoxious, petty criminal youth. The doctrine underwent a serious transformation at the hands of the Pennsylvania court. After its transatlantic voyage, *parens patriae* emerged in the *Crouse* decision as both the duty and license for the state to raise children seen as not being reared properly. The Quakers had been provided invaluable legal justification for their social intervention. As other state appellate courts addressed the legitimacy of their Houses of Refuge, the *parens patriae* doctrine was cited as the authorization for these institutions.[4] The doctrine would eventually become the legal foundation for juvenile courts, as we will see.

The *Crouse* decision also initiated what is known today as the *quid pro quo* (or "this for that") exchange: Because the intention of the state intervention is benevolent in that only treatment is dispensed, youth must surrender or exchange all rights they would have against a malevolent state that dispensed only punishment (Schultz and Cohen 1976). The concept of *quid pro quo* continues to be a major facet of juvenile court operation today.

Reformatories and Separate Trial Dockets

Further support for separating juveniles from adults occurred with the development of industrial or reform schools and reformatories in the mid-nineteenth century. These facilities had appeared already in England earlier in the century. Some Houses of Refuge actually evolved into reformatories, which were meant to house young criminals, including serious offenders. Reformatories inherited not only the Refuge's buildings, but also their educational and vocational programs approach to rehabilitating youth. Moreover, in addition to those who committed crimes, reformatories incarcerated children being brought up to lead an idle or vicious life—just as Houses of Refuge had. Laws instigated by the Quakers to enhance the childrearing intervention powers of the state (i.e., to replace unfit parents) survived the demise of Houses of Refuge (Dorne and Gewirth 1995).

Thus, although the Quakers themselves fell out of the forefront in directing juvenile-oriented correctional policy, their fundamental beliefs continued to steer policies regarding youth for some time. In fact, most of their beliefs are alive and well today.

A good deal of the reform school activity was centered in the midwest, especially Chicago. Although the Chicago Reform School movement mirrored the principles and operational methods of the Quakers, its success in the appellate courts was less even. In fact, the Illinois Supreme Court condemned virtually everything the Pennsylvania Supreme Court had praised in the *Ex parte Crouse* ruling. In *People v. Turner* in 1870, the Illinois court questioned the ability of the state to act as a surrogate parent and the legitimacy of the *parens patriae* doctrine in justifying substitute state parenthood. The court also objected to the idea that idleness and poverty inevitably lead to crime and that incarceration was possible even though no crime had been committed. Exacerbating matters was the fact that the incarceration was of indeterminate length. Nevertheless, a dozen

Many reformatories and reform schools were former Houses of Refuge. How punitive should reform schools be toward juvenile offenders?

years later the same court reversed its position. The court endorsed *parens patriae* and insisted that reform schools were benevolent and constructive enterprises that were equivalent to regular public schools. The court also placed little significance in the notion that children enjoy liberty and that they should be free from state intervention even in the absence of criminal behavior.[5]

Complementing the correctional separation of youth and adults was the development in Massachusetts of a system of probation (or community supervision) for juvenile offenders (Ryerson 1978). Even more important, perhaps, was that state's introduction of separate trial dockets for youth, which was adopted in other northeastern states as well. Here, both juvenile and adult offenders were prosecuted by the same court but at separate hearings. Different trial times were given to defendants based on their age. At this point, the notion of separating youth from adults had spread from the correctional component of the criminal justice system to the court stage.

The Emergence of Juvenile Court

The nineteenth-century theme of separation culminated in the juvenile court movement of the 1890s. A group of socially prominent women from Chicago (referred to in the literature as both the Chicago women and the child savers[6]) lobbied extensively throughout the decade to secure a separate system for juveniles. Among these advocates for a new juvenile court were Jane Addams and Julia Lathrop of the Settlement House movement. The Chicago women faced many of the social ills that had plagued the Quakers: immigration, urban poverty, and crime. They also viewed these problems in much the same way as the Quakers had. Poverty and social structure contribute to or evolve into crime. Youth must be separated from corrupting adults and negative urban surroundings in order to be rehabilitated (or socialized properly). The state, now represented by the Chicago women, needed to serve as replacement parents for those not doing the job correctly. Finally, education, in addition to therapeutic intervention, would "cure" juveniles of their problems, which manifested themselves in obnoxious and criminal behavior (Fox 1970a; Platt 1972).

One extra tool available to the Chicago women was the recent emergence of the field of psychology. The plan was to have their juvenile system managed by those with professional expertise in treatment who would be able to help youth to turn their lives around. The child savers were also inspired by thoughts of social justice (President's Commission 1967). As one examiner of the juvenile court movement explained:

> The juvenile court is conspicuously a response to the modern spirit of social justice. It is perhaps the first legal tribunal where law and science, especially the science of medicine and those sciences which deal with human behavior, such as biology, sociology, and psychology, work side by side. It recognizes the fact that the law unaided is incompetent to decide what is adequate treatment of delinquency and crime. It undertakes to define and readjust social situations without the sentiment of prejudice. Its approach to the problem which the child presents is scientific, objective, and dispassionate. The methods it uses are those of social case work, in which every child is studied and treated as an individual. (Lou 1927:2)

Overall, there were many important similarities between the Quakers and the Chicago women, ranging from their viewpoints to their motives. Much like the Quakers, the child savers have been credited with selfish reasons (such as trying to control the poor and immigrants) for launching the juvenile court movement (Fox 1970a; Platt 1972). One serious difference between the two groups is that the Chicago women aimed their reform at a broader juvenile population (i.e., all children with problems, whether poor, troublesome, or criminal). In addition, they developed their intervention at a broader level (i.e., separate courts and correctional components). The child savers were convinced that waiting until the correctional period to show benevolence to children was wrong. Instead, compassion needed to occur earlier in the court process (Platt 1972).

In 1899, the Chicago women finally convinced their legislative representatives (the Cook County legislature) to pass the first Juvenile Court Act, authorizing them to channel youth *en masse* into their juvenile justice system. The act was written so as to apply to virtually every child whose behavior could be perceived as criminal or problematic. It would not be unfair or extreme to say that nearly every child in existence at some point would have qualified for the system's intervention. A *delinquent* was defined as anyone who:

> violates any law of the State; or is incorrigible or knowingly associates with thieves, vicious or immoral persons; or without just cause and without the consent of its parents, guardians, or custodians absents itself from its home or place of abode, or is growing up in idleness or crime; or knowingly frequents any policy shop or place where any gaming device is operated; or frequents any saloon or draw shop where any intoxicating liquors are sold or patronizes or visits any public pool room or bucket shop; or wanders about the streets in the night time without being on any lawful business or lawful occupation; or habitually wanders about any railroad yards or jumps or attempts to jump onto a moving train; or enters any car or engine without lawful authority; or uses vile, obscene, vulgar, profane or indecent language in any public place or about any schoolhouse; or is guilty of indecent or lascivious conduct.[7]

The child savers were determined not to let the potential absence of any specific conduct per se (such as that the youth did not actually commit a particular crime) stand in the way of their helping any juvenile who appeared to need help.

The Legal Foundation of Juvenile Court

The original Juvenile Court Act provided for a jury trial of six members, perhaps due to a fear that the Illinois Supreme Court would strike the act down and follow its ruling in *People v. Turner*. It soon became the norm, however, for youth to be processed without any constitutional rights or safeguards (such as counsel or jury trial). In fact, the second Juvenile Court Act from Cook County deleted the reference to jury trial. Moreover, as the idea of juvenile courts spread throughout the country, which it did at a remarkable pace (all but two states had juvenile courts by 1925), the standard legislation omitted any reference to defendants' possession of rights.

Here lies another significant difference between the juvenile court and the House of Refuge movement. As we have already seen, the latter housed primarily poor youth that had not been given any rights. However, processing poor youth in this manner did not mark a radical departure from traditional poor law policy. Nevertheless, juvenile courts were prosecuting criminal offenders this way also. Some offenders were charged with serious crimes such as murder and rape. This certainly did constitute a break in legal tradition. It also arguably amounted to a statutory nullification of each state's constitution. To be fair, adult offenders during the first half of the twentieth century did not enjoy the abundance of rights that are the hallmarks of criminal courts today. Until the creation of juvenile courts, however, juveniles enjoyed the same defendants' rights as comparably situated adults. State constitutions did not differentiate rights by virtue of age. Without amending their constitutions, however, one state legislature after another simply passed new juvenile court laws that stripped juvenile criminal defendants of the rights they had enjoyed previously. Thus, a mere law or legislative act ended up negating various constitutional provisions.

Before long, juveniles challenged the outcome of the juvenile court laws. As it had done in the House of Refuge movement, the Pennsylvania Supreme Court would be the first appellate court to review the legitimacy of juvenile courts' prosecuting defendants without any rights. The Pennsylvania court upheld this aspect of juvenile court procedure in *Commonwealth v. Fisher* in 1905. This decision reads like a repetition of the 1839 *Crouse* opinion. It granted juvenile courts critical appellate court approval to operate without the interference of constitutional rights:

> To save a child from becoming a criminal, or from continuing a career in crime, to end in maturer years in public punishment and disgrace, the Legislature surely may provide for the salvation of such a child, if its parents or guardians be unable or unwilling to do so, by bringing it into one of the courts of the state without any process at all, for the purpose of subjecting it to the state's guardianship and protection. The natural parent needs no process to temporarily deprive his child of its liberty by confining it in his own home, to save it and to shield it from the consequences of persistence in a career of waywardness; nor is the state, when compelled, as *parens patriae*, to take the place of the father for the same purpose, required to adopt any process as a means of placing its hands upon the child to lead it into one of its courts. When the child gets there, and the court, with the power to save it, determines on its salvation, and not its punishment, it is immaterial how it got there. The act simply provides how children who ought to be saved may reach the court to be saved.[8]

Although the same basic words had appeared in *Crouse,* what the Pennsylvania Supreme Court said and did in *Fisher* was radical. For one thing, the court transported the *quid pro quo* formula (i.e., the juvenile's trade of rights for the state's protection and treatment) from the welfare-oriented Houses of Refuge—where the state would not seem to have had any reason to hurt young people since they had not done anything criminal—to the juvenile justice system—where the state also promised to be nice to young folks, although many of them would have committed crimes, sometimes serious ones. Thus, even though the Quakers had proven to be fairly harsh and punitive with a population of youth who primarily had been hurting themselves and not others, the Pennsylvania court was willing to believe that juvenile court officials would not be harsh or punitive with a juvenile population, many of whom had seriously hurt others. The Pennsylvania Supreme Court also stretched the *parens patriae* doctrine—now twice removed from its original context of estate management—so as to allow its legislature to take constitutional rights from juveniles charged with criminal behavior. The *Fisher* decision used *parens patriae* to bestow on juvenile court complete power—with virtually no controls or checks and balances—over essentially all children. Equally fascinating is the fact that as the operation of juvenile courts was challenged in state after state throughout the country, nearly every appellate court cited *Commonwealth v. Fisher,* together with its version of *parens patriae,* as the guiding and controlling precedent for denying rights to juvenile defendants.

The Reasons Juvenile Defendants Had No Rights in Juvenile Court

Throughout the first half of the twentieth century, five basic reasons for stripping juvenile defendants of their constitutional rights were offered by various sources. These sources ranged from authors of articles and books that explained and defended juvenile court practice to appellate court opinions (such as *Fisher*) that upheld that practice.

First, constitutional rights were *unnecessary.* Juveniles did not need rights because the juvenile system was benevolent and rehabilitative and not punitive (the basis for the *quid pro quo* exchange). The system was seeking to help rather than to hurt youth. Moreover, the juvenile system was not adversary like the adult system. In criminal court, the state positions itself as the adversary or enemy of the accused. Two distinct interests are at work in this system: the state's (to convict and punish) and the defendant's (to escape from the state's mission). In the juvenile system, however, there was only one interest at stake, namely, the youth's. The state was seeking only what would promote the best interests of the child.

Second, rights were *inappropriate* because the inquiry in juvenile court was directed to the youth's condition or problem rather than to any conduct per se. Rights are appropriate in criminal court because the contest there involves allegations that certain behavior has occurred. Thus, defense attorneys appropriately challenge (by confrontation and cross examination) those who have made allegations about their clients. Similarly, juries are appropriate in determining the credibility of the accuser and the validity of the charges. In juvenile court, however, the conduct that brought the youth to the attention of the system was viewed as a mere symptom of the problem. At best the conduct was a secondary concern that might be ignored altogether. In other words, proving a burglary charge was not what juvenile court was all about. Instead, juvenile court was about finding what prompted the juvenile to commit a burglary. The focus of juvenile court was on the learning, behavioral, or emotional disorder (or whatever) that contributed to or caused the misbehavior. It probably would have been more accurate to use the term "juvenile clinic" instead of juvenile court. Thus, defense attorneys who lack diagnostic expertise, and juries, who may be even worse, are inappropriate for the nature of the inquiry conducted in juvenile court.

Third, rights were *harmful* for a variety of reasons. For one thing, defending rights can be costly and time-consuming. Even worse, rights might enable a youth who needed help to escape from the system. Rights are geared to limit or to prevent the state's intervention, not to facilitate it. Juvenile court proponents considered rights counterproductive, since arming a youth with rights, like the right to counsel, could frustrate the court's ability to diagnose a problem and to prescribe a solution. A third way in which rights were harmful concerned the juvenile court's desire for informality and secrecy. Juvenile courts were designed to function like informal clinics rather than formal public courtrooms. That is, the inquiry into the youth's problem needed to be free flowing and receptive to all sources and types of information, much like a visit to a doctor's office. Formal rules of evidence would limit the consideration of information, which would harm the court's investigation and the likelihood of discovering the problem. In addition, juvenile courts were designed to operate behind closed doors so as not to publicly brand the youth as an offender. Revealing the identity of a juvenile defendant could compromise the rehabilitation effort, since the community might never forgive or forget one it knows to have committed a crime. Providing the juvenile with the right to a public and jury trial (where even the media might attend) was perceived as undermining the goals of juvenile justice. Finally, rights were harmful in a public relations way. That is, granting juveniles rights would speak negatively of the image of juvenile court. After all, rights are associated with criminal court because of its desire to hurt and maybe seriously harm the offender. Extending rights to juvenile defendants would suggest that the juvenile justice system actually must be hurting children. It must really be a clone of the criminal justice system. Such an association with the adult system could sabotage the identity, mission, and survival of the juvenile court.

Fourth, rights were *undeserved* or *uncalled for,* meaning juveniles were not entitled to rights. Adults have rights by virtue of their right to liberty, which cannot be taken from them without due process of law or rights. Juveniles, on the other hand, do not enjoy a right to liberty. They cannot even run away from home until they are 16 years old. Instead, juveniles are seen as having a right to protective custody, which is precisely what juvenile court is trying to guarantee the youth.

Fifth, rights were *inapplicable* because of the unique vocabulary used in juvenile justice. Constitutional rights are granted to those who are arrested, prosecuted, convicted, sentenced, punished, and imprisoned. As we know from Chapter 1, none of these phenomena happen to youth processed by the juvenile justice system. Consequently, rights do not apply to the events experienced by those defendants.

Combined, these five reasons resulted in juvenile court officials enjoying substantial powers for more than six decades. These reasons served as a formidable, coherent rhetoric or philosophy in rationalizing and justifying the appropriateness of stripping juvenile defendants of their constitutional rights. Even today, after the U.S. Supreme Court eliminated the idea that juvenile defendants deserve no rights (see Chapter 3), most of the five reasons are alive and well. They continue to serve as a basis for denying some rights to juveniles. In fact, the only reason that can be viewed today as having been laid to rest is the one dealing with rights as *inappropriate.* In light of what transpires today in juvenile court, there is little chance of anyone's confusing it with a clinic.

The Juvenile Justice System, 1899–1967: An Overview

Prior to the U.S. Supreme Court's intervention in the last part of the 1960s, juvenile court officials enjoyed almost absolute control over the fates of the young people they processed. Whether this power was abused depended on the location of the juvenile court, or, more accurately, on the integrity of the two people who truly ran the show: the judge and the probation officer. These two individuals accounted for virtually all the meaningful power rendered by juvenile court. There is no way to gauge exactly what most juvenile courts were like or what they were doing to young people during this period. Suffice it to say that some truly helped children, while others truly hurt some or most of the youth they encountered. Generally, the following represents the imbalance of power in favor of the state that likely characterized most (and perhaps the vast majority of) juvenile courts throughout the country before the Supreme Court intervened in the late 1960s.

The Law

Like adults, juveniles were subject to the provisions of the criminal law. Beyond that, however, juveniles also answered to laws that covered behavior illegal only for youth (status offenses). These laws were written in such vague and broad language as "growing up in idleness or crime or vice" or "living in conditions injurious to one's health or welfare." Theoretically, these laws could be describing any juvenile living in an urban area, which is precisely what juvenile court workers wanted. In the event that a criminal charge that brought a juvenile to court could not be proved (assuming that even mattered), the availability of broad and vague status offense provisions guaranteed that court officials could find nearly everyone "guilty" of at least something. This ability was critical if the child needed help and would have had to have been officially adjudicated in order to receive that help. The laws were sufficiently comprehensive to ensure that the court would not witness any needy child falling through the cracks and being denied help.

The Police

Law enforcement officers experienced little, if anything, in the way of controls over their behavior with youth. Probable cause to arrest (required to arrest adults) was not needed with young people, since no arrest occurred. Instead, juveniles were taken into custody. No standard of evidence necessary for doing so was identified. This suggests that police needed only a good reason or perhaps a benevolent or protective purpose. Whatever occurred in the way of a search and seizure was not an issue, as there was no exclusionary rule in juvenile court that would block the use or admission of "illegally" seized items as evidence (assuming any evidence was relevant or necessary). The same applied to any confessions secured by police through interrogation. Probably the only development that might cause police to be careful in their acquiring evidence from juveniles was the prospect that an offender's case could be transferred to criminal court, where the exclusionary rule, among other controls, was observed.

The Court

Traditionally, the juvenile court process has begun very shortly after "arrest," perhaps within only hours. The powers shared by judges and probation officers have been absolute. The front end of the process was controlled by the probation officer (PO). This official, alone, decided whether to detain the youth (pending the inquiry), how thoroughly to investigate the situation, whether to refer the case to court, and what to recommend to the judge in the way of an outcome or disposition (which was almost always followed). Pretrial detention, which in some places ran indefinitely, could be imposed without a hearing on the mere word or opinion of the PO. Typically, there was no right to bail, as juveniles have no right to liberty. Depending on how well the police had developed the case, coupled with the extent of the PO's curiosity and integrity, there would be a more or less thorough investigation of the circumstances surrounding the individual. This inquiry could include questioning victims, witnesses, arresting officer(s), the offender, family, neighbors, and school authorities; examining the youth's court record, if any, including delinquent history and previous dispositions as well as any prior matters involving parents and siblings; consulting the school record to discover discipline problems and academic abilities; and developing a treatment plan, ranging anywhere from allowing the young persons to return home to placement in a variety of facilities or—failing that—recommending the juvenile be sent to the adult system.

Juvenile courts were founded more as clinics than as courts. Does the juvenile court in this photo have the atmosphere of a clinic or a courthouse?

Based on what the PO determined, the case would be dismissed (due to either no evidence or, more likely, no problem with the youth), handled informally by the PO, or sent forward to the adjudicatory level. Inasmuch as only those juveniles who supposedly had a problem were referred to the judge, these cases entered the adjudicatory stage or "trial" with a significant prejudice. POs would deliver the case file and treatment plan to the judge (even in urban areas there might be only one judge) some time prior to the hearing. The judge may or may not have read the material before the child's appearance at court.

The juvenile's "day in court" was probably closer to five minutes or so. There was no trial per se. The PO had already done all the work, and, if there wasn't a problem, the case would not have been referred to court. Juveniles typically appeared with a parent or two, and they, plus the court workers, would be the only ones in the courtroom or judge's chambers. There was no need for victims or witnesses to appear or to testify (the police or the PO had already heard from them), so offenders had no opportunity to confront and cross-examine their accusers. Poor juveniles were not provided counsel. Even those who could afford to retain counsel could be denied these services until after adjudication. Judges could simply tell defense lawyers that the hearing was private and that their input was not desired or allowed until a disposition was to be imposed. If judges had any lingering doubts or curiosity, they could question defendants or demand an explanation (the privilege against self-incrimination did not exist). The right to jury trial was not granted. Most (perhaps all) defenses were unavailable to defendants. Even a self-defense situation could mean a youth needed some help—possibly unrelated to the incident itself (e.g., school attendance problems).

The defense of infancy was ignored. Common law had held that children younger than 7 years of age could never be convicted of crime because of their irrebuttable inability to form *mens rea* (intent). These children were irresponsible and could not legally be punished. Offenders between the ages of 7 and 14 could be convicted, but the prosecutor had a special burden to overcome. It was thus a rebuttable or challengeable presumption that these children could not form intent. Anyone older than 14 years of age was treated, presumptively, as a responsible adult. Juvenile court law eradicated these age groups. All children were now considered irresponsible and in need of help. Moreover, since juveniles were being neither convicted nor punished, the concept of responsibility was irrelevant. As a result, juveniles of all ages were vulnerable to adjudication. Finally, preponderance of evidence was cited as the standard of proof required to adjudicate in juvenile court. Whether that standard or any was observed most likely depended on what POs and judges thought was best at the time. Court records typically reflected only that the individual was adjudicated delinquent without specifying the nature or level of offense.[9]

Sentences or dispositions were indeterminate, lasting until the juvenile was 21 years old or rehabilitated, whichever occurred first. The potential length of commitment supposedly was unrelated to the current number or severity of charges. The prior record and previous dispositions were important in determining whether commitment was appropriate or necessary. Most courts had an obligation to remove the child from his or her home only as a last resort and to impose the least restrictive disposition. The extent to which courts adhered to this mandate would be difficult to ascertain. Offenders typically had no right to appeal an adjudication in juvenile court.

The Corrections

Juveniles assigned to community supervision were subject to the considerable discretionary powers of POs, who held the juveniles' fates in their hands with minimal, if any, oversight from the court. A young person who ignored the PO's directives (which may or may not have been consistent with the court's disposition order) could receive a weekend (or more) in detention. Violation of a dispositional provision exposed the juvenile to another summary hearing that could culminate in institutionalization. The extent to which POs abused this lofty power would be difficult to verify.

The institutions to which youth were committed also enjoyed extensive control over inmates (although the same can be said about adult prisons during this period). Juveniles encountered a full gamut of possibilities. Some of the facilities—especially some privately run operations—could boast of serious and sincere efforts to rehabilitate youth and were among the finest accomplishments of the juvenile justice system. Other juvenile institutions—most notably some state training and industrial schools—deservedly earned reputations as the full equivalent of any adult prison and offered little, if anything, in the way of rehabilitation. Thus, the regimens to which youth were exposed ranged from therapeutic counseling and positive educational and recreational measures to simple warehousing and physical beatings (by either staff or other inmates). Successful completion of a rehabilitation program was supposed to signal eligibility for release from the facility. This release could occur within months, or could take years, and was subject to the staff's evaluation of the child's progress (or lack thereof) in treatment. The juveniles' cooperation (and perhaps games playing) with the authorities, then, should have been instrumental in their gaining freedom.

All in all, the juvenile justice system in its first six-plus decades was one marked with significant powers, little if any accountability, and virtually no outside scrutiny. How well juvenile court did the job it was created to do, rather than simply exploit both its powers and the youth involved, depended pretty much on luck and location, influenced mostly by the integrity of the system's personnel.

Summary: Key Ideas and Concepts

- The Quakers' role in social reform in early America
- America in transition in the early nineteenth century
- The dual nature of the Quakers' intentions in reforming youth
- The four major beliefs of the Quakers
- The type of youth committed to Houses of Refuge
- Houses of Refuge as expansion of state control over children and parents
- The manner in which youth were committed to Houses of Refuge
- The manner in which youth were treated in Houses of Refuge
- The *parens patriae* doctrine as it was originally applied
- The role played by the *parens patriae* doctrine in juvenile court
- The trade of rights for treatment or the *quid pro quo* exchange
- Further separation of youth from adults in the late 1800s
- Similarities between the child savers' and Quakers' beliefs and intentions
- The breadth of the Juvenile Court Act
- The five reasons defendants had no rights in juvenile court
- The operation of the informal juvenile justice system for six decades

Discussion Questions

1. Discuss how America was changing in the early nineteenth century and how the Quakers responded to that change.

2. Compare the four pivotal Quaker beliefs to current ideas in these areas.

3. Explain the role played by Houses of Refuge in initiating the separation of youth from adults.

4. Discuss the appropriateness of the Pennsylvania Supreme Court's use of the *parens patriae* doctrine and the *quid pro quo* exchange in both the *Crouse* and *Fisher* decisions.

5. Explain how most of the child savers' work had been completed before their efforts in creating juvenile court.

6. Discuss the appropriateness of the expansion of state control over youth and parents as represented in the reforms of both the Quakers and the child savers.

7. Which, if any, of the five reasons defendants had no rights in juvenile court have merit?

8. Discuss the implications of the informal way in which juvenile justice operated for more than six decades.

Endnotes

1. Society for the Reformation of Pauperism in the City of New York, "Report on the Subject of Erecting a House of Refuge for Vagrant and Depraved Young People," reprinted in Society for the Reformation of Juvenile Delinquents, *Documents Relative to the House of Refuge*, p. 13 (N. Hart. ed., 1832).
2. For boys this meant to 21 years of age, while for girls it was 18 years of age.
3. *Ex Parte Crouse*, 4 Wharton 9, 11 (Pa. 1839).
4. See, e.g., *Roth v. House of Refuge*, 31 Md. 329 (1869); *Ex parte Ah Peen*, 51 Cal 280 (1876); *House of Refuge v. Ryan*, 37 Oh State 197 (1881); *In the Matter of the Petition of Alexander Ferrier*, 103 Ill. 367 (1882).
5. See *In the Matter of the Petition of Alexander Ferrier*, supra note 4. Remarkably, the Illinois Supreme Court yet again reversed its position a mere six years later in *County of Cook v. The Chicago Industrial School for Girls*, 125 Ill 540 (1888). In this case the state court objected to the denial of rights to female youth committed to this early type of reform school, despite the good intentions of the women who ran the school.
6. The term *child savers* was taken from a book with the same name written by Anthony Platt. Platt (1972) examined the efforts of these individuals in establishing the first juvenile court.
7. Revised Laws of Illinois, 1899, p. 131.
8. *Commonwealth v. Fisher*, 62 A 198, 200 (Pa. 1905).
9. Most of the account of the typical adjudicatory hearing was drawn from research conducted by the senior author concerning life in juvenile court before the *In re Gault* decision of 1967 (see Chapter 3). The research was presented as a paper at the American Society of Criminology November 1987 conference in Montreal, Canada. The title of the paper is "*In re Gault* and the Juvenile Court: What Twenty Years of Constitutional Domestication Have Wrought." (Sanborn 1987a) ✦

United States Supreme Court Intervention: The Legal Framework of Juvenile Justice

Focus of Chapter 3

Chapter 3 is dedicated to explaining the way in which the U.S. Supreme Court decided to revise juvenile court operation. Important here is the balance the Court determined was necessary in juvenile court. There would be neither too few nor too many rights granted to juvenile defendants. This balance-only formula the Supreme Court pursued allowed juvenile courts to be cleaned up without being eliminated.

Key Terms

- Bill of Rights
- domino theory
- double jeopardy
- Fourteenth Amendment's due process clause
- Warren Court

The Need for Changes in Juvenile Court Procedures

From the beginning, juvenile courts have been both condemned and praised. Some commentators have been impressed and pleased by the juvenile court's mission, while others have been concerned and dismayed by the court's abuse of its powers. With some exceptions, juvenile corrections have been lamented from the start. It seems as though few observers see this branch of the juvenile system as having been granted adequate resources to make it effective. Negative comments about the juvenile system began to circulate not long after its founding and were especially prevalent during the 1950s and 1960s. Some addressed the powers of the court; others focused on the failure to deliver services (Allen 1964; Comment 1966; Handler 1965; Ketcham 1965; Notes 1966, 1967; Paulsen 1957; President's Commission 1967). These criticisms eventually played a critical role in the U.S. Supreme Court's decision to alter the operation of the juvenile system in the 1960s.

Prior to that intervention, the Supreme Court had been given two opportunities to change the direction of

Did the U.S. Supreme Court grant juvenile defendants adequate rights in juvenile court?

juvenile court, but declined to do so on both occasions. In the 1930s a juvenile from New York complained about the imbalance of power in juvenile court. His challenge was unsuccessful throughout the New York court system, and his appeal to the Supreme Court was denied (*People v. Lewis* 1932). Similarly, in the 1950s a Pennsylvania boy objected to being processed by juvenile court without any rights. He experienced the same results as the New York youth (*In re Holmes* 1954). To be fair, the Supreme Court during this period was not inclined to require an abundance of rights for defendants in criminal courts. The point is, however, that although it was made aware of the way in which juvenile court processed cases, the Supreme Court elected not to introduce any rights for defendants within the juvenile court's jurisdiction during the first half of the twentieth century.

Establishing the Legal Framework of Juvenile Justice in *Kent v. United States*

The Supreme Court first examined an issue directly related to the juvenile justice system in *Kent v. United States* in 1966. The case involved a youth from Washington, D.C., whose multiple burglary and rape charges were transferred to criminal court for trial. We will discuss what *Kent* required of juvenile court in Chapter 12, which deals with transfer to adult court. More important than what the Court ruled in *Kent* was the fact that the Court had already accepted for review another juvenile case, *In re Gault* (1967), which promised to have a far greater impact on the future of juvenile court. Gault involved a youth's request to be granted six constitutional rights during the adjudicatory hearing. Whereas the *Kent* case involved relatively few juveniles destined to be transferred to adult court (and supposedly only those in Washington, D.C.), *Gault* promised to affect the nature of processing defendants in juvenile court throughout the country. Moreover, the Supreme Court knew that the success of the juvenile in *Gault* would signal the beginning of juvenile defendants everywhere seeking to be given all the rights that had been offered to adults. By 1966 and 1967 the list of rights for adults was extensive and ever growing. Thus, the Supreme Court that wrote the *Kent* decision clearly anticipated *Gault* and what would follow *Gault.* Despite *Kent's* limited focus (transfer to adult court in D.C. only), the Supreme Court spent more time with this case analyzing the national juvenile justice story and establishing a legal framework for the system than in ruling what must happen when a juvenile is transferred to criminal court.

Two other items help explain the *Kent* decision. First, *Kent* would mark the first words uttered by the nation's highest court about a reform movement that was at that point 67 years old. As mentioned earlier, numerous commentaries had surfaced documenting the legal abuse experienced by many defendants at the hands of juvenile court. The purported savior of children was frequently characterized as arbitrary and harsh. Second, the Supreme Court of the 1960s was known as the Warren Court (after its chief justice, Earl Warren). The Warren Court had prided itself on the extensive cleanup of the criminal court by granting defendants there numerous constitutional rights. It had to be difficult for the justices to imagine how adjudicatory hearings in juvenile courts were operating so fundamentally differently than trial in criminal courts and how this situation had continued during the Warren Court era.

We have provided the background to help explain why the Supreme Court in *Kent* went well beyond the parameters of the narrow issue the case presented. The Court developed a legal framework in *Kent* that would thereafter guide its evaluation of the rights that juveniles must be granted during trial in juvenile court and that continues to exist today. Although the ruling was critical in suggesting that certain rights had to be extended to juvenile defendants, it was just as critical, ultimately, in denying important constitutional rights sought by youth processed in juvenile court.

Anticipating future requests for rights at the adjudicatory hearing, the Supreme Court in *Kent* addressed and rejected what seemed to be the only two options when it came to granting rights to youth. First, juveniles could have been given *no rights*. This result would simply have continued the status quo and clearly would have supported the idea that juvenile court is nothing like adult court. Second, juveniles could have been given *all the same rights* that adults had been granted in criminal court. This result would have contradicted the first option and clearly would have suggested that juvenile courts are so much like criminal courts that no reason exists to distinguish the rights given to defendants in both systems. In other words, as Figure 3.1 shows, juvenile courts are either different from criminal courts (indicating the appropriateness of Option 1) or are the same as criminal courts (indicating the appropriateness of Option 2).

Neither of these options pleased the Supreme Court, however.

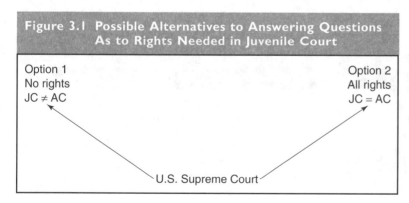

Figure 3.1 Possible Alternatives to Answering Questions As to Rights Needed in Juvenile Court

Option 1
No rights
JC ≠ AC

Option 2
All rights
JC = AC

U.S. Supreme Court

Both would present serious philosophical and practical problems. The difficulty with the first option was that the "no rights" choice would have perpetuated not only juvenile justice philosophy, but also the legal abuse characteristic of its court system. This outcome had to have been repugnant and unacceptable, especially to the Warren Court. At the same time, the second option, which equated the rights of juvenile and adult defendants, was fraught with serious implications. Equating the rights of the two defendants could have generated a domino theory. That is, granting equal rights would have made the systems equal (a complete "criminalization" of juvenile court), and would thereby have eliminated any philosophical justification for the separate existence of juvenile court. Moreover, to the extent that the two courts would have operated identically, there would have been no practical benefit to juvenile court's separate existence. That is, there would have been no saving of resources. The Supreme Court appears to have believed that the second option would have culminated, ultimately, in the demise of juvenile courts, an outcome that would have been a disaster not only for the masses of juvenile defendants who would have been forced into the criminal court, but for the criminal court as well, as it would have been threatened with a massive influx of defendants (see Figure 3.2).

The Court responded to this dilemma by creating Option 3. Because the extremes presented in Options 1 and 2 were undesirable, the Court simply steered a middle course between them, as shown in Figure 3.3. That is, it extended youth *some* rights (so juvenile court somewhat equals adult court), but not *all* rights enjoyed by adult defendants (so juvenile court somewhat does not equal adult court). What the Court intended was to clean up the juvenile court (by granting *some* rights) without sterilizing it out of existence (by granting *too many* rights).

The Supreme Court announced in *Kent* (and from then on) that defendants were entitled to fundamental fairness (i.e., the middle road or compromise position) in juvenile court. Precisely what fundamental fairness meant was impossible to determine until the Court would interpret a situation to see whether the issue or practice measured up to fundamental fairness. A good illustration of the Court's commitment in *Kent* to steering a middle course in juvenile justice

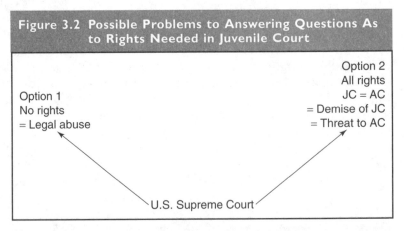

Figure 3.2 Possible Problems to Answering Questions As to Rights Needed in Juvenile Court

Option 1
No rights
= Legal abuse

Option 2
All rights
JC = AC
= Demise of JC
= Threat to AC

U.S. Supreme Court

Figure 3.3 Supreme Court Solution to Answering Questions As to Rights Needed in Juvenile Court

Option 3
Middle/compromise course
Some rights
JC = AC and
JC ≠ AC

Option 1

Option 2

Too extreme

U.S. Supreme Court

Too extreme

was its analysis of the *quid pro quo* exchange (i.e., juveniles give up rights in order to receive treatment)—a hallmark of the system. If the Supreme Court had felt allegiance to Option 1 (no rights), its probable description of the exchange would have been something like "Who can quarrel with the idea that youth would surrender mere procedural protections when the outcome of the intervention in juvenile court actually benefits the child?" Had Option 2 (all rights) been its preference, the Warren Court's most likely reaction would have been a challenge like "The very thought that a child charged with crime must surrender valuable safeguards, without ever having a say in that surrender, merely to receive certain rehabilitative services from the state is an outrage. Juveniles should not have to pay (with their rights) in order to receive some kindness from the state." As it turned out, the Court gave neither of these responses. Instead, it chose a middle ground, neither totally endorsing nor completely condemning *quid pro quo* (see Figure 3.4). The Court suggested that the application of the exchange—the complete absence of rights—was flawed in that it was too extreme. It needed to be adjusted. That is, at least some rights had to be given back to juvenile defendants.

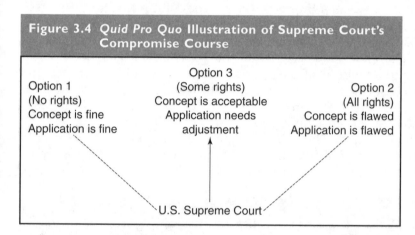

Figure 3.4 *Quid Pro Quo* Illustration of Supreme Court's Compromise Course

To conceptualize this legal framework another way, visualize a seesaw superimposed among the three options. Endorsing the extreme positions of Options 1 and 2 would place the seesaw with one end or the other squarely on the ground (like a heavy person would force a lighter rider to sit precariously in the air). This situation would result in an imbalance. *No rights* were too few and gave the state too much power, while *all rights* were too many and gave the state too much incentive to dissolve juvenile court. The Supreme Court wanted the seesaw to be perfectly parallel to the ground. The objective was to provide just enough rights to protect the youth from legal abuse without making juvenile court too inefficient and financially unattractive. Within only a few cases (and a few rights granted), the Supreme Court would announce that the appropriate balance had been achieved.

In re Gault and the Modification of Juvenile Court Procedure

The Supreme Court handed down *In re Gault* less than a year after *Kent.* It is the landmark juvenile justice case. The *Gault* decision was interesting in that it granted juvenile defendants four rights simultaneously, whereas adult defendants secured the rights given to them one at a time (or one per case). On the basis of a delinquent adjudication (for an obscene phone call), Gerald Gault had been committed to the Arizona State Industrial School for up to a six-year period. He was 15 at adjudication and would not have to be released until he was 21. Gault challenged his adjudication and requested six constitutional rights from the U.S. Supreme Court. He was granted four of them: notice of charges, counsel, confrontation and cross-examination of witnesses, and the privilege against self-incrimination. This meant that all defendants thereafter processed by all juvenile courts throughout the country would have to be granted these four rights, unless youth waived or surrendered these rights. (We will spend more time with this material in Chapter 13, which deals with the adjudicatory hearing.)

Gault continued and further developed the legal framework introduced in *Kent*. After reviewing some of the history and major principles of juvenile justice, the Supreme Court turned its attention to the *parens patriae* doctrine early in the opinion. Considering the importance of the doctrine, it was appropriate for the Court to do so. The Court's analysis of the doctrine reinforces the middle ground aspect of the legal framework (see Figure 3.5). If the Court had used Option 1 (no rights), its view of *parens patriae* would have echoed the opinions from the Pennsylvania Supreme Court cases of *Crouse* and *Fisher* (see Chapter 2). Thus, *parens patriae* would have been portrayed as the unassailable and legitimate authority and duty for the state to raise any children it believes are not being raised properly. If Option 2 (all rights) had been used, the Court would have acknowledged that *parens patriae* had nothing to do with what juvenile courts did to youth in America and was simply a convenient excuse for the state to strip juveniles and their parents of rights. The Supreme Court selected neither extreme position and instead cast the doctrine as murky in meaning, of dubious relevance, and of debatable constitutionality.[1]

To be sure, these descriptions are far from complimentary (like Option 1 would have been), but they are far from fatal (like Option 2 would have been). The Supreme Court seems to have been giving juvenile court workers a wake-up call and a warning. Although the juvenile court was on a shaky foundation and was about to be cleaned up by the Supreme Court, juvenile courts would not be forced to close their doors or to fear extermination.

Gault granted juvenile defendants four rights that provided youth the chance of receiving at least fundamental fairness at the adjudicatory hearing. Obviously, this is important. But *Gault* is actually more important for what it did *not* do than for what it did. Although four constitutional rights were "returned" to juvenile defendants, and although juvenile courts were made somewhat more like criminal courts (or criminalized), the Supreme Court refused to put juvenile and adult defendants on the same legal level (from fear of the domino effect). What the Court did was ingenuous, and the maneuver allowed it to clean up juvenile court without inflicting fatal damage.

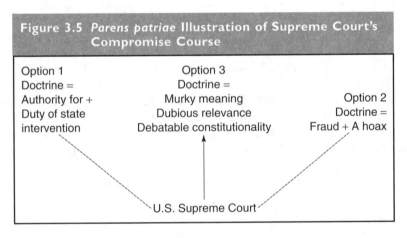

Figure 3.5 *Parens patriae* Illustration of Supreme Court's Compromise Course

| Option 1 Doctrine = Authority for + Duty of state intervention | Option 3 Doctrine = Murky meaning Dubious relevance Debatable constitutionality | Option 2 Doctrine = Fraud + A hoax |

U.S. Supreme Court

Was the U.S. Supreme Court correct in its belief of the domino effect that occurs by giving juveniles too many rights?

Through *Gault,* the Supreme Court was extending to juveniles four of the same rights it had already granted to adults. The implications were problematic. If juveniles needed or deserved four of the same constitutional rights, how could the Court prevent the logical extreme from occurring, in which youth would need or deserve all the same rights adults had been or would be given? The Court invented the solution to this problem in *Gault.* The answer was to declare that the constitutional standard that requires rights in juvenile court was *different* than the constitutional standard that requires rights in adult court. The *Gault* decision clearly signaled that thinking juvenile court was about to be transformed into a clone of criminal court was a mistake. That was neither the intention nor the desire of the Supreme Court.

Establishing a Legal Framework in *Gault*

Adult courts are obliged to guarantee defendants numerous trial-related constitutional rights, most of which are mentioned in the Fifth and Sixth Amendments of the Constitution (as are the four rights granted in *Gault*). These two amendments (and eight others) are part of the Bill of Rights, the first ten amendments to the Constitution that control many aspects of the operation of the federal and state governments, particularly the criminal courts. Defendants in state and federal criminal courts enjoy several rights because these courts must adhere to the relevant provisions of the Bill of Rights. Thus, defendants in criminal court have a Sixth Amendment right to counsel and a Fifth Amendment right to silence (or to not incriminate themselves). As a result of rather creative thinking by the Supreme Court in *Gault,* juvenile defendants were also given a right to counsel and silence, but *not* because of the Fifth or Sixth Amendments (despite the fact that those rights are mentioned in those amendments). *Gault* did not make juvenile court answer to the Bill of Rights. Had it done so, the Court would have been hard pressed to prevent *all* of the Bill of Rights from applying to and controlling juvenile court. This move would have amounted to the Court's adopting Option 2, and would have risked inviting the implications of the domino theory. Instead, the Supreme Court created a constitutional standard just for juvenile defendants and juvenile courts. The Supreme Court cited the Fourteenth Amendment's due process clause (often translated as fair treatment) as the source of the rights juvenile defendants would be given.

What rights are located in this constitutional provision? No one has any idea, except for the Supreme Court. That is because, unlike the Bill of Rights, the due process clause of the Fourteenth Amendment neither contains nor specifies any particular rights. Herein lies the brilliance of the *Gault* decision. Rights perceived to clean up juvenile court without seriously hurting it could be found to be a part of and required by due process. These rights would be extended to juvenile defendants. Rights perceived to constitute a threat to the survival of juvenile court could be found *not* to be a part of or required by due process. These rights would be denied to juvenile defendants. This constitutional standard allowed

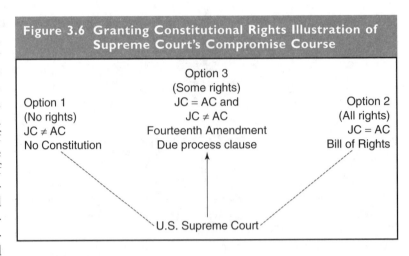

Figure 3.6 Granting Constitutional Rights Illustration of Supreme Court's Compromise Course

Option 3
(Some rights)
JC = AC and
JC ≠ AC
Fourteenth Amendment
Due process clause

Option 1
(No rights)
JC ≠ AC
No Constitution

Option 2
(All rights)
JC = AC
Bill of Rights

U.S. Supreme Court

the Supreme Court to carefully measure what rights would have a beneficial or a detrimental effect, which would then determine whether juvenile courts would be obliged to grant a particular right.

Gault told the country's juvenile courts that, for the moment, the due process clause required the four rights that were being given to young defendants. Although Justice Black agreed with the outcome of the case, he disagreed with the Court's reasoning. He did not believe in creating a special constitutional standard to govern juvenile courts. Justice Black was the only member of the Court who argued that the Bill of Rights should apply equally to juvenile and criminal courts, because he believed both sets of defendants experienced similar hardships and penalties. Justice Black thus openly endorsed Option 2 (all rights). It was obvious that the majority of justices in the *Gault* case did not share Black's opinion. He was forced to put his views in a separate concurring opinion (i.e., he agreed with only the result of granting juveniles the four rights involved). Moreover, no other justice signed his name to Black's opinion. Justice Black noted in his concurrence that he thought the case would prove problematic for juvenile courts, despite the Supreme Court's imaginative handling of the issue: "This holding strikes a well-nigh fatal blow to much that is unique about the juvenile courts in the Nation."[2]

Similarly, Justice Harlan voiced his concern that *Gault* could be read by some as an indication "that the Court is concerned principally with the wisdom of having such (juvenile) courts at all."[3] He was worried that granting juvenile defendants the right to confrontation and cross-examination and the protection against self-incrimination "might radically alter the character of juvenile court proceedings."[4] Justice Harlan split his vote. He agreed that juvenile defendants should be granted notice of charges and counsel but dissented against the extension of the other two rights. Justice Stewart went the farthest in concern about the implications of *Gault*. He viewed the decision as serving "to convert a juvenile proceeding into a criminal prosecution."[5] Stewart was the only justice to vote against extending all four rights at this time to juvenile defendants (he favored Option 1). He defended his position by suggesting that reuniting juvenile defendants with their constitutional rights could also end in reuniting youth with harsh punishments or the criminal justice system (the domino theory).

Putting *Gault* and the Legal Framework Into Context

As with all compromise verdicts, the *Gault* decision met criticism from all corners. Rehabilitation and crime control individuals complained that *Gault* went too far and undermined juvenile court by giving defendants too many costly rights. Due process proponents perceived *Gault* as not going far enough by refusing to equate the legal status of juvenile and adult defendants. At the very least, *Gault* contributed significantly to the Supreme Court's project of "cleaning up" juvenile court (much like the Warren Court had done in criminal court). Nevertheless, the compromise position assumed in *Gault* is seriously inconsistent, which, in the world of law and justice, is a major problem. The inconsistency stems from the Supreme Court's wanting it both ways. It wanted juvenile court to closely mirror criminal court without becoming an exact replica. In some ways, being much but not exactly like criminal court is as incongruous as being a little pregnant.

For example, the Supreme Court's insistence that juvenile courts provide defendants with notice of charges and the ability to confront and cross examine accusers is fundamental to justice and due process. At the same time, it poses no serious threat to the basic tenets of juvenile justice philosophy. If one is not notified of the charges being brought by the system, there is little, if any, chance of preparing a defense to those charges. Similarly, if one cannot challenge and refute accusations brought by others, there is virtually no chance of ensuring justice to the accused (beyond relying solely on the integrity of the evidence gatherer). Consequently, there is not one forum in this country in which an individual charged with misbehavior, ranging from a school rule violation to a traffic citation, that would deny these basic rights to the accused. Juvenile courts never should have denied these basic rights to defendants. Besides causing only slight inconvenience in slowing down the process, granting these protections does nothing to damage the "helping" image or benevolent purpose of juvenile court. After all, despite its clinical orientation and focus on the youth's problem, juvenile courts necessarily had to be concerned about the manifestations of the problem (the youth's behavior). If the behavior had never occurred, there would have been serious question about inferring the existence of a problem. Moreover, if the behavior had never really occurred, juvenile courts lacked both the authority and any legitimate reason to adjudicate youth and to subject them to the court's intervention.

The same argument cannot be made for providing counsel and the protection against self-incrimination, however, unless counsel is supposed to be nothing more than a passive bystander who merely oversees the process to assure its basic accuracy. There is no indication in *Gault* that the Supreme Court had intended to discourage or prohibit advocate-oriented defense attorneys from practicing in juvenile court. In fact, while discussing the juvenile's right to counsel, the Supreme Court drew a direct comparison between juvenile and criminal courts:

> A proceeding where the issue is whether the child will be found to be "delinquent" and subjected to the loss of his liberty for years is comparable in seriousness to a felony prosecution. The juvenile needs the assistance of counsel to cope with problems of law, to make skilled inquiry into the facts, to insist upon the regularity of the proceedings, and to ascertain whether he has a defense and to prepare and submit it.[6]

The Court issued similar remarks while recognizing the juvenile's right to silence:

(J)uvenile proceedings to determine "delinquency," which may lead to commitment to a state institution, must be regarded as "criminal" for purposes of the privilege against self-incrimination.[7]

The problem here is primarily philosophical. These two rights go well beyond what is necessary to ensure fundamental fairness, and, even more important, they serve as significant weapons youth can use to escape the system. The fact is that these two rights together exist in only one other forum—the criminal court. Granting these two rights clearly communicates that the Supreme Court must have believed that juvenile courts "hurt" (at least some) defendants much like criminal courts. The only context in which defendants had been granted these rights before *Gault* had been in criminal court, where the state had marshaled its forces in an attempt to seriously damage offenders. A reasonable inference, then, is that the Supreme Court perceived juvenile courts as inflicting similar damage on their populations. To be sure, the Supreme Court's view might be accurate. Nevertheless, an inescapable question is raised by this perception: If juvenile courts hurt their clients to the extent that youth must be armed with these two dramatic rights (that serve to prevent juvenile courts from helping youth), why don't juvenile courts have to answer to the Bill of Rights like criminal courts must?

In the end, the *Gault* decision floated two opposite propositions. The first is that juvenile courts are very much like criminal courts in that they are the only two forums in which defendants have the rights to counsel and silence. The second is that juvenile courts are very much unlike criminal courts, since the former answers only to the Fourteenth Amendment's due process clause while the latter is controlled by the Bill of Rights. Logic tells us that these two propositions cannot be simultaneously true. The *Gault* decision tells us otherwise.

The Legacy of *Gault*

The inconsistent holding was not the only problem in *Gault*. The decision (much like *Kent's*) reads like a roller coaster, alternately praising and then condemning juvenile courts. Throughout the opinion, the Supreme Court noted the many documented failures of rehabilitation in the juvenile system. Nevertheless, the Court perceived benefits to juvenile court processing for youth. For each of the four rights granted in *Gault*, the Supreme Court apologized and explained that granting the right would not damage juvenile court operations. Exactly what the Supreme Court wanted in and expected from juvenile courts was unstated and unclear (beyond wanting them to survive). Overall, the *Gault* decision was disjointed and weak.

In re Winship and the Burden of Proof

As testimony to the weakness of the *Gault* opinion, New York's highest appellate court, the Court of Appeals, decided two years after *Gault* (in 1969) that the traditional standard of proof in juvenile court—a preponderance of evidence—was still sufficient to adjudicate a youth delinquent. The New York court explained that four factors influenced its decision, namely, that juvenile court proceedings did not produce a criminal conviction; affected no right or privileges of the juvenile; were designed for the salvation, and not the punishment, of the child; and were surrounded by a cloak of protective confidentiality. The New York court's ability to discover four factors such as these suggests that *Gault* never happened. If nothing else, *Gault* had condemned such thinking and refused to allow these elements of traditional juvenile justice philosophy to be used in denying the extension of rights to defendants only two years earlier. The New York court seems to have completely ignored *Gault*.

Even more interesting, perhaps, was the response of the U.S. Supreme Court to this issue one year later in *In re Winship* (1970). The New York youth appealed the state court's decision, seeking to raise the level of proof needed to adjudicate delinquents in juvenile court. The Supreme Court first reviewed the purposes served by criminal court's traditional requirement that charges be proved beyond a reasonable doubt in order to convict:

- Reducing the risk of convictions resting on factual error

- Protecting the interests of the accused facing loss of liberty and the stigma of conviction

- Commanding the respect and confidence of the community in applying the criminal law[8]

To be sure, these purposes are vital in a system that openly seeks to "hurt" its clients significantly and in which, therefore, there should be no real doubt about whether the innocent "are being condemned,"[9] to quote the Supreme Court in *Winship*. The question remained whether these concerns could be present in a juvenile system whose entire reason for existence had been to help and not to hurt offenders. The Supreme Court resolved the issue summarily by noting simply: "The same considerations that demand extreme caution in fact-finding to protect the innocent adult apply as well to the innocent child."[10]

Accordingly, the *Winship* decision required that all adjudications of delinquents in juvenile court from this time forward be based on proof beyond a reasonable doubt. Like it had in *Gault*, the Supreme Court apologized for adding a right to the juvenile court process and promised that there would be no adverse effect on the rehabilitation mission of the system.

As in *Gault*, the Court's ruling in *Winship* is interesting for its implications. *Winship* added yet another constitutional right associated directly with criminal court. Together, *Gault* and *Winship* bestowed on juvenile defendants five constitutional rights, three of which are trademarks of criminal courts only. *Winship* furthered the notion that the Supreme Court viewed juvenile courts as being equal to adult courts, at least with respect to what the state was doing to offenders. Thus, the Court's decision to hold juvenile courts answerable to only the due process clause of the Fourteenth Amendment instead of to the Bill of Rights becomes even more difficult to understand and defend. In his dissent in *Winship*, Chief Justice Burger lamented:

> The Court's opinion today rests entirely on the assumption that all juvenile proceedings are "criminal prosecutions," hence subject to constitutional limitations. This derives from earlier holdings, which, like today's holding, were steps eroding the differences between juvenile courts and traditional criminal courts.[11]

Importantly, *Winship* marked the end of the Supreme Court's "assault" on the adjudicatory hearing (Chief Justice Burger's term for Supreme Court intervention). Evidently, the five constitutional rights granted juvenile defendants achieved fundamental fairness, or the balance the Supreme Court wanted in the *quid pro quo* exchange. Actually, there remained only one very critical constitutional right that had yet to be provided juvenile defendants: the right to jury trial. This right was the *big one,* however, since, more than any other right, it would trigger the domino effect.

McKeiver v. Pennsylvania and the Right to Jury Trial

In *McKeiver v. Pennsylvania* (1971), the Supreme Court directly faced the jury trial issue. *McKeiver* was a consolidation of cases from Pennsylvania and North Carolina. The Pennsylvania Supreme Court had ruled against two youth from Philadelphia who had demanded jury trial in juvenile court. The U.S. Supreme Court quoted the decision at length because it provided helpful precedent for the highest court to rule the same way. This marks the third occasion that the Pennsylvania Supreme Court played an instrumental role in the history of juvenile justice. It was the first appellate court to uphold both the House of Refuge movement (*Crouse*) and the juvenile court system (*Fisher*), and now it helped prevent the destruction of juvenile court by refusing to grant the right to jury trial (*McKeiver*).

The Supreme Court also denied juvenile defendants the right to trial by jury. According to Justice Blackmun, the author of *McKeiver,* the one legal reason that supported this conclusion was that "the juvenile court proceeding has not yet been held to be a 'criminal prosecution,' within the meaning and reach of the Sixth Amendment."[12]

Technically, this statement was correct. *Gault* had not held juvenile court answerable to either the Fifth or the Sixth Amendments (but rather to the Fourteenth Amendment). *Gault* had held the door open for a ruling precisely like this (and probably to allow this exact outcome). On the other hand, one has to wonder why juvenile courts must provide defendants three of the rights located in the Sixth Amendment (and another from the Fifth Amendment) because of just how "criminal" the prosecution is in juvenile court, and yet does not have to grant a fourth Sixth Amendment right that applies in criminal court. Just three years before *McKeiver,* in *Duncan v. Louisiana* (1968), the Supreme Court had extended the right to jury trial to defendants facing felony charges in criminal court. The Court required this right as being "fundamental to the American scheme of justice."[13] A fair translation of the Court's words is: no jury, no justice. Not granting juvenile defendants a parallel right to jury trial suggests, then, that justice is not paramount or imperative in juvenile court, which seems to contradict the need for counsel, silence, and proof beyond a reasonable doubt.

Justice Blackmun spent the last five pages of his opinion identifying 13 other reasons that juveniles could legitimately be denied jury trial, none of which offers a sound legal principle as to how this can be done. The bottom line of the decision, the real motivation behind the ruling, emerged in the final two sentences penned by Justice Blackmun, which echoed the Supreme Court's domino theory:

> If the formalities of the criminal adjudicative process are to be superimposed upon the juvenile court system, there is little need for its separate existence. Perhaps that ultimate disillusionment will come one day, but for the moment we are disinclined to give impetus to it.[14]

Despite the import of *McKeiver*, the decision is both weak and fractured. Only three other justices signed their names to Blackmun's writings, making *McKeiver* only a plurality (as opposed to a majority) opinion. Even Justice Harlan, who agreed only with the result of the case in a separate concurrence (he had voted against giving adults the right in *Duncan*), wondered how anyone who believed in jury trials per se could endorse anything Justice Blackmun had said about this constitutional right.

Assuming the accuracy of the domino theory, *McKeiver* probably saved juvenile court's life. To reach this result the Supreme Court had to minimize the comparability *Gault* and *Winship* had portrayed between juvenile and adult courts. Accordingly, *McKeiver* stressed what supposedly was different or unique about juvenile courts. According to *McKeiver*, juvenile courts are apples while criminal courts are oranges. Since only oranges are criminal prosecutions, they are the only forums in which jury trials are constitutionally required. This position makes what happened in the next Supreme Court decision, *Breed v. Jones* (1975), difficult to comprehend.

Breed v. Jones and Trial in Both Juvenile and Adult Court

The fact situation of *Breed v. Jones* was interesting. A juvenile defendant in California was adjudicated delinquent in juvenile court, but his disposition or sentence resulted in his being transferred to adult court for trial. Ultimately, the youth was convicted in criminal court as well. He appealed this practice and claimed double jeopardy was violated by virtue of his being subjected to *two trials*. Double jeopardy is a Fifth Amendment provision that prohibits the state from doubling up either prosecutions or punishments against a defendant for a single offense. Importantly, double jeopardy does not prohibit all successive trials. A civil trial can follow a criminal trial, even when an acquittal occurred in the latter, as in O. J. Simpson's case. Rather, only successive *criminal prosecutions* can violate double jeopardy. In light of the Supreme Court's ruling in *McKeiver* that the adjudicatory hearing was *not* a criminal prosecution, it would seem obvious that the California procedure of two trials in the two different systems would not offend double jeopardy. *McKeiver* had clearly held:

adjudicatory hearing ≠ criminal prosecution

Thus, the California youth must have experienced only *one* criminal prosecution (in criminal court, of course) and surely not two criminal prosecutions.

Nevertheless, the U.S. Supreme Court found this practice to be in violation of double jeopardy. Moreover, all nine justices viewed it this way, including the four who had made up the *McKeiver* plurality. To rule this way, the Court had to equate the adjudicatory hearing to a criminal prosecution (since *two* are needed to be *double* anything), which amounts to a direct refutation of *McKeiver*. Not only did the Court do this, but it also wrote that the equivalency was obvious and simply could not be denied:

> Jeopardy denotes risk. In the constitutional sense, jeopardy describes the risk that is traditionally associated with a criminal prosecution. . . .

* * *

> We believe it is simply too late in the day to conclude . . . that a juvenile is not put in jeopardy at a (juvenile) proceeding whose object is to determine whether he has

committed acts that violate a criminal law and whose potential consequences include both the stigma inherent is such a determination and the deprivation of liberty for many years. . . .

*   *   *

Thus, in terms of potential consequences, there is little to distinguish an adjudicatory hearing such as was held in this case from a traditional criminal prosecution. . . .

*   *   *

We deal here . . . with an analysis of an aspect of the kind of risk to which jeopardy refers. Under our decisions we can find no persuasive distinction in that regard between the (juvenile) proceeding conducted in this case . . . and a criminal prosecution, each of which is designed "to vindicate (the) very vital interest in enforcement of criminal laws. . . ."

*   *   *

We therefore conclude that (the youth) was put in jeopardy at the adjudicatory hearing.[15]

Based on this reasoning, it appears that *McKeiver* must have occurred "too early in the day." These views of the reality of juvenile court proceedings were noticeably absent when jury trials were being discussed.

The *Breed v. Jones* decision had minimal impact on the juvenile justice system. Only three states had operated this way, and the decision simply required juvenile court to transfer a youth to adult court *before* the adjudicatory hearing rather than after it. Actually, the decision ended up hurting juvenile defendants by making it easier to transfer them to criminal court (at least in the three states affected by the case). Prior to *Breed v. Jones,* the state would have had to establish proof beyond a reasonable doubt in order to adjudicate a youth (because of *Winship*) before the youth could ever see adult court. Acquittal in juvenile court would have prevented any further proceedings in either court. Moreover, there would also have been rules of evidence and other limits that apply to trial in juvenile court. As a result of *Breed v. Jones,* youth eligible for transfer from then on would be given only a transfer hearing (and not a trial), where the level of proof needed for the state to prevail is mere probable cause (rather than proof beyond a reasonable doubt) and where fewer rules of evidence apply. The "unconstitutional" process had ensured that the only youth who saw adult court were those against whom the state had a really solid case, as demonstrated by adjudication in juvenile court initially being required.

Despite the limited impact of *Breed v. Jones,* the case is of considerable significance, legally speaking. For one thing, *Breed v. Jones* clearly held:

adjudicatory hearing = criminal prosecution

at least as far as the double jeopardy clause is concerned. Even more important, the *Breed v. Jones* ruling did not rely on the Fourteenth Amendment's due process clause (as *Gault, Winship,* and *McKeiver* had). Instead, the Supreme Court classified the California transfer system as a violation of the Fifth Amendment's double jeopardy clause, to which juvenile courts were held directly answerable. This case was the one and only time in which the Supreme Court applied the Bill of Rights directly to juvenile court. It completely contradicted the very essence of the rationale *McKeiver* had used to deny jury trials.

The Overall Result of the Legal Framework

The U.S. Supreme Court arguably accomplished a worthy mission in its modification of juvenile court procedure. It cleaned up juvenile court without bringing about its demise. To achieve this outcome, however, the Supreme Court had to perform some clever maneuvering in its constitutional analysis of what juvenile court and its defendants are all about. The Supreme Court is responsible for constructing and supporting three seriously contradictory propositions about juvenile courts and their relationship to criminal courts:

1. Juvenile court = criminal court (counsel, self-incrimination, proof beyond a reasonable doubt)
   Juvenile court (due process clause) ≠ criminal court (Bill of Rights)

2. Adjudicatory hearing = criminal prosecution (*Breed v. Jones*)
   Adjudicatory hearing ≠ criminal prosecution (*McKeiver v. Pennsylvania*)

3. Juvenile court answers to Fifth Amendment (*Breed v. Jones*)
   Juvenile court does not answer to Sixth Amendment (*McKeiver v. Pennsylvania*)

This contradictory and fractured decision making by the Supreme Court, together with its construction of a special but watered-down version of constitutional rights for juvenile defendants, has contributed to some defendants being subjected to sloppy justice in the juvenile system. To be sure, the juvenile system was never known as a hallmark of justice, and historically the consequences stemming from being processed by and adjudicated in the system were not severe. Now that is no longer true. As we will see later (Chapters 12 and 14), the consequences of a juvenile court adjudication today are very serious both for youth within the juvenile system and for those who end up convicted in criminal court (and have their juvenile record trail them into that forum). This reality should suffice to make sloppy justice in juvenile court intolerable. The first five U.S. Supreme Court decisions firmly established a legal framework for juvenile justice, contradictions included. The remaining Supreme Court cases in the field of juvenile justice have not changed that framework (or reduced the contradictions), and they will be examined throughout the remainder of the text (in the sections to which the cases relate).

Summary: Key Ideas and Concepts

- Establishing a legal framework for juvenile court
- Problems with granting youth no constitutional rights
- Problems with granting youth all constitutional rights
- Supreme Court decision to grant youth some constitutional rights
- Fundamental fairness the standard for the rights of youth
- *Quid pro quo* requiring adjustment only
- *Parens patriae* murky, dubious, debatable
- Juvenile courts not answering to the Bill of Rights

- Juvenile courts answering to the Fourteenth Amendment due process clause
- The brilliance of the *Gault* decision
- The *Gault* decision promoting opposite propositions
- *Winship* raising the burden of proof to adjudicate
- The implications of the *Winship* holding
- The Pennsylvania Supreme Court's role in juvenile court history
- The inconsistency between *McKeiver v. Pennsylvania* and *Breed v. Jones*
- *Breed v. Jones* hurting youth facing transfer to adult court
- The Supreme Court's contradictory propositions regarding juvenile court

Discussion Questions

1. Discuss the dimensions of the legal framework the Supreme Court has created for juvenile courts.

2. Consider the domino theory. What examples support the argument that the Supreme Court was influenced by such a theory? Is it accurate? Should it have influenced the way in which the Supreme Court determined the rights youth should have in juvenile court? Did juvenile defendants end up better or worse off as a result of the impact of the domino theory?

3. Should juvenile courts answer to a different constitutional standard than the one that applies to criminal court? If yes, why? If no, why not?

4. Discuss the implications of the rationale offered by the Supreme Court in *Winship* as to why adjudications in juvenile court must be based on proof beyond a reasonable doubt.

5. How has the Pennsylvania Supreme Court played a critical role in the history of juvenile justice?

6. Discuss the implications of the rationale used by the Supreme Court in the *Breed v. Jones* decision.

7. In what ways has the Supreme Court established contradictory positions in its legal analysis of the juvenile court?

8. Discuss how the Supreme Court's intervention into juvenile justice resulted in both preserving the *unique* character of juvenile court and also furthering the *criminalization* of juvenile court.

Endnotes

1. See *In re Gault*, 387 U.S. 1, 16–17 (1967).
2. *Id.*, at 60 (Black, J., concurring).
3. *Id.*, at 67 (Harlan, J., concurring and dissenting).
4. *Id.*, at 75 (Harlan, J., concurring and dissenting).

 5. *Id.,* at 79 (Stewart, J., dissenting).
 6. *Id.,* at 36, citation omitted.
 7. *Id.,* at 49.
 8. See *In re Winship,* 397 U.S. 358, 363–364 (1970).
 9. *Id.,* at 364.
10. *Id.,* at 365.
11. *Id.,* at 375–376 (Burger, C.J., and Stewart, J., dissenting).
12. *McKeiver v. Pennsylvania,* 403 U.S. 528, 541 (1971).
13. *Duncan v. Louisiana,* 391 U.S. 145, 149 (1968).
14. *McKeiver v. Pennsylvania, supra* note 12, at 551.
15. *Breed v. Jones,* 421 U.S. 519, 528, 529, 530, 531 (1975), citations omitted. ✦

The Nature of Juvenile Misbehavior

- Chapter 4: Juvenile Court Jurisdiction
- Chapter 5: Measuring Juvenile Crime
- Chapter 6: Patterns of Juvenile Crime

Focus of Section II

Section II explores the dimensions of offenses committed by juveniles, including both the quantity and types of misbehaviors involved. This section also examines the characteristics most often associated with juvenile misbehavior. The section begins with an in-depth coverage of the jurisdiction of juvenile court and details all the behaviors and individuals over whom juvenile court has authority or power. ✦

Juvenile Court Jurisdiction

Focus of Chapter 4

Chapter 4 explores the various factors and situations that affect the jurisdiction of juvenile court. Topics covered here include the acts youth commit that are subject to the court's jurisdiction and the ages of youth in various states that determine whether a case will go to juvenile or adult court.

Key Terms

- at-risk youth
- Becker hearing
- decriminalize
- family court
- jurisdiction

- juvenile delinquent
- mandatory exclusion
- retention age
- venue

Factors Influencing Jurisdiction

Jurisdiction is an important term. It refers to (for us) the juvenile court's authority to hear a case or—to put it another way—the court's power to demand someone appear before it to answer to it. Jurisdiction (and another important word, venue) can also be used as a synonym for a geographical location such as a state or the District of Columbia, as has been done in this text. The three factors that affect jurisdiction in juvenile court are geography, age, and act.

Geography

The first factor affecting jurisdiction is *geography,* or where the event took place. What this *usually* means in juvenile court (and *always* means in adult court) is that jurisdiction is determined by the county or district in which the event occurred. In criminal court, a change of venue should take place only when so much pretrial publicity has occurred that a fair trial is not believed to be possible where the crime happened. The Scott Peterson prosecution in California is an example of a criminal court trial moved due to publicity. In juvenile court, the typical absence of both jury trials and pretrial publicity makes a change of venue for fair trial reasons much less likely. Nevertheless, three states (CO, LA, WA) specifically provide for a change of venue in order to ensure a fair trial in juvenile court. So, much like in adult court, typically County A's juvenile court would have jurisdiction over events that occurred in County A, but not over those that transpired in County B (unless the two counties share the same court).

Not surprisingly (unlike criminal court), juvenile court is sensitive to where the youth *resides* or is *currently found,* if either of these locations differs from where the event took place. Consequently, venue in juvenile court is frequently divided among these three possible locations. Thus, the trial (and even more likely the disposition) of the case can be held in a county other than the one in which the event happened. The venue issue is irrelevant to the District of Columbia, which has only one district or court in which to prosecute juvenile offenders. In the *delinquency category,* four jurisdictions (AK, FED, ME, MA) have adopted criminal court provisions in this area, while two states (NV, RI) do not identify where venue lies in delinquency cases. Fifteen states have explicitly limited venue in juvenile court to the location of the event and thus have chosen to follow the guidelines used in adult court.[1] The remaining 30 states have juggled the three main variables (youth resides, youth is found, event occurred) and have divided venue in three ways. New Hampshire allows a choice between where the youth resides or is found. Second, 10 states provide a choice among all three variables.[2] Finally, 19 states offer an option between where the youth resides and where the event occurred.[3]

Interestingly, whereas Alabama and Ohio declare that a case must be moved to where the youth resides if other cases are pending there, Oklahoma holds that a current adjudication and disposition take precedence over any other prior court orders (including those from where the child resides). Most states (30) continue to hold onto the traditional provision of allowing trial to occur in a juvenile court other than the one in which the event took place, and 28 states still hold that at least disposition can (and perhaps should or must) be sent to where the child resides.[4] Nevertheless, these provisions are subject to change. Nineteen states have already adopted or have followed criminal court standards for venue. Moreover, the current tendency when legislatures modify the venue provision is to adopt the standard used in criminal court (i.e., where the event occurred). This is another illustration of the *criminalization* of juvenile court. For example, Arizona (1997) and Louisiana (1991) recently adopted the where-the-event-occurred standard as the only venue provision for trial, and Washington (1997) no longer allows even the disposition to be moved to the county in which the youth resides (although it can be modified there). Idaho has gone even farther by requiring not only the consent of all parties before venue can be changed to where the child resides, but also a guilty plea from the youth or a "written notice of intent to enter an admission to the petition." Similarly, although Virginia theoretically allows prosecution either where the child resides or where the event occurred, movement of the adjudicatory hearing to where the youth resides requires the consent of the defendant and the prosecutors of both courts. A prosecutor's motion to move the trial to where the child resides is also now required in South Dakota.

Only 44 states have identified venue specifically in *status offense* cases. The remaining eight jurisdictions are only one district in size (DC), have no status offense jurisdiction (DE, FED, ME), follow adult court standards (AK, MA), or do not identify venue in juvenile court (NV, RI). Half of the states have adopted a venue provision for status offense issues that differs from that for delinquency cases.[5] Not surprisingly, perhaps, because of the nature of status offenses, venue for these misbehaviors is even more likely than delinquencies to be located where the youth resides,[6] or to be divided between where the youth resides or is found.[7] Nevertheless, many states also provide the area in which the event occurred to have jurisdiction, in addition to where the child resides,[8] while eight states actually restrict venue to where the status offense occurred.[9]

Age

The second factor that affects jurisdiction is age, or the youth's age either at the time of the event or at trial. Depending on the behavior, juvenile court statutes may or may not mention a *minimum* age. A *maximum* age *must* be identified so that we know where juvenile court jurisdiction stops and criminal court jurisdiction begins (for most people). With respect to a minimum age, only 17 states hold that one applies to youth charged with criminal conduct (i.e., a misdemeanor or felony). The minimum ages specified in these states range from a low of six (NC), seven (MD, MA, NY), or eight (AZ, WA) years of age to as high as 10[10] or even 12 (OR) years of age. This means that any youth below these ages could not be adjudicated *delinquent* for criminal behaviors in these states. As we will see shortly, that does not mean that these juvenile courts have no jurisdiction or authority over these children for these actions. Moreover, as we will discuss in Chapter 12 regarding transfer to criminal court, it is also possible that some offenders who are too young to be prosecuted as delinquents in juvenile court may be prosecuted as criminals in adult court. One behavior over which juvenile court typically has jurisdiction and for which there *must* be a minimum age is *truancy* (or unauthorized absence from school). This minimum typically is either six or seven years of age but can be as young as five (VA).

The maximum age of juvenile court jurisdiction ranges from 15 to 17. Only a relatively small number of states (13) have elected to end jurisdiction when the youth is either 15 or 16, however. Interestingly, Vermont gives juvenile and adult courts concurrent jurisdiction over all 16 and 17 year olds. Thus, juveniles of those ages can be prosecuted in both courts in Vermont. Table 4.1 outlines the maximum age distribution from around the country.

Obviously, the vast majority of jurisdictions (39) consider adulthood to begin

| Table 4.1   Maximum Ages of Juvenile Court Jurisdiction |||
Age 15	Age 16	Age 17
CT, NY, NC	GA, IL, LA, MA, MI, MO, NH, SC, TX, WI	AL, AK, AZ, AR, CA, CO, DE, DC, FED, FL, HI, ID, IN, IA, KS, KY, ME, MD, MN, MS, MT, NE, NV, NJ, NM, ND, OH, OK, OR, PA, RI, SD, TN, UT, VT, VA, WA, WV, WY

at the age of 18. One interesting note is that any state that observes common law in the age capacity (GA, MA, MO, NJ, RI) will declare that people reach their birthday the *day before* the actual anniversary date.

Picking the maximum age only partially resolves the age question. What also must be determined is *which* age should be determinative. This issue is especially important for those youth who are close to the maximum age. The three choices for this maximum age are:

1. at the time of the event/offense;

2. at the point of arrest or charging; and

3. at the time of prosecution in juvenile court or transfer to adult court.

Each of these stages would be a logical selection. The time of the event or offense may seem most appropriate, as the court would be addressing the youth's condition and accountability determined at the time the behavior occurred. On the other hand, if the youth has passed the maximum age by the time of charging or prosecution (perhaps by many years), he or she has become an adult. This makes juvenile court's handling of the case appear inappropriate. Even more critical, perhaps, is that unless this defendant is transferred to criminal court for prosecution, it is possible that the juvenile court could be prohibited from responding with anything more than a probation sentence. Some states forbid commitments to juvenile facilities if youth are beyond a certain age (see Chapter 14). For older defendants even probation would not be possible, since in most states the juvenile court's authority over all individuals ends by the age of 21 (see later parts of this section).

Most of the country agrees that the youth's age at the time of the event or offense is the operative age for determining juvenile court jurisdiction over *delinquency*. In fact, only a handful of states provide that the age at either arrest or charging (DE, OR, WI) or trial (AZ, WA) should be controlling. Of course, this opens the door in these few states for the prosecutor to sit on the case and simply wait for the youth to "age out" of juvenile court. Doing so would guarantee prosecution in criminal court, which is not a certainty if the prosecutor has to pursue a transfer hearing instead (see Chapter 12). In Arizona and Washington prosecutors can openly adopt this tactic.[11] In Wisconsin, however, any such questionable move by a prosecutor is subject to what is called a Becker hearing. This hearing examines whether the prosecution was intentionally "delayed so as to avoid the juvenile justice system."[12] Even some jurisdictions that have opted to use the age at the offense or event have clearly communicated that if the accused is not discovered, arrested, or prosecuted until clearly of adult age, such as between the ages of 18 and 21, trial will occur in criminal court.[13] Most statutes simply do not address this "What if?" and the absence of cases (and case law) makes it impossible to determine what most states are supposed to do when the issue arises.

Most statutes are silent about the critical age for *status offenses* (such as truancy, running away, incorrigibility) in juvenile court. It is more likely for the court to focus on the age of the status offender at the time of the proceedings (e.g., MD), since a youth's passing a certain age would make him or her no longer liable for the behavior and would seem to make little sense (such as prosecuting a truant at the age of 19). In addition, a status offender's exceeding the maximum age limit should mean the juvenile court would not have jurisdiction over the youth. Criminal court could not have jurisdiction in most situations either, since typically the behaviors are *not crimes*.

Adding some confusion to the age element is the fact that some juvenile courts have limited jurisdiction over some *adults*. It is often emphasized that felonies are excluded from juvenile court's jurisdiction in this situation (DE, HI, OH, VA). Moreover, this jurisdiction is concurrent (or shared) with adult court in some states.[14] If a trial proves necessary, the proceeding might have to be moved to adult court (AL, VA), or the adult defendant might be required to waive the right to jury trial in order to keep the matter in juvenile court (TN). Nevertheless, some states go so far as to hold that jury trial for adults is a possibility (MD, MN), even though the typical juvenile defendant is denied this right in these locations. Most of the offenses for which adults can find themselves prosecuted in juvenile court are misdemeanors such as compulsory education violations (CA, IN, RI, UT), nonsupport (DE, HI, OH, RI), certain family offenses (DE, HI, NY, OH), and interfering with the custody of a child (AL, DE, IN, UT).[15] The offenses that most commonly fall within juvenile court jurisdiction are contributing to the delinquency of a minor and neglect and abuse.[16] Juvenile court will also "prosecute" a variety of family-related matters that involve adults as well as children (see next section).

The final aspect of the age variable is the age to which juvenile court *retains* jurisdiction. That is, assuming there is an adjudication or some other arrangement through which the juvenile court gains some control over the youth,[17] for *how long* (or *to what age*) does juvenile court retain or keep that control? Typically, this outermost age to which juvenile court can keep a youth on probation or in an institution ranges from 18 to 25 (see Table 4.2).

All jurisdictions work with a statutorily identified maximum retention age, which in many states must be considered only a *presumptive maximum age* because it can be adjusted, sometimes significantly. Fourteen jurisdictions have created multiple ages, typically for older or more serious offenders. New Hampshire has the youngest retention age of 17 for most of its juvenile offenders. At the same time, it has estab-

Table 4.2 Statutorily Identified Retention Age of Juvenile Court Jurisdiction	
Age	**State(s)**
17	NH
18	AZ, DE, IA, KY, MA, NC, VT
19	AK, FL, MI, NE, OK, TN
20	MS, ND
21	AL, AR, CA, CT, DC, FED, GA, ID, IL, IN, LA, ME, MD, MN, MO, MT, NV, NM, NY, OH, PA, RI, SC, SD, TX, UT, VA, WA, WV, WY
23	KS
25	OR, WI
Until court order expires	CO, HI, NJ

lished not only an upper level of 18 for youth adjudicated at the age of 17, but also an extended jurisdiction age of 21 for older and serious offenders. Similarly, five states (DE, IA, KY, MA, VT) join Arizona in establishing a rather young cutoff age of 18 and, not surprisingly, allow another year (i.e., to 19) of juvenile court jurisdiction for those youth who were at or above the retention age at disposition or who were institutionalized for having committed rather serious offenses (in Vermont these are youthful offenders). Although the retention age in North Carolina is also 18, sentencing guidelines in that state provide for sentencing and jurisdiction to continue until 19 and 21 years of age for certain serious offenders. Like New Hampshire, Delaware has an extended jurisdiction provision through which certain serious offenders can be retained by juvenile court to the age of 21. Massachusetts has the same expiration age for its youthful offenders. Like Vermont, Oklahoma raises its jurisdiction over more serious youthful offenders one year (from 19 to 20 years of age). Florida and Michigan both have a relatively young retention age of 19 for most of their juvenile offenders, but allow juvenile court to hold onto some of their worst offenders to 21 (MI) or to 21 or 22 years of age (FL) for different offenders. Finally, four jurisdictions (CA, FED, MT, TX) have 21 as the retention age for most offenders, but both California and Montana will go as high as 25 for their most significant delinquents, while 40 years is the maximum sentence possible for offenders who have been given a determinate juvenile court sentence in Texas. In the federal system, 21 years of age is the maximum retention age for both probation and commitment sentences, provided the individual was younger than 18 at the time of disposition. For defendants between ages 18 and 21 at sentencing, however, probation can last at most three years, while commitments for Class A, B, and C felonies can last five years.

True to juvenile court tradition, most jurisdictions (30) provide that all or nearly all of their youth are subject to the court's control until the age of 21. Interestingly, though, 16 states have adopted a younger retention age for most of the youth who will be processed in their juvenile courts. Also interesting is the recent move in several states to exceed the traditional limit of age 21. Three states simply raised their age of retention to 23 (KS) or 25 (OR, WI). Other states with multiple ages (CA, FL, MT) have recently accomplished similar results by increasing the maximum possible age of retention, at least for their worst offenders. Finally, perhaps most intriguing is the fact that the disposition, rather than the youth's age, determines the juvenile court's retention of jurisdiction (i.e., until the disposition order expires) in three states (CO, HI, NJ).

The retention ages discussed above apply to delinquents and to most status offenders. Fifteen states, however, identify a younger maximum retention age for status offenses. These states have selected 17 (WY), 18,[18] or 19 (IL, MN) years of age as the oldest ages any youth can be controlled via status offense behavior. Delinquent behavior in these states calls for a higher age of retention.

Act

The third factor that affects juvenile court jurisdiction is an *act*. That is, some behavior is required. This text focuses on only two of the categories over which juvenile courts typically have jurisdiction: delinquent acts, which are mostly *crimes* if committed by adults, and *status offenses*, which usually are acts illegal for youth only (and usually are *not crimes*).

Before we analyze delinquencies and status offenses, it is important to note briefly that juvenile courts typically have jurisdiction over other behaviors (even though they will not be the focus of this text). Most common among these behaviors is the abuse, neglect, or dependency many children suffer at the hands of their parents. At least 38 jurisdictions address this problem in their juvenile courts together with juvenile misbehavior.[19] Going hand-in-hand with the neglect and dependency issue is adoption and custody, or the more likely termination of parental rights, which are listed among the items of jurisdiction in at least 34 jurisdictions.[20] Otherwise, juvenile courts can also have jurisdiction over other family-related matters, including support,[21] paternity,[22] visitation,[23] divorce and annulment,[24] and judicial consent to marriage, employment, or enlistment in the military.[25]

In fact, juvenile courts in a number of states actually are known instead as family court.[26] This title reflects the broad number of family issues addressed in that forum. In other states the juvenile and family courts are interchangeable (PA, NJ, VT), while in Virginia the name of the court is *juvenile and domestic relations*. Although many states have used another court to handle family-related issues, it is important to realize just how much material can be sent to juvenile court to be resolved. It is especially in these family-oriented capacities that juvenile courts have jurisdiction over adults as well as children, even though the context is not criminal behavior per se.

Juvenile Delinquency

The first set of acts that fall under juvenile court jurisdiction are known universally as *delinquent acts*, which is why youth who commit these behaviors are known commonly as juvenile delinquents. A few states, however, also refer to the individual as a juvenile, youth, or public *offender*, or as a juvenile or law *violator*.[27] These titles emphasize that most youth within these categories are actually *young criminals* and would be called criminals if they were adults. Consequently, *delinquency* typically is thought to be a synonym for *crime*. Crime, in turn, refers to offenses classified as either felonies or misdemeanors. Crime does not include lesser illegal behaviors such as infractions or ordinance violations (like the everyday traffic ticket). Adults are subject to penalties for committing these lesser behaviors, but are not considered or branded criminals if they are found guilty of having committed them. To be sure, all 52 jurisdictions include felonies within their definitions of delinquency (although some jurisdictions exclude the most serious felonies from prosecution in juvenile court—see Chapter 12). Similarly, all 52 jurisdictions include misdemeanors, too, within their definitions of delinquency, albeit with some limits. Minnesota and South Dakota exclude petty offenses from their definitions of delinquency. Minnesota has a separate special title of petty offender for this individual. Rhode Island requires multiple misdemeanor incidents (and also ordinance violations) before a youth will be labeled a delinquent, while Texas excludes both the first two DUIs (driving under the influence) that a youth commits and nonjailable misdemeanors from the delinquent category.

So far, the definitions of delinquency and crime parallel each other closely. What is important to realize, however, is that in most locations, the parameters of delinquency are broader than those of crime. That is, there are behaviors for which a juvenile can earn a delinquent title for which a comparably situated adult would *not* be called a criminal. For example, most states include ordinance violations and infractions within the delinquency category, although there are some limits.[28]

Although a number of these states (AL, CA, HI, ID, VA) specifically exclude curfew violations from this grouping, some other states (CT, GA, KY, ND, TN, WV) similarly insist that ordinance violations not be categorized as delinquency if they involve behaviors illegal only for juveniles (such as curfew violations). In addition, while Colorado and Florida extend the delinquency label only to ordinance violations that can result in jail time for an adult, Iowa similarly limits the violations to those that would be a public offense for an adult. Finally, numerous jurisdictions (AL, GA, LA, MO, NE, VA) label some offenses applicable only to children as status offenses.

Delinquency is also broader than crime in the numerous jurisdictions that equate offenses for which only minors can be held liable with delinquent acts. Examples are the purchase or possession of either alcohol (IN, IA, KS, ME, NM, WY) or a handgun or firearm (AR, FED, KS, OH, VA). Even behaviors such as running away from home (IN, MI), truancy (IN, MI, MS), and incorrigibility (IN, MI) can be labeled delinquent. Somewhat esoteric is the Kansas statute's inclusion of purchasing a pari-mutuel (betting) ticket, and Ohio's adding tattooing, body piercing, and ear piercing within the delinquent category. Finally, unlike the definition of crime, many states extend delinquency to violations of (juvenile) court orders.[29]

Some states have narrowed the definition of delinquency so as to exclude some noncriminal behaviors (in addition to the examples mentioned previously). One way this has been done is to identify certain traffic infractions and ordinance violations as completely separate categories within juvenile court jurisdiction (DE, GA, WI, WY), even ones dealing with alcohol use or possession (MD, MN). Similarly, some states provide that juvenile courts and adult courts can or will share jurisdiction over these types of traffic and ordinance violations.[30] A few states have gone so far as to give adult court jurisdiction over any offense dealing with alcohol (AK, ID), curfew (AK, NJ), tobacco (AK, ID, IA, MO), or even inhalants and marijuana (ID). It is becoming common to strip juvenile court of jurisdiction over traffic (and perhaps boating) violations (NJ, OH, OK, RI) unless the violation is a felony (AK, CA, IA, MO, ND, TN) or a DUI,[31] or if the youth is below the age of 16[32] or 14 (ID, KS) years of age. Similar provisions have been associated with fishing, gaming, parks, and recreation offenses as well.[33] Despite these developments, it is still true that many more behaviors are called delinquencies than are labeled crimes.

One interesting and unique feature of criminal conduct for youth is that many jurisdictions still require more than just behavior before they can be declared to be delinquents. Not only must they physically commit the illegal acts themselves, but they must also be in need of care, rehabilitation, or supervision before they can be officially adjudicated delinquent (see Chapter 13).[34]

Status Offenses

In addition to delinquencies, juvenile court has jurisdiction over numerous behaviors that are illegal only for youth. These age-related behaviors are referred to as status offenses since it is the *status of age* that makes the conduct illegal. Although the vast majority of these status offenses (such truancy or running away) have no connection to crimes, some status offenses (such as possession of a handgun) actually are categorized as misdemeanors (CO, TX).

Separating Delinquents and Status Offenders

For the first six decades of juvenile court's existence, *all* juvenile misbehavior was classified as delinquency. Today, only three states (IN, MI, SC) have continued this trend of calling all juvenile offenders delinquents. In 1962, New York was the first state to create a special name for status offenders. California followed this example shortly thereafter. The initial motivation to distinguish status offenders from delinquents was twofold, focused primarily on benefiting status offenders. First, there was a desire to develop a title that would carry *less stigmatization* than can result from a delinquent label. To the extent that the public considers "delinquent" to be a synonym for criminal, it is arguably both unfair and detrimental to place that same stigma on status offenders who have not committed a crime. Moreover, whereas delinquents (or criminals) hurt other people, status offenders tend to hurt only themselves and thus should not be equated with delinquents. A second motivation was to offer status offenders *better treatment*, by confining them in their own facilities, apart from the corrupting influences of their delinquent counterparts. Of course, these motivations were critical in the initial development of the juvenile court itself (i.e., to not refer to juvenile offenders as criminals and to separate them from adult inmates).

Should juvenile court have jurisdiction over status offenders? Should these offenders be processed elsewhere?

Between 1967 and 1974, two major developments added more impetus to separating status offenders from juvenile delinquents and probably account for the great majority of states that finally followed New York's and California's lead. First, the *Gault* and *Winship* rulings from the U.S. Supreme Court (see Chapter 3) granted a number of constitutional rights to *juvenile delinquents*, or those charged with *criminal behavior.* The constitutional rights identified in the Fourth, Fifth, and Sixth Amendments in the Bill of Rights are associated specifically with *criminal charges.* As we will see in later chapters, many jurisdictions have elected *not* to extend some of the *Gault* and *Winship* provisions to status offenders. Second, Congress passed the Juvenile Justice and Delinquency Prevention Act of 1974[35] that called for, among other things, a separation of the two populations. Congress allocated federal dollars to states to reward their cooperation in removing status offenders from institutions containing delinquents.

Interestingly, although all states prohibit at least some behaviors (such as truancy) only for children, not all states grant juvenile court jurisdiction over these behaviors. Shortly after the 1974 Congressional Act there was a movement to decriminalize status offenses, or to remove these misbehaviors completely from the sanctioning power of juvenile court. This movement questioned the appropriateness of the juvenile justice system's controlling (and punishing) behavior that was not criminal. This system associated status offenders with juvenile delinquents (even if separately) and perhaps compounded the troubles and problems of status offenders by formally processing them in a justice system. Nevertheless, only Delaware (1976) and Maine (1977) implemented this strategy.[36] These states join the federal jurisdiction (where almost all status offenses are irrelevant since they cannot be federal crimes) as the only three locations that do not have their juvenile courts processing at least some status offenders. Of the remaining 49 jurisdictions, only 17 states have a detailed and separate section of their juvenile court act dedicated exclusively to the processing of status offenders.[37] Most of the country, then, simply intersperses status offense material among delinquency provisions, sometimes not clearly identifying how, if at all, the former must be handled differently than the latter.

Special Titles

Altogether, 45 jurisdictions have created a special title for their status offenders.[38] Some use multiple labels, which can make matters quite confusing. Most jurisdictions (27) begin the title with the words *children* (ch), *juveniles* (j), *persons* (p), *youth* (y), or perhaps *families* (f) and then refer to them as being in *need of* something like the following:

- **Supervision:** AL(ch), DC(ch), MD(ch), MS(ch), OK(ch and j), NV(ch), NY(p), SD(ch), VA(ch), WY(ch)

- **Services:** AR(f), CT(f), FL(ch), LA(f), MA(ch), NH(ch), NM(f), VA(ch), WA(ch)

- **Protection or services:** MN(ch), WI(ch)

- **Assistance:** IA(ch and f), NE(j)

- **Aid:** AK(ch)

- **Care:** KS(ch)

- **Intervention:** MT(y)

- **Care or supervision:** VT(ch)

- **Care and treatment:** MO(ch)

- **Special supervision:** NE(j)

Consequently, acronyms such as *chins* (children in need of supervision/services) are popular in many jurisdictions. New York started this acronym phenomenon with the variation *pins* (persons . . .). Oklahoma refers interchangeably to *chins* and *jins*. Also fairly popular is *fins* (families . . .). Texas has implemented the acronym *cins*, which stands for "conduct indicating a need for supervision," while the title used in Illinois, "minor requiring authoritative intervention," is similar to this approach but does not produce a convenient acronym per se.

Another 11 states have developed a sometimes less than flattering single-word title to capture all their status offenders, such as *dependent* (AZ, CO, OR, PA), *unruly* (GA, ND, OH, TN), *incorrigible* (AZ), *undisciplined* (NC), or *wayward* (RI). California and New Jersey have also not chosen the acronym route in this title game. Both delinquents and status offenders are *wards* of the court in California. Whereas the former become so by virtue of *section 602* of the juvenile court act, status offense wards are linked with *section 601*. New Jersey regards their troubled status offenders as those with a *juvenile-family crisis*. Finally, four states have ignored the special title pursuit and refer to those who commit these misbehaviors simply as *status offenders* (HI, ID, KY, WY); another five states also use status offender as an additional or secondary title (CO, GA, NE, TX, VA).

A new designation—at-risk youth—has arisen in recent years. Currently, four states (CA, TX, WA, WI) mention this individual in their statutes. Whereas Wisconsin has earmarked this classification for youth having particular problems with their education, the other states commonly portray this child as a status offender in the making (CA, TX, WA), a drug and alcohol experimenter (CA, WA), or a predelinquent (TX) who does not require court intervention or placement at this time, but easily could in the future unless serious preventive measures are taken now.

Title Confusion

Apart from the jurisdictions that have added the at-risk youth category, seven states use multiple titles to refer to their status offense population. In Colorado and Georgia, the status offender title merely seems to be an alternative way to refer to the dependent (CO) or unruly (GA) youth. Iowa has both children and families in need of assistance, but the latter is described only as breakdown situations between youth and their parents, with no definitions or remedies identified. Arizona pretty much just divides its status offense population into those younger than (dependent) or older than (incorrigible) eight years of age. Nebraska, Texas, and Virginia use overlapping categories that can be confusing.

In Nebraska, jin*a* (*assistance*) refers to a youth who works or lives in a dangerous, unhealthy, or immoral situation, while jin*ss* (*special supervision*) refers to the traditional runaway or truant, but also includes those who deport themselves in ways so as to injure or endanger their own or others' morals or health. Meanwhile, the status offender in Nebraska is one who does any of the behaviors defined under *jinss* or possesses alcohol. Despite the seeming similarity between the *jina* and *jinss*, the latter requires a higher standard of proof to be adjudicated than the *jina*. The child in need of *services* in Virginia parallels Nebraska's *jina*, while the child in need of *supervision* is the typical truant or runaway, and the status offender is one who commits an act that is prohibited by law but that is not an offense for an adult. Although the status offender and the supervision category seem to overlap, the status offender is allotted dispositions reserved for the child in need of services. By far, the Texas formula is the most confusing. Although running away, truancy, disobedience in school, and committing a misdemeanor punishable by a fine only are contained within both the *cins* and status offender categories, other misbehaviors in these two areas are dissimilar. Moreover, truancy and running away also are included within the at-risk youth description.

Besides single states' using multiple titles, the lack of uniformity among states is another source of confusion in the title game, especially in the relationship between status offenders (who have done something wrong) and children who are abused or neglected by their parents. In some states, children in need of *assistance* (MD), *services* (IN), or *care* (LA, MT) are neglected or dependent (or victims) rather than status offenders. Just as confusing is the fact that many states' titles for status offenders include not only these youth, but also some truly dependent children as well.[39] Of course, the most misappropriated title is that which refers to *all* (CO, OR, PA) or *some* (AZ) status offenders as dependent.

The Illegal Status Behaviors

Although *truancy* (or skipping school) is illegal for juveniles (depending on their age) in every jurisdiction (except federal), several states have elected either *not* to prosecute this matter in juvenile court, at least initially (AK, DE, IA, ME, OR, WA), or not to include this behavior within the status offense category (CO, IL, UT).[40] The remaining 42 jurisdictions consider truancy as a status offense. Although 16 traditionally has been the maximum compulsory education age for youth, it can be as young as 15 (ME) or as high as 18, which is becoming increasingly popular (IN, NY, UT, WA, WI), especially if the child has not completed the 12th grade (KS, OR). Typically, the truancy must be habitual rather than a single incident, but the days requirement can range from as few as three (DE, MN), four (CA), or five (AZ) to as many as 15 (FL), and that is within a 90-day period only. Some states differentiate elementary from secondary requirements (CO, MN). The recent trend adopted by numerous states is to insist that the youth and the parents be referred to truancy centers or boards in the community and to pursue mediation in an all-out effort to avoid referring the matter to juvenile court (CA, FL, LA, MN, NV, WA, WI).

Only six jurisdictions fail to include *incorrigibility* within the status offense category (AK, DC, FED, ME, TX, VA); Utah calls these youth *ungovernable*. Incorrigibility minimally means a youth's refusal to obey the reasonable and proper orders of parents. Sometimes the wording includes "or any lawful authority," which would seem to include obeying school rules as well. That might explain why only 15 states specifically and separately refer to school disobedience as a status offense situation.[41] Although most jurisdictions require the incorrigibility to be habitual or persistent,[42] unlike truancy, habitual violations in this category are not universally required. Related to incorrigibility, numerous states continue to use traditional juvenile justice language and to prohibit youth from deporting themselves so as to injure or endanger the health or morals of themselves or others;[43] being in circumstances or conditions that would produce similar results;[44] regularly being found in places where it is unlawful to be (MI, NC, OH), such as a bar (GA, LA) or billiard room (SC); engaging in illegal or injurious occupations (MN, NE, OH); associating with vicious, criminal, notorious, or immoral persons (MI, OH, RI); indecent or immoral conduct (CT, MI); or leading an immoral or vicious life (RI).

Running away from home has been recognized officially as an illegal act for youth in all but 12 jurisdictions.[45] Some states prohibit this behavior without classifying it as either a delinquency or a status offense (IA, NY, UT). Some states refer to this conduct as "truant from home" (NE, OH, WI). It can include situations in which youth refuse to live with their parents (IL, NM) or where the family refuses to let the youth live with them (NM). In Minnesota, the child must be unmarried and absent from home without the consent of the parents, while in Oklahoma there has to be no intent on the child's part to return home. As with truancy, for running away to result in serious juvenile court intervention, exhausting alternatives and efforts at reconciliation could be a prerequisite (IL, MI, NJ, TN, WI). The number or length of departures from home is not typically specified. However, some states require that the running away be more than once (IA, VA), continued (LA), persistent (FL, MA), or habitual (AK, KY, MO, NE, NH, OH, WI), while the duration requirement could be more than 24 hours (NJ, NM, NC), 72 hours (WA), or simply a substantial length of time (OK, TX).

A status offender actually may have committed a crime or a delinquent act, but is disqualified for one reason or another from being labeled or adjudicated delinquent. Many states include within the status offense category those who have done a delinquency but are:

- younger than eight years old (AZ);
- younger than 10 years old (KS, LA, MN, MS, PA, TX, WI);
- incompetent to stand trial and/or not guilty by mental disease (AZ, MN, WI);
- pressured by parents to do wrong (AK, IA, LA);
- not in need of treatment/rehabilitation (GA); or
- simply viewed by the court as a status offender (MS, MT).

Although only two states (MS, MT) have committed officially to allowing the status offense category to serve as a kind of a catchall for "inappropriate" delinquency situations, it is quite possible that nearly all locations with status offense jurisdiction would allow this development. For example, in an Iowa case a 13-year-old boy was charged (both as a delinquent and a status offender) with two counts of sexual abuse (where the victims were 5 and 6 years old) and was adjudicated by the court as a status offender despite the criminal nature of the misbehavior.[46] Similarly, an Ohio case that began as a delinquency ended with a status offense adjudication based on its being a "lesser included offense."[47] This downgrading of the incident most likely would result when a prosecutor or a judge (or perhaps a PO) would believe the youth should not be burdened with a delinquency adjudication, or when a prosecutor wanted to pursue a status offense outcome because of its less demanding procedures and burden of proof (if applicable) (see especially Chapter 13) or as a plea bargaining arrangement with the defense (see Chapter 11).

Finally, status offenses can include a variety of behaviors that are grouped simply as offenses for children[48] or that are spelled out as alcohol possession,[49] curfew,[50] tobacco possession (NH, VA), handgun possession (CO, LA), or inhalant use (TX). It is important to remember, however, that some of these juvenile-only offenses are not regarded as either delinquencies or status offenses (DE, MN, SD), and that they may not be within juvenile court jurisdiction at all (KY, WI). It is also possible for ordinance violations to be treated as status offenses (NH, RI, TX, WY) instead of as delinquencies. Multiple ordinance violations in Rhode Island will convert the youth to a delinquent, however. Finally, status offenses can also include some esoteric misbehavior such as playing a pinball machine (SC).

As with delinquencies, status offense adjudications in numerous jurisdictions require not only proof of the misbehavior itself, but also proof (perhaps even at the clear and convincing level—MI, ND) that the youth is in need of care or rehabilitation.[51]

Mandatory Exclusion

Just as critical as who belongs within the jurisdiction of juvenile court is the subject of which juveniles do *not* belong within the court's jurisdiction, despite their young age. Many *crimes* committed by *juveniles* have been *excluded* from juvenile court jurisdiction

A courtroom in a juvenile court where preliminary hearings are given to adult offenders who victimize young children. Is juvenile court the place to conduct these types of hearings?

due to their severity (and perhaps due as well to the youth's advanced age and record). In these cases juveniles *can be transferred* to criminal court for prosecution by judges or prosecutors who have been given *discretionary power* over these youth by the legislature. This discretionary exclusion involves being transferred to adult court. It is the subject of Chapter 12 and will be explored in great depth there. Although thousands of youth are affected by discretionary exclusion, even greater numbers of youth have been subjected to mandatory exclusion from juvenile court. These youth *cannot be prosecuted* in juvenile court for *any crime* because, although chronologically they are juveniles (or at least most of the country would regard them as such), the legislatures have *conferred adult status* on these individuals. That is, despite their age, these youth *were adults, legally,* when they committed their crimes. This is why criminal court has jurisdiction over them and also why these offenders *cannot be prosecuted* in juvenile court.

Mandatory exclusion, thus far, can occur in three ways:

1. Implementing a maximum juvenile court age below 17 years old

2. Allowing a previous transfer to and/or conviction in criminal court to mean this person is an adult

3. Permitting youth to "strike out" of juvenile court

First, with respect to juvenile court's maximum age limit, the vast majority of jurisdictions (39) and the public at large consider 18 years of age as the initiation of adulthood. This age confers a number of rights and privileges (voting, smoking) typically associated with adulthood. Jurisdictions that endorse this position when crime is involved would have a maximum juvenile court age at 17 years old (so adult court would start at 18 years of age). As we saw earlier in this chapter (see Table 4.1), however, 13 states have adopted maximum juvenile court ages of 15 and 16. They have elected to identify adulthood (for purposes of criminal prosecution at least) as beginning at the ages of 16 or 17. These states have exercised mandatory exclusion of "juveniles" from juvenile court jurisdiction. They have conferred adult legal status (again, for crime) on individuals typically regarded as juveniles. The 16- and 17-year-olds in these states are considered *adults* when they commit their offenses and *must go,* if anywhere, to criminal court for prosecution.

More than half of the country considers a juvenile (usually regardless of age) who is convicted in criminal court to be an adult from that point onward.[52] This rule can apply even if the youth is found not guilty by reason of insanity (DC) or is given a deferred conviction (OK) in adult court. Only a few states have required this conviction to be on the felony level (AZ, DE, MI, MN). Many states have imposed serious stipulations, however.

Florida requires the convicted youth to be given an adult sentence rather than a juvenile court one (which Florida permits for most juvenile defendants in criminal court—see Chapter 12) in order to be considered an adult henceforth. A number of states (KS, OR, PA, VA) insist that a youth convicted in adult court of an offense that was less serious than the offense that qualified for transfer can or must be given a juvenile court disposition and thus is legally a juvenile rather than an adult.[53]

Five states (CA, DE, HI, RI, WA) allow a judicial transfer (to adult court) alone to confer adult status on a youth. While California stipulates that this transfer must be based on the youth's delinquent record or treatment history, Rhode Island holds that the youth must first be transferred to the second tier of its juvenile court (see Chapter 12) before the waiver to adult court converts the defendant into an adult.

The logic behind permitting these previous transfers and adult convictions to place the juvenile on the same legal status as an adult is kind of a "you can't go home again" rationale. If the juvenile court judge has determined that the individual does not belong in juvenile court any longer or if the criminal court finds sufficient intent and behavior to convict the individual of a crime, returning him or her to juvenile court for future crimes seems to make little sense. Of course, the determination that a youth "belongs" in criminal court is based, in part at least, on the assumption that the youth actually committed the offense. That is why most jurisdictions require the conviction in adult court so as to confirm that assumption. Nevertheless, in the early days of juvenile court, the norm was for youth to have to *pass through* juvenile court on their way to adult court, regardless of their previous criminal history. It would not be strange at this point for more states to embrace provisions like these, especially if there is a felony conviction in adult court.

To date, Florida is the only state that allows youth to, in effect, "strike out" of juvenile court. In this state, youth who have witnessed three separate felony adjudications, coupled with three separate commitments following these adjudications, have struck out of juvenile court and are considered adults.

We will review what can happen to these mandatory excluded "juveniles" and to youth transferred to adult court in Chapter 12. For the next several chapters, however, our focus will be on those youth processed by the juvenile justice system.

Summary: Key Ideas and Concepts

- Three factors that influence juvenile court jurisdiction
- Juvenile court venue affected by where the youth resides
- Variation in the maximum juvenile court age
- Variation in how the relevant age of the defendant is determined
- Variation in the retention age of juvenile court jurisdiction
- Juvenile court jurisdiction over adults
- The multifaceted nature of juvenile court jurisdiction
- Juvenile delinquency broader in scope than crime
- Separation of status offenders from juvenile delinquents

- Special labels or titles for status offenders
- Variety of status offense behaviors, including delinquent behavior
- Conferring adult status on juveniles

Discussion Questions

1. How does venue of a juvenile court case differ potentially from that for a criminal court case?

2. Should there be a minimum age for juvenile court jurisdiction, and, if so, what should that age be?

3. What should be the maximum age for juvenile court jurisdiction?

4. What are the implications of the lower maximum ages some states observe?

5. Which of the three possible stages should determine the relevant age for a juvenile defendant?

6. Should prosecutors be able to delay prosecution so that the juvenile defendant becomes disqualified from juvenile court?

7. To what age should juvenile court retain jurisdiction over youth?

8. What are the implications in having a relatively young or old retention age?

9. Should juveniles be labeled delinquent for committing violations or infractions? Should juvenile court have jurisdiction over these behaviors?

10. Discuss the reasons behind separating status offenders from delinquents. Was this separation a good or a bad idea?

11. Describe the ways in which mandatory exclusion occurs. Should juveniles be subjected to mandatory exclusion and, if so, in what situations?

12. What aspects of juvenile court jurisdiction are unique?

Endnotes

1. These states are: AL*, AZ, CO*, DE, HI*, KS*, LA*, MS*, NE*, NY*, NC*, OK, TX*, WA, WV.
2. These states are: CA*, FL*, IN*, IA, KY*, NM*, SD, UT*, WI*, WY.
3. These states are: AR*, CT, GA*, ID, IL*, MD*, MI, MN*, MO*, MT, NJ, ND, OH, OR*, PA*, SC*, TN*, VT, VA*.
4. The states designated in footnotes 1, 2, and 3, above, with an * are the ones that allow or insist that the disposition should be transferred to the court in which the child resides.
5. The states designated in footnotes 6, 7, and 8, below, with an * are the ones that have a venue provision for status offenders that differs from the one applying to delinquents.
6. These states are: AR*, CT*, MD*, MT*, WA*.
7. These states are: CO*, FL*, IL*, IA*, KS*, KY*, MO*, NH, NJ*, NM*, PA*, VY*, VA*, WI*.
8. These states are: AZ*, CA, GA, ID, IN, LA*, MI, MN*, ND, OH, OK*, OR, SC, SD, TN, UT, WY.
9. These states are: AL, HI, MS, NE, NY, NC, TX, WV.
10. These states are: AR, CO, KS, LA, MN, MS, PA, SD, TX, VT, WI.
11. See, e.g., *McBeth v. Rose*, 531 P.2d 156 (Ariz. 1975); *State v. Nicholson*, 925 P.2d 637 (Wash. App. Div. 2 1996).
12. *State v. Annala*, 484 N.W.2d 138, 140 (Wis. 1992). See *State v. Becker*, 247 N.W.2d 495 (Wis. 1976).

13. Many jurisdictions identify 18 (DE, MA, NH, NC, TX), 19 (AL, FL, TN, WV), 20 (ND, OH), or 21 (DC, FED, IL, MD, MT, PA, RI, SD, UT, VA) years of age as being too old to be prosecuted in juvenile court.
14. These states are: DE, IN, NY, RI, TN, UT.
15. Other miscellaneous offenses for which adults can be tried in juvenile court include court order violations (AL, HI, WI), sale of alcohol to minors (DE, UT), criminal confinement of a child (IN), and obstructing a PO (AL).
16. These states are: AL, CO, DE, HI, IN, MD, MN, NH, OH, RI, TN, UT, VA, WI.
17. There are other arrangements such as diversion, consent decrees, and so on (see Chapter 9) in which the juvenile court continues to exercise control over an individual despite the absence of an adjudication.
18. These states are: FL, KS, LA, NJ, NM, NY, OK, SC, TN, TX, VA, WI.
19. These jurisdictions are: AL, AK, AZ, AR, CA, CO, CT, DE, DC, FL, GA, HI, IL, IN, IA, KS, KY, LA, MD, MN, MO, NE, NY, NC, ND, OH, OK, OR, PA, RI, SC, SD, TN, UT, VT, VA, WA, WV.
20. These jurisdictions are: AL, AK, AR, CA, CO, CT, DE, DC, GA, HI, IN, IA, KS, KY, LA, MD, MN, MO, NE, NY, NC, ND, OH, OK, OR, RI, SC, TN, UT, VT, VA, WA, WV, WI.
21. These states are: AR, CO, CT, DE, HI, MD, NY, OH, SC, TN, UT, VA.
22. These jurisdictions are: AR, CO, CT, DC, IN, MD, NY, OH, OK, RI, SC, TN, UT, VA.
23. These states are: AR, DE, MO, SC, VA.
24. These states are: DE, NY, OH, RI, SC, VT.
25. These states are: AL, AZ, CO, DE, GA, HI, MN, ND, OH, RI, SC, TN, UT.
26. These jurisdictions are: DE, DC, HI, MI, NY, RI, SC.
27. These states are: CA, CO, HI, ID, KS, KY, MT, NE, OR, WA.
28. These states are: AL, AZ, AR, CA, CO, CT, FL, GA, HI, ID, IL, IN, IA, KY, LA, MA, MI, MS, MO, NE, NV, NJ, NM, NC, ND, OH, OK, OR, PA, RI, SC, TN, UT, VA, WA, WV.
29. These states are: CO, CT, FL, GA, LA, ME, MT, OH, OK, TX, VA, WI, WY.
30. These states are: AZ, HI, IL, IA, NE, OK, UT, WI, WY.
31. These states are: AL, AZ, IN, ME, ND, TN, TX, VT.
32. These jurisdictions are: DC, IN, KY, MD, MO, UT, WA, WI.
33. These states are: AK, AR, CO, ID, IA, KS, NM, SC, SD, WA.
34. These jurisdictions are: AL, DC, GA, IN, MD, NH, NY, ND, PA, TN.
35. 42 U.S.C.S. Section 5001 *et seq.*
36. Recently, Texas has allowed its justice or municipal courts to address truancies and some misdemeanors if juvenile court waives jurisdiction.
37. These states are: AK, CO, FL, IL, IA, KS, KY, LA, MA, MN, NH, NM, NY, OR, SD, WA, WY.
38. Three jurisdictions do not have status offense jurisdiction (DE, FED, ME), three states suggest all juvenile offenders are delinquents (IN, MI, SC), and Utah refers to youth by virtue of their specific behavior (e.g., ungovernable, runaway, truant) rather than by creating a special title for these individuals.
39. These states are: AK, IA, KS, MN, MO, NE, TN, VT, VA.
40. Utah does not have a special status offense title for this behavior.
41. These states are: CA, CO, CT, HI, KY, LA, MA, MI, MS, NY, OH, RI, TX, UT, WY.
42. These jurisdictions are: AR, CA, DC, FL, GA, IN, LA, MD, MA, MI, NE, NV, NH, NJ, NY, NC, ND, OH, OK, PA, RI, TN, WV, WY.
43. These states are: AZ, HI, MD, MI, MN, MO, NE, NJ, OH, OR, SD, WA, WV.
44. These states are: CO, IL, IA, KS, LA, MI, MN, NE, NJ, ND, OH, OR, SD, VA.
45. These jurisdictions are: AL, AR, CA, DE, DC, FED, HI, ME, MD, ND, PA, VT.
46. See *In Interest of W.R.C.*, 489 N.W.2d 40 (Iowa App. 1992).
47. See *In re Felton*, 706 N.E.2d 809 (Ohio App. 3 Dist. 1997).
48. These jurisdictions are: AL, AZ, CO, DC, GA, KS, LA, MD, MO, MT, NE, ND, OH, SC, SD, TN, TX, VA, WY.
49. These states are: GA, LA, MT, NE, ND, SC, TX, WV.
50. These states are: CA, GA, HI, ID, TX, VA.
51. These jurisdictions are: AL, DC, GA, IN, IA, MD, MI, MS, NV, NH, NY, ND, PA, TN, VT, VA.
52. These jurisdictions are: AL, AZ, CA, CT, DE, DC, FL, ID, IN, KS, LA, ME, MI, MN, MS, MO, NV, NH, ND, OH, OK, OR, PA, RI, SD, TN, UT, VA, WI.
53. Nevada limits the provision to convictions of murder, attempted murder, or a lesser included offense, while in Oregon the youth convicted in adult court must be at least 16 years old and the juvenile court judge must specifically order the mandatory exclusion. Interestingly, Oregon is the only state that allows the juvenile court judge to revoke the mandatory exclusion. ✦

Chapter 5

Measuring Juvenile Crime

Focus of Chapter 5

This chapter explores the extent of juvenile offending and some recent trends. It examines the various methods experts use in attempting to answer the question: Who does how much of what? In answering this question we will look at the four characteristics by which juvenile crime tends to be analyzed: age, gender, race, and social class.

Key Terms

• cohort	• Part I crimes
• Federal Bureau of Investigation (FBI)	• Part II crimes
• index crimes	• self-report surveys (SRS)
• invariant hypothesis	• socioeconomic status (SES)
• National Crime Victimization Surveys (NCVS)	• Uniform Crime Reports (UCR)
	• victimization survey

On April 20, 1999, at Columbine High School in Littleton, Colorado, a horrible tragedy occurred. Two students shot and killed 12 fellow students and a teacher. The event captured the attention of a shocked nation throughout endless hours of on-scene television coverage. It also reignited the controversy over the easy availability of guns and reinforced the public's perception of the escalation of juvenile crime, especially involving violence. Columbine is one of many highly publicized school shootings that have taken place around the nation in recent years.

Juvenile crime must certainly be out of control. Oddly enough, it is not. In fact, it has been declining since 1994. So has adult crime. The media reaction to school shootings may be attributed to the events' shock value and viewer ratings. The political reaction may be a delayed response to the significant increase in juvenile crime between 1987 and

1994, an increase that in some cases outstripped the increases in adult crime. This period of increase followed a slight decline in juvenile crime from 1980 to the mid-1980s. Nevertheless, official data collected by government agencies indicate juvenile crime has declined over the past ten years or so.

Measuring Juvenile Delinquency

There are four methods of measuring crime in the United States, one official and three unofficial. The one official method is the Uniform Crime Reports (UCR) produced by the Federal Bureau of Investigation (FBI). It is official because it is the product of law enforcement agencies reporting crime and it is used as *the* acceptable measure of crime in the United States.

The three unofficial measures are victimization surveys, self-report surveys, and cohort studies. A victimization survey asks a sample of people whether they have been the victims of certain specified crimes. A self-report survey asks a sample of people whether they have ever committed certain specified crimes. Finally, a cohort study examines the delinquency of a group of people who have at least one characteristic in common, over a period of time.

The vast majority of juvenile crime is nonserious. Should crimes such as graffiti be processed in juvenile court?

Uniform Crime Reports

In 1930 Congress authorized the FBI to collect nationwide data on crime in the United States (Inciardi 1987). With that, the Uniform Crime Reports were born, a product of voluntary reporting by police departments around the nation. In recent years some 10,000-plus agencies, representing approximately 95–98 percent of the nation's population, report crime data. The UCR is divided into two major categories: reported crime and arrests.

Reported Crime

Reported crime is divided into Part I and Part II crimes. The eight Part I crimes—murder and nonnegligent manslaughter, forcible rape, robbery, aggravated assault, burglary, larceny/theft, auto theft, and arson—constitute the index crimes. It is the index crime rate that provides the public with its overall perception of crime in America. For instance, if the crime rate rises 6 percent from one year to the next, that figure reflects changes in the index crimes. The word *rate* is the most meaningful quick measure of crime, since it takes into account variations in populations. For instance, if we know the homicide rate is 8.2, that means there are 8.2 homicides for every 100,000 people in the general population. This statistic allows comparison of crime from one time to another or from one place to another even if overall populations change.

Part II crimes (there are 21 of them) are presumed to be less serious than Part I crimes. Examples that support this assertion are vandalism, disorderly conduct, drunkenness, and vagrancy. However, the Part II crimes also encompass drug abuse violations—unlawful possession, sale, use, growing, and manufacturing of illegal drugs—which are the basis for many mandatory prison sentences around the country. Because Part II crimes are not collectively reported the way Part I crimes are, the public is generally not aware of their extent. It is also to be noted that two Part II "crimes" include juvenile status offenses, such as curfew violations and running away.

According to Cohen (1981), there are several reasons why the crime data reflected in the UCR need to be accurate:

- Crime is among the major factors that we believe reflect the nation's social health.

- Crime rates are frequently cited by the media. Often, the recitations on television news broadcasts are accompanied by graphic depictions of victims or their survivors.

- UCR data are used by researchers, theorists, and other scholars.

- Crime data often form the basis for legislation and policy.

As useful as the UCR are to the nation as a whole, critics have pointed to a number of flaws that compromise their accuracy:

- It is obvious that not every crime is reported to the police. Victims of some crimes believe it is not worth the trouble to call the police. A home break-in from which nothing is stolen may be shrugged off. Anecdotal information supports the assertion that some victims of rape do not report the crime (Chesney-Lind 1998). For over 20 years victimization surveys have supported the claim that the UCR significantly underreport crime.

- Victimless crimes are not reported to the police. The individuals involved in drug deals do not report their transactions.

- Law enforcement agencies have been known to manipulate the data for various reasons (Seidman and Couzens 1974). When there is need for greater department resources, the data are inflated.

- Variations in methods of reporting contribute to the distortion of crime data. Although the FBI provides uniform definitions of the UCR crimes as well as a guidelines handbook, no one can determine the degree of compliance among the thousands of reporting agencies. Therefore, reporting Event A as a Part I or Part II crime may simply be a discretionary act by a police department.

- Among the states, definitions vary on what could constitute the same crime. Larceny is a good example. Whether an offense is grand larceny (a Part I felony) or petty larceny (a Part II misdemeanor) depends on the amount of money or value of the stolen goods. The dividing line between felony-misdemeanor can be in the hundreds or thousands of dollars.

Irrespective of the views of critics, the UCR does provide a significant number of benefits. The reports are the official statistics of the criminal justice system. No other method of collecting crime data is as extensive or covers as much of the nation's population. Because much of the data are converted into rates, we can make geographic and time comparisons. The UCR, assuming errors are constant or nearly so, can provide crime trends over time. They can also show any seasonal trends that exist.

Arrest Data and Juvenile Crime

The second major part of the UCR consists of arrest data, the only way official statistics can inform us of juvenile crime. Arrest data in the UCR provide three key identifiers: age, gender, and race.

Table 5.1 Age Distribution of Juvenile Arrests, 2002

Offense	Under 10	10–12	13–14	15	16	17	Under 18
Total	19,904	120,097	370,225	306,678	381,909	425,379	1,624,192
Percent distribution	*0.2*	*1.2*	*3.8*	*3.1*	*3.9*	*4.3*	*16.5*
Murder and nonnegligent manslaughter	0	17	84	140	274	458	973
Forcible rape	42	336	865	562	672	884	3,361
Robbery	85	789	3,449	3,408	4,532	5,630	17,893
Aggravated assault	699	4,350	10,797	7,948	9,722	10,765	44,281
Burglary	1,153	5,804	15,432	11,515	13,349	14,590	61,843
Larceny/theft	3,538	25,799	65,753	46,317	53,323	54,131	248,861
Motor vehicle theft	65	1,006	7,156	7,698	8,531	8,008	32,544
Arson	552	1,350	1,826	855	671	597	5,851
Violent crime	826	5,492	15,195	12,058	15,200	17,737	66,508
Percent distribution	*0.2*	*1.2*	*3.4*	*2.7*	*3.4*	*4.0*	*14.9*
Property crime	5,308	33,959	90,167	66,385	75,874	77,406	349,099
Percent distribution	*0.5*	*2.9*	*7.7*	*5.7*	*6.5*	*6.6*	*29.8*
Crime index	6,134	39,451	105,362	78,443	91,074	95,143	415,607
Percent distribution	*0.4*	*2.4*	*6.5*	*4.9*	*5.6*	*5.9*	*25.7*
Other assaults	2,813	20,123	48,761	31,230	33,653	32,416	168,996
							(continued)

Table 5.1 Age Distribution of Juvenile Arrests, 2002 (*continued*)

Offense	Under 10	10–12	13–14	15	16	17	Under 18
Forgery/counterfeiting	34	70	353	479	984	1,732	3,652
Fraud	102	225	851	885	1,611	2,760	6,434
Embezzlement	2	20	68	72	259	584	1,005
Stolen property	138	982	3,924	3,550	4,600	5,625	18,819
Vandalism	2,656	10,049	20,274	13,179	14,988	14,900	75,955
Weapons	438	2,166	6,043	4,615	5,379	6,647	25,288
Prostitution/vice	2	24	139	170	281	479	1,095
Sex offenses (except rape and prostitution)	427	2,144	4,655	2,352	2,128	2,171	13,877
Drug abuse violations	284	2,609	18,943	23,031	36,904	51,983	133,754
Gambling	0	32	139	200	308	435	1,114
Offenses against family	343	612	1,487	1,279	1,406	1,445	6,572
Driving under influence	113	23	234	631	3,810	10,403	15,214
Liquor laws	152	752	9,228	15,826	30,702	49,354	106,014
Drunkenness	87	143	1,449	2,101	3,245	6,504	13,529
Disorderly conduct	1,487	14,502	40,325	27,667	27,941	27,126	139,048
Vagrancy	10	62	330	297	369	451	1,519
All other offenses	3,118	15,459	57,448	54,407	70,007	81,586	282,025
Suspicion	6	52	236	220	359	451	1,519
Curfew and loitering	523	5,127	23,420	23,323	29,066	21,696	103,155
Runaways	1,126	5,470	26,556	22,721	22,896	11,580	90,349

Source: Uniform Crime Reports (2003), Table 38.

In referring to juveniles, the data reported in the UCR use either the term "under 18" or the age bracket 10–17. Table 5.1 is instructive in that it includes index and nonindex crimes and the total number (estimated) of juveniles arrested in 2002. This is our best indication of the amount of illegal activity for juveniles during that year.

Table 5.2 presents the percentage of arrested juveniles who are female, the percentage who are under 15, and the percentage changes for all offenses over several time periods. A striking piece of information—one that should alert us—is that almost one-third (31.4 percent) of all juveniles arrested are *under* age 15. A slightly higher percentage (32.3) holds for violent offenses for the same age group. At present, though, the nation has experienced a significant decline in serious juvenile crime since it peaked in 1993.

Table 5.2 Juvenile Arrests by Age Group and Gender, 2002

Most Serious Offense	2002 Estimated Number of Juvenile Arrests	Percent of Total Juvenile Arrests		Percent Change		
		Female	Under Age 15	1993–2002	1998–2002	2001–2002
Total	1,624,300	28.9	31.4	−10.9	−19.3	−3.0
Crime index total	415,607	29.7	36.3	−33.3	−21.8	−3.5
Violent crime index	66,508	18.4	32.3	−29.3	−16.9	−3.0
Murder and nonnegligent manslaughter	973	10.4	10.4	−64.3	−35.6	1.5
Forcible rape	3,361	3.2	37	−26.5	−13.8	−1.4
Robbery	17,893	8.8	24.2	−38.4	−20.7	−0.9
Aggravated assault	44,281	23.6	35.8	−23.0	−15.0	−4.4
Property crime index	349,099	31.9	37.1	−34.0	−22.7	−3.6
Burglary	61,843	11.2	36.2	−39.2	−26.1	−4.4
Larceny-theft	248,861	39.4	38.2	−28.7	−22.9	−3.0
Motor vehicle theft	32,544	17.2	25.3	−50.4	−15.2	−5.7
Arson	5,851	11.4	63.7	−23.2	−11.3	−10.2
Nonindex						
Other assaults	168,996	32.1	42.4	13.8	−1.7	1.4
Forgery/counterfeiting	3,652	35.7	12.5	−42.5	−31.3	−17.3
Fraud	6,434	32.8	18.3	−18.5	−20.0	−7.2
Embezzlement	1,005	41.3	8.9	73.1	−18.2	−25.4
Stolen property	18,819	15.7	26.6	−45.3	−26.1	−5.4
Vandalism	75,955	13.5	43.3	−33.3	−22.2	−1.9
Weapons	25,288	11.0	34.2	−46.8	−24.1	−5.2
Prostitution/vice	1,095	66.6	15.1	26.9	−5.7	4.2
Sex offenses	13,877	9.2	52.1	−8.9	9.1	0.6
Drug abuse violations	133,754	16.1	16.3	59.1	−10.6	−7.2
Gambling	1,114	3.0	15.4	−38.6	−8.2	16.3

(continued)

Table 5.2 Juvenile Arrests by Age Group and Gender, 2002 (*continued*)

Most Serious Offense	2002 Estimated Number of Juvenile Arrests	Percent of Total Juvenile Arrests		Percent Change		
		Female	Under Age 15	1993–2002	1998–2002	2001–2002
Offenses against family	6,572	39.2	37.2	48.0	−12.3	−6.3
Driving under influence	15,214	19.4	2.4	45.5	−5.8	4.1
Liquor law violations	106,014	33.7	9.6	16.8	−21.9	2.9
Drunkenness	13,529	21.6	12.4	−2.2	−26.4	−6.8
Disorderly conduct	139,048	30.1	40.5	8.8	−15.5	2.7
Vagrancy	1,519	23.5	26.5	−40.3	−37.0	−15
All other offenses	282,025	26.9	27.0	7.9	−19.9	−2.9
Suspicion	1,171	28.7	25.1	−42.9	−9.1	49.3
Curfew and loitering	103,155	31.3	28.2	35.2	−32.7	−4.7
Runaways	90,349	59.8	36.7	−37.4	−27.3	−7.7

Source: Adapted from Uniform Crime Reports (2003), Tables 32, 34, 36, 38, 41, 43.

Table 5.3 focuses on gender and arrest trends between 1994 and 1998, and between 1998 and 2002. As the table indicates, there was an increase in female arrests (10.9 percent) and a decrease in male arrests (2.2 percent) between 1994 and 1998. In the 1998–2002 period, there was an overall decline in arrests for both males (21.2 percent) and females (14 percent). What can be seen throughout Table 5.3 is that for nearly all offenses, arrests of female juveniles increased more or decreased less than arrests of male juveniles during the past decade.

Table 5.3 Percent Change in Juvenile Arrests for Select Offenses by Gender, 1994–1998 and 1998–2002

Offenses	1994–1998		1998–2002	
	Male	Female	Male	Female
Murder	−48.7	−34.0	−36.6	−24.2
Forcible rape	−8.7	−16.0	−15.3	+73.6
Robbery	−29.1	−26.4	−20.9	−18.4
Aggravated assault	−17.6	+7.5	−16.9	−8.2

(*continued*)

Table 5.3 Percent Change in Juvenile Arrests for Select Offenses by Gender, 1994–1998 and 1998–2002 (*continued*)				
	1994–1998		1998–2002	
Offenses	Male	Female	Male	Female
Burglary	−18.1	−4.7	−26.2	−25.4
Larceny-theft	−17.1	−6.1	−28.3	−12.9
Motor vehicle theft	−41.7	−27.1	−14.5	−18.3
Other assaults	+3.6	+28.7	−4.1	+3.8
Stolen property	−27.8	−19.5	−28.8	−7.9
Vandalism	−19.9	−4.9	−23.7	−10.8
Weapons	−30.8	−20.1	−25.6	−9.2
Sex offenses	−5.2	−3.7	+8.9	+12.3
Drug abuse violations	+23.3	+42.6	−12.8	+2.9
Driving under the influence	+32.9	+74.7	−7.6	+2.4
Liquor laws	+35.4	+47.3	−25.1	−14.8
Disorderly conduct	+12.6	+43.4	−18.2	−8.4
All other offenses (except traffic)	+16.3	+34.2	−21.8	−14.0
Curfew and loitering	+44.4	+60.4	−32.4	−33.4
Violent crime index	−22.2	−.2	−18.4	−9.5
Property crime index	−20.8	−7.6	−26.1	−14.1
Crime index	−21.1	−6.9	−24.8	−13.6
Total	−2.2	+10.9	−21.1	−14.0
Source: Adapted from Uniform Crime Reports (1999, 2003), Table 35.				

Table 5.4 gives further indication that girls are prominently involved in delinquency. Interestingly, juvenile girls account for a higher percentage of arrests for all females than do boys in arrests for all males, except for those under ten years of age.

Table 5.5 depicts the racial proportion of juvenile arrestees for serious crimes and select other offenses. For now, note that the arrest percentages for black youth exceed their percentage in the general population of juveniles (15 percent). We will discuss gender and race in some detail later in this chapter.

Table 5.4 Number and Percentage of Arrests by Age and Gender, 2002

Age	Gender				Total	
	Male		Female			
Under 10	16,157	.2	3,747	.2	19,904	.2
10–12	87,842	1.2	32,255	1.4	120,097	1.2
13–14	245,308	3.2	124,917	5.5	370,225	3.8
15	207,784	2.7	98,894	4.4	306,678	3.1
16	273,085	3.6	108,824	4.8	381,909	3.9
17	324,117	4.3	101,362	4.5	425,379	4.3
Under 15	349,307	4.6	160,919	7.1	510,226	5.2
Under 18	1,154,193	15.3	469,999	20.8	1,624,192	16.5
Over 18	6,405,242	84.7	1,790,067	79.2	8,195,309	83.5

Source: Adapted from Uniform Crime Reports (2003), Tables 38, 40.

Table 5.5 Distribution of Juvenile Arrests for Select Offenses by Race, 2002

Offense	Number of Arrests				Percent Distribution			
	White	Black	Native American	Asian	White	Black	Native American	Asian
Murder	446	487	23	16	45.9	50.1	2.4	1.6
Forcible rape	2,079	1,207	37	32	62.0	36.0	1.1	1.0
Robbery	6,895	10,537	91	355	38.6	58.9	0.5	2.0
Aggravated assault	26,877	16,217	535	556	60.8	36.7	1.2	1.3
Violent crime index	**36,297**	**28,448**	**686**	**959**	**54.7**	**42.8**	**1.0**	**1.4**
Burglary	44,680	15,558	689	827	72.4	25.2	1.1	1.3
Larceny/theft	173,910	65,667	3,443	5,182	70.1	26.5	1.4	2.1
Motor vehicle theft	18,949	12,428	445	665	58.3	38.3	1.4	2.0
Arson	4,711	1,026	48	52	80.7	17.6	0.8	0.9
Property crime index	**242,250**	**94,679**	**4,625**	**6,726**	**69.6**	**27.2**	**1.3**	**1.9**
Other assaults	106,119	58,518	1,942	2,062	62.9	34.7	1.2	1.2

(continued)

Table 5.5 Distribution of Juvenile Arrests for Select Offenses by Race, 2002 (*continued*)								
	Number of Arrests				Percent Distribution			
Offense	White	Black	Native American	Asian	White	Black	Native American	Asian
Stolen property	10,612	7,761	134	262	56.5	41.4	0.7	1.4
Weapons	16,945	7,751	207	336	67.1	30.7	0.8	1.3
Drug abuse violations	97,766	33,208	1,152	1,368	73.2	24.9	0.9	1.0
All other arrests	210,704	62,641	3,261	4,578	74.9	22.3	1.2	1.6
Curfew and loitering	70,738	29,717	1,083	1,516	68.6	28.8	1.1	1.5
Runaways	68,371	16,603	1,214	4,039	75.8	18.4	1.3	4.5
Crime index	278,547	123,127	5,311	7,685	67.2	29.7	1.3	1.9

Source: Uniform Crime Reports (2003), Table 43.

A Cautionary Note on Arrest Data

Some who read arrest data produced in the UCR are probably quick to draw conclusions about crimes and people. For instance, in 2002 about 1.6 million juvenile arrests were recorded by the FBI. What might we conclude from that arrest figure? Snyder (1999) cautions that the following be kept in mind before drawing conclusions:

- The number of arrests does not necessarily equal the number of individuals arrested. Some are arrested more than once a year.

- The number of people arrested does not equal the number of crimes committed by the arrestees. The arrest of a single person may represent a series of crimes committed by that person. On the other hand, the arrest of a number of people can relate to a single crime.

- An arrest is identified by the most serious offense in multiple offenses. For instance, an arrest logged as aggravated assault could also include, but not count, drug possession.

- A measure of police performance commonly used is the clearance rates, or the proportion of crimes known to the police that are resolved by arrests. But a single arrest could clear 40 crimes or multiple arrests could clear a single crime.

Thus far, we have discussed the official measurement of crime, which is inextricably tied to law enforcement. The remaining three methods of measuring crime are unofficial but nonetheless make valuable contributions to our understanding of crime and delinquency.

Victimization Surveys

In 1966, the President's Commission on Law Enforcement and the Administration of Justice authorized a victimization survey, one that asked a sample of people whether they had been the victim of crime. The major reasons for this undertaking were to serve as a supplemental piece of information to the UCR and to respond to questions about the accuracy of the official data (Bartol and Bartol 1998). In the ensuing years several pilot surveys were carried out, but since 1973 the federal government has produced the results of national victimization surveys on an annual basis. Officially, they are now called National Crime Victimization Surveys (NCVS).

Over the years the sample size and interview periods have varied. Essentially, the members of households age 12 and over are interviewed several times over a multiyear period. The interviews are carried out by the Census Bureau for the Bureau of Justice Statistics. The first of a series is done in person. Then repeat contacts are made, in person or by telephone, every six months over a three-year period. In 1997, approximately 80,000 people in 43,000 households were contacted (Rand 1998).

What have we learned over the years from the NCVS? First, according to the victims since 1973, less than 40 percent of all crimes are reported to the police (Bastion 1993). As late as 1997, the figure for all crime reported to the police was 37.4 percent (Rand 1998). Table 5.6 reflects the percentages of selected crimes reported to the police in 1996.

Second, the NVCS provides data on household income of victims, marital status in households of victims, and the existence of any victim-offender relationship when a crime took place. The NCVS also provides data on victimization by age grouping and gender (see Table 5.7).

Table 5.6 Crimes Reported to Police by Victims, in 1997, by Percent

Rape/sexual assault	30.5%
Robbery	55.8
Aggravated assault	59.1
Burglary	51.8
Motor vehicle theft	79.8
Theft	27.9
Source: Adapted from Rand (1998).	

Table 5.7 Victimization Rates by Gender and Age (rate per 1,000 persons in each age group in 1998)

Gender and Age	Rape/Sexual Assault	Robbery	Aggravated Assault
Male			
12–15	0.0	8.9	18.2
16–19	0.4	17.2	28.6
Female			
12–15	7.0	6.6	6.1
16–19	10.0	5.2	8.9
Source: Adapted from Bureau of Justice Statistics (2000c), Table 4.			

Self-Report Surveys

Prior to the 1960s juvenile delinquency was almost universally believed to be a lower-class phenomenon. Cohen (1955) supported this assertion by stating that all statistical analyses of juvenile delinquency point to this conclusion. The reason for that kind of thinking is now obvious. The only available data were official statistics. Researchers probed only the data that existed in the juvenile court and police files.

It would be difficult to determine what percentage of juveniles commit delinquent acts if we had to rely solely on the measures discussed thus far. We may get closer to an answer if we ask juveniles whether they have committed juvenile or adult offenses. The method used to tap into this data is self-report surveys (SRS).

The first requirement of an SRS is a large number of respondents. This requirement alone puts the vast majority of crime and delinquency SRS in schools. An adult SRS is a rarity. Several have been done in adult prisons, but they have had a specific agenda, such as the Rand Corporation's research on career criminals in the late 1970s and early 1980s (Petersilia et al. 1978). Furthermore, survey respondents in adult prisons and juvenile training schools are official offenders. The purpose of SRS is to learn about the delinquent behavior that has not become official. In addition, one of the objectives of the SRS is to learn about personal and social variables of respondents.

Self-report surveys can be carried out in a number of ways. They can be anonymous or subjects can be identified. Anonymity is preferred since researchers believe subjects will be more forthcoming and can be asked questions that relate to family structure, parental education, family income, and so on. Surveys can also be done through interviews or in writing. Because interviewing several thousand high school seniors is a labor-intensive task, the anonymous, written (multiple-choice) survey is the preferred one.

From the 1960s on, self-report surveys became a significant aspect of delinquency research. Short and Nye (1958) used an anonymous survey with high school students (boys and girls) and juveniles incarcerated in a training school. They concluded that delinquency in the school group was uniform among the social classes, but in the training school it was disproportionately weighted at the lower socioeconomic status (SES). In general, among schoolchildren the same results have occurred over and over. There is no clear relationship between delinquency and SES (Chamblis and Nagasawa 1969; Elliott and Voss 1974; Gold 1966; Gould 1969; Williams and Gold 1972). The years of these studies were marked by civil strife and civil rights, antiwar protests, urban riots, and illegal drugs. The researchers were mostly sociologists who were often accused of being significantly left of center politically and underdog fighters, a veiled claim that the research had been slanted toward a desired effect. Nevertheless, some researchers put forth a contrary view. Cemkovich et al. (1985) argued that most self-report studies miss the hardcore chronic offender. Elliott and Voss (1974) demonstrated with an SRS that there is a clear SES distinction when high-frequency delinquents are compared. Research during the 1990s, though, seems to confirm the original no-relationship conclusion (Tittle and Meier 1990; Wright et al. 1999).

No researcher has made an outright claim that no relationship exists between SES and delinquency. Conclusions are modified by the phrases "it seems" and "it appears." Because a significant portion of crime and delinquency theory is based on SES, a concrete finding of no relationship between the two could dismantle many theories (Tittle and Meier 1990).

Criticism of SRS

Regardless of one's view on this issue, there are several compelling reasons for questioning the accuracy of self-report studies. The major criticism is aimed at the construction of the survey instrument itself. Critics have argued that an overrepresentation of questions that relate to minor offenses such as truancy, drinking alcoholic beverages, and petty theft will almost guarantee a conclusion that there are no SES differences among those who admit to delinquent behavior. In fact, under these circumstances one would conclude that all youth are delinquent. The choice of questions in designing the survey is thus the critical element. As it turns out, the most common offenses reported by teens are truancy, drinking alcoholic beverages, fighting, petty theft (shoplifting), and damaging property.

Another criticism is the tendency of surveys to overlap elements of behavior that have a common thread. It is not uncommon to find survey questions that use overlapping terms such as "shoplifting," "theft under $5," and "theft between $5 and $50" (Elliott and Ageton 1980). This terminology can confuse respondents or result in multiple answers for a single act.

Overrepresentation of one or two categories of behavior can distort the collective results of SRS. In one instrument with 21 items, 11 are related to alcohol consumption and the use of illegal drugs (Siegel and Senna 1991). In this instrument, the three questions that relate to alcohol ask youth if they have ever:

- got drunk on beer;
- got drunk on hard liquor; and
- got drunk on wine.

The delinquent act for an underage person is *drinking,* not necessarily getting drunk. A teen who imbibed all three beverages could answer truthfully *never* to the questions. And why have three types of alcoholic beverages? Would not one question about alcohol consumption do?

Finally, the form of responses on SRS has come under attack. Some SRS use terms like "often," "sometimes," and "occasionally," which can lead to a wide variety of interpretations (Elliott and Ageton 1980). Also, many SRS instruments attempt to become more precise by using specific numerical instances of behavior. It is common to see "never," "once," "2–5 times," and "more than 5 times." It is also common to apply the SRS to high school juniors and seniors. Can youthful memories be accurate enough to mark the "2–5" column or the "5 or more" column for behavior like drinking? And "more than 5 times" can mean 6 or 600.

Validation of SRS

Among the criticisms of SRS is that respondents, especially juveniles, are not truthful in answering questions. There are several ways to validate SRS responses but, unfortunately, each is flawed. Researchers can ask peers about their friends' behavior, but that would eliminate anonymity. Responses on the SRS could be checked against police records, with the same effect on anonymity. In fact, anonymity is lost in any test of validity other than a collective check. In this case the SRS is anonymous but the researcher provides the respondents' identities to police authorities for a records check. The police provide group responses, such as 23 percent of the respondents have been arrested for shoplifting. This method of validating the SRS is rather crude and therefore of little utility.

Finally, assuming an SRS is most often issued in high schools, two groups of teens who some would say are potentially or in reality the most delinquent of all (chronic truants and dropouts) rarely participate in surveys of this kind. The National Center for Education Statistics, in the U.S. Department of Education, reported that in 1992 381,000 (4.5 percent) of all high school students had dropped out of grades 10–12. The percentage of dropouts varies by race and ethnicity. The Center reported dropout rates for 1998 of 5 percent for whites, 14 percent for blacks, and 30 percent for Hispanics.

Despite shortcomings in self-reports, there should be no thoughts of abandoning them. Together with other forms of measuring crime (UCR and NCVS), they broaden the scope of identifying such behavior among the nation's population. Further, researchers and theorists are able to create particular banks of data and information by the way SRS instruments are constructed. Hirschi (1969) made a significant contribution to the development of control theory through his monumental SRS with school teens and their social attachments to parents, school, and peers in the 1960s.

We now add another method of measuring delinquency, this time focusing on identifying youth who persist in law-violating behavior.

Cohort Studies

A fourth method of measuring crime is by studying cohorts. A cohort is a group of people who have at least one thing in common. A freshman class at a university is a cohort—their common characteristic is the fact that they are freshmen. Cohorts are studied over time. A researcher might want to know how many freshmen drop out by the time they are seniors, or track their grades over that time period. In the area of crime, cohort studies have been carried out almost exclusively on juveniles.

The first major study of this kind was performed by noted criminologist Marvin E. Wolfgang and his colleagues (1972) in Philadelphia. They examined the delinquency of 9,945 boys born in Philadelphia in 1945 who continued to live there from ages 10 to 17. The study revealed, among other things, that a small fraction of the boys committed a disproportionate amount of the crime committed by all the boys in the cohort, a finding that was startling and inspired further research. This study group is known as *Cohort I*.

Wolfgang and his colleagues (Tracy et al. 1985) continued cohort research in Philadelphia by selecting boys *and* girls who were born in Philadelphia in 1958 and who continued to reside there from ages 10 to 17. Not only did this group include girls, but it was also much larger than Cohort I. Containing 13,160 boys and 14,000 girls, it is referred to as *Cohort II*. Delinquency rates and patterns in Cohort II resembled those of Cohort I.

Wolfgang et al. (1987) managed to identify a 10 percent sample of Cohort I boys and examined their criminal behavior until age 30. This study clearly pointed out the criminal careers of some of the high-delinquency youth of the cohort.

In the mid-1970s Donna Hamparian and her colleagues (1978) essentially replicated the Cohort I study with one major exception: The youth selected for their cohort study (boys and girls) had already been charged with a violent offense. These juveniles were born in a five-year period (1956–1960) in Columbus, Ohio. Among other cohort studies are one conducted in London, England (West and Farrington 1977), and another in Racine, Wisconsin, in which Lyle Shannon (1982) tracked the delinquent histories of three cohorts born in 1942, 1949, and 1952.

Interestingly, whether cohorts of juveniles are studied in Philadelphia or Columbus, and whether they are studied in the 1950s, 1960s, or 1970s, several findings reveal common threads regarding youthful law violations.

Cohorts I and II

The sources of data collected by Wolfgang et al. (1972) were the official records of the police, schools, and juvenile court. Our focus will be on police data. Delinquency was measured by police *contacts*, whether they resulted in arrest or diversion.

In Cohort I about one-third (35 percent) of the 9,945 boys had at least one police contact. Of that one-third, 46 percent had only one contact, and 35 percent had two to four contacts. A small group—627, or 18 percent of the delinquents and 6 percent of the total cohort—had five or more contacts and were responsible for 52 percent of all the delinquent offenses. These 627 youth were referred to as *chronic delinquents* in this and subsequent cohort studies carried out by Wolfgang and his colleagues.

The chronics were responsible for:

- 71 percent of the homicides committed by cohort youth;

- 73 percent of the rapes;

- 82 percent of the robberies; and

- 69 percent of the aggravated assaults.

The researchers in Cohort II used the same methodology as that in Cohort I. In some respects the cohorts proved to be similar, but in some ways they differed. For instance, the youth in the two cohorts were raised in very different social environments. The period at risk (10 to 17 years old) for youth in Cohort I was 1955–1962, a time of relative tranquility. America was enjoying a prosperous postwar economy, and the overall crime rate was low. For juveniles, the homicide rate reached 5 per 100,000 juveniles only once during the at-risk period. The at-risk period for youth in Cohort II was 1968–1975, a period notable for drug use, urban riots, the civil rights movement, and antiwar protests. The crime rate in the nation had begun to escalate in 1963 and the juvenile homicide rate rose from 6.9 in 1968 to 9.6 in 1975 (Bureau of Justice Statistics 2000).

In Cohort I, 71 percent were white, while 29 percent were nonwhite. In Cohort II, we see a result of the demographic shifts that took place in American cities after World War

II, as the percentage of white males declined to 47 percent while the percentage of nonwhite males rose to 53 percent (see Table 5.8).

Socioeconomic status was measured by family income, divided into two groups, high and low. In Cohort I, 70 percent of white boys were classified as high SES, while for nonwhites it was 16 percent. Substantial within-group upward shifts occurred in SES from Cohort I to Cohort II. In Cohort II, 79 percent of the white boys were classified high, as were 27 percent of the nonwhite boys (see Table 5.9).

In terms of delinquent behavior, we see several significant shifts from Cohort I to Cohort II. The overall prevalence rates (police contacts) were about the same in both cohorts except for the chronics, which were 18 percent in Cohort I and 23 percent in Cohort II (see Table 5.10).

Cohort II youth committed more offenses and more serious offenses than Cohort I youth. Cohort I youth committed 1,027 offenses per 1,000 youth, while Cohort II youth committed 1,159. Also, Cohort I youth committed 247 UCR index offenses per 1,000 youth, while Cohort II youth committed 455. The differences between the cohorts are dramatic when we view the ratio of Cohort II to Cohort I UCR violent index crimes, as shown in Table 5.11.

In 1964, Sellin and Wolfgang developed a crime-seriousness scale that provides numerical values for crimes; the higher the number, the more serious the crime. Tracy et al. (1985) analyzed the seriousness of crimes committed by males in Cohort I and Cohort II using the Sellin-Wolfgang scale. In Cohort I, less than 1 percent fell at the upper end of the scale, whereas in Cohort II it was 20 percent. They also compared the

Table 5.8 Males in Cohorts I and II, by Race (percentage)

Race	Cohort I	Cohort II
White	71	47
Nonwhite	29	53

Source: Tracy et al. (1985).

Table 5.9 Males in Cohorts I and II, by Race and High SES (percentage)

Race	Cohort I	Cohort II
White	70	79
Nonwhite	16	27

Source: Tracy et al. (1985).

Table 5.10 Prevalence of Male Delinquency in Cohorts I and II (police contacts, in percentages)

Contacts	Cohort I	Cohort II
At least 1	35	33
Only 1	46	42
2 to 4	35	35
Chronic	18	23

Source: Tracy et al. (1985).

Table 5.11 Ratio of Violent Index Crimes, Cohort II: Cohort I (for Males)

Crime	Rates
Homicide	3:1
Rape	1.7:1
Robbery	5:1
Aggravated assault	2:1

Source: Tracy et al. (1985).

Table 5.12 Comparing the Chronics of Cohorts I and II (Males)	
Cohort I	**Cohort II**
1. The 627 chronics were 6 percent of the total cohort and 18 percent of the delinquents.	1. The 982 chronics were 7.5 percent of the total cohort and 23 percent of the delinquents.
2. The chronics accounted for 5,305 offenses, or 52 percent of all offenses committed by the cohort.	2. The chronics accounted for 9,240 offenses, or 61 percent of all offenses committed by the cohort.

3. Percent of all juvenile offenses for selected crimes.

	Cohort I	Cohort II
Homicides	71%	61%
Rapes	73	75
Robberies	82	75
Aggravated assault	69	65

Source: Tracy et al. (1985).

chronics of the two cohorts in terms of crimes committed and their levels of severity (see Table 5.12).

A significant finding in the research is that the chronics in both cohorts committed more than their share of crimes, irrespective of race and SES. For instance, nonwhite chronics committed 65 percent of all offenses committed by nonwhites in both cohorts. High-SES chronics committed 35 percent in Cohort I and 50 percent in Cohort II of all offenses committed by high-SES youth.

The Philadelphia cohort studies were unique measures of delinquency at the time and inspired further research of the same kind. We now discuss two other cohort studies on youth in Columbus, Ohio, and Racine, Wisconsin.

The Violent Few

Donna Hamparian and her colleagues (1978) carried out a cohort study in Columbus, Ohio. The cohort consisted of boys and girls born there from 1956 to 1960 (a five-year total) who had been arrested at least once for a violent crime by age 18 (violent crimes included in this study went far beyond index crimes and included such offenses such as schoolyard fighting and purse snatching). The total cohort consisted of 1,138 boys and girls. The cohort was disproportionately male by a 6:1 ratio; it was disproportionately black, as is the proportion in the local general population; and it was disproportionately low SES. The researchers used income to measure SES and found only 14.3 percent of the cohort to be above the median household income. Race and SES were significantly related: 98 percent of black youth were categorized as very poor, while 77.2 percent of white youth were above the median income. An interesting finding of the study was that 12.2 percent of the youth had siblings who were also in the study. There were 62 pairs and 7 sets of three siblings in a study that covered only five years. One-third of the youth lived in mother-only households.

The study focused on 811 youth born in 1956–1958, which the researchers labeled Subset 1 since some of the youth born in 1959–1960 had not reached 18 when data collection started. The 811 youth accumulated 3,373 arrests, an average of 4.2 per youth, and were charged with 4,445 offenses. Twenty-nine percent of the subset desisted after the one violent arrest that had earned them a spot in the study, which means that 71 percent were recidivists, a figure well above that in the Philadelphia Cohort I of 53.6 percent.

The chronics in the Columbus study (five arrests or more) constituted 33.6 percent of the total cohort, while those in Philadelphia Cohort I had made up 18 percent. The 811 subset youth were arrested 985 times for violent crimes, tallying 1,087 charges. Only 3.8 percent of them had three or more violent arrests, but they accounted for 10.4 percent of the violent arrests.

Among the chronics there was no race distinction in terms of violent arrests—blacks averaged 1.23; whites averaged 1.15. Almost 19 percent of the males were violent recidivists; for the females it was 5.5 percent. Finally, only 7.9 percent of the youth above the median income were violent recidivists.

Hamparian et al. (1985) also followed the cohort into adulthood. About 12.5 percent of the cohort were "total chronics." They were responsible for about half of juvenile arrests and more than 45 percent of all arrests.

Shannon's (1982) cohort study in Racine, Wisconsin, consisted of youth born there in 1942, 1949, and 1955. The total number of youth in the three cohorts was 6,127; of them, 4,079 lived in Racine continuously until the data collection in 1974 (for Cohorts 1 and 2) and 1976 (for Cohort 3).

The study revealed a now-common, recurring theme. About 5 to 7 percent of each cohort were responsible for over half of all nontraffic police contacts. About 20 percent of each cohort were responsible for about 80 percent of all such contacts. About 8 to 14 percent of each cohort were responsible for all the cohorts' felonies, and 5 percent was responsible for 75 percent of the felonies.

While the rate of first police contacts for males was high—70 to 80 percent for the three cohorts—more than 50 percent had fewer than five contacts, and more than half of the females did not have a second.

Shannon concluded, as have other cohort researchers, that a small, hardcore group of offenders are continuously and seriously involved in crime.

Critique of Cohort Studies

The major criticisms of cohort studies are their compartmentalization (they are done with a relatively small group of individuals within a defined geographical space) and their lack of generalizability (ability to be generalized nationally). They are also done retrospectively. That is, after the subjects have reached a predetermined age, the researchers go into various data banks and collect historical information. When the studies discussed here were done, computers for storing data were not available. The researchers had to locate and read through thousands of paper files, many no doubt stored for years in cardboard boxes. Also, the information logged in the various records was done years—in some cases, *many* years—before the researchers examined them. The individuals who wrote the information in the records (clerk-staffs of police, schools, and juvenile courts) had no idea about their work becoming part of a research project ten years later. Practitioners in the criminal and juvenile justice systems have long known about the inaccuracies in official records. We may safely assume that these problems were probably worse 20 or 30 years ago than they are today.

Nevertheless, on the positive side, we can also assume with some degree of confidence that in any community a small group of youth commit a disproportionate amount of juvenile offenses. We can also assume that the majority of youth in a community do not have contact with the police, and among those who do, a substantial proportion have no more than one contact.

Evaluating Measures of Juvenile Delinquency

We have explored four methods of measuring juvenile delinquency: Uniform Crime Reports (UCR), victimization surveys (NCVS), self-reports surveys (SRS), and cohort studies. Each has strengths and each has weaknesses. Each also lends a unique aspect to crime reporting. The UCR, in addition to being the official measurement of crime, is the only true national count. The NCVS purports to provide national victimization data on crime, but its credibility as a national measure is only as good as the U.S. Census Bureau's sampling methods. However, the NCVS does supply information not available through other methods. Victims in some cases can give descriptions of perpetrators, provide their race and gender, and note the time of the day of the offense. The NCVS also offers an idea of the percentage of crimes not reported to the police. Both the UCR and the NCVS can give us an insight into crime trends over time.

Self-report surveys are unique in that they report delinquent behavior by the "offenders" themselves. Although the potential for flawed reporting is always present because of the variations in the questions asked, an SRS can provide information not found in other forms of measurement. While Hirschi's (1969) 400-plus item questionnaire may have been tedious, it included scores of questions about parents, schools, and peers. Cohort studies, like the Philadelphia studies, are unique in that not only do they acquire information from police, schools, and the juvenile court, but they also trace delinquent careers over time. They provide the age of onset of delinquency and usually include race, SES, and gender characteristics of offenders.

Age and Delinquency

Someone once said, "Crime is a young man's game." This particular aphorism has been bandied about in academic and nonacademic circles for decades. Perhaps the first to implant this assertion into the literature were Travis Hirschi and Michael Gottfredson (1983). A few years later, they wrote a criminology text (Gottfredson and Hirschi 1990) in which *age* occupied about half of a chapter and was also scattered throughout the text. They are credited with developing the invariant hypothesis, which says that no matter what the place (city, state, or nation) or the era, crime peaks in the late teens. This assertion is generally accepted without challenge in the literature (see Sampson and Laub 1995). If we separate property crime from violent crime, there are slight variations. For property crime a sharp decline follows the peak, but for violent crime a leveling off follows the peak until about age 25, then there is a decline. This information can be depicted in a line graph as shown in Figure 5.1.

Researchers have used UCR arrest data, self-reports, cohort studies, and even victimization surveys to test the hypothesis. The last source is the least reliable because victims who experience stranger-to-stranger crime often have to guess at the offender's age. Moreover, many property crimes are not witnessed by victims.

Arrest data tend to support the invariant hypothesis. In their book, Gottfredson and Hirschi (1990) use UCR arrest data for their graphs in depicting crime in the United States. Snyder and Sickmund (1999) produce many graphs of juvenile offending, also using UCR data. These graphs follow the patterns displayed in Figure 5.1.

Self-reports are used infrequently to test the hypothesis. Osgood et al.

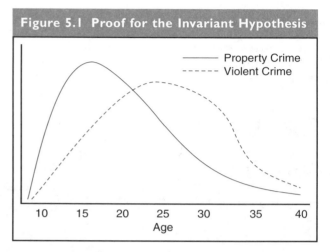

Figure 5.1 Proof for the Invariant Hypothesis

——— Property Crime
- - - - Violent Crime

Age

(1989) compared SRS and arrest rates of 17- to 23-year-olds from 1975 to 1985. Their data show substantial decline from age 17 to 23 for almost all offenses. The limitations in using self-reports for this purpose parallel the general weaknesses of SRS. Much depends on the types of questions used on surveys, the memories of those surveyed, the age range of the subjects, and the year of the offense (or their age at the time of the offense). To test the hypothesis researchers would have to perform *prospective* longitudinal surveys—that is, follow the same group of subjects over a period of time.

Cohort studies (*retrospective* longitudinal studies) may be the best method of testing the invariant hypothesis. Rather than taking a snapshot view of offending in one year and determining the ages of those arrested, cohort studies track the *same subjects* over time. Thus, for example, in 1955 the Cohort I boys became 10 years of age, in 1956 they became 11, and so on. This method can indicate not only when offending *peaks* but also the age of the *onset* of official delinquency. The Philadelphia studies, in general, agree with the hypothesis. Wolfgang et al. (1987) state that the peak age of arrests is 16. Almost 13 percent of the follow-up sample's offenses occurred at age 16. From that point there is a steep decline to 8.1 percent at 17 and 5.6 percent at 18. Overall, 42.6 percent of the sample's offenses were committed from ages 15 to 19.

Tracy et al. (1985) report the same offending pattern for the two Philadelphia cohorts. In the 15–17 age group, 64 percent of Cohort II's offenses and 60 percent of Cohort I's offenses were committed. They also report that both index and nonindex crimes increase from ages 10 to 16.

Does it matter when the delinquent career begins? Apparently not. For both Philadelphia cohorts, Tracy

Burglary is a crime committed by many juveniles. Should there be a special response to offenders who commit this offense?

et al. (1985) reported that the earlier the start, the more offenses delinquents accumulated, and the earlier the start, the more likely that delinquents would accumulate index crimes. Yet the peak age of offending remained 15–17.

A major flaw in Gottfredson and Hirschi's (1990) argument is their use of *all* offenses in the UCR reports. This approach does indeed support the curve of the invariant hypothesis. Moreover, they argue that the thesis applies to white-collar crimes as well as to street crimes. Only two offenses that are commonly referred to as white-collar crime appear in the UCR, embezzlement and fraud.

Table 5.13 consists of data from the FBI's report titled *Age-Specific Arrest Rates and Race-Specific Arrest Rates for Selected Offenses 1965–1992*. The year 1977 was chosen

Table 5.13 Age-Specific Arrest Rates for Selected Crimes by Gender, 1977 (per 100,000)

Offense	Gender	15	16	17	18	19	20	21	22	23	24
						Age					
Murder	Total	7	14	19	23	23	23	26	24	23	24
	M	13	26	35	41	40	40	46	42	40	43
	F	2	2	2	6	6	6	6	7	7	6
Robbery	Total	215	283	311	300	255	221	212	194	171	146
	M	390	519	575	555	470	405	386	353	317	265
	F	32	37	37	39	37	36	36	36	27	28
Burglary	Total	1,298	1,412	1,273	1,039	772	603	520	440	382	332
	M	2,393	2,630	2,387	1,958	1,454	428	968	822	717	619
	F	155	147	121	101	80	70	68	58	51	48
Larceny/theft	Total	2,166	2,334	2,173	1,851	1,471	1,235	1,131	1,016	921	818
	M	2,978	3,269	3,066	2,568	2,026	1,647	1,492	1,331	1,192	1,061
	F	1,318	1,363	1,248	1,119	913	817	768	703	653	578
Forgery/ counterfeiting	Total	41	62	88	102	106	105	116	116	112	105
	M	57	89	122	139	140	136	155	152	148	141
	F	23	34	52	65	72	73	77	79	77	69
Gambling	Total	13	16	24	31	30	34	37	38	37	38
	M	24	30	45	57	55	62	68	67	68	69
	F	1	1	3	4	4	6	6	9	7	7
Drug abuse	Total	673	1,075	1,358	1,513	1,407	1,277	1,165	1,012	903	786
	M	1,062	1,773	2,319	2,622	2,425	2,216	2,021	1,757	1,561	1,359
	F	267	351	364	382	376	325	302	268	253	218

Source: U.S. Department of Justice, Federal Bureau of Investigation (1993).

since that was the year Gottfredson and Hirschi (1990) used to support the invariant hypothesis. Collapsing the data as they did presents a different picture than we get by looking at offending peaks by crime. For instance, in Table 5.13, for males in 1977 murder peaks at age 21, as does forgery and counterfeiting; robbery peaks at 17, and burglary and larceny/theft at 16. Other UCR data not depicted in Table 5.13 show that gambling arrests peak after 35, while motor vehicle theft is clearly in ages 15–16 and weapons offenses peak at 17–18.

Guns are used by many juveniles in committing crimes. Should these offenders receive harsher dispositions in juvenile court or be sent to adult court?

The age-specific data are able to indicate trends, subtle as some may be. For three violent index crimes (for males)—murder, forcible rape, and aggravated assault—from 1965 to 1992, we can see a downward trend in peak offending from the early 20s to the late teens. In fact, for these three offenses plus robbery, for the last four years of the report (1989–1992), the peak is 18. Until 1977, male gambling arrests numbered in the hundreds annually. Since then the number of arrests has declined to the low 20s and even lower in the age groups (over 35) that once were highest. This trend no doubt reflects the steady growth of legalized gambling across the country.

The point we make here is that although the invariant hypothesis has a distinct value in the study of crime, including age-specific arrest rates adds a valuable dimension to the total picture.

The National Center for Juvenile Justice assembles another source of information regarding the age of juvenile offenders. In its *Juvenile Court Statistics 1999*, (Puzzanchera et al. 2003b) the center reported that during that year the delinquency case rates (per 1,000 juveniles in each age group) increased with the age of the offender. As Table 5.14 shows, this trend was apparent throughout most of the 1990s.

These numbers add support to the idea that as juveniles age, their involvement in delinquent activity increases as well.

Table 5.14 Delinquency Case Rates by Age During the 1990s				
Age at Referral	**Case Rates**			**Percent Change**
	1990	**1995**	**1999**	**1990–1999**
10	6.3	6.1	5.3	–15%
11	11.1	12.0	10.7	–4
12	22.0	25.5	23.0	5
13	41.3	49.4	44.0	7
14	65.4	79.5	68.4	5
15	83.5	101.6	92.1	10
16	99.9	121.5	111.6	12
17	96.9	118.5	113.7	18

Source: Puzzanchera et al. (2003b).

Gender and Delinquency

Several of the cohort studies we have discussed can provide some insight into male-female differences in juvenile offending. The 1958 Philadelphia Cohort II study revealed an overall male-to-female arrest differential of 4:1; however, the male-female ratio for index crimes was 9:1, and for violent index crimes it was 14:1 (Tracy et al. 1985). In 2002, girls constituted 28.9 percent of all juvenile arrests, 29.7 percent of the index crime total, and 18.4 percent violent crime index total. The boy-girl index and violent index crime ratios have closed considerably since the 1970s.

From another perspective, 22 percent of all females arrested in 1998 were juveniles (in 2002 it was 20.8 percent), but in terms of rates, *girls* exceeded *women* in several categories of crime. For instance, for Part I violent crimes one arrest occurred for every 794 girls and for every 1,099 adult women. For larceny, the offense that tallied the greatest number of arrests, there was one arrest for every 105 girls and for every 337 women. These arrest differentials held up for most offenses (Greenfeld and Snell 1999). As compelling as these data may be, one needs to be cautious in drawing any firm conclusions from them. The girls in the UCR were ages 10–17, while the age range for women extends from 18 to, literally, the end of life. Consequently, the adult group contains an increasing number of seniors, a group that grows each year but is hardly a group at risk for crime.

Some support for the disproportionate share of girl offending among females is provided by the FBI's age-specific, race-specific arrests report referred to earlier. Table 5.15 reflects the relevant data for selected crimes. The four index crimes (robbery, burglary, larceny/theft, and motor vehicle theft) support the disproportionate share of juveniles among female offenders. In fact, if all index crimes are collapsed into one rate, female crime peaks at age 15–16. As Table 5.15 shows, some nonindex crimes peak later (forgery/counterfeiting, fraud, and drug abuse peak beyond age 18).

The national overall crime rate has declined considerably since 1994. This trend holds true for juvenile males but not for juvenile females. We will discuss two time frames,

Table 5.15 Age-Specific Arrest Rates, 1992 (per 100,000 females)

Age	Robbery	Burglary	Larceny/ Theft	Motor Vehicle Theft	Forgery/ Counterfeiting	Fraud	Drug Abuse
15	58	135	1,530	164	27	62	106
16	48	129	1,585	145	43	46	156
17	42	111	1,432	96	70	74	196
18	41	102	1,306	63	93	197	300
19	33	92	1,061	48	101	293	312
20	31	73	895	38	101	358	316
21	30	65	821	34	84	386	341
22	28	66	789	30	90	400	365

Source: U.S. Department of Justice, Federal Bureau of Investigation (1993).

1994–1998 and 1998–2002. During the period 1994–1998, offenses by girls (as measured by arrests) in some instances *increased* while they *decreased* for boys. For instance, there were 27,176 *fewer* male arrests in 1998 than in 1994, but there were 43,305 *more* arrests of girls in 1998 than in 1994. Between 1998 and 2002, there were 251,500 fewer arrests for boys (a 21 percent decline), but only 60,998 fewer arrests for girls (a 14 percent decline).

Between 1994 and 1998, juvenile arrests of females *increased* for some offenses while they *decreased* for males; for other offenses the female declines were less than for males. For instance, for aggravated assault, girl arrests *increased* 7.5 percent while the rate for boys *decreased* 17.6 percent. For other assaults, girl arrests increased 28.7 percent while for boys the increase was 3.6 percent. Girl arrests for drug abuse increased 42.6 percent, while the increase for boys was 23.3 percent. Interestingly, between 1998 and 2002, girl arrests for forcible rape *increased* 73.6 percent, while for boys it *decreased* 15.3 percent. Similarly, in other assaults, while arrests for boys *declined* 4.1 percent, the rate for girls *increased* 3.8 percent (see Table 5.2).

The numbers accumulated by the National Center for Juvenile Justice corroborate this trend of greater involvement in delinquency by girls. As shown in Table 5.16, throughout the 1990s the domination by boys diminished in each offense category. Reinforcing this trend are data showing a higher percentage change in case rates for females than for males in each offense category in the 1990s, as shown in Table 5.17.

Finally, although, as expected, delinquency case rates for both genders increased with age, the increase was greater for girls than for boys. While the female case rate averaged an increase of 75 percent from one age to the next, for boys the increase average was 57 percent. Also,

Table 5.16 Percentage of Offenses Committed by Males

Offense	1990	1995	1999
Delinquency	81%	78%	76%
Person	80	76	73
Property	81	78	76
Drugs	87	86	84
Public order	81	78	75

Source: Puzzanchera et al. (2003b).

Table 5.17 Percentage Change in Case Rates by Gender, 1990s

Offense	Male	Female
Delinquency	4%	39%
Person	24	80
Property	−25	0
Drugs	128	178
Public order	42	93

Source: Puzzanchera et al. (2003b).

Table 5.18 Case Rates by Age and Gender, 1999

Age	Male	Female
10	8.8	1.7
11	16.6	4.4
12	34.0	11.7
13	62.6	24.5
14	97.3	37.9
15	134.3	47.6
16	167.5	52.1
17	173.8	49.3

Source: Puzzanchera et al. (2003b).

while case rates for males increased through age 17, the peak age for girls was 16, as shown in Table 5.18.

Perhaps crime is no longer just "a young man's game." It may be too soon to draw any firm conclusions about trends in female delinquency. The 1990s was a mixed decade, beginning with a leftover increase in crime from the 1980s and ending in a decline. The first several years of the new millennium will tell us more.

Race and Delinquency

Blacks have long claimed to be singled out for special attention by the criminal and juvenile justice systems. In the late 1990s racial profiling on the nation's highways, especially in New Jersey, emerged as a political issue. In the eyes of many, racial profiling lent some credence to the claims of discrimination in the criminal justice process.

Advocates of antidiscriminatory practices point to the fact that blacks constitute 15 percent of the juvenile population yet far surpass that percentage in arrest rates for most, if not all, offenses. For instance, in 2002 the percentage of juveniles arrested for murder who were black was 50 percent, for robbery 58.1 percent, for forcible rape 36 percent, and for aggravated assaults 36.7 percent (see Table 5.5).

Once again, the data from the National Center for Juvenile Justice add support. In 1999 blacks were disproportionately represented in all four offense categories, as shown in Table 5.19. The numbers for blacks appear disproportionate throughout all age groups, compared to whites and youth of other races—see Table 5.20.

In a way, the cohort studies can be used to corroborate or dispute the allegations of

Table 5.19 Racial Profile in Offense Categories, 1999

Offense	White	Black	Other Races	Total
Delinquency	68%	28%	3%	100%
Person	63	34	3	100
Property	70	26	4	100
Drugs	71	27	2	100
Public order	69	28	3	100
Juvenile population	79%	15%	6%	100%

Source: Puzzanchera et al. (2003b).

Table 5.20 Case Rates by Age and Race, 1999

Age	White	Black	Other Races
10	4.2	11.4	3.6
11	8.3	23.9	6.8
12	18.6	49.0	13.7
13	36.5	87.4	28.2
14	57.8	130.4	42.7
15	78.3	176.4	57.0
16	97.4	206.6	66.2
17	101.2	219.9	61.2

Source: Puzzanchera et al. (2003b).

discrimination, since the researchers in these cases used police records. The Philadelphia studies used police *contacts* for their base measure of delinquency, which could have included diversion of youth after being taken into custody (Tracy et al. 1985). Hamparian and her colleagues (1978), on the other hand, chose youth who already had an arrest for a violent offense and then recorded further arrests. As imprecise as these procedures may have been, they do cast some light on minority offending.

In Philadelphia in Cohort I (1945), 71 percent of the arrested youth were white, while 29 percent were nonwhite. In Cohort II (1958), 47 percent were white; 53 percent were nonwhite. Whether these data reflect a racial change in delinquency over time or are merely a reflection of demographic changes in Philadelphia during the 1960s–1970s remains an unanswered question. Hamparian et al. (1978) found in the Columbus cohort that black chronics made up approximately four times their proportion in the general population—54.8 percent to 15.4 percent, respectively.

Social Class and Delinquency

The Philadelphia and Columbus researchers interfaced delinquency with socioeconomic status, using family income as the measure of social class. The cohort studies found a consistent inverse relationship between SES and delinquency. In terms of frequency and seriousness, lower-income youth were more delinquent than higher-income youth.

We must inject one cautionary note in viewing the relationship between SES and delinquency, at least in these cohort studies. There are significant correlations between race and SES. In general, SES can be measured in a number of ways, using multiple variables. In the Philadelphia cohorts (I and II), over 70 percent of whites were classified high SES, while nonwhites were less than 30 percent (Tracy et al. 1985). In the Columbus study, Hamparian et al. (1978) reported that 98.6 percent of the very poor were black, while 77.2 percent of the whites were above the median income level.

Official data depict the disproportionate share of minorities in crime. Cohort studies also used police data and came to the same conclusion. Agencies that report official data do not make social class distinctions, but researchers who look beyond arrest data have included SES and consistently report a positive correlation between low SES and crime. We also know there is a positive correlation between race and SES. Those who take a closer look at these relationships raise several cautionary notes. Official data are the product of the police, who are often accused of discriminatory practices. Definitions of SES are variable and are chosen by researchers.

Juveniles Preying on Juveniles: Juveniles as Victims

One final facet of juvenile offending is that youth very often victimize other youth. This makes sense, inasmuch as young people spend a good deal of their time with and around each other. This tendency is most obvious in school, but the topic of school crime will be addressed at length in the next chapter (Chapter 6). Not surprisingly, nonfatal violent victimization rates for youth between the ages of 12 and 17 (per 1,000 persons in age group) parallel the juvenile crime rate over the last 25 years. Obviously the numbers have

Table 5.21 Nonfatal Violent Victimization Rates, Ages 12 to 17, 1976–2000

1976	86.7	1981	93.2	1986	86.9	1991	111.4	1996	96.1
1977	92.8	1982	84.9	1987	96.1	1992	119.0	1997	92.8
1978	92.2	1983	84.9	1988	98.1	1993	128.0	1998	85.4
1979	87.9	1984	87.3	1989	102.4	1994	122.7	1999	69.0
1980	83.2	1985	90.6	1990	104.0	1995	105.8	2000	58.9

Source: Adapted from Bureau of Justice Statistics (2004), Table 3.6.

improved considerably in recent years. In fact, there was a 32 percent decline in the victimization rates between 1976 and 2000, and an even greater reduction (47.1 percent) between 1991 and 2000.

The NCVS provides information not only about the juvenile offender, but also about juvenile victims. Data on personal crimes are compiled concerning the victimization of several age groups. The two groups we care about are youth ages 12–15 and 16–19. As shown in Table 5.22, between 1996 and 2002, a steady decline occurred in the victimization rates of these two groups, corroborating the numbers reported above.

Although the trends represented in the table are encouraging, it needs to be noted that victimization rates are still highest among youth, especially the 16–19 group. Only those between ages 20 and 24 have a rate in crimes of violence (47.4) that comes close to that of juvenile victims. As we go well into adulthood, rates decrease consistently from 26.3 (25–34 years old) to 18.1 (35–49 years old) to 10.7 (50–64 years old) (Bureau of Justice Statistics, 2003b, Table 35). Obviously, the youth in today's society are disproportionately exposed to crimes of violence, and the numbers have been that way for quite some time. In fact, between 1996 and 2001, the two highest rates of victimization in crimes of violence (by a fairly wide margin) were the two age groups involving juveniles.

The 2002 NCVS data also detail the victimization rates by race and gender in addition to age. While the rates for males are slightly higher than those for females in both age groups, the rates in terms of race depend on the age of the victim. For younger youth, whites have a higher rate of victimization than blacks, but the reverse is true for older youth. Table 5.23 discloses these trends. Several numbers in the victimization rates stand out, especially rape and sexual assault of blacks in the older age

Table 5.22 Victimization Rates for Persons 12–15 and 16–19, All Personal Crimes, 1996–2002

	12–15	16–19
1996	98.3	105.2
1997	90.7	99.7
1998	84.4	93.4
1999	77.5	78.9
2000	61.9	67.3
2001	55.6	58.8
2002	45.3	58.8

Source: Adapted from Bureau of Justice Statistics (1999, 2000a, 2000b, 2001, 2002, 2003a, 2003b), Table 3 (in each).

	White		Black		Male		Female		Total	
Offenses	**12–15**	**16–19**	**12–15**	**16–19**	**12–15**	**16–19**	**12–15**	**16–19**	**12–15**	**16–19**
Crimes of violence	47.5	56.6	39.6	73.9	46.1	58.4	42.6	58.1	44.4	58.2
Rape/sexual assault	2.0	3.4	3.0	18.1	0.0	0.8	4.3	10.4	2.1	5.5
Robbery	2.6	4.2	4.5	4.3	4.9	4.9	0.9	3.2	3.0	4.0
Aggravated assault	5.3	10.9	4.7	21.1	5.4	16.3	4.5	7.4	5.0	11.9
Simple assault	37.6	38.1	27.4	30.4	35.8	36.3	32.8	37.1	34.3	36.7
Purse snatching	1.2	0.8	0.0	0.0	1.8	1.2	0.0	0.0	0.9	0.6

Table 5.23 Victimization Rates for Age Groups 12–15, 16–19, by Race and Gender

Source: Adapted from Bureau of Justice Statistics (2003b), Tables 3, 4, 9.

group, simple assault of whites, aggravated assault of the older males and older blacks, and the overall crimes of violence rate among blacks in the older age group.

The final piece of the puzzle concerns the relationship of juvenile offender to juvenile victim. Data from previous surveys suggest that in juvenile crime, offenders share similar age, race, and gender characteristics as victims, and this occurs to a greater extent than the relationship between offender and victim in adult crime (Whitaker and Bastian 1991). The NCVS data from 2002 support this contention. For juvenile victims (between the ages of 12 and 19), 71.4 percent of the offenders in crimes of violence were younger than 20 years of age; 56.8 percent of the offenders were younger than 18. In crimes of robbery the two figures were 65.9 percent and 41.5 percent, respectively, and in assault offenses the numbers were 75 percent and 61.2 percent, respectively (U.S. Department of Justice 2003, Table 41). Moreover, the rates of victims-offenders who are either well-known or casual acquaintances in both crimes of violence and assault are highest among the 16–19 age group and are second highest among the 12–15 age group. In the older group the rates for well-known and casual relationships in crimes of violence were 19.6 and 10.1, respectively; the numbers in assault crimes for this group were 15.5 and 8.3, respectively. For the 12–15 group, the rates for well-known and casual relationships in crimes of violence were 15.9 and 8.9, respectively; the numbers in assault crimes for this group were 14.7 and 8.1, respectively. Interestingly, the only other age group that had double-digit rates in the offender-victim relationship was young adults (20–24), who tended to be well-known to the offender in crimes of violence (12.3) and assault (10.0) (U.S. Department of Justice 2003, Table 35).

The final consideration in the juvenile as victim belongs to the family. In addition to the offender-victim relationship identified above, juveniles between 16 and 19 years of age

Table 5.24 Child Maltreatment Victimization Rates, 1990–2001

Year	Child Population	Victim Rate	Estimated Number of Victims
1990	64,163,192	13.4	861,000
1991	65,069,507	14.0	912,000
1992	66,073,841	15.1	995,000
1993	66,961,573	15.3	1,026,000
1994	67,803,294	15.2	1,032,000
1995	68,437,378	14.7	1,006,000
1996	69,022,127	14.7	1,012,000
1997	69,527,944	13.8	957,000
1998	69,872,059	12.9	904,000
1999	70,199,435	11.8	829,000
2000	72,293,812	12.2	879,000
2001	72,941,000	12.4	903,000

Source: U.S. Department of Health and Human Services (2003), Table 3.3.

Table 5.25 Victimization Rates by Maltreatment Type, 1997–2001

Types	1997	1998	1999	2000	2001
Physical abuse	3.3	2.9	2.5	2.3	2.3
Neglect	7.5	6.9	6.5	7.3	7.1
Medical neglect	0.4	0.4	0.4	0.5	0.3
Sexual abuse	1.7	1.5	1.3	1.2	1.2
Psychological maltreatment	0.9	0.8	0.9	1.0	0.9
Other abuse	1.8	4.1	4.4	2.7	3.2

Source: U.S. Department of Health and Human Services (2003), Table 3.5.

also tend to be disproportionately victimized by family members as well. Their victimization rate (3.1) at the hands of relatives in 2002 was second highest to the 20–24 group (4.2). The younger juvenile group's rate was 1.1 (U.S. Department of Justice 2003, Table 35). The numbers from the U.S. Department of Health and Human Services are even more disturbing. This government agency publishes reports of various forms of child abuse and neglect. The latest report, *Child Maltreatment 2001,* details identified cases of abuse between 1990 and 2001. Interestingly, the rates during this time period look similar to the juvenile crime rate numbers, as shown in Table 5.24.

The agency also computed the rates for various types of maltreatment for the years 1997–2001. Table 5.25 reveals these rates for that five-year period.

Like the cases in which the offender and victim are both juveniles, these cases of child maltreatment are headed to juvenile court in many states. Usually, but not always, the offenders in these child maltreatment cases are adults. If the offense involves serious injury to the victim, chances are the prosecution will take place in criminal court, although the juvenile court could very well serve as the location of the preliminary hearing (as we discussed in Chapter 4). Although the statistics in most of these examples of child maltreatment have been improving, they still represent serious numbers of juvenile victims. Combining well-known and acquaintance offenders with family offenders produces staggering numbers of juvenile victims every year. Many of these juvenile victims will reappear in juvenile court in the future, but it could very well be as a defendant.

Summary: Key Ideas and Concepts

- Official and unofficial measurements of delinquency
- Serious weaknesses in official data sources
- Decrease in overall serious juvenile crime in recent years
- Increase in female delinquency
- Disproportionate arrests of minority youth
- Unreported crime detected by victimization surveys
- Widespread delinquency discovered via self-report surveys
- Limitations of self-report surveys
- Cohort studies show small portion of youth commit large portion of crime
- Limitations of cohort studies
- Controversy concerning crime peaking in late teen years
- Disproportionate arrests of low-income youth
- Improvement in victimization rates in recent years
- Serious variation in victimization rates by age, race, and gender
- Juveniles committing crimes primarily against other juveniles
- Juveniles as victims within the family

Discussion Questions

1. Of all the sources of crime information, which provides the best picture of juvenile crime? Why is this the case?

2. Describe the juvenile crime picture portrayed by UCR, victimization surveys, self-report surveys, and cohort studies. What is the story of juvenile crime in terms of crime rates, violence, and offender characteristics?

3. Discuss the various limitations involved in the major sources of juvenile crime data. Do the limitations outweigh the information for any of these sources?

4. Is there something about juvenile crime that one source provides that the others do not? What do self-report surveys and cohort studies suggest that official crime data do not reveal?

5. What, if any, comfort can be drawn from the cohort studies?

6. To what extent do discriminatory practices influence the arrest data on which delinquency theories rely? ✦

Chapter 6

Patterns of Juvenile Crime

Focus of Chapter 6

The previous chapter discussed the quantity aspect of juvenile offending, or: Who does how much of what? This chapter discusses some of the various patterns in which the juvenile offending occurs.

Key Terms

- gang
- National Incident-Based Reporting System (NIBRS)
- Office of Juvenile Justice and Delinquency Prevention (OJJDP)
- pattern
- serious violent juvenile (SVJ)
- superpredators
- zero-tolerance laws

Considering Patterns

The term pattern can refer to a number of things, including the environment within which juvenile offenses occur. One location that comes to mind almost immediately is the public school, primarily because of all the media attention to school shootings and bomb threats. Patterns related to location of juvenile offenses are included in some statistics. Starting in the mid-1990s, the National Crime Victimization Survey (NCVS) and the National Center for Educational Statistics (NCES) started collecting student reporting on crime, and the recent enhancement to FBI data called the National Incident-Based Reporting System (NIBRIS) reports 53 pieces of information on a crime incident, including the date and time of day of the offense.

Pattern also refers to crime committed by groups of juveniles. In Chapter 5 we stated a "truism" that crime is a young man's game. We can add another: that youth commit crimes in groups (Erickson 1971; Hindelang 1971). A lone juvenile offender is a rarity.[1] A certain kind of group that commits crime raising special fears among citizens is the gang. Gangs have been part of the urban landscape for centuries. The gang label has been attached to the Mafia, prohibition bootleggers, motorcycle groups—and adolescents.

Another pattern of offending involves illegal and legal drugs. Possessing, selling, and using illegal drugs are illegal for anyone, while buying or possessing alcohol is a juvenile status offense. In addition to discussing the extent of juvenile drug and alcohol activity, we will discuss criminal behavior linked to drugs. In the past 20 years, illegal drugs have been significantly associated with gangs and violence.

Guns and violence are two words that defined a decade of crime in America. With the appearance of crack cocaine on urban streets in the mid-1980s, drug turf wars and violence soon became part of the American landscape. Juvenile violence rates, especially gun-related ones, rose dramatically during this period.

Finally, we discuss an ongoing study of the serious violent juvenile (SVJ), which is being carried out in a number of different locations in the nation. While the subject itself does not define a pattern of delinquency, some preliminary findings have revealed a variety of characteristics and attributes of serious violent juvenile offenders.

Crime in the Schools

A recent Census Bureau survey found that teens claimed to have been victims of 2.7 million school crimes in 1998. However, fewer than one-tenth of the crimes were categorized as serious. In fact, many public officials have grossly exaggerated school crime. The perception of dangerous public schools stems from the few, but highly publicized, school shootings that captured the nation's attention in the 1990s. Americans sat transfixed before their television sets on April 20, 1999, as the Columbine High School shootings unfolded. Columbine followed a number of other high-profile shootings during the decade. The public belief that schools are dangerous places was significantly reinforced by two school shootings in the San Diego, California, area in March 2001.

So, how dangerous *are* schools? To answer the question we must seek out the relevant data. The FBI's Uniform Crime Reports do not provide us with the locations of crimes. Self-report surveys ask individuals to disclose their criminality but have not asked, on any scale, the time and location of the self-admitted offenses. That leaves us with victimization surveys. In 1995, the NCVS (Chandler et al. 1998) included a *School Crime Supplement (SCS)*, which focused on approximately 10,000 students, ages 12 to 19. The survey related to victimization in schools (defined as occurring in the building, on school grounds, or in school buses), the presence of gangs, the availability of drugs, and the presence of guns. More than one-third of the students (37 percent) reported the existence of gangs in their schools, and these respondents indicated that two-thirds of these gangs were involved in criminal activity—namely, carrying guns, selling drugs, and committing acts of violence (Howell and Lynch 2000). The researchers then reanalyzed the 1989 NCVS data and teased out crime statistics that related to schools. The overall victimization rates were about the same for the two years—14.5 percent in 1989 and 14.6 percent in

1995. Property victimization rates were 12.2 percent and 11.6 percent, respectively. Comparing the two time periods for violent victimization rates, they rose slightly from 3.4 percent to 4.2 percent.

One interesting finding in the SCS was the relationship between the presence of gangs at school and the presence of drugs and guns there as well. According to the SCS data, the percentage of students who reported gang presence at school nearly doubled between 1989 and 1995 (Chandler et al. 1998). Moreover, students' perception that gangs existed at their school (versus none identified) significantly affected the reports of knowing a student who had brought a weapon to school (25 percent versus 8 percent), seeing a student with a gun at school (12 percent versus 3 percent), alleging that drugs (marijuana, cocaine, crack, or uppers/downers) were readily available at school (35 percent versus 14 percent), and expecting to be violently victimized at school (8 percent versus 3 percent) (Howell and Lynch 2000).

Crime does indeed take place in schools. The Bureau of Justice Statistics (BJS), in collaboration with the NCES, began annual reporting on the subject starting with 1996 data (Kaufman et al. 1998). In 1996, students ages 12 to 17 were victims of 255,000 incidents of serious, nonfatal crime at school. Also in 1996, 5 percent of 12th graders reported injuries from weapons such as knives, guns, or clubs; another 12 percent reported injuries without weapons.

The most recent report from this group, *Indicators of School Crime and Safety: 2003* (DeVoe et al. 2003) reveals that the situation in schools is improving. In 2001 students between the ages of 12 and 18 were the victims of about 2 million nonfatal crimes of violence or theft at school, but much more than half (62 percent) of these incidents involved thefts. Between 1995 and 2001, there was a decrease (from 10 percent to 6 percent) in the overall number of students who reported victimization in school, and the decrease pertained to both thefts (from 7 percent to 4 percent) and violent encounters (from 3 percent to 2 percent) (DeVoe et al. 2003). A total of 161,000 violent crimes occurred at school compared to 290,000 away from school. Interestingly, although the proportion of students who reported being in a fight at school declined from 16 percent to 13 percent and the proportion of secondary students who reported carrying a weapon declined from 12 percent to 6 percent between 1993 and 2001, secondary students who were threatened or injured with a weapon on school property remained between 7 and 9 percent in 1993, 1995, 1997, 1999, and 2001. Table 6.1 reveals the improving picture for students at school or going to and from school in recent years.

Not surprisingly perhaps, as the age of the student and the size of the student body increased, so did the number of violent incidents involving both students and teachers. Not all

Table 6.1 Number of Nonfatal Crimes Against Students, Ages 12 to 18, Select Years					
	Year				
Offense	**1994**	**1996**	**1998**	**2000**	**2001**
Theft	2,371,500	2,028,700	1,562,300	1,246,600	1,237,600
Violent	1,424,000	1,134,400	1,153,200	699,800	763,700
Serious violent	322,400	225,400	252,700	128,400	160,900
Total	3,795,500	3,163,000	2,715,600	1,946,400	2,001,300

Source: DeVoe et al. (2003), Table 2.1.

data were positive, inasmuch as an increase occurred from 5 percent to 8 percent in students between the ages of 12 and 18 who reported being bullied during the previous six months at school between 1999 and 2001 (DeVoe et al. 2003). Moreover, the number of incidents reported by students increased at each grade level. Not surprisingly, the percentage of reports on bullying decreased as the grade level of the student increased (see Table 6.2). The same trend occurred in victimization reports regarding nonfatal crimes as well (see DeVoe et al. 2003, Figure 3.1).

Table 6.2 Percentage of Students Reporting Incidents of Bullying During Previous Six Months, by Grade Level, 1999 and 2001

Grade	Year	
	1999	2001
Sixth	11%	14%
Seventh	9	13
Eighth	6	9
Ninth	5	9
Tenth	3	5
Eleventh	3	4
Twelfth	1	2
Total	5	8

Source: DeVoe et al. (2003), Figure 6.2.

So, to some extent at least, schools are dangerous places for children. Not only do we see some of the violence played out graphically on television, but school officials argue for protective hardware and promote zero-tolerance laws and rules for student misbehavior. These laws have forbidden the possession of virtually all drugs (including possibly aspirin) and any item resembling a weapon. Much of what has gone on among officials recently seems to support a 1978 study by the Department of Health, Education, and Welfare that asserted the risk of violence to teenagers is greater in school than anywhere else (Rubel and Ames 1986).

Much of what has transpired in this area has had one definite effect: The level of fear among students has risen significantly. A 1993 survey (Arnette and Walsleben 1998) revealed that 4.4 percent of students reported missing one day of school a month because of fear. Students also reported avoiding certain hallways, restrooms, and even schoolgrounds for the same reason. Although there was some decrease in the number of students who felt unsafe at school (or in transit) between 1995 and 1999, no subsequent decrease has occurred in these numbers, and in both 1999 and 2001 students reported being more afraid at school than away from school (see Table 6.3). A similar decrease (between 1995 and 1999), and then stabilizing (between 1999 and 2001), occurred among students who reported avoiding certain areas at school (DeVoe et al. 2003).

The differences in the rates reported by the various races are most likely related to the location of the school, inasmuch as urban schools witnessed the highest volume of complaints in these categories (DeVoe et al. 2003, Figure 13.2).

In responding to the situation at schools, Crews and Tipton (2000) of the Koch Institute argue that transforming schools into fortresses simply reinforces the existing levels of fear in students. They further hypothesize that these actions will dampen student enthusiasm, cause students to spend time and psychic energy worrying about being victim-

Table 6.3 Percentage of Students, Ages 12 to 18, Reporting Both Being Afraid/ Avoiding Places, by Race/Ethnicity, 1995, 1999, and 2001			
	Year		
Race	1995	1999	2001
White	8%/7%	5%/4%	5%/4%
Black	20/12	14/7	9/7
Hispanic	21/13	12/6	11/6
Other	14/11	7/5	6/6
Total	12/9	7/5	6/5
Source: DeVoe et al. (2003), Figures 12.1 and 13.1.			

ized, and heighten distrust. These outcomes could in turn affect academic performance and stifle creativity and intellectual development. Arnette and Walsleben (1998) go so far as to say that crime in school and reactions to it may be a major reason for the decline in achievement in American students.

The truth of the matter is that the media hype of school crime does not square with the facts. Indeed, school may be the safest place for children. The report that recorded 255,000 incidents of serious nonfatal school crimes also recorded 671,000 similar incidents *away* from school (Kaufman et al. 1998). On the face of it, this comparison may not be fair, since it is obvious that the at-risk time out of school far exceeds the at-risk time at school. In approximate terms, students are in school from September to June and usually attend school five days a week. Out of a 24-hour day, the school day is about 7 hours. So, something else is needed to compare in-school to out-of-school crime. That something is a blend of the National Crime Victimization Survey (NCVS) and the FBI's National Incident-Based Reporting System (NIBRS), an enhancement to the UCR. NIBRS collects information on the 8 index and 38 other offenses, as well as 53 pieces of information on every crime incident, including, for our purposes, the date and hour of the crime event (Rantala 2000). In the 1990s, an increasing number of jurisdictions in the nation started collecting the data required for NIBRS.

Researchers report (Juvenile Justice Bulletin 1999) that by asking victims to report their victimizations in six-hour blocks of time, we find that juveniles are at highest risk in the 4 hours following the school day. Researchers examining NIBRS data from 1991 to 1996 also divided the days of the year into two groups: school days (Monday through Friday during the school year) and nonschool days (weekends, holidays, and summer break). By blending NCVS and NIBRS statistics, the conclusion is that juvenile offending on school days peaks at 3 p.m. and tapers off by about 6 p.m. On nonschool days, juvenile crime tends to pattern itself after adult crime, peaking at about 8 p.m. to 10 p.m. (adult crime peaks later).

Thus, while crime does occur in schools, and very violent episodes have captured the nation's attention on a number of occasions, many experts argue that creating fortresses out of our schools is like killing an ant with a sledgehammer (Crews and Tipton 2000). Some school authorities are working with students, staff, and teachers to change the culture of the school. Programs focus on seeking out high-risk students and provide guidance and counseling. Programs also focus on empathy, impulse control, and anger management. Some programs provide classes on crime victims, consequences of fighting, and role-playing. Thus, the research of the past decade has started school officials on prevention programs.

Gangs

The word *gang* usually conjures up images of violent groups of males, such as the Hell's Angels motorcycle gang. The word *gang* has also been attached to adult mobsters of the Mafia or La Cosa Nostra version. While these groups of deviant adult males may fit the definition of gang, we focus our attention here on the juvenile or youth variation, which has a longer history than any other group designated as a gang.

Much information on youth gangs has been published since the mid-1980s, largely as a result of considerable media attention to the presumed relationships among gangs, guns, drugs, and violence. The federal government, largely through the Office of Juvenile Justice and Delinquency Prevention (OJJDP), has funded a great deal of research on youth gangs. A National Youth Gang Survey has been conducted under the auspices of OJJDP every year since 1995. Since the late 1980s, scores of government publications have reported on virtually every aspect of youth gangs across the nation. The primary sources of information for researchers on the subject of gangs come from:

Gangs are a major component of juvenile crime. What do you think accounts for the recent drop in the number of gangs and gang members?

1. ***Police departments.*** Researchers send surveys to police departments and make follow-up telephone calls. Arrest data are another source of information, since pertinent crime information can be classified as gang-related.

2. ***Prosecutors.*** Some cities that have been plagued by gang crime have set up special prosecutorial units that focus on gang-related defendants. One tactic is *vertical* prosecution, in which a prosecutor (or team) stays with a case from start to finish.

3. ***Gang members.*** Interviews with gang members, on the street or in detention, are another source of information. This method has the usual drawbacks associated with self-reports (see Chapter 5).

Definition of Gangs

A major sticking point in collecting data about gangs is how they are defined. If a group of adolescents is directly responsible for the death of a person, how do we know whether the crime is gang related? For instance, the adolescents who did the killing may have done so for reasons unrelated to their gang. So at the very least, we must have an acceptable definition of *gang* from the outset. This definition is crucial for researchers, as well as for practitioners, since the appropriate identification of gang-related crime plays into not only research reporting but also official system handling of the adolescents.

Though varying to some degree, modern researchers include some common elements in their definitions—elements that originated with researchers of an earlier era (Thrasher 1927; Miller 1975; Klein 1995). For Block and Block (1993), the elements that constitute a youth gang are:

- a name and specific symbols;
- a geographic territory;
- a regular meeting pattern; and
- an organized, continuous course of crime.

Howell (1998) uses elements that have been borrowed from researchers and theorists. A youth gang:

- is self-formed;
- is united by mutual interests;
- controls a particular territory or enterprise;
- uses symbols in communication; and
- is collectively involved in crime.

Curry and Decker (1998) identify six typical elements associated with a gang:

- A group, meaning at least more than two individuals
- Symbols that are associated with membership in the group, such as clothes and hand signs
- Special communication that assumes verbal and nonverbal forms
- Some permanence, meaning that gangs must persist usually for at least a year
- Turf or territory that is claimed to be under the gang's control
- Crime and illegal behaviors

Maxson (1998) adopts a broader perspective, presenting a gang as a group of adolescents or young adults who see themselves (as do others) as a gang and who have been involved in enough crime to be of considerable concern to law enforcement and the community. Finally, and interestingly, in the SCS students were most likely to mention having a name (80 percent), spending time with others (80 percent), and wearing clothing or other items (70 percent) that would indicate gang membership as the most obvious indicators of gang presence. Beyond these criteria, tagging or marking turf (56 percent) and violent gang activity (50 percent) were cited by the students. The least frequently mentioned indicators were territory or turf (47 percent), tattoos (37 percent), and a recognized leader (33 percent) (Howell and Lynch 2000).

We can see that there are enough variations among these definitions to cause differential reporting on the presence and activities of gangs.

A Brief History of Gangs in America

There is some evidence that youth gangs in America emerged as the Revolutionary War ended (Howell 1998). Gangs also appeared in southwestern America after the Mexican Revolution of 1813. Youth gangs are usually associated with poverty-stricken urban slums. Asbury (1928) contended that the first recognized gangs in America were located in the Five Points slum area of lower Manhattan in the early 1800s. The area was filled with tenement houses, saloons, and dance halls. The most frequent hangouts of the gangs were the many green grocers in the area. Asbury (1928) claimed the first known organized gang was the Forty Thieves, which originated from Roseanna Peers' grocery store. The known gangs of the time were Irish immigrants who sported colors, fought each other, committed thefts, and were very violent.

Gang researchers offer four periods in American history to denote the growth and activity of gangs: the late 1880s, the 1920s, the 1960s, and the 1990s. The last period is the one of interest to us. It covers roughly the decade from the mid-1980s to the mid-1990s. This period is notable for a resurgence in drug trafficking and gun violence. It was also a period of violent gangs in a number of Chinatowns across the country, a phenomenon unheard of prior to these times.

There is little doubt that from the public's perspective, drug-dealing gangs—those that would shoot to kill if a drug deal went wrong—were the scourge of inner-city neighborhoods. To a degree that perspective is correct. The Bloods and Crips of Los Angeles and the Vice Lords and Black Gangster Disciples of Chicago were notorious in this respect during this period (Howell 1997). So was the gang Born to Kill, made up of Vietnamese refugees, that purportedly supplied 75 percent of the heroin infused into New York City (*New York Times* March 3, 1989). The Jheri-Kurl gang, made up mostly of males from the Dominican Republic, operated in the Washington Heights section of New York City and reportedly ran a $5.2-million-a-year drug operation (*New York Times* October 24, 1991). The violence associated with drug trafficking is significantly related to the ready availability of guns. During the period 1987–1990, the increase in gang-related homicides was connected to the use of high-caliber guns, and in Los Angeles from 1979 to 1994 the proportion of homicides involving guns rose from 71 percent to 95 percent (Howell 1997).

There is also little doubt about the perceived relationships among gangs, drugs, and gun violence. But does reality square with perception? Vigil (1988), writing about Chicano gangs in California, stated that at the end of 1987 gangs had killed 205 people and that 60 percent of victims had been innocent bystanders. Many deaths were the result of a drive-by shooting, in which youth in autos shot at targets as they drove by a designated spot. Given the times, it was easy to associate these killings not only with gangs but also with drug deals gone wrong. Like school shootings, these events received considerable media attention and, as in the school situations, the media reports gave the public an impression of frequent gang-related, drug-related shootings.

Some researchers have questioned the extent of the relationships among gangs, drugs, and gun violence. Howell (1997) claims that in reality in the late 1980s, the amount of violent crime connected to drug sales was only 5 percent and that firearms were used in only 10 percent of violent crimes. These findings also emerged in a number of American cities. The difference between perception and reality may be explained if we make a distinction among types of gangs. Most gangs are loosely organized groups of youth whose level of crime is limited to fighting other gangs and engaging in property crime. Well-organized "corporate" gangs such as the Bloods and Crips, which are businesslike in drug trafficking, tend to be older, are more likely to be heavily armed, and are likely to use gun violence in pursuit of their business goals.

Gang Migration

Another widespread public perception about gangs is that they are migrating rapidly around the country, primarily to spread drugs. This perception gained some support through the media, which in turn repeated what police departments reported. For instance, the *New York Times* (October 15, 1991) reported that the Las Vegas police estimated the presence of about 5,000 gang members in the city at the time, up from 1,500 three years prior. The police attributed the growth to migration from Los Angeles. In general, though, researchers believe that gang migration is overrated and that when it does occur, it is for reasons other than expanding drug markets. Maxson (1998) refers to a study of this phenomenon by the University of Southern California in 1992. Of the 792 cities in which the survey was conducted, law enforcement officials in 700 claimed to have migrant gangs. The researchers claimed that this actually was the case in only 22 percent of the cities. When gang members do migrate, the reasons are more often for family or economic reasons (jobs).

The Extent of Gangs

Regardless of whether migration explains the spread of gang problems, there is no doubt that more and more communities are reporting the presence of gangs. National surveys that estimate the number of cities reporting gang problems, the number of gangs, and the number of gang members reveal how gangs have escalated in prominence during the last two decades, as shown in Table 6.4.

A recent study sponsored by OJJDP traced the growth of gang problems from the 1970s through the 1990s. In the 1970s the data on gangs included (Miller 2001):

- 19 states reported gang problems.

- The population of gang-riddled cities equaled 25 percent of the population of all cities.

- The population of gang-riddled counties equaled 40 percent of all counties' populations.

- Only California and Illinois reported large numbers of cities with gang problems.

- The top four states contained about three-quarters of all gang cities.

- Only eight states reported five or more gang cities.

- Only six states reported more than five gang counties.

By the 1990s the figures had changed dramatically:

- All 50 states and the District of Columbia reported gang problems.
- The population of gang-riddled cities equaled 60 percent of the population of all cities.
- The population of gang-riddled counties equaled 90 percent of all counties' populations.
- Four states (CA, IL, TX, FL) reported at least 125 cities with gangs (OH had 86).
- All 50 states reported five or more gang cities.
- 47 states reported more than five gang counties.

Table 6.4 Numbers of Cities Reporting Gangs and Numbers of Gangs and Gang Members, 1975–2000			
Year	Cities Reporting Gangs	Number of Gangs	Number of Gang Members
1975	6	27	55,000
1983	27	2,285	97,940
1988	68	1,439	120,636
1992	110	4,481	249,324
1994	282	8,625	378,897
1995	1,492	23,388	664,906
1996	3,847	30,818	846,428
1997	3,789	30,533	815,896
1998	3,420	28,707	780,233
1999	3,192	26,175	840,613
2000	2,788	24,742	772,550

Source: Curry and Decker (2002), Figures 1.7, 1.8, 1.9.

What had also changed by the late 1990s was that more gangs were located in smaller cities and towns and that the South, which had been last in reporting gang problems in the 1970s, became the second highest region identifying gang problems by the late 1990s (Miller 2001).

These data were corroborated by the seventh annual national gang survey of 2001. The gang survey (also sponsored by OJJDP) contacted 3,018 respondents, including 1,216 larger city police departments (populations of 25,000 or more), 661 suburban sheriff and police departments, a random sample of 398 smaller cities' police departments (populations between 2,500 and 25,000), and a random sample or 743 rural police and sheriff departments. Of those that responded to the survey (2,560 departments, or 85 percent), the 2001 results were (Egley and Major 2003):

- 100 percent of cities with populations of 250,000 or more reported gang activity.
- 85 percent of cities with populations between 100,000 and 249,000 reported gang activity.
- 65 percent of cities with populations between 50,000 and 99,000 reported gang activity.
- 44 percent of cities with populations between 25,000 and 49,999 reported gang activity.
- 20 percent of cities with populations between 2,500 and 24,999 reported gang activity.

Table 6.5 Estimated Number of Youth Gangs and Gang Members by Area Type, 1996, 1998						
	Gangs			Gang Members		
Area Type	1996	1998	Percent Change 1996–1998	1996	1998	Percent Change 1996–1998
Large city	12,841	12,538	–2%	513,243	482,380	–6%
Small city	8,053	8,413	4	92,448	94,875	3
Suburban county	7,956	6,040	–24	222,267	176,610	–21
Rural county	1,968	1,716	–13	18,470	26,368	43
Total	30,818	28,707	–7	846,428	780,233	–8
Source: National Youth Gang Center (2000), Table 9.						

- 35 percent of suburban counties and 11 percent of rural counties reported gang activity.

The survey estimated that 3,000 jurisdictions in this country witnessed gang activity in 2001. More important, perhaps, 42 percent of cities with a population of at least 25,000 reported an increase in the number of gang members, while 45 percent reported an increase in the number of gangs from 1999.

As Table 6.4 revealed, however, one positive sign in recent times is that the estimated number of gangs and gang members has decreased. The 1998 National Youth Gang Survey (see Table 6.5) reported that between 1996 and 1998, the numbers declined for both gangs (7 percent) and gang members (8 percent) (the numbers for 2000 show further decline in both categories). All communities, except small cities and rural counties witnessed fewer numbers in both categories during this time span.[2]

Although the general numbers of gang members are available, estimates of the percentage of youth who are members of gangs are not traced as consistently, and they vary considerably from one location to another. Research that has attempted to isolate that figure has produced estimates from as low as 7 to 10 percent (Esbensen and Huizinga 1993; Esbensen and Osgood 1997) to as high as 25 to 30 percent (Mays et al. 1994; Thornberry and Burch 1997).

Gang Characteristics ✤

Another positive sign, in terms of juvenile offending at least, is that most gang members are adults and that this tendency became even more prominent between 1996 and 1998. During this period the proportion of adult gang members increased from 50 to 60 percent. The 1998 NYGS reported that the age distribution of gang members shifted somewhat toward the end of the 1990s, as shown in Table 6.6.

In terms of gender, a decline occurred in the proportion of gang members that were female (from 10 to 8 percent) between 1996 and 1998. Interestingly, as the population of the area increased, the proportion of female gangs tended to decrease during this time span, as shown in Table 6.7.

Research in certain cities (Denver, Rochester) has disclosed that girls can make up as much as 20 to 33 percent of gang members (Bjerregaard and Smith 1993; Campbell 1990; Esbensen and Huizinga 1993; Esbensen and Osgood 1997). In addition, the number of female-dominated gangs tends to increase as the population of the area increased, as indicated in Table 6.8. We will return to the topic of gender in connection to gangs later in this chapter.

Only once thus far has the national gang survey focused on the social class of gang members. According to the *1996 National Youth Gang Survey* (National Youth Gang Center [NYGC] 1999), half of gang members were from the underclass. The other half were distributed among the working (35 percent), middle (12 percent), and upper middle classes (3 percent) (Egley 2000).

In terms of race, Hispanic youth were reported to constitute a majority of gang members, while Asians were the least numerous gang members (see Table 6.9).[3] Interestingly,

Table 6.6 Age Distribution of Gang Members, 1996 and 1998

Age	Percentage of Gang Members	
	1996	1998
Younger than 15	16%	11%
15–17	34	29
18–24	37	46
Older than 24	13	14

Source: NYGC (2000), Figure 4.

Table 6.7 Gender of Youth Gang Members by Area Type, 1996 and 1998

Area Type	1996		1998	
	Male	Female	Male	Female
Large city	92%	8%	93%	7%
Small city	80	20	88	12
Suburban county	91	9	90	10
Rural county	87	13	89	11
Total	90	10	92	8

Source: NYGC (1999), Table 15; NYGC (2000), Table 14.

Table 6.8 Female-Dominated Youth Gangs, by Population Size, 1998

Population Size	Total Gangs	Female-Dominated Gangs	
		Number	Percent
250,000 or more	5,283	120	2%
100,000 to 249,999	3,123	46	2
50,000 to 99,999	2,234	29	1
25,000 to 49,999	2,203	34	2
10,000 to 24,999	751	13	2
Less than 10,000	320	3	1
Overall	13,914	245	2

Source: NYGC (2000), Table 18.

Table 6.9 Race/Ethnicity of Juvenile Gang Members, 1998

Race/Ethnicity	Number of Gang Members	Percent
Black	184,467	34%
Hispanic	255,254	46
White	64,828	12
Asian	34,296	6
Other	9,672	2
Total	548,517	100

Source: NYGC (2000), Table 19.

Table 6.10 Multiracial/Multiethnic Juvenile Gangs by Area Type, 1998

Area Type	Total Gangs	Mixed Gangs	
		Number	Percent
Large city	9,982	3,204	32%
Small city	316	171	54
Suburban county	3,858	1,733	45
Rural county	420	178	42

Source: NYGC (2000), Table 23.

between 1996 and 1998 a slight increase occurred in gang membership in both the Hispanic (from 44 to 46 percent) and Asian groups (from 5 to 6 percent). During this time period there was a slight decline in gang membership among blacks (from 35 to 34 percent) and whites (from 14 to 12 percent). While Hispanic gang members outnumbered other groups in large cities (47 percent of members), suburban counties (47 percent), and small cities (46 percent), blacks were dominant in rural counties (36 percent). No area was dominated by white gang members, but they were most prominent in small cities (30 percent) and rural counties (27 percent) (NYGC 2000). The 1998 survey also discovered that more than one-third (36 percent) of gangs are mixed or multiracial/multiethnic (the estimate in 1996 was 46 percent). Gangs were most likely to be mixed in the Midwest and in small cities (see Table 6.10).

Gangs and Crime Estimates

If defining a gang is a difficult task, estimating the number of crimes committed by gangs is not surprisingly even more difficult. The most recent available estimate was made in 1996. It was based on 1993 crime data collected by the 1994 National Institute of Justice (NIJ) Gang Survey. Two estimates were taken, as shown in Table 6.11. The first was termed "conservative" because some of the survey sources had not identified any gang-related crime despite having reported the presence of a gang problem. The second was called "reasonable" in that the numbers were adjusted to compensate for the lack of reporting from several sources. The "truth" most likely lies somewhere between the two estimates.

Not surprisingly, most jurisdictions reported at least some gang participation in a good proportion of the major offenses committed within their boundaries. Still, the num-

Table 6.11 Estimates of the Crimes Committed by Youth Gangs by Jurisdiction Size, 1993

Size of Jurisdiction	Number of Crimes	
	Conservative Estimate	Reasonable Estimate
Cities over 200,000	26,731	51,155
Cities 150,000–200,000	10,382	46,616
Cities 25,000–150,000	8,497	89,232
Smaller cities	1,284	3,156
Selected counties	390,172	390,172
Total	437,066	580,331

Source: Curry et al. (1996), Exhibits 2, 3.

ber of jurisdictions making claims regarding the level of gang participation in numerous crimes between 1996 and 1998 showed a decline in gang involvement—see Table 6.12.

With respect to gang homicides, the *1998 NYGS* (NYGC 2000) examined 1,216 cities (population greater than 25,000) that had reported gang problems and gang homicides between 1996 and 1998. In all, 436 cities participated in the survey, and, among them, 237 cities reported a gang problem together with a homicide in all three years. The trend in gang-related homicides was encouraging, as nearly half (49 percent) of the cities reported

Table 6.12 Jurisdictions Reporting Proportion of Gang Involvement in Crimes, 1996 and 1998

Offense/Level of Gang Participation	1996		1998	
	Number	Percent	Number	Percent
Aggravated assault				
Most/all*	440	33%	147	12%
Some	516	39	515	43
Few	344	26	473	40
None	35	3	69	6
Robbery				
Most/all	198	15	39	3
Some	413	31	362	30
Few	573	43	580	49
None	139	11	215	18

(*continued*)

Table 6.12 Jurisdictions Reporting Proportion of Gang Involvement in Crimes, 1996 and 1998 (*continued*)

Offense/Level of Gang Participation	1996		1998	
	Number	Percent	Number	Percent
Burglary[†]				
Most/all	394	30	157	13
Some	559	42	539	45
Few	342	26	426	36
None	40	3	69	6
Motor vehicle theft				
Most/all	404	30	136	11
Some	427	32	491	41
Few	438	33	442	37
None	64	5	126	11
Larceny/theft				
Most/all	505	38	209	17
Some	601	45	591	49
Few	211	16	347	29
None	22	2	51	4

Source: NYGC (1999), Table 24; NYGC (2000), Table 29.
*The 1996 NYGS used the following terms to convey the level of gang participation: high, medium, low, and not involved.
†The 1998 NYGS referred to the burglary category as also including breaking and entering.

a decrease in gang homicides, while another 15 percent reported no change. Nevertheless, more than one-third (36 percent) of the cities experienced an increase. However, over the three-year span, the total number of gang homicides fell from 1,293 to 1,260 to 1,061. Moreover, the tendency was for few cities to report very high numbers. Only two cities reported more than 50 gang homicides in any of the years. Most (383 cities) had between 1 and 10 gang homicides in any of the three years, and another 45 cities had between 11 and 50. Los Angeles and Chicago dominated the cities with 173 and 180 gang homicides, respectively, in 1998. Nevertheless, both Los Angeles (41 percent) and Chicago (19 percent) witnessed a decline in these homicides between 1996 and 1998 (Curry et al. 2001).

In 2001, gang-related homicides were reported in 69 percent of cities with a population of at least 100,000 and in 37 percent of locations with a population between 50,000 and 99,999. Most of the homicides in Los Angeles (59 percent) and Chicago (53 percent) were identified as gang-related in 2001. Interestingly, the homicides of this nature (698) in these two cities outnumbered gang-related homicides (637) that occurred in 130 other gang-riddled cities with a population of at least 100,000 (Egley and Major 2003).

Gangs, Drugs, and Violence

The reemergence of gangs on a large scale in the mid-1980s is largely attributed to crack, a derivative of cocaine. The use of crack swept across the nation during the 1980s, fueling drug market rivalries and inevitable violence. The stark difference with regard to drugs and gangs is dramatic when we compare Miller's (1977) national gang survey, where the word "drugs" does not appear, to the massive number of recent surveys in which "drugs" is almost synonymous with "gangs." During this period, the media devoted much time and space to the subject. Moreover, research in Rochester (Thornberry et al. 1993), Denver (Huizinga 1997), and Seattle (Hill et al. 1999) found that gang youth were three to ten times more likely than nongang juveniles to be involved in selling drugs. Similarly, in the *1998 NYGS*, the jurisdictions surveyed reported gangs to be involved in most/ all (27 percent) or at least some (45 percent) of drug sales. Relatively few jurisdictions claimed that gangs were responsible for only few (25 percent) or none (3 percent) of drug sales (NYGC 2000). Thus, the gang-drugs connection is clear.

Drugs play a major role in juvenile crime. What measures can be used to more effectively stop the use of drugs by juveniles?

Although homicides by juveniles increased dramatically in the relatively small window of 1985–1993 (Cook 1998), the question remains as to whether these homicides were related to gangs and drugs. There are mixed views on this matter. According to Howell and Decker (1999), with the advent of crack cocaine, gang warfare with guns over markets grew dramatically. Howell (1997), however, believes the proportion of juvenile homicides attributed to drugs and gangs is highly overrated. In Pasadena and Pomona (in suburban Los Angeles), for instance, violence in drug-related crimes occurred in only 5 percent of cases, and firearms were used in only 10 percent of juvenile drug offenses (Maxson 1995). Other studies in Los Angeles have confirmed the marginal contribution of drug trafficking to gang violence (Klein et al. 1991; Meehan and O'Carroll 1992; Hutson et al. 1995). The same was found in Chicago (Block and Block 1993).[4] The larger reason for the killing epidemic is more related to the ready availability of guns (Block and Block 1993; Howell 1997). Whereas at one time disputes and differences were settled with fists and clubs, they are now resolved with guns. Moreover, research has found that gang members are more likely (31 percent versus 20 percent) than other juveniles to carry guns most or all of the time, while one-third of gang members assert that disrespect is a reason to shoot someone. In addition, arrestees who admitted using a gun in the commission of a crime were more common among juveniles who sold drugs (42 percent) or who were gang members (50 percent) than among other youth (33 percent) (Decker et al. 1997). In St. Louis, disrespecting gang colors or driving through rival neighborhoods or flashing gang signs explained most gang violence (Decker and VanWinkle 1996). This study also found that more than four-fifths (81 percent) of gang members admitted to owning a gun, that the average number of guns possessed by these youth was four, and that two-thirds had used their gun at least on one occasion, but rarely was there a drug connection to the use of a gun. Similarly, in Chicago during the 1980s, a good deal of violence and homicides was concentrated in areas connected with boundary disputes among rival Latino street gangs (Block et al. 1996).

Girls in the Gang

Girls as gang members have been given little attention in the past. Thrasher's (1927) study of 1,313 gangs in Chicago in the 1920s revealed only six gangs that could be called girl gangs. Until recently, girls associated with gangs were "attachments," often referred to as Debs or Auxiliaries, and were used by males for comfort and sex. Howell (1998) reported that in Chicago from 1965 to 1994, females constituted only 1 percent of gang offenders. In the 1970s Campbell's (1984) research in Brooklyn, New York, made it clear that an increasing number of females were essentially doing what male gangs do. According to Moore and Hagedorn (2001), female gang members now constitute 37 percent of drug arrests of identified gang members. In the mid-1990s, in New York City, when many of the Latin Kings went to prison, the Latin Queens became a prominent presence in themselves. They remained in touch with the imprisoned males, established branches of the gang, and, interestingly, became involved in neighborhood problems and downplayed violence (Moore and Hagedorn 2001).

Like males, female gang members are more criminal than similarly situated female nongang members (Howell 1998).[5] In Cleveland, researchers located very good matches of gang and nongang youth. The two groups were similar with respect to age, gender, ethnicity/race, education, work, and being raised in two-parent homes. Gang members were far more likely to steal automobiles, assault others, carry concealed weapons in school, sell and steal drugs, intimidate and assault witnesses, and be involved in homicides and drive-by shootings. The Cleveland findings essentially mirrored those in four other sites (Huff 1998).

Juvenile Violent Crime

Murder has always taken a front seat in any serious discussion of crime. It has no particular status in the Uniform Crime Reports, other than being listed as the first index crime, but the deliberate killing of another human being always is defined as the most egregious of all crimes.

In the decade of the 1990s, homicide became a major topic of public and political discussion for a hitherto benign group of individuals—juveniles. In 1984 the homicide rate for the 14–17 age cohort was 8.5 per 100,000 youth. That rate then increased annually, peaking at 30.2 in 1993. And though it has declined since then, the rate of 12.9 in 1998 is still higher than the 1976 rate of 10.6.

Has the nation experienced a growth of superpredators, or morally impoverished youth, as some writers have claimed? Or are there other reasons that explain this sudden and abrupt window of violence by juveniles from 1987 to 1993? According to Cook (1998), the 15–19 cohort of nonwhites was very lethal in 1990. Yet, they were not so in 1985 when they were 10–14 years of age. Some scholars claim that the only way to understand this violent window of time is to include guns and drugs.

Guns

Gun control is a major political issue in America. The availability of guns, both legally and illegally, is all too common. Surveys of schoolchildren reveal they can acquire a handgun in little time (Chandler et al. 1998). This claim is supported by official data. The Uniform Crime Reports include a weapons violation charge, a charge that includes firearms and their ammunition, silencers, explosives, and certain knives. In 1974, juveniles made up 16 percent of weapons violations arrestees; in 1993, they accounted for 23 percent. Further, between 1985 and 1993 juvenile weapons arrests increased by more than 100 percent, from just under 30,000 to more than 61,000 (Greenfeld and Zawitz 1995). In Los Angeles, while the proportion of gang-related homicides in 1979 that involved a firearm was 71 percent, by 1994 it had risen to 95 percent (Hutson et al. 1995). Similarly, in Chicago between 1987 and 1990 a significant rise occurred in gang-related homicides, but no increase occurred in the number of gang assault incidents (Block and Block 1993). If we were to compare the period 1982–1985 to 1990–1992, gun homicides by 13- to 24-year-olds rose from 55 percent to 72 percent (Cook 1998). The *New York Times* (April 9, 1996) reported data from a number of social and health groups on this topic. At that time gunfire was the second leading cause of death among young Americans ages 10 to 19. Between 1992 and 1993 that form of dying increased 7 percent, while the increase for all other age groups was 4.8 percent.

Other sources of information also support the homicide weapons-gun connection to juveniles during this lethal time window. In 1996, the juvenile courts in the nation handled approximately 2,400 homicide cases (Stahl et al. 1999). The trends here parallel the trends already discussed. Between 1987 and 1996 there was an increase of 74 percent of homicide cases, but the increase between 1992 and 1996 was only 11 percent. In this time period, there were 41,200 weapons cases. Between 1987 and 1996 there was an increase of 109 percent, but from 1992 to 1996 there was a *decrease* of 3 percent. Also, according to OJJDP (Juvenile Justice Bulletin 2000), while an increase occurred in juvenile homicides during 1987–1993, they declined to just 20 percent above the 1987 level during the 1993–1997 period. Yet the *proportion* of homicides by firearms in that period did not decline.

Victimization rates, though measured beyond the juvenile age span, support the gun "hypothesis" of the window of violence. For people 12 years of age and older, the rate of nonfatal handgun victimizations in 1992 was 4.5 crimes per 100,000, a figure that supplanted the record of 4.0 in 1982 (Rand 1994). Further, in 1992 victims reported 930,700 handgun crimes; the annual average for 1987–1991 was 667,000.

Recently, the number of youth involved in the use of firearms has been decreasing, according to data collected by the Bureau of Alcohol, Tobacco, and Firearms (ATF). Over the last few years ATF has been collecting data that involve trace analysis requests concerning the use of firearms. The number of cities participating in the data collection has grown

Table 6.13 Percentage of Juveniles as Gun Possessors	
Year	Percentage
1998	11.3%
1999	9.3
2000	7.6

Source: Bureau of Alcohol, Tobacco, and Firearms (1999, 2000, 2002).

from 17 (in 1997) to 50 (in 2000). As Table 6.13 indicates, between 1998 and 2000 juveniles were consistent in their use of semiautomatic pistols (between 56.7 and 57.7 percent), revolvers (between 27.1 and 29.5 percent), and rifles or shotguns (between 12.3 and 14.8 percent). More important, the numbers show decreasing gun possession by juveniles while committing crimes.

Drugs (and Guns and Race)

Some criminologists, such as Alfred Blumstein (1995), believe the lethal window under discussion was not due simply to the availability of guns. Professor Blumstein attributes the dramatic increase in gun crimes among adolescents to the advent of crack cocaine in the middle 1980s. Trafficking in crack resulted in a constant flow of money and inevitably led to conflict over drug markets. The easy availability of guns, plus the conflicts that were assured because of economic competition, yielded gun deaths and injuries.

While illicit drug *use* among whites is as high as, or higher than, among blacks, most trading and selling takes place in the inner city. That completes the drugs-guns-race connection. According to Blumstein (1995), it is what accounts for the disparate racial differences in drug arrests and gun homicide arrests starting around 1985. In fact, the drug arrest rates for white juveniles were slightly higher than for black youth from 1970 to about the mid-1980s. Nevertheless, from that point on the black rates escalated dramatically while the rates for whites declined (see Blumstein 1995, Figure 5). The same pattern essentially held for homicide arrests. From 1976 to 1987 the white homicide arrest rate was 8.1 (per 100,000 juveniles), and it rose to 13.6 by 1992. For black youth the rate was 50.4 in the first period and 111.8 for the second period. From 1976 to 1985, 59 percent of juvenile homicides were gun related. This figure doubled from 1985 to 1992 (Blumstein 1995).

Drug use among adolescents and young adults has been surveyed annually since 1975, and the survey was extended to include eighth- and tenth-grade students in 1991. The survey, conducted by the National Institute of Drug Abuse (NIDA), is reported in an annual publication, *Monitoring the Future*. It monitors daily, yearly, and lifetime use of many drugs among the target population. The results offered mixed encouragement. The good news is that only cigarettes (among tenth and twelfth graders) were identified as being used daily by more than 10 percent of youth. Also good news is that only marijuana, cigarettes, and alcohol tend to be reported by more than 10 percent of youth on an annual basis. Finally, the numbers within the last few years show a decline among virtually all groups in the use of virtually all drugs. Nevertheless, the bad news is that the percentage of users is higher today than it was in 1991 for all groups for all drugs (Johnston et al. 2003). Table 6.14 reveals trends in the percentage of users of various drugs since 1991.

Table 6.14 Trends in Annual Use of Various Drugs for Eighth, Tenth, and Twelfth Graders									
	1991			**1997**			**2002**		
Drug	**8th**	**10th**	**12th**	**8th**	**10th**	**12th**	**8th**	**10th**	**12th**
Any illicit drug	11.3	21.4	29.4	22.1	38.5	42.4	17.7	34.8	41.0
Marijuana/hashish	6.2	16.5	23.9	17.7	34.8	38.5	14.6	30.3	36.2
Inhalants	9.0	7.1	6.6	11.8	8.7	6.7	7.7	5.8	4.5
Hallucinogens	1.9	4.0	5.8	3.7	7.6	9.8	2.6	4.7	6.6
LSD	1.7	3.7	5.2	3.2	6.7	8.4	1.5	2.6	3.5
PCP	—	—	1.4	—	—	2.3	—	—	1.1
Ecstasy	—	—	—	2.3	3.9	4.0	2.9	4.9	7.4
Cocaine	1.1	2.2	3.5	2.8	4.7	5.5	2.3	4.0	5.0
Crack	0.7	0.9	1.5	1.7	2.2	2.4	1.6	2.3	2.3
Heroin	0.7	0.5	0.4	1.3	1.4	1.2	0.9	1.1	1.0
Other narcotics	—	—	3.5	—	—	6.2	—	—	7.0
Amphetamines	6.2	8.2	8.2	8.1	12.1	9.5	5.5	10.7	11.1
Barbiturates	—	—	3.4	—	—	5.1	—	—	6.7
Tranquilizers	1.8	3.2	3.6	2.9	4.9	4.7	2.6	6.3	7.7
Cigarettes*	14.3	20.8	28.3	19.4	29.8	36.5	10.7	17.7	26.7

Source: Johnston et al. (2003), Table 2.2.
* Percentages for cigarettes were based on previous 30-day use rather than annual.
— Indicates data are not available.

The NIDA offers a number of facts that it believes puts drug use among juveniles into perspective. These facts include the following:

- By the end of eighth grade, nearly one-third (32 percent) of youth have tried an illicit drug (if inhalants are included), and by twelfth grade, more than half (55 percent) have done so.

- 8 percent of students have tried cocaine by their senior year of high school. More than one in every 25 seniors (3.8 percent) has tried crack.

- Over one in every 16 high school seniors (6 percent) in 2002 smoked marijuana daily. Among those seniors, one in every six (16 percent) had been daily marijuana smokers at some time for at least a month.

- Three in ten high school seniors (29 percent) consumed five or more drinks in a row at least once in the two weeks prior to the survey.

- More than one-fourth (27 percent) of high school seniors in 2002 were current cigarette smokers, and 17 percent were already current daily smokers.

- Despite the substantial improvement in the U.S. drug situation in the 1980s and the 1990s, it is still true that this nation's secondary students show a level of involvement with illicit drugs that is as great as has been documented in any other industrialized nation in the world. (Johnston et al. 2003, 34)

What should make matters even worse is that the surveys are done at schools, meaning that dropouts (constituting approximately 15 to 20 percent of eligible students)—perhaps the worst drug abusers (Fagan and Pabon 1990; Altschuler and Brounstein 1991)—are not included within the survey data.

The numbers are also much worse among juvenile offenders than among nonarrestees. Since 1997 juveniles arrested in nine cities have been monitored to detect the presence of drugs (especially marijuana, cocaine, methamphetamine, opiates, and PCP).[6] The data are collected under the auspices of the *Arrestees Drug Abuse Monitoring* (ADAM) *Program*. Since 1999, most participating cities have kept track of both male and female juvenile arrestees. Table 6.15 discloses the results from 1999 to 2002. By a wide margin, the drug most often detected has been marijuana. There has been no pattern between the use of drugs and the type of offense committed. Nevertheless, one noticeable pattern is that a much higher percentage of arrested youth who were not in school were involved with drug use compared to arrested youth who were attending school. Often the difference between the two groups was as great as 35 percent. Another discernable pattern was that the percentage of drug use among arrestees increased as age increased. Although most often males had a higher involvement with drugs than females, the number of arrested girls was frequently too low to form any firm conclusions. Finally, there was no consistent pattern in terms of race. Overall, white arrestees tended to have the lowest rate of drug use compared to blacks and Hispanics (especially in Cleveland, Denver, and San Antonio), but in some cities (including Portland and San Diego), whereas white youth had a lower rate of involvement than Hispanics, they had a higher rate than blacks.

Table 6.15 Percentage of Drug Use Among Male/Female Arrestees, in Nine Cities, 1999–2002

City	1999	2000	2001	2002
Birmingham	45.5/—	41.5/16.7	47.3/13.6	62.2/62.5
Cleveland	62.0/—	56.7/—	55.1/—	60.2/—
Denver	62.2/46.9	66.5/65.4	64.6/66.7	—
Los Angeles	53.9/—	62.1/38.3	—	—
Phoenix	68.5/45.5	59.6/45.6	65.7/43.5	71.6/53.2
Portland	43.3/37.7	51.0/44.7	48.1/52.5	—
San Antonio	56.1/24.8	53.5/25.6	52.0/23.1	50.5/25.5
San Diego	56.8/47.7	47.3/43.1	53.2/43.5	52.5/38.5
Tucson	55.8/41.0	53.6/44.4	53.1/61.1	—

Source: ADAM (2000, 2001, 2003a, 2003b).
— Indicates data are unavailable.

Serious Violent Juveniles (SVJ)

The term *serious violent juvenile (SVJ)* is being used more and more often in the juvenile delinquency/justice literature. There are now ongoing projects in a number of areas, dealing with thousands of juveniles and crime incidents, to determine the factors that contribute to serious and violent juvenile offenders. Spurred no doubt by the significant increases in serious juvenile crime starting in the mid-1980s, Congress, in one of its regular amendments to the Juvenile Justice and Delinquency Prevention Act of 1974, directed the OJJDP in 1992 to study juvenile violence in a variety of settings around the country. Included are three ongoing long-term studies in Denver, Colorado; Pittsburgh, Pennsylvania; and Rochester, New York. Four new areas have been added: Washington, DC; several southern rural areas; Los Angeles; and Milwaukee.

Among the specific objectives handed down by Congress to ascertain are (1) individual risk factors of SVJ, (2) characteristics of areas that contribute to violence, (3) access ability to firearms and their use, and (4) conditions that contribute to youth violence. Researchers at several sites have interviewed youth at 6- to 12-month intervals, which presumably helps retrospective recall. The interviews have focused on serious offenses such as rape, robbery, aggravated assault, and gang fights.

Some preliminary results of the research reveal some unusual patterns (Kelly et al. 1997):

- According to self-reports, violence in males peaks at the 15–17 range.
- Youth as young as 10, and females, report higher levels of crime than expected.
- The peak age of offending varies by gender and, to a lesser degree, site. Girls in Denver peak at 14–15 and then decline. For boys, the peak offending period is 16–18. For Rochester, girls the peak offending age is 13–14, followed by a decline. For boys, there is a unique pattern. Offending first peaks at 14, then declines through 15–17, then rises again at 18. In Pittsburgh males only, the pattern is similar to that for Rochester males. There is a peak at 13–14, then a decline through 15–16, then another peak at 17.
- In Rochester, in the 12–14 age group, girl offending is about the same as it is for boys. And at 13, girls *exceed* boys in their offending.
- Seven percent of the Pittsburgh boys as young as 10 were involved in a violent crime.
- At all three sites, by age 16, 40 percent of males reported one or more violent acts.

Risk factors for SVJs fall into several categories: those that relate to the individual, those that relate to criminal history, and those that relate to neighborhoods (OJJDP 1999). Being male is probably the most obvious individual characteristic. Other individual characteristics that presumably contribute to later SVJs are early signs of aggressive behavior such as bullying, hyperactivity and risk-taking behavior, early initiation (age 12–15) of violence, and antisocial behavior. Early involvement in criminal behavior is predictive of SVJ. In Pittsburgh, 85 percent of youth admitted to serious offenses by 14, as did 65 percent in Denver and Rochester. An interesting finding (Juvenile Justice Bulletin 1998) is that behavior problems of eventual SVJs begin early (at age 7), moderate to serious problem behavior appears by age 9.5, and although serious delinquency starts at age 11.9, the first court appearance, on average, is not until age 14.5. A study team in South Carolina reports similar findings (OJJDP 1999). The average age of the first referral to juvenile court for a homicide group was 14; for an assault and battery group it was 14.2; and for serious assault charges it was 14.1. Those in the homicide and assault groups did not have juvenile justice records prior to their arrests.

The researchers in the SVJ study (OJJDP 1999) also scrutinized neighborhood characteristics of juvenile offenders and juvenile victims of violent crime. In Washington, DC, the census tract, which was recorded as 41 percent below the poverty line (DC as a whole was 17 percent below), was the highest risk zone for assault, rape, and robbery of juveniles. It was also noted that 86 percent of the households in this census tract were single-parent and female-headed. In Milwaukee, the highest rates of juvenile victimization occurred in census tracts designated "dangerous neighborhood." Ninety percent of homicide offenders came from single-parent households. The South Carolina researchers in this study examined rural areas in four states. Juvenile violence was associated with family disruption, ethnic heterogeneity, and poverty.

Juvenile homicides have occurred under certain conditions and circumstances. For example, in Los Angeles, 73 percent of juvenile homicides occurred in public places, whereas in Washington, DC, they were clearly associated with schools. With regard to the latter, the researchers noted the lack of after-school supervision—75 percent of the boys had no adult supervision after school. In fact, the researchers pointed out that suspension from school simply adds hours of unsupervised time.

Firearms have also played a major role in juvenile homicides. In Washington, DC, 85 percent of juvenile homicide victims were killed with a firearm, while in Los Angeles it was 91 percent. In Milwaukee, 40 of the 48 (83 percent) juvenile homicide offenders used a gun to kill.

The SVJ project is a lengthy, prospective, longitudinal study. It is too early to draw any significant conclusions, but a review of the cohort studies we discussed in Chapter 5 may demonstrate that the earlier studies were on the right track. In the Washington, DC, SVJ group, 7 percent of the youth were responsible for committing 36 percent of all delinquent acts, 21 percent of juvenile assaults, 44 percent of all drug deals, and 44 percent of all property crimes. Also, in the SVJ studies thus far, race, SES, and poverty have been found to be related to serious delinquency. The SVJ project is far more sophisticated than the cohort studies of the 1950s–1970s and should provide not only much more valuable information, but also some keys to prevention and treatment.

Summary: Key Ideas and Concepts

- Patterns or environments in which juvenile crime occurs
- Delinquency a group thing
- Media hype of school crime
- School crime incidents decreasing recently
- Schools as safer than the streets

- Various information sources on juvenile gangs
- Difficulty and variation in defining *gang*
- Decrease in numbers of gangs and gang members
- Widespread presence of gangs in various communities
- Most gang members are adults
- Significant but decreasing number of female gang members
- Hispanics most numerous gang population
- Significant number of gangs of mixed races/ethnicities
- Decline in reports of crime estimates involving gangs
- Declining use of guns by juveniles
- Declining use of drugs by juveniles
- Decline in juvenile arrests evidencing the presence of drug use
- Complex relationship among gangs, drugs, and guns
- Serious violent juveniles studies confirming cohort findings

Discussion Questions

1. Are schools safer or more dangerous today since various highly publicized incidents of school violence in recent years? Have the media exaggerated the school violence problem?

2. Do zero-tolerance laws work? Are they appropriate for the school setting? Are there any circumstances of these laws that could be characterized as extreme?

3. How would you define *gang*? What deficiencies exist in the definitions included in the text?

4. Are gangs the main cause of the violence represented in juvenile crime? If not, what is?

5. What impact has drugs had on juvenile crime? How about guns?

6. Do gangs, drugs, and guns go together?

7. What should we expect the serious violent juvenile studies to ultimately say about juvenile crime?

Endnotes

1. Although some offenses, such as assaults, tend to not involve group behavior, most illegal activities, including drug offenses, burglary, and vandalism, typically occur in groups (Erickson 1971; Erickson and Jensen 1977).
2. The most recent complete survey was the 1998 survey published in 2000. Since then, only highlights have been available.

3. Youth classified as *other* (including American Indian and Haitian, among others) made up 2 percent of gang members in both 1996 and 1998.
4. One study in San Diego contended that drugs were related to a rise in gang violence and homicides between 1985 and 1988 (Sanders 1994). It is possible, of course, that different cities would experience differences in the connection between drugs and gang violence.
5. With respect to males, this phenomenon is pointed out by Huff (1998).
6. Originally, 13 cities participated in the monitoring. After two years, Indianapolis, St. Louis, San Jose, and Washington, DC, were no longer included in the data collection. There are no data available from Los Angeles for the last two years. For 2002, besides Los Angeles, data are lacking from Denver, Portland, and Tucson. ✦

The Gatekeepers of Juvenile Justice

- Chapter 7: Policing Juveniles
- Chapter 8: Juvenile Court Personnel
- Chapter 9: The Intake Process

Focus of Section III

Section III addresses the critical "gatekeeping" stage of the juvenile justice process. Both police (Chapter 7) and intake workers (Chapter 9) serve in the important role of screeners, determining whether youth require the attention of the formal system. As we will see, most youth are found not to require that attention. Besides this essential use of discretionary power by these officials, Section III focuses on the other juvenile court workers who make the court what it is and especially on the characteristics that make these court workers unique. ✦

Policing Juveniles

Focus of Chapter 7

Chapter 7 examines the relationship between police and youth. In this chapter we will discover the special role played by police vis-à-vis juveniles. Despite the fact that the founders of juvenile court did not seek the development of a police force that focused exclusively on youth, several aspects of policing youth differ significantly from those for policing adults. We will also learn the rights youth enjoy during the policing stage.

Key Terms

- chivalry hypothesis
- exclusionary rule
- field investigation
- Fifth Amendment
- Fourth Amendment
- gatekeeper
- *in loco parentis*
- intake officer
- interrogation

- *Miranda* warning
- order maintenance
- policing authorities
- presumption of release
- service
- station adjustment
- stop and frisk
- totality of circumstances

Policing: The Underdeveloped Component

Policing was the one-third of the system that juvenile justice advocates did not develop at the turn of the twentieth century. Unlike juvenile courts and juvenile corrections, juvenile policing remains relatively underdeveloped today. Although the child savers believed that special courts and facilities were necessary to deal with juvenile offenders specially and separately, they did not identify a need for separation during the policing stage. The child savers were content with relying on the police who arrest adult offenders to be the same persons who refer most problem children to the juvenile system. It was *after* apprehension by police and referral to court that separation and special handling were believed to be required.

This is not to say that jurisdictions have not developed specialized police units that deal extensively or exclusively with children. School resource officers (SROs) patrol only hallways instead of streets. Larger police departments may have units that focus on curfew violators, runaways or missing children, and school or gang violence (some of which overlaps with adult targets). They also may have what are called juvenile police officers or juvenile aide officers, but those individuals tend to process only youths who are apprehended by rank- and file-cops. Again, the police officer who is pursuing most juvenile delinquents and status offenders in the community is the same individual who is seeking adult offenders as well.

Unique Police Service and Prevention Roles

Although juvenile policing clearly borrows heavily from officers who work regularly in criminal justice, it has many unique elements. For one thing, besides regular cops (including SROs), juveniles are monitored by more policing authorities than adults are. Status offense laws confer policing-like powers on school officials and parents. Quite naturally, since youths answer to more laws than adults, they also answer to more policing

Most police encounters with juveniles do not involve law enforcement. What impact does the police service role have on juveniles' attitudes toward the police?

agents. School officials and parents account for significant numbers of youths who end up referred to and processed by juvenile courts. Despite this fact, we examine only "regular" law enforcement officers for the most part in this chapter.

Police officers have three basic roles to play in the community (Wilson 1968): law enforcement (literally enforcing laws, making arrests, etc.), order maintenance (preventing or stopping disturbances), and service (assisting people in trouble). Although police officers have some unique powers and responsibilities when reacting to juveniles via their law enforcement and order maintenance capacities, their basic roles in these two categories do not vary by whether an adult or a juvenile is involved. The police behaviors entailed in dispersing a crowd, arresting, searching and seizing, and interrogating are essentially the same for juvenile and adult suspects. The same is not true of the police officer's service role, however.

Even regular cops have a unique role when it comes to the service aspect of policing juveniles.

This role has two major manifestations. First, police have a special responsibility to *protect children*. Besides the laws that authorize the police to intervene in situations in which the youth's health or welfare is threatened (see Chapter 4), society has expectations for police who encounter endangered children. Whereas police officers could possibly justify ignoring troubled adults (such as the homeless and those involved in domestic conflicts), the same failure to respond when children are involved could be fatal to both the child and the officer's career. Not surprisingly, a recent study of police-juvenile encounters discovered police extending support in various ways to youth in about 25 percent of the interactions (Myers 2002).

The second unique aspect of the service role involves *delinquency prevention*. Chapter 16 will explore prevention programs in detail. Suffice it to say here that police are equipped with special laws (such as truancy and curfew laws) and powers to help particular youths avoid getting into trouble. They also conduct special programs (such as the DARE antidrug initiative, the GREAT antigang program, and the Police Athletic League— PAL) that attempt to educate youth regarding potential problems and choices they will face in life and to occupy their free time in prosocial, law-abiding activities. Police in many locations also engage in proactive prevention measures geared to stop gang activities and gun use, which might be grouped under patrols focused on truancy and curfew violations (Fritsch et al. 1999). Operation Ceasefire in Boston involves police engaging violent gangs and telling them they will not tolerate violence. Proactive measures associated with this operation (such as arresting gang members for drug and alcohol use) have been credited with serious reductions in homicides, gun use, and violence (Braga et al. 2001).

Police in some towns have aligned themselves with other representatives from the community, such as school officials and drug abuse counselors, to form a multidisciplinary unit that attempts to identify at-risk youths and to refer these young people to group and individual counseling (Wyrick 2000). Similarly, police have teamed up with probation officers in Anchorage, Alaska, to enhance the level of supervision of juveniles on probation. Although the intensified supervision has not resulted in a reduction of crime, the number of probation violations discovered has increased (Giblin 2002). A police-PO linkage in Baton Rouge (gun offense cases) and in Riverside, California (gang offenses), was developed not only to expand the probationary supervision of juveniles, but also to assist in extending treatment-oriented services to them (Howell 2000; Lizotte and Sheppard 2001). In Indianapolis, police have helped coordinate and host restorative justice conferences in which youthful offenders and victims communicate with each other about the effects of crime. This intervention has been found to be effective in reducing recidivism (McGarrell et al. 2000). In other cities (such as Tacoma, Washington) police have been known to counsel truants concerning the problems that result from not getting an education and to transport truants to truancy centers (Baker et. al 2001).

The special service role of police has had a long history. In fact, the introduction of women to the field of policing in the early 1900s came about largely because of a desire to provide youth with special attention and handling (Fogelson 1977). These special service responsibilities can contribute to police officers' experiencing a *role conflict* that does not tend to occur with the policing of adults. Much like probation officers (see Chapter 8), police officers can feel conflict from having to serve as both protectors and law enforcers where problem children are concerned. The special police service role also is a response to the widely held belief that it is critical for children to develop positive attitudes toward police officers.

Juveniles' Attitudes Toward Police

Research studies that have examined attitudes of youth toward the police have found that poorer, black males hold the most negative views (Anderson 1994; Hurst and Frank 2000; Johnston et al. 1996; Leiber et al. 1998; Portune 1971). Negative views also are likely among youth who have poor school records (Portune 1971), who live in high-crime neighborhoods (Browning et al. 1994) or in urban surroundings (Hurst and Frank 2000), who have had negative previous contacts with police (Griffiths and Winfree 1982; Hurst and Frank 2000; Winfree and Griffiths 1977), who have recently been a victim of crime (Hurst and Frank 2000), or who have a delinquent history (Cox and Falkenberg 1987) or a commitment to delinquent norms (Leiber et al. 1998).

Also a factor in young people's attitudes is the context or neighborhood within which they live. That is, they are socialized in their community and can share attitudes held by members of that community. Critical to the development of a poor juvenile attitude toward police is a negative perception in the neighborhood that police are there mostly to impose legal authority and social control. This perception of unfairness and police discrimination can lead to resentment and resistance among all the inhabitants of the affected community (Leiber et al. 1998). The fact that attitudes and views can be converted into behavior, both verbal and physical, has serious implications for what can happen particularly to these juveniles during encounters with police. The research in this area has contributed to developing new approaches to delinquency prevention and even to modifying police practices, particularly in urban neighborhoods.

Community-Oriented Policing

Although it has not been developed purely as a strategy to address juvenile delinquency, *community-oriented policing* is considered particularly well suited to promoting delinquency prevention and to improving relationships with youth and the surrounding neighborhood (Leiber et al. 1998). This brand of policing encourages officers to become more integrated with community life and, especially in the juvenile context, to form partnerships with the school system, the juvenile court, social service providers, and health and mental health agencies to address myriad problems experienced by youth. Community policing was given a huge boost when Congress passed the Violent Crime Control and Law Enforcement Act of 1994. That act helped create the Office of Community-Oriented Policing Services (COPS). Since then, COPS has funded numerous initiatives across the country that seek to develop community policing strategies that will result in reducing juvenile crime, drug and weapons offenses, and street and school violence, among other social problems involving youth. For example, COPS partnerships have joined police with students, school administrators and faculty, bus drivers, school support personnel, parents, and local businesses to combat bullying, drug dealing and use at school, various types of assaults on school property and on routes to and from school, vandalism and graffiti, loitering, and thefts (Rich et al. 2001; Varano and Bezdikian 2001).

One of the most significant ventures sponsored by COPS was the Youth Firearms Violence Initiative (YFVI). This project used community policing approaches to foster youth-focused programs aiming to decrease violent firearms crimes and reduce the number of firearms-related drug offenses. Of the 10 cities involved in the project, San Antonio reported the most significant reduction (41 percent) in gun crimes (Dunworth 2000). Other initiatives have involved police aligning with youth groups, such as the Boy Scouts and Girl Scouts, in an attempt to reduce the risk of children becoming involved in crime. Police volunteer to teach and conduct joint activities with youth groups in order to promote wholesome development and to provide protection from delinquency and victimization (Chaiken 1998). In Chapter 16 we will return to a discussion of delinquency prevention programs.

Curfew Laws

Many cities today have curfew laws that restrict youth activities in the public domain, usually during the late-night hours. Typically, curfews affect those under the age of 18, but they can be drafted to apply only to those younger than 16. Also typically, curfews begin around 11 p.m. (and may extend to midnight on the weekends) and last until 6 a.m. In some locations juveniles are allowed to be out during the prohibited hours if they are returning from work or certain activities or are with their parents (Stuphen and Ford 2001). The rationale for these laws is to limit opportunities for getting into trouble. Curfew laws have been credited with decreases in burglaries, simple assaults, and thefts in some locations (McDowall et al. 2000). For the most part, however, research on curfew effectiveness has not found decreases in crimes committed by youth during curfew hours that can be attributed to the curfew laws themselves (Males 2000; Reynolds et al. 2000). Research has also discovered that juveniles cited for curfew violations are prone to be arrested at a later date for criminal behavior (Hirschel et al. 2001). The probable explanation for the ineffectiveness of curfew laws is that juveniles do not tend to be particularly criminally active during the early morning hours to which curfews apply. Curfews might be more productive if they focused on the after-school time period, as is the case in a minority of areas that have these laws (Bannister et al. 2001).

Detecting Youth Misbehavior

Before examining the dynamics of policing juveniles, it is important to note that many—perhaps most—delinquent and status offense events go *undetected* (Williams and Gold 1972). Juveniles get away with most of the illegal behaviors they commit. Many of the offenders' parents do not learn of the event and the victims (if any) of these behaviors rarely discover the perpetrator. Even when these offenses are detected, most probably remain *unreported* to the authorities. Parents may ignore or accept their children's misbehaviors. Victims and witnesses may do the same or, if they know the offender, may call the parent instead of the police. The incident and damage may be resolvable without having to involve the system. Similarly, school officials may choose to work informally with a truant or delinquent and not report him or her to juvenile authorities. In short, *people exercise discretion* in electing whether to contact the police. In fact, unless they have a specific legal duty (usually because of their job or status), citizens are not obligated to report crimes. This means that the police and the system will only selectively know juvenile offenders.

Historically, most police encounters with juveniles that have culminated in arrest have come about via citizen reporting rather than routine police patrol (traffic offenses are an exception to this rule). In the past, citizen-initiated reports have accounted for two-thirds to three-fourths of juvenile arrests (Black and Reiss 1970; Lundman et al. 1978). The presence of modern, proactive police units that focus on juveniles (such as curfew, gangs, drugs, and serious offenders) have probably reduced the gap between citizens and the police with regard to who brings a youth to the attention of the police (see Klein 1993; Owens and Wells 1993).

Interestingly, one recent analysis of regular police patrol units found that half of the police-juvenile encounters were initiated by the police rather than by a citizen complaint (Worden and Myers 1999). The initiation of the encounter can be critical inasmuch as police have been found to be less likely to arrest when they are the ones to have begun the interaction (Worden and Myers 1999). This study found the typical police-juvenile encounter to involve a minor incident (such as theft or curfew violation) in which a single officer interacted with a single youth in a public location, such as a park or mall, usually between the afternoon and nighttime hours of any day of the week, and to involve individuals who did not know each other previously (Worden and Myers 1999).

Although it is likely that victims will not be present when police encounter youth (Worden and Myers 1999), the presence of witnesses and victims at or near a crime scene is important in a couple of ways. First, the citizen's account of what supposedly happened can easily end up as the officer's entire field investigation. That is, the witness account could provide an officer with sufficient evidence to believe that (1) an offense has occurred and that the juvenile committed it; (2) the youth should be detained and the accusation investigated; and, (3) ultimately, the youth should be taken into custody. Second, although it is likely that victims will request an arrest in few police-juvenile encounters (Worden and Myers 1999), the desires of a victim can be a critical factor in determining whether an arrest will occur. Victims appear to be more likely to request that the officer admonish the youth or to force the juvenile to leave the area (Worden and Myers 1999).

Field Investigations and Stops and Frisks

The presence of victims and witnesses can affect the amount of evidence an officer has that implicates the youth. Between the statements secured from these individuals (as well as from the youth) and the evidence garnered from physical evidence and direct observations of the officer, it can be expected that police will have evidence of offending in about half of the cases involving youth (Worden and Myers 1999). Some of this information is gathered by an investigation conducted by the police. A field investigation involves as many as three behaviors by the police: a stop (or a brief detention) of the youth, a frisk of the youth (or a pat down aimed at weapons and even for drugs), and an interrogation or questioning related to the officer's suspicions. Although there has not been any case law from the U.S. Supreme Court in field investigations, it seems reasonable to assume that the standards governing these police behaviors with adults would apply equally to juveniles. That means that as a result of *Terry v. Ohio* (1968), police would need at least *reasonable suspicion* to believe an offense has occurred or is occurring and that the juvenile is involved with that offense before a stop is permissible. In addition, police would have to be able to identify an *articulable* or *identifiable reason* as to why they feared for their safety before a pat down or frisk for weapons or drugs is permissible. As far as interrogation is concerned, unless the youth is clearly in custody (translated usually as "not free to leave"), police can ask questions (including ones that can get the youth into serious trouble) without reciting *Miranda* warnings (from *Miranda v. Arizona* 1966) (of the right to silence and counsel). The longer the detention or the more intimidating its nature (e.g., several officers surrounding the youth), the more likely a court will ultimately find that the juvenile was actually in custody and should have been given a *Miranda* warning. One recent study disclosed that police search and interrogate youth in nearly 25 percent of encounters (Worden and Myers 1999).

In terms of time, the detention can persist as long as is "reasonable" to accomplish a "reasonable" inquiry by the police. Again, these circumstances exist for adults as well. One issue that might require an answer from the Supreme Court is whether juveniles are equally entitled not to respond to police questioning and not to be arrested merely for that fact alone. It is certainly possible that police interrogation of status offenses such as truancy and running away from home (and even curfew violations) might require more in the way of responses from juveniles than would inquiries of criminal activities such as burglary and robbery.

The Decision Not to Arrest a Youth

Depending on what the officer hears from all parties involved or finds via a frisk or search of the youth and the surrounding area (such as a vehicle), there may be grounds for an arrest. Typically, that does not mean an arrest has to or will occur. In the past, the vast majority of police encounters with youth (perhaps as many as 85 percent) have *not* resulted in an arrest (Black and Reiss 1970; Lundman et al. 1978). In keeping with the times, it might seem reasonable to think that today police are more reluctant to resolve incidents with juveniles informally (i.e., without an arrest). Nevertheless, recent numbers suggest that police continue to arrest in less than 15 percent of their encounters with youth (Crowe 1991; Myers 2002; Worden and Myers 1999). In lieu of arrest, police most frequently threaten to arrest juveniles (or to issue a citation), request or command that they leave the area and discontinue their behavior, or merely release the juveniles (Worden and Myers 1999). Police rarely do not exercise any authority whatsoever with juvenile suspects (Myers 2002).

Before proceeding, it is important to note that many states refer to this interference into a youth's life as being *taken into custody* and insist that, except for gauging its legality, this event not be called an arrest.[1] Although physically the two are identical, not calling the experience an arrest allows individuals to report later that they have never been arrested. Thus, the difference between the two is not merely semantic.

Taking juveniles into custody is different from arresting adults in a number of ways. For one thing, because of the juvenile system's rehabilitation mission, police are specifically expected to exercise *discretion* when they encounter youth in situations that can culminate in arrest (IJA/ABA 1980). Discretion means the police have choices or options in deciding how to respond to an incident. Not all encounters have to culminate in arrest, even when there is sufficient evidence to arrest. To be sure, police practice discretion in determining whether to arrest adults as well. Nevertheless, the juvenile system's special mandate and the sheer nature of dealing with children provide police much more leeway. For example, in an encounter with a 12-year-old an officer's explanation of "I'm taking a chance on this kid" would likely elicit much less public criticism than if he were discussing a 25-year-old suspect. Of course, 30 years ago there was less criticism about "cutting juveniles a break" than there is today. Not surprisingly, police are more likely to exercise this discretion when nonserious offenses and nonchronic offenders are involved. This discretion to arrest establishes the police as a critical gatekeeper to the juvenile justice system. That is, in most cases, *they* decide which youth will be forced to experience juvenile court. In addition, it is this discretion or authority to choose whether to arrest a youth that also enables police to *discriminate*, or to treat equally situated youth unequally because of some prejudicial factor such as race, gender, or ethnicity. We will see throughout the remainder of this text that other important workers in the juvenile justice system (such as POs, prosecutors, and judges) have similarly critical discretionary powers, which can also result in discriminatory responses from the system.

Fortifying this expectation of discretion is the fact that police have more options in arresting youths when compared to adults. With the adults, police have only two choices: to arrest or not to arrest. For juveniles who have not committed serious offenses (e.g., no felonies qualify in KY), there is an important middle ground. Instead of just ignoring the conduct or merely warning and releasing the youth (which can be done with adults, too), police can select (or combine) three approaches with youth short of formal arrest and processing:

1. Solicit the help and attention of parents.

2. Refer the youth to a community agency or group.

3. Require the youth to report periodically and directly to the officer.

A recent study discovered police taking youth home to their parents in nearly 16 percent of their encounters (Myers 2002). The last two situations are examples of police diversion, which is kicking the juvenile's case out of the formal system while keeping tabs on him or her via an informal system (for more on diversion, see Chapters 9 and 16). Many states specifically identify the police officer's authority to divert appropriate juvenile cases.[2] These situations could also be referred to as station adjustments, which simply means that formal processing is not being pursued at this time. Both could require the consent of the youth and/or the parents. Suffice it to say, police diversion is consistent with the rehabilitation mission of juvenile court, and police are more likely and more able to engage in this personal monitoring of the informal resolution of a case when a juvenile is involved.

Police may feel that less serious violations and offenses do not require even continued informal control of the youth and that appropriate parental discipline is all that is necessary to correct a problem. This is where the role of the parent in the juvenile system begins its critical and unique course. We will see this parental role as also having a potential significant impact at the interrogation stage and at each important decision-making stage of the juvenile court process. When police take juveniles to their homes (as opposed to the police station), a clear message is sent to the child and the parents. This situation does not have to culminate in an arrest (or even in informal processing) if the officer has a viable alternative via the parent. A parental reaction of gratitude for bringing the youth's behavior to light, coupled with a promise of suitable discipline, is likely to convince an officer that an arrest is unnecessary. A parental response of denial that the youth could have done anything wrong and that the wrong must lie with the officer is likely to convince an officer that the parent is probably the source of the youth's problem, rather than its solution. Minimally in this situation, a station adjustment or even an arrest could appear necessary. In other words, parental response can be what brings about a juvenile arrest, especially in the nonserious offense or nonchronic offender category. The interaction between parents and police could also transpire at the police station and be just as critical there as at the youth's residence. It also cannot be ruled out that the *parent* may actually *want* the child arrested and taken out of the house. This situation may stem from legitimate reasons (e.g., the youth is beating up the parent or siblings) or illegitimate ones (e.g., the parent simply and selfishly wants nothing to do with the child). A belligerent attitude from the parents or their refusal to appear at the police station could guarantee their child's arrest, as could their demand that the youth be arrested.

Grounds and Evidence for Arrest (Taking Into Custody)

Juveniles can be arrested in every situation that applies to adults and then some. Like adults, young people can be taken into custody for committing a crime (delinquency), for being a fugitive from justice or an escapee from an institution, for violation of probation or parole, or via a court order. A court order usually involves an arrest warrant or a judge's ordering arrest because of the youth's failure to appear at court for a scheduled hearing (or for ignoring some other obliged performance or appearance). Unlike adults, juveniles in California, Idaho, and Virginia can be arrested for misdemeanors even though the crimes were not committed in the officer's presence. Also unlike adults, juveniles are eligible for being taken into custody for a variety of status offenses,[3] ranging from truancy[4] to incorrigibility[5] to running away from home.[6] Stemming from society's duty to protect children in general, police may also take youth into custody when illness or injury or danger to the youth's health, morals, or welfare is possible,[7] when the youth has no parent or is abandoned,[8] when the youth may abscond or leave the jurisdiction,[9] and when the youth is mentally ill or dangerous.[10]

How much evidence of wrongdoing an officer needs before arresting a juvenile is sometimes unclear. For delinquencies or crime the standard used by most jurisdictions since the *Gault* decision is the same as that applied to adults: *probable cause* (juvenile statutes often phrase it as the law of arrest). However, some jurisdictions use terms that can be regarded as synonyms for *reasonable suspicion* (a less demanding standard than probable cause), such as *reasonable cause* (CA, ID, IL) or *reasonable grounds* (AZ, CO, DC, GA, HI, NE, UT, WI), making it uncertain whether police always need the same amount of evidence to arrest youth as they need to arrest adults. Even more uncertain situations arise in the few states (NC, NH, SC) that fail to identify any standard of evidence. What reinforces the notion that some jurisdictions might require less evidence to arrest a delinquent (compared to a criminal) is that most of the country employs terms like *reasonable cause* or *grounds* or *belief* to identify what is required to take various status offenders or medically or physically threatened children into custody.[11] Many states omit mention of any level of evidence required to take children from these special groups into custody.[12] Nevertheless, five states (IN, KS, MS, VA, TX) appear to require probable cause to take all juveniles into custody, regardless of the offense or situation.

Police officers are not the only individuals empowered to arrest juveniles. Like their counterparts in criminal court, juvenile probation officers (POs) have law enforcement powers, especially over youth under their supervision (i.e., youth who have been temporarily released to the community prior to trial, sentenced to probation after adjudication, or paroled from an institution). Consequently, POs typically have the authority to take juveniles into custody for any behavior that would violate a condition of release, probation or parole, or any court order.[13] Similarly, some statutes mention the PO's ability to arrest those who are escapees from a facility or perhaps about to flee the jurisdiction (or be removed from it).[14] Interestingly, many states have gone even further in the PO's capacity to arrest and equate POs with police, empowering them to arrest for status offenses or crimes committed by those *not* under supervision.[15] Finally, consistent with the system's overall concern for the physical well-being of the child, several states provide that POs can take juveniles into custody when they appear to be runaways or in a dangerous situation that could threaten injury or illness.[16]

Of course, whenever police do not need probable cause to arrest some juveniles, they have greater authority to interfere with young people than they have with adults. More important, perhaps, is the fact that the legality of the arrest on lesser evidence will not be a problem even if a "nondelinquent" arrest ends up unintentionally yielding criminal products such as weapons or drugs. Except in the five states that always require probable cause to arrest youth, delinquency adjudications can be obtained when the evidence justifying the initial arrest was much less than probable cause, at least when the basis for the arrest was not a delinquency.

One unresolved issue in arresting juveniles is whether police need a warrant to arrest youth in their homes. Most arrests (of youth and adults) occur outside of the home and without a warrant. In *Payton v. New York* (1980), the U.S. Supreme Court ruled that adults could not be arrested in their homes without a warrant unless there was an emergency. The decision relied heavily on adults' right to privacy in their own homes. What makes it uncertain whether this ruling would apply to juveniles is that the latter do not tend to be perceived as having a similar right to privacy in their parents' homes. An even more interesting wrinkle would be whether the parents' agreement that the police can take away and arrest their child would affect the need for a warrant. Arguably it is the youth's constitutional right not to be removed from home without a warrant, rather than the parents' feelings or desires, that should control the outcome.

Whatever level of evidence is required to arrest juveniles (and whether a warrant is needed for a home arrest), if it is later determined that the police lacked sufficient evidence to arrest (or lacked a needed warrant), the arrest would be illegal. The police would have committed a constitutional violation by arresting the youth. As we will see shortly, police can also commit constitutional violations during searches and interrogations. Any evidence of wrongdoing that is secured via unconstitutional police actions has been obtained illegally. Illegally seized evidence is subject to the exclusionary rule in criminal court (via *Mapp v. Ohio*, 1961). That means, with some exceptions, that the illegally seized evidence cannot be used (or is excluded) against defendants at trial. The U.S. Supreme Court has not yet extended the exclusionary rule to juvenile court proceedings. In none of the handful of cases it has reviewed has the Court found that there had been an illegal seizure of evidence involving youth prosecuted in juvenile court.[17] Nonetheless, it appears that all jurisdictions have adopted the exclusionary rule in juvenile court, making a Supreme Court declaration on the issue somewhat redundant or unnecessary. Most states have statutes or case law formally requiring juvenile courts to use the exclusionary rule.[18] Actually, even without an official endorsement it would be surprising today to find any appellate court not holding the exclusionary rule relevant to and binding on adjudicatory hearings in juvenile court.

Factors That Can Affect the Decision to Arrest

The factors that can influence an officer's decision to arrest a youth are almost too plentiful to identify and involve many items that are difficult to measure (such as demeanor). Some factors, such as offense and record, tend to be more important than others, such as youth's or parents' demeanor, but the latter can at times actually explain why the youth was arrested. Most of the factors are legitimate, but some (such as race, gender, and class status) suggest unfairness. Many of the factors can be gleaned from a police report that describes the police-youth encounter, but, unless the actual interaction is observed, the true and full context of the arrest may remain unknown. We say all this to emphasize that the nature of arresting juveniles defies research and analysis and prevents a complete understanding of all that is involved. Many of the factors mentioned in the following sections are fairly obvious and will not be further described. Some factors may have been unintentionally omitted.

Factors Related to the Offense

- Seriousness of the offense (felony, misdemeanor, violation)
- Type of offense (especially cruel, violent, problematic)
- Time of day (school hours, after school, early morning)
- Youth acted alone or with others
- Gang-related incident
- Amount of evidence linking youth with offense
- Use of a weapon

Typically, felonies are less likely to be ignored by police than misdemeanors or mere violations (Sealock and Simpson 1998). However, some misdemeanors (such as cruelty to animals or prostitution) may not be as legally serious as felonies but may actually appear to the officer as more problematic. Moreover, some jurisdictions mandate arrest even in some misdemeanor situations. For example, Arizona demands an arrest if a felony or breach of the peace is committed in the officer's presence (or after fresh pursuit). Oregon requires the arrest of juveniles caught with a firearm in a public building or court facility.

Not surprisingly, one study found that possession of a weapon made arrest more likely (Myers 2002; Worden and Myers 1999). Similarly, juveniles who are cutting school or perpetrating crimes at 3 a.m. could be perceived as representing a bigger problem (possibly related to the youth's family) than juveniles who get involved in a more serious offense on the way home from school. Youth who commit crimes with others may appear more dangerous than loners or may suffer from an all-or-nothing decision—namely, "If I'm going to arrest one of you, I'm going to arrest all of you." Juveniles who commit offenses with weapons or in furtherance of a gang's objectives have an increased likelihood of arrest. Although the strength of the evidence is rarely examined as a factor, it can exert substantial influence on the officer's decision to arrest (Worden and Myers 1999).

Factors Related to the Youth's Record or Status

- Previous delinquent or status offense record
- School or work record
- Program or treatment history
- Number of and nature of previous police contacts
- Probation, parole, furlough, or escape status

The police may not be able to determine the status of some of these factors until after the youth is transported to the police station. Nevertheless, an officer's awareness of one of these items (such as that the youth is an escapee) alone might be *the* factor that precipitates an arrest. Interestingly, Illinois law specifies education and employment status together with program history (which could include juvenile court intervention or community social service history) as factors to be considered in the arrest decision.

Factors Related to the Offender

- Race, gender, age
- Class status
- Demeanor, reputation, condition (drunk or high)
- Gang member
- Belligerent or resisting arrest

An extensive amount of research has been dedicated to determining whether the race or gender of the offender affects the decision to arrest. Although the results are mixed, most research has found that race is a factor in the arrest decision (Conley 1994; Wordes et al. 1994). Whether the race factor stems from outright racism or from the interaction of numerous other potential factors is nearly impossible to discern (Tracy 2002). Interestingly, a recent study found that police were likely to have more evidence against minorities who also were involved in more serious offenses, which could explain a greater arrest rate. Specifically, police were more likely to observe minority suspects commit illegal acts, more likely to discover physical evidence against minority youth, and more likely to encounter witnesses who claimed to have seen minority juveniles commit an offense (Worden and Myers 1999).

Gender has also been found to play a part in the arrest decision. The chivalry hypothesis has frequently been offered as an explanation. This hypothesis suggests that police will act paternally toward girls and be less likely to arrest girls in delinquency situations (Worden and Myers 1999), but they will be more likely to arrest girls in status offense contexts (Bishop and Frazier 1992; Chesney-Lind 1973).

The class status of the offender has not received equal attention in the research, but some research has found lower-class youth to be more likely to being arrested (Sampson 1986; Sealock and Simpson 1998). Again, whether disproportionate arrests would stem from discrimination or from other variables (such as the police saturation of lower-class neighborhoods) would be difficult to determine. Interestingly, older juveniles do not appear to be substantially more likely to be arrested than younger ones (Myers 2002).

It is a fairly safe bet that police will be less likely to ignore or to divert even less serious offenses when the accused is intoxicated or high, is too polite or too arrogant or defiant, or has a bad reputation in the community (including possibly being a gang member). Similarly, juveniles perceived as having "gotten away with things" in the past could be more prone to arrest. Although only a small percentage of police-juvenile encounters involve disrespect displayed by youth (Worden and Myers 1999), perhaps the single most offender-related factor critical to police arresting a youth is his or her demeanor (Lundman 1994, 1996a, 1996b). This is not to say that an adult suspect's demeanor is unimportant. Rather, it appears that a youth's demeanor can be even more important than a comparably situated adult's demeanor. Cops appear prepared to take "more lip" from an adult (who may at least have earned an attitude) than from a juvenile. Moreover, the recommendations of a national committee were for the police to ignore an adult's demeanor while considering and giving weight to a youth's attitude when deciding to arrest (NAC 1976).

A youth's resisting arrest may be poor demeanor in the extreme, but it can serve as both an independent authorization to arrest a youth (it is illegal to resist arrest) and a factor in whether the youth should be arrested. In fact, a police officer's using force in effecting the arrest may make the decision to arrest all the more necessary, as the officer's actions could have legal ramifications. Essentially, the rule on the use of force for police is the same whether the arrestee is a juvenile or an adult. Police are allowed to use only that amount of force *necessary to overcome the arrestee's resistance* (including when flight is involved). Any more force than that is excessive or unreasonable and therefore illegal. Police can use deadly force only when the suspect threatens them or others with the same. Interestingly, the U.S. Supreme Court case that resolved the use of deadly force on suspects involved a juvenile who had just burglarized a house. Prior to this case, police shoot-

Should the police be required to use less force when arresting juveniles?

ings of youth, many of whom were blacks who had stolen cars, had caused a number of incidents of urban unrest. These shootings had been "legal" at the time because officers were allowed to shoot fleeing felons. These were individuals who had committed felonies (such as auto theft) and were fleeing police apprehension. The Supreme Court put an end to the common law–based fleeing felon rule in *Tennessee v. Garner* (1985).

Factors Related to the Complainant

- Present at the scene
- Able to identify the perpetrator
- Desire to prosecute
- Relation to the accused
- Level of blame in the offense
- Prominence in the community, social class
- Race, gender, age

The complainant can be *the* most important factor in any arrest decision, regardless of the offense and the offender's record. The failure of a complainant to remain at the scene of a crime, or the complainant's inability to describe or identify an assailant, effectively may guarantee that no arrest will ever be made in an incident. The complainant's refusal to prosecute can derail an arrest even when the suspect is in custody (Black and Reiss 1970). In misdemeanor cases the police must typically have the complainant's cooperation in order to arrest, since an officer's having probable cause to believe the offense occurred is not sufficient to take the youth into custody. Interestingly, however, one recent study found that victims' requests to arrest had no detectable effect on the outcome (Worden and Myers 1999).

The desire to prosecute could be seriously influenced by whether the victim is partly to blame or is related to the perpetrator, and by the personal characteristics of the complainant (i.e., race, gender, and age). Not all victims are equally inclined to prosecute their assailants. The complainant's personal and social characteristics could in turn affect the officer's reactions to this individual's desires. One recent study found that police are more inclined to investigate cases and arrest youth when the complainant is a minority (Worden and Myers 1999).

Factors Related to the Location of the Offense

- Crime level
- Police patrol level
- Class status, community resources
- Offender is a community member
- Bystanders (especially if hostile)
- Fractured or cohesive community

The impact of a crime is not uniform among all communities. Crime is relative. The extent of police presence in neighborhoods is also relative and tends to be a response to the area's crime level. Both can certainly affect the number of arrests brought about in any location, especially in urban centers where black youth could far outnumber white youth (Sampson 1986). Moreover, behavior that tends to be ignored in some areas may be viewed as outrageous in others. Similarly, the extent of the community's resources may influence whether certain offenses will be tolerated or prosecuted. Community resources can also affect the number of programs available to police that provide a plausible alternative to arrest. Even in situations in which the complainant is not particularly anxious to prosecute, an arrest could result when bystanders demand it or an active neighborhood watch organization presses for one (especially if the complainant is encouraged to rethink the situation).

Factors Related to the Parents or Home

- Belligerent parental attitude
- Parent not home or not located
- Parents or home present a problem
- Parent fails or refuses to appear at police station

As suggested earlier, if the parents appear to be more of a problem than a solution to the youth's behavior, arrest becomes a more likely outcome. The inability to produce a parent could require at least a trip to the police station, if not an arrest.

Factors Related to the Officer

- Race, gender, age
- Class status
- Alone or working with a partner
- Training (especially regarding juvenile system) and experience
- View of juvenile system and diversion
- Previous contact with accused
- Workload
- Laziness or incompetence

Obviously, the police officer does not enter the encounter with the youth on totally neutral grounds. The officer's race, gender, age, and class status can influence his or her reaction to youthful misbehavior and the extent of his or her tolerance of such behavior and tendency to act in a discriminatory manner. The fact that one officer is working with another officer could affect the ability of either to act discriminatorily. The mere presence of a second officer, especially if the officers vary by race or gender (and perhaps even by age or class status), could eliminate an opportunity for a racist or sexist response. Similarly, the presence of a supervisor at the scene could affect an officer's behavior (Myers 2002). Previous encounters with a particular child could ensure an arrest in a situation that would otherwise result in the officer's use of discretion to ignore a misbehavior (Myers 2002).

The officer's previous experiences (including childhood, education, parenting, juvenile system contacts, and so on) will influence reactions to juvenile delinquency, as will prior training and support or distrust of community programs and the juvenile system. For example, a perception that neither diversion programs nor the juvenile court itself has any valuable lesson to provide a youth could encourage an officer to view arrest, in general, as an unproductive activity. Similarly, officers' views of their role in policing could influence whether they elect to arrest or "work" with youth (Myers 2002). The timing of the encounter could be critical, in that the officer's workload could influence the decision to arrest. For example, one recent study found arrests to be less likely to occur on weekend days because workloads were heavier and there was less time to process arrests (Worden and Myers 1999). Of course, lazy and incompetent officers and those who are alone at the encounter may find it easier to simply ignore certain juvenile behavior, especially if considerable paperwork is involved or the juvenile system seemingly will do nothing about the youth's conduct.

Factors Related to the Police Organization

- Enforcement priorities
- Department policies (e.g., community policing)

The police do not act in a vacuum but rather react to the community they serve. Again, the police department might tolerate certain illegal behaviors, even when committed by youth. A legalistic-oriented police department, however, could promote a tendency to arrest on the part of its officers (Smith 1984). It is also likely that an officer's having ties to the community (via community policing initiatives or prevention programs) will affect the propensity to arrest or to divert offenders. Finally, the police department's organization will influence whether police-juvenile encounters usually involve regular patrol or specialized juvenile units. Specialized units can be more likely to consist of detectives prone to investigation of incidents and who know more about the prior records of youth. Regular patrol officers tend to engage youth in the heat of the moment on the street. Although the structure of police departments could affect decisions to arrest, it has not been researched for the most part (Worden and Myers 1999).

Factor Interaction

Not only are the potential factors numerous, but the way they operate and interact can also be complex and confusing. For example, as noted previously, the offender's gender can work in opposite directions. Girls may not be as likely as boys to be arrested for delinquencies, because of the officer's chivalrous view toward females, but they may be more likely to be arrested for status offenses, because of the officer's paternalistic or protective view. Moreover, the outcome could depend on the age of the girl. Similarly, two relatively similar officers could look at two equally offending 12-year-olds in opposite ways.

These juveniles could be perceived as too young to get involved formally with the juvenile system or as simply getting an early jump on a delinquent career and thus desperately needing official intervention. White police officers surely could be motivated by racism in arresting a black youth (where a similarly situated white youth would be diverted). Nevertheless, the white officer could exercise a kind of "reverse" or "inverted" racism and not arrest black youth as readily, thinking that delinquent behavior is more common and accepted in black communities. Of course, black police officers might tolerate more or less from black juvenile offenders than from white offenders and be just as racist as the white officers. Finally (although there are many more examples we could discuss), the race of the complainant may confuse things, perhaps in unexpected ways. Black juvenile delinquents are more likely to victimize other blacks. Interestingly, black victims prosecute more black defendants than white victims do white defendants, *and* police not only encounter more black victims but also tend to listen more to the desires of black victims (Black and Reiss 1970; Lundman et al. 1978; Worden and Myers 2002).

One of the most expansive analyses of arrest data that looked specifically at race was recently conducted using 1997 and 1998 NIBRS master files from 17 states that involved several violent crimes (Pope and Snyder 2003). The results are interesting not only because they failed to find a so-called race effect behind the arrest decision, but also because they identified offense tendencies between whites and nonwhites.

Perhaps most intriguing, besides the absence of a race effect, is that compared to nonwhites, whites were:

- less likely to have multiple victims;
- more likely to act alone;
- less likely to possess a nonpersonal weapon, such as a firearm, knife, or club;
- less likely to offend against an adult;
- equally likely to offend against females;
- less likely to offend against members of another race;
- equally likely to injure victims; and
- more likely to commit crimes against family members.

In the end, pinpointing the legitimate or illegitimate factors that affect the arrest of youth is a difficult, if not impossible, task. Not surprisingly, no research study has attempted to address nearly half of the factors identified in this section. Also not surprisingly, research studies largely contradict each other when proposing that one or even multiple factors explain the arrest decision.

Because the topic has already been covered extensively, the actual results of research into the various arrest decision factors will not be presented here. Students are encouraged to consult these sources to determine for themselves how well (or how badly) the studies have addressed and accounted for the numerous factors that could affect the arrest decision. Although the results of research studies conflict and fail to consistently pinpoint the various factors, an inescapable fact is that minority youth disproportionately experience arrest. Appendix A outlines the ratio of minority youth arrested in 38 jurisdictions, only two of which do not report a disproportionate rate for minorities.

Table 7.1 Characteristics of Violent Crimes by Juvenile Offenders, 17 States, 1997 and 1998

Offense Characteristics		Percentage of Offenders		
		White (*n*=71,246)	Nonwhite (*n*=31,659)	All (*n*=102,905)
Was offender arrested?	No	64.1	69.6	65.8
	Yes	35.9	30.4	34.2
Number of victims	One	82.8	79.8	81.8
	More than one	17.2	20.2	18.2
Number of offenders	One	67.1	54.4	63.2
	More than one	32.9	45.6	36.8
Location of incident	Indoors	21.7	32.8	25.1
	Outdoors	78.3	67.2	74.9
Most serious weapon	Personal	84.0	77.0	81.8
	Nonpersonal	16.0	23.0	18.2
Victim age	Juvenile	62.1	57.6	60.7
	Adult	37.9	42.4	39.3
Victim gender	Female	46.8	47.6	47.0
	Male	53.2	52.4	53.0
Victim race	White	96.7	34.0	77.4
	Nonwhite	3.3	66.0	22.6
Was victim injured?	No	53.9	53.6	53.8
	Yes	46.1	46.4	46.2
Was offender a family member?	No	76.2	82.8	78.3
	Yes	23.8	17.2	21.7
Was offender an acquaintance?	No	31.4	33.3	32.0
	Yes	68.6	66.7	68.0
Was offender a stranger?	No	87.9	77.2	84.6
	Yes	12.1	22.8	15.4
Offender gender	Female	26.5	27.7	26.8
	Male	73.5	72.3	73.2
Offender race	White			69.2
	Nonwhite			30.8

Source: Pope and Snyder (2003), Table 1.

Procedures Following Arrest

Although the police who arrest a youth may not be "special" juvenile officers, the procedures they must follow after an arrest frequently are unique. If the encounter can result in a citation (similar to a traffic ticket) instead of an arrest, which is possible in some jurisdictions for low-level misdemeanors and violations such as curfew, the matter can be resolved right on the street. Texas law provides for warning notices in lieu of taking juveniles into custody. An arrest, however, typically means the youth will not be "cut loose" on the street, but rather will be transported to the police station or district for further processing. When processing arrested juveniles, police in many states face three obligations they do not have after they arrest adults.[19]

First, a number of jurisdictions hold that juveniles cannot be transported to a police station at all (e.g., NY), that transport is permissible only when a special room in the station has been earmarked only for juveniles (e.g., TX), or that any visit to a station must be

for processing only, which must be done within a severely limited time frame (e.g., KY, SC). Similarly, it is common for police to be prohibited from holding young people in the station (especially in lockup) altogether or beyond a limited number of hours (AZ, MS, NH, NJ, OH).

Second, police are usually obligated to notify the parent(s) of the youth's arrest and custody (or at least to make a good faith effort to do so) within a brief period. Although some statutes are not specific in describing the allotted time,[20] Arizona has established a 6-hour limit, while Arkansas and New Mexico police have 24 hours.

Should the police be allowed to take juvenile arrestees to the same area of the police station as adult arrestees?

Other states use terms like "immediately,"[21] "as soon as possible or practicable,"[22] "promptly" (LA, OH, TX), "without unnecessary delay" (UT), or "in the most expeditious manner possible" (VA).

For the most part, these directives apply equally to delinquents and status offenders. A few states are more protective of status offenders, however, by specifying that parental notification must occur immediately (MT, NJ) or as soon as possible (WY).

Besides notice of arrest or custody, police in many jurisdictions are required to notify parents of related items, such as why the youth was arrested,[23] the youth's right to silence,[24] the youth's right to counsel,[25] the parent's right to visitation,[26] the location of detention,[27] why the youth was held in detention,[28] and the right to and timing of a detention hearing.[29]

Finally, and consistent with the other obligations, if police cannot (due to the parents' failure to appear) or will not release the youth to the parents,[30] the police must immediately notify a juvenile PO of this development (KY, MT, NH). In addition, the police are usually under obligation to turn the youth over to juvenile court authorities within a specified and limited number of hours (AK, AR, KY, ME, NH, RI). Some states qualify this obligation with terms like "immediately,"[31] "without delay,"[32] "with all reasonable speed,"[33] "as soon as possible" (MN, WY), "directly" (DE, MO, NY), "forthwith" (FED, ID), "promptly" (LA), "in the most expeditious manner possible" (AL), or "with all practicable speed" (VA). Status offenders minimally should enjoy limits similar to those granted delinquents in this regard. In fact, a few states actually require the police to take the status offender home (CT, NY, NJ).

These unique obligations are intended to ensure that the vast majority of juveniles will be reunited with their families as soon as possible, and that the police do not have a long time (in intimidating surroundings) to coerce statements from arrested youth. Most juveniles are released within a short time to their parents. In fact, there is a presumption of release of delinquents and status offenders to the parents, usually by the police or at least by juvenile authorities.[34] Parents are typically required to sign a form promising to appear in juvenile court with the youth on the day assigned by court personnel.[35] A summons to appear in court will never materialize for some of these juveniles if the police decide not to proceed with the case (perhaps because of a lack of evidence or a desire to divert the matter). Serious or chronic offenders (and juveniles whose parents do not appear at the station) are more likely to be escorted by the police to juvenile detention or to an intake officer (the initial gatekeeper of the juvenile court system). This individual will decide how to proceed with the case (including whether to detain or to prosecute the defendant; see Chapter 9). Parents who did not appear at the police station will still be able to retrieve their children from intake/detention, provided there are no independent reasons for holding the youth in detention pending trial (see Chapter 10).

Search and Seizure and Interrogation

During their encounter with police, juveniles can experience two significant police activities: searches and seizures and interrogations. Just as with adults, an arrest is not necessary to trigger either of these activities. Searches and interrogations can occur before, during, or after an arrest. The suspect might be handcuffed while being questioned and searched even though an arrest has not transpired (Myers 2002). One recent study found that searches occurred in less than a quarter of police encounters with youths (and more frequently with boys than girls), while interrogations occurred in nearly half (Myers 2002; Worden and Myers 1999). Nevertheless, *when* a search or interrogation occurs is critical in determining the legality of the activity and what exactly police are or are not permitted or forced to do.

Search and Seizure

The Fourth Amendment in the Bill of Rights is the major source of control over police behavior. It requires probable cause for police to arrest and, with some exceptions, both probable cause and a warrant for police to search and seize. To date, no court or legislature in this country has distinguished search-related Fourth Amendment protections of adults versus juveniles on the street.[36] In other words, juveniles walk around and drive through their communities on a legal footing equal to that of their adult counterparts. Police have no greater searching power over juveniles in the public arena. A search of juveniles or of automobiles they are driving would require their consent, probable cause to believe contraband or stolen property is located in the vehicle, or an arrest or some other exception to the warrant requirement (assuming a warrant has not been secured).

Juveniles do not enjoy the same Fourth Amendment status as adults, however, *at home* or *at school*. Generally, parents can give permission to police to search their children's rooms or belongings—in other words, they can substitute their consent for their child's and thereby surrender the youth's constitutional rights. The parents' responsibility for the welfare of their children and the youth's diminished expectation of privacy in his or her parents' homes combine to justify parents' authority over children in this respect.[37] Of course, parents face no legal obstacles or constraints in conducting their own search of their children's rooms. The Fourth Amendment places restraint only over government agents, which typically means only law enforcement agents of some sort. Children, on the other hand, are not authorized to permit police to search their parents' rooms, beyond those utilized and shared by the family in general. Although the U.S. Supreme Court has yet to address this issue, it is unlikely that the Court would modify this broadly recognized parental permission power.

A youth's expectation of privacy is seriously diminished in elementary and secondary schools as well. In fact, school desks and lockers are viewed as school property in which the child has *no* privacy expectation. Consequently, school authorities would need no evidence per se of wrongdoing or the presence of contraband in order to search these locations or to permit the police to do so.[38] Some state courts prefer school officials to have some reasonable basis for searching desks or lockers,[39] but this appears to be a standard voluntarily adopted by these jurisdictions rather than a position the Supreme Court would interpret as required by the Fourth Amendment. The use of stationary metal detectors (like those used in airports and courthouses) and portable handheld metal detector wands for random searches of youth for weapons are permitted without any suspicion that any of the individuals are carrying weapons.[40] Similarly, the Supreme Court has declared that random, suspicionless drug testing of student athletes and of students who participate in extracurricular activities is not a violation of students' Fourth Amendment rights.[41]

Beyond a doubt, the Supreme Court's decision in *New Jersey v. T.L.O.* (1985) has had the greatest implications for a youth's right to privacy (and freedom from searches) in the school context. In that case, TLO had been accused of violating a school rule by smoking in the girls' lavatory. At the time (unlike today) it was neither illegal nor a school rule violation for a student to possess cigarettes. TLO's school also permitted smoking, but only in designated areas, which did not include lavatories. The teacher who discovered the incident turned TLO and her companion (who subsequently admitted doing wrong) over to the assistant vice principal (AVP). TLO not only denied the violation but also denied being a smoker. The AVP believed—incorrectly—that if he were to find cigarettes in TLO's purse, that would refute both of her denials. This assumption was patently absurd, because even if TLO had cigarettes in her purse, while it might make her appear to be a smoker (of course, she could have been holding them for someone else), it would not prove or even corroborate that she indeed smoked one of those very same (or someone else's) cigarettes in the lavatory. Only if the AVP had intended to match the brand of cigarettes in TLO's purse with the brand of cigarette from the lavatory (which was not his intent) would there have been *some* corroboration that *someone* smoked in the lavatory the same brand of cigarettes TLO possessed in her purse. For true corroboration, the AVP would have needed to link TLO's DNA with saliva taken from the spent cigarette from the lavatory, which still meant that any cigarettes in the purse were irrelevant. Despite this reality, the AVP, without *any* evidence that there were cigarettes in the purse, searched it without her permission. This fishing expedition proved fruitful in that he found not only cigarettes, but also some marijuana in the purse. TLO was adjudicated delinquent on the drug possession charge. She appealed this adjudication to the New Jersey Supreme Court and won a reversal on the basis of her claim that the search of her purse was illegal.[42]

Neither the state court nor eventually the U.S. Supreme Court had an objection to school authorities' searching students when it comes to school rule violations (instead of only in criminally related events). As a result of *T.L.O.*, then, youth in school are subject to being searched in situations that could not be applied to adults (in college). However, the N.J. Supreme Court had two objections to the search. The first objection concerned the amount of evidence that should be required before a school official can search a student's private possessions (book bags, purses, clothing). The state court appeared to have two options in identifying the proper status of a school person who searches students. The court could easily have equated school officials with parents (especially since the former operate *in loco parentis,* or in place of the parent). In this case no evidence at all would be required before conducting a search. At the other extreme, school officials could have been equated with the police. That probably would have meant requiring at least probable cause, if not a warrant, to justify school searches. Instead, the court compromised. In effect, it created a third level of evidence especially for school authorities: reasonable grounds (akin to reasonable suspicion). As a result of the state court ruling, the following formula had been established:

Person	Level of Evidence
Parent	None
School official	Reasonable grounds
Police	Probable cause (and warrant)

Applying the reasonable grounds standard to TLO's situation, the N.J. Supreme Court ruled that the AVP's search was illegal because he had no idea (let alone reasonable grounds to believe) that cigarettes were in TLO's purse. At best, the AVP acted on a hunch or an instinct, since no information had been supplied to him that cigarettes were in that particular (or any) purse.

The state court's second problem with the search complemented the first. Even if the AVP had had reasonable grounds to believe cigarettes were in the purse (for that matter, even if the purse had been open, clearly revealing the pack of cigarettes), the AVP's search and seizure of the cigarettes was unlawful since TLO's possession of them violated *neither* a school rule *nor* a law. For a search and seizure to be lawful, there must be evidence as to the location of an item, and the possession of the item must be illegal or at least evidence of a crime (or, for youth, at least evidence of a school rule violation). Because TLO's possession of cigarettes was neither unlawful nor evidence of *any* wrongdoing, the New Jersey Supreme Court declared the search unconstitutional.

The state of New Jersey appealed its highest court's ruling to the U.S. Supreme Court. The state won a reversal there, which thus reinstated TLO's adjudication. Although the Supreme Court agreed that the Fourth Amendment controlled the searching activities of school authorities (at least when directed at students' personal belongings), the Court made the unprecedented move of not requiring *any* level of evidence per se in the school search area. So, instead of demanding criteria such as reasonable grounds or suspicion or probable cause (which are usually associated with searching activity), the Supreme Court insisted only that school searches must be *reasonable* in themselves. In the majority's view, the AVP's actions were reasonable. It was reasonable for the AVP to think that TLO had cigarettes (assuming the accusation of her smoking in the lavatory was accurate), a purse is the reasonable place for cigarettes to be located, and TLO's possession of cigarettes could reasonably be interpreted as supporting the claim that she had smoked one of them in the lavatory earlier that day.

Despite the fact that the Supreme Court extended the Fourth Amendment to the schoolhouse, its minimal standard of basic reasonableness and permission of searches in school rule violations potentially opens students' private possessions to extensive searching. In effect, *T.L.O.* gives schoolteachers and administrators permission to act on hunches and instincts (albeit only reasonable ones) rather than on any particular proof of wrongdoing on the part of any one student and to search in a great variety of situations. For example, *T.L.O.* could serve as grounds for either a teacher's "reasonably" searching *every* student in a classroom for drugs after entering the room and believing the odor of marijuana was in the air. Similarly, a teacher "reasonably" could seize a youth's diary after hearing accusations that this student violated a school rule of spreading rumors about others (or of having uncharitable thoughts of others). Finally, even if the Supreme Court were to determine that a particular search was conducted unreasonably, the *T.L.O.* ruling specifically refused to commit itself to holding that any such evidence or information seized unlawfully would be excluded from a juvenile court prosecution. Lower courts have divided on this issue.[43] The suggestion from the Supreme Court was that the exclusionary rule would not be implemented in the school search context.

Interrogation

Constitutional controls. The *Miranda v. Arizona* (1966) decision regulates the interrogation or questioning of suspects in the criminal justice system. As a result of that case, the U.S. Supreme Court required adult suspects interrogated *by police* while *in custody* to be warned prior to questioning of their Fifth Amendment right to silence. Two warnings regarding this right were mandated: a reminder of the right to silence and a caution that statements could be used against one in court. The Court added two more warnings concerning the suspect's right to counsel that would be granted free of charge to the indigent should police ask incriminating questions. Warnings do not have to be given when only demographic questions are asked (such as name and address) or when the person is not in custody at the time of the questioning. For the most part, only police (or prosecutors) are obligated to Mirandize suspects. Since *Miranda* was delivered, the Supreme Court has introduced numerous exceptions or limits to its application.

Although the Supreme Court had an excellent opportunity to announce whether *Miranda* warnings were required when police acquire statements or confessions from youth who are prosecuted in juvenile court (assumedly, *anyone* who is prosecuted in criminal court would have a right to have been given *Miranda* warnings), it purposely refused to do so. In *Fare v. Michael C.* (1979), a youth who had been Mirandized did not trust the police when they offered him the assistance of a lawyer. He thought the police might dress up one of their officers and present this person as an attorney. Instead, Michael C. asked to see his probation officer, the one person he did trust and who had told the youth to contact him should Michael get into trouble. Michael's request was neither wise (the PO could have testified as to what the youth had revealed to him) nor legally required (police have no obligation to contact POs during interrogation). Without ever consulting anyone else, Michael ultimately confessed to the homicide with which he was charged. The juvenile court declared the confession was admissible and adjudicated Michael C. delinquent.

Michael C. appealed to the California Supreme Court and won a reversal of his adjudication.[44] The California court examined the way in which the confession was secured and determined there was a violation of *Miranda*, based along Fifth Amendment grounds of a right to silence. The California court phrased the situation as follows:

asking for a probation officer = asking for silence, help, or advice

Michael C.'s request to see his PO (a "trusted guardian figure") was tantamount to his asking to remain silent; thus the denial of that request amounted to a constitutional violation, according to the California Supreme Court. Several years earlier, the same court had similarly ruled that a youth's asking to see his parents constituted an invocation of a right to remain silent.[45] In both cases, the California court opined that a youth in custody is more likely to "call for help from the only person to whom he normally looks—a parent or guardian"[46] than from an attorney.

The state of California appealed this ruling to the U.S. Supreme Court, which reversed the previous court's decision. Although the focus of the Court purportedly remained on the right to remain silent, the Supreme Court rephrased the situation as follows:

asking for a probation officer ≠ asking for a lawyer

Consequently, the Court found that the police had committed no *Miranda* violation, since Michael C. had asked to see the wrong person. In this 5–4 ruling, the majority insisted on a strict, technical reading of *Miranda* that allows the suspect to ask for silence and for only one person's presence—a lawyer's. In a footnote (#4, p. 717), the Court noted that it had not yet ruled that *Miranda* applied to juvenile court proceedings, nor was it about to do so at this point. The one certain result of *Fare v. Michael C.* is that if *Miranda* applies to juveniles, it applies to them in the same context that it does to adults. The Supreme Court was not willing to adjust *Miranda* for youth. Juveniles must abide by the specific provisions of *Miranda* and will not be extended any extra considerations when they invoke or waive their rights.

It appears that, despite the Supreme Court's position, most jurisdictions (via statute or court decision) require police to give juveniles *Miranda* warnings preceding any custodial interrogation.[47] In fact, it would be surprising to find any jurisdiction that would allow the proceeds of a custodial interrogation to be used in the absence of *Miranda* warnings—at least in delinquency matters. It is quite possible that *Miranda* warnings would not have to be given to status offenders (e.g., NY, WI),[48] but several jurisdictions do require these juveniles to be advised of their rights at interrogation.[49]

Like adults, youths must be in custody before *Miranda* warnings are required. So, juveniles at home or in school or who voluntarily show up at a police station have been considered not in custody and thus not deserving of warnings.[50] Similarly, the exceptions to and limits of *Miranda* warnings that the Supreme Court has implemented in criminal court should apply equally to juvenile court. Thus, a statement secured in violation of *Miranda* can be used to impeach juveniles who take the stand and testify at an adjudicatory hearing.[51] *Miranda* warnings should not have to be given to youth when the safety of the public is in question (the public safety exception to *Miranda*).[52] Similarly, should police fail to Mirandize a youth *before* securing an initial statement, Mirandizing the youth *after* the first statement and *prior* to obtaining a second statement means the second statement is admissible.[53]

Accompanying *Miranda* warnings is a constitutional requirement that all confessions and statements be given voluntarily by youths (and adults).[54] To measure the voluntariness of a child's statement courts use a totality of circumstances test, perhaps best developed in *West v. United States* (1968) by the Fifth Circuit Court of Appeals. Included in the test are numerous factors to be examined by a judge relating to the context or atmosphere within which police secured the statement, such as:

• the youth's age, education, intelligence, and awareness of and ability to understand rights, the situation, and the charges;

• the length and conditions of the interrogation, including time of day and whether the youth was questioned in the presence of a parent or an attorney; and

• the youth's ability to confer with a parent or adult prior to the interrogation.

Not any one of these factors determines the voluntariness issue. Instead, the judge will look at *all* (totality) of these circumstances to gauge whether the youth talked voluntarily.

Two serious issues surround juveniles' surrender of their right to silence (and counsel), with or without the benefits of *Miranda* warnings. First is the question of whether youths generally can understand their rights, which would undermine the intelligence of any waiver of rights, if not its voluntariness. A number of studies have documented youths' inability to understand constitutional rights *and* the significance of surrendering them (Ferguson and Douglas 1970; Grisso 1980, 1981; Holtz 1987; Robin 1982). Despite these findings, no special procedures are constitutionally required in Mirandizing youth so as to ensure an understanding of rights, apart from encouragement from courts that police communicate with youth in noncomplicated language. Second is the question of whether juveniles, who are told or commanded by their parents to talk to the police, have voluntarily waived their rights when they provide a statement to the authorities. Although it surely is conceivable that some children would be talking to the police against their own will or desires (i.e., involuntarily), in this context appellate courts have refused to declare these waivers involuntary.[55] According to these courts, only police (or government agents) can render the surrender of someone's rights involuntary. The U.S. Supreme Court would almost certainly agree with this position. Although this view is not unreasonable, the fact remains that some youths are (in their eyes at least) involuntarily waiving their rights. The additional fact that statements given in this context can also be used to convict juveniles in criminal court (perhaps even in a capital case) only serves to underscore how parents can dramatically and adversely affect both their children's rights and the outcomes of proceedings against them. Compounding matters as well is that, although a couple of courts ruled some time ago that youth must be advised of the possibility that they could be tried as adults,[56] the modern approach adopted by most appellate courts is that juveniles and their parents are not entitled to any such warnings (which the U.S. Supreme Court would likely endorse).[57]

One interesting and unresolved issue is whether the U.S. Supreme Court would require school officials to Mirandize youth in school who are suspected of criminal activity (it is doubtful warnings would be necessary for status offenses and rule violations). Doing so would assume, of course, that *Miranda* warnings are required when police interrogate juveniles. Although the answer might appear obvious—that only police need to Mirandize—the *T.L.O.* holding complicates the matter. Arguably, the two items triggering the *Miranda* requirement (i.e., custody and police agent) are present in the school situation. Schoolchildren, at least all those younger than 16, are legally obligated to attend and to remain at school. They are in quasi-custody since they are not simply free to leave the premises at will (i.e., not without serious legal consequences, such as an eventual status offense prosecution and even institutionalization). The *T.L.O.* decision certainly suggested that school officials are quasi-police and not regular private citizens or parental figures. If they were parent-like, the constitution would not control their behavior at all in searching youths (i.e., they would not need any evidence or to act reasonably). Since the Court implemented quasi-controls over school officials, they must have been perceived as quasi-police. With quasi-custody and quasi-police in place, it is difficult to understand why quasi-*Miranda* warnings would not be necessary. To put it another way, if the Fourth Amendment exerts some control over school officials (via *T.L.O.*), why wouldn't the Fifth Amendment also exert some control over the same people (via some warnings)? The U.S. Supreme Court most likely would try to avoid this outcome, but it would have some interesting explaining to do regarding why *T.L.O.* would not influence the issue as noted above.[58]

Statutory controls. Statutory controls are those procedures police must observe because legislatures have determined on their own accord that interrogation of juveniles must occur in a certain way. These controls are neither constitutionally mandated (except perhaps by the state constitution) nor universal in practice (few of these measures are followed in a majority of jurisdictions). They represent extra steps police must take in some locations when interrogating only youths and not adults. Two of these controls have been covered already and will only be repeated here: notifying parents of the youth's arrest and presence at the police station, and transporting the youth quickly to juvenile court or detention authorities. These two controls are commonly required throughout the country.

It is possible also that police are prevented from interrogating juveniles in a police vehicle or station (AR, NY) unless the station contains a juvenile processing office (NY, TX). Some states require that the youth consult with the parent (or perhaps an attorney) prior to questioning (IN, LA, MA, MO, VT) or that, depending on the youth's age, the parent must be present during the interrogation (CO, CT, IA, ME, MT, NC, OK). Six states even prohibit some juveniles from waiving rights on their own (IA, LA, MA, MT, NJ, NY). Other states have been less demanding, instead forcing the youth to request to see his or her parents before the police would have to include them in the process (AL, AR, CA). Of course, some jurisdictions require neither consultation with the parent (CA, GA, IL) nor the parent's presence at interrogation (AL, AR, CA, DC, FL, GA, IL). Finally, some states have gone so far as to allow parents to be denied access to their children (IL), or for juveniles either to be denied access to their parents (GA, IL, MD, OR) or not to be told their parents are present at the station (CA).

Although the extent of some of these controls is somewhat limited, violation of these provisions can be as hazardous as constitutional violations. That is, police failure to observe these requirements has led to several court rulings that the statements could not be used in juvenile or criminal court.[59] Appellate court reaction to statutory violations has not been uniform, however. Georgia and Illinois insist that a statutory violation is just one factor to consider in the totality of circumstances regarding the admissibility of a statement secured after such a violation.[60] Interestingly, other appellate courts have determined that juveniles who ultimately are prosecuted in criminal court are not entitled to any special juvenile justice provisions, so violations of these provisions would not affect the admissibility of statements in a criminal prosecution.[61]

Fingerprints and Photographs

Fingerprinting and photographing adult arrestees has been standard operating procedure for decades. With juveniles the story has been quite different. Historically, juvenile justice has been dedicated to limiting the ability of law enforcers to create and maintain print and photo records of juveniles. The purpose of this policy was to minimize both the stigmatizing of juvenile offenders and the opportunity for employers (and others) to discover these records and to discriminate against those who have been arrested. Printing and photographing juveniles had frequently required a court order and had tended to be directed at only the oldest and most serious offenders. Beyond a doubt, the failure to put juveniles through this process enabled some of them to escape detection for crimes they committed, even when they left prints at the scene of a crime. To say that times have changed is an understatement. It appears that only Maryland and Michigan still have the traditional provision that prosecutors must ask for a court order to document youths.

A good deal of change occurred during and since the 1990s when no fewer than 16 jurisdictions not only abolished the court order requirement but also eliminated or lowered the age requirement, increased the type of eligible offenses, and/or mandated prints and photographs in some situations.[62] Interestingly, many jurisdictions have yet to include a print or photo provision in their juvenile court statutes.[63]

As proof that the pendulum has swung the other way, eight states now require fingerprinting in all felony arrests (AL, AR, FL, KS, MO, NV, OR, TN). These states (except Tennessee) also insist on printing many or all misdemeanants. Even more impressive are the three states that have required all detained youth (ID), all adjudicated youth (NJ), all juveniles adjudicated of felonies or crimes involving drugs or violence (FED), or all arrested youth (OK) to be fingerprinted. North Carolina, South Carolina, and Virginia mandate printing in some felony arrests, usually the most serious and violent, but North Carolina (10) and Virginia (14) also have established minimum ages for these provisions to take force.

Nonmandatory printing has become fairly widespread as well. Seventeen states allow juveniles who are taken into custody for *all* crimes (i.e., all felonies and misdemeanors) to be printed.[64] While Iowa and Ohio exclude simple and minor misdemeanors, respectively, from this measure, and South Carolina requires a petition to have been filed against the youth, Hawaii limits this provision to those who are at least 12 years old, and another five states (IN, NE, NJ, ND, OH) have established a 14-year-old minimum age. Another 10 states permit the printing of all felony arrests,[65] while Georgia, Illinois, and North Dakota have no minimum age requirement for more serious felonies. Class A and B felony charges authorize printing of youth at a younger age (11) in New York than Class C, D, and E felonies do (13). The magic number for printing of felons in North Carolina is age 10, while 14 provides a green light for felons in Indiana and Utah. Youths charged with the most serious or violent misdemeanors (or those associated with weapons) are subject to be printed in five states regardless of their age (AR, KS, LA, MS, TX). In Florida, 12-year-olds must be printed regardless of the severity of the misdemeanor.

Other new features have appeared as well. For one, if latent prints are discovered at the scene of the crime, juveniles connected to the crime (as possible suspects) may be printed for investigative purposes in many states.[66] To ensure that the fingerprint records are put to good law enforcement use, it is now common for local police agencies to be allowed[67] or even to be required[68] to forward these records to a centralized state agency. Consistent with traditional juvenile justice philosophy, however, if the youth's case is diverted (TX, WY) or results in no adjudication, many states call for the destruction of the fingerprint records.[69]

Most states have the same rules for photographing juveniles as for fingerprinting them.[70] A few states have slightly narrower (IN, MN, ND, UT) or broader (AL, NV) provisions regarding photographing juvenile suspects. Interestingly, however, Vermont requires either a court order or transfer of the case to criminal court in order to photograph juveniles.

Despite the liberalization in printing and photographing delinquents, it is still relatively rare for status offenders to be allowed to be photographed or printed. Nevertheless, some states do permit this activity (ID, MO, NE, NM), at least for photographs (NV, NJ), while Michigan requires it when a status offender is held in custody.

Other Identification Methods

Besides fingerprints and photographs, police may seek other features about juveniles in order to identify them as perpetrators of the crimes under investigation. As evidence that juvenile court statutes are starting to reflect advances in modern identification techniques, permission is being granted for securing blood samples from juveniles, especially in sex crimes where DNA analysis could help prove guilt and/or HIV could be a concern of the victim.[71]

Otherwise, police may also want hair, saliva, or urine samples; may want voice and handwriting samples; or may want to put the youth in a lineup for viewing by witnesses. Most statutes do not address these areas, so it is difficult to ascertain whether procedures in obtaining the items are unique when juveniles are involved. On the constitutional level, there is no reason to believe that juveniles' rights would differ from those of adults, which are minimal. Assuming that the suspect is lawfully in custody, there are no Fourth Amendment protections applicable to seizing these identification items, nor are there any Fifth Amendment protections concerning the suspect's right not to self-incriminate. The lack of a right to privacy when in custody dispenses the Fourth Amendment controls, and the fact that these identification items do not deal with testimony (i.e., forcing the suspect to confess or verbalize guilt) erases any Fifth Amendment controls. Actually, the only applicable constitutional right in this entire area is a Sixth Amendment right to counsel when suspects who have been charged with a crime are placed in a lineup.[72] The few cases that have addressed the topic have ruled that juveniles also have a right to counsel at lineup identifications.[73] Of course, it is always possible that some states require more in this regard. For example, North Carolina law requires a court order for police to obtain these nontestimonial identification items. It also permits such court orders only if the crime investigated is punishable by more than two years of incarceration.

The Decision to Refer the Case to Juvenile Court

Depending on the dynamics of the case, plus the results of the police investigation into the case, the police will ultimately make a decision whether to refer the matter to juvenile court. Just because an arrest has been made does not mean that a referral to court must result. Many things could change between the initial encounter with the youth and the final referral decision. These changes range from a lack of sufficient evidence to go forward with the case to an attitude adjustment on the part of the child or parent or even a change of heart by the victim or arresting officer.

Simply put, all those factors that emerged when the decision to arrest was made resurface and influence the court referral decision as well. The fact that a "second" decision is necessary for a case to see juvenile court (much like in criminal court) complicates research that attempts to understand and explain what motivated the referral decision. The arrest-referral decisions involve a process, which means a continuing development exists involving many possible changes, some of which may be both undetected and immeasurable. What is known is that over the last couple of decades, the number of referrals to juvenile court has been increasingly steadily. In fact, between 1980 and 1990 the referral rate rose from 58 percent to 64 percent, while between 1990 and 2001 the proportion of arrests that resulted in a referral to juvenile court rose from 64 percent to 72 percent. These increases were virtually identical in urban, suburban, and rural areas (Snyder 2003).

Over the last several years the police choice of informal processing versus referral to adult court versus referral to juvenile court has shown a lesser inclination of police to handle the case themselves and a slightly greater likelihood to refer the matter to juvenile court (Snyder 1997, 1998, 1999, 2000, 2002, 2003; UCR 2002). Again, urban, suburban, and rural police have referred almost identical percentages of their cases to juvenile court during most of these years (see Table 7.2).

Throughout the 1990s, law enforcement agencies were responsible for referring more than four out of every five delinquency cases that reached juvenile court. The remainder of the cases were referred by parents, schools, probation officers, social service agencies, and victims. Table 7.3 shows that police have been the major referral source throughout

Table 7.2 Percentage of Cases Resolved by Police Decisions

Disposition of Case	Year						
	1996	1997	1998	1999	2000	2001	2002
Informal process	23%	25%	22%	23%	20%	19%	18%
Refer to adult court	6	7	7	6	7	7	7
Refer to juvenile court	69	67	69	69	71	72	73

Table 7.3 Percentage of Cases Referred to Juvenile Court by Police Agencies, 1990–1999

Year	Offense				
	Person	Property	Drug	Public Order	Total
1990	86%	91%	92%	69%	86%
1991	81	89	88	69	84
1992	85	90	93	71	86
1993	87	91	94	70	87
1994	87	91	94	69	86
1995	88	91	94	69	87
1996	87	91	93	68	86
1997	86	91	93	65	85
1998	86	90	92	63	84
1999	86	91	91	63	83

the decade, especially in drug and property crimes (Puzzanchera et al. 2003b). Between 1990 and 1999, with the exception of liquor violations (92 percent), law enforcement was the referral source of less than half of all runaway cases (40 percent), truancies (10 percent), and ungovernability cases (11 percent) (Puzzanchera et al. 2003b).

Summary: Key Ideas and Concepts

- Police an underdeveloped component of the juvenile justice system
- More policing authorities for juveniles
- Unique police service role in protection and prevention for youth
- Critical attitudes of juveniles toward police
- Most delinquent activities go undetected or unreported

- Impact of citizen presence at crime scene
- Nature of field investigation
- Controls over stops, frisks, and interrogations
- Use of decision to not arrest
- Idea that juveniles are not arrested per se
- Police with significant discretionary power, which can lead to discrimination
- Police with many more options to arrest for youth
- Critical and unique role played by parents at this stage
- Parents possibly wanting youth arrested
- Unique grounds or reasons for taking youth into custody
- Less evidence needed to arrest some youth
- POs with arresting power
- Whether police need a warrant to arrest a youth at home
- Uncertain status of the exclusionary rule in juvenile court
- Extensive number of factors that can affect the decision to arrest
- Difficulty in determining the factors that affect any particular arrest
- Rule on police use of force with youth
- Unique police duties following arrest of youth
- Controls over search and seizure
- Unique search and seizure situations for youth
- Constitutional and statutory controls over interrogation of youth
- Question whether juveniles understand *Miranda* warnings
- Fairness problem when parents tell their children to talk to the police
- Question whether school officials are required to Mirandize youth
- Unique situation with fingerprinting and photographing youth
- Uncertain status of techniques used to identify youth

Discussion Questions

1. What is unique about the service role that police play when dealing with juveniles?
2. What needs to be done to improve juveniles' attitudes toward police?
3. What are the implications of most youthful illegal behavior being undetected or unreported?

4. What is involved in a field investigation?

5. What is unique about police exercise of discretion with juveniles?

6. What are the implications of police diversion of juveniles?

7. Discuss the role of the parent at the policing stage and the implications for juveniles.

8. Discuss the situations in which juveniles are subject to be taken into custody and by whom.

9. Should police be required to have an arrest warrant to arrest a youth at home? Why or why not?

10. Should the exclusionary rule apply to juvenile court proceedings? Why or why not?

11. Discuss the factors that can affect the decision to arrest youth. Which should be relevant and which irrelevant? Which would seem to apply more to juveniles than to adults?

12. What is meant by factor interaction in the arrest context, and how might it affect research into this topic?

13. Discuss how well or how badly research studies have accounted for the relevant factors that can affect the arrest decision.

14. Describe the three obligations police face after arresting youth.

15. Describe the situations in which searching juveniles is unique.

16. Discuss the appropriateness of the U.S. Supreme Court's rulings in *New Jersey v. T.L.O.* and *Fare v. Michael C.*

17. What controls should apply when police interrogate youth?

18. Can juveniles understand their constitutional rights regarding interrogation? Regarding searches?

19. What should be the role of the parent at interrogation?

20. Should school officials be required to Mirandize youth? Why or why not?

21. What standards should apply to fingerprinting and photographing youth?

Endnotes

1. The states that do not refer to this activity as an arrest are: AK, CO, FL, GA, ID, IL, IA, KY, LA, ME, MN, MS, MO, MT, NE, NJ, ND, OH, OK, OR, SC, SD, TN, TX, WI.
2. The states that mention an officer's authority to divert cases are: CA, FL, IL, KY, MI, NH, NC, TX.
3. The states that identify all status offenses as being eligible for taking a youth into custody are: AZ, CA, GA, HI, ID, IN, LA, NV, NC, OH, RI, TX, VA, WY.
4. The jurisdictions calling for truants to be taken into custody are: DE, DC, FL, ID, KS, KY, LA, MN, UT, WI.
5. The states calling for cases of incorrigibility to be taken into custody are: AZ, CA, ID, IL, NC, WA.
6. The jurisdictions calling for runaways to be taken into custody are: AL, AK, AZ, CO, DC, FL, GA, ID, IL, IA, KY, ME, MD, MA, MN, NE, NH, NJ, NM, NY, NC, ND, OH, OK, OR, PA, SD, TN, UT, VT, VA, WA, WV, WI, WY.

7. The jurisdictions allowing illness, injury, and danger situations to result in taking youth into custody are: AL, AZ, AR, CA, DC, GA, IL, KS, ME, MD, MI, MN, MS, MO, MT, NE, NH, NJ, NC, ND, OH, OK, PA, RI, SD, TN, UT, VT, VA, WA, WV, WI, WY.

8. The states that allow youth without a parent to be taken into custody are: AL, CO, MS, MO, NM, SD, WY.

9. The states that call for youth who may leave the jurisdiction to be taken into custody are: GA, MS, NM, OH, PA, WV.

10. The states that allow mentally ill or dangerous youth to be taken into custody are: KS, NE, OK, SD, UT, WY. It is important to remember that many other states may allow youth to be taken into custody in all of the various situations identified in this section and simply have not specified such in their statutes.

11. The jurisdictions that use this type of wording when taking status offenders into custody are: AL, AK, AZ, AR, CA, CO, DC, FL, GA, HI, ID, IL, IA, KS, KY, LA, ME, MD, MN, MO, NE, NH, NJ, NM, NY, NC, ND, OH, OR, PA, RI, SD, TN, UT, VT, WA, WV, WI, WY.

12. The states that fail to mention a level of evidence required to take status offenders into custody are: CT, DE, IN, MA, MI, MT, NV, OK, SC.

13. The jurisdictions that allow POs to take youth into custody for violations are: AL, AK, AZ, CA, CO, CT, DC, FL, GA, HI, IA, KS, KY, LA, ME, MA, MN, MT, NM, OK, OR, PA, SD, TX, UT, VA, WA, WI.

14. The jurisdictions that allow POs to take escapees into custody are: DC, FL, GA, KY, NH, NM, NC, ND, OH, PA, TN, WI.

15. The states that equate the arresting powers of POs and police are: CA, CO, HI, LA, MI, MO, NV, NC, OR, RI, TX, VA.

16. The states that allow POs to take runaways and youth in danger into custody are: AR, FL, IN, MI, NE, MO, NH, OH, OK, OR, PA, RI, TN, UT, VA, WI.

17. *New Jersey v. T.L.O.* (1985) and *Fare v. Michael C.* (1979) are the only U.S. Supreme Court cases that have involved contested seizures of evidence, and on both occasions the Supreme Court ruled the seizures lawful.

18. The jurisdictions that officially have recognized the use of the exclusionary rule in juvenile court are: AL, AK, AZ, CA, CO, DC, FL, GA, HI, IL, IN, IA, LA, ME, MD, MA, MI, MN, MS, MO, NV, NJ, NM, NC, ND, OH, OK, OR, PA, RI, TN, TX, UT, VT, WA, WV, WI.

19. Even where legislation does not address these duties, which means that a state is not listed here, local practices are likely to require them.

20. The jurisdictions that require notification but do not mention a time limit in which the police must notify the parents are: AL, AK, CA, CT, DC, FED, FL, GA, MA, MN, MS, MT, NJ, NC, ND, OK, PA, SD, TN, WA, WY.

21. The states that require notice immediately are: DE, HI, IN, KY, MD, MI, NE, NV, NY, VT, WV, WI.

22. The states that require notice as soon as possible or practicable are: ID, IL, IA, ME, MO, OR, SC.

23. The jurisdictions that require police to inform parents as to why youth were arrested are: AL, CA, DE, DC, ID, KY, MD, MN, MT, NM, NC, ND, OH, TN, TX, UT, VA, WY.

24. The jurisdictions that require police to inform parents on the youth's right to silence are: FED, MO, ND, TX, VA, WY.

25. The jurisdictions that require police to inform parents of the youth's right to counsel are: DC, FED, MN, MO, NM, ND, TX, VA, WY.

26. The jurisdictions that require police to inform parents of their right to visitation are: DC, MN, MS, MO, OH, TN, UT.

27. The states that require police to inform parents of the location of detention are: CA, ID, IL, IN, ME, MN, MT, NM, VT, WI.

28. The states that require police to inform parents as to why the youth was held in detention are: IN, MD, MN, MS, MO, NM, NC, OH, TN, VT, WI.

29. The jurisdictions that require police to inform parents about the right to and timing of a detention hearing are: AZ, AR, CA, CO, DE, DC, HI, ID, IL, IN, IA, KS, ME, MD, MA, MI, MN, MS, MO, NJ, NM, ND, OH, OR, PA, RI, SD, TN, TX, UT, VT, WA, WI, WY.

30. If police are requesting detention (see Chapter 10), they may be required to give juvenile court authorities their reason for seeking detention (DC, HI, MN, MO, MT, NC, OH, OK, SC, TN, UT, WY), and/or a probable cause affidavit supporting the arrest (CA, DE, FL, HI, LA, ME, MN, MO, MT, NM, NC, OH, OK, PA, SC, SD, TN, TX, UT, VT, WI, WY).

31. The states that require police to turn youth over to court officers immediately are: CT, GA, IA, MA, MI, MS, MO, MT, OK, SC, VT, WV.

32. The states that require police to turn youth over to court officers without delay are: CA, CO, FL, HI, IL, KS, NE, NV, OR, UT, TX.

33. The jurisdictions that require police to turn youth over to court officers with all reasonable speed are: DC, MD, NM, NY, ND, OH, PA, SD, TN.

34. The jurisdictions that operate with a presumption of release to parents are: Al, AK, CA, CO, CT, DE, DC, FED, FL, GA, HI, ID, IL, IN, IA, KS, LA, MD, MA, MI, MN, MS, MO, NE, NH, NJ, NM, NY, ND, OH, OR, PA, RI, SD, TN, TX, UT, VA, WA, WV, WI, WY.

35. The jurisdictions that require parents to sign a promise to return to court are: AL, AK, AR, CA, CO, CT, FED, HI, ID, IN, IA, KY, LA, ME, MD, MA, MI, MN, MO, MT, NV, NJ, NM, NC, ND, OK, PA, RI, SC, SD, TN, TX, UT, VA, WY. Recent California law (1996) prohibits release until a judge is involved in cases where the youth is 14 years old and the crime is a felony in which a firearm was used. Oklahoma law has gone so far as to assign parents responsibility for costs and damages caused if the child commits any delinquent acts after being released.

36. It should be remembered that it is somewhat unclear as to whether police need probable cause to arrest in all jurisdictions even for criminal or delinquent behavior.

37. See, for example, *United States v. Stone*, 401 F.2d 32 (4th Cir. 1968); *Taylor v. State*, 491 So.2d 1042 (Ala. Crim. App. 1986); *Grant v. State*, 589 S.W.2d 11 (Ark. 1979); *Tolbert v. State*, 161 S.E.2d 279 (Ga. 1978).

38. See, for example, *In re Donaldson*, 269 Cal App2d 509, 75 Cal Rptr 220 (1969); *People v. Overton*, 229 NE2d 596 (NY 1967); *State v. Stein*, 456 P2d 1 (KS), *cert denied*, 397 US 947 (1969); *Isiah v. State*, 500 MW2d 637 (WI), *cert denied*, 510 US 884 (1993); *Zamora v. Pomery*, 639 F2d 662 (10th Cir 1981).

39. See, for example, *State v. Joseph T.*, 336 SE2d 728 (WV 1985); *Commonwealth v. Snyder*, 597 NE2d 1363 (MA 1990); *S.C. v. State*, 583 So2d 188 (MS 1991).

40. See, for example, *In re F.B.*, 658 A2d 1378 (Pa Super 1995); *In re S.S.*, 680 A2d 1172 (PA Super 1996); *People v. Pruitt*, 278 Ill App3d 194, 662 NE2d 540 (1996), *appeal denied*, 667 NE2d 1061 (1996); *People v. Dukes*, 151 Misc.2d 295, 580 NYS2d 850 (NY Crim Ct 1992); *State v. J.A.*, 679 So2d 316 (Fla App 3 Dist 1996).

41. See *Vernonia School District 47J v. Acton*, 515 US 646 (1995); *Board of Education of Independent School District Number 92 of Pottawatomie County v. Earls*, 536 U.S. 822 (2002).

42. *T.L.O. v. New Jersey*, 463 A.2d 934 (N.J. 1983).

43. See, for example, *State v. Young*, 216 S.E.2d 586 (GA. 1975), *cert denied* 423 U.S. 1039 (1975) for a ruling that the exclusionary does not apply to school searches (even when a crime is involved), and *In re Dumas*, 515 A.2d 984 (PA. Super. 1986) for a ruling that the exclusionary rule does apply to school searches.

44. *In re Michael C.*, 579 P.2d 7 (CA. 1978).

45. *People v. Burton*, 491 P.2d 793 (CA. 1971).

46. *In re Michael C.*, *supra* note 44 at 9, quoting *People v. Burton*, *supra* note 45, at 797–798.

47. The jurisdictions that officially require *Miranda* warnings via statute or case law are: AL, AK, AZ, AR, CA, CO, CT, DC, FL, GA, HI, ID, IL, IN, IA, MD, MA, MO, MT, NH, NM, NY, NC, ND, OH, OK, PA, SD, TN, TX, VT, WV, WI.

48. See, for example, *Matter of James J.*, 644 N.Y.S.2d 171 (N.Y.A.D. 1 Dept. 1996); *In re Michael J.*, 650 N.Y.S.2d 6 (N.Y.A.D. 1 Dept. 1996); *In Interest of Thomas J.W.*, 570 N.W.2d 586 (WI. App. 1997).

49. The jurisdictions that do not require status offenders to be Mirandized are: AL, AZ, AR, CA, DC, HI, MO, MT, NC, OK, TX, WV.

50. See, for example, *In re Juvenile Action No JV-501010*, 852 P.2d 414 (AZ. Ct. App. 1993); *State v. Smith*, 546 S.W.2d 916 (IA. 1996).

51. See, for example, *In re Larson*, 254 N.W.2d 388 (MN. 1977); *In re Noble*, 547 P.2d 880 (WA. App. 1976).

52. See, for example, *In re J.D.F.*, 553 N.W.2d 585 (IA. 1996).

53. See, for example, *State ex rel Juv. Dept. v. Charles*, 779 P.2d 1075 (OR. App. 1989, *modified* 786 P.2d 1277 (OR. App. 1990).

54. See, for example, *Rincher v. State*, 632 So.2d 37 (AL. Crim App. 1993), *cert denied* 632 So.2d 41 (AL. 1994); *Shelton v. State*, 699 S.W.2d 728 (AR. 1985); *People v. Shawn D.*, 24 Cal. Rptr.2d 395 (CA. App. 6 Dist. 1993); *In re J.D.F.*, 553 N.W.2d 585 (IA. 1996); *Green v. State*, 605 A.2d 1001 (MD. App. 1992); *People v. Ward*, 466 N.Y.S.2d 686 (N.Y.A.D. 2 Dept. 1983).

55. See, for example, *Burnham v. State*, 453 S.E.2d 449 (GA. 1995); *Harden v. State*, 576 N.E.2d 590 (IN. 1991); *Ingram v. State*, 918 S.W.2d 724 (AR. App. 1996); *In re Eric F.*, 698 A.2d 1121 (MD. App. 1997); *Matter of James O.O.*, 652 N.Y.S.2d 783 (N.Y.A.D. 3 Dept. 1996).

56. See, for example, *State v. Lehnes*, 324 N.W.2d 409 (S.D. 1982), *cert denied* 459 U.S. 1226 (1983); *State v. Benoit*, 490 A.2d 295 (N.H. 1985).

57. See, for example, *State v. Perez*, 591 A.2d 119 (CT. 1991); *In re Jonathan M.*, 700 A.2d 1370 (CT. App. 1997); *Marine v. State*, 607 A.2d 1185 (DE. 1992); *In re V.W.B.*, 665 P.2d 1222 (OK.Crim. App. 1983); *C.M.B. v. State*, 594 So.2d 695 (AL. Crim. App. 1991); *Tingle v. State*, 632 N.E.2d 345 (IN. 1994); *People v. Smith*, 635 N.Y.S.2d 824 (N.Y.A.D 4 Dept. 1995), *appeal denied* 664 N.E.2d 1270 (N.Y. 1995).

58. See *S.A. v. State*, 654 N.E.2d 791 (IN. App. 1995) and *In re Navajo County Juv. Action No. JV91000058*, 901 P.2d 1247 (AZ. CT. App, 1995) for rulings that school officials do not need to Mirandize students at school.

59. See, for example, *Rhoades v. State*, 896 S.W.2d 698 (AR. 1994); *In re Rambeau*, 266 Cal.App.2d 1, 72 Cal.Rptr. 171 (1968); *In re Schirner*, 399 A.2d 728 (PA. Super. 1979); *In re L.R.S.*, 573 S.W.2d 888 (TX. Civ. App. 1978); *State v. Strickland*, 532 S.W.2d 912 (TN. 1975), *appeal dismissed*, 425 U.S. 929, *cert denied*, 429 U.S. 805 (1976) for rulings that failure to comply with statutory requirements renders the statement inadmissible in juvenile court. See, for example, *Palmer v. State*, 626 A.2d 1358 (DE. 1993); *Anthony v. State*, 954 S.W.2d 132 (TX. App.—San Antonio 1997); *Daniels v. State*, 174 S.E.2d 422 (GA. 1970); *People v. Montanez*, 652 N.E.2d 1271 (IL. 1995), *cert denied*, 116 S.Ct. 2514 (1996); *State v. Walker*, 352 N.W.2d 239 (IA. 1984); *People v. Jordan*, 386 N.W.2d 594 (I. App. 1986); *State v. Wade*, 531 S.W.2d 726 (MO. 1976); *Comer v. State*, 776 S.W.2d 191 (TX. Crim. App. 1989); *State v. Giles*, 395 S.W.2d 481 (W.V. 1990); *People v. Pico*, 678 N.E.2d 780 (IL. App. 1 Dist. 1997) for rulings that failure to comply with statutory requirements renders the statement inadmissible in adult court.

60. See, for example, *In re J.D.G.*, 429 S.E.2d 118 (GA.App. 1993); *Lattimore v. State*, 454 S.E.2d 474 (GA. 1995); *State v. McBride*, 401 S.E.2d 484 (GA. 1991); *In re V.L.T.*, 686 N.E.2d 79 (IL. App. 2 Dist. 1997); *People v. Brown*, 601 N.E.2d 1190 (IL. 1992); *People v. Williams*, 655 N.E.2d 1071 (IL. App. 1 Dist. 1995), *appeal denied*, 660 N.E.2d 1279 (IL. 1995); *People v. Johnson*, 603 N.E.2d 624 (IL. App. 1 Dist. 1992), *appeal dismissed*, 606 N.E.2d 1231 (IL. 1992). See also *People v. Brooks*, 459 N.W.2d 313 (MI. App. 1990); *People v. Abiodun L.*, 660 N.Y.S.2d 761 (N.Y.A.D. 3 Dept. 1997).

61. See, for example, *Boyd v. State*, 853 S.W.2d 263 (AR. 1993); *Colyer v. State*, 577 S.W.2d 460 (TN. 1979); *Misskelley v. State*, 915 S.W.2d 702 (AR. 1996); *State v. Lundy*, 808 S.W.2d 444 (TN. 1991); *State v. Dutchie*, 969 P.2d 422 (UT 1998).

62. The jurisdictions that changed their policy regarding the printing and photographing of juveniles are: AL, AK, AR, CT, FED, GA, HI, IA, NV, NJ, NY, NC, OR, PA, SC, VA.

63. The jurisdictions that do not have a relevant provision in their statutes are: AZ, CA, CO, DE, DC, KY, ME, MA, NH, NM, RI, SD, WA, WV, WI.

64. The states that allow all arrests to result in printing youth are: CT, HI, ID, IN, IA, MO, NE, NJ, ND, OH, OK, PA, SC, TN, VT, VA.

65. The states that allow all felony arrests to be printed are: AL, AK, AR, KS, LA, MN, MS, MT, TX, WY.

66. The states that allow prints to be taken for investigative purposes are: AL, IN, IA, NV, NJ, ND, TN, VT, WY.

67. The states that allow police to forward records to a centralized state agency are: AL, AR, CO, GA, ID, IL, IA, LA, ME, MD, MN, MS, NE, ND, PA, TX, WY.

68. The states that require police to forward records to a centralized state agency are: FL, KS, NV, NJ, NY, NC, OK, OR, SC, UT, VA.

69. The states that call for destruction of records in this context are: AL, CT, FL, GA, IN, IA, NV, NC, OR, PA, SC, TN, TX, VT, VA, WY.

70. The states that have the same provisions for printing and photographing youth are: AR, CT, FL, GA, ID, IA, KS, LA, MS, MO, MT, NY, NC, OH, OR, PA, SC, TN, TX, VA, WY.

71. The states that permit blood samples to be taken from youth are: AL, MD, MN, NY, OR, VA, UT.

72. See *United States v. Wade*, 388 U.S. 218 (1967); *Gilbert v. California*, 388 U.S. 263 (1967); *Kirby v. Ill.*, 406 U.S. 682 (1972).

73. See, for example, *In re Carl T.*, 1 Cal.App.3d 344, 81 Cal.Rptr. 655 (1969); *In re Holley*, 268 A.2d 723 (R.I. 1970); *In re Stoutzenberger*, 344 A.2d 668 (PA. Super. 1975). ✦

The Juvenile Court Personnel

Focus of Chapter 8

Chapter 8 examines the individuals who are most responsible for determining what happens to youthful offenders in the juvenile court. In this chapter we will see how differently these individuals operate in juvenile court compared to their counterparts in the criminal court. These differences are significant. They explain, in part, how the juvenile system remains unique. These differences also account for a good deal of the fairness problems that plague the juvenile court today. Finally, the chapter discusses the newly emerging role of the victim in juvenile court, together with the implications of giving this person a voice in determining outcomes in juvenile court.

Key Terms

- appointed or assigned counsel
- defense attorney
- guardian *ad litem*
- judge
- master
- *parens patriae* figure
- parental liability
- probation officer

- prosecutor
- public defender
- referee
- retained counsel
- vertical prosecution
- victim impact statements
- victim-offender mediation

A Unique Place to Work

The traditionally different philosophy and environment of juvenile court make it a unique place to work for many of the individuals who have practiced in that forum.

Judges, prosecutors, and defense attorneys can experience role conflict and confusion that is not present in their work in criminal court. Juvenile court can serve uniquely as a training ground or as a dumping ground for all three types of workers. The relative lack of serious cases (and usually jury trial) makes this court a good place to learn one's trade, while the relative lack of visibility also makes it a good place to hide. Lawyers who are known as masters or referees are allowed to perform duties (such as conducting trials) that are not permitted in criminal court (where only judges can perform such duties). The parents also have a unique role in juvenile court. Unlike criminal court, where they are mostly irrelevant, parents can make all the difference in the world in juvenile court—as we have seen already in the policing stage. Although they are not unique to juvenile court, victims have been recently elevated to an influential status in the decision making that occurs in juvenile court. Finally, although they, too, are not unique to juvenile court, probation officers certainly have had and continue to have a different role there than they have in criminal court. The history of juvenile court confirms the multifaceted and powerful role POs used to play (see Chapter 2). This chapter explores just how unique the role these individuals play still is in the juvenile court process.

The Prosecutor

In the criminal justice system, the prosecutor is the individual charged with representing the state and victim in a role that has four primary areas of responsibility:

1. Identifying the appropriate charges to bring against the accused, including deciding whether the case can be or should be prosecuted

2. Determining the need for pretrial detention of the accused and presenting that position to the judge

3. Assembling the case together with prosecuting or presenting the state's evidence at trial (or negotiating a plea with the defense instead)

4. Gauging the public interest in sentencing the defendant, assuming conviction, and recommending to the judge a term of probation or incarceration

In earlier chapters we saw how the prosecutor historically has not played a role in juvenile court. Prosecutors were not only unnecessary (POs could do their work), but they were also dangerous, since their presence would suggest that the state had an interest in the proceedings that was both independent of and opposed to the child's. *In re Gault* changed the juvenile court landscape by granting defendants a right to counsel. That development (Fox 1970b; Purdom 1970; Skoler 1968) and a worsening juvenile crime rate (Laub and MacMurray 1987; Rubin 1980, 1985b) combined to make the prosecutor appear to be a necessary participant in juvenile court proceedings.

Most jurisdictions have responded to these events by including a regular criminal courtlike prosecutor among their juvenile court personnel. Thus, in many jurisdictions the local prosecutor's office works in both adult and juvenile courts. In these situations it is not unusual for the prosecutor's office to require a stay in juvenile court as part of the training process. Prosecutors may be forced to "cut their teeth" in the juvenile system.

The thinking here is that any errors these rookie prosecutors commit would have less devastating results in juvenile court than in criminal court.

The prosecutor might be known as the *district attorney, county attorney/prosecutor, state's attorney, prosecuting attorney, commonwealth attorney, attorney general,* or *solicitor.* A number of states also provide that juvenile court can allow someone other than this prosecutor to operate there. For example, instead of the district attorney, New York statutes refer to corporation counsel or the county attorney as being allowed to prosecute cases in juvenile court. Georgia, Hawaii, Ohio, and Tennessee hold that the juvenile court can ask *any* attorney to serve as prosecutor. Other states declare that the regular criminal prosecutor does not always have to appear in juvenile court, depending on the severity of the offense and record, and especially if a status offense in involved.[1] Similarly, several jurisdictions explain that the prosecutor should appear only at the request of the juvenile court.[2] Finally, some states have a juvenile prosecutor who does not appear to be drawn from the "regular" prosecutor's office (CT, MS, NM).

In short, although prosecutors certainly are no longer irrelevant, their inclusion in various juvenile courts across the country has not been uniform. Consequently, depending on the jurisdiction and the particular case before the court, a regular prosecutor (albeit possibly a rookie), a prosecutor who has been specially indoctrinated in juvenile court philosophy (and may not be familiar with criminal court), an attorney whose primary business is not prosecuting criminal behavior, or someone else altogether (such as a PO, the arresting officer, the victim, not to mention a judge) could be functioning like a prosecutor at various stages of the juvenile court system. Unlike in criminal court, then, in juvenile court a full-fledged criminal prosecutor may not be the person representing the state at critical decision-making points, such as charging and diversion, trial, and sentencing.

As a group, juvenile prosecutors (or the juvenile court unit of the prosecutor's office) vary tremendously across the country. They can range from one- and two-person operations to large units staffed by dozens of attorneys. The atmosphere in these offices can vary as well, from laissez-faire (this is only "kiddie" court) settings to rehabilitation-oriented places, from those staffed by individuals who could be confused with social workers to conviction-thirsty operations containing people who might seem to belong in adult court. Some of these prosecutors might work regularly in criminal court and visit juvenile court only one day a week, or simply be on rotation in juvenile court for a few months, after having spent months or years in adult court.

An example of how some juvenile courts have been "criminalized" is that some prosecutors' offices today employ one or more individuals (in a unit, perhaps) who are responsible for prosecuting particularly serious or chronic offenders only. This is often referred to as vertical prosecution because the prosecutors are usually responsible for "walking" the case through the juvenile system and perhaps seeking transfer of the case to criminal court. In other words, these prosecutors concentrate on a few cases only and ensure that the cases do not fall through the cracks by monitoring every development in the court's processing of the cases, from preliminary hearings until sentencing. If these prosecutors are organized into a group, they are likely to be known as the Serious/Habitual Offender Unit.

Considering the history and philosophy of juvenile court and its maintaining mostly a dedication to rehabilitation, it is not surprising that some locations are still reluctant to use criminal court-oriented prosecutors to perform prosecutorial tasks in juvenile court. This reluctance can have serious repercussions at the adjudicatory hearing, which we will review in Chapter 13.

Regardless of who performs as the prosecutor, there are several possible tasks this individual can fulfill in juvenile court. For example, the prosecutor is recognized as needed today in juvenile court in order to:

- represent the state's interests and balance representation vis-à-vis defense counsel (Rubin 1980, 1989; Shine and Price 1992);

- guarantee that only legally sufficient cases are brought to court (Shine and Price 1992);

- impress upon the child the seriousness of the crime (IJA/ABA 1980; NAC 1976, 1980);

- remove role conflict for judges, who without prosecutors must perform the prosecutor's job as well as their own (Finkelstein et al. 1973; Skoler 1968);

- make juvenile court more formal and due process oriented (Rubin 1985a; Shine and Price 1992);

- ensure that all court officials are accountable and fulfill their roles (Laub and MacMurray 1987; NAC 1976, 1980); and

- assist the rehabilitation effort (Shine and Price 1992).

Some confusion exists about the proper role for prosecutors, particularly at the intake and dispositional stages. We will see in the next chapter that at intake, controversy exists as to whether the PO or the prosecutor should control the decision to file a petition against the youth. Whereas some experts believe the charging power rightly belongs to the prosecutor (Bahlmann and Johnson 1978; Fox 1970b; Hicks 1978; IJA/ABA 1980; Shine and Price 1992), others prefer the prosecutor to exercise only reviewing powers at intake (NAC 1976; Rubin 1985a). As we will see in Chapter 14, the dispositional issue involves the conflict between the prosecutor's dual responsibilities to both the child and the community. National commissions and experts have advised the prosecutor to seek justice while not losing sight of the needs of the child or the philosophy of the juvenile court (IJA/ABA 1980; NAC 1976, 1980; Rubin 1985a; Shine and Price 1992). Prosecutors have been asked not to assume the stance taken by criminal court prosecutors and not to seek the most severe sentence at disposition (Fox 1970b; NAC 1976; Rubin 1985a). At the heart of these controversial points is the question of to what extent the prosecutor should replace the PO as the major proponent of actions and decisions in the juvenile court process. Recently, the prosecutor's role conflict in juvenile court has been exacerbated by an increase in both the number and severity of juvenile offenses and the development of a "get tough" punitive response to young criminals prosecuted in juvenile court.

A pivotal issue facing juvenile justice is the extent to which the prosecutor's role in juvenile court should and does differ from that individual's role in criminal court. Research has shown that juvenile court workers continue to want and expect prosecutors to act differently in juvenile court by pursuing the rehabilitation of the youth. Specifically, most court workers expect juvenile prosecutors to act like their criminal court counterparts only at the charging and trial stages. That is, the prosecutor's behavior in deciding which statute was violated, deciding whether to prosecute, and conducting the actual trial should not differ from one court to another. However, most workers believe that both the detention and disposition stages call for a different approach by the juvenile prosecutor. That is, rather than focusing on only the youth's dangerousness and potential threat to society, the prosecutor at the detention hearing should be influenced by the child's best interests and situation at home (see Chapter 10). Similarly, at sentencing, rather than simply seeking the harshest disposition possible, the prosecutor should either help fashion a disposition geared to the child's best interests or not obstruct the PO's attempt to devise the proper treatment plan (see Chapter 14). Whether prosecutors actually fulfill these expectations depends on which juvenile court is examined, however. Prosecutors vary from those who are concerned primarily with the welfare of the youth to those who seek to protect the community to the same extent as their criminal court counterparts. Again, the location of the court and such other factors as the amount of juvenile crime, local politics, and the policies of the prosecutor's office influence how prosecutors behave in juvenile court and determine whether they act differently than the way criminal court prosecutors behave (Sanborn 1995a).

The same factors also determine whether juvenile prosecutors experience role conflict, by being torn between representing the best interests of the child or of society. So, for example, a pro-society, punitive-oriented prosecutor who works in a similarly oriented juvenile court should have no role conflict. A pro-child, rehabilitation-oriented prosecutor should also have no role conflict in a juvenile court that matches that orientation. However, a mismatch of these orientations could produce serious role conflict (Sanborn 1995a). Of course, criminal court prosecutors are not perceived as having any role conflict in this respect, since the only "client" they represent is society.

Research has discovered a certain amount of conflict between the prosecutor and the PO, at least in some juvenile courts. This conflict involves disagreement as to who should control the charging and diversion decision (together with the decision whether to transfer the youth to criminal court—see Chapter 12). In addition, there is conflict concerning the prosecutor's authority to challenge the severity of dispositions recommended by the PO (Sanborn 1995a). This situation is unfortunate according to most court workers, who believe that juvenile prosecutors should enjoy a special and close relationship with all other court workers (including POs, of course), since the mission of all these individuals supposedly is to promote the best interests of the child. Thus, another feature that is supposed to distinguish the juvenile from the criminal court prosecutor is not present in all juvenile courts (Sanborn 1995a).

Finally, research has found that while most court workers believe that prosecutors need special training to work effectively in juvenile court, this training rarely, if ever, exists (Sanborn 1995a). Only Mississippi mandates the special training of juvenile prosecutors via its statute. Juvenile prosecutors also face the prospect of being considered as occupying a lesser status. To be sure, some juvenile courts are the training grounds for prosecutors, and, in that context, juvenile prosecutors in some locations would rightly be regarded as rookies who do not know much yet. Nevertheless, even in courts where veterans are employed in the prosecutorial role, there can be a perception that these individuals just do not match up against their counterparts in criminal court. Juvenile court's traditional identity as "kiddie court" no doubt plays a role in court workers' viewing juvenile prosecutors in this light (Sanborn 1995a).

The Defense Attorney

In the criminal justice system, the defense attorney is the individual charged with representing the accused and serving as that person's advocate. The primary responsibilities of the defense attorney are challenging the prosecutor at every stage of the process as an *adversary* and providing damage control to the defendant (i.e., getting the best possible results for the client). These responsibilities ideally require a broad range of knowledge on the defense attorney's part, including knowledge of:

- criminal law and criminal procedure;
- the rights of the accused;
- the case against the defendant;
- the opponents in the case (prosecutor and judge);
- the typical results in a case with this type of charge and record; and
- the defendant's wishes and definition of best possible results.

Prior to the *Gault* decision, the defense attorney played a marginal role at best in juvenile court. Not only were defense attorneys generally not assigned to indigent juveniles, but even wealthier defendants were frequently not permitted to avail themselves of the services of a lawyer they themselves had hired.[3] Consequently, defense attorneys rarely appeared in juvenile court before 1967, with the exception of some jurisdictions, such as California; Washington, DC; and New York (Coxe 1967; Notes 1966; President's Commission 1967; Skoler and Tenney 1964). Again, the PO was believed to be able to serve in this capacity while simultaneously prosecuting the case. The U.S. Supreme Court finally came to a different conclusion in *Gault,* by extending the right to counsel to juvenile defendants, particularly those facing incarceration.

Like adult court, juvenile court draws defense attorneys from three primary sources. Retained counsel are hired by defendants (or by parents) who have sufficient financial resources to purchase the services of counsel. A public defender (PD) (or perhaps legal aide) represents poor defendants regularly, possibly as a full-time job. Like prosecutors, as a group, juvenile PDs (or the juvenile unit of a public defender's office) vary tremendously across the country, ranging from one- and two-person operations to large units staffed by dozens of attorneys. Also similar is that the atmosphere in these offices can vary from laissez-faire (this is only "kiddie" court) settings to rehabilitation-oriented places, from those staffed by individuals who could be confused with social workers to adversarial operations containing people who might seem to belong in adult court. Some of these PDs might work regularly in criminal court and visit juvenile court only one day a week or may simply be on rotation in juvenile court for a few months after having spent months or years in adult court. Finally, appointed or assigned counsel are private practitioners (who also could be retained by nonindigent defendants) who are assigned to represent one or more indigent defendants in a particular case (and are assigned on a case-by-case basis).

This group of assigned counsel could serve as *the* source of representation for poor defendants in jurisdictions operating without a PD's office. Otherwise, they are usually appointed in multiple-defendant cases where a PD already represents one of the defendants and cannot represent two (or all) of them because of a potential conflict of interests among the defendants. In fact, they could be known as *conflict counsel.*

Some of the retained counsel who work in juvenile court regularly represent adult defendants as well. They can constitute some of the best defense attorney representation available. Nevertheless, as in adult court, there is no way to guarantee that a defendant will hire an attorney with adequate experience in defending criminal charges. It is very likely, moreover, that the really big-name, big-money defense attorneys—the supposed cream of the crop—never appear in juvenile court. Similarly, some of the PDs who represent juvenile defendants are extremely capable, knowledgeable, and dedicated and would provide better representation than some private counsel. At the same time, however, as in the prosecutor's office, juvenile court can serve as the training or dumping ground for PDs who are either just learning the process or already burned out. These same comments can be made about private lawyers assigned to a poor defendant's case. Juvenile court is simply a particularly good place to learn the ropes, hide out, or tread water. The only consolation with respect to assigning private attorneys to cases in juvenile court (as well as in adult court) is that judges have the authority to not assign any more cases to those attorneys who perform miserably. Judges lack this direct control over the appearance of retained counsel and PDs.

Regardless of who serves as the defense attorney, there has been serious controversy and debate as to the proper role for this person in juvenile court. In adult court, there is no debate. The defense attorney's role is singular: to work as an *advocate,* pursuing outright acquittal or the next best possible solution for the defendant. Some experts insist the defense attorney in juvenile court should also operate as an advocate (Federle 1990; Guggenheim 1996). Others have suggested that the defense attorney should serve as a *guardian* and assist the court in determining the treatment plan best suited to the child's interests (Coxe 1967; Ketcham 1967; Kravitz 1973; Noyes 1970; Rosenberg 1980). In *Gault,* the Supreme Court did little to resolve the confusion, because the opinion seemed to support both advocates and guardians (1967, 36–38).

The guardian role coincides well with juvenile court treatment philosophy because the guardian does not attempt to secure acquittal at all costs. Many experts consider this type of representation as a subversion of the child's rights, however (Costello 1980; IJA/ABA 1980; Notes and Comments 1979). The advocate is true to both the lawyer's ethical duties and the defendant's rights, but, according to other experts, this role undermines the juvenile court's treatment purpose by enabling delinquent, treatment-needy youth to escape the system's help (Bogen 1980; Rosenberg 1980). Thus, the defense lawyer appears to be caught in a Catch-22 situation in juvenile court: Whereas the guardian is a traitor to the child's legal interests, the advocate is a traitor to the child's treatment interests (and to juvenile court as well). The defense attorney ends up trapped between the ethics of the legal profession and the philosophy of juvenile court (Levin 1968).

Research into this difficult topic has disclosed some interesting findings. First, juvenile court workers are divided as to the proper role for the defense attorney at both trial and sentencing, but tend to agree that the role should differ between the two stages. Few workers endorse a "pure guardian" role at the adjudicatory hearing. Instead, the vast majority prefer that defense counsel act either as a "modified advocate" or as a "pure advocate." The modified advocate is an attorney who neither always seeks acquittals (like a pure advocate) nor automatically assists the court (like a pure guardian) but rather assumes a "commonsense" approach. This approach translates into the defense lawyer's balancing the child's legal and treatment interests and fighting the prosecution only when:

- the youth is innocent;
- the charges or dispositions are serious; or
- the defendant insists on not being helped by the system.

At disposition, however, the vast majority of the workers expect defense counsel to perform as a pure guardian or as a modified advocate. Thus, while defense attorneys could appropriately fight the case at trial, they should cooperate with rather than battle the juvenile court at disposition (Sanborn 1987b).

Research has also disclosed defense attorneys that operate in these various capacities, frequently as a result of a number of factors:

- The stage of the court process (trial versus sentencing)
- The location of the court (and the severity of the juvenile crime problem)
- The defense attorney's belief in the juvenile system and its rehabilitation capabilities (and commitment to same)
- The seriousness of the offense, record, and disposition
- The type of defense attorney (PD, retained, or assigned)
- The desires of the parents (especially if counsel is retained)
- The prosecutor's tendency to play hardball and attempt to hurt juveniles
- The previous experience of the defense attorney in juvenile or adult court
- The judge's tolerance of the advocate role (Sanborn 1987b)

In short, defense attorneys do not always act like advocates in juvenile court—especially, but not only, at the disposition hearing. In addition, juvenile court judges are not always receptive to the advocate role, even at trial. Although defense representation is not always what it should be in adult court, there is definitely no expectation there (from anyone) that defense attorneys act like guardians or modified advocates at either trial or sentencing. In fact, performance along these lines in adult court could result in a lawsuit being filed against the defense attorney for rendering ineffective assistance of counsel and disbarment as well.

Research found that most juvenile court workers perceive role conflict for the defense attorney, regardless of the role chosen by that person in juvenile court. This is especially the situation for the guardian (and especially with respect to legal ethics). However, the guardian role does enable the defense attorney to be most cooperative with the greatest number of people in juvenile court: the prosecutor (who wants to adjudicate or to help the youth and not lose the case outright), the judge (who probably would want the same for the defendant, assuming guilt), the PO (who wants to implement a treatment plan that cannot happen without an adjudication), the parent (who might want the same result as the PO), and the victim (who might want restitution, which could be part of the treatment plan). Of course, at the other extreme, the advocate potentially stands in the way of all of these desires.

In the end, unlike defense attorneys who work in criminal court, those who practice in juvenile court have three possible paramount concerns or objectives:

- Promoting the child's legal interests only (i.e., serving as the advocate who seeks acquittals, etc.)

- Promoting the child's treatment interests only (i.e., serving as the guardian who seeks the court's intervention and rehabilitation)

- Balancing the child's legal and treatment interests (i.e., serving as the modified advocate who uses the "commonsense" approach)

Like prosecutors, to be effective in the juvenile system, defense attorneys need to develop special relationships, especially with POs, and require special training in order to comprehend the differences among the various dispositional options available to the court. Whether they enjoy these relationships and receive this training depends largely on the location of the juvenile court. Also like prosecutors, defense attorneys in the juvenile system can be perceived as occupying a lesser status than those who appear in criminal court (Sanborn 1987b).

The Judge

In the criminal justice system, the judge is the individual charged with serving as the neutral referee and overall dispenser of justice who will ultimately be responsible in deciding the defendant's guilt (unless the case is a jury trial) and punishment. Unlike prosecutors and defense attorneys, who must be proactive in assembling and readying a case for trial, the judge is the passive recipient of and ruler on both requests and motions put forth by opposing counsel before trial and the evidence, objections, and motions offered by opposing counsel during trial. After ruling on the appropriateness of the various motions and objections and receiving all the evidence, the judge eventually determines whether the state has offered sufficient proof to sustain a conviction. If the case is resolved by a guilty plea instead of by trial, the judge's obligations are narrowed to determining the intelligence and voluntariness of the guilty plea and the appropriateness of whatever arrangements have been made between prosecution and defense (see Chapter 11).

Historically, judges in juvenile court played a much more expanded role than that played by their counterparts in adult court. Many juvenile courts were simply two-person operations: the judge and the PO. These two people shared, to some degree, the responsibilities of the prosecutor and defense attorney. Jury trials were not part of the routine in juvenile court. Thus, the juvenile court judge has traditionally been vested with formidable adjudicating power, greater than the corresponding power criminal court judges have enjoyed.

Although granted immense power, the juvenile court judge was instructed to act in a unique way, primarily like a benevolent parent or *parens patriae* figure concerned mostly, if not solely, with the best interests of the child (Dunham 1958; Lou 1927; Mack 1909). This paternal expectation continued unchallenged until the *Gault* decision in 1967. In *Gault*, the Supreme Court indicated that the judge should be more of a neutral umpire or referee than a parental figure, at least during the adjudicatory hearing. The implication of *Gault* was that judges legitimately could be paternal only during the pretrial and postadjudication stages of the court's operation (Graff 1973). Thus, *Gault* created a potential conflict for the judge in deciding whether to promote a traditional *parens patriae* attitude or a criminal court–like legalistic atmosphere during trial.

Should juvenile court judges work exclusively in juvenile court or should they be allowed to rotate between juvenile court and criminal court?

Today, research has shown that juvenile court workers believe that there still is a clearly unique responsibility for the juvenile court judge. This distinct job involves being particularly active and assertive, especially at disposition, in understanding both the youth and the rehabilitation programs available to the juvenile system and in individualizing the court's response so as to further the rehabilitation and best interests of the child. Whereas most workers want judges to operate like neutral factfinders at trial, they do not want judges to parallel their criminal court counterparts at detention and disposition. Rather than looking only at the youth's potential dangerousness and the protection of society, the judge should be concerned about the child's welfare, problems at home, and the parents' ability to care for and supervise the juvenile at the detention stage (see Chapter 10). The judge's special responsibility at disposition involves being active in conducting a thorough investigation into the child's needs, an inquiry that should focus on myriad aspects of the youth's life rather than on merely the crime and record (see Chapter 14). Similarly, the hearing to decide transfer to adult court (see Chapter 12) requires a special judicial expertise in deciding which youth are beyond the rehabilitative capacities of the juvenile system (and thus belong in criminal court) (Sanborn 2001a).

Research has also revealed that court workers believe that judges experience conflict at the adjudicatory hearing. One result of that conflict is that some judges, at least occasionally, adjudicate defendants who are not guilty beyond a reasonable doubt in order to channel them officially into rehabilitation programs (see Chapter 13) (Sanborn 1994c, 2001a).

Judges who work in juvenile court will vary considerably in a number of ways:

- Those in their first job as a judge (the training ground phenomenon) versus veterans who have served on the bench for years

- Those who are *parens patriae* oriented versus those who are legalistic and criminal court-like

- Those who truly want to work in juvenile court versus those sent there as banishment or punishment or to retire

- Those who work exclusively in juvenile court versus those who are borrowed for a day or two from adult court

- Those who work *alone* as the juvenile court judge (who may or may not also work in adult court) versus those who work in multijudge operations

To be effective, juvenile court judges need special training to be able to distinguish among the dispositional options available to the system and the type of offenders appropriate for the treatment programs (Rubin 1985a). In addition, judges need to enjoy a special relationship with the PO in order to achieve the rehabilitation mission. Juvenile courts vary in the extent to which these special relationships and trainings occur. Some juvenile courts continue to operate much like they did in the pre-*Gault* era, at least with respect to a special partnership between the judge and the PO. Also consistent with the past is that judges assigned to juvenile court can view themselves or be viewed by others as occupying a lesser status compared to judges from criminal court (Sanborn 2001a).

So, unlike the prosecutors, defense attorneys, and judges who dominate criminal court proceedings, their counterparts in juvenile court can experience serious role conflict and can be expected to act differently. The prosecutor can be torn between promoting the rehabilitation of the child versus protecting the community, and is supposed to act differently at detention and disposition. The defense attorney can be torn between promoting the child's legal interests versus treatment interests, and is supposed to act differently at disposition, and perhaps at trial as well. The judge can be torn between promoting neutrality versus parental concern for the youth's treatment needs, and is expected to act differently at possibly all stages, but especially at disposition. All three of these juvenile court personnel tend to be seen as:

- requiring special training;

- occupying a lesser status than comparable criminal court personnel; and

- needing to have a special relationship with the PO.

Referees and Masters

The criminal justice system has "inferior judicial officers" known by various titles, such as justices of the peace, commissioners, magistrates, and district justices. For the most part, these individuals are assigned only two tasks in criminal court: (1) to preside over pretrial matters such as bail and a variety of defense and prosecution motions; and (2) to adjudicate minor offenses such as ordinance violations, summary offenses, and some misdemeanors. Historically, inferior judicial officers have been central to the entire operation of the juvenile court in many jurisdictions. In some locations they function as *the* juvenile court judge. Altogether, 32 states use these officials in some capacity under an assortment of names, including referees,[4] masters,[5] commissioners,[6] magistrates (CO,

OH), and associate juvenile court judges (GA, IA). Interestingly, Delaware uses both masters and commissioners in juvenile court. Whereas the master in that state is a nonlawyer limited to hearing cases in which neither a felony nor incarceration is involved, the commissioner is an attorney empowered to conduct all delinquency trials. The title for this official in Texas (referee or master) depends on the county in which the juvenile court is located.

Typically, the referee or master must be a lawyer who is admitted to the state bar, but a handful of states do not mandate a law degree for any of these officials (NV, NJ, OR, WV). As indicated before, Delaware does not require a degree for its masters. Ohio allows the same but only for officials hired before 1995, and Michigan allows nonlawyers to be involved if the issue is a misdemeanor or a status offense. Statutes in Alaska, Washington, and Wyoming are silent about the law degree requirement. The referee is almost always empowered to conduct preliminary hearings and pretrial matters. The one exception is that several states specifically prohibit masters presiding at transfer hearings to decide whether the youth should be prosecuted in criminal court.[7] The controversy surrounding the presence of these referees in juvenile court is twofold: (1) the quality of justice provided by those who are nonlawyers, and (2) the problems that result when these officials conduct trial. We will explore these issues in Chapter 13.

Important to note here is that using masters results in serious financial and administrative rewards for juvenile courts. These officials are to juvenile court what adjuncts are to colleges:

- They are part-time workers paid a lesser salary than judges, possibly only for those hours on the clock, and possibly without vacation, pension, or other benefits having to be provided (e.g., offices, support staff, drivers, and a car).

- They free the judges of the court system from having to do considerable legwork and busywork, meaning that fewer judges can be maintained on staff or that they can be used primarily in adult court and then borrowed for juvenile court.

- They are untenured employees who can be fired summarily for poor performance—unlike judges, who typically would have to be impeached or removed by a state judicial conduct commission (or defeated in the next election).

In short, the savings that can be realized from employing referees are considerable.

Probation Officers

In the criminal justice system, the probation officer, or PO, tends to be exclusively a postconviction figure. That is, POs do not become relevant until the defendant is convicted, whereupon they inherit two tasks: (1) constructing the PSI (presentence investigation), which compiles the offender's past history to help guide the judge's sentencing decision; and (2) supervising the offender in the community (assuming there is no incarceration) and reporting violations and problems to the court.

We have already seen that, historically, the PO was the most critical juvenile court worker. POs literally ran the system. Although their powers have been reduced significantly, especially with the inclusion today of prosecutors and defense attorneys, POs are still the backbone of the system. Their responsibilities are extensive, running the full course of the juvenile court process and far exceeding what POs typically do in criminal court. In addition, the PO in juvenile justice is much more likely to be considered an officer of the court rather than a corrections officer like in criminal justice. Juvenile POs (JPOs) are more likely to answer directly to and work closely with the juvenile court judge rather than a department of corrections or state agency.[8] It would not be unusual, in fact, for the chief JPO to serve also as the juvenile court administrator.

Most jurisdictions refer to this person simply as the PO[9] or the JPO.[10] A few states, however, use terms such as *probation service* (NM, NY, SC) or *probation counselor* (RI, WA) instead. It is also fairly common for states not to use the probation title at all for this official and instead to have a *juvenile* or *juvenile court officer* (AZ, IA, MI, MO); a *court, youth,* or *juvenile services officer* (KS, NH, SD, TN); a *juvenile caseworker* (ME, WI); a *juvenile department* or *youth counselor* (AK, OR); or a *juvenile supervisor* (ND). Finally, some jurisdictions do not use any title, so it is difficult to ascertain what POs are called in these locations (DE, DC, FED, MD, MS, NC). Two of these jurisdictions (DE, FED) also do not spell out any PO duties in the statutes or court rules.

Although POs' tasks permeate the court process and do not neatly divide into stages, we will present their duties as such here. During the precourt stage, as we have seen, just like adult POs, JPOs have law enforcement powers, particularly over juveniles under court supervision. Unique to JPOs, however, is the charging and diversion power they enjoy in juvenile court. Even though their authority may no longer be absolute like it once was (see Chapter 9), only JPOs can actually determine whether (and what) charges will be brought against a defendant or exert serious influence over a prosecutor's decision in this regard.

Historically, POs have had a much greater presence during the processing and trial of a case in juvenile court than in criminal court. Of course, prior to *Gault,* POs were the ones prosecuting the case in juvenile court. Despite the changes brought about by *Gault,* a handful of states specifically mention an expectation that JPOs will be *present* at court hearings (KY, MA, OR, SC, TN). It is still possible to see POs acting as prosecutors in status offense cases and even in minor delinquency cases (e.g., violations or misdemeanors) (NJ, WA), or where violations of probation are alleged. And in a handful of states, POs are allowed to serve as juvenile hearing officers (or as masters and referees). While some states suggest this role as a possibility without clearly stating it (AZ, DE, NJ, OR, WV), others openly acknowledge the PO's capacity to function like a judge in juvenile court (CA, MI, NV, ND). California and Nevada do not require POs to have a law degree in this context, but both limit the PO's authority to minor cases (such as misdemeanors, violations, and traffic offenses) that involve limited sentencing powers (small fines, restitution, short periods of probation). North Dakota requires POs to have a law degree to serve in a judicial capacity, but does not delineate the types of cases they are entitled to hear. Michigan provides that if POs are lawyers, they can conduct trials as a judge or referee (without identifying the type of cases), while nonlawyer POs are restricted to presiding at preliminary hearings.

During the court processing of a case, POs are much more likely to be involved in two major potential investigations: transfer to adult court (see Chapter 12), and juvenile court disposition (see Chapter 14) for those not transferred. The latter investigation is not unique to JPOs, since adult POs are also responsible for conducting a presentence investigation, albeit *after* conviction rather than during the processing of the case. As part of their traditional charging power, JPOs in some locations are *the* court official authorized to launch a transfer attempt.[11] Moreover, it would not be strange for the PO's analysis and recommendations to carry more weight or influence with the judge than the prosecutor's desires to see the case transferred to criminal court (Sanborn 1994a). To the extent that the PO has serious influence at the transfer stage, conflict with the prosecutor (or the defense attorney) could result (see Chapter 12).

Unless there is a special division of the prosecutor's office or a specially created department, JPOs are also likely to be responsible for "victim management" in juvenile court (CA, OH). With the recent ascendancy of the victim in the power structure of juvenile court (which we address momentarily), victims are now entitled to some basic considerations in that system. Minimally, POs can be required to keep victims posted as to how the case is or is not progressing through the system, to inform them of various services available, and to ascertain the extent of the victim's damages, injuries, and losses for inclusion in the disposition report (or as a separate victim impact statement).

Assuming the youth is adjudicated, one of the first and unique tasks for JPOs today in the postcourt stage is to tell the school of this development (as well as the disposition handed down) (see Chapter 15). If the disposition is probation, the PO will have a variety of duties that parallel those of an adult PO, a topic that will be explored in Chapter 16. Unlike adult POs, JPOs are expected to be active participants in and actual dispensers of rehabilitation for their clients. Thus, JPOs have both treatment and law enforcement duties that can cause role conflict (assuming the JPO is committed to both duties). Potentially, the role conflict—or the perception of it by the juvenile—could undermine the rehabilitation effort.

Unique to the juvenile system is that even when youths are sentenced to commitment in a facility, they may be assigned to JPOs' caseloads in order to monitor their progress in rehabilitation programs (ME, NE, SC). JPOs might also be expected to help design a youth's parole or aftercare plan (WV). JPOs in some states operate some commitment facilities as well (CA, KS, NV, SC).

JPOs are obligated to report to the court on all measures taken with a juvenile and how well he or she did in various treatment programs, which is unique to juvenile court (see Chapter 15). Unlike criminal courts, juvenile courts provide for what are known as review or modification hearings, which are geared to determine the success or failure of the rehabilitation program. Based on that determination, the disposition may be adjusted to better promote the youth's treatment. Chapter 15 will explore this topic at length. Suffice it to say here that JPOs are responsible for providing the analyses and reports used by the juvenile court in conducting this review process. Like adults, juveniles who are alleged to have violated the conditions of their probation/parole are subject to having a violation of probation or parole (VOP) petition filed against them by the JPO, or by the prosecutor following a request by the JPO.

In legislatures' attempts to determine how juvenile courts fare in treating delinquents, it is becoming common for statutes to demand that JPOs collect and compile statistical data and to keep meticulous records in cases in which they are involved.[12] They could also be responsible for ultimately destroying the court records of juveniles (CA, KY, NM, NC). Finally, in testimony to the all-inclusive nature of the duties and tasks historically assigned to JPOs, statutes still regularly and broadly declare that JPOs must perform "such other functions" as are designated either by statute or the juvenile court judge.[13]

Parents and Victims

The final two major players in the juvenile court system are *not* court officials: They are the *parents* of young offenders and the *victims* of these offenders. Whereas the parent has always been a critical figure in juvenile court, the victim's attainment of prominence is recent. Both have been the subject of recent legislation that has significantly affected their roles in the juvenile court process.

The Parent

Everything dealing with the role of the parent is unique to juvenile court. There is simply no corresponding role for such an individual in criminal court. Well over half of the states seriously expanded the role of the parent in juvenile court during the late 1980s (CA, ID, KY, ME, MS) or the 1990s.[14] Alaska (1996), Maryland (1997), Texas (1995), and Wyoming (1997) went so far as to include this expanded role of the parent in their purpose clauses. Today, the treatment of the parent is listed as a primary mission of juvenile courts in Alaska and Texas. Exacting parents' responsibility for the behavior of their children has been announced as a major juvenile court goal in all four states. The California purpose clause identifies a parent's duty to financially support the juvenile while he or she is a ward of the juvenile court.

The parents' role today tends to be identified in juvenile court statutes referred to as *parental responsibility laws* (e.g., CO), which generally apply to both delinquency and status offense cases. The parental role can be divided into two broad categories: financial responsibilities and behavioral obligations. Parents have always had financial liabilities for the costs of prosecuting their children in juvenile court—at least those parents who have had some financial means to absorb some of the costs. What has changed recently, however, is that virtually every financial aspect of the system's handling of the juvenile is subject to being recovered from parents. Additionally, there may be (at least theoretically) no ceiling on the recoverable dollar amount. In 1997, Florida even extended the parents' liability to costs associated with prosecuting their children as adults. As examples of how far some states have been willing to go to recoup their costs from offenders' parents, a number of esoteric items have been identified as involving reimbursable costs, such as any investigation involved to seal the youth's record (CA), any experts employed in the case (WA), the return and extradition of a defendant back to the state (IN), appellate transcripts (WA), expenses associated with helping the youth become competent to stand trial (KS), and any attorney hired by the victim (MT).

A majority of jurisdictions do not hesitate to include virtually all the major costs in both proving the youth's guilt and discovering and remedying the child's problem within parental liability provisions (see Table 8.1). It is possible, if not probable, that some jurisdictions not listed in the table regularly collect some of these costs from parents without a special provision permitting such in their juvenile court statute.

Often these parental liability provisions state that only those parents who can afford to repay the juvenile court are actually obligated to do so and that perhaps only *some* rather than *all* of the expenses are recoverable. Sometimes the wording in the statutes is vague and may apply more broadly than identified in Table 8.1. For example, Alabama and Delaware statutes say parents are liable for all treatment or service costs incurred by their children, which might include placement of youth in institutions in these states. Moreover, in some states, the parents' duty to

Table 8.1 Parental Financial Liability Provisions for Delinquency and Status Offense Cases	
Costs/Expenses	**States Applying**
Treatment/services	All but: CO, FED, ME, MN, NJ, NY, WV
Counsel/defense attorney	All but: FED, ME, MN, NJ, NY, WV
Placement/removal from home	All but: AL, DE, FED, MN, NY
Court costs	AL, AR, DC, IN, IA, KS, KY, MD, MS, MO, NV, NM, ND, OK, OR, PA, SD, WY
Examinations of youth	CO, CT, DE, DC, GA, HI, IA, LA, ME, MS, MO, MT, NE, NV, NC, ND, PA, UT, WI, WY
Detention	AR, CA, DE, GA, ID, LA, MT, NV, OK, OR, SC, SD, WA, WI
Transportation of youth to court	IA, ME, NV, ND, PA, TN
Probation costs/fees	AZ, AR, CA, CO, CT, GA, IL, IN, KS, LA, MI, MT, NC, OK, TX, WY

pay for counsel also includes administrative fees or costs (CA, OR, TN) and the appointment of a guardian *ad litem* (an attorney who safeguards the youth's interests in general) (IL, IN, IA, MD, NM, NC, WY). Probation costs often are capped at so many dollars per month,[15] but Georgia and Indiana both require "up front" money from parents to offset the costs of probation.

On the behavioral side, an increasing number of jurisdictions have recently legislated that parents must attend all court hearings in which their children are involved.[16] Parental attendance has always been the expectation and desire of juvenile court officials, but frequent failure of parents to appear at these proceedings has prompted many jurisdictions to legally demand it. In addition, parents are being ordered by statutes to pick up their children from police stations (CA, OR) and to ensure that their children go to school (CA, IN, MN, VA).

Perhaps the most controversial performance aspect is the juvenile court's imposition of "sentences" on parents that mirror actions that can be taken against delinquents. For example, like their children, parents can be ordered to submit to a variety of medical or mental examinations in 18 states. Penalties against parents, such as community service or fines and restitution, are available in 34 states. Several of these states require proof that the parent shares some of the blame or fault for the delinquent act before these sanctions can be implemented. This usually means that parents must have contributed to the delinquency in some way or completely ignored their children's crime-prone behavior. Although most states do not mention any limit on the possible restitution order, several identify fairly high amounts, such as $4,000 (MO, NM), $5,000 (DE, ND, SC), or even $10,000 (MD). Other states simply announce the potential for "full" restitution for *all* the losses and damages suffered by the victim(s) (AZ, WV). Arkansas law provides that

Table 8.2 Parental Performance Liability Provisions for Delinquency and Status Offense Cases

Provision	States Applying or Requiring
Examine parent	AR, FL, GA, IN, IA, LA, MD, MI, MO, MT, NH, NM, NC, OR, SD, WV, WI, WY
Community service	AR, CA, FL*, NV, NH, PA, TN, TX*, WY
Restitution/fines	AL, AK, AZ, AR, CA, CO, CT, DE, FL*, GA, HI, ID, IL, KY*, MD, MI, MS, MO*, MT, NV, NH, NJ*, NM, ND, OK, OR, PA, RI, SC, TN*, TX*, WV, WI, WY*
Probation partner	AL, AK, AZ, CA, DE, GA, ID, IL, IN, KS, KY, LA, MI, MN, NE, NV, NH, NM, NC, OH, OR, SD, TX, VT, WA, WY
Perform acts	All but: AK, AR, CT, DE, FED, FL, KS, KY, ME, MA, NJ, RI, WA, (SC*)
Participate in treatment	All but: FED, MA, OH, VT (NJ*, TN*)

* State requires fault on part of parent.
( ) Applies to status offenders only.

the juvenile court judge can impose restitution up to $10,000, but amounts higher than that require providing the parents the right to a jury determination.

As Table 8.2 reveals, 26 states have made the parent an active partner in a probation disposition. The partnership usually entails an obligation on the parents' part to closely monitor the child's activities (including compliance with all conditions of probation), to frequently communicate with the PO as to the child's progress on probation, and to report any violations of probation committed by the youth. Alabama allows the parents' agreement to become a probation partner to serve as a prerequisite for putting the youth on probation. A number of states are forcing parents to put up a probation bond that is forfeited if the child is found to have violated probation or to pay a fine in this situation (KY, OH, OK, WY). Even more common is the provision (present in 39 jurisdictions) that parents can be ordered to perform whatever "reasonable" acts the court believes are necessary to promote the child's rehabilitation. Typically, "reasonable" is left undefined. It might overlap other provisions identified in Tables 8.1 and 8.2. In some states (AL, GA, SD), an *order of protection* that delineates numerous responsibilities of the parents can be made part of the disposition order. Most of these responsibilities refer to general care of the child and cooperation with the juvenile court in the youth's rehabilitation effort.

Finally, all but four jurisdictions permit the judge to order the parents to participate in the youth's treatment program or to engage in training and counseling sessions of their own.[17] Thus, the juvenile court's rehabilitation target has been expanded to focus specifically on parents. This expansion has had two major dimensions: teaching parents how to parent, and offering support initiatives designed to help preserve the family. For example, Colorado law addresses both Parental Responsibility Training Programs as well as an Intensive Family Preservation Program.

Parents' failure to satisfy any of the financial or behavioral obligations imposed by the juvenile court can result in a civil judgment against them[18] and their being held in contempt of court.[19] The latter can result in the imposition of fines, community service, or jail time. Interestingly, Indiana identifies termination of parental rights as a possible outcome of parental noncompliance with court orders.

As we will see throughout the remainder of the text, parents play a critical role and seriously influence decision making at all major stages of the juvenile court process. Simply put, parents are a two-edged sword throughout juvenile justice. In Chapter 9 we will review how parents can be perceived by juvenile court as the alternative to which youth can be diverted from the system. Financially able parents can purchase private alternative remedies for their children. Similarly, cooperative parents can make a sentence of probation appear appropriate and workable and thus eliminate the need to institutionalize the youth. These parents provide their children with very serious *legal advantages* by eliminating the need for a system response altogether, or at least by reducing the severity of the system's reaction to juvenile offenders.

In other situations, parents can be perceived as the major contributor to the child's problem, making the system's need to intervene into the youth's life all the more apparent. Dysfunctional and poor families may be physically and financially unable to resolve their children's problems by themselves. Uncooperative parents may simply refuse to help the system help their children. Moreover, some parents simply want their children both convicted and removed from home (see Chapters 13 and 14). These parents provide their children with serious *legal disadvantages* by creating the system's need to respond or at least by exacerbating the severity of the system's reaction to juvenile offenders. The parents tend to be critical players, especially at intake, detention, trial, and disposition. Juvenile court statutes tend to identify the parents as a factor for decision makers to consider at these vital stages of the juvenile court process. Needless to say, all of this material and parental influence is unique to the juvenile system.

The Victim

Like parents, *victims* experienced greatly expanded roles in juvenile court via legislation that was rampant during the late 1980s (CO, ID, MI, MO, NJ, PA) and the 1990s.[20] Ten states have what is, in effect, a victim's bill of rights in juvenile court.[21] Alaska (1998), Maryland (1997), Vermont (1996), and Wisconsin (1995) have gone so far as to include this expanded role of the victim in their purpose clauses. Today, ensuring the youth's accountability to the victim (and community) is listed as a primary mission of juvenile courts in Maryland. Protecting the rights of victims and treating them with respect and dignity are among the paramount concerns of Vermont's and Wisconsin's juvenile courts.

Unlike parents, however, until recently victims were almost completely ignored in juvenile court, apart perhaps from needing their testimony in order to adjudicate a youth. Before *Gault*, many POs did not want or need more than a police report of the victim's account (if even that was required), so in most cases victims would not have been connected to any juvenile court proceedings per se. Even though *Gault* made victim testimony at an adjudicatory hearing all the more possible (assuming the youth demanded a trial), victims were still considered mostly irrelevant to juvenile court processing. To be sure, victims were largely ignored (and perhaps mistreated) in criminal court until recently as well. But they were probably never considered as irrelevant as they were inconvenient to criminal court workers, since the victim meant one more person who had to be accommodated and factored into the court process. Nevertheless, in criminal court, victims have historically been much more necessary and likely to testify at trial and even at sentencing. In juvenile court, it was quite likely that even victims who had had to testify at an adjudicatory hearing would be quite ignorant of the existence or outcome of a disposition hearing (or of any development after their testimony).

The most plausible explanation for the differences in victim experiences in the two courts is that whereas the victim supposedly has always been relevant to the *punishment* of a criminal offender (e.g., in proportion to the amount of damage and injury suffered by the victim), the victim has not been considered relevant to the *treatment* of a juvenile offender. In other words, traditional juvenile justice thinking would have held that the victim's version of the impact of a crime should not have any influence on determining the nature of the disposition most appropriate for the youth. Although what happened to the victim was important to the extent that it disclosed how serious the youth's behavior and problem had become, the victim was not seen as having a role to play (or any expertise) in finding a suitable treatment-oriented disposition. Currently, the pendulum has swung in the opposite direction. The victim today is a serious player in the juvenile courts of many jurisdictions. This movement is more a result of the expansion of victims' rights in general (in both juvenile and criminal courts) than a development of the current drive for restorative justice. The recent rise of restorative justice (which in former times was called victim-offender mediation) deals primarily with a sentencing strategy of mending the wounds caused by the offender's act (see Chapter 16). Independent of any such motivation, juvenile court statutes have seriously accommodated and empowered victims throughout the juvenile court process (Sanborn 2001b).

Juvenile courts must accommodate victims in three general ways: provide them information, take basic care of them, and permit them to attend juvenile court hearings. Some of the information that must be made available to the victim is generic, such as the availability of financial assistance or medical and social services,[22] the right to pursue civil damages (CA, FL, WI, WY), the general workings of juvenile court (AZ, FL, MI, SC, TX, UT), or the prosecutor's office phone number (AZ, MI, WY). Much of the information subject to disclosure, however, marks a serious departure from traditional juvenile justice operations, and includes the items covered in Table 8.3. Requiring the disclosure of this information has made the juvenile courts' operations in these jurisdictions somewhat less secretive (and maybe less puzzling), at least to the victim.

Legislatures are also directing juvenile courts to take care of victims in a number of ways, including simply treating them with respect (CA, MD, UT, VA) and considering their situations when scheduling or postponing hearings (AZ, UT, WY). To enhance their comfort and convenience, victims also have been guaranteed separate waiting rooms in the courthouse,[23] as well as a right to refuse an interview with the defense attorney (AZ, WY), and to demand a speedy or expedited trial (AZ, FL, MI, MN, NV, UT). Beyond the courthouse, legislation has demanded that employers not retaliate against victims for missing work due to appearing in juvenile court (FL, MI, MN, TX, UT, WY). To better protect victims of juvenile crime, some statutes insist that the victim's identity and residence remain confidential (AL, LA, MI, MN, NV, UT) and that victims be entitled to increased law enforcement protection (AZ, FL, TX, UT, WY), including possibly a restraining order against the defendant (CO, IL) or even placing offenders in detention if they make threats against victims (MI, WY). Finally, juvenile courts have been mandated to better compensate victims by considering them to be entitled to restitution,[24] by ordering POs to guarantee that restitution is actually paid by the offender (ID, MD, MI, MN), and by guaranteeing the return of stolen property.[25]

A final measure of accommodation involves granting victims a right to attend all hearings in juvenile court[26] and even to bring along an attorney (CO, CT, FL) or another supportive person (CT, MN, OK, PA, VA, WI, WY). A handful of states have identified specifically the right of victim attendance at a number of proceedings that formerly victims were neither aware of nor present at, including diversion (DE), detention (AZ, UT), appeal (MI, MN, VA), vacating an adjudication (MI), reviewing or modifying a disposition (CO, UT), and parole (AZ, TX, UT).

By far the most controversial and significant revision in the role of victims in juvenile court has been

Table 8.3 Information Provided to Accommodate Victims in Juvenile Court

Type of Information	Jurisdictions
Hearing dates and outcomes	AZ, AR, CA, CT, FL, HI, IL, IA, LA, MD, MI, MN, MT, NV, NH, NJ, OK, SC, SD, TX, UT, VT, VA, WI, WY
Cancelled hearings	AZ, FL, LA, MI, MN, TX, UT, VA, WY
Youth's name/address	AK, CA, CT, HI, ID, IL, IA, ME, MI, MN, MT, NV, NH, NJ, OR, RI, SC, SD, VT, WA, WI, WY
Status of investigation	FL, MN, WA, WI
Youth's arrest/rearrest	AZ, FL, LA, MD, MN, WY
Youth's release from custody	AK, AZ, FL, IA, KS, LA, MD, MI, MN, MT, NH, TX, VA, WY
Youth's escape from custody	AZ, FL, IA, LA, MI, MN, NH, WY
Youth's court records	AK, AZ, CA, CO, CT, IN, IA, KY, MD, MT, UT, WI
Close of case	AZ, MD, MI, NH, WI
Youth's HIV test results	KY, OR, UT, WI

their empowerment, by allowing them to have input into how cases are resolved. This development complements but goes far beyond merely permitting victims to attend all the various proceedings. Victims are being given a voice on decisions reached throughout the entire juvenile court operation. Louisiana has given victims a right to retain counsel in order to confer with the police and the court on the proper outcome of the case. Victims today are permitted to provide victim impact statements (VIS) or to offer a *victim statement of opinion (VSO)* regarding what should happen to offenders at detention (AZ, FL, MT, TX, UT), diversion,[27] filing a petition (AZ, LA, MI, MN, MT), plea bargaining,[28] transfer to criminal court (MD), disposition,[29] vacating adjudication or modifying disposition (AZ, MI, MN, UT), parole (AZ, FL, SC, TX, UT), and expunging records (UT, WY).

At the diversion and filing petition stage (see Chapter 9), the Iowa statute declares that the view of the victim *shall be* considered, while other jurisdictions allow the victim to appeal the PO's decision not to file a petition[30] or to divert the case (MT, NJ). Maryland and New York have granted victims actual veto power over the diversion decision. Similarly, Arizona has held that the juvenile court shall not accept a plea bargain unless the victim has been given a chance to comment and voice an opinion on its appropriateness. In that state as well, failure to notify victims and allow them to be present and to be heard at parole hearings are grounds for victims to have the release set aside until given such an opportunity. Half of the states have adopted provisions allowing victim input at disposition, together with a mandate in four states that the judge *shall* take the victim's view into consideration in deciding the disposition (CA, CO, TX, VT). Minnesota even provides for a community impact statement that is designed to emphasize the deleterious effects of the youth's offense on the community at large.

These measures of victims' input into the processing of cases in juvenile court constitute an important example of the *criminalization* of juvenile justice (Sanborn 2001b). To the extent that victims end up actually influencing the outcome of a case and derailing what was otherwise an appropriate treatment-oriented disposition or outcome, there is reason to question the amount of the system's continued dedication to the rehabilitation of youthful offenders in these jurisdictions. To the extent that victims' desires and influence in the ultimate disposition handed down are not reflected accurately in the court records and databases, research as to what factors determine juvenile court dispositions will be seriously compromised (see Chapter 14).

Personnel Overview

The personnel we have discussed in this chapter are not the only individuals who play a part in how cases are processed in the juvenile justice system. They are, however, the persons who exert the most significant and continuous influence over how cases are resolved and what happens to youth in juvenile court. Judges, prosecutors, and defense attorneys are drawn from the same basic pool of individuals (i.e., lawyers) who work in criminal court (and some work there as well). Their roles in juvenile court certainly can differ, however, and masters and referees who conduct trial in juvenile court enjoy no comparable powers in criminal court. POs who work in juvenile court are expected to have a different perception of their role when juveniles are under their supervision. Their jobs in juvenile court are also more varied. The parents' role in juvenile court is completely unique. There is no comparable counterpart in the adult system. Only victims (as they continue to be granted powers in juvenile court) have basically the same role, regardless of the system in which they appear.

What should juvenile court judges do to ensure that prosecutors and defense attorneys are competent and prepared to work a case?

Summary: Key Ideas and Concepts

- Juvenile court a unique place to work
- Variation in who serves as a prosecutor in juvenile court
- May not be a regular prosecutor in juvenile court

- Various responsibilities of the juvenile court prosecutor
- Various tasks performed by the juvenile court prosecutor
- Prosecutorial role conflict at intake and disposition
- Special prosecutorial role at detention and disposition
- Lack of training for a juvenile court prosecutor
- Broad knowledge juvenile court defense attorney needs to fulfill role
- Three sources from which to secure a defense attorney
- Role conflict for the juvenile court defense attorney
- Pros and cons of the guardian defense attorney
- Pros and cons of the advocate defense attorney
- Possible different defense attorney role at trial versus disposition
- Role conflict for the juvenile court judge
- Special judicial role at detention, transfer, and disposition
- Varieties in types of judges in juvenile court
- All juvenile court workers requiring special training, which may not occur
- All juvenile court workers occupying a lesser status than criminal court counterparts
- All juvenile court workers as needing to have special relationships among one another
- Controversy in using masters or referees in juvenile court
- Advantages in employing masters and referees in juvenile court
- Unique roles and powers of the juvenile court PO
- Various titles for the juvenile court PO
- Unique role of the parent in juvenile court
- Extensive financial responsibilities of the parent in juvenile court
- Parental behavioral responsibilities in juvenile court
- Positive and negative juvenile court reaction to youth due to parents
- Victims historically ignored in juvenile court, even more than in criminal court
- Juvenile court duty today to accommodate victims in various ways
- Increase in victims' rights in juvenile court
- Victims' rights contributing to the criminalization of juvenile court

Discussion Questions

1. In what ways can the juvenile court serve as a unique place to work?

2. How does juvenile court differ as to who may be the individual prosecuting the case?

3. What conflict can a prosecutor experience in juvenile court, and at which stages of the process is this conflict most likely to emerge?

4. What is the proper role for the prosecutor in juvenile court?

5. What conflict can a defense attorney experience in juvenile court?

6. What is the proper role for the defense attorney in juvenile court? What factors should influence the choice of role for the defense attorney?

7. What conflict can a judge experience in juvenile court?

8. What is the proper role for the judge in juvenile court?

9. Should masters and referees work in juvenile court, and, if so, in what capacities?

10. In what ways do the responsibilities of the PO differ in juvenile court compared to criminal court?

11. What are the implications of the PO's having so many responsibilities in juvenile court?

12. Describe how the role of the parent is unique in juvenile court. What are the implications of that role?

13. What types of responsibilities do parents have in juvenile court?

14. In what ways can parents provide a legal advantage or legal disadvantage to their children?

15. Discuss the ways in which victims must be taken care of today in juvenile court.

16. What are the implications of giving the victim a say in how the case against a youth will be resolved in juvenile court?

17. Discuss the developments described in this chapter that support the idea that juvenile court is being criminalized.

Endnotes

1. The states that hold that a regular prosecutor need not appear in juvenile court are: AZ, CA, DE, NH, NY, VA, WA, WI.
2. The states that provide for the prosecutor to appear at the request of the court are: AL, GA, HI, MA, MI, NM, NY, PA, RI, TN.
3. Sanborn (1987a) reported that many juvenile court workers who had been employees in the juvenile court system prior to the 1967 *Gault* decision recalled how lawyers who frequently appeared to represent youth were routinely told to wait outside the courtroom until after the adjudication stage. It was only at disposition that these attorneys were allowed to participate in the process.

4. The states that refer to this person as a master are: AL, CA, CT, IN, MI, MN, MS, NJ, ND, OK, OR, TN, TX, WV.
5. The states that refer to this person as a referee are: AK, DE, MD, MT, NV, NM, PA, RI, TX.
6. The states that refer to this person as a commissioner are: AZ, DE, MO, UT, WA, WI, WY.
7. The states that prohibit masters from conducting transfer hearings are: AL, AK, CO, MD, MI, NJ, NM, TX, WI, WY.
8. JPOs work directly or closely with a juvenile court judge in the following jurisdictions: AL, AZ, AR, CA, CO, CT, DC, GA, HI, ID, IL, IN, IA, KS, MA, MI, MN, MO, MT, NV, NY, NC, ND, OH, PA, TX, UT, WA, WV.
9. The states that refer to this person as a PO are: AK, AR, CA, GA, ID, IL, IN, KY, LA, MA, MI, MN, MT, NE, NV, NJ, PA, TN, TX, UT, VA, WI, WY.
10. The states that refer to this person as a JPO are: AL, AZ, CO, CT, FL, HI, ND, OH, OK, VT, WV.
11. JPOs will initiate a transfer petition in the following jurisdictions: AZ, CA, DC, FL, HI, ID, IN, IA, MD, MS, MO, ND, PA, RI, TX, UT, VA, WI.
12. JPOs are under special orders to keep correct records in AL, IL, IN, KY, ME, MO, NC, OH, TN, VA, WI.
13. JPOS have been told to perform the "other" functions in AL, AK, AZ, AR, GA, IL, IN, KY, MI, MO, MT, ND, OK, OR, PA, SC, TN, VT, WI. It is beyond the scope of this text but still important to note that in many jurisdictions JPOs also have to perform such tasks as pursuing the civil commitment of youth, making mental health referrals, and petitioning for matters such as the youth's emancipation or the termination of parental rights.
14. The jurisdictions that adopted provisions regarding parents in the 1990s are: AL, AK, AZ, CA, CO, CT, DE, DC, FL, GA, IA, KS, KY, LA, MD, MI, MN, MO, MT, NV, NH, ND, OK, OR, PA, RI, SC, SD, TN, TX, VT, VA, WA, WI, WY.
15. Examples of states that have capped the dollar amount for probation costs are Indiana and Texas at $15, Illinois and Oklahoma at $25, Arkansas at $30, and Louisiana at $100.
16. The jurisdictions that demand the attendance of parents at all hearings are: AK, CO, DC, GA, KS, KY, MI, MN, NY, PA, SC, SD, TX, UT, VT, WA, WY.
17. Three (MN, OH, VT) of the six jurisdictions that fail to mention the judge's authority to order the parents to participate in treatment may nevertheless grant the judge this power via their statutory provision that identifies the judge's ability to order the parents to perform "reasonable acts."
18. The states that allow the judge to impose a civil judgment against parents are: CA, KS, MO, NV, NH, SD, TN, VA.
19. The jurisdictions that allow the judge to hold parents in contempt of court are: AL, AZ, AR, CO, DC, GA, ID, IL, KS, KY, LA, MD, MI, MN, MT, NE, NV, NH, NM, NC, OH, OK, OR, PA, SC, SD, TN, TX, UT, VA, WA, WI, WY.
20. The states that adopted provisions concerning the victim in the 1990s are: AL, AK, AZ, AR, CA, CO, CT, FL, GA, ID, IL, IA, KY, LA, MD, MI, MN, MT, NV, NH, NJ, NM, ND, SC, SD, TX, UT, VT, VA, WI, WY.
21. The 10 states with a victims' bill of rights in juvenile court are: AL, AZ, ID, MI, MN, ND, TX, UT, VA, WY.
22. Victims must be told about medical and social services in AZ, CA, FL, IA, LA, MD, MI, MN, SC, TX, UT, WY.
23. Victims must be provided separate waiting rooms in CA, FL, LA, MD, MI, MN, TX, UT, WY.
24. Victims are entitled to restitution in AK, CO, HI, ID, IA, MD, MI, MN, NM, OK, OR, UT, WY.
25. Victims are guaranteed the return of stolen property in AZ, FL, KY, LA, MD, MI, TX, UT, WY.
26. Victims are permitted to attend all juvenile court hearings in AK, AZ, CA, CO, FL, KS, KY, LA, MI, MN, NJ, OK, OR, PA, SD, TX, UT, VA, WI, WY.
27. Victims can give a VIS or VSO at diversion in AL, AZ, FL, IA, KY, MI, NE, NJ, WI.
28. Victims can give a VIS or VSO regarding a plea bargain in AZ, FL, LA, MI, MN, MT, NH, WY.
29. Victims can give a VIS or VSO at disposition in AK, AZ, CA, CO, CT, FL, GA, IL, IA, LA, MD, MI, MN, MO, MT, NH, NJ, NY, SC, TX, UT, VT, VA, WI, WY.
30. Victims can appeal a PO's decision not to file a petition in CA, DC, HI, KY, ME, MD, MT, NV, NY, NC, VA. ✦

The Intake Process

Focus of Chapter 9

Chapter 9 addresses the critical intake stage, in which POs review the youth's history and current charges to determine whether formal court processing is necessary. Like the police, POs are acting as gatekeepers to the juvenile system. We will see, again, that there are viable alternatives to formal court intervention and that significant numbers of youth are diverted from the juvenile justice system.

Key Terms

- case rates
- court of last resort
- diversion
- individualization
- informal adjustment

- intake
- labeling theory
- net widening
- preliminary inquiry

Intake Objectives

The intake stage entails a number of goals or objectives. They include identifying whether juveniles constitute a risk to themselves or others, determining whether youths should be placed in detention for the time being (while not overcrowding detention) or released to the community with or without conditions, ascertaining the existence of probable cause to believe the youth committed the offense alleged, and developing a risk and needs assessment (Mears and Kelly 1999). During intake, a vast amount of information regarding the youth is likely to be collected. Included within these data are such items as offense history, past indications of violence or aggressive behavior, mental health and medical needs, substance use and abuse, family problems, problems with peers and neighborhood, educational and vocational deficits, and the youth's amenability to the various treatment programs available to the juvenile system (Mears and Kelly 1999). How well these goals will be achieved and how well the information will be collected will vary depending on the location of the juvenile court and the abilities of its staff (Mears and Kelly 1999).

POs as Intake Workers

Statutes commonly refer to POs' duties to *receive complaints* concerning juvenile misbehavior (from police, parents, schools, or private citizens).[1] Typically, a juvenile's first contact with a PO is known as intake. Intake is the initial decision-making stage within the juvenile court system. It is staffed by individuals who may be known as probation officers (POs) or who may be given a special title such as intake officer (IO) or intake worker.[2] Another title used is *assessment officer* (FL, MT). These special titles do imply that the focus of these individuals' work is limited explicitly to the precourt investigation (and perhaps supervision) of cases against juveniles. A modern development is to have intake run by a child department or agency (such as a Department of Juvenile Justice). Another recent innovation that challenges traditional juvenile justice philosophy is staffing intake with prosecutors (SD, WA, WY). This approach is another example of the criminalization of juvenile court. Intake involves screening cases to see whether they should proceed further into the court process, much like prosecutorial screening accomplishes in criminal court. Unlike in criminal court, however, the juvenile screening process does not involve grand jury proceedings, in which the accused is indicted as part of the charging process.[3]

In some juvenile courts, the intake process takes place at the detention center. With whom should the intake decision rest: the probation officer or the prosecutor?

The Uniqueness of Intake

Intake has a number of other unique aspects. For one thing, although their authority is diminishing somewhat in some locations, POs have been major players at this screening stage. In the adult system, prosecutors alone play the role of screening agent. Second, the focus of intake is not restricted to the offense and record as it tends to be in adult court. Instead, the family and the entire living environment (e.g., neighborhood, peers, school) are examined as well, and could be *the* factors that influence whether a case is processed through the system. In juvenile court, a social work or rehabilitation mentality has ruled at this stage, rather than the crime control perspective that dominates in criminal court. In addition, the emphasis at intake historically has been the opposite of that at adult court screening. Cases are supposed to be diverted or *sent home* unless the family cannot resolve the problem. Juvenile court was established as a court of last resort, one that would replace or substitute for the family only when necessary. Intake, then, would have been better referred to as *out-take*. To be sure, the prosecutor in adult court also sends cases home, but the emphasis is reversed, such that cases there will be *prosecuted* unless extenuating circumstances would justify nonprosecution.

Intake's emphasis on the youth's problem leads juvenile court in a direction that differs from the focus on offense and record in criminal court. In the latter forum, *equality* or *equal justice* is ideally supposed to rule. Regardless of whether criminal courts fully achieve that objective, there is little debate over whether equal justice should be the goal of the adult system. For example, few individuals would disagree with the following proposition:

equal crime and record = equal punishment

Again, this goal is supposed to influence criminal court proceedings and has been the major impetus behind the widespread adoption of sentencing guidelines.

In juvenile court, individualization, rather than equality, has been the objective of the system. In short, simply because two youths have the same offense and record does not mean they have the same problem, or:

equal crimes and records ≠ equal problems

For example, two juveniles guilty of the same behavior could differ significantly. One could be a leader and the other a follower in the criminal episode. Even more important, perhaps, one could have a substance abuse problem the other does not share.

Not only is it possible for the problems of two youths (whose behavior is equal) to differ considerably, but the solutions to handling two youths with equal problems could also differ tremendously. In other words:

equal problems ≠ equal solutions

For example, two youths just starting delinquent careers and otherwise equal in whatever problems have steered them in this direction could nevertheless be in very different situations that call for very different solutions as far as intake is concerned. The one youth could have a family who is now aware of behavioral problems and is willing and able to address and remedy the source of the problem. This situation could contrast dramatically with a second youth who lives in a single-parent household with a drug-dependent parent who denies the existence of a problem and who has previously produced delinquent offspring. Whereas the first juvenile arguably does not require juvenile court's attention (assuming the offense is not serious), the second appears to need juvenile court's help (perhaps even if the offense is not serious). The same perspective could arise in a case with two drug-dependent youth. One could have parents who can privately purchase (perhaps more effective) services in the community, while the second could be financially destitute and thus dependent on juvenile court for substance abuse counseling. This difference in circumstances could result in different responses from intake personnel.

The juvenile court's pursuit of individualization in lieu of equality (at least in terms of offense and record) opens the door for treating similarly situated individuals (in terms of behavior) very differently and perhaps discriminatorily. The modern trend of criminalizing juvenile court, with prosecutors increasingly gaining control of intake, could reduce or even eliminate these historically unique aspects of the process. That is because prosecutors are supposedly influenced more by legal factors (crime and record) than social factors (family problems and limitations).

Intake Options

Ideally, the IO should turn away cases that have no legal merit (i.e., insufficient evidence). However, it is difficult to guarantee that the IO will do so, especially if the youth is perceived as having a problem. Cases with legal merit may still be completely dismissed, especially if the charge and record are not serious or the problem has been or is being resolved. Even some cases that go forward for the moment may still never be officially prosecuted. Instead, the case may be diverted out of the system. Diversion usually means the defendant will not be formally adjudicated (or have a delinquent record for this case), but there will be strings attached. That is, the youth will have to perform a number of tasks to earn a dismissal of the case.

Essentially, the IO has three choices at intake:

- Take no action at all—perhaps just counsel and advise the youth and the family *or* refer the youth and family to services outside the system with no strings attached.

- Divert the case outside the system *with* strings attached (i.e., with a diversion agreement via a diversion program).

- File a petition (or recommend that the prosecutor file), which is juvenile court's version of a complaint or charging document.

In other words, the system ignores the incident (option 1), diverts the case (option 2), or prosecutes the youth (option 3).

The *no action* option means the system is not pursuing the matter at this time. Of course, an absence of legal merit could forever make prosecution of the charges implausible. Depending on the youth's performance in the near future, however (perhaps misbehaving at home or school or at an agency to which the youth has been referred, or commiting a new offense), the charges that resulted in "no action" could resurface (assuming the statute of limitations, if any, has not expired). We will explore what the *prosecution* option means throughout the remainder of the text. This leaves the *diversion* option to consider in this chapter.

Diversion is designed almost exclusively for an offender who does not yet have a delinquent (or criminal) record. It is the embodiment of what is called labeling theory, which proposes that a youth's self-concept (and future behavior) is less negatively affected by permitting the offender to avoid an official delinquent label and record. In other words, labeling theorists suggest that adjudicating and officially stigmatizing youth can actually end up encouraging more criminal behavior, provided the youth internalizes that label and acts out on it (i.e., "You say I'm no good, I believe that and I'm going to act that way"). Besides reducing stigma, diversion accomplishes other important goals. For one thing, it reduces the juvenile court's caseload, which saves considerable time and money for the system. Simply put, juvenile court could not engage in 100 percent prosecution (just like adult court could not). Valuable resources that the system conserves via diversion can be spent on youth with more serious problems and behavior. Moreover, diversion can result in the diverted youth's receiving quicker (no trial is needed) and better (superior community resources and services) treatment.

Diversion is not without its critics and problems. The problem most frequently identified is net widening. This means that community resources are co-opted by (or become a satellite of) the juvenile justice system. The latter becomes huge by virtue of these community agencies working with, and to some respect under, juvenile court. Also, the number of youth who can be subjected to at least some control of the juvenile court expands accordingly. To some extent, diversion also has to be blamed for encouraging some crime. It is certainly plausible that some youth will regard diversion not as an attempt to bolster their self-esteem, but rather as proof that juvenile court need not be taken seriously because it does not hurt juveniles. Finally, it is possible that due process problems attend diversion, at least for those youth who arguably would never have been adjudicated for what they were supposed to have done, if they actually did anything wrong.

Chapter 16 will cover the nature of diversion programs in depth. Suffice it to say here that IOs/POs will be the ones supervising diverted youth and monitoring their progress in the diversion program (and perhaps even running the diversion program itself).[4] IOs/POs are responsible for making referrals of cases to (and also coordinating) private and public agencies in the community whose services will be used for both diverted and adjudicated youth.[5]

Intake Decision Making

After the IOs receive a referral, they conduct what is popularly known as a preliminary inquiry[6] or a preliminary investigation[7] in which records and reports are gathered and investigated to get a feel for the situation. These reports should encompass the current charge, but can also include the youth's school record, social history, family and neighborhood environment, and previous encounters with social service agencies or juvenile court. In conjunction with this investigation, IOs will hold what is commonly referred to as an *intake conference*,[8] typically with the child and the parent (and maybe the police and the victim). A few states have noted the defendant's right to counsel[9] and silence[10] at the intake conference. Historically, attorneys would have been viewed as interference at this point (and probably still are), and their attendance could still be discouraged. If pushed to a U.S. Supreme Court decision, it is quite probable that defendants would not be granted such a right (just as adults have no such right at the charging stage). Although a right to silence formally exists, a youth's exercise of that right could necessitate filing charges. Many states specify that a youth's statements cannot be used at *any* subsequent proceeding,[11] while other jurisdictions prohibit their use at the trial stage.[12] The difference between these positions is important: In the latter situation, juveniles' statements are admissible at nontrial hearings such as detention, transfer, and disposition.[13]

The youth's and the parents' attendance at intake is usually voluntary,[14] but failure to appear would almost certainly result in a formal charge or petition being filed (DC, HI). The same would hold true if only the parent fails to attend, since the IO would be seriously handicapped in conducting the preliminary inquiry. The conference begins with an explanation of the charges and the potential outcomes (diversion, adjudication, disposition) of the juvenile court process. The participants then discuss the youth's behavior in the alleged incident, the parents' ability and willingness to resolve the problem, and community resources available to assist in the solution. Most jurisdictions continue to instruct their IOs to be guided in this decision making by the youth's (and the public's) best interests and the need for help or treatment.[15] In fact, Georgia notes that a petition shall not be filed unless the court has determined and endorsed upon the petition that filing one is needed to promote the best interests of the child and the public.

In addition, some legislatures have officially identified the factors IOs are to consider at this stage. Although most jurisdictions do not spell out the criteria to be used, the few that do highlight how many considerations can come into play:

- The age of the youth (and perhaps maturity and capabilities)
- The offense involved, including such elements as extent of injury, use of a weapon, and amount of violence and threat to the community
- The youth's prior record, including previous diversions or adjudications
- Other offenses pending against the youth
- Whether co-defendants will be prosecuted for the offense
- The prospect for the youth to cooperate in the diversion effort, including whether the youth might reoffend or retaliate against the victim
- The prospect of the success of the diversion, as well as the adequacy of community resources and services, and the time it will take to work with the youth on diversion
- Whether the youth would need to be removed from the home to complete the diversion
- Previous problems the child has had at home, in school, and in the community, including gang affiliations, substance abuse problems, chronic truancy, etc.
- The attitude of the defendant and the parents
- The attitude of others affected by the case (e.g., victim, police, prosecutor)
- Any chronic family problems, including dependency history, social services history, and drug dependency and criminal tendencies of the parents

Even this may not represent an exhaustive list of possible factors, and not all factors may be used and weighed equally by all IOs within a particular juvenile court, or among all juvenile courts within one state or jurisdiction. Thus, uniformity among jurisdictions should not exist. For example, of the 13 jurisdictions with detailed factors in their juvenile law, Washington, DC, and New York (which have identical provisions) focus almost exclusively on items related to offense and record. Hawaii and Montana combine these items with an in-depth analysis of the youth. California, New Jersey, and Tennessee combine offense and record factors with ones that deal with the family's strengths and weaknesses and the attitudes of all parties toward diversion. Florida, Indiana, and Michigan concentrate mostly on the youth's character and attributes. Finally, Kansas, Rhode Island, and South Carolina emphasize all three major areas of offense and record, youth character, and the family situation.

Unlike the old days when the IO's discretion at intake was virtually unlimited (i.e., just about any charge could be "buried"), today a number of developments have seriously curtailed the IO's decision-making power. Most critical, perhaps, is that prosecutors may actually be calling most or all of the shots at this stage. We have already noted some states where prosecutors make all the decisions at the intake stage (SD, WA, WY). Even where IOs still manage the intake process, some states have recently mandated that all crimes (FL, IN), or ones committed by juveniles with prior records (AZ, NM, VA, TX), or certain serious, violent, weapons offenses (CA, MD, TX) must be brought by the IO to the prosecutor to allow the latter to consider whether to file a petition. In addition, certain violent offenses might make the filing of a petition mandatory (DC, TX, VA, WA). These mandatory referrals to prosecutors and filings of petitions may still mean that the case can be diverted (unless the legislature has specifically declared otherwise or diversion is prohibited once a petition is filed). For instance, a prosecutor's choice to "undercharge" the youth (i.e., to charge an offense less serious than the one for which the defendant could plausibly be charged) at a level below the mandatory filing threshold would allow the prosecutor to avoid filing a petition and to divert a case.

Similarly, some jurisdictions have disqualified certain juvenile offenders from the diversionary pool. Thus far, 15 jurisdictions have eliminated various offenses (usually serious or violent ones) or juveniles with previous records (diversion or adjudication) from diversion eligibility. Of course, other locations may unofficially consider these situations as inappropriate for diversion, but states have decided formally to prohibit IOs/prosecutors from diverting cases in the following instances:

- Violent offenses and crimes against persons (CA, CT, DC, GA, KS, MI, MN, NC, TX, VA, WA)
- Previous adjudication (depending upon severity of offense) (CA, CO, CT, KS, MN, MT, OK, VA, WA)
- Previous diversion (AZ, CA, CO, CT, KS, MN, WA)
- Firearms (CA, CT, KS, NC, TX, WA)
- Drugs (CA, CT, NC, TX)
- All felonies (AZ, OK)

Offenders not mentioned in these lists are eligible diversion candidates. Beyond disqualification via offense and record, three other serious, potential obstacles could stand in the way of a youth's receiving a diversionary outcome, assuming the IO supports diversion in the first place. First, many jurisdictions have adopted a policy in which the prosecutor must either originate or at least consent to any youth's being put on diversion.[16] In some jurisdictions a serious offense must be present for this consent to be required. For example, the following states have identified only certain serious offenses as requiring a green light from the prosecutor:

- GA: designated felonies
- MD: crime and handgun/felony
- NV: felony or gross misdemeanor, disorderly persons
- NJ: crime 1°, 2°, 3°, 4°, repeat offenders
- OK: felony sex offense, felony offense, and firearm or second felony
- TX: previous felony adjudication

A few states actually require a judge's consent,[17] again perhaps only for very serious charges. Finally, a growing number of states have made the victim's opinion either a factor (AL, NE, NJ) or the deciding vote (MD) in determining whether diversion will occur. Similarly, it is becoming common for victims to be allowed to appeal an IO's (and sometimes a prosecutor's) decision to divert or not file a petition to either a prosecutor[18] or a judge.[19] In fact, Virginia provides that when a victim appeal involves a felony or class 1 misdemeanor, the judge's finding of probable cause that the offense occurred means a petition must be filed. Even arresting officers are being given a greater voice in some jurisdictions. Their recommendation can be a factor in the diversion deliberation (NJ), or they actually can appeal an IO's decision not to file a petition to a judge or prosecutor (ME, MD, RI).

Most of the country has not distinguished the intake process and diversion decision for delinquents verses status offenders (apart from disqualifying some serious delinquents). Nevertheless, there are some differences for status offenders at the intake stage. For one thing, someone other than the IO, such as a juvenile department, may be authorized to conduct the review (CO, FL, MD). Victims may be denied any right to appeal a decision to not file a status offense petition (DC, VA) or may have to appeal to an IO instead of to a prosecutor (MD). A number of states have granted IOs more power to divert a status offense case compared to a delinquency (AR, CT, MA, NY). Moreover, several states (FL, KY, NV, NM, UT, VA, WA) demand that to file a status offense petition, previous services to the youth and family had to have either failed or been refused.

The Essence of Diversion

Diversion, which should be a relatively simple phenomenon, has instead become quite complex and confusing.[20] The confusion ranges from when diversion can happen to what to call it to what it can include. Addressing these items in reverse order, some observers suggest that diversion includes any measure or sentence that represents less than what the system theoretically could have done to the offender. Thus, an offender who could have been incarcerated but was not might be considered as having been diverted from institutionalization to probation (or community control). If these are the parameters of diversion, the concept loses its meaning. Remember, diversion was previously defined as kicking the case out of the system to allow the defendant to avoid acquiring a delinquent record. Diversion "to probation" does not provide for that avoidance of a record and consequently does not belong among examples of diversion.

There is no uniformity around the country as to the term by which the diversionary experience is known. The most frequently used term (and perhaps one that could be understood virtually everywhere) is informal adjustment.[21] The term literally means that the charges are being adjusted or resolved informally or without trial. Otherwise, this phenomenon is also known as:

informal probation (ID)	informal supervision (AK, CA, NV, TN)
informal agreement (LA)	diversionary agreement (AR, KY, MI, WA)
arbitration agreement (DE)	adjustment (AK, AZ, DC, NM, NY)
consent agreement (UT)	diversion (AZ, FL, IL, NH, NJ, NC, SD)
nonjudicial supervision (CT)	first-time offender program (OK, TX)
consent adjustment (MT)	formal accountability agreement (OR)
informally screened (OH)	nonjudicial adjustment (IL, UT)
informal action (SD, VA)	nonjudicial handling (FL)
pretrial diversion (MN, TN)	deferred prosecution (TX, WI)
informal disposition (ID, MT)	

Adding to the confusion are states that use more than one term to apply to this situation,[22] suggesting there are multiple diversion options when, in reality, there is only one. Even more confounding are the three states (KY, MT, TN) that actually have two different but almost identical diversion efforts. For example, Kentucky has a diversionary agreement that the IO monitors, while its juvenile court judge can grant an informal agreement (but the two do not appear to have any distinguishing features). The same applies to Tennessee, which has an informal adjustment that can run no longer than nine months, and also pretrial diversion that can last 12 months and requires a judge's approval, but otherwise the two diversions are the same. Finally, in Montana, while an informal disposition cannot involve probation or detention, a consent adjustment without a petition can entail numerous conditions (including detention).

Uniformity is also lacking regarding *when* diversion can occur. A few states provide simply that diversion can either precede or follow the filing of a petition (CO, KY, LA, MN, TN). However, most jurisdictions are adamant that diversion *must* occur before a petition is filed (or in lieu of a petition).[23] The suggestion here is that the decision to file a petition is equivalent to a commitment to prosecute the case that cannot be undone. However, some of these states also provide that, even after a petition is filed, the prosecutor can withdraw the petition or the judge can dismiss it with the purpose of placing the youth in a diversion program.[24] Even more confusing is the notion that diversion can occur *after* the youth is adjudicated delinquent—or, in other words, as a disposition or sentence (CO, ID, WV). Implied here is that the charges will then be retroactively dismissed by the judge (WV) or that juveniles will be allowed to "*un*-adjudicate" themselves by successfully completing a diversion program (and the delinquent record would then simply evaporate).

Exactly what is required for diversion to happen varies as well. We have already seen that certain offenses and records are disqualified and that the approval of one or more persons will be necessary. Assuming these hurdles have been overcome, other requirements remain in most jurisdictions. For example, numerous states insist that before a youth is put into a diversion program, proof must be presented that the youth committed an offense.[25] A number of states provide for a *special conference*—beyond the intake one—in which diversion is specifically negotiated between the IO and the youth.[26] In fact, all of these states, some of which are silent about a right to counsel generally at intake (MI, OR, UT, WA), identify this right at the *diversion conference*. In light of what diversion requires of a youth, and its potential impact on the youth in the future, it makes sense that before a case is resolved in this manner, the youth be entitled to consult with an attorney. A perfect example of the significance of diversion is that many states demand that the youth admit to having done what is alleged, typically holding that a denial of guilt would require an adjudicatory hearing to be held.[27] Interestingly, California does not require the youth to acknowledge guilt and furthermore holds that it is illegal to exclude youth from diversion when they deny involvement in an offense.

Being Put on Diversion

Most jurisdictions emphasize that diversion must be voluntarily accepted by the youth,[28] and must be intelligently accepted as well (IA, LA, ME, MI, SD). That is, the youth would have to realize that diversion could require the performance of a number of tasks and will constitute a waiver of the right to trial, including any speedy trial (CO, MS, NM) (see Chapter 13). Thus, the youth is giving up any chance of absolute vindication of the charges. Despite the important impact of diversion, few states appear to have insisted that youth be warned in detail of both the rights they are surrendering and the consequences they are accepting via diversion (GA, WA). To help ensure that the diversion is accepted voluntarily, most states also demand that the parent consent to this informal resolution of the case.[29] Finally, to help ensure that a youth is not taken advantage of while performing the tasks diversion will require, a growing number of states hold that the terms accepted by all parties must be placed in a written agreement.[30] It is quite probable today that most juvenile courts are using a written agreement even without a legislative command to do so.

Diversion Tasks

A few states note that the diversionary experience, in some cases, might involve no tasks on the part of the youth, aside from agreeing to stay out of trouble.[31] If this is the extent of the youth's obligations, there would seem to be nothing to distinguish this situation from that in which the IO takes "no action." There are two critical distinctions, however. First, even though the youth given no extra responsibilities on diversion would seem to have been given a "free ride," there will be a court record of the fact that a diversion has occurred. That means, unlike the youth with a "no action," the diversion youth has actually received an *adverse finding* (an assumption of the youth's guilt will exist) and would likely be ineligible for "another" diversionary effort if arrested a second time. Second, unlike the "no action" youth, the diverted juvenile would have the charges and case kept alive during the diversionary period. In fact, technically, this youth has "served time" for that offense. Thus, once the youth survives the diversion period without any other problems, the offense(s) that brought about the diversion could not resurface against the youth. The "no action" youth who is rearrested, on the other hand, could face trial on both the charges that led to the "no action" outcome *and* the charges that led to the second arrest.

Not all jurisdictions specify what diversion can entail. Unlike the old days, when a diversion could have been regarded as a "free ride," the current atmosphere seems to favor requiring the diversion period to be a meaningful experience. For example, California demands the diversion include "constructive assignments" to help juveniles "learn to be responsible for their actions." A few states say simply that any "reasonable" conditions can be imposed (DE, LA, ME, MD, NM, UT). In other jurisdictions, conditions usually include restitution and/or community service;[32] some type of counseling, education, job training, or even substance abuse treatment;[33] or counseling by a PO.[34] In fact, the conditions imposed via diversion can exceed those possible at disposition following adjudication. For example, while statutes often limit the amount of restitution a judge can impose by way of disposition following adjudication (see Chapter 14), it is not illegal for parties at diversion to agree to compensate a victim for all losses incurred in an amount that exceeds the possible sentence.

Diversion supervision should not be as intensive as that given to a youth who has been adjudicated delinquent. It is frequently referred to as informal probation. One of the latest versions of restitution is to refer the victim (if agreeable) and the youth to a restorative justice center or to victim-offender reconciliation (KS, ME, MN, MT, NE, NC, WA). The possibility of imposing a fine on the youth has been mentioned by only two states (UT, WA), while three others permit the suspension of a driver's license (IA, MD, MT). It appears that status offenders can also be subjected to these "reasonable" conditions, although Hawaii specifically prohibits any restitution orders in status offense cases.

Somewhat more controversial, and much less universal, is the issue of whether brief periods of detention are permitted in diversion programs for delinquents. The country is clearly divided, with a few states allowing some usually brief confinement,[35] some clearly prohibiting any detention,[36] and some not permitting detention unless it is otherwise permitted by the juvenile code (GA, MO, ND, TN). Similarly, few states thus far have specifically mentioned the possibility of imposing either house arrest (MT, WA) or a special curfew (WI) on youth via diversion. Nevertheless, these conditions could be implemented on a widespread basis.[37] Chapter 16 will explore the nature of diversion programs in greater depth.

Perhaps the most interesting development in this area is the court's authority to impose conditions on parents as well as on juvenile offenders. A growing number of jurisdictions have decided to require parents to pay for the diversion program, pay restitution, and/or attend counseling (particularly parenting-skill classes) as part of the diversion agreement.[38] In fact, the parents' failure to agree to these conditions can lead to a refusal to place the youth on diversion (FL, IN).

Another recent development within diversion has been the adoption of what are known variously as *teen*,[39] *youth* (AK, KS), or *neighborhood* (HI) *courts*. These courts will be described in greater detail in Chapter 16. They take diversion cases out of juvenile court and place them into community channels to be resolved. Community residents (often high school students) "adjudicate" the diverted youth and assign minimal sanctions. Typically, only nonserious offenses qualify for these courts—usually less serious offenses than those eligible for traditional diversion programs. In a few states, only status offenders (and perhaps some misdemeanants) are eligible for special diversion programs (OH), such as teen court (TX, WV) or a juvenile conference committee (AL).

The Length of Diversion

States vary in how long they allow a diversion program to run. Different diversions within the same state can have different time limits as well (and states may identify the limit for one program and not others). For example, California and Tennessee allow a longer limit for diversions in which a judge is involved. Moreover, some jurisdictions allow the diversionary period to be extended for a "good cause," such as completing a counseling program or paying restitution. Sometimes the length of the extensions is not specified. Table 9.1 demonstrates how much variation there is across the country, showing that the most commonly selected limit is six months. Delaware simply states that the diversion period shall not run beyond the period of time set by the court. Typically, then, youth will have somewhere between 6 and 12 months to satisfy the conditions agreed to in the diversion agreement.

Table 9.1 Time Limits For Diversion Programs (in months)*	
A.	Jurisdictions With Only One Time Limit Identified
	3: OK, UT
	6: AL, AK, AR, CA, CT, IL, IA, KY, ME, NJ, NC, OR, TX
	9: AR
	12: CA, CT, IL
B.	Jurisdictions With Original Periods and Extensions Identified
	2 + 2: NY, UT
	3 + 3: GA
	3 + 6: TN
	3 + ?: AZ, HI, MD
	6 + 3: PA
	6 + 6: CO, DC, IN, LA, MS, MO, TN, WA, WV
	9 + 6: ND
	12 + 24: WI

* States mentioned more than once have different limits for different programs.

Failure, Successful Completion, and Impact of Diversion

Three events could put an end to the diversion prior to the expiration of the time limit. If the youth completes the conditions earlier than expected, the PO can either suspend the remaining time or ask the court to do so. If the juvenile is not performing the tasks adequately (e.g., not attending counseling sessions), the PO can seek to terminate the diversion and to file (or refile) a petition containing the original charge (as well as a petition for subsequent charges, if any).[40] Finally, numerous jurisdictions specify that the youth and the parents are always free to reconsider the diversion agreement and to request its termi-nation.[41] Such a request could result in a petition being filed.

When POs attempt to file a petition on a diverted youth, they must demonstrate to the court (usually during the diversion time period) exactly how the youth failed in the diversion. This demonstration is much less formal than a trial and, depending on the judge's view of the juvenile's performance on diversion, could lead to an adjudicatory hearing on the charges that led to the diversion. Interestingly, in Kansas the admission required of the youth to enter diversion is equivalent to a guilty plea (it is phrased as a "stipulation to the charges"). Thus, assuming the diversion failure is proved, there is no need for a trial on the original charges. The youth stands adjudicated delinquent on those charges by virtue of the guilty plea and proof of the diversion failure. On the other hand, successful completion of the diversion tasks should mean that the charges (or petition) will be dismissed. It is difficult to imagine a petition being filed in this context. Nevertheless, only 21 states officially commit to this outcome,[42] while Nevada asserts that successful completions are grounds for a judge to dismiss a petition.

Youth placed on diversion are not considered adjudicated and thus will not have a delinquent record when they complete their programs (and the charges are dismissed). There will be a court record of the diversion, however, which usually disqualifies these juveniles from a second diversion effort. Some states do allow for multi-

Youth Studies Center: Should there be a limit on qualifying for diversion? Why do you think diversion fails in some cases?

ple diversion experiences, however, especially if only misdemeanors are committed (AZ, CO, CT, KS, NM). Similarly, a previous trip to teen court might preserve a subsequent diversion opportunity for youth who are arrested for a second time (again, most likely depending on the severity of the second offense). Although a diversion is not an adjudication, many jurisdictions announce that the diversion is material for the judge to consider at the disposition for any future offense adjudicated by juvenile court (AZ, HI, LA, OR, RI, UT, WA). In fact, Hawaii instructs its juvenile courts to inform all parties that an informal agreement is tantamount to an admission of the child's complicity in the offense, and that the diversion can be used at a later disposition hearing for a subsequent adjudication. Similarly, Washington openly identifies diversion as part of an offender's "criminal history." Inasmuch as diversions are certain to be noted in the youth's court file or record, they most likely will play a part in every juvenile court's reaction to a youth who continues to commit offenses after having been given a break via diversion.

Legally speaking, then, diversion should not be regarded as a free ride. It is likely to require certain tasks from the youth and can be used against a juvenile who gets into trouble again. In Iowa, schools are informed if any students who are 14 or older are put on diversion by virtue of committing an aggravated misdemeanor or felony. Diversion is certainly better for a juvenile's record than an adjudication, but it constitutes a more adverse finding than either a "no action" or an acquittal after trial.

Most research that has examined diversion has reported that juveniles placed in this alternative programming recidivate less frequently than those formally processed by the system (Campbell and Retzlaff 2000; Davidson et al. 1990; Frazier and Cochran 1986b; Gilbert 1977; Lipsey, Cordray, and Berger 1981; Pogrebin et al. 1984). Nevertheless, some studies have found no reduction of recidivism (Elliott et al. 1978; Lincoln 1976; Rojek and Erickson 1982) and that any intervention by the juvenile court (including diversion) increases labeling of the youth (Elliott et al. 1978; Lincoln 1976; Lipsey et al. 1981). One lesson learned from these examinations is that matching the youth to a specific program is critical to any chance of success in the diversion effort (Campbell and Retzlaff 2000).

Modern Aspects of Diversion

There is little doubt that states are taking diversion more seriously today. Several recent changes have made diversion less automatic and less trivial. Prosecutors have been granted significant authority in determining whether diversion will occur. Serious offenses and records have been disqualified by legislatures. Conditions or tasks can be as severe as those accompanying disposition following adjudication (such as full restitution to the victim). In fact, some observers have complained that diversion is just as intrusive or even more intrusive than formal processing by the system (Frazier and Cochran 1986b; Rojek and Erickson 1982). Parents are being required to perform some of the same tasks as their children and to bear some of the responsibility for monitoring their children's progress on diversion. Diversion lengths have been extended in some states to give juvenile court a longer period of control over the youth. Diversion records are being factored into dispositions for subsequent offenses committed by diverted youth. Finally, legislatures are starting to require juvenile court officials to keep detailed records and statistics on whom the court diverts and how well these juveniles perform on diversion as well as after completion of the diversion program (GA, MI, MN, NV, TX). The results of the data analysis could eventually have a serious impact on both how generously diversion is allocated and how leniently diversion is administered in the future. Official figures continue to show, nevertheless, that diversion remains an option frequently used by juvenile courts across the country.

Research on Who Is Diverted

The decision making surrounding the diversion option is complex. We have already seen that an incredible number of factors can influence this decision. Most likely, the two legal factors, offense and prior record, will be most influential. Many research studies have confirmed this finding (Bell and Lang 1985; Cohen and Kluegel 1978; Fenwick 1982; Grisso et al. 1988; McCarthy 1989; McCarthy and Smith 1986; Minor et al. 1997; Schwartz and Barton 1994; Sheldon and Horvath 1987; Thornberry 1973). However, research that examines only the juvenile court record of the current and prior offenses may not capture the full or true essence of the legal factors. For example, some misdemeanor offenses, such as reckless endangerment of others, could actually involve a near disaster in which one or more people barely escaped serious or near fatal injury and could be much more serious than many felonies. Moreover, not all crimes otherwise equal are truly equal, especially when committed with one or more fellow conspirators or in a gang-related situation (for instance, robbery is very different when committed by one versus several persons). Similarly, not all offenders are equally culpable. It is quite possible for multiple-offender crimes to involve different types of delinquents (for example, those who are leaders versus those who are followers) who play different roles in the offense (such as the lookout versus the gun-wielding thief). Despite these differences, all defendants involved in the criminal incident could be charged with the same offense. Even single-offender crimes can differ tremendously (such as a robbery with a gun versus a knife), while the charge can be the same (armed robbery). Finally, although statutes do not address this item, the type of offense that suggests serious potential underlying problems in the youth (prostitution, huffing glue or solvents, mutilation of animals) may be nondivertable in practice even though the law has not included the offense(s) within the disqualified group and even though the offenses are not particularly heinous (or even felonies).

Also, prior record could mean more to the court than a simple tally of previous arrests, diversions, or adjudications. The youth's having a court history pertaining to a dependency finding, including perhaps a placement outside of the home, could be relevant to determining whether a diversion program is the appropriate solution in a case.

Any factor other than offense and record is usually considered extralegal or nonlegal. The list of these nonlegal factors is lengthy and can include the following:

- **Child characteristics**

age*	emotional, medical, psychological problems
gender	substance abuse history
race/ethnicity	demeanor and cooperation
school record	willingness to admit offense*
work history	consent to diversion*

- **Family characteristics**

class status	demeanor and cooperation
court history	consent to diversion*
ability to help court	social service history
criminal and substance	abuse history

- **Situational characteristics**

court resources	victim consent to diversion*
community resources	defense attorney advice
program availability	IO and prosecutor orientation
strength of case	co-defendants' disposition

Strictly speaking, factors marked with an asterisk (*) could be identified as legal factors, since statutes frequently require these items in order to divert the case.

The factors associated with the child are self-explanatory. The final three are distinct but interrelated, and any one of them could preclude diversion. They deal with the youth's attitude during the intake process (or the way he or she "comes off" to the IO), and whether the youth will both offer an acknowledgment of guilt and accept the proposed terms of the diversion agreement.

While a couple of the family characteristics parallel the child's, most have to do with the family's financial or physical ability (assuming parents exist, of course) to resolve the youth's problems without formal court intervention and any prior history the family has had with either the juvenile justice system (previous children with delinquent problems or previous findings of dependency, neglect, or abuse of this child or others) or community agencies that address family problems. Moreover, a criminal past or drug dependency on the part of one or both parents could be perceived by the court as preventing diversion in some (or all) cases.

Finally, situational factors include the resources that are available generally to the juvenile court, whether as part of the juvenile system or in the local community. For example, an abundance of programs in the community coupled with relatively limited court resources could easily promote a high rate of diversion (with the reverse holding true as well). The lack of programs for girls as opposed to boys could have an impact, as could the temporary inability of a program to accommodate a particular youth at the moment of diversion. When crimes involve multiple defendants, it is possible for the IO (and/or the prosecutor) to prefer diversion to be all or nothing. That is, everyone is placed on diversion, or, if that is impossible because of the circumstances of one or more co-defendants, everyone is prosecuted, even though one or more of these youth would have been diverted had they committed the same offense alone or with only diversion-eligible defendants. Of course, either a victim's opposition to a proposed diversion plan, or a defense attorney's recommendation to the youth or parent to reject the diversion offer, could work to prevent diversion from happening. On the other hand, a weak case against the youth (e.g., possible illegally seized evidence or a reluctant witness or victim) could encourage a decision to divert what would otherwise be a case bound for prosecution.

A final consideration is the orientation of the IO and prosecutor (e.g., crime control, rehabilitation, due process). All the legal and extralegal variables are filtered through very different sets of eyes. For example, the same weak case that might tempt a rehabilitation or crime control person to divert the case could prompt a due process–oriented individual to dismiss it outright or to refer it to court so that the child's rights can be vindicated.

Some extralegal factors can be easily identified (e.g., gender and age), while others can be impossible to ascertain via court records (e.g., family ability and willingness to help, child's and parent's demeanor). The presence of some extralegal variables (e.g., race, gender, ethnicity, and social class) would raise concerns of fairness in the diversion decision, while the impact of others (e.g., age, cooperation of youth and parent) could be less controversial. The attempt to isolate the more controversial factors from the influence of other variables (such as separating race from parental ability and cooperation) to determine whether the diversion decision is being made "fairly" could prove impossible. To make an informed conclusion in this regard, research would need access to information that is often nonexistent or even immeasurable.

These complexities could explain why research studies are all over the map in trying to determine the extralegal factors associated with the diversion decision. For example, race has been found (Bishop and Frazier 1996; Dean et al. 1996; Leiber 1995; Leiber and Mack 2002, 2003; Leiber and Stairs 1999; Liska and Tausig 1979) and not found (Bell and

Lang 1985; McCarthy and Smith 1986; Cohen and Kluegel 1979; Sheldon and Horvath 1987) to be a decisive factor. Socioeconomic (or class) status should be a factor in some cases, particularly those in which parents can purchase a solution to the child's problem outside the system, but research has tended to find that it is not a factor (Tittle and Meier 1990). Race and the sociodemographics of the community (e.g., rate of poverty or minority population) can combine with items like the stability of the family and attitudes of the juvenile court workers towards race, crime, and the effectiveness of the juvenile system to affect those who are put on diversion (Leiber and Stairs 1999). Gender could easily be a factor, especially since some diversion programs are gender oriented. Again, the research findings conflict (*yes:* Cohen and Kluegel 1979; Rowe et al. 1995; Triplett and Myers 1995; *minimal:* McCarthy and Smith 1986; Shelden and Horvath 1987). Research has also found age (Leiber and Mack 2002; McCarthy 1989; Schwartz and Barton 1994) and demeanor (Bell and Lang 1985; Fenwick 1982) to influence the diversion outcome.

Some of the more advanced research is attempting to gauge the interactive effect of numerous factors. There have been interesting discoveries, such as that prior record may matter, depending on race and age, and that family stability may matter for one race but not another (Leiber and Mack 2002). The other extralegal factors remain unexamined, mostly because of their immeasurability or noninclusion in court records and databases scrutinized by researchers. In short, we do not know more than we think we know about the potential effect of extralegal variables on the diversion decision.

The Formal Prosecution Option

Cases that result in neither "no action" nor diversion are destined for further court processing. This does not mean that trial or adjudication is inevitable, however. For the moment, however, it does mean that a *petition* must be filed to enable further proceedings to occur. The petition is juvenile court's version of a criminal complaint or information. In fact, Washington uses the adult court term, *information,* rather than *petition.* In some states, the petition must include the same contents as a complaint or information (ME, MA, NE, WA). Most jurisdictions continue to use the traditional petition format that replicates most of what is contained in a complaint, but can also require information not found in a complaint. Typically, any petition issued by juvenile court should detail the following (although some statutes do not identify all of these items):

- Name, age, address of the youth
- Name and address of (each) parent
- Statement of facts (as to what the youth is alleged to have done)

Obviously, the criminal court complaint would not be concerned about the parent(s) of the offender. It is becoming more common for petitions to state also (like a complaint) the statute or law supposedly violated by the youth.[43] Some jurisdictions require *unique information* to be included in the petition, such as whether filing a petition is truly in the best interests of the child or the public,[44] or whether the defendant is being held in detention.[45] It is also possible that the victim's or petitioner's name and address would be cited in the petition (AK, KS, MT, OR).

Historically, in criminal court, only the prosecutor has been authorized to file an information or complaint. It is also becoming the norm in juvenile court for prosecutors alone to have the authority to file a petition, especially in delinquency cases.[46] Some of these jurisdictions suggest, however, that someone other than the prosecutor could file a delinquency petition (IA, LA, MD, NE, NV, SC). When status offenses are involved, it is even more likely that someone other than a prosecutor (especially a PO or the complainant) would be allowed to file a petition,[47] or that the petition would not require a prosecutor's approval (VT). Utah allows either the prosecutor or the judge to file a petition in juvenile court. Nevertheless, many states have maintained the traditional position that the IO or PO or perhaps even the complainant, a school official, or the arresting officer can file a petition is juvenile court.[48] Washington allows nonprosecutors to file petitions in delinquency cases involving misdemeanors but not felonies. It is possible that some of the 11 jurisdictions that do not specifically identify who is authorized to file a petition would also allow someone other than a prosecutor to do so.[49] In the end, this means that some prosecutions that could not be initiated in criminal court could be launched in juvenile court, since the prosecutor's approval is not always and everywhere required.

Most jurisdictions give a deadline for filing a petition when the youth is held in detention (see Appendix C). The same does not apply when the youth has been released. Only a handful of jurisdictions have established a petition-filing deadline in these cases (see Table 9.2). Comparing Table 9.2 and Appendix C discloses that the deadline for filing a petition is shorter for juveniles who have been detained than it is for youth who have been released. If the deadline is violated for detention cases, the most likely remedy required would be to release the youth from confinement. That would leave the door open for the charges to remain alive or, at worst, to be refiled against these youth at a later date. With respect to released juveniles, only Maine declares that violating the deadline (which is nine months) would result in not being able to prosecute a youth (ever) for the offense involved. In addition, Maine allows the prosecutor to be granted an extension by the court of unspecified length upon a showing of "good cause." In other words, these deadlines do not tend to carry serious consequences for prosecutors who ignore them.

A number of jurisdictions have adopted special prosecution measures (see Chapter 13) for certain serious offenders who are kept within the juvenile justice system instead of being transferred to criminal court (see Chapter 12). These special prosecutions allow significantly harsher and longer dispositions than those allotted the "ordinary" juvenile offender. Consequently, prosecutors who have decided to pursue these special measures must prepare a special petition that identifies the prosecutor's intentions and warns the youth of the potential outcome of the prosecution. These petitions may (1) identify the youth

Table 9.2 Deadline for Filing Petitions In Released Cases		
Jurisdiction	**Clock Starts**	**Deadline**
AL	Complaint received	14 days
DC	Complaint received	7 days*
ME	Complaint received	9 months
MD	Complaint received	25 days
MI	Diversion conference	30 days
MS	Complaint received	10 days
NC	Complaint received	15 days[†]
WI	Complaint received	20 days

* excludes Sundays and holidays
[†] can be extended 15 days

as a serious, habitual, or violent offender (CO, FL, IL, NV, PA); (2) concentrate on the behavior as a designated or serious felony (GA, NY); or (3) address the state's intention to seek extended control or confinement over the youth (KS, MN, MT). In some of these states, the petition also notifies defendants of a right to jury trial that does not exist for ordinary offenders (IL, KS, MN). Similarly, Washington calls for a special petition for any offense that involves a firearm, while Texas prosecutors who allege that a youth is a habitual offender must list all prior felony adjudications on the petition.

The Numbers at Intake

Delinquent Youth

As recently as 1989, half of the cases referred to intake were dismissed or handled informally. Since the beginning of the 1990s, we have seen a fairly steady decline in cases resolved in these ways and a corresponding increase in the percentage of cases resulting in formal prosecution. Between 1992 and 1999, 17–23 percent of all cases were dismissed, 23–26 percent were processed informally (i.e., diversion), and between 51 and 57 percent were formally prosecuted (see Table 9.3).

Between 1990 and 1999, the percentage of delinquency cases resulting in a formal petition increased 7 percent (from 50 to 57 percent). An increase was witnessed in all offense categories, with the exception of drug offenses. The biggest increase occurred in public order offenses (from 50 to 59 percent). The percentage of property offenses prosecuted climbed 7 percent (from 47 to 54 percent), while person offenses increased 5 percent (from 55 to 60 percent) and drug offenses declined 5 percent (from 66 to 61 percent). These data show that, despite the recent decline, drug crimes were the most likely to be prosecuted in juvenile court during these years. The number of prosecuted drug offenses increased 152 percent between 1989 and 1998, an increase greater than that for any other offense (Puzzanchera et al. 2003a).

In terms of an offense profile for 1999, petitioned cases consisted mostly of property offenses (40 percent), followed by person offenses and public order offenses (24 percent each), and drug crimes (12 percent). Nonpetitioned cases had the same pattern. Property offenses made up nearly half (45 percent) of the cases not prosecuted in juvenile court, followed by public order offenses (23 percent), person offenses (22 percent), and drug crimes (10 percent) (Puzzanchera et al. 2003b).

Year	Dismissal	Informal Processing	Formal Processing
1992	23	26	51
1993	23	24	53
1994	22	23	55
1995	21	24	55
1996	20	24	56
1997	19 (335,400)	24 (423,700)	57 (996,000)
1998	19 (327,800)	24 (429,300)	57 (1,000,300)
1999	17 (279,100)	26 (432,000)	57 (962,000)

Table 9.3 Percentage of Delinquency Cases Resolved by Types of Processing, 1992–1999

Source: Adapted from Butts (1994, 1996); Butts et al. (1996b); Stahl (1998, 1999, 2000, 2001, 2003).
Note: In the parentheses of the last three years reported are the whole numbers of cases with which these percentages dealt.

Both males (from 52 percent to 60 percent) and females (from 38 percent to 49 percent) experienced an increased likelihood that their cases would be formally prosecuted between 1990 and 1999. These numbers demonstrate that males have been and continue to be more likely than females to be prosecuted in juvenile court. In 1999, while males were most likely to be prosecuted for person and drug crimes (63 percent each), females were most likely to face trial for public order offenses (54 percent).

Whites (from 45 percent to 54 percent), blacks (from 60 percent to 65 percent), and youth from other races (from 51 percent to 53 percent) all experienced an increased likelihood of being formally prosecuted between 1990 and 1999, a pattern that held true for nearly every offense category. During this period, blacks were more likely than whites and

Figure 9.1 Juvenile Court Processing of Delinquency Cases, 1999

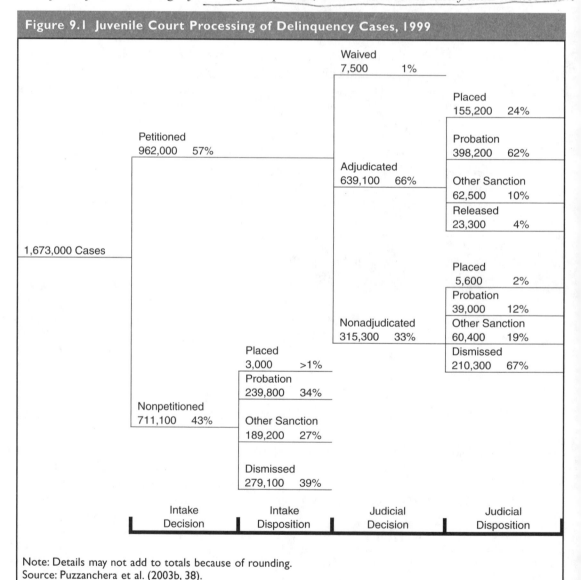

Note: Details may not add to totals because of rounding.
Source: Puzzanchera et al. (2003b, 38).

youth from other races to have their cases petitioned. In 1999, blacks (65 percent) experienced a much greater likelihood than whites (54 percent) and those from other races (53 percent) to be prosecuted in juvenile court. In fact, a higher percentage of blacks ended up being charged in all four offense categories (between 60 percent and 80 percent) than whites (between 53 percent and 57 percent) and youth from other races (between 48 percent and 58 percent). The biggest difference occurred in drug crimes, where blacks (80 percent) far outdistanced whites (54 percent) and youth from other races (56 percent) in the chance of facing trial for these charges. While whites (57 percent) and youth from other races (58 percent) were most likely to be prosecuted for person offenses, blacks were most likely to be charged with drug offenses.

Both those 15 years old and younger (from 47 percent to 55 percent) and those 16 and older (from 54 percent to 61 percent) witnessed an increased likelihood of being formally prosecuted between 1990 and 1999. In 1999, those in the older group (between 58 percent and 64 percent) were more likely than those in the younger group (between 52 percent and 59 percent) to be prosecuted in each of the four offense categories. This pattern held true for the entire decade (Puzzanchera et al. 2003b). These data show that older juveniles have been and continue to be more likely to be forced to face trial. Both age groups shared a pattern of being least likely to be prosecuted for property crimes and most likely to be prosecuted for drug offenses (Puzzanchera et al. 2003b).

Figure 9.1 provides an overall picture of how delinquency cases were resolved in 1999. Only the first column deals directly with the intake stage. It offers a good indication of how many cases that were not petitioned still ended in the juvenile system exercising some control over youth. The remaining columns show us how cases headed for processing through the juvenile system were resolved during that year.

Status Offenders

Between 1988 and 1997, the number of status offense cases formally prosecuted in juvenile court increased 101 percent (see Table 9.4).[50] Truancy and liquor violations (26 percent each) accounted for more than half of the cases petitioned in 1997. The miscellaneous category, which includes curfew violations and illegal behaviors such as smoking, experienced the sharpest rise in the percentage of status offense cases prosecuted. In 1997, they made up 20 percent of the petitioned cases, while running away (15 percent) and ungovernability (13 per-

Table 9.4 Number of Status Offense Prosecutions and Percent Change, 1988–1997

	Year			Percent Change
	1988	1993	1997	
All Offenses	79,000	112,300	158,500	101%
Runaway	12,400	19,900	24,000	93
Truancy	20,600	33,700	40,500	96
Ungovernable	12,900	14,900	24,000	65
Liquor	26,200	27,800	40,700	56
Miscellaneous	6,900	16,000	32,100	367

Source: Puzzanchera et al. (2000).

cent) charges were least likely to culminate in a juvenile court adjudicatory hearing (Puzzanchera et al. 2000).

Not only did youths age 15 and younger account for a majority (55 percent) of the status offense petitions filed in 1997, they dominated all offense categories but one (see Table 9.5). The younger juveniles were involved in 74 percent of truancy cases, 71 percent of ungovernability cases, 62 percent of runaway cases, and 53 percent of the miscellaneous charges. Older youth constituted a majority only in liquor violations (73 percent). This offense pattern was also reflected in the offense profile for 1997. While most younger juveniles were involved in truancies, most older youth were engaged in liquor violations.

These age-related status offense patterns held throughout the 1990s. Table 9.6 discloses the younger group's dominance of all offense categories, except liquor violations.

Table 9.5 Offense Profile of Petitioned Status Offenses by Age, 1997

Status Offense	Age	
	15 Years and Younger	16 Years and Older
Runaway	17%	13%
Truancy	34	15
Ungovernable	17	9
Liquor	12	42
Miscellaneous	19	21
Total	100%	100%

Source: Puzzanchera et al. (2000).

Table 9.6 Status Offense Profile During the 1990s

Age	Runaway	Truancy	Ungovernability	Liquor
10	0%	1%	1%	0%
11	1	3	3	0
12	4	6	6	1
13	11	14	14	2
14	22	23	22	7
15	28	30	25	16
16	25	16	20	33
17	10	7	9	42
Total	100%	100%	100%	100%

Source: Puzzanchera et al. (2003b).

Despite the younger group's dominance of those prosecuted for status offenses in juvenile court, the case rates against juveniles actually worsened or increased with each advancing year. That is, the rates of status offense prosecution per 1,000 youth in each age group increased as the age increased. This trend has existed for some time, as shown in Table 9.7. Note that the rate for each age group increased over the three time periods.

Males were involved in 59 percent of petitioned status offense cases in 1997, and accounted for a majority of the liquor violations (68 percent), ungovernability (55 percent),

Table 9.7 Petitioned Status Offense Case Rates, by Age, 1988–1997

Age	Year		
	1988	1992	1997
10	0.1	0.2	0.2
11	0.3	0.4	0.5
12	0.9	1.3	1.5
13	2.1	3.1	3.7
14	4.1	5.7	6.9
15	5.6	7.8	9.7
16	5.8	7.9	11.5
17	6.5	8.9	12.2

Source: Puzzanchera et al. (2000).

Table 9.8 Offense Profile of Petitioned Status Offenses by Gender, 1997

Status Offense	Male	Female
Runaway	10%	22%
Truancy	23	29
Ungovernable	13	14
Liquor	30	20
Miscellaneous	24	15
Total	100%	100%

Source: Puzzanchera et al. (2000).

and truancy cases (53 percent) that were prosecuted. Females (60 percent) dominated the runaway cases, as shown in Table 9.8. This gender distribution pattern remained virtually the same, within a percent or two, throughout the 1990s (Puzzanchera et al. 2003b). The number of petitioned cases increased for both males (from 46,900 to 92,700, or 98 percent) and females (from 32,000 to 65,800 or 105 percent) between 1988 and 1997. The biggest increase for both males and females between 1988 and 1997 was for the miscellaneous offenses, which experienced more than a 300 percent increase in both. Otherwise, while males witnessed their next largest increase in runaway prosecutions (105 percent), females experienced their second largest increase in liquor violations (108 percent) during this period.

Finally, the case rate for males (6.3) was higher than it was for females (4.7). The difference was greatest for older youths, especially those age 16 (13.7 versus 9.2) and 17 (16.0 versus 8.2) (Puzzanchera et al. 2000).

In 1997, whites were involved in a majority (78 percent) of the status offense cases that were formally prosecuted, a much higher percentage than that for blacks (18 percent) or youth from other races (4 percent). The difference was especially pronounced in liquor violations, where whites accounted for 90 percent of petitioned cases (see Table 9.9). In the other four categories, whites made up between 73 percent and 75 percent of the prosecutions. As in the situation of gender, this race distribution stayed the same, within a percent or two, throughout the 1990s (Puzzanchera et al. 2003b). However, the case rate for blacks (6.7) was higher than it was for both whites (5.4) and youth from other races (4.0). Between 1988 and 1997, the number of petitioned cases increased 96 percent for whites (from 63,000 to 123,500), 122 percent for blacks (from 13,000 to 28,900), and 104 percent for youth from other races (from 3,000 to 6,100).

Table 9.9 Offense Profile of Petitioned Status Offenses by Race, 1997

Status Offense	White	Black	Other Races
Runaway	14%	19%	15%
Truancy	24	33	21
Ungovernable	13	18	7
Liquor	30	8	26
Miscellaneous	19	21	31
Total	100%	100%	100%

Note: Details may not total 100% because of rounding.
Source: Puzzanchera et al. (2000).

Summary: Key Ideas and Concepts

- POs losing historically uncontrolled power over intake
- Social work or rehabilitation mentality prevailing at intake
- Different emphasis on diversion in juvenile court versus criminal court
- Pursuit of individualization in juvenile court, rather than equality
- Implications of pursuing individualization
- Three options available to the intake officer
- Influence of labeling theory on diversion
- Goals of diversion versus problems of diversion
- Nature of the preliminary inquiry
- Numerous and varied factors affecting diversion decision
- Prosecutorial control of intake and diversion
- Offenses disqualified from diversion
- People who can serve as obstacles to diversion
- Potential differences for diverting delinquents versus status offenders
- Confusion as to what qualifies to be called diversion
- Variety and confusion of names for informal adjustment
- Rights surrounding the diversion decision
- Tasks that can be required via diversion
- Placing conditions on parents via diversion
- Teen courts as examples of diversion

- Reasons for early termination of diversion
- Consequences of failing on diversion
- Legal impact of diversion
- Recent changes to dimensions of diversion
- Difficulty in researching factors related to diversion
- Unique aspects of the juvenile court petition
- Nonprosecutors filing petitions in juvenile court
- Special petitions as examples of juvenile court's second tier

Discussion Questions

1. What are the implications of using a social work mentality at the intake stage?

2. Do the advantages of diversion outweigh the disadvantages? How or why not?

3. Who should control the diversion decision—the PO or the prosecutor? What are the implications of either one of these individuals controlling the decision?

4. Should certain offenses be excluded from the opportunity of diversion? If no, why not? If yes, which offenses?

5. Should the victim have a vote as to whether diversion should occur? If so, how much impact should the victim's position have?

6. What rights should a youth have at the diversion stage?

7. What, if any, conditions should be possible in the diversion situation? Should detention be one of them, and if so, with what limits?

8. What are the implications in having a parent agree to and participate in diversion? Should parents be allowed to reject a diversion opportunity for their children?

9. Should diversion be used for subsequent sentencing purposes in juvenile court? Why or why not?

10. Should nonprosecutors be allowed to file a petition in juvenile court? Why or why not?

Endnotes

1. The states that authorize POs to receive complaints from these sources are: AL, AZ, AR, CA, FL, GA, IL, IN, IA, KY, MD, MO, NJ, NM, NY, ND, PA, TN, VT, VA.
2. These individuals are called intake officers or workers in AL, AR, GA, IN, IA, KS, MD, MS, NC, OH, OK, RI, SC, SD, TN, TX, UT, VA, WI.
3. An indictment may be required to prosecute some juveniles in criminal court in some states (e.g., FL, TX), but states do not require an indictment to prosecute an offender in the juvenile system. The one exception to this rule is that Texas requires an indictment to prosecute offenders in juvenile court who are eligible for determinate sentencing there.

4. The jurisdictions that assign the PO to monitor the diversion program are: AL, AZ, AR, CA, CT, DC, FL, GA, HI, ID, IL, IN, IA, KY, LA, ME, MD, MS, MO, MT, NV, NH, NJ, NM, NY, NC, ND, OK, OR, PA, RI, SD, TN, TX, UT, VA, WA, WV, WI, WY.

5. The states that require POs to refer youth to community agencies are: AL, AR, CA, FL, GA, IL, KS, KY, MO, MT, NM, NC, ND, PA, RI, SC, TN, VT, WI.

6. The jurisdictions that refer to this stage as a preliminary inquiry are: AL, AK, DC, ID, IN, IA, KY, MD, MI, MS, MO, MT, NM, OK, SC, UT.

7. Six states (AR, CT, CO, RI, SD, TX) call this process a preliminary investigation. In addition, while Maryland calls this proceeding a jurisdictional inquiry, North Carolina refers to the process as a preliminary determination.

8. The jurisdictions that refer to this meeting as an intake conference are: AL, AR, CA, DC, FL, HI, KS, ME, MD, NJ, NC, OH, SC, TN, TX, VA, WA. Other names given this meeting are intake inquiry (WI), initial interview (CT), child interview (IN), preliminary conference (IL), preliminary probation conference (NY), and arbitration conference (DE).

9. The states that recognize a youth's right to counsel at this stage are: AK, AR, CT, CO, DE, GA, HI, IN, IA, MS, MO, RI, TN, WI.

10. The states that recognize a right to silence at this stage are: AK, AR, GA, IN, IA, MO, RI, TN, WI.

11. The states holding that a youth's statement cannot be used at all at a later stage are: DE, IN, ME, MI, MT, PA, SC, TN, TX, VA, WI.

12. The jurisdictions that prohibit the use of any statement at a subsequent trial are: CA, CT, DC, GA, HI, IL, LA, ME, MD, NV, NY, ND, OR, RI, UT.

13. Alaska openly admits intake statements as evidence at trial, but juveniles are warned specifically of this possibility.

14. The jurisdictions that make all parties' appearance at intake voluntary are: AK, AR, DE, DC, HI, IL, IA, NY, NM, UT, WI.

15. The jurisdictions that instruct IOs to be guided by the youth's (and perhaps the public's) best interests are: AL, AK, AR, CA, CO, CT, DC, FL, GA, HI, ID, IN, IA, KS, ME, MD, MI, MS, MO, MT, NE, NV, NM, NY, ND, OH, OK, PA, RI, SC, TN, TX, UT, VT, VA, WV, WI, WY.

16. The jurisdictions that give prosecutors supervisory power over diversion decisions are: AZ, AR, CA, CO, DC, FL, ID, KY, LA, MN, MT, OK, SC, SD, WA, WI.

17. The states that require a judge's consent to diversion are: KY, MT, NJ, NY, TN, UT.

18. The jurisdictions that allow victims to appeal this decision to a prosecutor are: CA, DC, FL, IA, ME, MD, MT, NV, NC.

19. Five states (HI, NJ, RI, VA, WA) allow victims to appeal this decision to a judge.

20. Four jurisdictions (FED, MA, VT, WY) have no statutory provision or court rule on diversion, and some other locations (e.g., OH) have little information on the practice in their juvenile code.

21. The states that refer to diversions as informal adjustment are: AL, AK, CO, GA, HI, IL, IN, IA, KY, ME, MD, MS, MO, MT, ND, OK, PA, RI, SC, SD, TN, UT, VA, WY.

22. The states that use more than one term here are: AK, AZ, FL, ID, IL, MT, OK, SD, TX, UT, VA.

23. The states that insist the diversion must occur before a petition is filed are: AL, AK, AZ, CA, FL, GA, HI, ID, IN, ME, MI, MS, MT, NV, NH, NM, NY, NC, OH, OK, PA, RI, SC, SD, VA, WV, WI.

24. Eight states (AL, CA, GA, ID, MS, NV, NH, WI) allow diversion after a petition is filed, although the statute suggests otherwise.

25. The states that demand proof of an offense prior to diversion are: AL, CA, CO, FL, HI, IN, IA, ME, MD, NC, OR, TN, TX, VA, WA, WI.

26. The states that provide for a special diversion conference are: AL, AK, MI, MS, MO, OR, RI, TN, UT, WA.

27. The states that demand the youth admit committing the offense before diversion is permitted are: AL, AZ, AR, CT, GA, HI, ID, IA, KS, MS, MO, NV, ND, OK, PA, RI, SD, TN, UT, WV, WI.

28. The jurisdictions that insist that diversion be voluntary on the youth's part are: AL, AZ, AR, CT, DC, FL, GA, HI, IA, LA, ME, MI, MS, MO, MT, NV, NC, ND, OR, PA, RI, SD, TN, TX, WA, WV.

29. The states that require a parent to consent to diversion are: AL, AK, AR, CA, CT, FL, GA, HI, IN, IA, LA, ME, MD, MI, MS, MO, MT, NV, NH, NJ, NC, ND, OR, PA, SD, TN, TX, UT, WV, WI.

30. A written agreement is required in: AR, DE, GA, IL, IA, LA, MI, MT, NV, NJ, OR, UT, WA, WI. In North Carolina, a written agreement is discretionary.

31. The states that allow no tasks be required of youth on diversion are: AK, AZ, CA, GA, MS, MT, PA, WA, WV.

32. The states that provide restitution or community service as a condition of diversion are: AK, AZ, CA, CO, CT, DE, FL, GA, HI, ID, IL, IA, KY, ME, MD, MN, MS, MT, NV, NJ, NY, NC, OR, TX, UT, VA, WA, WI.

33. The jurisdictions that provide for counseling-like activities on diversion are: AL, AZ, AR, CA, CO, CT, DC, GA, HI, ID, IL, IA, KY, MD, MN, MS, MT, NJ, NC, OR, TN, TX, UT, WA, WI.

34. The states that call for supervision by a PO on diversion are: AL, AR, CA, CO, CT, ID, IL, IA, MD, TX, WI.

35. The states that allow for brief detention during diversion are: AL, CA, HI, ID, IL, IA, MS, MT, NC.
36. The states that prohibit detention during diversion are: AK, NJ, NY, PA, TX, WA, WI.
37. Other possible conditions include book reports, jail visits, and letters of apology, among other tasks.
38. The jurisdictions that permit parents to be required to attend counseling are: AL, AZ, CA, DE, DC, FL, HI, IN, KS, MN, MS, NJ, NC, SC, TX, UT, WI.
39. The states that call this diversion teen court are: AR, CO, FL, IL, MS, NM, NC, OK, TX, WV, WI.
40. The jurisdictions that call for a PO to file a petition when diversion is not completed successfully are: AL, AZ, AR, CA, CT, DC, GA, HI, IA, KY, LA, MD, MI, MS, MO, NJ, NM, NY, NC, OR, RI, TN, TX, VA, WA, WV, WI.
41. The states that allow the youth and parent to withdraw from diversion are: AR, IA, MS, MO, NV, NJ, OR, RI, TN, WI.
42. The states that demand the petition be dismissed when diversion is completed successfully are: AK, AZ, AR, CA, CT, DE, IA, KY, LA, ME, MI, MN, NJ, NM, NC, OK, TN, TX, UT WI.
43. The jurisdictions that require the statute involved to be listed on the petition are: AZ, AR, CA, CO, DE, DC, FL, GA, IN, IA, KS, LA, MD, MO, MT, NH, NJ, NM, NY, OH, OK, RI, SD, TX, VA, WI, WY.
44. The jurisdictions that require a statement that court intervention is in the youth's best interests are: AL, DC, GA, IL, IN, MT, NY, ND, PA, VT.
45. The states that require the petition to reflect whether the youth is in detention are: Al, AZ, AR, CA, KY, MT, NV, NM, NY, ND, PA, TN, VT, VA, WI, WY.
46. The jurisdictions in which only prosecutors can file a petition are: AZ, AR, CA, DE, DC, FL, IL, IN, IA, LA, ME, MD, MI, MS, MT, NE, NV, NM, NY, OK, SC, SD, TX, VT, WA, WI, WY.
47. The states that allow someone other than a prosecutor to file a petition in some cases are: AR, CA, CT, IL, IN, IA, MD, NV, NJ, NY, OR, WI.
48. The states that allow a complainant to file a petition are: AL, GA, ID, KS, MN, NH, NJ, NC, ND, OH, RI, TN, WV.
49. The jurisdictions that do not identify who is authorized to file a petition are: AK, CO, CT, FED, HI, KY, MA, MO, OR, PA, VA.
50. Unlike the data for delinquencies, which cover 1999, the most recent reports with detailed information for status offenses are for the year 1997. In addition, there is no recent graph (like Figure 9.1) for the nationwide processing of status offenders. The only graphs available are those that depict what happened to a typical 1,000 petitioned runaway, truancy, ungovernability, and liquor law violation cases. They will not be presented in this text. ✦

The Juvenile Court: The Preliminary Stages

- Chapter 10: Detention
- Chapter 11: The Pretrial Stage
- Chapter 12: Transfer to Criminal Court

Focus of Section IV

Section IV explores the initial stages of the official juvenile court process. First, we discuss the important detention decision. As Chapter 10 examines, the decision to detain a youth pending trial is critical to this individual, not only in the deprivation of liberty experienced via detention, but also in the effect detention has on the youth's trial and sentencing. During the pretrial stage, the case involving the youth must either be prepared for trial or informally resolved, often through plea bargaining. We will see in Chapter 11 how well (or not) plea bargaining and other accommodations fit in juvenile court. Finally, some cases seemingly headed for processing in juvenile court are channeled, instead, into criminal court. Chapter 12 analyzes the decision to transfer a youth to criminal court, arguably the most important decision made regarding the fate of the alleged delinquent. ✦

Detention

Focus of Chapter 10

Chapter 10 examines the nature of the decision to detain a youth pending trial in juvenile court. In this chapter we will see how detention for juveniles differs from that for adults. We will see also that bail has traditionally been denied to juveniles and that this is not necessarily to their disadvantage. The chapter explores the rationales for detention, some of which are unique to the juvenile system, and analyzes the detention hearing. The decision to detain youth is one of the most important in the juvenile system. There is not only the potentially adverse effect of confinement, but also the likelihood of a significant, negative impact on later stages of the case, particularly at trial and sentencing.

Key Terms

- detention
- Detention Diversion Advocacy Project
- detention hearing
- Juvenile Detention Alternative Initiative
- mandatory initial detention
- presumptive detention
- preventive detention
- risk (or needs) assessment
- shelter care

POs as the Gatekeepers to Detention

In Chapter 7 we saw how JPOs, unlike their adult court counterparts, serve as a reception committee for youth arrested by the police and that this stage in the process is referred to as intake (see Chapter 9). While the PO is considering whether to charge the youth by filing a petition, the question of detention will arise for some youth. With status offenders the term shelter care is typically used instead of detention. Historically, detention was defined as the temporary, pretrial custody of a delinquent in a physically secure setting, meaning that the youth was placed in a secure or jail-like structure and was unable simply to walk out of the facility at will. Shelter care, on the other hand, usually involved a location that was not characterized by locked doors or cells. Although shelter care has retained this feature, the dynamics of detention today not only make the traditional definition obsolete, but also make it difficult to develop a comprehensive description of its current practice.[1]

Usually the PO or a staff member of the detention facility will be the one who makes the initial decision to detain a youth (awaiting review by a judge or master or referee).[2] Some states, however, authorize the police (AK) or a prosecutor (WY) to determine whether to allow the child to remain at home pending trial.

Humane Detention

Because of the potential trauma surrounding the removal of a child from the home, statutes have promoted the notion that detention should be the exception and not the rule in juvenile court. This same idea surfaces at the disposition hearing when the sentencing decision is reached (see Chapter 14). Moreover, when detention is required, legislatures have announced that juveniles should be confined in a humane setting. For example, the California and Nevada statutes instruct that "any detention home must be constructed and conducted as nearly like a home as possible and must not be deemed to be or treated as a penal institution." Similarly, the Georgia legislature has gone so far as to declare that detention should reflect the following values:

• Respect for the privacy, dignity, and individuality of the child and the family

• Protection of the psychological and physical health of the youth

• Tolerance of diverse values and preferences

• Assurance of equality of treatment by race, class, ethnicity, and gender

• Avoidance of regimentation, depersonalization, and stigmatization

In short, detention in juvenile justice is designed to differ physically and spiritually from jail in criminal justice.

Moreover, as we saw in Chapter 7, most jurisdictions continue to subscribe to traditional principles by announcing that there is a presumption of release to parents for juveniles taken into custody by the police, and most jurisdictions have contributed to the probability of this release by allowing the parents to sign a written promise to return the child to court for future hearings. This written promise enables juvenile court to find the parents in contempt of court if they fail to produce the child at a later date.

Nevertheless, not all detention centers look and operate equally. Although the county runs most, some are operated by the state, some are operated by the court, and still others are privately run. It would be reasonable to expect serious differences among these facilities just by virtue of the body that oversees its operation (Dedel 1998). One recent study reported that detention centers were operating adequately when it came to food, clothing, hygiene, recreation, and living accommodations. Problems existed, however, in such areas as living space, health care, institutional safety, and control of suicidal and assaultive behavior by inmates (on staff and other inmates) (Allen-Hagen 1993). Perhaps the most critical problem facing detention centers is overcrowding. Between 1985 and 1992 the average daily population in public detention centers rose 72 percent. During this period there was a 642 percent increase in the number of overcrowded detention centers. The situation has not improved—in 2000 more than 60 percent of juveniles were admitted to an overcrowded detention center (Lubow and Barron 2000; Wordes and Jones 1998).

To some extent this overcrowding has to be the result of expanding those eligible to be held in detention from the traditional group awaiting trial, disposition, or a bed in a facility to juveniles who are serving short sentences of incarceration (see Chapter 14). Also contributing to the overcrowding is the fact that between 1984 and 1994, the average length of stay in detention increased from 12 to 15 days (Wordes and Jones 1998). Finally, simple overuse of detention and the absence or misuse of alternatives to secure detention have been credited with overcrowding many detention centers (Lubow 1997).

The Detention Alternative Movement

Although detention in the juvenile system is relatively humane and rarely imposed, it carries enough of a stigma and adverse consequences for youth that a recent movement has emerged seeking to develop alternatives for those who would otherwise be bound for a detention center. The Detention Diversion Advocacy Project (DDAP) began operation in San Francisco in the early 1990s. The project targeted juveniles headed to or already held in secure detention. Project representatives constructed a release plan that was presented to the juvenile court judge. The plan included services (tutoring, drug and family counseling) that would be offered youth during the pretrial period. The objective was to send the youth home or to an alternative, less restrictive detention site, offer the services, and encourage the youth to meet certain goals, such as achieving good grades in school, staying off drugs, and paying restitution to the victim. A project representative maintained daily contact with the youth in the community and provided the youth and the family with constant support. A 1999 evaluation of the project revealed encouraging results. There were 271 youth in the project and 542 in a comparison group. The project group had more males, more older juveniles, and more who had experienced previous placements in the system as opposed to the comparison group (which had, however, more youth with more than three previous referrals to court). Nevertheless, the performance of the project youth surpassed that of the comparison group on many outcomes, as shown in Table 10.1.

The DDAP relied on case management, which "seeks to integrate services across a cluster of organizations, to ensure a continuity of

Table 10.1 Outcomes of Detention Diversion Advocacy Project

Outcomes	Project Youth	Comparison Group
Recidivism rate	34%	60%
Two or more subsequent referrals	14	50
Return on a violent charge	9	25
Two or more subsequent petitions	5	22
Subsequent placement	18	24

Source: Shelden (1999).

care, and to facilitate development of client skills" (Shelden 1999, 5). The DDAP involved a variety of service providers and extended intensive supervision for the entire pretrial period, including placement in community-based programs (Shelden 1999).

Another group, the Annie E. Casey Foundation, has funded the Juvenile Detention Alternative Initiative (JDAI) in four sites (Cook County, Multnomah County, New York City, and Sacramento County) with four objectives:

- To eliminate the inappropriate or unnecessary use of secure detention
- To minimize failures to appear and the incidence of delinquent behavior
- To redirect public finances to responsible alternative strategies
- To improve conditions in secure detention facilities

The JDAI built on reforms that had been launched in Broward County, Florida, where the average daily detention population between 1987 and 1992 was reduced from 160 to 56 youth. Except for Cook County, each site achieved substantial reductions in detention admissions between 1994 and 1996. Cook County did achieve a reduction in the last year of the project, but this followed an increase in admissions between 1994 and 1995. Including Cook County, admissions were down for all four sites by 7 percent at the end of 1996, which meant a reduction of 14 percent for the other three sites. Sacramento County experienced the largest reduction (15.5 percent) in the two-year project (Lubow 1997). By the end of the project in 1998, all but New York City had absorbed the JDAI innovations into their juvenile justice policies (Stanfield 1999).

Detention Settings

Alleged delinquents can be located in a variety of settings while being considered, legally, as under a detention order (which makes detention difficult to define). Every state has something in the way of a secure or nonsecure detention home, center, or facility. In many states, detention exists in "levels," referring to the amount of physical control over the youth or the security of the setting. The more secure the facility, the more likely it is to:

- resemble a jail, which warehouses inmates more than offering treatment-oriented programs;
- be characterized by relatively harsh conditions;
- be populated by the worst juvenile offenders in terms of current offense and prior record; and
- be county- or state-run.

None of these descriptions is universal or necessary, however. Some secure detention homes look like schools, are new and clean, offer serious educational and recreational programs, and house status offenders. Nevertheless, many states completely prohibit putting status offenders in detention,[3] and those that permit it typically restrict it to serious situations, as we will see.

Many states provide numerous alternatives to these centers under the umbrella of detention. Examples of these alternatives range from child welfare licensed facilities[4] to foster, group, or private homes[5] to the defendant's own home (often referred to as house arrest)[6] to the rather ambiguous "any other suitable place."[7] Detention sites identified less commonly in the statutes include work camps (AK), holdover (AR, CO, KY, ME) or youth residential (KS) facilities, and community diversion programs (ID, MT, NV). Some jurisdictions even permit delinquents to be placed in shelter care with status offenders, especially if the crime involved is not particularly serious or violent and the youth is rather young in age or small in stature.[8]

The presence of these alternatives makes detention a varied phenomenon. It includes not only placement in a juvenile jail-like facility (as well as adult jail, which we will consider presently), but also being sent home or to someone else's house. Obviously, then, not all detention experiences are equal, or even similar, making detention difficult to study and understand. Moreover, the lack of universal terms in this area makes researching and analyzing detention even more difficult. For example, whereas Montana equates home detention with shelter care placement, Tennessee denies that shelter care is the same as detention. Whereas Maine specifies that group, foster, and private homes are actually instances of conditional release rather than detention, Minnesota holds that "all liberty restrictions affecting the defendant's physical freedom or living arrangements" (including the youth's home) are included within the parameters of detention. Sometimes the names used to refer to a public detention center can be misleading as well. For example, in San Francisco the Youth Guidance Center serves as the detention center. For the most part, shelter care is less amorphous in that it remains limited to smaller or larger (i.e., foster versus group homes) residential, nonsecure facilities (perhaps referred to as community-based shelters).

Besides the *release whenever possible policy*, traditional juvenile justice philosophy called for POs to select the *least restrictive setting* for those youth bound for detention. Nineteen jurisdictions continue to endorse this requirement specifically in their statutes, although Minnesota's provision here applies only to status offenders.[9] The least-restrictive-setting mandate creates an affirmative duty on the part of the decision maker to establish, typically on the record or transcript of the detention hearing, that holding the youth in a less secure or restrictive location than the one chosen is inappropriate and likely to undermine the reasons behind detaining the youth in the first place. Like the presumption of release, the least-restrictive-setting directive arises again at the disposition hearing (see Chapter 14).

Juveniles in Jail

Selecting the location of detention becomes especially controversial in two situations: placing the delinquent in jail and committing the status offender to either a detention center or jail pending an adjudicatory hearing. Incarcerating juveniles with adults, however briefly, seems to violate the very essence of juvenile justice philosophy and the need for a separate system for youth. Congress agreed with this sentiment when it passed the Juvenile Justice and Delinquency Prevention Act (JJDP) of 1974. What the act sought to prevent were two situations. First, it prohibits the placing of any youth in adult facilities, such as jails and lockups. Second, the act prohibits placing status offenders in secure detention, so as to reduce both stigma and the chances of physical harm to these youth.

Room conditions at a detention center can be similar to a jail cell. Are detained youth pressured to plead guilty in order to secure release from detention?

Perhaps placing delinquents in jail seems less egregious when the juvenile defendant is forced to stand trial in criminal court rather than in juvenile court. The 1974 act was subsequently amended to allow jail if the youth is certified to or convicted in adult court. In this situation the youth is considered legally an adult and thus entitled to all the rights and disadvantages associated with being an adult defendant. For juveniles who have been subject to mandatory exclusion from juvenile court, because of age or record (see Chapter 4), the only legal option is to detain them (assuming release is not possible) with "fellow" adults, since adult status has been conferred on them. Juveniles excluded from juvenile court via transfer to adult court (see Chapter 12) present more of a choice, since these individuals are juveniles chronologically, were originally under the juvenile court's jurisdiction, and likely began their detention experience in the juvenile system (i.e., before the transfer hearing).

Thus, although transfer is possible in every jurisdiction, only 34 jurisdictions provide that transferred juveniles are subject to being jailed (see Table 10.2). Nine of these states demand, moreover, that these youth be held separately from adult inmates,[10] while California and Ohio insist on special supervision as well. In Florida and Georgia, juveniles transferred to adult court can be jailed only if their crimes are felonies (FL) or are violent or capital (GA). While Wisconsin places a minimum age of 15 on those who can be jailed, Minnesota and Oregon have selected 16 as the cutoff. Jailing these adult court-bound juveniles in California, Georgia, and New Jersey requires a special determination (via a hearing or court order) that allowing them to remain in detention is detrimental to society, to the defendant, or to other juveniles held in detention. Similarly, youths who have been transferred from juvenile court in Nevada can petition the court to be held in juvenile detention rather than in jail, while prosecutors in Colorado have the authority to permit this result as well. With all these caveats in mind, the point is that substantial numbers of chronological juveniles who have been transferred to criminal court, together with those who have been sent there via mandatory exclusion, are subject to being jailed, perhaps for a considerable length of time, while awaiting trial.

Even more jurisdictions (40) have authorized the jailing of delinquents who will be prosecuted in the juvenile system (see section B in Table 10.2). The JJDP Act currently permits the jailing of delinquents for limited periods and for specific purposes, which numerous states have adopted. Most jurisdictions justify this practice as a sometimes necessary evil to facilitate the processing of a charge against a youth, especially with respect to fingerprinting and photographing the accused (FL, OH, SC), or to hold the youth temporarily for transport to a distant detention center. Not every county or political subdivision has a detention center available, so transportation to the nearest one could be lengthy. A number of jurisdictions use a minimum age requirement in the jail context while mandating the physical separation of these delinquents from adults (see Table 10.2). Moreover, the statutes typically stress that the separation must apply also to visual and sound contact, dining arrangements, and educational and recreational programs. For most of these juveniles, jail will be a brief experience. Statutes tend to permit this jailing to last somewhere between three and six hours, with 24 hours reserved usually for locations that are far removed from major population centers. In addition, nine states call for extra supervision of delinquents in jail, with Florida prohibiting more than 15 consecutive unsupervised minutes and Ohio demanding direct supervision at all times. Finally, eight states specify that jailing delinquents is allowed only when no alternative juvenile detention facility is available (see Table

Table 10.2 Jailing Juveniles

A.	Jurisdictions Jailing Defendants Transferred to Adult Court
	AL, AK, AZ(s), AR, CA(s), CO(s), DC, FL(s), GA(s), HI, IL(s), IA(s), KS, LA, ME, MD, MN, MS, MT, NV, NJ, ND, OH(s), OK, OR, PA, SC, SD(s), TN, TX, UT, VA, WI, WY
B.	Jurisdictions Jailing Juvenile Delinquents
	AL(s), AK(s), AZ(s), AR(s), CA(s), CO(s), DC(s), FL(s), HI(s), ID(s), IL(s), IN(s), IA(s), KS(s), ME(s), MA(s), MI(s), MN(s), MS(s), MT(s), NE(s), NV(s), NH(s), NJ, NM, NY, ND(s), OH(s), OK(s), OR, PA(s), SC(s), SD(s), TN(s), TX(s), VT(s), VT, VA(s), WA(s), WI(s)
C.	Minimum Age for Jailing Juvenile Delinquents
	10 years of age: SC
	12 years of age: IL
	14 years of age: CA, IA, MA, MN, SD, VA
	15 years of age: MI, WI
	16 years of age: DC, NE

(s) = Youth must be held in own cell or separate from adults.

Table 10.3 Additional Controls Over Jailing Delinquents

A.	Time Limits
	3 Hours: CA, (status offenders + misdemeanors), OH (misdemeanors)
	5 Hours: OR
	6 Hours: AK, AZ, CA (felonies), CO, FL, GA, HI, IL, IN, IA, KS, ME, MS, MT, NH, OH (felonies), OK, SC, SD, UT, VA
	24 Hours: AK, AR, HI, IA, LA, ME, MT, NH, OK, WA
	48 Hours: TN (serious offenders)
	Brief: NJ
B.	Supervision
	AL, CA, FL, ID, IL, IN, ME, OH, WI
C.	No Juvenile Facility
	HI, IA, ME, MT, NV, NJ, ND, TN
D.	Menace to Other Delinquents or Society
	CA, DC, HI, ME, MI, MT, ND, TN, UT, VT, VA, WI

10.3). One recent development that may reduce the number of juveniles held in jail in this context is that a few states (IN, MO, OK, TN) have already given a green light to construct detention centers and jails in the same building or on the same grounds, provided there is spatial separation between the facilities as well as distinction between program activities and staff. Not surprisingly, most statutes officially prohibit the jailing of status offenders.[11]

Table 10.4 Juveniles in Local Jail			
Year	As Juveniles	As Adults	Total
1993	1,000	3,300	4,300
1994	1,600	5,100	6,700
1995	1,800	5,900	7,700
1996	2,400	5,700	8,100
1997	2,098	7,007	9,105
1998	1,548	6,542	8,090
1999	860	8,598	9,458
2000	1,489	6,126	7,615
2001	856	6,757	7,613
Source: Adapted from Beck (2000); Beck and Karberg (2001); Beck et al. (2002); Gilliard (1999).			

Despite these controls that point to the limited, emergency situations surrounding the jailing of most delinquents, at least a dozen states have sanctioned the use of jail for delinquents who are perceived either as a serious threat to public safety or as a menace to others in a detention center (see Table 10.3). While the time these youth spend in jail is likely to be much shorter than that experienced by their fellow adult inmates, it could extend anywhere from a week (AL) to a month or more (MI).

All told, significant numbers of juveniles end up incarcerated in jails yearly. Each year an average daily count of the juvenile population in jail reveals thousands of youth held there. Extrapolating this number to a yearlong count would mean that hundreds of thousands of juveniles experience jail each year in this country (see Table 10.4).

Juveniles Eligible for Detention

Another unique and controversial feature of detention is the breadth of individuals eligible for some form of pretrial custody. Historically, most states have denied the right of bail to all juvenile defendants, regardless of the severity of the offense and prior record. Even with some recent changes in this regard, only 21 states currently provide for the youth's ability either to post bail or to be released via a bond to the parents. Utah applies this option only to defendants who are nonresidents of the state.[12] Similarly, only 10 states officially identify the possibility for youth to be released on their own recognizance (ROR). To qualify for this release, juveniles in New Jersey must be 14, while those in Wisconsin must be 15.[13] A number of states specifically extend a right to bail to status offenders as well.[14]

The Traditional Absence of Bail

The absence of *bail* is consistent with traditional juvenile justice philosophy. The "no bail" policy is a benefit, inasmuch as juveniles typically do not need to put up any money to secure their release pending trial. Instead, juveniles are usually released to their parents, without money being involved at all. In fact, of all the rights currently denied to juvenile defendants, the right to bail is the one not actively pursued by defense attorneys because of their belief that prosecutors could use (i.e., misuse) bail as a weapon to detain more juveniles (Sanborn 1992a). Nevertheless, the denial of bail is a two-edged sword in juvenile justice. Whereas most defendants do indeed seem to benefit from its absence, some youth who would have been able to "purchase" their pretrial freedom in adult court are denied that opportunity in most juvenile courts.

The prohibition of bail supports the system's philosophy in a number of ways. First, granting bail promotes the criminalization of the system. It suggests that, like criminal court, juvenile court is something that can be and should be avoided through money and that freedom is a purchasable commodity in both systems. Second, juveniles ideally are held in detention only when a good reason exists (remember the presumption of release). Consequently, only those who "need" to be held are supposedly held in custody. Thus, allowing release via bail would undermine the purposes served by detention and possibly endanger the youth and/or the community. Finally, juveniles have not been entitled to rights (beyond bail) because of their right to custody and not to liberty (see Chapter 2). Since the availability of bail connotes a right to liberty, granting this right is not only underserved or uncalled for, it could lead to questioning of the legitimacy of denying other rights (such as jury trial) to juvenile defendants. Besides these philosophical problems, there is a practical obstacle to granting juveniles the right to bail. The vast majority, except perhaps entrepreneurial drug dealers, do not have the resources to post bail personally. Moreover, bail bondsmen typically refuse to lend the money directly to juveniles, since they have neither the collateral nor the ability to be held legally liable for any contract (prior to the age of 18) entered into with a bail bondsman.

Before proceeding with the reasons or criteria behind holding juveniles in detention, we must mention two more subtle and more serious potential downsides to the absence of bail. The first involves the ability to use detention in a discriminatory manner. To be sure, bail is associated with problems in adult court, especially since reliance on money or property means class discrimination can account for some of the defendants held in jail. Nevertheless, the standardization of bail amounts (i.e., standard rates for certain crimes, often posted in police stations and lower courts) should at least reduce the possibility of some defendants being singled out for arbitrary handling. In the juvenile system, however, the lack of standardized bail rates, coupled with ambiguous detention criteria (which we explore shortly), creates a decision-making process that would appear vulnerable to discriminatory handling (much like the problems we discussed at the intake stage in Chapter 9). Interestingly, Minnesota pointedly has directed its decision makers not to consider race, color, gender, sexual orientation, religion, national origin, class, public assistance status, family structure, or residential mobility at the detention stage.

A second and related difficulty is that, unlike in the adult system, where a defendant's presence in jail may simply reflect a lack of money or property or favorable employment history, a youth's presence in detention is not likely to be interpreted merely as a poverty situation. The juvenile cannot be "just" a poor kid, since money is not a prerequisite for release to the parents. Instead, a juvenile held in detention, especially in a secure or non-secure facility, suggests that a rather significant problem exists, with either the defendant or the family. This interpretation can create serious fairness problems for detained youth at both the adjudicatory and dispositional stages (see Chapters 13 and 14).

Detention Criteria

Because of its potential adverse impact on subsequent stages (and whatever possible discriminatory use and adverse effects custody may have on the youth personally as well), detaining an offender looms as one of the most critical decisions made in the juvenile system. Complicating matters are the broad *detention criteria* used in determining the pretrial custody issue. Basically, three general criteria or reasons support the notion of holding a youth in detention. Each criterion is associated with one of the three major juvenile justice models:

Model	Criteria
Crime control	Prevent crime or harm to the community
Rehabilitation	Prevent harm to the youth
Due process	Prevent flight

In the juvenile system, these criteria are not always clearly demarcated or separated from one another. For example, a rehabilitation-oriented person could promote detention in order to prevent another incident, viewing this occurrence as actually as harmful or even fatal to the youth or to potential victims. This same individual could be worried about the juvenile's fleeing the jurisdiction, not necessarily because this behavior would frustrate the justice system from a due process view, but rather because flight would result in the youth's not receiving treatment or help. Similarly, the fact that the child has no parents, or only irresponsible ones, could qualify the youth for detention under all three criteria. Juvenile court statutes do not tend to differentiate detention criteria for delinquents versus status offenders.

Preventing crime. The first and most widely observed criterion is to prevent crime or harm to others. In the statutes it is usually represented as the youth's constituting a *threat to the person or property of others.* Fifty jurisdictions (all but LA and OH) specifically cite this criterion and frequently offer phrases of explanation, such as:

- clear and substantial threat of serious nature (AL);
- immediate or imminent harm (AR, HI, IL);
- strong probability of crime (CT, MI); or
- serious or substantial risk of bodily harm (FL, IA, NY, WI).

Focusing on the offense or the youth's delinquent record, numerous jurisdictions cite three other related reasons in support of detention: violating conditions of release, probation, or a court order;[15] having other charges pending against the youth;[16] and preventing harm or intimidation of a witness.[17] Actually, intake officers presented with juveniles in any of these three situations could recommend detention in every jurisdiction, even if the statute failed to include these specific provisions. Several states that otherwise prohibit placing status offenders in a detention center permit this practice for a limited time when the youth violates release conditions, probation, or a court order.[18]

A few states have decided that a particular offense alone qualifies the juvenile for detention. Thus, domestic violence in Florida, murder and a Class A or B felony in Indiana, an offense transferable to adult court in Massachusetts, and an assault and battery on a school official in South Carolina are all that an intake officer needs in order to justify detention in those states. Similarly, a number of jurisdictions have associated the level of offense with the level of detention. For example, secure detention in Virginia requires minimally a felony or a Class 1 misdemeanor. Similarly, South Carolina and Tennessee identify numerous crimes, most involving weapons, serious injury, or violence, as eligible for secure detention. Recently, nine jurisdictions have adopted measures that not only focus exclusively on the circumstances of the crime, but also have eliminated the intake officer's discretion to release the accused prior to a detention hearing (which we will review shortly). This constitutes mandatory initial detention, such that only a judge, master, or referee ultimately is authorized to allow the youth to return home, and only after a hearing at which a prosecutor is likely to be allowed to protest that release (see Table 10.5). It would not be surprising to see more jurisdictions adopt this policy in the near future.

As of now, no state has gone so far as to indicate that *no one* has the discretion to release any particular juveniles pending trial. Detention has not become completely mandatory anywhere yet. Colorado and Wisconsin have come closest to this point, however, by adopting presumptive detention. In Colorado, juveniles who have committed offenses identified by this state (see Table 10.5) have created a rebuttable presumption of being dangerous to either themselves or the community. Consequently, the burden is on them to prove they warrant release pending trial. Similarly, Wisconsin lists 20 offenses; the use of a handgun, rifle, or shotgun during a felony; and the mere possession of the latter two weapons as grounds for which the perpetrator is *considered* to present a substantial risk of physical harm to another person. Wisconsin juveniles involved in these incidents are not only eligible for secure detention, but also share the burden experienced by Colorado juveniles to gain their release. Presumptive detention, like mandatory initial detention, could easily become a trend of the future, depending on the juvenile crime rate in the next several years.

To help juvenile court officials operationalize detention criteria, many states have included factors in their statutes that decision makers should consider when ordering pretrial custody. First, we consider the factors linked primarily with the *prevent crime* criterion. (Actually, it is virtually inevitable that these items, regardless of whether they are mentioned in the stat-

Table 10.5 Jurisdictions Practicing Mandatory Initial Detention	
State	**Criteria**
AR	Unlawful possession of a handgun, unlawful discharge of firearm from vehicle, any felony committed with a firearm, criminal use of a prohibited weapon
CA	Defendant age 14 or older and personally uses a firearm in a felony or attempted felony.
CO	Crime of violence, felony against a person committed with a firearm, possession of a dangerous or illegal weapon, carrying a concealed weapon, prohibited use of a weapon, illegal discharge of a firearm, illegal possession of a handgun
CT	Serious juvenile offense or when a take-into-custody order is issued
DC	Homicide, forcible rape, armed robbery, 1° burglary, escape from secure custody
NV	Any offense and firearm
NY	Designated felony
SC	Violent crime
TX	Any offense and firearm

ute, would influence intake officers.) They include the nature of the offense[19] and prior record;[20] the current or past use of force, violence, or weapons;[21] the presence of a parent who is willing and able to supervise the youth;[22] the probability of the youth's committing an offense dangerous to others;[23] and a history or recent record of violence.[24]

Two comments about these factors are useful. First, Louisiana, which does not officially list the criterion of threat to the person or property of others, mentions both the nature of the offense and the youth's prior record as factors to guide the detention decision. This means that only Ohio has refrained officially from directing its intake officers to consider the prevention of crime as a purpose behind detaining delinquents. Second, the parent emerges as a potential major factor in this criterion as well as in the other two major criteria (and especially in the desire to prevent harm to the youth). As we have noted previously, the parent in the juvenile justice system represents what can be *the* factor or variable that explains many decisions at numerous stages of the process. This is dramatically true at detention. Just as an otherwise divertible case may not be removed from the system at intake because of the parent, an otherwise releasable youth, whose offense and record are fairly innocuous, may experience detention because of primarily, if not exclusively, the parent (or the lack of one).

Before leaving the *prevent crime* criterion, we must note that this reason amounts to what is called preventive detention in criminal court. That is, the youth is held in pretrial custody to prevent a "second" offense. Preventive detention has been openly and widely practiced in juvenile court from its inception (again, today only Ohio has seemingly failed to embrace it). In contrast, the adult system has for the most part been forbidden to use it. It tends to be limited to federal racketeering and organized crime,[25] and recent statutes permitting a "cooling off" period in domestic assault and violence cases. Beyond that, preventive detention is not *openly* practiced in criminal justice. To be sure, bail may be set at a level beyond the reach of the accused so as to prevent release and the possibility of further misdeeds rather than to assure the adult defendant's presence at trial. Nevertheless, the only officially recognized, due process–compatible reason to detain an adult defendant (beyond the already noted exceptions) is to ensure appearance at trial. The same is not true for juvenile defendants. The U.S. Supreme Court has sanctioned preventive detention of these individuals explicitly. This approval occurred in *Schall v. Martin* (1984).

Schall v. Martin involved a group of juveniles from New York who challenged the state's statute that authorized preventive detention when it was believed that a "serious risk" existed that the youth would commit a crime prior to trial. The juveniles' suit was successful at both the District Court and the Second Circuit Court of Appeals. Both lower federal courts found serious due process problems with preventive detention in general, and they declared the practice unconstitutional. Combining the findings of the two courts, the unfairness of preventive detention stemmed from the following:

1. It amounts to "punishment" before adjudication or conviction (or a violation of the presumption of innocence).

2. It amounts to "punishment" for a future crime that has not occurred yet (and may never have happened).

3. No one can predict future behavior, so there is no way to know whether the future crime will ever happen.

The word *punishment* has to be placed in quotes in this context because punishment cannot legally exist until there has actually been an adjudication or conviction.

In addition, three other aspects particular to the New York statute and situation (but present in other states as well) were found by the lower federal courts to violate due process:

1. Juveniles could be held five days by a judge without a finding that there was probable cause to believe the youth committed the offense that led to arrest (adults cannot be held longer than 48 hours without this finding).

2. There were no limits—with respect to severity of offense and record—as to which juveniles could be held in preventive detention (giving POs and judges virtually unlimited discretion and the ability to discriminate against certain youth).

3. More than half (and perhaps more than two-thirds) of the juveniles held in preventive detention were released from detention at some point before trial, had their cases thrown out by prosecutors or dismissed at trial by judges, or were placed on probation after an adjudication (thus questioning the need for and legitimacy of preventive detention).

Having lost at both federal courts, the state of New York appealed these rulings to the U.S. Supreme Court and won. Writing for the Court, Justice (now Chief Justice) Rehnquist offered two justifications for upholding the practice of preventive detention:

1. It served a legitimate and important state objective in preventing crime (suggesting, then, that it is a necessary measure despite the numbers ultimately released on probation even after an adjudication).

2. There were adequate safeguards accompanying preventive detention in that defendants were given a hearing, the right to counsel, and the right to a written explanation by the judge as to why preventive detention was necessary.

The Court relied on a number of questionably sound "findings" in reaching these conclusions:

- Juveniles are dangerous—perhaps even more than adults because of their high recidivism rates.

- Juveniles have an interest in freedom, but it is "qualified" since they "are always in some form of custody," and whatever their liberty interest is, it may be subordinated to the state's *parens patriae* obligation.

- Juveniles must be protected from themselves and others (which is not actually preventive detention).

- Every jurisdiction practices it (all did then), so it must be acceptable.

- There was no indication that preventive detention was used as punishment.

This last finding was made despite testimony from the attorney representing New York at the Second Court of Appeals that juvenile court judges granted probation to adjudicated youth who had experienced preventive detention because this group was perceived to have been "sufficiently punished" or to have served enough time by the time of the disposition hearing.[26]

In upholding preventive detention (via the New York statute), *Schall v. Martin* has resulted in granting states a green light to deny juveniles bail, to hold them for an unspecified amount of time during the pretrial period because of an unverifiable suspicion that a "second" undisclosed offense will occur before trial (and regardless of whether the original offense was serious or a first-time occurrence), and to offer them a judicial finding of probable cause at some point substantially beyond the time limit for which an adult must be provided the same protection. There have been no other U.S. Supreme Court cases in the detention area.

Preventing harm. Unique to the juvenile court setting is the second major detention criterion, *preventing harm to the youth*. Statutes tend to use these exact words or to cite the general related category of *no parent*. Between these two standards, 47 jurisdictions (all but FL, LA, MA, NJ, NY) call for the detention of youth in these situations, while Florida permits detention in this context *only* if the youth requests it. Besides the five states that do not grant judges the authority to detain via this criterion, Utah, Wisconsin, and Wyoming fail to mention harm to the youth per se. Nevertheless, these three states join 22 others that identify the lack of a parent as a legitimate reason to detain.[27] Moreover, four states (CA, IN, UT, VA) include within the "no parent" provision a situation in which the parent simply refuses to take the child home,[28] while Washington and West Virginia insist that the parent must be considered responsible in order for the youth to be released. Although the no parent provision is rarely linked specifically with holding status offenders in shelter care (FL, WI, WY), it would be surprising if this factor did not contribute to the pretrial custody of these individuals. In fact, California and Texas, which severely restrict placing status offenders in detention centers, permit it when the parent is absent.

Statutes frequently demand some level of proof to support this criterion, such as reasonable grounds or serious threat of substantial harm,[29] immediate or imminent harm to the youth,[30] the strong probability of harm (CT), or reasonable grounds of threat to the physical, mental, emotional health or well-being of the child (DE, HI). Similarly, statutes often cite factors for judges to consider in determining whether the prevent-harm criterion warrants detention in any particular case. Examples of these factors include the defendant's character, reputation, and mental condition (AR, DC, HI, MI); the home situation (DE, IL, MI); the victim's or community's attitude toward the youth (IL); the presence of a parent who is willing and able to care for and protect the child;[31] a youth who is on drugs or is self-destructive (CA, DC, SD); the probability of the youth's committing an offense dangerous to self (KY, TX, UT); and a history or recent record of harm (KS, OK). In Colorado and Oklahoma, status offenders who are seriously self-destructive can end up in a detention center. Finally, although it tends not to be mentioned specifically in the statutes, a youth involved in a gang-related crime for which retaliation from a rival gang is a prospect could also experience detention under this criterion.[32]

Again, it can be seen how the parent and family can be a critical variable in detaining a juvenile for a number of reasons. Judges could also use this criterion to justify a particular case of detention ("I can't allow this youth to return to his home") when the real concern is to protect the community. This potential for deception can wreak havoc with research studies in their attempt to determine the reasons behind juvenile detention.

While only Montana and Virginia (if there is no parent) have it as a statutory requirement, it would not be unlikely to find that some delinquents (except perhaps gang members) detained to prevent harm from happening to them are held in shelter care or perhaps in a foster or group home, rather than in a detention center.

Preventing flight. *Preventing flight*, or ensuring the defendant's appearance at trial, is the third major criterion for detaining juveniles. It is the one criterion that is both due process compatible and shared by the adult court. It is also the one criterion that could be the most likely reason a status offender can be held in a detention center.[33] Only 47 jurisdictions cite this provision as a reason to detain youth. Although five states (CO, KY, RI, VT, WV) omit any official reference to this criterion, it is highly doubtful that the prospect of flight or being a fugitive or escapee does not affect either the setting of bail or the decision to release the youth pending trial in these states. Some of the 47 jurisdictions that focus on the child's possible failure to appear at trial also include other situations, such as being a runaway from home,[34] being an escapee from a program or facility,[35] being a fugitive (typically from and wanted by another state),[36] being removed from the jurisdiction,[37] and the parent's refusing to promise to return the youth to court (MI, MN).

Minnesota provides that a parent's failure to sign the promise-to-appear form creates a presumption that the child will fail to appear at trial. Here is another example of how a parent's behavior or condition can lead to a juvenile's detention. Chances are good that judges in other states would use the same presumption operating in Minnesota, regardless of whether the state statute officially recognizes this conclusion. Similarly, the failure of a state to include a specific reference to any of the above situations as a cause for detention in its statute would certainly not prevent a judge from considering any of these situations as grounds to believe the youth would not appear at an adjudicatory hearing. The factors associated with the prevention-of-flight criterion are fairly obvious and include the youth's ties to the community,[38] any escape or failure to appear history,[39] a parent's willingness and ability to assure the child's presence at trial,[40] and the youth's promise to appear (CA, GA).

Beyond the three major criteria, a handful of states provide for the defendant's ability to request detention (FL, IN, SC, WA, WI), but this request would probably result in detention (perhaps in shelter care or a foster or group home) in many jurisdictions. Another five states (AZ, DE, SC, VT, WV) cite an ambiguous "in the interests of the child and the public" reason, expanding the judge's rather broad powers to detain youth. Finally, although currently no jurisdiction appears to permit detention purely to further the juvenile court's mission or interests, juveniles used to be detained when their presence was required for tests or examinations by court personnel. Although it is possible that such examinations still occur today while the youth is in detention (and may have been the motivation behind the detention), this purpose is probably no longer cited as the primary one for holding a youth in pretrial custody. In fact, Florida and Georgia have gone so far as prohibiting detention when the goal is merely to have more convenient access to the defendant or to facilitate further investigation or interrogation.

Statutes can use factors to limit or prevent detention as well as to sanction it. We have already seen how the severity of the offense can affect the location or level of detention. Similarly, *age* can influence the detention decision as well, although few states actually mention this factor. Nevertheless, while 10 years of age is a minimum requirement for detention in Illinois, those younger than 11 years old must commit certain offenses to qual-

ify for detention in New Jersey. Only youth age 10 or older can experience secure detention in New York, and a special court order is needed in Oregon to detain children below
the age of 12. New Jersey and South Carolina also specifically prohibit detaining juveniles
in facilities that have reached the maximum population capacity.

In the end, the picture presented by the detention criteria in the juvenile justice system is complex and problematic. For one thing, the criteria and factors are sufficiently
broad and vague to guarantee that *virtually any* child the PO and the judge want to detain
in most, if not all, jurisdictions can be detained for one reason or another. Moreover, this
same feature also enables discriminatory decisions to be made without being obvious
as such. Similarly, many of the factors are simply not measurable (e.g., the home situation
or the parent's ability to supervise or provide care), which means that research studies
may never be able to ascertain precisely which factors drive the detention decision in
juvenile court.

Detention Research

The vast majority of empirical research in the detention area has been aimed at identifying the factors related to decision making at this stage. Not surprisingly, the findings
have been very mixed. Some studies have found that race (McGarrell 1993; Wordes et al.
1994), gender (Bortner 1982; Chesney-Lind 1988), class status (Cohen 1975b, 1975c), and
family affiliation (McCarthy 1987; Schutt and Dannefer 1988) *are* associated with detention decisions in juvenile court. Other studies have found that race (Bookin-Weiner 1984;
Tracy 2002), gender (Frazier and Bishop 1985; Teilmann and Landry 1981), class status
(Bailey 1981; McCarthy 1987), and family affiliation (Dungworth 1977; Sumner 1971)
are not associated with detention decisions. The juvenile's previous record (Frazier and
Cochran 1986a; Schutt and Dannefer 1988) and the availability of space within detention
centers (Krisberg et al. 1984; Lerman 1977) are the only two factors that have been found
to be *consistently associated* with youth's being detained.

With ever-expanding definitions of detention, broad and amorphous criteria and factors, and the virtual impossibility of record data (on which research studies tend to rely
solely for their information) to reflect all the nuances surrounding the decision to detain,
the detention picture in juvenile court is unlikely to become any clearer in the future. As
with the arrest situation, students are encouraged to consult the research to determine
how well (or how badly) the studies have addressed and accounted for the numerous factors that could affect the detention decision.

Regardless of whether research studies can pinpoint the factors that explain the detention decision, an inescapable fact is that minority youth disproportionately experience
detention in the great majority of states (at least 43) (Leiber 2002). Although some states
can supposedly explain the disproportionality by virtue of the offense, most states (at
least 29) cannot.[41] The disproportionate ratio of minorities also applies to confinement in
adult jails and lockups in many states. Appendix B spells out the ratio of minorities experiencing confinement.

Risk (and Needs) Assessments

One device adopted by some jurisdictions that is designed to make the detention decision more rational and less arbitrary is the risk (or needs) assessment instrument (RAI). The RAI attempts to remove subjective impressions from this decision-making stage by assigning points to a variety of factors usually associated with the need to detain youth. The issue then becomes which factors are assigned points and which are not. For example, Florida has chosen to restrict the RAI primarily to the areas of preventing crime and flight, instead of preventing harm to the child. Points in this state are allotted to:

- previous history of failure to appear;
- prior offenses;
- offense committed pending trial;
- any unlawful possessions of firearms;
- theft of motor vehicles or possession of same;
- community control status when taken into custody; and
- any aggravating or mitigating factors.

After points are assigned to these items, the decision supposedly becomes clear and easy. There are either enough points to justify detention (also indicating the level of detention), or there are insufficient points and the juvenile must be released.[42]

The RAI might decrease some of the inequality that has marked detention decisions in the past. Ideally, all those who have similar situations in their records will be assigned equal points and will experience equal results. However, there can never be a guarantee that the assignment of points will always be equal. Moreover, the RAI is not immune from creating other problems. For example, setting the overall points needed to detain at *too low* a level could mean serious (and unnecessary) increases in the number of juveniles detained, while setting the point level *too high* could mean serious (and unnecessary) increases in the number of potentially dangerous offenders released to the community. Even if the point threshold is set at the most ideal and sound spot, decision making by points will mean the detention of at least some juveniles who otherwise would have been released under a more flexible and discretionary system, with the reverse being true as well. Of course, if the points are enforced so as to allow some discretion, it is possible that the problem sought to be avoided by points is still present.

One additional focus that has been added to the RAI in some juvenile courts is to gauge the youth's needs at this point as well. Juvenile courts in some states have implemented a Juvenile Assessment Center (JAC) to centralize the screening of youth and to better coordinate the justice and human service system activities young people require (Rivers and Anwyl 2000). The needs assessment will be reviewed in Chapter 16.

Detention Hearing

For juveniles who are detained pending trial, three determinations must be made within a relatively short period of time. These three related but independent matters are:

Determinations	Court Process
1. Decision to prosecute case	Filing petition
2. Judge's finding need to detain	Detention hearing
3. Judge's finding legal basis for case	Probable cause finding

In Chapter 9 we discussed the decision the PO and prosecutor reach to file a petition, formally charging the youth with an offense. Suffice it to say here that when a youth is held in custody, most jurisdictions have established a time limit within which this decision must be made (see Appendix C). The purpose of the time limit is to prevent juveniles from experiencing prolonged detention while court officials decide whether to prosecute or even whether there are grounds to prosecute. States divide as to whether the petition must be filed prior to or shortly after the judge's finding either a need to detain or probable cause for the offense.

Not all jurisdictions have committed to limiting the time in which a petition must be filed (consult Appendix C). Statutes vary not only as to the number of hours they identify and whether only court days (as opposed to weekends or holidays) count, but also as to the starting point. The earliest the clock begins is when the youth is taken into custody. The latest is the detention hearing. The range as to when the petition must be filed against a detained youth, then, is considerable throughout the country (and unknown in a good part of it). So far only Utah has distinguished the type of detention to which the youth is subjected as related to a time limit for filing a petition. Whereas juveniles in a detention center in that state must have a petition filed against them within five days or 120 hours from the initiation of detention, POs have 30 days to file a petition against a youth placed in home detention or granted a conditional release.

The failure to file a petition within the time allotted could result in the court's granting the PO a continuance to comply with the statute, although only Colorado specifically mentions that possibility. Barring that event, at a minimum juvenile authorities are required to release the defendant from custody (or maybe reduce the level of custody) when the time runs out—although, again, statutes rarely spell this out. Even if the juvenile is released from a detention facility (and perhaps put on home detention or conditional release), that does not mean the case is finished. The petition could still be considered alive while the youth's category is simply switched to having been released from custody.

The bond room is where detained juveniles await hearings in juvenile court. What factors should judges consider in detaining juveniles?

Contemporaneous with the petition-filing situation is the determination by a judge or master as to whether the original decision to detain should stand or be ended. One positive aspect of detention in the juvenile system is that nearly all jurisdictions require a detention hearing (Nebraska appears to be alone in demanding only a court order) within a specified, relatively limited number of hours (see Appendix D). This means that a second, independent decision maker must also be convinced that detention is appropriate (assuming it was in the first place). The detention criteria must survive two analyses. Many juveniles will be released at this point (or foster or group home detention might replace secure detention). For some youth this could mean that the judge was simply harder to convince than the PO that custody was necessary, or perhaps an inflamed neighborhood has calmed down in the interim. For others, critical situations could have changed (an alternative not previously available now is), or maybe a parent finally appeared or agreed to both take the child home and bring him or her back to court.

Once again, the time limits vary considerably from one jurisdiction to another (consult Appendix D). Five states put an absolute cap on the overall number of hours permitted, while nine provide for extensions. While four states use no description or simply "good cause" as the basis for granting an extension to the time limit, the other five list particular situations in which an extension is warranted.[43] Most statutes that specify time limits for the shelter-care hearings provided status offenders have established the same standard that applies to delinquent cases. It is possible, however, that a slightly shorter or even a slightly longer time period will be associated with shelter-care hearings.[44] Five states also have specified a quicker time frame for those defendants being held in jail.

It should be safe to assume that the court will have to release the defendant from custody if the hearing is not held on time. Ten jurisdictions detail this obligation in their statutes,[45] provided that the youth is neither already under the court's supervision (which means the court can legally hold on to the child independent of the current charge) nor the cause of the delay. Once again, merely because the juvenile has to be released does not mean that the case is over or that the state is prevented from prosecuting the charges.

Besides the time requirements, every jurisdiction mandates the presence of the parent at the detention hearing. All the statutes carry provisions for notifying the parents of the hearing and threatening them with various consequences for failure to appear when summoned (usually a contempt of court finding). Nevertheless, the notice may not reach the parent on time (or may have incorrect information), or the parent may simply choose to ignore it. While the parent's failure to appear might be used as grounds for postponing the hearing, most jurisdictions have decided to allow the detention hearing to proceed without the parent.[46] Other states require a second hearing if and when the parent appears or is brought to court.[47]

The third virtually simultaneous determination that must usually be made in these first few days after detention has begun is the *probable cause finding*. That is, it must be shown that there is probable cause to believe the youth committed the offense at issue. As we saw in Chapter 7, police need this level of evidence in order to arrest, at least for delinquencies or crimes. But when an arrest is followed by pretrial detention, there is a significant interference with the youth's liberty that logically would seem to demand more than only a police officer's say-so. For adults in this situation, the U.S. Supreme Court has required that a judge also be convinced that there is probable cause to link the offender with the offense (*Gerstein v. Pugh* 1975). This determination must occur within 48 hours of the arrest (*Riverside v. McLaughlin* 1991). Thus far, the Supreme Court has not been asked whether these requirements apply to the juvenile system. The closest the Court has come to addressing the issue occurred in *Schall v. Martin* (1984). Without identifying any requirements per se for juvenile court, the Court simply noted it was satisfied with New York's standards, which called for a probable cause hearing sometime between four and seven days of the child's custody. In short, we do not know whether there is a constitutional mandate for a probable cause finding in the juvenile detention context, and, if there is one, when it must occur. Juvenile court statutes reflect this uncertainty.

Of course, there is no controversy here if the youth has been taken into custody via a warrant or court order. In both of those situations, judicial authorization that there is a probable cause basis for interfering with the juvenile's liberty has already occurred. Nevertheless, just as important is the fact that, like adults, most juveniles are taken into custody by police without judicial authorization or a finding that probable cause exists.

The extent to which juvenile court statutes adopt the same standards required in adult court is somewhat of a puzzle. Only 38 jurisdictions have officially announced a probable cause requirement (or something like it) at the detention stage,[48] and nine of these jurisdictions officially demand probable cause in status offense cases as well.[49] A few states use wording like *reasonable cause* or *reasonable grounds* (GA, NC, UT) or a *prima facie* case (CA) to convey the same meaning as probable cause. Whether the remaining 14 jurisdictions similarly require probable cause in this context is difficult to discern.

Even more complex is the timing behind and the process by which probable cause is found for detained youth. In the adult system, the universality of the requirement has produced what would be recognized as a *Gerstein* hearing (reflecting the name of the Supreme Court case), which must occur within 48 hours in every state. The lack of one standard in juvenile court, however, has led to a variety of ways in which juvenile courts address (and ignore) the issue. The dominant practice throughout the country is for juvenile court to use the *detention hearing* to resolve both the *need to detain* and the *probable cause* matters. This practice is logical because of the history of the court, in which hearings were kept to a minimum (in fact, to only one). Nevertheless, a handful of states have established a hearing whose sole purpose is to focus on the probable cause finding.[50] But even some of these states (MN, NJ, WV) suggest or do not rule out that the two matters can be merged into one hearing in certain situations. Meanwhile, the third consideration of filing the petition in detention cases also needs to be accommodated during this same time period. The result is that states divide into six possible progressions through which these three detention-related matters are handled (and some states are flexible enough to use two different progressions).[51]

It seems most of the country uses progressions 1 and 5, wherein the petition must be filed either shortly before (or by) the combined detention/probable cause hearing or shortly afterward. The vast majority of these jurisdictions allow the combined hearing to occur (sometimes substantially) beyond the adult court's time limit (with notable exceptions like AK, AZ, CT, FL, TX). Few states operate under the progressions 3 and 6. Three of them (MN, MS, NM), however, have explicitly adopted the constitutional limits found

Progressions					
1	2	3	4	5	6
Petition	Petition	PC	DH	DH/PC	Petition
DH/PC	DH	Petition	Petition	Petition	PC
	PC	DH	PC		DH

in criminal court. Finally, progressions 2 and 4 place the greatest barriers and result in none of these juvenile courts' complying with a 48-hour probable cause finding deadline. In the end, fewer than a dozen jurisdictions guarantee a detained juvenile a judicial determination of probable cause within two days of custody, especially if the youth is taken into custody on a Friday. Instead, the probable cause finding can be delayed for up to one week (NY), ten days (RI, WV), two weeks (MI), or even a month (CO). Ultimately, if probable cause is not established, the juvenile should be released from detention and the case should be closed (subject to future rearrest and detention if probable cause eventually materializes). Seventeen jurisdictions specifically demand this outcome.[52] Obviously, this result may come about only after the youth has spent an appreciable amount of time in detention.

Constitutional Rights at the Detention Hearing

How the detention hearing operates depends on the location of the court, especially with respect to the rights granted the youth. There has not been a U.S. Supreme Court case to identify which, if any, constitutional rights the defendant has at this stage. The only comment in this regard by the Supreme Court was the observation in *Schall v. Martin* that New York had provided sufficient rights to those placed in preventive detention (including a hearing, notice of charges, and the advice of the rights to silence and counsel). Whether any of these rights are constitutionally mandated remains uncertain. However, *Schall v. Martin* apparently has had an impact, since the four rights mentioned in the case are the four most often contained in statutes and court rules. For example, the right to a hearing has been mostly resolved. Every state but one already grants that right. Nebraska, alone, allows detention to occur by virtue of a court order only (which would entail judicial authorization without the necessity of holding a hearing). Even though a detention hearing will occur virtually everywhere, statutes and court rules offer relatively little guidance as to the procedure that must be followed.

First of all, 14 states make no mention of the juveniles' rights at the detention hearing.[53] Of the 38 jurisdictions that do address the particular rights allowed, the right to counsel is identified most frequently. While 34 of these jurisdictions explicitly state that the right exists, the remaining four states (KY, MS, OR, UT) strongly imply that it does. Actually, it is difficult to imagine that any juvenile court in the country would deny the right to counsel to a youth who has requested representation at this critical stage. Nevertheless, a mere seven states (IL, KS, NJ, NY, TX, WA, WV) insist that either a detention hearing cannot take place without a defense attorney or a second hearing must occur if the youth was without counsel at the first detention hearing, and Missouri holds that the lack of counsel may cause the detention hearing to be postponed. It would not be surprising, then, to find that some, and perhaps many, defendants are not represented by counsel at the detention hearing. Moreover, even defendants who are represented by counsel may not have had any discussion with their attorney prior to the hearing, as one national study discovered (Puritz et al. 1995). Thus, the quality of the representation given to juveniles facing detention hearings may leave a lot to be desired. The status offender's right to counsel at detention is even less clear. While some states simply mention the court's duty to advise these youths of a right to counsel (LA, MN, WY), the New York statute suggests that the parents must hire their own attorney, and Illinois guarantees only a guardian *ad litem.*

Besides the uncertainty as to whether the right to counsel even exists, the following dimensions would be critical in explaining the lack of counsel:

1.   The ease by which eligible juveniles can waive (or even be encouraged to waive) their right to counsel (see Chapter 13)[54]

2.   The extent to which those youths who can afford to retain counsel (usually via their parents) are forced to do so at this point (instead of being provided a public defender)

3.   The judge's willingness or duty to appoint counsel should able parents refuse or fail to retain counsel

4.   The availability and monitoring of the detention hearing by the public defender

If the third and fourth situations were characteristic of a juvenile court, there could be 100 percent representation of youth at the detention hearing.

The right not to incriminate oneself follows counsel as the next most frequently mentioned safeguard. Twenty-one states officially announce it as a right at the detention hearing.[55] Three of these states extend status offenders a right to silence too (LA, NY, WI). Texas goes so far as to hold that any statement made by a youth at the detention hearing cannot be used in subsequent proceedings. Despite the relative "silence" of statutes as to the presence of this right, it is virtually impossible to think that a juvenile court would not advise a defendant of this right during a detention hearing (or that a statement secured from a youth who had not been so warned would be admissible later at trial). Thus, it is probably a right that does not need to be identified to be operable at this point. Nevertheless, it is not impossible for juveniles to waive their right to silence at this hearing, perhaps without having had the chance to discuss this decision with counsel. The presence of attorneys is absolutely vital in this context, inasmuch as their absence could mean that conversations usually and more appropriately held between defendant and defense attorney would occur instead between the judge and the youth (or the parent). Although judges would be required to have given defendants a basic warning about the right to silence before any such conversation with them, it would not be remarkable for unrepresented youth to fail to appreciate the potential significance of that conversation and to understand that they may be waiving their constitutional rights in answering the judge's questions.

Only 18 jurisdictions demand that juveniles be notified of the charges against them at the detention hearing,[56] three of which provide the same right to status offenders (LA, MN, WY). Many other states accomplish this same end by insisting that the petition be served on the youth at this time. As with the protection against self-incrimination, it is difficult to believe that juveniles would not be entitled to this right everywhere and would be unaware of the charges they face by the end of the detention hearing. Minimally, then, it is reasonable to expect juveniles to be granted the rights to a hearing, counsel, silence, and notice of charges at the detention hearing.

Beyond these four rights, few constitutional protections have been given widely to detention-bound youth. Thirteen states recognize the defendant's right to confront and cross examine witnesses,[57] while the same number of jurisdictions guarantee the youth's right to be heard and to present evidence,[58] and 6 states (CA, MI, NY, TN, WI, WY) specifically include calling witnesses. While New York reserves the right to withdraw these safeguards if good cause is shown, Mississippi stresses that these rights may be limited in their extent but not their existence. In California, exercising the right to confront and cross examine may not only require a delay of five judicial days (or potentially up to eight days total), but also excludes the victim from the questioning. Some of these jurisdictions would operationalize these rights only at the separate probable cause hearing rather than during the detention hearing. Three states (IL, MS, NC) guarantee status offenders a right to cross examine witnesses and to present evidence.

To summarize, the nature and conduct of the detention hearing varies considerably from state to state. There may or may not be a probable cause finding, which may or may not require the testimony of witnesses. The detention hearing can range, then, from an informal proceeding (as Georgia calls it) in which the only evidence about the offense is the police report describing how and why the youth was taken into custody (e.g., CT, NM) to a formal preliminary hearing resembling a criminal court trial (e.g., KY). Judging from the history of juvenile court and the dearth of rights and requirements in the statutes, it seems fair to infer that the informal type of hearing is far more prevalent than the formal one. Many of the adolescents who continue to be held in custody after the detention hearing will not get "another" chance to challenge the case against them until trial (except possibly in those few states that offer a subsequent separate probable cause hearing). This translates into a potentially appreciable period of pretrial detention based on what is often a shaky probable cause foundation. Nevertheless, the expedited trial given to most detained juveniles probably results in their experiencing no more pretrial custody without being able to fight the charges than that to which a comparably situated adult is subjected.

The Need to Detain

Although detention hearings may not involve a serious testing of the evidence relating to the offense, they are intended to closely examine the need to detain the child until trial. In fact, it is the latter inquiry that often overshadows and even preempts the former. It would be compatible with juvenile justice philosophy if, in a case in which there was a youth who "clearly needed to be held," the judge would choose to ignore the fact that probable cause had not been established and simply assert that it had been. A judge more concerned about legalities might grant the prosecution an extra day or two in order to get a probable cause case together. An explanation for this behavior is that once a juvenile is held in detention (and not later released), a seriously adverse label or stigma attaches, which can prejudice virtually all subsequent stages of decision making. Again, since money usually is not an issue in securing postarrest freedom, detaining youths suggests they (or their families) have a "problem." Youths who remain in detention until the detention hearing may still be perceived as having a problem when they appear before the judge. Although judges typically would have an obligation to determine that probable cause exists (and many would scrupulously insist on its presence), some judges reasonably could fear that releasing the youth because of a lack of probable cause (which might be the only available option) could worsen the problem. This fear could certainly influ-

Should juveniles be held in jail? In what situations and under what circumstances?

ence judicial determinations on the probable cause finding (as well as other determinations made later at the adjudicatory and dispositional stages) (Sanborn 1992a).

With respect to ascertaining a need to detain the juvenile, statutes typically provide that any "probative" or pertinent evidence is allowed to be considered.[59] In all jurisdictions, juvenile court judges would be permitted at this hearing to review all records pertaining to the youth's delinquent past and any relevant social data, such as school performance, family history, and conditions and even the situation in the neighborhood. Nearly half of the country has associated an evidentiary level directly with the need-to-detain question. This means that the person(s) seeking the youth's detention would have to produce a certain amount of proof that detention is indeed necessary:[60]

Level of Proof	Jurisdiction
Probable cause	IN, MS, MO, NV, NM, OK, OR, SC, WI
Clear and convincing	AL, AR, FL, GA, NH, NC, VA
Prima facie	CA
Reasonable cause	AZ, MN, UT
Preponderance	AK, ME, NE

Complementing this proof is the requirement, operating in almost half of the jurisdictions, that the judge explain on the record the reasons behind holding the juvenile in custody.[61] As many as 50 percent of youth initially held by the PO are released by a judge at the detention hearing (Rubin 1998).

Even if the defendant is not released, that does not mean he or she will remain in detention until the adjudicatory hearing. For one thing, if youth is not granted a trial within the expedited deadline provided detainees, his or her release (or a reduction in the level of detention) until trial becomes mandatory (which we will examine presently). Moreover, statutes usually announce that, if and when the conditions originally warranting detention cease to exist prior to the adjudicatory hearing, release (or level reduction) is required. Eight states formally guarantee this reconsideration of the need to detain by demanding periodic detention review hearings.[62]

Release Conditions

If the defendant is released by the judge at the detention hearing or sometime thereafter (and for that matter even if the intake officer never detained the youth in the first place), there can still be strings attached to the youth's liberty. After being taken into custody juveniles are routinely released to the community with conditions or restrictions. In fact, Maine has declared that the child's refusal to agree to the conditions constitutes a reason to detain (a policy probably observed in numerous states). Although only 35 jurisdictions have either specifically identified restrictions or generally granted the judge authority to impose "reasonable" ones,[63] release with conditions is no doubt universally practiced. Colorado has institutionalized the restrictions into what it calls a *preadjudicatory service program*, which merely mentions conditions that are also typically imposed on released youth around the country. The possible conditions include everything available in an *informal agreement*, with the notable exception of restitution (conditional release does not amount to the youth's agreeing either to admit guilt or to compensate any victims):

- Avoid certain people and/or places (including victims).
- Attend school and/or work.
- Participate in various counseling programs.
- Submit to drug and alcohol testing.
- Observe a curfew (beyond any ordinance standards).
- Report periodically to a PO (by phone or in person).
- Agree to monitoring by a PO (at home and school).

Electronic monitoring may also be added to the conditions (as Colorado and Indiana do), meaning that, in some situations, conditional release and home detention could be indistinguishable. The nature of these conditions results in juvenile court's having rather serious controls and powers with which to interfere in juveniles' lives, possibly without needing any official determination that an offense has been committed.

Addressing the Charges at Detention

With respect to the youth's custody status, then, the judge has two choices: to continue or reduce the level of detention or to release the youth with or without conditions. This custody issue may be the only serious inquiry made at the detention hearing. Nevertheless, the judge must decide the fate of the charges as well. Essentially, the judge has three options:

1. Dismiss the charges and case.
2. Informally resolve the case.
3. Continue the case—most likely for an adjudicatory hearing, but possibly for a transfer hearing instead.

The first option is supposed to occur when probable cause to prosecute the charges is lacking. As we discussed earlier, this option may not happen when either the probable cause examination is not very demanding or a traditional juvenile court judge is unwilling to exercise this choice because the need for detention appears to be substantial. Nevertheless, cases tend to end at this stage when there is a failure to sustain the probable cause requirement (especially when the need to detain is marginal). The second option involves resolving the charges without the necessity of holding an adjudicatory hearing. It includes efforts to divert the case or to secure a guilty plea, both of which we will explore in the next chapter.[64] Once again, the need-to-detain question tends to dominate the focus of the detention hearing so much that attempts to answer the merits of the charges, together with the child's possibly significant treatment needs, typically go unaddressed. Moreover, a prosecutorial desire to transfer the case to criminal court would usually prevent an informal resolution at this time. Interestingly, only eight jurisdictions even mention the availability of informal resolution at this stage (CA, DC, MI, NH, UT, WV, WI, WY). This does not mean that an informal resolution is impossible at the detention hearing—only that it is unlikely. The unattractiveness of dismissal and informal resolution adds great momentum to detention cases proceeding forward to the trial level. If nothing else, continuing the case for trial allows the detention hearing judge to avoid having to make a difficult or unpopular decision, while it allows the juvenile court staff to have more time to put a treatment plan together.

The Numbers at Detention

Delinquent Youth

During the 1990s an average of more than 300,000 delinquent-charged youth were securely detained every year (Snyder and Sickmund 1999). After a slight decline following a peak in 1994, the number of youth held has increased slightly each year and, in 1999, surpassed the 1994 peak, as shown in Table 10.6.

The type of offense that led to detention showed some consistency between 1990 and 1999. Although the percentage detained declined in all offense categories, drug offenses witnessed the sharpest decline. Also, despite the decline in each offense category, the increase in percentage of cases reaching juvenile court contributed to an overall increase of 11 percent in the number of cases (or an increase of 33,400 youth) in which detention occurred during the 1990s (Harms 2003). In 1999, detention was equally likely to be imposed in person, drug, and public order offenses (23 percent each) and least likely to happen in property offenses (16 percent) (Harms 2003).

Table 10.7 shows the likelihood of the imposition of detention for each offense during the 1990s. The last column lists the percentage of the total 1999 detention population by virtue

Table 10.6 Delinquent Youth Held in Detention, 1990–1999		
Year	**Number of Youth Held**
1990	302,800
1991	293,900
1992	299,780
1993	309,900
1994	329,600
1995	318,900
1996	320,900
1997	326,800
1998	327,700
1999	336,200
Source: Puzzanchera et al. (2003b).	

of offense committed. Between 1990 and 1999 the detention population profile changed, with an increase in those committing person offenses (from 22 percent to 27 percent), drug offenses (from 9 percent to 13 percent), and public order offenses (from 20 percent to 26 percent), but a decline in the property offense category (from 49 percent to 34 percent) (Puzzanchera et al. 2003b). Although the percentage of female property offenders detained by juvenile court rose from 15 percent to 18 percent between 1995 and 1999 (Harms 2003), property offenders no longer make up approximately half of the detention population.

The biggest increase in detention cases between 1990 and 1999 involved female delinquents. A 50 percent increase occurred in the detention of girls (compared to a 4 percent increase for boys), due largely to a significant increase in the percentage (102 percent) of person offense cases for girls that resulted in detention (compared to a 20 percent increase for boys) (Harms 2003). During this period, males (between 18 percent and 25 percent) were more likely to be detained than females (between 12 percent and 20 percent) in all four offense categories. Males accounted for 80 percent of all cases that ended in detention in 1999. Nevertheless, both genders experienced declines in the percentage detained for each offense category between 1990 and 1999, especially for drug offenses. In 1999, both males (18 percent) and females (12 percent) were least likely to be detained for property offenses, and while males were most likely to be held for person offenses (25 percent), females were most likely to be held for drug and public order offenses (20 percent each) (Harms 2003; Puzzanchera et al. 2003b).

In terms of race, the increase in detention (17 percent) for whites from 1990 to 1999 surpassed that for both blacks (3 percent) and youth of other races (2 percent). This increase is attributed to white youths committing more person and drug offenses. Although the overall number of juveniles held has increased, a decline has actually occurred in the proportion of juveniles of all races who have been detained. As shown in Table 10.8, the reduction in the rate of detention has been more marked for blacks (4 percent) and youth from other races (6 percent) than for whites (2 percent). Despite the recent, greater increase experienced by whites, in 1999 a higher percentage of blacks (25 percent) and youth from other races (23 percent) were held in detention compared to whites (18 percent), and this pattern held true in all four offense categories (Harms 2003).

The largest difference among races in 1999 concerned drug offenses. Whereas the detention rate for whites was 17 percent, the rate for blacks was 38 percent, and for those from other races it was 21 percent. Drug offenses also accounted for the sharpest decline in the use of detention between 1990 and 1999. Whites experienced a drop of 9 percent, while the reduction was 14 percent for both blacks and youth from other races. The over-

Table 10.7 Percentage of Delinquency Cases Involving Detention by Offense, 1990–1999

Type of Offense	Year		
	1990	1995	1999
All offenses	23%	17%	20% (100%)
Person	27	22	23 (27%)
Property	19	13	16 (36%)
Drugs	38	21	23 (13%)
Public order	27	19	23 (24%)

Source: Puzzanchera et al. (2003b).

representation of blacks in detention becomes clearest when the data show that despite black youth being involved in 28 percent of delinquency cases, they accounted for 36 percent of detained cases in 1999. Once again, drug offenses were associated with the most severe differences. Whereas blacks were involved in 27 percent of all drug cases processed by juvenile court, they were detained in 45 percent of drug prosecutions. Finally, while whites and youths from other races tended to be detained most often for person offenses (21 percent and 32 percent, respectively) and public order offenses (20 percent and 29 percent, respectively), not surprisingly blacks were held most frequently for drug offenses (38 percent) (Puzzanchera et al. 2003b).

The detention pattern in terms of age looks much like what would be expected. In 1999, detention was used more frequently for older delinquents. As the age of the offender increased in each offense category, so did the prospect of detention. Overall, 14- (21 percent), 15- (23 percent), 16- (22 percent), and 17-year-olds (23 percent) were much more likely than 10- (6 percent), 11- (9 percent), and 12-year-olds (13 percent) to be detained. Property offenses were least likely to result in detention, regardless of age. Among older youth (16 and 17), those committing person offenses were most likely to be detained. With respect to the detention population, 15- (23 percent), 16- (26 percent), and 17-year-olds (21 percent) accounted for 70 percent of those held prior to trial in 1999. There was virtually no change in the age profile of detention between 1990 and 1999, except for 17-year-olds, who witnessed an increase of 4 percent (Puzzanchera et al. 2003b). Finally, although the percentage of detained defendants younger than age 12 did not increase in the 1990s (there was a 1 percent decline), the actual number of juveniles detained from that age group increased 22 percent (Harms 2003). The increase of young offenders and girls in detention has placed new demands on detention centers, which some observers believe lack appropriate programs for these new inmates (ABA/NBA 2001).

Table 10.8 Percentage of Delinquency Cases Involving Detention by Gender and Race, 1990–1999			
	Year		
Gender/Race	1990	1995	1999
Male	24%	18%	21%
Female	18	12	16
White	20	14	18
Black	29	22	25
Other Races	29	21	23
Source: Puzzanchera et al (2003b).			

Status Offenders

Detention was rarely used for status offenders between 1989 and 1998. It was used most frequently for runaways (13 percent) and least often for truants (2 percent). A charge of ungovernability (8 percent) was only slightly more likely to result in detention than were liquor violations (7 percent). These percentages varied by no more than 1 percent throughout the 1990s (Puzzanchera et al. 2003b). The actual number of status offenders held in detention was last reported for the 1988–1997 period (see Table 10.9). These numbers reveal an overall increase in those detained, especially for liquor violations (103 percent), but a reduction in the detention for most of the offense categories (Puzzanchera et al. 2000).

Between 1990 and 1999, males (3–14 percent) were more likely than females (2–11 percent) to be detained in each of the offense categories. Both males (14 percent) and females (11 percent) were most likely to be held in runaway cases. Next to running away, liquor violations (male = 8 percent; female = 5 percent) and ungovernability (male = 8 percent; female = 7 percent) were the offenses most likely to result in detention. During the 1990s, the status offense detention population was dominated by white youth, who constituted approximately 70 percent of those detained in all offense categories (see Table 10.10).

Despite the white dominance of the detention population, black status offenders were more likely than whites or youths from other races to experience detention. The differences were most apparent in liquor violations, where blacks (14 percent) were twice as likely as juveniles from other races (6 percent) or whites (7 percent) to be detained. Liquor violations and running away (14 percent each) accounted for the offenses for which blacks were detained most often, while for whites (12 percent) and youths of other races (15 percent), running away was the most prevalent (Puzzanchera et al.

Table 10.9 Number of Detained Status Offenders by Offense and Percent Change, 1988–1997

Status Offense	Year			Change
	1988	1993	1997	
All Offenses	8,500	8,900	9,400	11%
Runaway	3,200	3,200	2,600	−18
Truancy	700	600	600	−8
Ungovernable	1,900	1,000	1,500	−23
Liquor	1,400	1,600	2,800	103
Miscellaneous	1,300	2,500	1,800	45

Source: Puzzanchera et al. (2000).

Table 10.10 Percentage of Status Offense Detention Population by Offense and Race, 1990–1999

Race	Offense			
	Runaway	Truancy	Ungovernability	Liquor
White	65%	71%	72%	69%
Black	31	25	26	27
Other races	4	4	2	4

Source: Puzzanchera et al. (2003b).

Table 10.11 Percentage of Status Offense Cases Involving Detention by Gender and Race, 1988–1997

Gender/Race	Year		
	1988	1993	1997
Male	10%	9%	6%
Female	12	7	5
White	10	7	6
Black	14	10	8
Other races	14	11	4

Source: Puzzanchera et al. (2000).

Table 10.12 Age Profile of Detained Status Offenders, 1988–1997

Age	Year		
	1988	1993	1997
10 or younger	1%	<1%	<1%
11	1	<1	1
12	4	5	3
13	11	8	6
14	20	17	16
15	27	25	21
16	23	27	28
17 or older	13	18	22
Total	100	100	100

Source: Puzzanchera et al. (2000).

2003b). Table 10.11 shows how the use of detention in status offense cases has declined in terms of race and gender over the course of the last several years.

In 1998, youths ages 15 and younger accounted for the vast majority of those held for running away (65 percent), truancy (73 percent), and ungovernability (66 percent). Liquor violations were the only offenses to break this pattern: 16- and 17-year-olds made up 73 percent of those detained (Puzzanchera et al. 2003a). The percentages throughout the 1990s are virtually identical to the 1998 numbers (Puzzanchera et al. 2003b). Despite these age patterns, half of the status offense detention population was 16 or older in 1997. In fact, studies indicate that the detention population has been getting increasingly older (see Table 10.12).

Expedited Trial Date for Detention Cases

As consolation to defendants whose cases have been sent to an adjudicatory hearing, the vast majority of jurisdictions provide an expedited trial date in detention cases. Forty-four jurisdictions have placed a specific time limit on when the trial is supposed to begin in this situation, while Alabama and Missouri request priority without a defined deadline (see Appendix E). The number of days permitted ranges from 3 to 180 (with one week to one month the typical allotted period), while the clock starts from the youth's being taken into custody until after a number of possible pretrial hearings. Obviously, the later the clock is turned on means the more time the prosecution has to initiate proceedings (and the more time the juvenile spends in detention). Moreover, many jurisdictions allow extensions of the deadline, sometimes for a considerable number of days or for an unspecified length of time, provided a usually undefined *good cause* is demonstrated (consult Appendix D). Finally, in some states the deadlines apply to secure detention only or vary by type of offense committed or by whether the defendant has requested a jury trial rather than a bench trial (an option available in a few states; see Chapter 13). Precisely how many jurisdictions apply these deadlines to status offense detainees is unclear. While in some states the statute clearly endorses the same deadline for status offenders (LA, NH, NY, WY), Florida demands a much quicker adjudicatory hearing for these defendants, but Minnesota allows twice the amount of days in which to try detained status offenders.

As in the violation of other deadlines, the failure of the prosecutor to begin the adjudicatory hearing on time (including extensions) does not require a dismissal of the case. Instead, the youth would have to be released from detention (perhaps with conditions).

Summary: Key Ideas and Concepts

- PO as gatekeeper to detention
- Detention in humane settings an exception, not the rule
- Variety in sites that can serve as detention and the impact of this on research
- Unique mandates for detaining versus releasing youth
- Ability to detain youth in adult jails and requirements for doing so
- Philosophical and practical obstacles to granting bail to youth
- Advantages and disadvantages of denying bail to youth
- Potential discriminatory result of lack of bail
- Detaining youth to prevent crime
- Particular offenses qualifying for (levels of) detention
- Particular offenses making initial detention mandatory or presumptive
- Critical role of the parent affecting all three criteria for detention of youth
- Due process problems with preventive detention
- U.S. Supreme Court belief in the constitutionality of preventive detention
- Unique detention criterion of preventing harm to youth
- Youths' ability to request detention and to be held if in their best interests
- Broadness and vagueness of detention criteria
- Conflicting results in research studies of detention factors
- Idea of making the detention decision via a point system, and potential problems
- Limited detention period before petition must be filed
- Judge reviewing initial detention decision as a second decision maker
- Parents' presence mandated at the detention hearing
- Question of when and whether probable cause finding is required in detention cases
- Requiring PO to satisfy a level of proof that detention is necessary
- Potentially demanding conditions accompanying release of youth
- Potential unique aspects of juvenile detention

Discussion Questions

1. What are the implications behind the PO serving as the gatekeeper to detention?

2. Discuss how well research studies have accounted for the variety in locations that can serve as detention for juveniles, and the potential impact that variety can have on findings.

3. Should juveniles be granted a right to bail? Why or why not?

4. Discuss the many ways in which a parent can affect the decision to detain a youth.

5. Should juveniles be subjected to preventive detention? Should their situation differ from that of adults in this context? Why or why not?

6. Should preventing harm to the youth be a criterion for detaining youth? If so, should there be any special requirements in detaining these youth, such as a special facility?

7. Discuss the U.S. Supreme Court's position in *Schall v. Martin*. Did the Court effectively respond to the lower federal courts in the position they held regarding preventive detention?

8. What are the implications of the broadness and vagueness of juvenile detention criteria?

9. Will a point system help or hurt the decision to detain youth? How?

10. Should juveniles be held in detention without a probable cause finding by the court? Why or why not?

11. What rights should youth have at a detention hearing? Should the detention hearing be a formal or informal testing of the evidence?

12. Discuss the unique aspects of juvenile detention and whether juveniles benefit or suffer from this uniqueness.

Endnotes

1. As one example of the confusion, Mississippi calls for detention hearings for both delinquents and status offenders and uses shelter care for abused and neglected children.
2. Jurisdictions that specify the PO makes the initial detention decision are: AL, AZ, CA, DC, HI, IL, IN, KS, LA, ME, MD, MI, MN, MO, MT, NE, NH, NJ, NM, NC, ND, OH, RI, SC, SD, TN, TX, VA, WI.
3. The states that prohibit placing status offenders in detention are: AL, AK, CT, FL, IL, MD, MT, NH, NJ.
4. The states that allow child welfare licensed facilities to operate as detention locations are: GA, MI, MT, NE, NM, NC, ND, OH, PA, SC, TN, VT, WI.
5. The jurisdictions that allow foster, group, and private homes to operate as detention locations are: DE, DC, FED, GA, ID, IL, HI, LA, ME, MA, MI, MN, MT, NE, NV, NH, NM, NC, ND, OH, PA, RI, SC, SD, TN, VT, VA, WI.
6. The states that allow the youth's home to serve as a detention location are: CA, DE, FL, IL, ME, MA, MI, MN, MT, NE, NV, NJ, UT, VT, WI.
7. The states that mention any suitable place as a detention location are: AK, IA, ME, MO, NM, ND, OH, PA, UT, VA.
8. The jurisdictions that allow delinquents to be placed in shelter care are: AZ, CO, DC, HI, IL, MN, MO, MT, NH, NJ, NC, PA, SD, TN, UT, VA, WI.
9. The jurisdictions that require the least restrictive setting in detention are: AK, AR, CA, DE, FED, FL, GA, HI, ME, MI, MN, MS, NC, OR, SC, SD, TN, UT, WI.
10. In Illinois this provision applies only to youths who are younger than 15 held in jails outside Chicago.

11. The states that prohibit jailing status offenders are: AL, AK, AZ, AR, CA, GA, ID, IN, IA, MA, MI, MS, MO, MT, NE, NV, NJ, NY, NC, ND, OH, OK, OR, PA, RI, SC, TN, TX, UT, VT, VA, WY.
12. The states that provide for bail or a bond for youth are: AR, CO, CT, DE, GA, KS, LA, MA, MI, MN, MT, NE, NM, OK, SD, TN, UT, VT, VA, WA, WV.
13. The states that provide for ROR are: DE, IN, MA, MN, NJ, OR, VA, WA, WV, WI.
14. The states that give a right to bail to status offenders are: GA, LA, MA, MI, OK, SD, VT, VA, WV.
15. The states that mention a violation of sorts as a reason to detain are: AK, CA, CO, FL, IA, ME, MA, MI, MN, MT, NC, OK, OR, SC, SD, TN, VA, WA.
16. The states that mention pending charges as grounds for detention are: IL, KS, KY, ME, MN, MT, NY, NC, OK, OR, SC, SD, TN, VA, WA.
17. The jurisdictions that mention preventing harm to or intimidation of a witness as grounds for detention are: DC, ME, UT, WA.
18. The states that permit placing status offenders in detention in these situations are: AR, HI, IA, KY, LA, MI, MS, MO, NE, NV, SC, TN, TX, WA.
19. The jurisdictions that mention the nature of the offense are: AR, CA, DE, DC, HI, IL, KY, LA, MI, MN, NJ, OR, VA.
20. The jurisdictions that mention the prior record are: AR, CA, CO, DE, DC, HI, IL, KS, KY, LA, MI, MN, NJ, OR, SC, SD, TN, TX, UT, VA.
21. The jurisdictions that mention current or past use of force or weapons are: DC, KS, MI, NY, OR, SC, SD, TN.
22. The states that mention the parent's ability and willingness to supervise the youth are: DE, GA, HI, ME, MD, MI, MO, NH, NM, OH, PA, TX, VA, WI, WY.
23. Kentucky, Texas, and Utah cite the probability of committing an offense dangerous to others as a reason to detain.
24. Kansas, Massachusetts, Oklahoma, and South Carolina cite the history of violence as a criterion for detention.
25. See Bail Reform Act of 1984, 18 U.S.C.S. 3141 section 3141 et seq.; *United States v. Salerno*, 481 U.S. 739 (1987).
26. See *Schall v. Martin*, 689 F.2d 365, 371 (2d. Cir. 1982).
27. The states that identify the lack of a parent as a reason to detain are: AL, CA, DE, GA, HI, IL, IN, ME, MD, MI, MS, MO, NH, NM, NC, ND, OH, PA, TX, UT, VA, WA, WV, WI, WY.
28. Florida and Georgia specifically prohibit detention if the reason is to allow the parent to avoid legal responsibilities.
29. This criterion is used in AL, ID, IA, VA.
30. The states that employ this criterion are: AR, CA, CO, IL, MI, MN, OH, WV.
31. The states that focus on the parent in this context are: CA, GA, IL, ME, MD, MO, NH, OH, PA, TX, UT, VA, WI, WY.
32. Colorado warns its detention administrators to be extra vigilant to prevent gang reunions and recruitment within their facilities.
33. The states that allow detention for status offenders in this situation are: IN, IA, KS, KY, MO, NV, NC, TX, WI.
34. The states that mention runaways are: LA, MI, MN, NC, OR, VA.
35. The jurisdictions that mention escapees are: AR, CA, DE, DC, FL, IA, KS, ME, MI, MN, MT, NC, OK, TN, VA, WI.
36. The states that mention fugitives are: AZ, AR, CT, DE, FL, IA, KS, MA, MN, MO, MT, NV, NC, OK, OR, SC, SD, TN, VA, WA, WI.
37. The states that mention being removed from the jurisdiction are: GA, MO, MT, NV, ND, OH, PA, TX, UT, WI, WY.
38. The jurisdictions that cite ties to the community are: AR, CA, DC, HI, IL, MI, NJ, OR.
39. The states that mention escape or failure-to-appear history are: AL, CA, CT, DE, IL, KS, LA, ME, MA, MI, MN, NJ, OR, SC, SD, TN, UT, VA.
40. The states that include the parent here are: CA, GA, IL, MD, MO, OH, PA, TX, UT, WY.
41. Nine states (AL, AK, AR, DE, HI, IN, MA, RI, WI) argue that the numbers can be accounted for by the seriousness of the offense, but 29 states (AZ, CA, CO, CT, FL, GA, IL, IA, MD, MI, MN, MO, NE, NJ, NM, NY, NC, ND, OH, OK, OR, PA, SC, SD, TX, VA, WA, WV) have failed to associate the disproportionate rate with offense severity (see Leiber 2002).
42. See, for example, *D.G.H. v. Gnat*, 682 So.2d 210 (FL. App. 1 Dist. 1996). Florida law does permit an IO to release a youth with points that qualify for detention, but the IO must secure the prosecutor's approval. Judges can also reach a decision not indicated by the points but must specify in writing the criteria relied on in place of the points.

43. New Jersey insists on the presence of counsel for the child at the detention hearing. If counsel is absent from the first detention hearing, it becomes necessary for a second hearing (or a "first official" one), which means a 48-hour extension is allowed to ensure the attorney's presence. In Oklahoma, transportation has been cited as a reason to grant a one-day extension. Utah is so concerned that a parent appear at the detention hearing that a 48-hour extension will be provided to guarantee the parent be present at this stage. Probable cause to believe the defendant committed the offense must be established at a detention hearing in Virginia. If witnesses are needed to sustain this proof, an extension of up to 72 hours is possible. Finally, in Wisconsin, a 48-hour extension can occur when the youth represents an imminent danger to self or others or when the parent is either unavailable or unwilling to supervise and care for the child. It is certainly possible that continuances or extensions for these reasons could be granted in other jurisdictions that have failed to mention their availability in a statute.

44. The states with the same standards for delinquents and status offenders are: CO, FL, GA, IL, KS, LA, NY, WA, WY. While the time period for status offenders is shorter in AK, OR, SD, TN, TX, it is longer in CT, KT, MN, NM.

45. The jurisdictions that require release here are: AL, CA, DC, IL, IN, IA, LA, MI, MO, PA.

46. The jurisdictions that permit the hearing to proceed without the parent are: AK, AZ, AR, DC, FL, HI, IL, IA, KS, MI, MN, MS, MT, NJ, NY, OR, SC, SD, TX, UT.

47. The states that require a second hearing here are: Al, CA, GA, NM, ND, OH, PA, TN, VT, VA, WI, WY.

48. The jurisdictions that require a probable cause finding are: AK, AZ, AR, CA, CO, CT, DC, FL, GA, HI, IL, IN, IA, KY, LA, ME, MA, MI, MN, MS, MO, MT, NE, NH, NJ, NM, NY, NC, ND, PA, RI, TN, TX, UT, VA, WA, WV, WI.

49. The jurisdictions that require a probable cause finding in status offense cases are: DC, IL, KY, MS, MO, MT, NE, NY, TN.

50. The states that offer a probable cause hearing are: CO, MI, MN, NE, NJ, NM, RI, WA, WV.

51. The other two progressions (PC—DH—Pet, and DH—PC—Pet) were not discovered in any state but could possibly be operating somewhere.

52. The jurisdictions that demand this outcome are: AK, AR, CA, CO, DC, IL, KY, LA, MN, MT, NE, NJ, NM, NY, VA, WV.

53. The states that do not mention any rights at the detention hearing are: AZ, CO, HI, ID, IA, ME, MD, MA, MT, NE, NV, OK, SD, VT.

54. South Carolina does not allow the defendant to waive the right to counsel without having conferred with counsel first at the detention hearing.

55. The states that recognize a right to silence at the detention hearing are: AL, AR, CA, FL, GA, IN, LA, MI, MN, NH, NM, NY, ND, OH, PA, TN, TX, VA, WV, WI, WY.

56. The jurisdictions that require notice of charges at the detention hearing are: AL, CA, DC, FL, GA, IA, KY, LA, MI, MN, NH, NM, NY, TN, UT, VA, WI, WY.

57. The jurisdictions that recognize the youth's right to confront and cross examine witnesses at the detention hearing are: AK, CA, IL, KY, LA, MI, MS, NY, NC, OR, TN, WI, WY.

58. The jurisdictions that recognize the youth's right to be heard and to present evidence at the detention hearing are: CA, DC, KY, LA, MI, MS, NY, NC, OR, TN, WA, WI, WY.

59. The states that allow any probative evidence to be considered at the detention hearing are: AL, AR, CO, HI, MN, MS, MO, NH, OH, SC, SD, TN, TX, UT, VA, WY.

60. As we discussed previously, another seven states have constructed similar controls by demanding certain amounts of proof be shown that the criteria to hold defendants have been satisfied by using terms such as *strong probability* (CT, MI), *serious* or *substantial risk* (ID, IA, NY), and *reasonable grounds* (DE, HI).

61. The jurisdictions that require the judge to explain the reasons for detention are: AL, AK, AR, CA, DE, DC, IL, KS, KY, MI, MN, MO, NH, NJ, NC, OH, OR, RI, SC, TN, WA, WI.

62. Eight states require review hearings. The first review hearing must typically be held within one week (NC, TX, UT), 10 days (OR, SC), or two weeks (CT, DE, NJ). Subsequent review hearings vary from 7 to 30 days after the initial review hearing.

63. The jurisdictions that have identified conditions for release or that require reasonable ones are: AL, AR, CA, CO, CT, DE, DC, GA, ID, IL, IN, IA, KS, KY, LA, ME, MI, MN, MO, NE, NH, NJ, NM, NY, NC, OR, SC, SD, TX, UT, VT, VA, WA, WI, WY.

64. If the youth were eligible, an informal agreement could not be ruled out here. However, since a petition is often already filed at this stage, there is some momentum not to go backward and dismiss or unfile a petition and grant the defendant an informal agreement. ✦

Chapter 11

The Pretrial Stage

Focus of Chapter 11

In Chapter 11 we examine the important, but often neglected, pretrial stage of the juvenile court process. During this stage critical issues must be resolved, including the defense's discovery of the state's case and the filing of any motions, such as to suppress illegally seized evidence. It is also possible for diversion to occur during this stage. And, if there is going to be a plea bargain, which is common and perhaps the dominant method of resolving cases in some juvenile courts, it will likely happen at this time. In other words, in any given juvenile court, most cases will not proceed beyond the pretrial stage and will not experience an adjudicatory hearing or trial.

Key Terms

* *Alford* plea
* arraignment
* charge bargains
* colloquy
* competency hearing
* consent decree
* dismissal bargain
* guilty plea
* nolo contendere plea
* nol pros bargain
* nonnegotiated guilty plea
* not guilty plea
* plea bargaining
* pretrial stage
* probable cause hearing
* sentence bargains
* trial penalty

An Underdeveloped Stage

In criminal court the pretrial stage is highly developed. Juvenile court tends to be the opposite, no doubt as a result of a historical antipathy to both legal trappings and adversarial proceedings. There are comparatively few and possibly even no pretrial hearings, depending on the youth's custody status and the jurisdiction.

The detention hearing frequently serves as the one all-purpose hearing provided to juveniles. It can combine functions served by a number of postarrest, pretrial proceedings in adult court, such as the bail hearing, initial appearance, arraignment, and preliminary hearing or grand jury proceeding. It is common for a detained youth to not encounter another hearing until the actual trial. This situation can create serious disadvantages for detained defendants, a topic explored in Chapter 13. Nevertheless, there are some notable exceptions to this situation. First, as previously noted, some states divide the need to detain determination and the probable cause findings into two proceedings, and in some states (CO, MI, NE, NJ, NY, RI, WV), a probable cause (or *preliminary*) hearing will follow the detention hearing rather than precede it. Otherwise, only a handful of states (FL, LA, NY, UT, WI) further subdivide these preliminary issues into a separate arraignment or *plea hearing* (New York calls it an initial appearance) in which detained youths are given a chance to respond to the charges against them. Most states, if they even expect or provide for such a plea opportunity from young defendants, conduct the arraignment through the detention hearing. Given the relative comprehensiveness of the detention hearing and the relatively short time between it and the trial, it is not surprising to see so few examples of intervening hearings.

Few pretrial hearings are available for the released population as well. It is common for a youth on released status to proceed from intake to trial without experiencing any hearing along the way. In fact, it appears that only 30 jurisdictions have any legislative or judicial provision dealing with pretrial hearings in any capacity. First, 22 jurisdictions use a variety of hearing titles to refer to what appears to be the same phenomenon—namely, to advise the released defendant of the charges contained in the petition and to solicit a plea or response to the charges. These hearing titles include *advisory, advisement, answer petition, plea, arraignment,* and *initial* or *first appearance.*[1] Twelve of these jurisdictions also associate these hearings with status offenders after the petition is filed.[2] Some states have identified a deadline by which this hearing must occur, ranging from 10 (NY) to 14 (WA), 15 (ID, LA), 20 (MN), or 30 days (UT, WI). Seven states (AZ, FL, GA, ID, IN, WV, WY) formally announce (and perhaps others allow) that this arraignment process can be combined with the adjudicatory hearing, perhaps eliminating any hearing for this group prior to trial.

Pleading

As suggested previously, it is common for a juvenile defendant never to be asked to formally plead. If given the opportunity, however, a youth should be permitted to tender the same three pleas available to adult defendants:

1. Not guilty (for a variety of reasons, ranging from simply not having committed the act to insanity)

2. guilty

3. nolo contendere

A not guilty plea denies guilt and indicates, for the time being at least, that an adjudicatory hearing will be necessary if the prosecution wants an adjudication. A guilty plea amounts to a self-conviction, a complete surrender of all trial-related rights. Here, the defendant dispenses with the need for the prosecutor to prove the charges. (We will return to guilty pleas later in the chapter.) An *Alford* plea is a controversial version of the guilty plea.[3] With the plea, the defendant pleads guilty but protests innocence. This contradiction could stem from the defendant's inability to acknowledge guilt while recognizing the wisdom or advantages in pleading guilty. Although infrequent in criminal court, *Alford* pleas are constitutionally sound and are unlikely to be rejected by the court, assuming there is sufficient evidence (independent of the guilty plea) to convict.[4] How juvenile courts stand on this issue is unclear, however. Only three states have identified a policy on *Alford* pleas, with Florida permitting them and Minnesota and Oklahoma forbidding them.

Finally, a nolo contendere plea literally means "no contest," or that the defendant will not challenge or refute the prosecutor's charges. Unlike in criminal court, where the plea is universally possible, only eight states officially have listed its availability in juvenile court (CA, DE, FL, KS, LA, MI, UT, WI), but most jurisdictions probably permit it. A *nolo* plea is the legal equivalent of a guilty plea in that the defendant stands convicted. Besides the benefit of never having to admit guilt per se, the *nolo* plea differs from a guilty plea in that the former cannot be used as evidence in a subsequent civil prosecution should the victim attempt to sue the defendant after the criminal trial. Its connection to postponing civil liability makes the nolo contendere plea less relevant to and less frequent in juvenile court.

Pretrial Issues

Nine jurisdictions offer a *pretrial* or *status conference* that could achieve the same purpose as an arraignment or serve as a clearinghouse for all pretrial motions and requests by the prosecution and defense.[5] The latter mission is exactly what Minnesota and Montana expect of their *omnibus hearing*. Three jurisdictions refer to a competency hearing when the defendant's ability to form intent or mens rea and to be culpable for an offense are drawn into question (DC, NY, WA). Finally, West Virginia appears to be alone in calling for a *preliminary hearing* for released defendants as well as for detained ones.

Some observations are important here. The absence of a specific statutory provision for a pretrial hearing *does not* mean that one cannot or will not occur. Local practice in a juvenile

A courtroom where pretrials are conducted. Are juveniles disadvantaged by not having the same type of pretrial processing as adults?

court might routinely involve a pretrial proceeding nowhere to be found in the statute or court rule. It would not be unusual (or unwise) for a juvenile court with a high volume of cases to create (on its own initiative) either an arraignment proceeding to weed out cases (through diversion or guilty pleas, perhaps) or a pretrial conference to resolve outstanding questions and issues prior to the adjudicatory hearing. It is equally important, however, that the lack of a statutory provision for such proceedings means that juvenile courts in those jurisdictions *are not* obligated to implement them. Also, the relative absence of these provisions in the statutes indicates that juvenile courts, on the whole, are probably offering much less than criminal courts in the way of pretrial evaluation and examination of issues and charges. The implications are twofold. First, juvenile courts can be the benefactors of a more expedient pretrial processing of cases than criminal courts, which seem to be bogged down endlessly in proceedings. Second, juvenile defendants may be the recipients of much less in the way of procedural due process, judicial scrutiny of pretrial matters, and defense attorney motions challenging various facets of the prosecutor's case, as compared to what must happen to adult defendants.

One thing that is certain and unique to juvenile court is that (except for serious cases in Texas) no charges are initiated via a *grand jury indictment.* A defendant's right to be indicted has not been constitutionally recognized in criminal court (except in the federal system and in some state constitutions), and where it is required, it has been limited strictly to criminal prosecutions. Except in the state of Washington, prosecutors in juvenile court typically do not file an *information* either (the alternative to indictment in criminal court), but the petition is basically the same document.

Regardless of whether hearings are provided for, a number of pretrial issues must be resolved in delinquency cases. The most common issues include:

- prosecutorial disclosure of evidence;

- defense discovery of evidence;

- motions from both sides for continuances;

- defense motions to suppress illegally seized evidence;

- defense disclosure of alibi or insanity defense;

- determination of defendant's capacity or competency; and

- various defense motions (e.g., joinder or severance, change of venue) or pleadings (e.g., double jeopardy, denial of speedy trial).

Almost every case should involve, to some extent, the defense attorney's attempt to discover the evidence the prosecution will rely on at trial. Prosecutors in criminal court have a constitutional obligation to disclose exculpatory evidence (i.e., evidence that tends to show the defendant did *not* commit the crime) to the defense (*Brady v. Maryland* 1963). Whether the Supreme Court would place the same burden on juvenile court prosecutors is uncertain, but a handful of states have already ruled this way (CA, MD, MN, NM, NY, OH). The extent to which this prosecutorial duty is observed is difficult to determine. Prosecutors must also disclose offense-related information to the defense that is controlled by state statute. This information includes such items as:

- physical evidence;

- laboratory analysis;
- witness statements;
- arresting officer's statement and report; and
- defendant statement.

Some jurisdictions appear to give juvenile defendants the same discovery rules and rights as those granted to adults,[6] while other states have given less discovery opportunity to juveniles.[7] For most of the country, it is basically impossible to discern what the discovery rules are in juvenile court, let alone how much they differ from adult court standards. Nevertheless, a few jurisdictions have detailed the possible consequences of a prosecutor's failing to disclose that to which the defense is entitled. Besides ordering disclosure and discovery, the trial judge is empowered to:

- issue a "reasonable order";[8]
- hold the prosecutor in contempt (FL, MN, NM);
- grant a mistrial (FL, MD);
- dismiss the proceedings (CA);
- continue the proceedings; and[9]
- prevent the use of the evidence.[10]

Many of these consequences could also be used to sanction a defense attorney who failed to disclose necessary information.

It is difficult to believe that a defense attorney would not be allowed to file a motion to suppress illegally seized evidence in juvenile court. Although the U.S. Supreme Court has not yet demanded that juvenile court adopt the exclusionary rule (applicable to criminal court via *Mapp v. Ohio* 1961), no jurisdiction has refused to recognize this constitutional right in juvenile court, at least for delinquents. While a handful of jurisdictions have applied to exclusionary rule to status offense cases (AL, DC, OK, TN, TX), some states appear to deny these youth this protection (HI, MT, ND, PA, VT). Whether defense attorneys file these motions proportionately to what they do in criminal court and whether judges rule on these motions with the same standards they use in adult court are different matters, however (a topic we return to in Chapter 13).

Criminal court rules routinely require defense attorneys to notify the prosecutor and court if they are pursuing certain defenses, such as insanity or alibi. The former defense requires extensive examination of the youth's mental capabilities, while the latter entails someone's vouching for the accused (which means the prosecutor will want to examine the veracity of the alibi). Several states have demanded notification of the insanity defense in juvenile court,[11] while even more jurisdictions insist on defense warnings of an alibi defense.[12] The insanity issue should be easy to address, since every jurisdiction authorizes extensive physical, medical, and mental examinations of juveniles whenever there is a question about the youth's welfare along any of these lines. Whether the insanity defense is allowed in juvenile court (see Chapter 13), whether defense attorneys will invoke the defense in juvenile court like they would in criminal court, and whether there will be a separate pretrial proceeding addressing *only* this issue (perhaps together with the juvenile's competency to stand trial) are matters that could make juvenile court's handling of the insanity defense (and competency to stand trial) different from criminal court's.

A variety of situations involve constitutional rights, since they could affect the defendant's ability to get a fair trial. They are governed by various rules of criminal procedure (and are usually resolved during the pretrial stage in adult court). For example, when there are multiple charges against a defendant or when there are multiple defendants in a single case, a fair trial may be threatened if all the charges are joined in one trial or all the defendants are prosecuted simultaneously (as opposed to severance of the charges or defendants into multiple prosecutions). Some states have openly embraced all rules of criminal procedure in juvenile court,[13] while other jurisdictions have adopted adult court joinder and severance rules in juvenile court.[14] Whether defense attorneys in juvenile courts in these locations take advantage of these rules and file appropriate motions and whether the remaining jurisdictions observe the same rules would be difficult to determine. Similarly, a change of venue could be necessary in situations where pretrial publicity has been so extensive as to make it unlikely to find an impartial fact finder at trial. Although juvenile courts are rather liberal in granting changes of venue when the youth's residence is an issue (as we discussed in Chapter 4), moving the location of a trial for any other reason is rarely recognized in juvenile court law. To be sure, the general absence of both extensive pretrial exposure of juvenile defendants and trial by jury may lessen the need to relocate the trial in the juvenile system.

Finally, defense attorneys may want to make a claim or pleading prior to trial about the inappropriateness or unconstitutionality of prosecuting the defendant, for a number of reasons. For example, the statute of limitations may have expired. That is, the state has a limited amount of time within which to prosecute alleged offenders for most crimes (but not murder). Failure to charge offenders within that time period usually prevents the state from prosecuting them. Presumably, juvenile defendants would be entitled to this same protection. Similarly, once charged, an adult defendant has a constitutional right to a speedy trial within a certain amount of time. The Supreme Court has not extended this constitutional safeguard to juvenile defendants, however, and fewer than half of the states have granted juveniles this right (see Chapter 13). Thus, defense attorneys in only some jurisdictions could file a pretrial motion establishing a violation of this right in juvenile court and expect to win that argument. A juvenile defendant might also have a claim of double jeopardy, stating that the case about to be prosecuted has already been prosecuted and resolved via an acquittal or an adjudication. In *Breed v. Jones* (1975) the Supreme Court determined that juvenile defendants do indeed have the right to be free from double jeopardy. The context of that case, as we saw in Chapter 3, involved an adjudication in juvenile court followed by a conviction in criminal court, however. Although it is impossible to guarantee that the Supreme Court would forbid two prosecutions or adjudications *within* juvenile court (rather than *between* it and adult court), it would seem that this practice would be found by the Court to constitute double jeopardy.

Informal Resolutions

Overall, then, although juvenile courts vary from one jurisdiction to another, there has been relatively little development in the way of creating pretrial hearings. If separate pretrial proceedings do exist, however (perhaps something like an arraignment or pretrial conference), they provide excellent opportunities for the case to be informally resolved (i.e., without conducting an adjudicatory hearing). Two caveats need to be mentioned here. First, separate pretrial proceedings *are not* a prerequisite to an informal resolution. They merely facilitate or increase the probability of one. Second, an informal resolution can occur anytime from before the petition is filed until after a trial has occurred. In Chapter 9 we discussed *informal agreements,* which usually involve resolving the case without filing a petition. However, informal agreements are possible even after a trial has been held. In fact, a youth could even be sentenced to one. So actually, a more precise, more comprehensive definition of an informal resolution is *resolving the case without relying on a trial-based adjudication.* This concept will become clearer in Chapters 13 and 14, which deal with adjudicatory and disposition hearings.

For now, we will focus on the possible pretrial informal resolutions, which should far outnumber instances of the like after trial has begun. These informal resolutions include:

- informal agreements;
- consent decrees;
- nol pros (with or without bargaining); and
- guilty pleas (with or without bargaining).

Informal Agreements

There could be a simple reason—perhaps detention got in the way or a defendant, parent, victim, or prosecutor was problematic at intake—that a case that otherwise could have resulted in an informal agreement at intake ended instead in a petition being filed and the case being sent forward. It is probably never too late in juvenile court for a petition to reverse its course and to be referred back to intake for an informal agreement, provided all necessary parties agree to that outcome. A petition does tend to gain forward momentum and only rarely proceeds backward. Nevertheless, the obstacle that detention can place in the way of resolving the case this way (not to mention other possible extenuating circumstances) makes taking "another" postpetition look at an informal agreement perhaps the only fair thing to do. If indeed the case finally results in an informal agreement during the pretrial stage, all the dimensions we reviewed in Chapter 9 would now apply equally.

Consent Decrees

Another type of informal agreement, virtually identical to an informal agreement, is frequently available, at least for "first-time," nonserious offenders. This clone of an informal agreement is widely known as a consent decree[15] but can also be called *continuance under supervision* (AL, IL), *deferred prosecution* or *deferred disposition* (CO, FL, OK, TX, WA), *continuance without finding delinquency* (MA, MN), *adjournment in contemplation of dismissal* (NY), *placing the petition on file* (RI), an *improvement period* (WV), or a *nonjudicial disposition* (CT), or it may simply not be given any name at all (UT). A number of states have linked consent decrees with their teen court programs (CO, FL, OK, TX, WI).

Consent decrees should be available for both delinquents and status offenders. Again, it needs to be noted that these pretrial examples of diversion can also surface at the disposition stage (see Chapter 14), following a guilty plea or a trial. Distinguishing the pretrial versions of this diversionary leniency from sentencing leniency may be difficult or impossible (compare Chapter 14).

A consent decree represents for the nonserious offender (possibly) another chance for diversion of the case. Assuming a first arrest or referral to juvenile court involves a nonserious offense (whatever that means in state law), the offender could be eligible for an informal agreement. If, after the informal agreement successfully expires, the youth reoffends, again not seriously, a second informal agreement would be unlikely in today's climate (in the past informal agreements could be given repeatedly to the same defendant). The youth's second arrest or referral could result, then, in the youth's "first" official appearance in juvenile court (or perhaps literally within the juvenile court building itself). If the circumstances are right (i.e., nonserious offense, workable defendant and family, and agreeable prosecutor), a consent decree could be granted. The same result would be likely for a true first offender whose offense was above the threshold for an informal agreement but nevertheless qualified for a consent decree. Perhaps a felony would be eligible for the latter but not the former. Like the informal agreement, a consent decree is a diversionary attempt inasmuch as successful completion of its terms means the youth does not have a delinquent record.[16] To the extent that a consent decree mostly replicates an informal agreement (and offers some defendants a second bite of the diversion apple), there is reason to wonder whether they both will survive. The answer will depend on how much a jurisdiction believes in or relies on diversion.

Consent decrees in many jurisdictions share numerous features with informal agreements, such as that certain crimes and records may be eliminated from eligibility,[17] the defendant and parent must agree to it (CT, FL, IL, MT), the prosecutor must agree as well (FL, IL, PA, WY), services must be performed by the youth (CT, IL, PA, WA, WY), and success means the petition will be dismissed.[18] As with the informal agreement, the consent decree offers potentially significant supervision of the youth in the community, with serious responsibilities and tasks imposed.

Nevertheless, there can be some important differences between the two forms of diversion. For one thing, although a consent decree ensures a nondelinquent record, the court record it produces is worse than that for an informal agreement. With a consent decree the youth has penetrated deeper into the system. The matter was not resolvable at intake (perhaps because the offense was too serious for an informal agreement). It would be in a defendant's legal interests to have an informal agreement the first time around in order to still be eligible for a consent decree on the second visit. Once a consent decree has been granted, however, the next visit to court means that an informal agreement is virtually impossible, a second consent decree is unlikely, and the prosecutor almost certainly will seek an adjudication.

Even more important, consent decrees frequently require an admission of guilt from the defendant, which, unlike the admission that might be necessary for an informal agreement, is actually the equivalent of a guilty plea in several states.[19] There can be a serious difference between a statement offered to a PO at intake (which cannot be used to convict the youth thereafter) and an acknowledgement of guilt offered to a judge at court. For example, whereas a violation of an informal agreement would, at worst, mean the youth would have to go to trial for the original charge, a consent decree violation can result directly in an adjudication, assuming the violation of the consent decree is proved (CO, IL, NM, UT, WA).

Because a consent decree is typically negotiated among court personnel, the prosecutor is likely to have more of a say in developing its terms than in an informal agreement.[20] To be sure, prosecutors are being given more control over the intake process and generally must sign off before an informal agreement can be reached. Nevertheless, the specific terms of the informal agreement are likely to be consummated between the PO and the defendant and parent, without interference from the prosecutor. The prosecutor's direct say in the formulation of a consent decree could, however, result in the youth's performing services unlikely to be associated with an informal agreement, especially along the lines of having to testify against co-defendants.

Finally, it is common for consent decrees to entail more intensive supervision of the youth by the PO and to last longer than an informal agreement. Both of these circumstances make sense inasmuch as consent decrees could easily involve a slightly different population than those eligible for informal agreements—namely, somewhat more serious and chronic offenders. So, for example, Connecticut, Washington, and Wyoming make community supervision a mandatory part of a consent decree, while West Virginia and Wyoming let consent decrees last for a full year. Illinois, Washington, and Wisconsin provide for a two-year consent decree period. Finally, the terms in Florida, Minnesota, Montana, and Utah are indeterminate. Unless the consent decree is the judge's disposition following adjudication (see Chapter 14), this informal resolution, like an informal agreement, is a dismissal bargain. That is, the youth surrenders a right to trial (and perhaps complete vindication) and agrees to perform certain services in exchange for an ultimate dismissal of the charges.

The Nol Pros Bargain

A third way the youth can negotiate a dismissal of the charges is the nol pros bargain, so named because of the prosecutor's *nolle prosequi* power (i.e., to decide *not to prosecute*). Here the prosecutor agrees to drop some or all of the charges against the youth. Actually, the nol pros is not always negotiated. For example, the prosecutor may unilaterally decide not to prosecute because of a lack of evidence (or perhaps some or all of the evidence has already been ruled by the court to have been illegally seized), a reluctant victim or witness, or the sheer volume of cases and a lack of manpower. Depending on the jurisdiction, the decision to withdraw the charges for these reasons may not occur until the case has reached the adjudicatory level. With or without discussions with the defense, the prosecutor may also nol pros the charges out of consideration for the accused, rather than from a concern about being able to prosecute and win the case per se. If the charges are not severe and the child appears to be a "good kid" (who perhaps simply would not agree to an informal agreement or a consent decree), the prosecutor may elect to nol pros. The prosecutor might do the same in the case of a defendant on the verge of adulthood whose case was not serious and for whom any juvenile court intervention would seem to be a waste of resources. Similarly, a prosecutor could decide the charges are not worth pursuing when a youth has left the jurisdiction, has just been transferred to criminal court on another case, has been newly arrested as an adult, or has been committed to an institution on another case. Finally, if the treatment programs available for dependent and neglected youth or status offenders seem more appropriate for the defendant, a prosecutor might withdraw the delinquent petition in order to channel the case into a more suitable forum.

It is likely, nevertheless, for a nol pros to be secured via an overt negotiation. That is, the prosecutor drops the charges in exchange for a number of possible services performed by the youth, including all of those available via an informal agreement and a consent decree. What distinguishes the nol pros bargain from the other dismissal bargains is that it is not designed to be a diversionary mechanism. Consequently, its audience is potentially much broader in scope. In fact, a nol pros bargain can be offered to a juvenile with a lengthy delinquent record (or who is facing a serious charge), or can be linked with a plea bargain so that the defendant ends up being adjudicated. For example, if a juvenile with several prior adjudications were involved in a series of burglaries with a group of more culpable adults, the prosecutor might offer the youth a nol pros for some or all of the burglary charges (i.e., some charges could be nol prossed while some could be plea bargained) in exchange for testifying against the adult co-defendants. Even a youth with no prior record in this situation (and maybe even acting alone) would probably be viewed as too serious an offender for either an informal agreement or a consent decree, but would be a prime candidate for a combined nol pros/plea bargain.[21]

It is in an office such as this near the courtroom that prosecutors and defense attorneys regularly negotiate pleas. Should plea bargaining be allowed in juvenile court?

Although the nol pros bargain often involves defendants who are "ineligible" for an informal agreement or consent decree,[22] these youths will likely be required to perform the services associated with those diversion efforts. Moreover, youths whose cases are nol prossed are often required to perform tasks particularly useful to the prosecutor (rather than those that benefit the defendant per se, such as counseling). Examples of services the prosecutor could seek include:

- information about or testimony against co-defendants;
- guilty plea(s) to other charge(s);
- cooperation from the defense attorney not to fight a collateral matter;
- youth's agreement to leave the jurisdiction permanently; and
- restitution to the victim.

Securing information, testimony, and guilty pleas from a defendant have already been covered. Interestingly, the prosecutor can trade a nol pros for the defense attorney's silence. For example, if the youth has a case for which a disposition has been prepared or if the prosecutor is about to request transfer of the juvenile to criminal court on another case, a nol pros may purchase the defense attorney's agreement not to fight these matters. Also interesting is that the prosecutor's goal may simply be to encourage the juvenile to leave the area and to stop bothering neighbors. Finally, the prosecutor may exchange a nol pros for a restitution amount that exceeds the limit identified in the statute. As we will see in Chapter 14, which deals with dispositions, some states place a maximum on the amount of restitution for which a juvenile (and/or the parents) is liable if adjudicated. One way to circumvent that limit in cases where the victim's losses exceed that limit is to arrange a settlement in which the defendant and/or parent agrees to pay an amount of restitution that exceeds the statutory limit in exchange for making some or all charges disappear.

Plea Bargaining

These prosecutorial objectives can also be accomplished through plea bargaining, (except in Mississippi, which has prohibited the practice in juvenile court). Whereas plea bargaining necessarily involves pleading guilty (another way in which an informal resolution can occur), not all guilty pleas are negotiated (as with nol pros cases). There are a variety of nonnegotiated guilty pleas, which we will review shortly. Chances are, however, that most guilty pleas are secured through overt bargaining, so we will examine them first. The mechanics of plea bargaining in juvenile court mirror what transpires in criminal court. That is, the youth pleads guilty, often phrased as *making an admission* in the statutes, in exchange for some *charge* or sentence consideration. The defendant, usually represented by defense counsel, is a necessary party to this exchange, as it is the defendant who ultimately must plead guilty or offer an admission.[23] On the other side of the exchange is a prosecutor (or the person acting like one), as in adult court. Nevertheless, just like in adult court, the judge may be the one with whom the defense negotiates the outcome of the case, unless, perhaps, state law prohibits the judge's participation in plea bargaining.[24]

Regardless of who represents the state, the dimensions of plea bargaining are the same in both courts. The two types of plea bargains are charge bargains and sentence bargains, both of which might be linked together and/or with a nol pros bargain. Charge bargaining can occur in four contexts. First, there is charge reduction, which involves lowering the severity of the offense (perhaps from a felony to a misdemeanor, or from a higher-degree felony to a lower one). Second, unique to juvenile justice is the ability to merge charge reduction and nol prossing by having the youth *admit to a status offense* in lieu of a delinquent charge. In this situation the charges have been reduced, inasmuch as a delinquency charge is replaced by a status offense, and have been nol prossed, to the extent that the result is a nondelinquent or noncriminal finding. Nevertheless, the youth in this situation is officially adjudicated (as a status offender) and is subject to a wide variety of dispositions (some of which are also available for delinquents), and has a court record that some jurisdictions allow to be factored into subsequent criminal court sentencing (see Chapter 12). Thus, referring to this scenario as a true or complete nol pros would be inaccurate in some jurisdictions. Third, the defendant could plead guilty "on the nose" (i.e., to the highest offense charged) if other related or nonrelated charges are either reduced or nol prossed. This deal could even involve reducing or eliminating charges against someone else the defendant does not want prosecuted fully or at all. Finally, the youth could plead guilty in exchange for the prosecutor's agreement not to pursue a discretionary charging choice. For example, the youth's guilty plea could purchase a *withdrawal* of (or a decision *not to implement*) either a *petition to prosecute* the juvenile as a *habitual offender* or to *transfer* the case to *adult court*. Except for the status offense and transfer situations, these charging arrangements are available in criminal court as well.

Sentence bargains may exist independently of or grouped with a charge bargain (just as in adult court). They focus on the outcome or disposition of the case, which can be *complete* or *incomplete*. *Complete sentence bargains* mean what they imply: a firm agreement between the two sides as to the precise disposition that will follow the guilty plea. In juvenile justice, any of the following could be the outcomes of a complete sentence bargain:

- Probation (with length and conditions specified)
- A specific commitment (perhaps with length specified)
- Remain in present commitment
- Suspended sentence
- No disposition

The judge would accept or reject the package. Accepting the package means the guilty plea would be entered with the understanding that the agreed disposition would follow. Rejecting the package would force the defendant to resume negotiations with the prosecutor, proceed to trial, or enter a guilty plea with uncertain results (unless both sides can steer the package to another, more receptive judge).

Incomplete sentence bargains do not guarantee a particular disposition outcome per se. Instead, the maneuvering falls short of that point. In juvenile justice, any of the following arrangements could be negotiated in this context:

- Let another judge sentence.
- Prosecutor and/or victim keeps silent at disposition.
- Prosecutor and/or victim endorses defense attorney disposition.
- Youth is referred to a specific institution (which may or may not accept the youth).
- Disposition is transferred to the county in which the youth resides or to some other jurisdiction.

In all these variations, the defendants are not guaranteed an ultimate outcome or what the disposition will be, and would not be entitled to withdraw the guilty plea if they are merely disappointed in the outcome. To be sure, the prosecutor who agrees to remain silent or to support the defense sentence request is obligated to do so. Nevertheless, if the defense request is for probation, there is absolutely nothing that binds the judge to honor that request per se. In the end, an incomplete sentence bargain could seriously backfire and could prove to be antithetical to the defendant's hopes. Both complete and incomplete sentence bargains can occur in criminal court as well.

Unique Aspects of Juvenile Court Plea Bargaining

Plea bargaining is a much more recent phenomenon in juvenile court versus criminal court; although criminal court plea bargaining can be traced to the twelfth century (Sanborn 1986), the juvenile court version emerged in the late 1960s. The reason for the late development is simple: Prior to the 1967 *Gault* decision, juveniles were denied the constitutional rights defendants needed both to demand trial and to offer something of value in exchange for consideration from the prosecution. We already know that the juvenile's inability to invoke a right to silence, to insist on confronting and cross-examining accusers, and to be represented by counsel in the pre-*Gault* era made "trial" a formality or a foregone conclusion in juvenile court. Moreover, POs at that time did not need to extend charge or sentence considerations to a juvenile in order to secure either his or her cooperation (i.e., a guilty plea) or an adjudication. Even if an admission were believed to be desirable or relevant to adjudicating the youth in what was a one-sided "hearing," a week or so in detention would be easily arranged and could loosen the youth's lips without having to include some reward as well.

Does Plea Bargaining Belong in Juvenile Court?

Despite the fact that *Gault* extended juvenile defendants the necessary rights with which to demand trial and thus made plea bargaining relevant to juvenile court, there is still a general disbelief that plea bargaining occurs there. A number of views contribute to this disbelief. First, the juvenile court process is generally less cumbersome than that in criminal court, so juvenile court would appear to be less dependent on plea bargaining to resolve cases. Second, the *parens patriae* philosophy would ideally encourage prosecutors and defense attorneys to seek the appropriate outcome for the youth rather than seek plea negotiation to avoid trial. Third, charge bargaining in juvenile court is perceived by many as worthless since dispositions are still *not* determined by the number or severity of adjudicated charges in most juvenile courts. That is, the defendant cannot guarantee a reduction in the sentence outcome by charge bargaining alone, which can happen in adult court.

Finally, plea bargaining is considered harmful to juvenile court for two reasons. The adoption of plea bargaining would contribute to the criminalization of juvenile court. In criminal court, plea bargaining serves, in part, to minimize the state's punishment of the offender. A transfer of this logic to juvenile court, plea bargaining to minimize the state's treatment or punishment of the youth, would create an image problem for the court. In addition, permitting sentence bargaining is dangerous, as it could interfere with arriving at the disposition best suited to the defendant's treatment needs. That is, the prosecutor's agreement with defense counsel to accept a particular sentence could prevent an alternative disposition more compatible with the youth's rehabilitation. It is for this reason, in fact, that some juvenile courts (CO, DE, DC) prohibit sentence bargaining (see Sanborn 1993a).

Is Juvenile Court Less Dependent on Plea Bargaining?

Given sufficient resources, it is true that a juvenile court could be much less dependent on plea bargaining than a comparable criminal court. To the extent that the following descriptions apply to a particular court, we could find close to a zero rate of plea bargaining there. This result would be unique to juvenile court (Sanborn 1984).

Juvenile court prosecutors do not need plea bargaining. If the prosecutor's office has adequate staffing (i.e., proportionate to that of criminal courts), it should need to plea bargain fewer cases in juvenile court compared to adult court for at least five reasons:

1. High diversion rate
2. No jury trial
3. No speedy trial rule
4. Quick bench trial
5. Process structured to convict

Although all of these elements are not characteristic of all juvenile courts, most of them should apply to most juvenile courts. We already know about the system's dedication to diversion and the *McKeiver* decision to deny the right to jury trial. The last three features will be explored in greater depth in Chapter 13. Suffice it to say here that most of the country does not require a prompt resolution of charges (at least for defendants not in custody) and provides an adjudicatory hearing that is usually a quick experience that transpires in a setting that is not designed to maximize fairness (or acquittals) (see Chapter 13). If juvenile court prosecutors so desire, they can afford to go to trial much more regularly than their criminal court counterparts. If juvenile court prosecutors want to maximize the severity and number of charges for which the defendant is adjudicated (to make the youth's record as damaging as possible), forcing virtually all cases to trial could be rewarding without threatening to collapse the system (see Sanborn 1993a).

Juvenile court defense attorneys do not need plea bargaining. On the other side, an adequately staffed public defender's office (or the sufficient availability of appointed and private counsel) would not desperately need plea bargaining or to have their clients plead guilty in juvenile court for at least five reasons:

1. High diversion rate
2. No jury trial
3. Quick bench trial
4. No trial penalty
5. Not much at stake

The first three reasons refer to the defense attorney's ability (matching the prosecutor's) to take the majority of cases to trial without an exorbitant cost in time and resources. Similarly, this ability on everyone's part to resort to trial (assuming there are enough judges to try the cases) should mean that juvenile court does not exact a trial penalty on defendants (Sanborn 1993a). That is, youth who demand trial should not be penalized or given a harsher disposition simply for exercising that right, since the juvenile system seemingly can afford to provide trials to all those who request one. In criminal court the trial penalty is believed to be one—and perhaps *the* major—inducement for defendants to plead guilty and to waive their right to trial. Not only would a trial penalty seem unnecessary and gratuitous in juvenile court, but it would also damage the court's image by suggesting that it is more concerned with how cases are processed than with what the youth's treatment needs are.[25]

Finally, except for defendants at risk of being institutionalized in secure state facilities, the juvenile version of prison (see Chapter 17), there is simply not that much at stake in juvenile court sentencing (especially compared to what can happen to defendants in criminal court). Defense attorneys do not face literally life or death choices for their clients—or, for that matter, prolonged incarceration threats (20 to 1,000 years) when deciding whether to go to trial or to plead guilty in juvenile court. The situation and choices are drastically different in adult court. Moreover, unlike standard adult prisons, many juvenile facilities may actually represent an improvement over the home and neighborhood in which the youth resides. Thus, there is little potential of dire results that would convince defendants and defense attorneys that a trial must be avoided at all costs in juvenile court. If the defense attorney also wants to minimize the severity and number of charges for which the defendant is adjudicated (to make the youth's record as clean as possible), and prosecutors are unwilling to negotiate, forcing virtually all cases to trial would seem to offer the counsel nothing to lose and everything to gain.

Are Juvenile Courts Just as Dependent on Plea Bargaining?

Some juvenile courts can and do have remarkably high rates of cases proceeding to trial because some combination of these features can make guilty pleas and plea bargaining less necessary there than in adult court. If neither prosecutors nor defense attorneys particularly need or want plea bargaining, less of it can be expected and allowed to occur in juvenile court without necessarily threatening its survival. But, as we have noted frequently, juvenile courts vary considerably. Many do not have anything close to adequate or proportionate staffing (see Chapter 8). Some have no more than one or two of each: judges (including masters and referees), prosecutors, and public defenders. These juvenile courts could be seriously dependent on plea bargaining (and other forms of informal resolution) just to keep afloat. Thus, incredibly high rates of plea bargaining could be characteristic of some juvenile courts for the simple reason of limited personnel. These juvenile courts might also be prone to exact a trial penalty on defendants who insist on an adjudicatory hearing.

Incentives for Plea Bargaining in Juvenile Court

Plea bargaining has no necessary relationship to staffing resources in either juvenile or adult court. In other words, plea bargaining makes perfect sense and could be routine in juvenile court, regardless of whether staffing is adequate. Both prosecutors and defense attorneys have several reasons to want plea bargaining even if they do not especially need it to conserve resources. If nothing else, plea bargaining could reflect a nonadversarial approach typically used by opposing counsel in juvenile court, and an ability to agree as to what should happen to and for a particular defendant, making trial unnecessary.

Juvenile court prosecutors want plea bargaining. Incentives for the prosecutor to negotiate for guilty pleas are numerous and can include:

1. securing information on co-defendants;

2. guaranteeing restitution to victim;

3. a bad or weak case;

4. clearing the docket;

5. the same results as a trial;

6. ensuring adjudication and/or disposition;

7. the best interests of the child; and

8. spare witnesses.

Just as a nol pros can be traded for information and sufficient restitution, so can guilty pleas. Perhaps the most common reason prosecutors pursue a plea bargain is a weak or bad case. Although the weak case might mean the evidence against the defendant is non-existent or insufficient, it is more likely an indication that the evidence is problematic (e.g., an admissibility obstacle) or that a witness is reluctant or unavailable. Plea bargaining also allows prosecutors to clear out the backlog in their caseloads. In fact, cases can seem to linger forever. A plea bargain may afford the opportunity to resolve matters that otherwise would grow stale, possibly disappear, and never be prosecuted. Without a trial penalty, most dispositions should be unaffected by the method of adjudication. In fact, it is not unusual in juvenile court for the disposition recommendation to have been completed prior to trial and before it is known whether there will even be a trial. Because the likely results often are known prior to adjudication, trial could easily be perceived as simply a longer and more complicated way to reach the same result as a plea bargain. At the same time, nothing is ever certain in juvenile court (or in criminal court). "Dead-bang," "good" cases can be lost because of unforeseen witness, judge, or evidence problems. Plea bargaining ensures adjudication will occur, and perhaps a particular disposition as well. It guarantees prosecutors will not lose total control of the case. Finally, plea bargaining spares witnesses the ordeal of having to testify in court (and possibly from even appearing there) and may give prosecutors flexibility in reaching a conclusion of the case that actually furthers the youth's best interests (Sanborn 1993a).

Juvenile court defense attorneys want plea bargaining. Incentives for the defense attorney to negotiate guilty pleas are equally numerous and can include the following:

1. Charge bargaining to help record

2. Avoiding transfer to criminal court

3. Sentence bargaining minimizes disposition

4. No defense or the same result as trial

5. Best interests of the child

6. Defendant actually welcomes result

7. Keeping control of case

8. Clearing the docket

Contrary to popular belief, charge bargaining is not worthless in juvenile court. Reducing the severity or number of charges helps the defendant in two ways. First, the fewer overall adjudications the youth has, and the fewer of these adjudications that involve felonies (especially those of the highest degree), the greater the chance of avoiding building a certification record. For youths destined to return to juvenile court, it is critical to have the most innocuous record possible, as that might be *the* factor that keeps them from being transferred to criminal court. In fact, defense counsel might trade a guilty plea directly to defeat a current transfer effort. Second, if the defendant is eventually transferred to adult court or commits a future offense as an adult, the juvenile court record can be factored into the criminal court sentence (see Chapter 12). The more felony adjudications the offender has, the lengthier the adult sentence can be.

Sentence bargaining in juvenile court may indeed be dangerous in that the youth might not receive an "appropriate" disposition. Accordingly, some juvenile courts prohibit it. Where sentence bargaining is permitted, however, it offers an attractive and effective opportunity for defense counsel to lessen the amount of supervision or interference juvenile court will impose on the child. Juvenile court dispositions are arranged along a hierarchy of increasing controls over the youth's behavior. Envision a ladder with a series of rungs (for more discussion of this disposition ladder, see Chapter 14). The more the juvenile recidivates or will not respond to treatment, the higher up the ladder the youth climbs (like being promoted to a higher grade in school). The highest rungs on the ladder are juvenile prisons and transfer to criminal court (about the worst outcomes for a youth). Thus, the farther down the ladder the defense attorney can keep the disposition via a sentence bargain, the greater the chance the youth will not be sent either to a secure state facility or to adult court for the next offense.

The vast majority of juveniles taken into custody are guilty. For many, if not most, there is neither a credible defense to launch nor a reason to expect better results via trial. These realities can prompt defense attorneys to seek a plea bargain, which also can allow counsel to appear reasonable (defense attorneys can cry wolf only so often without losing credibility). In addition, plea bargaining can provide counsel flexibility to fashion the most appropriate arrangement for the defendant, perhaps even to secure a result the youth endorses. Unlike the typical sentences in adult court, juvenile court dispositions can involve programs and settings the defendant perceives as beneficial and even desirable. A plea bargain might better ensure that result, as well as better ensure that defense counsel does not lose control of the case, which can occur via trial.

Even though no trial penalty may be associated with demanding a trial in juvenile court, insisting on an adjudicatory hearing can sometimes open a Pandora's box of sorts. A plea bargain can potentially enable the defense to circumvent *both* trial (where ugly facts about the defendant may surface) *and* a PO's investigation of the youth for disposition (where even uglier facts about the defendant and family may surface). In fact, a complete sentence bargain, if accepted, guarantees these results. Proceeding to trial, however, creates a greater opportunity for the PO's involvement, together with a possible discovery of damaging facts and circumstances, which, in turn, could end in a harsher disposition for the defendant than would have been negotiated by counsel.

Finally, like prosecutors, defense attorneys can be concerned about lingering cases that can require frequent visits to court. Plea bargaining can offer an opportunity to relieve defense counsel's obligation to one defendant, hopefully benefiting that client while allowing other defendants to receive more effective representation.

Juvenile court judges want plea bargaining. Prosecutors and defense attorneys are not the only ones with incentives to plea bargain. Judges and the court itself stand to gain from it as well in a number of ways:

1. Clear the docket.

2. Attend other cases.

3. No trial needed.

4. Judge avoids work and decisions.

5. Compensation for overcharging and overkill.

6. Admission helps defendant.

7. Defendant guaranteed help.

8. Defendant helped faster and better.

The first four judge-oriented incentives highlight the ability of plea bargaining to expedite the processing of cases (no trial needed), to allow the court to resolve outstanding matters (and ensure they do not fade away, which might frustrate victims and ignore the defendant's treatment needs), to focus on other cases where trial might be necessary, and to free up judges from time-consuming adjudicatory hearings. The higher the court's plea bargaining rate, the fewer judges are needed to work the juvenile division full time (perhaps enabling the county to divide a judge's responsibilities between juvenile and adult courts). Plea bargaining eliminates one and possibly two decisions the judge would otherwise have to make. Minimally, plea bargaining means the judge does not have to make a potentially difficult (and incorrect) choice in whom to believe: the police, the witness, or the juvenile. Many judges will welcome this result. If sentence bargains occur, especially complete ones, the judge also need not worry about being *the* person to designate the proper disposition.

The last four court-related reasons address the best interests of the child. Plea bargaining allows for manipulation (i.e., reduction) of the state's prosecution of the defendant in a way that could be either legally unavailable to a judge (who cannot simply make cases disappear) or politically unfeasible for a judge (who cannot indiscriminately exercise nullification or wholesale reduction of charges) in cases that go to trial. Treatment-oriented people can support plea bargaining, since an admission (or the guilty plea) is considered the first (often necessary) step along the path to rehabilitation. Moreover, unlike a trial (where an adjudication cannot be guaranteed), a plea bargain ensures not only that the defendant will receive some level of attention from the court, but also that this attention can begin sooner (no wait for trial and disposition), and possibly result in a better disposition than the court itself would have developed.

Juvenile court victims and defendants want plea bargaining. Finally, plea bargaining has something to offer victims and defendants too. Victims are not forced to testify, are ensured an adjudication (without a judge's questioning their veracity and credibility), and possibly secure a greater amount of restitution than either the statute provides or the judge would have granted. Besides reducing the charges and disposition (and maybe avoiding a negative label, like rapist), plea bargaining lets defendants avoid the trauma of trial and damning evidence. If the defendant retained counsel, the cost of a plea bargain might be less than that of a trial. An immediate release to community supervision or the earlier commencement of an institutional sentence (compared to waiting for trial and disposition) could provide extra incentives for a detained youth to plea bargain.

There are, then, important and numerous incentives on everyone's part to have a plea bargain, completely apart from resource limits and concerns (although they may be present as well). Thus, any particular juvenile court could experience a high rate of plea bargaining, just like adult courts tend to. Moreover, as in adult court, unless one of the major actors (prosecutor, defense attorney, judge, victim, defendant) refuses to cooperate, there is a good chance a plea bargain will result in juvenile court. One distinguishing aspect in this regard is the *role of the parent* in juvenile court plea bargaining. This person can be *the* determinative factor in whether a plea bargain will occur, despite the presence or absence of other significant incentives. Even if the defense attorney desperately wants to go to trial, failure to convince the parents of the wisdom of that choice could force counsel to seek the prosecutor's best offer for a guilty plea. The reverse is possible as well. Even if the defense counsel has an incredibly good plea bargain offer from the prosecutor, the parents' refusal to let the defendant plead guilty could force the case to trial (Sanborn 1984).

Is Plea Bargaining Less Problematic in Juvenile Court?

Plea bargaining in juvenile court may also be different with respect to the number and severity of *problems* the practice causes the system. The most serious problem linked with plea bargaining in adult court is the trial penalty, or defendants' receiving harsher sentences because their cases proceeded to trial. This potential result is what many critics point to as the unconstitutionality of plea bargaining (i.e., punishing the exercise of a constitutional right). It also triggers other serious problems, such as *role distortion* and *pressure on innocent defendants to convict themselves*. The former problem pertains to how plea bargaining in adult court makes everyone act in ways they should not: Prosecutors become all powerful by assuming the roles of judge and jury as well as their own role (they charge, convict, and sentence), judges become mostly irrelevant, defense attorneys become brokers rather than defenders since defending a client could cost the defendant years in prison (or death), and defendants become submissive pawns who waive rights that are just too costly to exercise. In addition, with such significant potential differences in the sentences accompanying guilty pleas compared to trial convictions, it is not unreasonable to think that some defendants who actually are innocent may accept the lesser of evils represented in a plea bargain.

These interrelated problems rarely accompany juvenile court plea bargaining. Where they do exist, however, they should be much less severe. For example, even in juvenile courts that use a trial penalty, the lack of extreme sentences should mean there cannot be a tremendous difference between guilty plea and trial adjudication sentences, which should mean less pressure for the innocent to self-convict and less likelihood that court personnel will experience significant role distortion. Moreover, both the PO's influence in developing dispositions (see Chapter 14) and the prohibition against sentence bargains in some juvenile courts should minimize sentence differentials in guilty pleas versus trials and defendants' fears of such differentials (Sanborn 1984).

Nonnegotiated Guilty Pleas

Even if a plea bargain cannot be worked out, that does not mean that a guilty plea will not be tendered or that the case must end in a trial. The defendant might still plead guilty, simply without any negotiation (or despite a failed negotiation attempt). Defendants can offer a variety of nonnegotiated guilty pleas that may or may not be specifically calculated to bring about a desired, plea bargain–like result. Depending on the jurisdiction, these nonnegotiated variations could account for a significant proportion of the guilty pleas registered in a juvenile court. Thus, we cannot assume that the guilty plea rate and the plea bargaining rate are absolutely the same. These nonnegotiated guilty pleas include the following:

- **Noncalculated**

  Straight guilty plea

- **Calculated**

  Mercy or contrition guilty plea

  Trade-seeking guilty plea

  Quick guilty plea

  Factual guilty plea

  Slow guilty plea

A *straight guilty plea* is offered with no strings attached and with no expectations of reward. Numerous motivations can explain why a defendant would be willing to waive rights without insisting on a payback per se, including:

- a need or desire to admit guilt;

- a confession or overwhelming evidence of guilt makes challenging the case impossible or foolish;

- a deal with the prosecutor is not particularly necessary, desirable, or possible (e.g., perhaps the case is definitely headed to probation, no matter what); and

- a desire or need to save time or money (the defense attorney is paid less, the case is over *now*, and a return to court for a time-consuming trial is not necessary).

In all these situations, surrender without reward could be plausible for a defendant, especially if the offense and record (and the likely disposition) are not serious.

It is quite possible, however, that the defendant and defense attorney hope to achieve just as much through a nonnegotiated guilty plea as might be attainable via a plea bargain. However, all these calculated guilty pleas are tendered without negotiation and thus also without any assurances that results will match expectations and calculations. In this respect, these guilty pleas are similar to incomplete sentence bargains. With the *mercy* or *contrition guilty plea*, defendants throw themselves at the "mercy" of the court, hoping that their demonstration of contrition or remorse makes them eligible for leniency or that judges are prone to give lighter sentences to defendants who have pled guilty (and who have not wasted valuable court resources) than to those who have demanded trial. In fact, there could be an obvious and verifiable pattern of sentence differentials between these nonnegotiated guilty pleas and trial convictions. This pattern could in turn create a reasonable expectation of reward on the defendant's part, which is why this arrangement has been characterized in the literature as an implicit plea bargain (Newman 1966). Nevertheless, the mercy or contrition guilty plea guarantees nothing. Defendants cannot complain about not having their expectations satisfied. If these defendants end up getting "slammed" by the court, they have no grounds for challenging or appealing the disposition, assuming it is otherwise legal (just like in the incomplete sentence bargain situation).

The *trade-seeking guilty plea* may represent a number of situations. For one thing, it may simply substitute for plea bargaining in some cases or jurisdictions. If negotiations with the prosecutor appear or prove to be impossible, defense attorneys may try to use a guilty plea as an introduction to pursuing an agreement with the judge as to the possible outcome of that plea (especially if the judge is neither legally permitted nor inclined to actively bargain cases *prior* to the entry of a guilty plea). The ensuing interaction between defense counsel and the judge could in fact be indistinguishable from the typical plea bargaining exchange.[26] Similarly, defense attorneys could hope that a guilty plea to one or more charges could convince the prosecutor and/or the judge (who might convince a reluctant prosecutor) to dismiss one or more of the other charges, since the latter may not seem to be an important factor in developing the ultimate disposition. The defense attorney could also attempt to trade the guilty plea for a delay in the disposition date, hoping that a successful, longer period at home after adjudication could convince the judge at disposition that institutionalization is not necessary. Actually, only the imagination limits the nature of arrangements that can be attempted by defense counsel via this guilty plea.

As its title suggests, the *quick guilty plea* is time-oriented. It can be geared to the charge or the sentence. It is quite possible for a juvenile defendant to be undercharged, especially during the pretrial stage. At this point a prosecutor may not have fully developed the charges, especially if communication with the complainant, witnesses, and arresting officer has been limited or nonexistent. Thus, a misdemeanor charge of unauthorized use of auto may represent an understatement of the youth's actual felony auto theft behavior. In this situation, defense counsel could urge the defendant to plead guilty quickly so as to avoid the higher charge. The quick guilty plea can also serve to silence victims (assuming they are not present in court) who could influence the judge's interpretation of both the charges to be adjudicated and the disposition to be entered. The quick guilty plea could be focused completely on disposition, in that defense attorneys could think it critical to get the defendant to the sentence as quickly as possible, especially if other matters, such as other criminal charges, are about to come to the court's attention.

Defendants in juvenile court are sometimes better off resolving charges sequentially rather than collectively. In the latter situation, the volume of cases can make the youth appear to be a worse offender who needs a serious response from the court. If sequential resolution is possible via a quick guilty plea, however, the later cases will not be adjudicated until *after* the defendant has begun the first disposition. This situation could encourage the next judge not to disturb the original disposition, since the open offenses preceded the court's current treatment effort and there would be no indication that the treatment is not working (assuming there are no "new" arrests) (Sanborn 1984).

With a *factual guilty plea*, the defendant admits to the facts only. That is, the youth acknowledges committing the *acts* charged. In many jurisdictions, for a youth to be adjudicated delinquent, it must be proved that he or she committed an offense *and* is in need of treatment, rehabilitation, or care (we return to this idea in Chapter 14). The factual guilty plea is the defense attorney's attempt to take advantage of this dual requirement. Provided neither the offense nor the defendant's record is serious (helped perhaps by other circumstances, such as a "good" family and a good school record), the defense attorney would argue that although the behavior was wrong, the youth is not really delinquent and should not be adjudicated. This is a guilty plea, in other words, that the defense attorney hopes will evaporate into a dismissal or a nondelinquent adjudication. If the attorney is successful, court records might not indicate that a guilty plea ever happened.

Similarly, the *slow guilty plea* is technically not a guilty plea and will not be registered as such. In fact, a trial will be recorded as the method of adjudication. With a slow guilty plea, the defendant takes the stand and testifies to a lesser offense than the one charged, which may actually be the truth. Since this admission occurs within the context of trial, it would not be recognized as a guilty plea per se. Moreover, there is one critical difference between the two. Whenever a defendant attempts to officially plead guilty to a lesser offense, a judge's disagreement with that maneuver should lead to an opportunity for the defendant to withdraw the plea. The defendant who tenders a slow guilty plea, however, risks the judge's disbelief and a resulting adjudication on the higher charge (without a chance to take back the admission). Nevertheless, the admission on the stand is a guilty plea that is simply much more dangerous than a comparable official guilty plea.

A final guilty plea situation is difficult to characterize: the *uncounseled guilty plea*, or one offered by the defendant without being represented by a defense attorney. This is not a rare event in some juvenile courts. This guilty plea is troubling inasmuch as it could be offered in ignorance (a defendant who does not understand his or her rights) or, even worse, out of fear (of parents or the judge). Judges might purposely or unwittingly encourage defendants to give up their right to trial (and/or a right to counsel). Parents might command their child to plead guilty to prevent a return visit to court. Ideally, judges are supposed to protect defendants when these conditions arise. When defendants appear in court without counsel, however, judges could very well turn out to be part of the problem instead of the solution (Feld 1993a).

Given the potential attractiveness of pleading guilty in juvenile court, it is not surprising that some juvenile courts witness high rates of guilty pleas, comparable to the norm in criminal court. It is also not strange that guilty pleas would account for a high percentage of adjudications, since adjudicatory hearings are a relatively recent phenomenon in the juvenile system. Because the critical research on pleading guilty and plea bargaining in juvenile court has focused on delinquents (Sanborn 1992b, 1993a), it is difficult to tell how much of the previous descriptions apply to status offenders as well. Most likely, the discussion explains what transpires in these cases too.

The Pleading Guilty Process

When an adult defendant pleads guilty, a well-detailed and regulated ritual unfolds. The U.S. Supreme Court required this ritual, known as a colloquy, in *Boykin v. Alabama* (1969). Following the defendant's offer of the guilty plea, someone (i.e., judge, defense attorney, or prosecutor) must ask the defendant a series of questions geared to show that the guilty plea is both *intelligent* and *voluntary*. This communication or colloquy with the defendant must be made on the record, and covers numerous inquiries associated with the two constitutional requirements of intelligence and voluntariness. With respect to intelligence, the court is required to ascertain that defendants:

- are competent to plead guilty (i.e., aware of the surroundings and the purpose of the court proceedings);

- know the nature of the charges against them and to which they are pleading guilty;

- understand the rights they have (e.g., trial, silence, etc.);

- comprehend the effects of a guilty plea as to both the rights surrendered thereby and the resulting conviction; and

- are aware of the possible penalty, sentence, and consequences attending conviction.

With respect to voluntariness, the court is obliged to determine whether:

- defendants are pleading guilty free from impermissible inducements (such as certain threats);

- any plea agreements or other pressures have prompted the guilty plea; and

- the agreements or pressures have overwhelmed the defendant's free choice in pleading guilty.

Often the guilty plea colloquy will pursue a third inquiry so as to ensure that an innocent person does not plead guilty. That is, the judge usually requires the prosecution to establish a *factual* basis for the guilty plea from one or more sources (e.g., defendant's statements, evidence summary, police report). Although this task is performed routinely in criminal court, it is not constitutionally required unless the defendant tenders an *Alford* plea (*North Carolina v. Alford* 1970).

Since the Supreme Court has not yet determined that *Boykin v. Alabama* applies to juvenile court, the nature of the colloquy, if any, to which a juvenile will be subjected after entering a guilty plea depends on the jurisdiction involved. The regulation of the guilty plea process varies immensely. At the one extreme, eight jurisdictions have not yet explicitly addressed the prospect of defendants' pleading guilty in juvenile court (see Table 11.1). Neither the appellate courts nor the legislatures in those jurisdictions have demanded any action by juvenile court judges when guilty pleas are tendered. Consequently, the existence and nature of colloquies following pleas of guilty in these locations rely on local standards and practices. At the other extreme, seven states have adopted the rules of criminal procedure from adult court, meaning the colloquies in both court systems *should be* indistinguishable. Between these extremes are 37 jurisdictions that have applied various levels of control over the juvenile court guilty plea process. Altogether, the country divides equally between jurisdictions whose standards in juvenile court differ significantly from those in criminal court and those whose standards are mostly the same in both courts (Sanborn 1992b).

Table 11.1 Regulation of the Juvenile Court Guilty Plea Process		
A. Jurisdictions With Standards Different From Adult Court		
No Standards	**Minimum Standards**	**Moderate Standards**
AR	AL	AZ
FED	CT	IL
MT	HI	IN
NJ	KY	KS
ND	MO	LA
PA	NH	MD
SC	WY	MS
VA		NV
		OR
		RI
		SD
B. Jurisdictions With Standards Similar to Adult Court		
Mostly Same	**Virtually Same**	**The Same**
CA	CO	AK
DE	DC	ME
GA	FL	MA
IA	ID	OK
NE	MI	VT
NM	MN	WA
NY	NC	WV
OH	TX	
TN	UT	
WI		

Jurisdictions in Part A of Table 11.1 either do not officially require a colloquy or have established a version of one peculiar to juvenile court. States in the *minimum* and *moderate* categories require at least three fewer inquiries than those mandated in adult court. They may allow a variety of things to happen that are unique to juvenile court, such as:

- mention the need to tell defendants their rights, but not necessarily in the context of a colloquy or clearly connected to the offering of a guilty plea;

- fail to identify any specific rights about which juveniles need to be advised;

- omit reference in the colloquy process to some or many of the constitutional rights guaranteed to youth;

- remove the colloquy requirement altogether when the youth is represented by counsel;

- do not specify that it is the defendant who is to be personally advised of rights and who must tender the guilty plea;

- permit the defendant to be uninformed or misinformed about the maximum possible disposition;

- ignore the voluntariness requirement of the colloquy or simply mention it;

- disregard the accuracy or factual basis inquiry or make it optional; and

- do not specify that either the colloquy or the terms of any plea bargain must be put on the record.

Moreover, even if the *Boykin* requirements have been adopted in these jurisdictions, it is likely that failure to adhere to all the requirements will not invalidate the guilty plea, as it would in adult court.[27]

The juvenile court colloquy in jurisdictions identified in Part B of Table 11.1 *should be* exactly the same as or mostly indistinguishable from the one offered in adult court. Besides the seven states that have adopted adult court rules of criminal procedure, 19 jurisdictions have enacted fairly identical standards within their juvenile court statutes and rules of procedure (requiring only one or two fewer inquiries than are necessary in criminal court). Nevertheless, although 26 jurisdictions have borrowed or created adult court-like standards, it is unclear in most of these locations whether appellate courts would react in the same way they do in adult cases when technical or serious errors are made during the guilty plea process in juvenile court (i.e., reversing the plea and the conviction).

It is consistent with traditional juvenile justice philosophy that, despite the critical importance of the guilty plea together with the increased vulnerability of a juvenile defendant, the process surrounding the acceptance of an admission in juvenile court remains largely underregulated or unregulated. Only three states (MN, RI, TX) require that the defendant be warned that the juvenile court guilty plea or adjudication can be factored into a criminal court sentence in the future. The Kansas Supreme Court, in fact, has held that no such warning is necessary, despite the extreme potential impact juvenile court adjudications have on criminal court sentences in that state (see Chapter 12).[28] Similarly, only Mississippi and West Virginia instruct their juvenile court judges to reject a guilty plea if facts are disclosed during its acceptance that would suggest the youth has a defense to the charges. Only Georgia and Wisconsin demand their juvenile court judges deliver special advice to defendants about the disadvantages of pleading guilty without counsel. Appendix F outlines the requirements for accepting guilty pleas that 37 jurisdictions have adopted in their juvenile court statutes, rules, and case law (excluding the 15 jurisdictions with either no standards or adult court rules). Nearly half of the jurisdictions have announced that status offenders enjoy the same rights as delinquents in the guilty pleas process.[29]

When the judge accepts the guilty plea, the case can proceed immediately to disposition, especially if a complete sentence bargain is agreeable to all parties. Without this type of agreement, however, the case will probably be postponed for an analysis of the defendant and a disposition hearing. Nevertheless, those youth being adjudicated delinquent for the first (and perhaps second) time for a nonserious offense may be perceived as not requiring an in-depth evaluation and may be placed on probation immediately (perhaps eliminating any need for the defendant to return to court for this case).

A guilty plea does not always guarantee a final resolution of the charges against the defendant. That is because a judge could either refuse to accept the guilty plea or allow the youth to withdraw it in a variety of situations:

1. The child will not admit guilt (i.e., an *Alford* plea).

2. The parent, defense attorney, or victim objects to the guilty plea or plea bargain.

3. The judge cannot agree to the sentence bargain.

4. The PO recommends against the sentence bargain.

5. The guilty plea or plea bargain does not appear to be in the defendant's best interests.

Only the third situation is reasonably likely to bring about a similar result in criminal court. Also unlike adult court, it is possible that the juvenile court statute or court rule could actually compel the judge to reject a guilty plea in some or all of these contexts (CA, IA, NY, MI, MN, OK). For example, Iowa law not only requires that the parent consent to the guilty plea, but also that the guilty plea further the best interests of the child. Assumedly, if the prosecutor reneges on the plea bargain, the youth would also be able to withdraw the guilty plea, like in adult court. Supreme Court case law has resolved this issue in criminal court (*Santobello v. New York* 1971), but has not yet addressed this situation in juvenile court. If the guilty plea is refused or withdrawn, the case likely reverts to square one, meaning that a new informal resolution, plea agreement, or adjudicatory hearing will be necessary.

Heading to Transfer or to an Adjudicatory Hearing

Some cases have relatively little prospect of being informally resolved and instead are destined for either a transfer to adult court or an adjudicatory hearing. This is most likely to occur when any of the following situations exist:

- The defendant actually is (or adamantly claims to be) innocent.
- The parent insists on proceeding to trial.
- The offense and record are sufficiently serious to prompt a prosecutor to demand nothing less than a transfer to adult court.
- Whether the youth is guilty or not, the defense attorney believes the defendant has an excellent or decent chance for acquittal.
- Opposing counsel (and defendant) do not need or want to reach an agreement.
- The disposition (regardless of the method of adjudication) is likely to be either so minimal or so serious that the defense has nothing to lose in going to trial.

Summary: Key Terms and Concepts

- Pretrial stage undeveloped in juvenile court
- Fewer and uncertain status of some pretrial hearings in juvenile court
- Uncertain or different status of *Alford* pleas in juvenile court
- Uncertain status of nolo contendere pleas in juvenile court
- Impact of the relative lack of pretrial hearings in juvenile court
- Uncertain status of prosecutorial disclosure of evidence to the defense in juvenile court
- Possible penalties for failure to disclose evidence for prosecutors and defense attorneys
- Uncertain status of defense disclosure to prosecution in juvenile court

- Similarities and differences between consent decrees and informal agreements
- Variety of reasons for prosecutors to nol pros a case
- Similarities and differences between a nol pros and other dismissal bargains
- Similarities and differences between a plea bargain and other negotiations
- Complete versus incomplete sentence bargains
- Juvenile court plea bargaining only a few decades old
- Belief that plea bargaining does not belong in juvenile court
- Juvenile court less dependent on plea bargaining than criminal court
- All parties in juvenile court able to operate without reliance on plea bargaining
- Juvenile court as dependent on plea bargaining as criminal court
- Prosecutors and defense attorneys want plea bargaining in juvenile court
- All parties in juvenile court stand to benefit from plea bargaining
- The parent as a potential inducement for or against plea bargaining
- Plea bargaining less problematic in juvenile court compared to criminal court
- Abundance of nonnegotiated guilty pleas in juvenile court
- Underregulated guilty plea process in juvenile court

Discussion Questions

1. In what ways can the pretrial stage in juvenile court be considered underdeveloped?
2. Should *Alford* pleas be allowed in juvenile court?
3. Should the rules of discovery and other criminal court rules of procedure apply equally to juvenile court? If not, why not?
4. Should the exclusionary rule have equal force in juvenile court? If not, why not? If yes, should status offenders also be extended its protections?
5. Discuss the various ways in which an informal resolution can occur in juvenile court.
6. What limits, if any, should be placed on the granting of a consent decree or a nol pros in juvenile court?
7. What elements of juvenile court plea bargaining are unique?
8. Discuss the various types of charge and sentence bargains that occur in juvenile court.
9. Explain why some people would think that plea bargaining does not or should not occur in juvenile court.
10. Discuss the various reasons that juvenile court and the various juvenile court workers may be less dependent on plea bargaining than criminal court.

11. Why would some prosecutors and defense attorneys want plea bargaining in juvenile court and practice it as frequently as in criminal court?

12. Why could judges, victims, and defendants prefer that a case be plea bargained rather than litigated in juvenile court?

13. In what ways could plea bargaining be less problematic in juvenile court than in criminal court?

14. Discuss the various nonnegotiated guilty pleas that can occur in juvenile court.

15. What are the implications for researching plea bargaining in juvenile court, in light of the variety of nonnegotiated guilty pleas that are possible there?

16. Discuss the status of the pleading guilty process in juvenile court. Should the rules governing the judge's acceptance of guilty pleas be the same in juvenile and criminal court?

17. What are the implications of the relative lack of standards in accepting guilty pleas in juvenile court?

Endnotes

1. The jurisdictions that offer juveniles these various hearings are: AK, AZ, CO, DC, FL, GA, ID, IN, KS, KY, LA, MN, NH, NM, NY, OR, RI, SD, UT, WA, WI, WY.
2. The jurisdictions that offer these hearings to status offenders are: DC, FL, IN, LA, MN, NH, NY, OR, RI, SD, WI, WY.
3. The *Alford* plea was named after a U.S. Supreme Court case, *North Carolina v. Alford* (1970).
4. In *North Carolina v. Alford,* the Supreme Court held that when defendants deny their guilt while pleading guilty, the state bears an extra burden of offering evidence (independent of the guilty plea) that a factual basis exists for the guilty plea or that the charges are accurate.
5. The jurisdictions that offer a pretrial or status conference are: CT, DE, DC, ID, IA, MI, MN, OH, VT.
6. The jurisdictions that have given juveniles discovery rights equal to those of adult defendants are: DE, DC, FL, ID, IN, LA, MD, MA, MN, NY, NC, SD, TN, WA.
7. The states that have given juvenile defendants less discovery rights than adults are: CA, IA, MI, OH, RI, UT, WI.
8. The judge can issue "reasonable orders" in CA, DC, FL, MD, NM, NY, OH, RI, SD.
9. The judge can continue the proceedings in CA, DC, FL, MD, MN, NM, NY, OH, RI, SD.
10. The judge can prevent the use of the evidence in CA, DC, FL, MD, NM, NY, OH, RI, SD.
11. Notification of the insanity defense is required in DE, FL, KS, MI, MN, NM, NY.
12. Warning of an alibi defense is required in DC, FL, KS, MD, MI, MN, NM, NY, NC, OH, RI.
13. Juvenile courts observe all rules of criminal procedure in AR, CO, ID, IN, KY, LA, ME, MA, NM, OR, WA.
14. Juvenile courts observe the joinder and severance rules from adult court in DE, DC, LA, MD, MN, NM.
15. Consent decrees are explicitly recognized in AL, DC, IA, MT, NV, NM, PA, WI, WY.
16. Montana violates the common understanding of a consent decree by allowing youths with prior adjudications to qualify for one.
17. Youths with prior records or who are accused of certain crimes are ineligible for consent decrees in CO, IL, MT, NY, OK, TX, WA, WI.
18. Successful completion of the consent decree means the petition is dismissed in CO, IL, IA, MT, NM, OK, PA, TX, UT, WA, WY.
19. The admission required for a consent decree is equivalent to a guilty plea in CO, IL, NM, OK, TX, UT, WA. Some states (FL, IA, PA, WV, WY) do not require an admission in order to be given a consent decree, and Montana's admission is not the same as a guilty plea.
20. In some jurisdictions it would be possible for the judge and defense attorney to negotiate a consent decree without the prosecutor's input. A consent decree may also be granted by the judge as a disposition in some locations, meaning the prosecutor may have little say in its dimensions.

21. For example, if a juvenile defendant facing five burglary charges secured a prosecutor's agreement to nol pros two of the charges in exchange for guilty pleas to the other three charges, this would mean the youth simultaneously nol pros bargained and plea bargained.
22. Youth who previously have received informal agreements and consent decrees would be ineligible for more of these diversion efforts, but could still be eligible for a nol pros agreement should the prosecutor be interested in such an outcome.
23. Idaho and Utah permit the prosecutor to plea bargain directly with the defendant, without the participation of a defense attorney.
24. The District of Columbia and Utah prohibit the judge's participation in plea bargaining.
25. Some research has documented the absence of a trial penalty in the plea bargaining exchange in juvenile court (Sanborn 1984, 1993a). West Virginia explicitly prohibits a trial penalty in juvenile court.
26. Massachusetts allows juvenile defendants to tender a guilty plea with a special request that, if the judge cannot agree to the special request, the juvenile has an opportunity to withdraw the plea.
27. See, for example, *In re Beasley*, 362 N.e.2d 1024 (Ill 1977), *cert denied, Beasley et al. v. Illinois*, 434 U.S. 1016 (1978), and *Interest of Jarrell*, 399 So.2d 583 (La 1981).
28. See *In re J.C.*, 925 P.2d 415 (Kan 1996).
29. Status offenders enjoy the same rights as delinquents in the guilty plea process in AZ, CA, DC, GA, ID, IN, IA, MI, MN, MS, MT, NE, NM, NC, OH, RI, SD, TN, TX, WV, WI. ✦

Chapter 12

Transfer to Adult Court

Focus of Chapter 12

Juveniles who commit crimes are usually subject to the jurisdiction of juvenile court. In a number of situations, however, youth can be tried in criminal court. Chapter 4 discussed how jurisdiction can be arranged to use mandatory exclusion to exclude from juvenile court all youths who have reached a certain age or who have accumulated a certain record. This chapter focuses on another way in which the state can force trial in adult court: the transfer of juveniles to adult court. Both mandatory exclusion and transfer expose juveniles to the punitive possibilities (including the death penalty) of the criminal justice system. Prosecution in criminal court can also result in both depriving youth of rehabilitative programs in the juvenile justice system and establishing permanent, debilitating criminal records. The stakes, then, are high, which is why transfer is considered the most important decision made in juvenile court.

Key Terms

- amenability hearing
- blended sentence
- certification
- combined sentence
- concurrent jurisdiction
- delayed judicial transfer
- delayed reverse transfer
- direct file
- discretionary exclusion
- extended juvenile jurisdiction prosecution
- judicial transfer
- *Kent* hearing

- offense exclusion
- presumptive judicial transfer
- prosecutorial transfer
- punishment gap
- recidivist impact
- regular judicial transfer
- reverse transfer
- second tier of juvenile court
- self-transfer
- sentencing guidelines
- transfer to adult court
- waiver
- youthful offender

The Prospect of Self-Transfer

Before we examine transfer process, we should note that many states permit self-transfer, in which juveniles can elect to send their own cases to adult court. A number of states have implemented a minimum age requirement of 12 (MO), 13 (IL, NC), 14 (NJ, VA, WV, WI), or even 16 (NH) for self-transfer, but other jurisdictions do not identify any particular age for this process.[1] Typically, the youth would have to petition the court to allow this transfer to occur. For very young children, Florida requires the consent of a parent or guardian *ad litem*. Although this chapter focuses on the state's forcing the case to be tried in adult court, it is important to remember that not all juveniles are prosecuted in criminal court against their will. In addition, some defendants do not fight the state's efforts to forcibly remove them from juvenile court. To be sure, most often juveniles would not want to be prosecuted in criminal court. Nevertheless, some defendants may prefer a trial to occur there instead of in juvenile court for one or more of the following reasons:

- To secure pretrial release via bail
- To be afforded more rights at trial
- To be eligible for more lenient sentencing

The What of Transfer

Although there is no one term that all jurisdictions use to refer to the phenomenon, transfer to adult court is the most commonly used across the country.[2] Waiver (not to be confused with a juvenile's waiver or surrender of rights) is another term used by many states,[3] as is certification.[4] Adding to the confusion is that 18 states use more than one term to refer to transfer, while Florida and Utah use all three major names. Less common terms one can encounter include *fitness* (CA), *bindover* (ME, SC, UT), *referral* (DE, NJ), *decline* (WA), *relinquishment* (OH), and *designated* (MI). Regardless of the wording used, all these terms mean that the juvenile defendant will be subject to the jurisdiction of (or prosecuted in) adult court rather than juvenile court.

Transfer must be distinguished from mandatory exclusion, which allows for *no alternative (or discretion)* as to where the youth's trial occurs because even before the current crime was committed, the "juvenile" was already legally defined as an adult. Transfer, on the other hand, involves the *discretionary decision* (or choice) to involve the jurisdiction of criminal court *instead of* juvenile court. In other words, the case *could have been* heard in juvenile court *but for* the decision of a court official (a judge or a prosecutor) to *transfer* the case or jurisdiction to adult court. Transfer, then, is the discretionary exclusion of a defendant who was legally defined as a juvenile at the time of the offense but whose *legal status changed* due to the decision of that court official. With mandatory exclusion, jurisdiction attaches *only* to criminal court, so there is no *transfer of jurisdiction* (or *change of legal status*) per se.[5]

The legislature is the source of all exclusion power. The legislature establishes the boundaries of juvenile and adult courts and determines which age can, and whether a certain record will, confer adult status on "juveniles" and thus subject them to mandatory exclusion from juvenile court (see Chapter 4). However, legislatures cannot, by themselves, individually choose any other particular defendant, younger than the juvenile court's maximum age, to be tried in adult court. Consequently, legislatures in all 52 jurisdictions have elected to share their jurisdictional decision-making power with judges and prosecutors by granting these officials the authority to transfer or to select certain juveniles, who otherwise are within juvenile court jurisdiction, for prosecution in criminal court.

The Why of Transfer

The founding of juvenile court was marked by optimistic beliefs that the difficulties of all youth could be resolved in that forum (Mack 1909; Lou 1927). Nevertheless, from virtually the first day of its operation, juvenile court relied on transferring its most troublesome cases to the adult system (Tannenhaus 2000; Whitebread and Batey 1981; Wizner 1984). Juvenile court officials recognized and acknowledged early on that they were faced with some youths who had problems or had committed wrongs that were beyond the rehabilitative or punitive capacities of the juvenile system. Transfer was designed to remove those with problems that the juvenile court could not or would not address.

Actually, each of the juvenile justice models supports transfer, but for different reasons. Those who are *rehabilitation* oriented have observed that some youths are simply beyond the treatment ability of the system and that valuable resources should not be wasted on them. Moreover, these offenders could also corrupt other juveniles and frustrate or impede the latter's chances of rehabilitation (Bishop and Frazier 1991; Bortner 1986; Feld 1978; Fagan and Deschenes 1990; Zimring 1981). Those from the *crime control* camp are more likely to cite the desirability of longer sentences (and possibly the death penalty) in adult court, the lack of security in juvenile facilities, and the deterrent efforts and public safety provided by an adult record (Bishop and Frazier 1991; Bortner 1986; Fagan and Deschenes 1990; Feld 1978, 1984; Zimring 1981, 1991). Finally, *due process*–driven people suggest that being adjudicated for serious offenses warrants serious justice (such as jury trial), which is more likely to materialize in criminal court than in juvenile court (Ainsworth 1991; Federle 1990; Feld 1990, 1993b; Sanborn 1996b). The logical extreme of this perspective is *total exclusion*, or the removal of all defendants from juvenile court, and the prosecution of all crime in criminal court.

Conversely, those who take the anti-exclusionary position oppose sending juveniles to adult court, citing three problems with prosecuting youths there. First, juveniles supposedly lack the competence to stand trial in criminal court. This means that they cannot participate adequately at trial because they cannot understand the proceedings and assist their attorneys (Bonnie and Grisso 2000; Steinberg and Schwartz 2000). Juveniles also supposedly lack the maturity needed to be held responsible and culpable for their behavior. This means they are unable to know and use legal rules, are unable to control their impulses, and are unable to resist peer pressure (Steinberg and Schwartz 2000; Zimring 1998, 2000). The second problem concerns the difficulties that arise when youth are incarcerated in adult facilities following conviction in criminal court (Bishop and Frazier 2000) (see Chapter 17). Finally, preliminary research has indicated that some juveniles will be arrested sooner, more often, and for more serious offenses after prosecution in adult court than supposedly comparable juveniles who are prosecuted in juvenile court

(Fagan 1991, 1995; Bishop et al. 1996). Other studies have suggested that juveniles prosecuted in criminal court have high recidivist rates (Podkopacz and Feld 1996; Myers 2001).

At the very least these propositions and research suggest that care should be exercised when deciding to transfer youth to criminal court and that penal policies in the criminal justice system need to be sensitive to incarcerating youngsters with adults. Whether youths continue to commit crimes, at an even greater rate, after prosecution in criminal court may be a reflection of lenient sentencing policies in adult court (see end of this chapter).

The When of Transfer

Historically, the reasons behind transfer have resulted in its being directed primarily against two populations: those who did not appear to be amenable to juvenile court treatment efforts (or the *beyond-rehabilitation group*), and those who appeared as worthy candidates for the harsh, punitive consequences (or justice) possible in the criminal justice system (or the *greater-punishment group*). Although the chronic serious offender could boast of membership in both of these groups, these populations do not necessarily overlap. For example, the first-time violent offender who arguably qualifies for adultlike punishments is not automatically beyond the treatment capacity of juvenile court, while the perpetual thief who has not been rehabilitated despite several efforts is neither targeted for nor guaranteed greater punishment if transferred.

For some time now, observers who insist that the only appropriate candidates for transfer are those from the greater-punishment camp have dominated the literature (Bortner 1986; Champion and Mays 1991; Feld 1983, 1984, 1987, 1988b; Zimring 1981, 1991). Consider the following observations:

> The primary justification for waiver is the need for minimum lengths of confinement that are substantially in excess of the maximum sanctions available within the juvenile court. (Feld 1984, 33)

> The justification for transfer is singular: transfer to criminal court is necessary when the maximum punishment available in juvenile court is clearly inadequate for a particular offender. (Zimring 1991, 276)

These statements ignore the fact that juvenile courts have also traditionally targeted for transfer the beyond-rehabilitation population (such as a perpetual thief), regardless of either the severity of the crime or the desire for lengthy incarceration.

The How (or Types) of Transfer: Judicial and Prosecutorial

For the most part, each of the populations subject to transfer has been assigned to a different court official or gatekeeper. While judges typically determine which juveniles are beyond rehabilitation, prosecutors usually decide which juveniles warrant greater punishment.[6] Consequently, transfer occurs two ways: *judicial* and *prosecutorial* (see Table 12.1).

Table 12.1 Types of Transfer			
A.	Judicial (Hearing Based)		
	1.	Regular (traditional amenability burden)	
		a.	Discretionary
		b.	Mandatory
	2.	Presumptive (altered amenability burden)	
		a.	Amenability burden on defendant
		b.	Nonculpability burden on defendant
		c.	Crime or factor weighs in favor of transfer
		d.	No amenability burden
B.	Prosecutorial (Charging Based)		
	1.	Forum oriented	
		a.	Concurrent jurisdiction
		b.	Direct file
	2.	Offense oriented	
		a.	Jurisdiction, child, delinquency ≠ offense
		b.	Crime = adult
		c.	Juvenile court does not have jurisdiction
		d.	Juvenile court has jurisdiction unless/except
		e.	Offenses are excluded from juvenile court jurisdiction
		f.	Juvenile court jurisdiction is excluded/divested
		g.	Criminal court has original jurisdiction
		h.	Juvenile must be charged or prosecuted as adult
		i.	Prosecutor shall direct file; mandatory direct file
		j.	Juvenile court shall transfer or waive

Although in some states judges are authorized to initiate a transfer consideration,[7] *judicial transfer* typically begins with a request made by prosecutors (in situations in which they cannot send the case to adult court by themselves). Most statutes that identify the person responsible for beginning this process specify the prosecutor.[8] Only a few states officially mention the probation officer's authority to pursue transfer (AK, MO, PA), but it is possible that many juvenile courts still rely on the probation officer to be the person seeking criminal prosecution of some juveniles. Regardless of who launches the process, judicial transfer has historically been a *discretionary* inquiry into the youth's amenability to treatment. A relatively recent innovation, however, is the requirement that a judicial transfer hearing be held in certain circumstances, usually depending upon the severity of the offense, the defendant's age, and his or her delinquent record. This *mandatory* hearing so far is available in only four states (DE, FL, MO, WA). The *only* mandatory aspect of this provision in these four states is the holding of the hearing itself. No added momentum toward ensuring transfer has been adopted by any of these states.[9] Moreover, if the prosecutor elects *not to charge* the qualifying offense, a transfer hearing need not be conducted.

The transfer request or petition to the judge would claim that the youth does not belong in the juvenile system because of a number of possible factors. Whereas probation officers are more likely to emphasize the youth's inability to respond successfully to treatment, prosecutors are more likely to focus on the defendant's current offense and delinquent record. Prosecutors cannot afford to ignore the offender's treatment history and capacity, however, inasmuch as these factors should influence the judge's ultimate decision.

We have seen that jurisdictions vary as to whether probation officers or prosecutors are the primary movers of transfer petitions. Regardless, agreement between these two officials (if not outright cooperation) may be critical in determining the success of any petition (Sanborn 1994a). Whereas Missouri law instructs the probation officer to consult the prosecutor in transfer decision making, Alabama and Florida law tell the prosecutor to consult the probation officer.

Unlike prosecutorial transfer, judicial transfer involves a hearing, often called a *Kent hearing* (after *Kent v. United States* from Chapter 3), which consists of two stages. The first stage is usually called a *probable cause hearing* because that is the level of evidence the state will have to satisfy in linking the juvenile and the offense. The second stage is typically referred to as the amenability hearing in which the youth's amenability (or suitability, responsiveness) to juvenile court treatment is examined.

The only exceptions to this two-stage format for judicial transfer exist in Massachusetts and New Mexico. Recently, these states introduced an innovative wrinkle to the judicial transfer process. Instead of forcing the judge to decide the youth's fate prior to trial (as is the norm in 46 jurisdictions), they place the judicial transfer decision at sentencing, after trial and adjudication or conviction. This process can be considered as delayed judicial transfer. What happens in both states is that the prosecutor initiates the proceeding by charging the defendant as an adult (if the prosecutor is pursuing transfer). Doing so appears to make this process prosecutorial transfer, and some authorities have interpreted it as such (Griffin et al. 1998). Nevertheless, both state statutes make it perfectly clear that there is no official or final commitment that the proceeding is actually adult or criminal until the juvenile court judge makes a simultaneous conviction and sentencing decision after trial and after using traditional judicial transfer-like criteria. Thus, the transfer decision making here belongs more to the judge than to the prosecutor. All that has happened in these states is that the judge's transfer decision has been delayed until after trial (rather than after a mere probable cause hearing). Unlike the vast majority of states, Massachusetts and New Mexico provide juvenile defendants a right to jury trial making their adjudicatory hearings the legal and functional equivalent of a criminal trial. So, again, unlike most jurisdictions, both states can postpone the juvenile versus adult conviction question until after the trial, and until after all the evidence seen by the judge is only that which is legally admissible at trial (unlike that which is admissible at a probable cause hearing).

The First Stage of Judicial Transfer: The Probable Cause Hearing

Legislatures have spent relatively little time in delineating the rights juveniles have at the transfer stage. If judicial transfer is involved (as opposed to prosecutorial), the rights identified in the *Kent* decision are assumed to be granted the youth. The four rights recognized by the Court in *Kent* were the right to a hearing, the right to counsel, the right for counsel to have access to the youth's juvenile court record, and a requirement that the judge write reasons that support the transfer decision. Nevertheless, juvenile court statutes are mostly quiet in this regard. A handful of jurisdictions have set time limits within which the prosecutor must file a motion to transfer and the transfer hearing must occur. Transfer motions must usually be filed within one to three weeks after filing of the initial juvenile court petition (DC, FL, MI, MS, NM, VT) or within a month after the arraignment (AZ, MN, NJ, RI); West Virginia holds the motion must be presented at least eight days before the adjudicatory hearing. The deadline for the transfer hearing can be as soon as within two weeks of either the filing of the transfer motion (DC, NM, WV) or arraignment (NC, WA) or as late as one month after the transfer motion is filed (AZ, AR, IA, MI, MN). Arkansas allows the state three months to hold a transfer hearing if the youth is not detained.

Half of the jurisdictions refer generally to a right to notice of a transfer hearing[10] or specify that the youth must be warned of its occurrence from three (GA, ND, OH, PA, TN, WI, WY) to five (CA) to ten days (ID, LA) before the hearing occurs. The process begins with the probable cause hearing that is the functional equivalent of a preliminary hearing in the adult system. Most states demand that the prosecutor first establish *reasonable grounds* (GA, ND), a *prima facie case* (PA), *prosecutive merit* (WI), or *probable cause*[11] to believe the youth committed the transferable offense. However, a few jurisdictions maintain that, for purposes of the transfer consideration, the court shall assume the child committed the act (DC, FED, MD), while South Dakota requires prosecutive merit be demonstrated but explains that showing probable cause is not needed to establish prosecutive merit. Usually, strict rules of evidence are not followed at the probable cause hearing so that hearsay[12] and even illegally seized evidence (AZ, DE, KY) can be admitted. A few states, however, are not as receptive to hearsay (AK, CT, SD) or illegally seized evidence (ME, MI, MN).

Statutes tend not to be clear as to whether the rights youth have at the transfer hearing apply to both the probable cause and amenability stages. Some of the rights might actually make sense only at the amenability hearing but will be identified at this point, nevertheless. The right mentioned most often, and certainly applicable to both hearings, is the right to counsel.[13] Illinois and Ohio declare that the youth must be represented by counsel. It is difficult to imagine any jurisdiction not extending this right to a juvenile. Confrontation and cross-examination of witnesses is another matter, however. Although more states have recognized this right[14] than have denied it (HI, IA, NH, NJ, WA), an important caveat must be noted. The nature of a preliminary hearing and the admissibility of hearsay suggest that this confrontation right might be observed only at the amenability hearing when the youth's treatment history is reviewed. Similarly, the right to present evidence acknowledged in many jurisdictions certainly could be limited to evidence concerning the youth's treatment potential (rather than to a lack of guilt).[15]

The right against self-incrimination is not recognized in a few states (IN, NV, WI), but again, this most likely applies to the amenability stage, and the norm is for juveniles to have the right granted them.[16] Moreover, any statement secured from a youth at a transfer hearing should be inadmissible at any subsequent trial in juvenile or adult court (IA, MS, VA, WY). Otherwise, juveniles facing transfer have been given the right to compulsory process (or bringing in their own witnesses),[17] the right to be present at the hearing,[18] the right to have a record kept of the hearing,[19] and the right to a transcript of the proceedings (AZ, MI, WV).

The Second Stage of Judicial Transfer: The Amenability Hearing

Barring unusual circumstances, the prosecutor should almost always prevail at the probable cause hearing. The same is far from true at the second stage, the amenability hearing, which operates much like a sentencing hearing. In fact, while both Alabama and Michigan refer to this stage as *disposition* or *sentencing*, all the judicial transfer decisions in Massachusetts and New Mexico are actually made at sentencing after trial and adjudication. Like sentencing, judicial transfer involves a judge's analysis of several criteria, typically patterned after the criteria the Supreme Court referred to in the Appendix to the *Kent* decision. These factors are usually identified in the juvenile court statute. However, three states that use judicial transfer do not list any factors (GA, NV, WA), while Nebraska, which does not practice judicial transfer, nevertheless instructs *prosecutors* to use judicial transfer-like criteria when they decide to put offenders younger than 16 in criminal court.

Altogether, 46 jurisdictions cite factors for judges (or prosecutors) to consider (Connecticut, Montana, and New York do not use judicial transfer). Most likely, these factors are detailed in a transfer report submitted to the court by the PO. While some jurisdictions mandate the completion of this report,[20] in other states it is discretionary for the court to order one.[21] Although it is inconceivable that defense counsel would not be provided with a copy of this report, fewer than half of the jurisdictions specifically mandate the delivery of the report to the defense attorney (or youth), usually one to seven days before the transfer hearing.[22] Similarly, a few states (MI, NH, NC, OK, RI) refer to defense counsel's right of access to the youth's juvenile court record, one of the rights the Supreme Court guaranteed in *Kent v. United States* Again, it would be unusual for the defense attorney to be denied an opportunity to review both the court record and the PO's transfer report.

Factors Considered at the Amenability Hearing

Many states continue to instruct their juvenile court judges to gauge the transfer decision according to the best interests of the child and the public.[23] Some juvenile court workers in Michigan refer to the amenability stage as the "best interests" hearing. Most of the factors judges are directed to consider at transfer are related to the current offense and prior delinquent record of the youth. In fact, Illinois, Michigan, and Minnesota tell juvenile courts to give greater weight to these two factors than to any others. Otherwise, the facilities and programs available to the juvenile court, the youth's previous treatment history, and basic characteristics of the child make up most of the remaining factors judges are expected to review at transfer.

Of the 46 jurisdictions citing factors, only West Virginia fails to mention the offense itself, while only that state, Delaware, and Maryland omit any reference to the delinquent record. Delaware does join 35 other jurisdictions, however, in holding that the protection of society is a factor worthy of consideration at transfer.[24] Many states have borrowed or adopted two other offense-related factors from the Appendix of the *Kent* decision: whether the offense was committed in a aggressive, violent, premeditated, willful manner,[25] and whether it was directed against persons or property, with greater emphasis given to crimes against persons, especially if injury resulted.[26] Other offense-oriented factors include the use of a deadly weapon,[27] participation with others or a gang,[28] the degree of participation or culpability,[29] the number of offenses (KS, VA), whether the offense was committed during an escape from a facility (OK) or while under the court's supervision (AZ, OH), and whether the maximum punishment for the offense in criminal court would exceed 20 years imprisonment (VA). Beyond the youth's delinquent court record, a handful of jurisdictions refer to related factors, such as police record (MI, NE, NH, OK), escape history (DC, VA), previous transfers to (MD, WI) or convictions in (DE, WI) criminal court, and whether there is a repetitive pattern of offenses (MO, VA).

The third set of factors that have attracted the attention of the legislatures involves the facilities available within the juvenile justice system to rehabilitate the youth. Only four states have not officially designated this rehabilitation potential as a transfer criterion (AL, DE, ID, WV), and it is difficult to imagine any juvenile court judge not considering this relevant factor. Not only would this factor concern the likelihood of rehabilitation in the juvenile system, but it would also involve whether this rehabilitation can occur before jurisdiction over the youth expires,[30] and perhaps even the adequacy of punishment in juvenile facilities (CO, IL, MI, MN), and whether a juvenile disposition will deter the offender (ME, MA) or diminish the offense (ME). Some states have phrased this consideration as whether the youth needs adult sanctions, supervision, or facilities,[31] or similarly as an examination of resources available in the adult system (MS, OR, PA, VA, WI). Closely related to the resource question, and a variable that would seem impossible to ignore, is the youth's previous treatment history and response to prior juvenile court interventions (as well as the youth's willingness to participate now in a juvenile treatment program). Nevertheless, only 28 jurisdictions refer to treatment history as a factor,[32] while 7 states specifically mention previous commitments.[33]

Various characteristics of the juveniles themselves also emerge as critical factors, especially their physical and mental maturity and capacity, which can also include an analysis of the youth's home, environment, emotional attitude, and pattern of living.[34] Although the child's age should almost always be important (and may disqualify the youth for transfer), only 19 jurisdictions specifically cite age as a factor in transfer.[35] In addition, the youth's school record (MI, NE, OK, UT, VT, VA, WV), intellectual functioning (FED, NC, ND), demeanor (AL, AR), or personality (WI) could play a role in the transfer decision. A few states also mention the juvenile's ability to distinguish right from wrong (OK) and the probable cause of the delinquent behavior (AK, LA, NE). Finally, it is likely that, if the youth suffers from a serious mental disability so as to be civilly committable, transfer would not be legally possible. Nevertheless, only 10 jurisdictions specifically cite this prohibition.[36]

Miscellaneous factors can sometimes influence a transfer consideration, especially since many states hold that *any other factors* the court chooses to examine are also appropriate.[37] Co-defendants headed to adult court can be important,[38] as can be the victim's view of the desirability of transfer.[39] The PO's recommendation should be critical, although only California and Iowa mention this as a factor. Even the strength of the state's case can have an impact since some statutes cite probable cause for the crime (FL, IN, NJ) or the prosecutive merit of the complaint (NH, OK, OR, SC, SD, WI) as transfer criteria. Of course, the prosecutor's decision to pursue judicial transfer could be seriously influenced by the strength of the evidence and whether the case would survive the more exacting analysis that should occur in criminal court (especially in a jury trial). Finally, while Pennsylvania juvenile courts have been told to consider the transfer's impact on the community, juvenile courts in Missouri have been instructed to be sensitive to racial disparity in transfer decisions.

Weighing the Amenability Factors: Regular and Presumptive Judicial Transfer

In analyzing the factors, treatment history becomes especially controversial when the state seeks to transfer a first offender, probably facing either a serious charge or a number of less serious ones. The challenge here is the ability to determine amenability to treatment when the system has never had an opportunity to work with the youth. Nevertheless, a number of states specify (AL, AR, CA, PA, SC), and most other jurisdictions likely believe, that the absence of treatment history is not an obstacle to transfer. Similarly, most statutes refuse to specify precisely how many criteria must suggest nonamenability before transfer is warranted. Nevertheless, Kentucky law requires at least two factors to be sustained before transfer is permitted, while an appellate case in Louisiana invalidated a transfer in which only three of the six statutory factors favored waiver (*State v. Collins* 1997). Ohio is the only state that identifies factors that militate both for and against transfer. Ohio law also requires the judge to indicate which factors to send a youth to adult court outweighed the factors to keep the youth in juvenile court.

The more common position among jurisdictions is that as long as all criteria are considered, a single criterion could justify a finding of nonamenability.[40] Moreover, some factors can favor juvenile court treatment and still not prevent certification to adult court. Jurisdictions typically have chosen either a *preponderance of evidence*[41] or *clear and convincing*[42] as the standard of proof needed for establishing nonamenability. A handful of states, however, have chosen to phrase the burden as *reasonable grounds* (GA, ND, PA, TN) to believe transfer is appropriate or that *sufficient, adequate,* or *substantial evidence* (IL, KS) exists to support a transfer decision. Historically, the burden of proof to demonstrate nonamenability has fallen on the state, since it is the party that is attacking the assumption that allegedly delinquent children will be prosecuted in juvenile court. This is regular judicial transfer, which is still the norm for most juveniles facing this type of transfer.

Recently, however, numerous jurisdictions (18) have shifted the burden from the state to the defendant, requiring him or her to prove amenability to treatment in juvenile court. This is known as presumptive judicial transfer because transfer is *presumed unless* defendants can sustain the burden on them. A number of states have quantified the youth's burden of proof as *clear and convincing* (IL, MN, NV, RI), as *preponderance of evidence* (AK, ME, PA), or as *reasonable grounds* (ND). Similarly, New Jersey requires the juvenile to show that the probability of successful rehabilitation before age 19 substantially outweighs the reasons for transfer. The presumptive version is usually limited to older youths who have accumulated a significant delinquent record or who have been accused of committing a serious crime.

Presumptive transfer has been developed in other ways as well. Some jurisdictions simply state that the presence of certain circumstances (ranging from crime and record to the age and vulnerability of the victim to the defendant's playing a leading role in organizing an offense) creates an expectation of transfer. Instead of a treatment amenability burden, Utah requires all defendants labeled as serious youth offenders to establish, by clear and convincing evidence, that they had a lesser degree of culpability than co-defendants (in multiple-offender cases) *and* that their role in the offense was not committed in a violent, aggressive, or premeditated manner.[43] Finally, in cases involving certain serious offenders, West Virginia allows judges to transfer when prosecutors show mere probable cause that the offense was committed, eliminating altogether the traditional treatment amenability criteria in these cases.[44]

Presumptive transfer adds momentum to the likelihood of transfer. To that extent, it can be regarded as a lack of trust in the judge or as an attempt to force the judge's hand to grant transfer. However, it can also be interpreted as a compromise or an alternative to adopting prosecutorial transfer. In presumptive transfer the prosecutor has neither the amenability burden characteristic of regular judicial transfer nor the substantial power represented in prosecutorial transfer.

Admittedly, the dividing line between *regular* and *presumptive* judicial transfer is at times difficult to draw and will become only more so as jurisdictions continue to revamp the regular version so that it, too, will increase the likelihood of transfer. Ideally, the term *presumptive transfer* should be limited to situations in which the amenability burden itself has been altered significantly, rather than merely modified so as to be easier to overcome. *So far* this alteration would apply, then, to instances in which the amenability burden has been shifted completely to the defendant, replaced with a nonculpability burden that also rests on the defendant, restructured to identify crimes or factors as calling specifically for transfer, or eliminated altogether.[45]

Judges who decide to transfer a youth to adult court are usually required to observe the fourth right mentioned in the *Kent* decision: to write reasons justifying the waiver.[46] Whereas Illinois explicitly does not require written justification for transfer, Arizona, Michigan, and Minnesota also require written reasons for cases that were *not* waived to adult court. Although some states require the juvenile to postpone any appeal of a transfer to criminal court until after a conviction in that forum, several jurisdictions do provide for an immediate appeal of any decision to certify a youth. Also, in many jurisdictions the prosecution is provided a right to appeal a judge's decision to not certify a juvenile to criminal court, and in some a second transfer hearing can be held without violating double jeopardy (see Chapter 15). For youths kept in juvenile court, it is becoming common to allow them to object to the same judge conducting both the transfer hearing and the subsequent adjudicatory hearing (CA, DC, SC, TN, VA, WY). In this situation the would-be trial judge would have had access to prejudicial information (such as prior record) that usually is not admissible at trial (see Chapter 13).

Judicial transfer has been praised for subjecting the waiver decision to a thorough, two-sided analysis before a neutral and impartial factfinder who will exercise restraint (Sanborn 1994a; cf. Podkopacz and Feld 1995). At the same time, however, judicial waivers are portrayed as subjective judgments made inconsistently and with too much discretion, using vague criteria and producing mere predictions and hunches as to potential rehabilitation or dangerousness (Bortner 1986; Fagan et al. 1986, 1987; Feld 1978, 1981, 1983, 1987, 1988b, 1989a; Hamparian et al. 1982). Moreover, some judges simply will not send juvenile defendants to adult court (McCarthy 1994; Sanborn 1994a), which probably explains, in part, the recent dramatic increase in prosecutorial transfers.

Prosecutorial Transfer

Prosecutorial transfer results from a charging decision made by the prosecutor. Charging by its very nature is discretionary. Prosecutorial transfer will not involve the rights juveniles are thought to have when facing transfer due to the *Kent* decision. The right to a hearing and counsel and the other *Kent*-related rights are required in judicial transfer situations only. Prosecutorial transfer focuses on one or more of three factors: severity of offense, criminal history, and age. There are two possible versions. The first is *forum oriented*, in that it allows the prosecutor to bring charges against the defendant in *either* juvenile *or* criminal court—in other words, to *select the proper forum or court* to hear the case. In states with this approach, legislatures have granted concurrent jurisdiction over juvenile crimes (depending perhaps on age and record) to both courts. The concurrent jurisdiction can be either *broad* and extend to virtually all offenses (e.g., Nebraska) or relatively *narrow* and apply to only a few crimes or situations (e.g., Georgia). A few states identify this practice as the prosecutor's authority to direct file charges in adult court. Both the concept of concurrent jurisdiction and the wording used in the statutes tend to be pretty straightforward. The prosecutor simply selects the court in which to prosecute the youth, since both courts have or share jurisdiction over the charges.

The second type of prosecutorial transfer is *offense oriented*, in that it provides that *charging certain offenses* (depending perhaps on age and record) automatically triggers criminal court jurisdiction over the juvenile defendant. These crimes have been excluded from juvenile court jurisdiction and *cannot* be prosecuted there. The extent of the offense exclusion can be *narrow* and apply to, perhaps only one or two of the most serious crimes (e.g., Kentucky) or can be *broad* and extend to a variety of felonies (e.g., Mississippi). The concept of offense exclusion is no more complicated than concurrent jurisdiction. With the former, the prosecutor's selection of charges to prosecute also simply and simultaneously selects the court in which the offender has to be prosecuted. Nevertheless, it is described in the statutes with such different and varying wording that comprehending what it entails becomes difficult. Even single jurisdictions use multiple descriptions.

Statutes have phrased this prosecutorial charging power in three ways. The first focuses on definitions of people and behavior and holds that certain crimes are *excluded* from the definition of what is a *child* (DC, IL, KS, MN, NM, OH, OK, SC) or *delinquent act* (MS, NV, PA), or holds that certain crimes convert the *child* into an *adult* (MA, NY, OK, RI). A second way looks at court jurisdiction and maintains that juvenile court *does not have jurisdiction, has jurisdiction unless/except,* or *jurisdiction is excluded/divested* when certain crimes are charged.[47] Another way of making the same statement is to declare that *adult court has original jurisdiction* over certain crimes (GA, IA, LA, ND, UT, WA, WI) or that certain crimes mean the youth *will have to be charged as an adult or must be subject to criminal proceedings.*[48] Florida and Montana add to the confusion by referring to the necessary prosecution of some charges in adult court as *mandatory direct file.* This term joins two otherwise incompatible notions, since *direct file* means the prosecutor can choose between courts, but adding the word *mandatory,* actually converts this situation into offense exclusion, which would not allow the prosecutor to pursue these charges in juvenile court.

In both of the first two ways of phrasing offense exclusion, charging the excludable offense automatically invokes the jurisdiction of criminal court. Thus, prosecution would need to be initiated by either a preliminary hearing or a grand jury proceeding, as with all other cases in adult court. If the prosecutor can demonstrate sufficient probable cause for only a lesser-included, nonexcluded crime, however, jurisdiction of the case reverts back to juvenile court. Finally, the third phrasing of offense-oriented prosecutorial transfer specifies that *juvenile court shall transfer or waive* the case to adult court because of the crime charged by the prosecutor.[49] Some states (IL, OH, TX) and some observers (Griffin et al. 1998) call this version mandatory transfer, which is misleading since the transfer becomes mandatory *only if* the prosecutor charges the excluded offense. In this version of offense exclusion, the jurisdiction of juvenile court is limited to finding probable cause to believe the defendant committed the excluded offense. Thus, the preliminary hearing occurs in juvenile court instead of in criminal court, which happens in the first two versions. Again, the transfer is not mandatory inasmuch as the prosecutor's failure to charge the qualifying offense *or* the judge's failure to find probable cause for the excluded offense keeps the case in juvenile court.

A number of observers have seriously misinterpreted offense exclusion and, instead of identifying it as a second version of prosecutorial transfer, have listed it actually as a third and distinct type of transfer (Champion 1989; Fritsch and Hemmens 1995; Torbet et al. 1996). The confusion and misinterpretation here stems from a false assertion that, unlike concurrent jurisdiction, offense exclusion represents "automatic" or "mandatory" removal from juvenile court because the legislature designates that excluded crimes *must* be prosecuted in criminal court (Allen 2000; Dawson 2000; Feld 1987, 1989a; Osbun and Rode 1984; Sorrentino and Olsen 1977; Whitebread and Batey 1981; Wizner 1984). This is clearly erroneous because the exclusion here is *discretionary* rather than *mandatory*. Transfer occurs, *if, and only if,* the excluded offense is charged rather than a lesser-included crime that does not have to be prosecuted in adult court. For example, if murder (or any other Class A or first-degree felony) were the only offense excluded from juvenile court, a charge of manslaughter (or any other Class B or second-degree felony) would be subject to prosecution in juvenile court. Charging crimes is *necessarily* a *discretionary* act, and prosecutors can *choose* to keep any case in juvenile court simply by *selecting* a nonexcluded offense for prosecution. Moreover, no one can force the prosecutor to charge an excluded offense.

Many observers have also labeled offense exclusion inappropriately as legislative transfer or legislative or statutory exclusion (Bishop and Frazier 2000; Dawson 2000; Feld 2000; Griffin et al. 1998; Snyder and Sickmund 1995; Torbet et al. 1996). For one thing, this label is uninformative, inasmuch as *all* exclusion from juvenile court is legislatively or statutorily based. Moreover, because the prosecutor actively controls this type of transfer, it should not be called legislative. In offense exclusion the legislature has authorized the prosecutor to transfer by virtue of the charge, much like it has empowered the judge to transfer because of nonamenability to treatment. The former is no more legislative in nature than judicial transfer, and neither should be referred to as legislative transfer or exclusion. Finally, using *legislative* as the term for this transfer wrongly implies that it is nondiscretionary and that therefore it cannot be discriminatory.

Historically, the two types of prosecutorial transfer have been structured differently. Whereas offense exclusion states have tended to limit prosecutorial discretion by allowing the transfer of no more than one or at most a few specifically designated crimes, concurrent jurisdictions have been more inclined to grant prosecutors broad transfer power by making all crimes committed by those above a certain age as triable in adult court. The current trend is for the two types to be structured more similarly. While offense exclusion now regularly includes an expansive list of crimes, concurrent jurisdictions frequently identify specific offenses for which jurisdiction is shared with adult court (see the following section, "Current Standards"). Moreover, today nine states practice both forms of prosecutorial transfer (see Appendix H).

To be sure, the two types of prosecutorial transfer can still require different outcomes. For example, while an excluded offense cannot be tried in juvenile court, there is no jurisdictional bar or obstacle to prosecuting any juvenile for *any* crime in juvenile court under concurrent jurisdiction. Nevertheless, prosecutors actually operate similarly in both methods of transfer. Once the statutory requirements are met (offense, age, record), prosecutors wanting to channel the case into the adult system simply file the appropriate charges in that forum via either offense exclusion or concurrent jurisdiction. This is all that is necessary (and ultimately the securing of an information or an indictment) to prosecute the matter in criminal court through prosecutorial transfer. In both types the defendant is afforded none of the rights identified in *Kent v. United States* Similarly, prosecutors desiring, instead, to retain the case in the juvenile system would have no charging difficulties in concurrent jurisdiction, and would simply have to charge an offense less serious than that for which exclusion is required in offense-oriented transfer. Most important, both forms of prosecutorial transfer result in prosecutors enjoying considerable discretion in serving as gatekeepers to the two court systems (Sanborn 2003, 2004).

Prosecutorial transfer can be said to represent both dissatisfaction with juvenile court rehabilitation (Feld 1987, 1989a), and a distrust of juvenile court judges (Champion and Mays 1991; Feld 1987; Jensen 1994; McCarthy 1994). In addition, prosecutorial transfer can be viewed as being cheaper to administer (no transfer hearing is required), as promoting deterrence, and as placing the transfer power where it belongs, especially for serious offenses where prosecutors can directly serve the public interest (McCarthy 1994; Sanborn 1994a, 1996b). Additionally, to the extent that prosecutorial transfer focuses more on offense and record (as opposed to amenability), it is credited with being more equitable and consistent, and as relying on more objective criteria than judicial waiver (Bishop and Frazier 1991; Fagan and Deschenes 1990; Feld 1987, 1989a). Both forms of prosecutorial transfer actually result in merely shifting discretion from the judge to the prosecutor, however, and the potential for abuse, unequal application, and lack of impartiality exists (Sanborn 1994a; Singer 1993). Promises of greater deterrence from prosecutorial transfer apparently have not materialized (Lee 1994; Jensen 1994; Jensen and Metsger 1994; Singer and McDowall 1988).

One caveat needs to be noted before we cover the specific provisions for judicial transfer. Thus far, we have been discussing judges and prosecutors who decide to transfer juvenile defendants to criminal court for trial. The only exception involved the Massachusetts-New Mexico version of trial-before-transfer decision. In a similar but still unique design, Michigan has implemented what it calls a designated proceeding. Michigan has retained traditional judicial and prosecutorial transfer for juveniles who are at least 14 years old. The designated proceeding is directed at youth younger than 14, and no minimum age is identified. Prosecutors can designate any case involving a *specified juvenile violation* (numerous serious offenses subject to concurrent jurisdiction for those 14 and older) and can request the judge to designate *any other criminal charge*. A juvenile case that is designated has been converted, permanently, into a criminal proceeding. Nevertheless, the trial occurs in juvenile court. Like Massachusetts and New Mexico, Michigan guarantees juvenile defendants a right to jury trial. Thus, it can secure an adult conviction via the juvenile court process (once it is officially, internally transformed) since the rights observed are the same in both courts. Unlike the other two states, however, Michigan commits (unalterably) to declaring the proceeding criminal prior to trial. Assuming there is a conviction (which must be criminal), the judge then utilizes judicial transfer-like criteria in determining whether the sentence will be within the auspices of juvenile or adult court.

Current Standards in Judicial and Prosecutorial Transfer

Until recently, it could be said that the judicial version was the more popular and available method of transfer. Historically, it was the only transfer mechanism in most states and accounted for the vast majority of juveniles certified to adult court. Today, the preference domination by the judicial method is no longer as clear. To be sure, legislatures have tended and continue to grant judges transfer powers affecting potentially many more youths than those who fall within the parameters of prosecutorial transfer. That is, compared to prosecutors, judges can transfer younger defendants who have committed a much broader range of offenses and who may not have a prior record (compare Appendix G and Appendix H).

Nevertheless, recent changes in legislation have done much to equalize the availability of the two types of transfer (see Table 12.2). Currently, judicial transfer is possible in only two more jurisdictions than its prosecutorial counterpart (48 compared to 46). Moreover, the list of offenses subject to prosecutorial transfer has grown so extensively that continued high rates of serious offending by youth could mean that prosecutor-based waivers will eventually far outnumber the transfers authorized by judges (as has happened already in Florida).

Most of the country (28 jurisdictions) has set a minimum age for transfer (see Table 12.2). This minimum age ranges from 10 to 14 and means that no one younger than those ages can ever face trial in adult court in any of these states, regardless of the severity of either the prior delinquent record or the current criminal charge. Some 36 jurisdictions permit youths younger than 14 to be prosecuted in adult court, including 24 states that have set no minimum age at all. Of course, this lack of a minimum age would be unrealistic or unenforceable at some point. For example, it is difficult to imagine a 5-year-old being criminally prosecuted, even for murder. Nevertheless, the fact that a state has a minimum age requirement for being adjudicated delinquent (see Chapter 4) does not necessarily prevent prosecution and conviction of youth below this age in criminal court. For example, in Pennsylvania, 10 is the youngest a juvenile can be declared delinquent. Children younger than 10 in that state can and have been prosecuted in adult court for murder, however.[50]

Finally, the lack of a minimum age identified for transfer in the juvenile court statute may conflict with what the state's penal code identifies as the minimum age for criminal court prosecution. For example, Georgia law clearly establishes no minimum age for concurrent jurisdiction when crimes punishable by death or life imprisonment are involved. Nevertheless, the penal code states that 13 is the minimum age for criminal responsibility.

Similarly, Idaho has no minimum age for judicial transfer of excluded offenses. Despite that juvenile provision, the minimum age for criminal prosecution is listed as 14 in the penal code. The legislatures in these states have not yet reconciled these inconsistent provisions. Until then, the no minimum age standard for transfer to adult court may actually be just false advertisement.

Connecticut's and Montana's recent decisions to join

Table 12.2 Minimum Age for Transferring Juvenile Offenders to Criminal Court	
Minimum Age	**Jurisdiction**
None	AK, AZ, DE, DC, FL, GA, HI, ID, KS, ME, MD, MI, NE, NV, NH, OK, OR, PA, RI, SC, SD, TN, WA, WV
10	IN, VT, WI
12	CO, MO, MT
13	FED, IL, MS, NY, NC, WY
14	AL, AR, CA, CT, IA, KY, LA, MA, MN, NJ, NM, ND, OH, TX, UT, VA

Nebraska and New York in relying exclusively on prosecutorial transfer have left 48 jurisdictions that currently provide for regular judicial transfer, 18 of which have endorsed the presumptive version as well. The tendency among most (34) of the jurisdictions with judicial transfer has been to create two or more levels of juveniles subject to this certification method. The groupings vary by age, offense, or delinquent record. Simply put, the more serious the offense, the more likely the jurisdiction is to allow younger defendants, perhaps without delinquent records, to be transferred, to make the hearing mandatory, or to make the transfer presumptive. In addition, the more extensive the delinquent record, the less serious the current offense needs to be to qualify for transfer (and it could become presumptive as well). Violent offenses and those involving drugs, weapons, gangs, and school have been increasingly singled out for transfer, very often in a presumptive capacity. Appendix G summarizes the judicial transfer provisions operating throughout the 48 jurisdictions.

Interestingly, 18 jurisdictions have established no minimum age for judicial transfer (more than twice as many as have done so for prosecutorial transfer). Moreover, nine of these states have also gone so far as to allow judicial transfer to apply to any crime or felony committed by very young persons. Altogether, 36 jurisdictions allow any crime or felony to qualify for judicial transfer, although the eligible ages vary considerably. The remaining jurisdictions with judicial transfer similarly omit a prior record requirement for certain serious offenses. In short, the potential pool of juvenile offenders subject to judicial transfer is immense.

Prosecutorial transfer is possible in 46 jurisdictions. Forty-two provide for offense exclusion and 13 practice concurrent jurisdiction, while nine allow both types of prosecutorial transfer. As Appendix H demonstrates, three variables tend to affect the scope of prosecutorial transfer: age, offense, and delinquent record. Like judicial transfer, prosecutorial transfer in many states exists on two or more levels according to these three variables. Compared to judicial transfer, older and/or more serious and/or more chronic juvenile offenders are likely to be included within the parameters of prosecutorial transfer. Similarly, in the nine states that have adopted both forms of prosecutorial transfer, the older, more serious, more chronic juvenile offender has tended to be linked with offense exclusion compared to those subject to concurrent jurisdiction.

Five of the seven jurisdictions with no minimum age for prosecutorial transfer have limited the eligible offenses to serious crimes such as murder. Only Nebraska has put no qualifier (besides a current felony charge) on extremely young offenders eligible for prosecutorial transfer. Overall, legislatures have been reluctant to give prosecutors *carte blanche* transfer power. Offense exclusion has tended to be limited to the most serious and violent offenses (and to those involving gangs and drugs). Concurrent jurisdiction has also focused on the more serious crimes or has given prosecutors power over all felonies, but only for older youth (with the notable exception of Nebraska). However, most of the states that have adopted offense exclusion have chosen not to require a prior delinquent record.

The result of the recent movement to expand the parameters of transfer to adult court is that there are now more certification provisions in place, potentially affecting a greater proportion of juvenile offenders than at any time in juvenile court history. Not only do all 52 jurisdictions provide for transfer, but 42 of them allow both judicial and prosecutorial transfer, 18 of which also practice presumptive judicial transfer. To say that the country is poised to permit the transfer of significant numbers of juvenile offenders to adult court is an understatement.

The Extent of Transfer to Adult Court

Nationally, the extent of certification varies tremendously, depending on a number of factors, including the geographical location, nature and amount of juvenile crime, political climate, power structure in juvenile court, and transfer laws and methods available (see Sanborn 1994a). Collectively, transfer to adult court most likely accounts for fewer juveniles being criminally prosecuted than mandatory exclusion does.

Our knowledge of the number of youth transferred to adult court is hampered by the fact that national data on prosecutorial transfers do not exist. Moreover, even if we knew how many juveniles were ushered into adult court by prosecutors, it would be difficult, if not impossible, to detect precisely how many of them were actually *transferred* there. The problem with determining the exact number of transfers is that 22 jurisdictions have *both prosecutorial transfer and mandatory exclusion* (by virtue of prior record) affecting potentially the same population of juvenile offenders.[51] Consequently, prosecutors' charging some youths in adult court in these jurisdictions would not automatically indicate whether the prosecutor was *forced* to process the case there (i.e., mandatory exclusion) or simply *elected* to charge an excludable offense or to direct file the case (i.e., transfer). For example, the mere presence in an Alabama criminal court of a 16- or 17-year-old charged with a felony involving a deadly weapon would not communicate, by itself, whether this defendant had been subjected to prosecutorial transfer via offense exclusion or to mandatory exclusion by virtue of having had a previous conviction in adult court.[52]

Data have been kept on judicial transfers, which are much easier to detect since a hearing on the matter is specifically required. The data clearly indicate that the number of juveniles judicially transferred to adult court decreased considerably in the late 1990s, following a sharp rise between 1989 and 1994. As Table 12.3 shows, between 1994 and 1999 there was a constant decline in the number of judicial transfers (Butts 1996; Stahl

1998, 1999, 2000, 2001, 2003). In all likelihood, the decline in the number of judicial transfers was offset by an increase in the number of prosecutorial transfer cases.

This trend in judicial transfer cases corresponds with the data presented in Chapter 5 on the rise and decline in rates of serious juvenile offenses during that span of years. Table 12.4 shows that crimes against property (40 percent) and those against persons (34 percent) are the offenses most frequently subjected to prosecution in criminal court. Some observers have criticized the fact that transfers are not restricted to the most violent youth who commit crimes against persons (Bortner 1986; Champion and Mays 1991; Feld 1987; Zimring 1991). There are at least two problems with this criticism. First, it ignores the potential dangerousness and violence present in some property crimes, such as residential burglary and arson. Second, it ignores that transfer has been aimed at youths who commit crimes repeatedly despite juvenile court intervention (the beyond-treatment juveniles), which certainly can apply to those who commit property crimes. Thus, judicial transfer seemingly continues to be aimed at both the beyond-rehabilitation and greater-punishment groups (discussed earlier in this chapter). The data also indicate that the youths most likely to be transferred are male (96 percent), slightly older (90 percent) (i.e., at least 16), and disproportionately black (44 percent).

Despite the number of youths subjected to judicial transfers, the percentage of delinquency cases petitioned in juvenile court that end in transfer to adult court has not been

Table 12.3 Number of Judicial Transfer Cases

Year	Number of Cases
1994	12,100
1995	10,400
1996	10,000
1997	8,400
1998	8,100
1999	7,500

Table 12.4 Characteristics of Waived Cases, 1990–1999

	1990	1994	1999
Total cases waived	8,300	12,100	7,500
Most serious offense			
Person	32%	44%	34%
Property	45	37	40
Drug	15	11	16
Public order	8	8	11
Gender			
Male	96%	95%	94%
Female	4	5	6
Age (years) at time of referral			
Under 16	10%	13%	14%
16 or older	90	87	86
Race/ethnicity			
White	45%	51%	54%
Black	53	45	44
Other	2	4	2
Predisposition detention			
Detained	57%	56%	35%
Not detained	43	44	65

Note: Totals may not equal 100% due to rounding.
Source: Puzzanchera (2003a); Stahl (2003).

extensive. In 1999, less than 1 percent of all property and public order offenses and slightly more than 1 percent of all drug crimes and crimes against persons were transferred by judges to adult court (Puzzanchera et al. 2003b) (see Table 12.5).

Juveniles who were 16 and older (1.5 percent) were much more likely than those 15 and younger (.2 percent) to have their cases transferred by judges. Not surprisingly, males (.9 percent) were more than four times more likely than females (.2 percent) to experience certification; black youth (1.1 percent) were more likely than whites (.7 percent) and youth of other races (.5 percent) to be transferred to adult court (Puzzanchera et al. 2003b).

Table 12.5 Percentage of Petitioned Delinquency Cases Judicially Transferred to Criminal Court, 1985–1999

Offense	Year			
	1985	1990	1994	1999
Total delinquency	1.4%	1.3%	1.4%	<1%
Person	2.5	2.0	2.7	1.1
Property	1.3	1.1	1.1	<1
Drugs	1.0	2.7	1.8	1.0
Public order	0.7	0.6	0.6	<.5

Sources: Adapted from Butts (1996); Puzzanchera (2003a); Puzzanchera et al. (2003b).

Research on Transfer to Adult Court

Although some studies have focused on the prosecutorial version (Clarke 1996; Singer 1993; Winner et al. 1997), the majority of research on the transfer decision has been directed at judicial transfer. This lopsided focus has two implications. First, most research has involved waiver decisions made based on the amenability of youth to juvenile court treatment. As we have seen, the variety and ambiguity of the factors that can influence the amenability decision make pinpointing the effect of the factors difficult, if not impossible. Second, judicial transfer usually involves decisions made by two, rather than only one court official. The first decision, albeit actually only a recommendation, concerns the PO's analysis of the youth's treatment capacity, coupled with an estimation of the system's capabilities and resources in addressing the youth's problems. The judge then decides whether to accept or to reject the PO's recommendations. What complicates matters is that neither the multiple POs who are responsible for the transfer reports nor the judges' inclinations whether to defer to POs tends to be examined in these transfer studies. In other words, it can be difficult to determine either who is really making the decision to transfer youth or why the decision occurred in judicial transfer cases.

The research has produced conflicting findings in identifying factors that do and do not affect the transfer decision. Although it is common for minorities to be overrepresented in the youth transferred to adult court (Barnes and Franz 1989; Bortner 1986; Clarke 1996; Houghtalin and Mays 1991; Kinder et al. 1995; Singer 1993; Winner et al. 1997), studies stop short of alleging that the transfer decision was based on race alone and not on other accompanying, critical factors. Some research has, in fact, found race not to be a significant factor in explaining transfer (Fagan et al. 1987; Podkopacz and Feld 1996;

Poulos and Orchowsky 1994). Whether or not the decision was racist, minorities seem to be disproportionately affected by certification practices and policies.

Factors that have been found to influence transfer outcomes include offense (Fagan and Deschenes 1990; Fagan et al. 1987; Nimick et al. 1986, Poulos and Orchowsky 1994), especially if numerous felonies or a weapon were involved (Podkopacz and Feld 1996); prior record (Clement 1997; Grisso et al. 1988; Poulos and Orchowsky 1994); age (Fagan et al. 1987; Podkopacz and Feld 1996; Poulos and Orchowsky 1994); previous placements (Podkopacz and Feld 1996; Poulos and Orchowsky 1994); and previous transfers (Lee 1994). The location of the juvenile court can be important. Urban courts appear less prone to transfer youth, possibly because of a greater tolerance to juvenile crime or an abundance of programs from which to draw when keeping youth in the juvenile system (Poulos and Orchowsky 1994). Consistent with that is that some judges are inclined to transfer to adult court more often than others (Podkopacz and Feld 1996). Finally, the PO report and psychologist recommendation have been found to be influential in the transfer decision (Podkopacz and Feld 1996).

Reverse Transfer: Sending the Youth Back to Juvenile Court

Just because a case has been transferred to adult court does not mean it has to stay there, at least in 17 states.[53] These jurisdictions permit the judge or even the prosecutor (CT, DE, GA, OK, SC) to send the case back to juvenile court. Typically, this reverse transfer (waiver, certification) is restricted to situations in which the prosecutor has transferred the case to criminal court. This makes sense, since in judicial transfer a judge has already made an evaluation of where the case belongs. Nevertheless, Mississippi provides for reverse transfer in judicial waiver cases, while Nevada allows reverse certification *only* in judicial transfer cases. In Nevada the juvenile court judge has to accept the reverse transfer for it to be finalized.

Reverse transfer is available in all four states (CT, MT, NE, NY) that have only prosecutorial transfer and no judicial transfer. Thus, judges in these states do have *some* veto power over prosecutors' decisions to transfer cases, albeit criminal court judges. Reverse transfer exists more often in situations where offense exclusion has occurred (perhaps as a consolation for an overzealous prosecutor or statute), but it also exists when prosecutors charged youths in adult court via concurrent jurisdiction (AR, MT, NE, VT, WY). Of course, in the five states in which the prosecutor can be the person who initiates reverse transfer, this move makes sense *only* when offense exclusion is involved. This maneuver compensates for the prosecutor's inability to charge the excluded offense *and* to keep the youth in juvenile court (i.e., for the absence of a concurrent jurisdiction choice). The prosecutor's desire to have the case sent back to juvenile court requires the adult court judge's approval in two states (CT, OK). The three other states (DE, GA, SC) permit prosecutors to make the decision by themselves. The prosecutorial authority possible in the latter situation comes close to converting offense exclusion into concurrent jurisdiction. Although the offense is indeed excluded from juvenile court, the prosecutor can actually end up prosecuting the charge there, albeit after the charged has been filed initially in adult court (and then reverse transferred).

Although it is common for reverse transfer to be possible for any case transferred by a prosecutor, some states limit the procedure to the least serious offenses or the youngest juveniles eligible for prosecutorial transfer (AR, CT, GA). Certain offenders in other states (DE, MD) can be disqualified because of their previous record (such as a previous transfer to or conviction in criminal court). States divide as to whether the adult court judge is supposed to consider the criteria used in traditional judicial transfer (DE, MD, NE, OK, PA) or is given no standards per se in deciding on reverse transfer (AR, CT, IA, MS, NV, NY, WY). While judges in some states (MT, WI) have been told to focus primarily on doing what promotes the protection of society, Georgia requires its judges to find *extraordinary cause*, and Nevada insists its judges have *exceptional circumstances* before reverse transfer is authorized. Some jurisdictions have placed the burden specifically on the juvenile to justify reverse transfer (MD, OK, PA, WI). Finally, although youths in most states are eligible for regular delinquent status if reverse transfer is granted, a number of jurisdictions require the youth to be placed in an *extended jurisdiction* status (AR; see next section) or to be classified as a *designated felon* (GA) or a *youthful offender* (OK, VT). These special classifications guarantee that, if adjudicated, these individuals will be eligible for more serious dispositions than the rank-and-file juvenile delinquent.

One final note on reverse transfer: If criminal court does not find probable cause for the transferred offense (which usually means only for crimes prosecutors have the power to transfer), the case should have to be sent back to juvenile court (much like the juvenile court's failure to find probable cause for the qualifying offense meaning the case cannot be sent to adult court). In this situation adult court loses jurisdiction over the case and it is *not* the same as reverse transfer, although it has been interpreted as such (Griffin et al. 1998). Similarly, if an appellate court were to find that the transfer to adult court was done illegally (which is usually because of some defect in the judicial transfer process), the case must also revert back to juvenile court (where it should be permissible to conduct a second transfer hearing). This situation should not be classified as reverse transfer either, but it has (Griffin et al. 1998). Both of these illustrations lack the essential characteristic of reverse transfer, which is a *discretionary choice* or *judgment* by the adult court judge that a particular case belongs more in juvenile court than in criminal court. The failure to find probable cause and a reversal of judicial transfer by an appellate court indicate that the transfer was *unauthorized* or *unlawful* and *legally must be returned* to juvenile court for further processing.

Transfer to Juvenile Court's Second Tier

Not only might the youth's transfer to adult court not be permanent, but the youth might also be transferred to somewhere other than criminal court. Thus far, eight states have created a second tier of juvenile court to which juvenile defendants may be transferred for trial and sentencing.[54] Most of these states refer to this second tier as an *extended juvenile jurisdiction prosecution* or *proceeding* (EJJP) (AR, IL, KS, MN, MT). A cautionary note is that some states (DE, NH) use the term *extended jurisdiction* to refer to juveniles over whom they have control until an older age than that available for the typical juvenile delinquent (see Chapter 14). There is no special second tier of the juvenile court in these states. Similarly, some states allow their juvenile courts to sentence juveniles in order to retain control over them well into their adulthood (CA, CO, NJ, OR, TX, WI). Again, these states have not implemented another tier of juvenile court from which to adjudicate and sentence these youth. Rhode Island, which was the first state to develop an internal transfer mechanism, calls this process *certification*, whereas juveniles sent to adult court are subject to waiver. It is easy to confuse these words in the state's statute. Connecticut and Ohio have chosen to call this maneuver a *serious juvenile repeat offender prosecution* and a *serious youthful offender disposition*, respectively.

Some aspects of second-tier processing are widely shared among the eight states. For one thing, in most of these states a youth has to be given a hearing before a juvenile court judge for this transfer to occur, and traditional judicial transfer criteria are used. Ohio, however, does not provide for a transfer hearing. An indictment or information filed by the prosecutor is sufficient. Another exception is that for some juveniles in Montana (those who commit an offense subject to prosecutorial transfer but who are too young to go to adult court), the prosecutor's designating the proceeding as an EJJP is all that is required for it to become one. Similarly, a Rhode Island prosecutor's charging a youth who is at least 16 years old with a felony (after the youth has already acquired two felony adjudications after the age of 16) requires certification to the second tier. Another similar provision can be found in Minnesota, where a case that was not sent to adult court, despite the fact that it had been one that was marked for presumptive judicial transfer, must be designated an EJJP (in this case there has been a transfer hearing). Illinois has gone almost this far by identifying any case that involves a juvenile over the age of 13 and a felony charge as a *presumptive* EJJP (assuming the prosecutor has pursued this outcome).

Another common feature is that most youths eligible for transfer to the second tier are those who are also subject to judicial and prosecutorial transfer to criminal court. The Arkansas, Montana, and Rhode Island statutes afford significant exceptions to this characteristic, however. These states have associated no minimum age either with any felony charge (RI) or with the most serious offenses (murder in Arkansas, prosecutorial transfer cases in Montana) that are subject to EJJP. Finally, trial and sentencing provisions are similar in the eight states. Unlike first-tier defendants (in all but Montana), EJJP youth in all eight states are afforded the right to jury trial. All juvenile defendants in Montana are entitled to jury trial. There is a penalty for EJJP defendants who exercise this right in Connecticut, however: Juveniles who demand a jury trial are transferred to criminal court in order to collect this right. Juveniles must waive the right to stay in juvenile court (which means they effectively do not have this right on tier two). If convicted, the result of this second-tier processing is regarded as a juvenile adjudication (rather than as an adult conviction), provided the youth successfully serves out the court's sentence.

Some states hold that if the youth is convicted of an offense less serious than the one that qualified for an EJJP, both the adjudication and sentence *must be* (CT, KS, MN, MT) or *can be* (IL) at the juvenile court level. Except for Rhode Island, the disposition in an EJJP is a combined or blended sentence. This means that the youth is given both a juvenile court disposition *and* an adult sentence. The latter is stayed or suspended while the juvenile court disposition is implemented. If the youth accomplishes the requirements of the implemented disposition, the adult sentence is dismissed. If the youth fails to fulfill the terms of the given disposition (has a new arrest, violates probation or institutional rules, or possibly fails to be rehabilitated), the adult sentence (typically together with an adult conviction) can be imposed on the youth, following a hearing that would document the failure. Instead of a combined sentence, Rhode Island allows the juvenile court judge to select *either* a juvenile *or* adult sentence for the youth.

Massachusetts also provides for a combined sentence option, while New Mexico forces judges to select a juvenile or adult sentence in the delayed judicial transfer procedure discussed earlier in this chapter. In that respect, these states could be regarded as the ninth and tenth jurisdictions with an EJJP setup, especially since the potential sentences in both states result from a joint jury trial/transfer proceeding. The critical difference between these two states and the other eight, however, is that in the delayed judicial transfer provision (i.e., MA and NM), the trial judge is able to both convict and sentence the defendant as an adult immediately rather than only after the youth has failed in a combined sentence situation. This is why the MA-NM provisions were linked with transfer to adult court rather than with transfer to a second tier of juvenile court. Moreover, inasmuch as Massachusetts and New Mexico extend a right to jury trial to all defendants in juvenile court, they have no need to develop a special second tier of juvenile court where that right uniquely exists for some juvenile defendants. As an interesting parallel, nevertheless, both Massachusetts and New Mexico provide juvenile defendants in the delayed judicial transfer a right to a jury made up of 12 members, whereas the regular juvenile defendant is provided a jury consisting of only six members. Finally, it is possible in some states (see below) for criminal courts to sentence youth convicted there to a combined sentence exactly like the one used in an EJJP. This, too, is not the same as transfer to a second tier of juvenile court, since these offenders have clearly been transferred, instead, to adult court.

The Juvenile's Future in Criminal Court

The trial juvenile defendants are given in criminal court does not differ from that given adult defendants. The anti-exclusion argument that juveniles lack the competence to stand trial in adult court could certainly prevent trial there. Ironically, individuals truly concerned about juveniles' lack of adjudicative competence should welcome trial in adult court, since the matter is likely to get a more demanding analysis there than in juvenile court (Sanborn 2003, 2004). If there is a difference in the criminal trial for juveniles, it will not surface until sentencing. Some juveniles have a chance of receiving a juvenile court disposition, despite a criminal court conviction.

Some states (e.g., MS) openly declare that a conviction in adult court means a criminal sentence must follow. For example, Massachusetts holds that defendants between the ages of 14 to 16 who are convicted of first- or second-degree murder must receive an adult sentence. In less than half of the jurisdictions (24), juveniles who commit a capital offense are eligible for the death penalty if convicted. While some states have not identified the age at which a juvenile who commits a capital crime qualifies for the death penalty,[55] a few have picked an age as young as 13 (MS) or 14 (AR, VA). Thus far, the U.S. Supreme Court has upheld the death sentences of youth who were 17 (*Stanford v. Kentucky* 1989) or 16 (*Wilkins v. Missouri* 1989) at the time of the murder. It is unlikely that the Court will permit the execution of anyone who was younger than 16 when the crime occurred. In

Thompson v. Oklahoma (1988), the Supreme Court overturned the capital sentence of a youth who was 15 at the time of the offense, mostly because of a lack of consensus that juveniles that young should be exposed the death penalty. Consequently, states that cite 16[56] or 17[57] as the qualifying threshold for capital punishment are the only ones in compliance with Supreme Court standards in juvenile cases. Juvenile murderers are rarely sentenced to death (and that assumes they are eligible for transfer to adult court in the first place) and are even more rarely executed for their crimes at some point later time. Between 1986 and 1996, nine individuals were executed for murders they had committed when they were 17 (Sickmund et al. 1997). All nine were from five states (GA, LA, MO, SC, TX) that consider age 17 to constitute adulthood. The maximum juvenile court age in these states is 16.

Even though juveniles may be exposed to adult sentences, this does not mean special allowances are prohibited. In all the death penalty states, juveniles can offer their youth as a factor that can mitigate their culpability and punishment. In addition, some states reduce the maximum sentences of incarceration for juveniles. For example, Louisiana does not allow any 14-year-old who was transferred to adult court by a judge to experience imprisonment beyond the age of 31. South Carolina limits the jail time for those younger than 18 who are convicted of Class 1 and 2 misdemeanors. While New York does not differentiate the maximum prison sentence (life) awaiting a juvenile or adult convicted of second-degree murder, there are serious differences in the maximums for other Class A felonies (15 years versus life), as well as for Class B (10 versus 25 years), C (7 versus 15 years), and D (4 versus 7 years) felonies. If juveniles are sentenced to prison, they must be at least 16 years old (AR, CA, MT, ND, TN) to serve any time in an adult facility. However, it is possible for juveniles as young as 14 (CO) to qualify for an adult facility. Even youths who are institutionalized with adults are likely be segregated from the adult inmates. Juveniles who are too young to be placed in prison are likely to start their sentence in a secure youth correctional facility or training school. Another possible location for these juveniles is a youthful offender facility, in which they may spend some of their adult years as well.

Special measures have also been developed for probation sentences. Some statutes seem to encourage a sentence of probation for juveniles (e.g., Michigan's designated proceeding). A couple of states have gone even farther by establishing special opportunities for youth placed on probation by criminal court. While Arizona targets those younger than 18 who have been convicted of a felony (but have no prior felony conviction), Iowa has disqualified any youth who is either convicted of a Class A felony or is subject to youthful offender processing (which we will consider shortly). What is possible in both states is that youths who successfully complete the probation sentence are eligible for the conviction to be set aside by the court.

Beyond what we have discussed already, many jurisdictions do not clearly disclose what can or must happen at sentencing for youth who are convicted in adult court. Of course, the best mandatory exclusion juveniles can hope for is youthful offender sentencing, as they become ineligible for juvenile court dispositions.

It seems reasonable to infer that silence in the statutes means no special juvenile provisions exist and that only criminal court sanctions are available to the judge. Nevertheless, there are exceptions to the general silence. Numerous statutes provide that, at sentencing, the door back to juvenile court has been left open.

This post-criminal-conviction return to juvenile court is much more likely to occur in prosecutorial transfer cases than judicial ones. This makes sense, since judicial transfer represents an analysis and decision by a judge that the youth does not belong in juvenile court. The return to juvenile court can be mandatory.

A number of jurisdictions (AR, KS, NY, VT, VA, WI) hold that youths convicted of charges that are less serious (often referred to as *lesser-included offenses*) than the offense that qualified for offense exclusion must be returned to juvenile court for disposition.[58] These states look at this situation as one in which adult court loses jurisdiction over the case since the conviction was not sustained at the level that had stripped juvenile court of jurisdiction in the first place. These youth are comparable to those who are returned to juvenile court before trial in adult court because of lack of probable cause to believe the excluded offense occurred. Both situations represent an adult court's having to return the youth to the juvenile system because of loss of jurisdiction over the youth. Colorado and Oregon call for the mandatory return to juvenile court when the conviction involves charges less serious than those that qualified for judicial transfer.

The potential for youth to return to juvenile court is not the norm, however. For one thing, many states emphasize that conviction on the offense exclusion or concurrent charges mandates an adult sentence (AK, GA, IL, KY, MT, ND, OR). Moreover, even convictions of lesser-included offenses can require adult sentences in many jurisdictions.[59] Nevertheless, many states have made the decision a discretionary one and have maintained the possibility of leniency by permitting adult court judges to sentence all youth convicted there to juvenile court dispositions (even if on the level of the excluded offense).[60] An important caveat in South Carolina is that the prosecutor must agree to the sentence. The convictions cannot involve life-earning or capital crimes in Florida and West Virginia.[61] Convictions of lesser-included offenses (than offense exclusion level) are even more likely (both in statutes and in reality) to permit the judge to invoke a juvenile sentence in some states[62] or to transfer the matter to juvenile court for disposition (PA).

When the option to sentence the youth is discretionary, the maneuver represents what can be called delayed reverse transfer. In the states that authorize it,[63] the matter is indeed transferred back to juvenile court (like the reverse transfer just covered), but it is delayed until after conviction and until sentencing, rather than occurring before trial. One important difference is that the delayed reverse transfer can amount to a criminal conviction (MI), whereas a pretrial reverse transfer would have to end at most in a juvenile adjudication.

Like other transfers in which a judge is the decision maker, delayed reverse transfer involves the use of criteria relating to the offense and the offender. While in Alaska youths have a burden of clear and convincing evidence that they can be rehabilitated in the juvenile justice system, Illinois requires prosecutors to convince the court that an adult sentence is more appropriate or necessary. Similarly, in Oklahoma the court can impose an adult sentence only if it finds by clear and convincing proof that the youth will not complete the rehabilitation plan or that the public will not be adequately protected if the juvenile is sentenced as a youthful offender. Instead of (or in addition to) imposing a straight juvenile court disposition, some states have chosen to impose a juvenile sentence only after an adult sentence is *stayed or suspended.*[64]

If the youth receives a juvenile disposition via adult court (with or without a suspended criminal sentence), that does not mean adult court loses all leverage or control over the offender. The suspended sentence acts as a constant reminder of what can happen to the youth if the juvenile disposition is not completed successfully. Eventually, these youths (as well as those given a straight juvenile disposition) undergo a *review hearing*, or process in which failure to satisfy the terms of the disposition can result in the imposition of the adult sentence. A number of states provide that the monitoring juvenile department (e.g., DJJ or DYS) (FL, MO) or someone such as the warden of an institution (WV) can report to the court that the juvenile disposition is simply not working out. If the court agrees, it is empowered to invoke the adult sentence.

Youthful Offender Sentencing in Criminal Court

Youth who are neither returned to juvenile court for sentencing nor given a juvenile disposition by criminal court may still be eligible for youthful offender (YO) sentencing. Although the YO term is associated usually with juveniles or young adults being prosecuted for the first time in criminal court, this is not always the case. For example, a number of states (MS, MT, NV, SD, UT) refer to their juvenile delinquents processed in juvenile court as YOs or as youth offenders (OR). Washington calls both juvenile delinquents and young adult first offenders YOs and has identified one of its juvenile institutions as a YO correctional facility. YOs in Ohio are juvenile delinquents who are transferred to the second tier of juvenile court.

Even if the YO label is associated with the adult system, it might refer only to juvenile inmates in adult facilities (NC), or to special rehabilitation-oriented institutions (GA), or programs (NJ) for juvenile and young adult inmates. Similarly, Indiana, Wisconsin, and Wyoming use the YO term in connection with the adjustment or reduction of criminal court sentences for young adults who agree to participate in (and complete) an adult boot camp or similar program.

That leaves 20 jurisdictions that use that YO status as a special method by which to address the presence of a juvenile or young adult in criminal court, typically for the first time. Fourteen jurisdictions connect YOs with juveniles who have been transferred to adult court (or to young adults facing their first conviction).[65] Even here there is considerable variation, however. Alabama extends YO eligibility to persons younger than 21, including youths transferred via offense exclusion (although the juvenile statute suggests otherwise). Alabama denies this opportunity to judicial transfer cases, however, which can produce quite an anomaly. That is, older youth who have committed the more serious offenses identified in offense exclusion (compared to the potential pool of judicial transfer cases) are eligible for adult court leniency denied to the possibly younger, less serious offenders transferred by a judge. Nevertheless, the appellate court has upheld this statute (*J.F.B. v. State* 1998). The most likely logic here is that, while the judicial transfer case has already been determined to be nonamenable to juvenile court treatment, no such finding has occurred in offense exclusion (or prosecutorial transfer) cases.

Arkansas restricts YO status to juveniles who are more amenable to rehabilitation programs in the juvenile system but does not appear to disqualify any youth because of crime and record, provided the youth is younger than 18. The age range in Colorado is between 14 and 18 but depends on the severity of the offense. Class 1 felonies are completely eliminated and Class 2 felonies are for juveniles who were at least 16 at the time of the offense. D.C. seems to open YO sentencing to all youth between the ages of 15 and 18, provided they were put on probation by the criminal court. The only restriction in Florida, South Carolina, and West Virginia is that the offense cannot be punishable by death or a life sentence (and no previous YO status). While Florida terminates YO eligibility at the age of 21, the operative age limit in South Carolina and West Virginia is 25 and 23, respectively. Iowa youth must be 15 or younger at the time of transfer.

All youth transferred to adult court in Kentucky are called youthful offenders, while in Massachusetts and New Mexico, YOs are those juveniles subjected to the delayed judicial transfer procedure described earlier in this chapter. Massachusetts and New Mexico also have juveniles transferred to criminal court via offense exclusion. Whereas the former does not give these youths a special label, in New Mexico they are known as serious youthful offenders. YOs in Oklahoma and Vermont are those transferred youth who are not given an adult sentence in criminal court. Finally, Virginia youth who are younger than 21 and who have not been charged with various murder and sexual assault offenses, qualify for YO treatment, provided the judge considers the offender "to be capable of returning to society as a productive citizen following a reasonable amount of rehabilitation" (VA. Code 19.2–311 B. 3).

Despite the variation in criteria, some operational consistencies exist among the jurisdictions that closely link YO status with transfer to adult court. First, traditional judicial transfer criteria, dealing with amenability to juvenile court treatment, are critical in determining whether a youth will secure a YO designation or an adult sentence in many of these jurisdictions.[66] In fact, in some states (AL, AR, FL, OK, VT) the YO determination operates just like the delayed reverse transfer discussed earlier. Sentencing is another facet of the YO process that is shared by many of these jurisdictions. Most call for setting a criminal sentence, which is then stayed or suspended while the youth serves a juvenile disposition.[67] It is common for the YO disposition to provide juvenile court 1 (OK, VT), 2 (NM), or even 4 years (MA) of extra or extended jurisdiction over the offender.

The *combination sentence* (i.e., suspending the adult while imposing the juvenile) is the mirror image or reverse situation of what transpires in juvenile court via the extended jurisdiction (transfer to juvenile court's second tier). The only difference is that criminal court sentences the YO, rather the juvenile court's second tier sentencing the delinquent. The sentences are indistinguishable. Besides this combination sentence, Massachusetts and Oklahoma allow the judge to select a juvenile or an adult sentence as well. This either/or selection is the only choice available to the sentencing judge in New Mexico. Finally, while Florida calls only for modifying the sentence for a YO (i.e., considerably reduced compared to a potential adult sentence), Kentucky imposes an adult sentence, but then reviews the youth's situation at the age of 18 to decide whether to continue the sentence or to discharge the youth.

The second way in which YO processing occurs involves young adults who are appearing in criminal court, usually for the first time. This version is available in eight jurisdictions.[68] We have already discussed six of these jurisdictions (AL, DC, FL, SC, VA, WV) in the content of juveniles transferred to criminal court. The provisions applicable to these youths do not appear to differ when young adults are arrested and prosecuted for the first time in criminal court. Consequently, we will not explore this latter aspect of YO status in these locations. However, two states extend the YO label to individuals who would be considered as juveniles by most of the country. Connecticut and New York have a maximum juvenile court jurisdictional age of 15 (see Chapter 4). Thus, the minimum criminal court age is 16. Not coincidentally, both states begin the youthful offender stage at the age of 16. It lasts until 18 in Connecticut and until 19 in New York. Both states exclude the most serious felonies as well as youth with previous YO findings or convictions. Similarly, South Carolina's range for YOs runs from 17 to 25. This state's maximum juvenile court age is 16. As with the other two states, YO status in South Carolina serves, in part, as compensation for having a relatively young threshold for criminal court jurisdiction.

With respect to sentencing, both Connecticut and South Carolina allow for a combined juvenile/adult court sentence, which is used by most jurisdictions with the other version of YO processing. New York, on the other hand (and South Carolina with older YOs), has opted to reduce the sentence (to four years maximum, if incarceration) to which a YO is exposed.

One final note of interest with respect to YO processing is that it shares some traits of juvenile court procedure. We have noted that most jurisdictions use judicial transfer-like criteria. This means, of course, that the (criminal court) judge ends up serving as the gatekeeper to YO status, which closely parallels the (juvenile court) judge's responsibilities. A number of statutes have identified other common characteristics:

- Defendant must waive jury trial (AL, CT)
- Closed trial (CT, NY)
- Is not a criminal conviction (AL, CA, CT, NY)
- Prints and photos not open to public inspection (AL, CT)
- No court record available to public (AL, CT, FL, NY)
- No disqualification from public office or employment (AL, CT, NY)

Use of the Juvenile Court Record in Criminal Court Sentencing

We saw in the first section of the text how juvenile courts were originally designed to respond to juvenile misbehavior with compassion and to pursue a mission of rehabilitation. Complementing this benevolent design was the fact that a juvenile adjudication did not have the same negative impact or onerous consequences as a criminal conviction. To ensure that adjudication was not permanently detrimental to the youth, and to minimize stigmatization and adverse labeling of the youth, records of the adjudication were typically sealed or expunged once offenders were no longer answerable to juvenile court jurisdiction (a topic we will cover in Chapter 15). The relative leniency of juvenile court was intended to follow youth into their adulthood. That is, former juvenile delinquents were supposed to enter adult criminality with a clean record. They were not to have their past held against them or to have it influence their sentence in criminal court should they continue to commit crimes. The result of this policy was what is referred to today in the literature as a punishment gap. Chronic juvenile offenders who appeared for the first time in adult court were considered first-time offenders, eligible for sentences reserved for those without a criminal history.

Juvenile court statutes in most jurisdictions continue to suggest that a juvenile record retains its traditional characteristics and is in no way comparable to a criminal record. All but 12 jurisdictions assert that a juvenile adjudication is not a criminal conviction.[69] Similarly, all but 14 jurisdictions insist that juvenile adjudications do not result in the civil disabilities or in the civil service disqualification that results from a criminal conviction.[70] Only seven jurisdictions have statutes that mention neither of these traditional traits.[71] Finally, 17 jurisdictions continue to declare that juvenile delinquents are not to be regarded as criminal or guilty by virtue of their adjudications.[72]

Although it might be reasonable to infer from these provisions that juvenile records are still not comparable to criminal records and that punishment gaps must still be necessary, this is no longer the case. To be sure, juveniles with "criminal pasts" can receive leniency in their first appearance in criminal court and can be treated like a first-time offender. We have seen that juveniles can be sentenced to a juvenile disposition in criminal court or can be subjected to a delayed reverse transfer to juvenile court. Failing that, youths may receive the benefits of YO sentencing. Despite all these leniency safety valves, juveniles in criminal court for the first time can be treated like recidivists because of their delinquency history. In other words, *factoring juvenile court records directly into criminal court sentencing* is a reality in many jurisdictions.

Actually, even juvenile court statutes warn of this potential outcome. All but seven states (AK, CA, HI, IN, KY, NH, UT) emphasize that a juvenile adjudication can be used in the sentencing of any subsequent adjudication or conviction. A variety of sources from criminal court (statutes, sentencing guidelines, presentence investigation reports) also clearly hold that sentencing can reflect a record accumulated in juvenile court. Only 17 jurisdictions lack a provision authorizing the use of a juvenile court record.[73] New Hampshire is the only state that has neither a juvenile nor a criminal court provision in this area. Moreover, case law in 46 jurisdictions (including New Hampshire) has thus far given judicial support for using juvenile court records in this capacity (only AR, DC, ME, MS, NM, VT lack an appellate court case), while 18 jurisdictions have appellate cases that have explicitly upheld sentencing offenders in criminal court for the first time as recidivists due to their juvenile record (Sanborn 1998, 2000).[74]

Only two states (AZ, GA) clearly prevent a juvenile adjudication from having a recidivist impact in criminal court sentencing. At most, a juvenile record in these states would disqualify offenders from receiving probation and would expose them to presumptive sentences of imprisonment. In 26 jurisdictions the exact impact of a juvenile record on criminal court sentencing is impossible to gauge.[75] These jurisdictions sentence criminals in terms of ranges (e.g., 10 to 20 years) and do not pinpoint just how much influence a criminal (or delinquent) history should have on the sentence. In other words, the precise number of "extra" years the offender would receive as a result of being a recidivist would not be revealed in the current sentence. Moreover, if the current prosecution involves multiple offenses, the defendant can receive a consecutive sentence, expanding the punishment by many years. It is within the judge's discretion to invoke a consecutive sentence, and the offender's having a delinquent record could influence this decision. Nevertheless, it is possible that the connection between juvenile adjudications and enhanced criminal sentences in this regard will not be disclosed.

A significant minority of jurisdictions (24) have granted juvenile adjudications open recidivist impact on criminal court sentencing. Most of these jurisdictions (13) have given points or criminal history classifications to juvenile adjudications via criminal court sentencing guidelines. The points or classifications that have been given to juvenile adjudications and records are:

- the same as those allocated for criminal conviction/history (DE, FL, KS, OR, PA, VA);

- the same for only the most serious offenses (AR, WA);

- fewer than those allocated for comparable criminal conviction (MI, MN, UT); or

- fewer than those given to criminal sentences (FED, MD).

Rather than assigning points to juvenile adjudications, the sentencing guidelines in North Carolina and Tennessee identify juvenile records as an aggravating factor that would expose the offender to an *extended sentence*. Similarly, six states that do not use sentencing guidelines have made juvenile records an *aggravating factor* that can influence criminal court sentence via:

- presumptive sentences (AK, CO);

- extended and consecutive sentences (IL, IN);

- consecutive sentences (NJ); or

- sentencing repeat violent offenders (OH).

Finally, three states (CA, LA, TX) allow juvenile adjudications to constitute a *strike* within three strikes sentencing. In fact, juveniles in these states can earn all but the final strike in juvenile court and can effectively strike out on the first conviction in criminal court. That is, an otherwise nonlife-earning crime can result in an offender's receiving a life sentence because he or she has a juvenile record.

Actually, striking out on the first pitch in criminal court is not limited to these three states. One study examined the potential "worst-case scenario" in each of the 24 jurisdictions that grant juvenile records open recidivist impact on criminal court sentencing. That is, assuming the current offense being prosecuted in criminal court is not a life-earning or capital offense, what is the most severe possible impact (a worst-case scenario for the defendant) a juvenile record can have on the adult sentence? As shown in Table 12.6, the 24 jurisdictions were divided into three categories, representing 20-year ranges of "extra" years or time a "first" offender could receive in a criminal court sentence for having a juvenile record.

While seven states limit the impact of a juvenile record on a criminal court sentence to less than 20 years of incarceration, in another six states an offender can receive between

Table 12.6 Potential Recidivist Impact of Juvenile Record

Moderate (<20 years)	Heavy (20–40 years)	Extreme (40 years–life)
AK	AR	CA
MD	CO	DE
MN	NJ	FED
NC	OR	FL
OH	TN	IL
PA	WA	IN
UT		KS
		LA
		MI
		TX
		VA

an extra 20 to 40 years of prison due exclusively to a juvenile record. By far, the most significant result is that in 11 jurisdictions a juvenile record can add 40 or more years of imprisonment to the sentence in criminal court. In some situations this would result in a life or even a life-without-parole sentence. Striking out on the first pitch is possible in all 11 jurisdictions (see Sanborn 1998, 2000). Moreover, the offender facing this sentencing may be a juvenile who has been transferred to criminal court.

Juvenile adjudications can also affect *capital sentencing* in criminal court. Of course, this is not an issue in the 13 jurisdictions that do not permit capital punishment.[76] Another five states (AL, CT, FL, NJ, NY) have refused to allow juvenile records to be considered in death penalty cases. That leaves 34 jurisdictions in which juvenile adjudications can be factored into this sentencing. These jurisdictions have allowed the juvenile record to influence capital sentence in one or more of three ways. First, a juvenile record can be permitted to reflect the *general character* of the accused.[77] This means that the judge or jury would be made aware that the defendant has a past not of exemplary character. A juvenile record has been allowed in 13 states to *neutralize* other *mitigating factors*.[78] This means if the defendant offers some evidence to mitigate or reduce culpability (e.g., youth), the state can produce the juvenile record to offset or to neutralize the mitigating factor(s). Finally, 20 jurisdictions have gone even farther by allowing juvenile records to serve as an *aggravating factor* in favor of imposing the death penalty.[79] Moreover, in some states (e.g., NC, PA) one aggravating factor is all that is required to impose the death penalty. Thus far, case law in 14 jurisdictions has upheld these various provisions that factor the juvenile record into capital sentencing (see Sanborn 1998, 2000).[80]

What this all means, of course, is that it is clearly inappropriate to think of juvenile court as "kiddie" court today. The consequences of juvenile court adjudications can be serious both within the juvenile system and in criminal court. That, in turn, means that fairness problems and other issues (such as denial of equal protection) are not inconsequential. What transpires in juvenile court truly does matter for both the present and future of each offender.

Research on Adult Court Sentencing of Juveniles

Studies that have examined the outcomes of sentences imposed on youth in criminal court have found mixed results. Some research has found that jail and prison terms are rarely given to youth convicted in adult court (Bortner 1986; Champion and Mays 1991; Fagan 1995; Hamparian et al. 1982). Other studies, however, have found juveniles being incarcerated at high rates and given much longer sentences than they could have received in juvenile court (Barnes and Franz 1989; Bishop et al. 1996; Clement 1997; Dawson 1992; Fritsch et al. 1996; Houghtalin and Mays 1991; Podkopacz and Feld 1996; Thomas and Bilchik 1985). However, even youth who are given lengthy sentences face a prospect of early release from adult prison, long before the expiration of the sentence (Fritsch et al. 1996).

These mixed results reflect the fact that the juvenile offenders who have been sent to criminal court have been mixed themselves. Nonviolent property offenders transferred to adult court because of a belief that they are not amenable to juvenile court treatment may not receive severe sentences in criminal court. This would especially be possible if the juvenile record is not known or is not seriously factored into criminal court sentencing in the particular state. Moreover, if the adult court judges have discretion, they may be reluctant to imprison a nonviolent young offender making a first appearance in the adult system. To be sure, if the only reason to transfer juveniles to adult court were to secure longer sentences than those available in juvenile court, transfer practices would have to be seriously questioned. As we saw earlier in this chapter, however, the reasons behind transfer are many and varied and do not rely exclusively, and often not primarily, on the sentencing outcome in criminal court.

Some Numbers on Youth Convicted and Sentenced in Criminal Court

Transferred youth tend to have been involved in more serious offenses than the general adult defendant population, which in some states includes chronological juveniles (16 and 17 year olds) who have been subject to mandatory exclusion (see Chapter 4). This makes sense because of the selectivity of transfer and its focus on serious offenders. Table 12.7 shows the offense profile of transferred juveniles and adults in adult court.

Again, due in part to the focused selection of the offenders, transferred youth tend to be subjected to harsher sentences than adult criminals. Overall, the difference for many offenses is considerable, as shown in Table 12.8.

Finally, as indicated in Table 12.9, the sentences handed down to youth convicted in criminal court often exceed those that would be possible (or desirable) in juvenile court. What is unknown about the data is the extent to which, if at all, juvenile records were actually considered or used (if permissible) to influence the criminal court sentence.

Table 12.7 Most Serious Offense for Transferred Youth and Adults Convicted in Adult Court, 1996		
Most Serious Offense	**Transferred Youth**	**Adults**
Gender		
Male	96%	84%
Female	4%	16
Race		
White	43	53
Black	55	45
Other	2	2
Violent Offenses	53	17
Murder	7	1
Sexual assault	4	3
Robbery	23	4
Aggravated assault	17	7
Other violent	1	1
Property Offenses	27	30
Burglary	19	9
Larceny	8	12
Fraud	1	8
Drug Offenses	11	37
Possession	3	15
Trafficking	8	22
Weapons Offenses	3	3
Other Offenses	6	14
Source: Levin et al. (2000), Table 5.1		

Table 12.8 Felony Sentences Imposed on Transferred Youth and Adults Convicted in Criminal Court, 1996						
Most Serious Offense	Transferred Youth			Adults		
	Prison	Jail	Probation	Prison	Jail	Probation
All offenses	60%	19%	21%	37%	23%	40%
Violent offenses	75	9	15	78	5	17
Property offenses	46	27	27	18	28	54
Drug offenses	31	36	33	34	28	38
Weapons offenses	55	20	25	39	17	44
Other offenses	37	43	20	22	37	41
Source: Levin et al. (2000), Table 5.2.						

Table 12.9 Mean Maximum Length of Felony Sentences Imposed on Transferred Youth in Adult Court, in Months, 1996			
Most Serious Offense	**Prison**	**Jail**	**Probation**
All Offenses	91	6	44
Violent Offenses	118	8	55
Murder	277	6	77
Sexual assault	105	7	67
Robbery	101	8	48
Aggravated assault	80	9	57
Other violent	79	5	48
Property Offenses	39	6	43
Burglary	41	5	45
Larceny	33	6	37
Fraud	27	5	41
Drug Offenses	30	6	29
Possession	21	6	36
Trafficking	32	5	27
Weapons Offenses	48	6	26
Other Offenses	48	6	33
Source: Levin et al. (2000), Table 5.3.			

Summary: Key Ideas and Concepts

- Transfer as the state forcing the case into the adult system
- Various reasons youth would elect to send themselves to adult court
- Variety of names given to the transfer phenomenon
- Important differences between mandatory exclusion and transfer
- Transfer a discretionary method of exclusion
- Legislature establishes exclusion but cannot transfer any particular defendant
- Transfer as old as juvenile court
- Transfer supported by all three juvenile justice models
- Some support total exclusion of juveniles or the abolition of juvenile court
- Transfer meant for beyond-rehabilitation and greater-punishment groups
- Anti-exclusion camp opposes exclusion due to three problems
- Judicial and prosecutorial the only two types of transfer
- Probable cause and amenability hearings the two stages of judicial transfer
- Transfer decision delayed until after trial in juvenile court
- Uncertain status of rights applicable to judicial transfer hearing
- Myriad factors used to gauge amenability to treatment
- Levels of proof to establish nonamenability to treatment
- Switching burden of proof to youth to show amenability to treatment
- Presumptive judicial transfer a compromise measure
- Various ways in which presumptive judicial transfer occurs
- Two types of prosecutorial transfer
- Serious confusion and misrepresentation over elements of offense exclusion
- Offense exclusion as discretionary and not mandatory exclusion
- Michigan designated proceeding converts juvenile court into adult court
- All jurisdictions have at least one form of transfer
- Only 10 states do not have both forms of transfer
- Different levels of judicial and prosecutorial transfer
- Ability of adult court to send a case back to juvenile court
- Reverse transfer versus adult court losing jurisdiction over a case
- Juvenile court transferring a case to itself (a second-tier prosecution)
- Second tier of juvenile court resembling prosecution in adult court

- Juvenile murderers as eligible for the death penalty
- Special adult court sentences for youth convicted there
- Mandatory and discretionary return to juvenile court following adult conviction
- Youthful offender as special adult court sentencing category for youth
- Multiple and confusing use of youthful offender designation and criteria
- Adult court imposing combination sentence
- Combination sentence as mirror of juvenile court second-tier disposition
- Factoring juvenile adjudications into adult court sentencing
- Striking out on the first pitch (or conviction) in adult court
- Juvenile adjudications factoring into death penalty sentencing

Discussion Questions

1. Should juveniles be permitted to transfer their cases to adult court? If not, why not? If so, at what age should this transfer be allowed?

2. Explain the differences between mandatory exclusion and transfer (or discretionary exclusion).

3. Discuss the various rationales for transfer. Are any inappropriate? Are some reasons more worthy or necessary than others? Should some be eliminated or revised?

4. For whom is transfer meant to occur? Is transfer appropriate for all the youth who have been targeted?

5. Identify the two types of judicial and prosecutorial transfer.

6. Do the arguments of the anti-exclusion proponents have merit? If so, which arguments, and why are they meritorious? Do any of these arguments mean that transfer should never occur? Should occur less frequently?

7. Is the delayed judicial transfer process better than the way in which most states conduct judicial transfer? Explain the differences and why one way is better than the other.

8. Should the amenability burden be switched to the youth? If so, when?

9. Should prosecutors have the discretion to transfer youths to adult court? If not, why not? If yes, under what circumstances?

10. Should criminal court have the discretion to send cases back to juvenile court? If not, why not? If yes, under what circumstances?

11. Should a juvenile court be permitted to transfer cases to a second tier of its court? If not, why not? If yes, why? Are there any potential problems in this structure?

12. Should juvenile murderers be eligible for the death penalty? If not, why not? If yes, why, and should there be a minimum age to qualify for the death penalty?

13. Should juveniles be eligible for special sentencing (such as youthful offender) in criminal court? If not, why not? If yes, should there be any restrictions on who qualifies for this sentencing?

14. Should the juvenile court record be factored into criminal court sentencing? If not, why not? If yes, should there be any limitations to the impact that the juvenile record can have in adult court?

Endnotes

1. No age requirement for self-transfer to adult court is identified in AK, FED, FL, ID, IA, LA, PA, WA, WY.
2. The jurisdictions that refer to this process as transfer are: AL, AZ, AR, CO, DC, FED, FL, GA, ID, KY, LA, MS, MO, NH, NC, ND, OH, PA, SC, SD, TN, TX, UT, VT, VA, WA, WV, WY.
3. The states that call this process waiver are: AK, AR, FL, HI, ID, IN, IA, MD, MI, NJ, OR, RI, TX, UT, WV, WI.
4. The states that call this process certification are: CO, FL, KS, ME, MN, MO, NV, NH, OK, PA, SD, UT.
5. Nevertheless, some authorities have identified mandatory exclusion as legislative transfer, which is inappropriate and confusing (Forst and Blomquist 1991; Whitebread and Batey 1981; Zimring 1981).
6. This is not meant to suggest that judges do not consider the offender's dangerousness and the need for greater punishment, or that prosecutors will not weigh the defendant's treatment potential and other circumstances unrelated to the offense that suggest that the case should stay in juvenile court.
7. Judges are authorized to initiate transfer proceedings in DE, ID, LA, MD, MS, MO, NC, OK, TN, WA, WI.
8. Prosecutors are identified as being responsible for beginning transfer proceedings in AL, AZ, AR, CA, CO, DE, DC, FED, FL, ID, IL, IN, IA, KS, KY, LA, ME, MD, MI, MN, MS, NV, NJ, NM, NC, OK, PA, RI, VT, VA, WA, WV, WI, WY.
9. A transfer hearing that is required is not related to whether the transfer itself is regular or presumptive. Although the four states that currently mandate a hearing have maintained regular judicial transfer in this regard, Massachusetts had coupled the mandatory hearing with presumptive judicial transfer before this provision was abandoned in favor of prosecutorial transfer. Florida also requires that the judge explain why certification is denied, assuming that it is the outcome of the hearing, but the amenability burden itself has not been altered or shifted to the defendant. Unfortunately, Florida's mandatory transfer hearing has already been mislabeled as presumptive transfer (Lanza-Kaduce et al. 1996).
10. Notice of the transfer hearing is required in AK, DC, IL, IA, KS, ME, MD, MI, MO, NC, OK, RI, TX, VA, WA, WV.
11. Probable cause to believe the crime occurred is required in AL, AK, AZ, CO, CT, DE, FL, IL, IN, IA, KY, LA, ME, MI, MN, NJ, NM, NC, OH, RI, UT, VT, VA, WV.
12. Strict rules of evidence are not followed in AL, AZ, CA, DE, FL, GA, HI, ID, IL, IN, IA, KS, MD, MA, MO, NV, NJ, NY, ND, OH, OK, OR, TN, TX, UT, WA, WV, WI.
13. The right to counsel is guaranteed in AL, AK, AZ, CO, CT, DC, GA, HI, ID, IL, IN, IA, KS, KY, LA, ME, MD, MI, MN, MS, MO, NH, NC, ND, OH, OK, RI, SC, TN, UT, WV, WI, WY.
14. Confrontation and cross-examination of witnesses is guaranteed in AL, AK, AZ, CO, CT, DE, FL, GA, ID, IL, IN, KS, KY, LA, ME, MN, MO, NC, ND, SD, TN, UT, WV, WI, WY.
15. The right to present evidence is recognized in AK, AZ, CA, DE, DC, GA, ID, IN, KY, LA, MD, MN, NC, ND, TN, UT, WV, WY.
16. The right against self-incrimination is recognized in AL, AK, AZ, CA, GA, IL, IN, KS, KY, LA, MI, NH, NJ, ND, OK, OR, TN, TX, WV, WY.
17. The right to compulsory process is granted in IN, KS, KY, LA, MN, NC, UT, WV, WY.
18. The right to be present at the hearing is granted in DC, LA, MD, MS, MO, NC, ND, TN, WV, WI, WY.
19. The right to have a record kept of the proceeding is recognized in AK, AZ, GA, ID, IL, KY, ME, MI, MN, OH, ND, TN, WV.
20. A transfer report is mandatory in AL, AZ, CA, DC, FL, ID, IA, MD, MO, RI, WA.
21. A transfer report is discretionary in MA, MN, MS, OH, TX, UT, VA, WI.
22. The jurisdictions that require the report to be delivered to defense counsel before the hearing are: AZ, CA, DC, FL, ID, IA, LA, MD, MA, MI, MN, MS, MO, NH, NC, OK, RI, TX, UT, VA, WI.

23. The best interests of the child and the public are required to be considered in AL, AZ, CO, GA, IN, IA, KS, KY, MI, NC, OR, RI, SC, SD, UT, WA, WI.
24. The protection of society must be considered in AZ, AR, CO, DE, DC, FL, GA, ID, IN, KS, KY, LA, ME, MD, MI, MN, MS, MO, NE, NH, NM, NC, ND, OH, OK, OR, PA, RI, SC, SD, TX, UT, VT, WI, WY.
25. These elements of the offense must be considered in AR, CO, FL, HI, ID, IL, KS, ME, MS, MO, NE, NH, NJ, NM, NC, OK, OR, SC, SD, TN, UT, VT, VA, WI, WY.
26. The person-versus-property nature of the offense must be considered in AR, CO, DE, FL, HI, ID, IN, KS, KY, ME, MS, MO, NH, NJ, NM, OK, OR, SC, SD, TN, TX, UT, VT, VA, WI, WY.
27. The use of a deadly weapon must be considered in CO, DE, IL, MI, MN, NJ, OH, UT, VA.
28. Participation with others or a gang must be considered in AZ, AR, FED, IL, KY, NJ, OH, TN, UT, WI.
29. The degree of participation or culpability must be considered in AZ, AR, CA, IL, MI, MN, PA, VA.
30. The expiration of the jurisdiction is a factor in AK, DC, HI, IL, KS, KY, ME, MS, NJ, NC, ND, OH, PA, RI, UT, VA.
31. The need for adult sanctions is a factor in AL, DE, HI, ID, ME, NE, OH, TN, WI.
32. Treatment history is a factor in AL, AZ, CA, DC, FED, FL, HI, ID, IL, IA, LA, MI, MN, MS, MO, NM, NC, ND, OH, OK, OR, PA, RI, TN, UT, VT, WY.
33. A previous commitment is a factor in AZ, DE, FL, OK, OR, VA, WY.
34. The youth's physical and mental maturity is a factor in AL, AR, CA, CO, DC, FED, FL, HI, ID, KS, KY, LA, ME, MD, MI, MN, MS, MO, NE, NH, NM, NC, ND, OH, OK, OR, PA, SC, SD, TX, UT, VT, VA, WV, WY.
35. Age is cited as a factor in CO, DE, DC, FED, IL, IN, IA, LA, ME, MD, MA, MO, NC, ND, PA, RI, VT, VA.
36. Mental disability is a factor in AL, DC, GA, HI, NM, ND, PA, TN, VA, WI.
37. Any other factors are considered in AR, VA, DE, HI, MA, MS, NM, ND, OH, PA, UT, WI.
38. The transfer status of co-defendants is a factor in DE, FL, HI, NH, OR, SC, SD, UT, WI, WY.
39. The victim's view on transfer is a factor in AZ, CA, CO, GA, MD, MA, MI, MN, PA.
40. Judges must consider all factors in AL, AK, AR, CA, CO, FL, ID, KS, MD, MI, MN, MO, UT, VA.
41. A preponderance of evidence is the level of proof in AK, AZ, CA, DC, FED, ME, MD, MI, OH, OR, PA, RI, UT, VA.
42. Clear and convincing is the standard of proof in AL, AR, LA, MN, MS, OK, WV, WI.
43. These defendants in Utah must not have been previously adjudicated delinquent of a felony involving the use of a deadly weapon. Utah has fashioned its presumptive transfer so as to be almost indistinguishable from the offense exclusion version of prosecutorial transfer. However, offense exclusion requires no more than probable cause for a crime to be established before juvenile court must transfer the case. To deny transfer in Utah a juvenile court judge can use relative nonculpability or nonviolence; this would not be possible in offense exclusion.
44. Like Utah's, this version of presumptive transfer is similar to offense exclusion. The major difference, however, is that in offense exclusion, probable cause means the case must go to adult court, while in these cases in West Virginia judges are not required to transfer when probable cause is established. Although West Virginia has not placed any specific, identifiable burden on defendants in order to stay in juvenile court, the ball is certainly in their court, inasmuch as prosecutors do not need to prove these youths are beyond the help of the juvenile system in order to secure transfer. The complete removal of the amenability consideration or hurdle would seem to reflect the legislature's desire to make transfer a presumptively safe bet, if not a sure one.
45. On the other hand, states that have maintained the traditional amenability burden, while perhaps simultaneously expanding the number of factors that the state can argue, suggest nonamenability, and reducing the number of factors the state must establish to prove nonamenability or requiring a transfer hearing per se or even explanations from the judge as to why transfer was denied would still be classified as practicing regular judicial transfer.
46. Judges must offer reasons justifying transfer in AL, AK, AZ, AR, CA, DC, FL, HI, ID, IL, IA, LA, MD, MA, MI, MN, MS, MO, NH, NC, OH, OK, OR, PA, RI, SD, TX, UT, VT, WA, WI, WY.
47. The states that phrase offense exclusion in this way are: AL, AK, IL, IN, LA, MD, MA, MS, NV, VA, WA.
48. The states that phrase offense exclusion in this way are: AL, AZ, CA, DE, FL, ID, IL, IA, MT, OK, OR, SC, UT, VT.
49. The jurisdictions that phrase offense exclusion in this way are: CT, GA, FED, IL, IN, KY, MI, MN, NJ, NC, ND, OH, SC, TX, VA, WV.
50. See *Commonwealth v. Kocher*, 602 A.2d 1308 (Pa. 1992).
51. Mandatory exclusion because of prior record obviously can involve youths who are within the age range of juvenile court jurisdiction. The presence of these individuals in adult court makes it appear that they were transferred there. This is not the case if mandatory exclusion has occurred. The jurisdictions in which this potential confusion can arise are: AL; CT, DE, DC, FL, HI, ID, IN, KS, LA, MN, MS, NV, ND, OH, OR, PA, RI, UT, VA, WA, WI. If the mandatory exclusion is because of age (rather than record), the

"adult" age of the defendant would automatically negate the possibility that transfer had occurred, and no confusion would exist.

52. A second minor problem with gauging the true extent of prosecutorial transfer is that cases involving offense exclusion may be neither recognized nor tallied as instances of transfer, and they may be identified instead as legislative transfers.

53. The states that practice reverse transfer are: AR, CT, DE, GA, IA, MD, MS, MT, NE, NV, NY, OK, PA, SC, VT, WI, WY. Two other states (NH, TN) technically provide for reverse transfer, but the provisions are so narrow they are virtually pointless. For example, in New Hampshire reverse transfer is limited to defendants who are 17 and who were out of the state at the time when proceedings were sent to adult court. Similarly, the statute in Tennessee states that if a youth is transferred by a nonlawyer judge (this was written for one judge in Memphis who fits this description), adult court will look into the appropriateness of sending the case back to juvenile court.

54. The eight states with a second tier are: AR, CT, IL, KS, MN, MT, OH, RI.

55. The states that do not mention a minimum age are: AZ, ID, MT, LA, PA, SC, SD, UT.

56. The states with a minimum age of 16 are: AL, DE. FL, IN, KY, MO, NV, OK, WY.

57. The states with a minimum age of 17 are: GA, NH, NC, TX.

58. There can be limitations in these provisions, however. While Arkansas and Vermont limit this opportunity to those younger than 16, Virginia mandates the return only in misdemeanor cases.

59. Adult sentences are required in this context in AL, AZ, CT, DE, DC, HI, IN, IA, LA, MN, MS, TN.

60. Juvenile court dispositions are possible in this context in CA, FL, ID, MI, MO, OK, SC, VA, WV.

61. Florida also excludes all youth who are convicted in adult court after being subjected to mandatory direct file or a mandatory transfer hearing in juvenile court.

62. Juvenile sentences are possible in this context in AK, CA, CO, GA, ID, MA, NM, OR.

63. Delayed reverse transfer can occur in AK, CO, FL, IL, MI, MO, OK, OR, PA.

64. The states that sentence youth this way are: ID, MA, MI, MO, OK, VA, WV.

65. The jurisdictions that use the YO title this way are: AL, AR, CO, DC, FL, IA, KY, MA, NM, OK, SC, VA, VT, WV.

66. The jurisdictions that use the criteria this way are: AL, AR. DC, FL, MA, NM, OK, SC, VT.

67. The jurisdictions that call for a criminal sentence are: AL, AR, CO, DC, IA, MA, OK, SC, VA, VT, WV.

68. The jurisdictions that use the YO status this way are: AL, CT, DC, FL, NY, SC, VA, WV.

69. The jurisdictions omitting this reference to a juvenile adjudication are: AR, CA, CT, FED, ID, IL, LA, NH, NJ, OH, VA, WV.

70. The jurisdictions that omit a reference to this characteristic are: AR, CA, CT, DE, FED, ID, KS, LA, ME, MI, NH, OR, WA, WV.

71. The seven jurisdictions are: AR, CT, FED, ID, IL, LA, NH, WV.

72. The jurisdictions that do not regard the juvenile as a criminal are: AK, DE, FL, HI, IN, KY, MA, MN, MS, MO, NV, NJ, NY, OH, OK, RI, SD.

73. The jurisdictions that lack this provision are: AZ, CT, DC, GA, ME, MS, MO, MT, NV, NH, NM, OK, RI, SC, VT, WV, WY.

74. The jurisdictions with an appellate court case are: AK, CA, CO, FED, FL, IL, IN, KS, LA, MI, NJ, NC, OR, PA, TN, TX, VA, WA.

75. The jurisdictions for which it is not possible to gauge an impact are: AL, CT, DC, HI, ID, IA, KY, ME, MA, MS, MO, MT, NE, NV, NH, NM, NY, ND, OK, RI, SC, SD, VT, WV, WI, WY.

76. The jurisdictions in which this is possible are: AK, DC, HI, IA, ME, MA, MI, MN, ND, RI, VT, WV, WI.

77. The juvenile record can reflect on general character in LA, MT, NV, OK, SC, SD, TN.

78. The juvenile record can neutralize mitigating factors in AZ, AR, CA, CO, ID, IN, KS, MD, NH, NM, OH, OR, WY.

79. The juvenile record can serve as an aggravating factor in CA, CO, DE, FED, GA, ID, IL, KS, KY, MS, MO, NE, NC, OR, PA, TX, UT, VA, WA, WY.

80. The appellate courts have upheld the law in AZ, CA, FED, GA, IL, LA, NE, PA, SC, TN, TX, UT, VA, WA. ✦

Juvenile Court's Trial and Sentencing Stages

- Chapter 13: The Adjudicatory Hearing
- Chapter 14: The Disposition Hearing
- Chapter 15: Postdisposition Hearings and Matters in Juvenile Court

Focus of Section V

Section V addresses the critical trial and sentencing stages of the juvenile court process. In these chapters we will discover how dramatically the adjudicatory hearing can differ from the adult court's criminal trial. Many individuals assume there is no difference, but this assumption is incorrect. The differences have implications when it comes to identifying the impact an adjudication should have for sentencing purposes, both within the juvenile system and in criminal court (as we discussed in Chapter 12). Disposition in juvenile court is also unique. We will see how social work criteria once again become influential in determining what should be done with young offenders. Finally, we will learn how issues and procedures that arise after disposition can influence and alter the juvenile court's response to the offender. ✦

Chapter 13

The Adjudicatory Hearing

Focus of Chapter 13

The focus of Chapter 13 is on the adjudicatory hearing or trial that occurs in juvenile court. Although some of its facets parallel what transpires in the criminal trial, many aspects of the adjudicatory hearing are truly unparalleled. Moreover, situations arise in the adjudicatory hearing that would not be permitted in criminal court. An appreciation of the differences between trials in juvenile and adult courts is critical in being able to put a juvenile court adjudication in its true legal context.

Key Terms

- adjudicatory hearing
- self-representation
- speedy trial
- waiver of counsel

Prosecutorial Case Preparation

If the case is not resolved during the pretrial stage or transferred to adult court, a prosecutor will have to prepare it for processing. A number of factors can affect the nature and extent of this processing:

- Whether a full-fledged criminal prosecutor is handling the case or someone else (or perhaps no one other than the complainant)
- The severity of the offense and the defendant's delinquent and treatment records
- The integrity and thoroughness of the prosecutor
- The prosecutor's office policies and practices, together with perspectives toward juvenile crime

It is becoming increasingly common for jurisdictions to insist that, if a trial ultimately is needed to resolve the case (meaning testimony will have to be elicited from witnesses), a prosecutor is the person to fulfill that task. In fact, Alabama and New Mexico specifically provide that a PO is *not* authorized to conduct questioning at trial. Nevertheless, many states extend prosecutors the discretion to not appear if the case involves less-serious felonies or misdemeanors (DE, NY, VA, WA). Moreover, several states still use the phrase that prosecutors will represent the state "at the court's request" (AL, GA, HI, NM, PA, RI, TN).[1] Although some states (ND, NM, WV) call for "regular" prosecutors to appear in both delinquency and status offense cases, it is quite likely that a different prosecutor (such as an attorney from the Department of Juvenile Justice) will pursue status offense adjudications (FL, MD). Moreover, some states (AZ, CA, GA, WI) link the appearance of any prosecutor with a status offender's being assisted by defense counsel. In Georgia, even a victim can play a role of prosecutor in a status offense case. Consequently, it is still common for there to be no prosecutor present during trial in juvenile court, or for the attorney who plays this role to be either a "rookie" or someone other than a regular criminal prosecutor. These situations can cause fairness problems for the defendant, which we will review in the section on judges.

A prosecutor's preparation for trial in juvenile court involves the same three major stages that occur in criminal court:

1. Assembling the evidence and disclosing parts of it to the defense

2. Examining the major obstacles to adjudication, together with anticipating and fighting any pretrial defense motions

3. Determining what should happen, what can happen, and what is the best way to reach the appropriate result

The first stage includes reading police reports of the incident and arrest and any interrogation of the defendant, as well as lab reports on ballistics, blood, or drug analysis, and interviewing potential witnesses (victim, eyewitness, police). In the second stage a prosecutor gauges the strengths and weaknesses of the assembled evidence, which encompasses:

- the willingness and ability of witnesses to testify and their credibility;

- evidence, whether testimonial or physical, and its sufficiency, legality, and admissibility;

- who the judge is, if known, and this person's tendencies to be sympathetic toward prosecution or defense (or neither);

- who the defense attorney is, if known, and this person's reputation and capabilities; and

- miscellaneous concerns such as the defendant's ability to file certain pretrial motions, the defendant's insistence on a jury trial, or the pressure of time limits in prosecuting the case.

In the third stage, prosecutors formulate an idea of what they want out of a case by evaluating the defendant's prior record (school, criminal, treatment history) and family and home situation, consulting the PO's recommendation and plan for the youth (if it has been completed), and perhaps ascertaining the victim's desires, all in the context of the current charges. The defendant's record and the PO's plan should also give the prosecutor a rough idea of what results are likely to occur if an adjudication is obtained.

The information garnered from these three stages should provide the prosecutor with an indication of whether a trial is plausible, necessary, or worthwhile or whether the same (or other desirable) results could

How does this courtroom differ from a criminal courtroom? Should juveniles be granted jury trials?

be reached through an informal resolution. In turn, this information, combined with traditional or routine practice in a particular juvenile court, should determine whether the prosecutor will approach the defense attorney (or the youth) with a proposal for an informal resolution or with simply an inquiry as to what the defense attorney wants or will accept in the case. The PO could also be brought into this discussion (unlike in adult court), and the judge could end up as a participant as well. As with adult court, this conversation could occur during the pretrial period or on the same day as the case is listed for trial.

The prosecutor's analysis of the case at the time of trial is unique in three ways. First, virtually all of the case processing by the prosecutor can occur on the day of trial in some jurisdictions. That is because the admissibility of evidence (i.e., whether there has been an illegal search and seizure or interrogation) may not be determined yet, and other issues may be outstanding as well (such as joinder or severance of charges or defendants). Several jurisdictions specifically provide that the adjudicatory hearing is the time and place to resolve pretrial matters (AZ, DC, OH, SD, WV, WY). Second, to determine the "appropriate" results, the prosecutor needs to consult items mostly irrelevant in criminal court, such as a school record or the family and home situation. Finally, juvenile court tends to put the cart before the horse by calling for a PO to develop a treatment plan that can be available to opposing counsel before the trial actually starts. The thinking here is that, assuming there is an adjudication, juvenile court wants to implement the proposed solution (again assuming treatment is necessary) as soon as possible following adjudication. (We revisit this material in Chapter 14.) The point is that because the PO recommendation is routinely adopted by the judge at disposition, both prosecutors and defense attorneys tend to know what they are up against prior to trial and can better gauge how necessary or beneficial a trial might be. This plan also provides the PO a unique and influential role in indirectly determining the method by which a case will be resolved in juvenile court.

Before we discuss the comparable tasks that *defense attorneys* must perform in preparing for trial, we must consider whether the accused will be represented by an attorney at the adjudicatory hearing and what kind of representation the youth can expect to receive in the juvenile system.

The Right to Counsel in Juvenile Court

To be sure, *In re Gault* granted juveniles charged with a delinquent act a right to counsel at the trial stage, meaning that indigent or poor defendants must be provided with counsel, while wealthy defendants can hire or retain their own lawyer. At least 40 jurisdictions speak to a right to counsel at all proceedings or critical stages, and the adjudicatory hearing certainly qualifies (see Appendix I). As in adult court, however, two things can stand in the way of the youth's being represented. First, the defendant may not qualify for appointed counsel, especially if he or she is not going to be institutionalized. The *Gault* decision emphasized the need for an attorney when a juvenile is removed from the home, and a subsequent adult case (*Scott v. Illinois* 1979), equally applicable to juvenile court, specifically authorized states to not appoint counsel in nonincarceration cases. Accordingly, five states specifically link the right to counsel to cases in which juveniles are committed to a facility (AL, MA, NJ, SC, TN). Second, the right to counsel is waivable in most jurisdictions, even in commitment situations.

A total of 25 jurisdictions *mandate* the presence of counsel in juvenile court in certain contexts. This policy differs from that in adult court, where the appointment of counsel is never mandatory and where defendants have a constitutional right to represent themselves (*Faretta v. California* 1975).[2] Nine jurisdictions insist on defendants being provided counsel (unless counsel has already been retained), regardless of the severity of the offense or the potential disposition.[3] It appears that in these locations juveniles *cannot waive* the right. Moreover, if the parents in these states are able but refuse to hire an attorney, counsel must be appointed, with the expenses then being assigned to the parents. The language in some statutes is compelling:

- No hearing on any petition can be commenced unless defendant is represented by counsel (IL).

- Counsel may not be waived by any child of any age (IA).

- The child shall be represented by counsel at all critical stages (MS).

Another nine states specify that counsel must represent a youth who is about to be incarcerated.[4]

Several states have associated the mandatory counsel provision with an issue involving the parents. For example, if there is no parent (or at least none present in court), seven states demand the appointment of counsel.[5] Otherwise, the absence of a parent has prompted some jurisdictions either to allow the judge to appoint a guardian *ad litem* for the child[6] or to demand this result,[7] unless an attorney is already available to represent the child. Similarly, as noted previously, parents may have interests that conflict with those of their children. One possible aspect of this conflict is that an attorney retained by the parents (and possibly even one appointed by the court) may end up representing the parents' interests (since they are the paying clients) instead of the youth's interests. Despite this ever-present problem, only nine states require the appointment of separate counsel to represent the child.[8] Otherwise, a conflict of interests with the parents has prompted some jurisdictions either to allow the judge to appoint a guardian *ad litem* for the child[9] or to demand this result[10]—again, unless an attorney is already available to represent the child.

Assuming there is a nonhostile parent present in court, 43 jurisdictions either do not guarantee a right to counsel or permit the youth to waive this right, provided incarceration is not involved. Even if the youth is removed from home, counsel can still be waived in 34 jurisdictions. A number of states specifically identify a defendant's right to self-representation in juvenile court (AZ, CA, MA, MI, SD, UT), while Minnesota allows it provided stand-by counsel is assigned. Waiver of counsel is thus a relevant topic in 43 jurisdictions. Waiving counsel is critical to juvenile defendants, since doing so means the case will be resolved without the youth's receiving legal assistance from someone who is supposed to advance his or her cause. One study has documented an abundance of juveniles not represented in juvenile court proceedings in a few jurisdictions (Feld 1993a).

The right to counsel in status offense prosecutions is somewhat more varied than it is in delinquency cases. While Hawaii does not mention the right, Alaska declares that the decision to supply status offenders with counsel is discretionary, depending on whether the judge believes doing so would promote the youth's welfare. A number of other states appear to require institutionalization before the right to counsel is activated (AZ, NJ, SC, TN, WA, WI), while Florida and North Carolina associate counsel with contempt charges against status offenders. Three states (KS, NM, OK) suggest that a guardian *ad litem* would suffice in representing status offenders. Juvenile courts commonly assign a guardian *ad litem* rather than a public defender or an appointed counsel to represent status offenders. The remaining 36 jurisdictions that process status offenders (see Chapter 4) appear to guarantee a right to counsel for these youth (see Appendix I).

Waiving the Right to Counsel

While New York has created a presumption that juveniles are *incapable* of waiving the right to counsel, a handful of states (AR, FL, MN, TN) have outlined a fairly demanding routine to be followed when a juvenile waives the right, including a thorough colloquy like the one that has to be followed in some locations when a youth pleads guilty in juvenile court (see Chapter 11). For example, the Arkansas statute details numerous considerations and inquiries to be made by the judge when a juvenile waives counsel. First, the judge must find by clear and convincing evidence after questioning the youth that:

1. the juvenile understands the full implications of the right to counsel;

2. the juvenile freely, voluntarily, and intelligently wishes to waive the right to counsel; and

3. the parent, guardian, custodian, or counsel for the juvenile has agreed with the juvenile's decision to waive the right to counsel.

The judge also has to examine the parents and their decision to agree with the child and find that:

1. such person has freely, voluntarily, and intelligently made the decision to agree with the juvenile's waiver of the right to counsel;

2. such person has no interest adverse to the juvenile; and

3. such person has consulted with the juvenile in regard to the juvenile's waiver of counsel.

Finally, the judge must consider several circumstances in determining whether the youth has freely, voluntarily, and intelligently waived the right to counsel, including:

1. the juvenile's physical, mental, and emotional maturity;

2. whether the juvenile understood the consequences of the waiver;

3. whether the parent understood the consequences of the waiver;

4. whether the juvenile and the parent were informed of the alleged delinquent act;

5. whether the waiver of the right to counsel was the result of any coercion, force, or inducement; and

6. whether the juvenile and the parent had been advised of the juvenile's right to remain silent and to the appointment of counsel and had waived such rights. (ARK Statute 9-27-317)

Beyond these requirements, a judge cannot accept a waiver of counsel by a youth in Arkansas if the parents have filed a petition against their children or if the youth is destined to be incarcerated, assuming adjudication occurs.

In addition, some states require that the defendant be warned of the specific dangers and disadvantages of proceeding without counsel (MI, MN, SD), that the youth consult an attorney prior to the waiver (AK, MN, NJ, NY, WV), or that the juvenile must talk to (TN) or secure the agreement of a parent (AK, AZ, LA, MA, MI, MT), who is not hostile to the youth (AR, NH, PA, VA), before the judge can accept a waiver of counsel, which must be made in open court and on the record (AR, CA, FL, MI, MN, NJ, TN). Despite these highly developed examinations of the waiver of counsel by juvenile defendants, most jurisdictions have done little in regulating this crucial decision beyond simply requiring that the waiver be voluntary and intelligent. Research conducted under the auspices of the American Bar Association has documented juveniles in several states waiving counsel often and without the benefit of consulting an attorney or of an exacting inquiry by the judge (ABA 2003; Albin et al. 2003; Brooks and Kamine 2003; Calvin 2003; Celeste and Puritz 2001; Cumming et al. 2003; Grindall 2003; Miller-Wilson 2003; Puritz and Brooks 2002; Puritz and Sun 2001; Puritz et al. 1995, 2002; Stewart et al. 2000).

It is the nonindigent juvenile defendant who may be most negatively affected by the ability to waive counsel. The poor defendant who qualifies for a public defender or an appointed counsel does not have to pay for the attorney's services and would seem to have no vested interest in declining those services, assuming there is no pressure from the judge to waive the right. The defendant whose parents are found to be wealthy enough to retain counsel, however, faces not only the same pressures as an indigent defendant but also a potential conflict with those parents who would be forced to pay for counsel out of their own pocket. There is thus a financial incentive for these parents to refuse to hire an attorney and then to encourage the child to waive the right to counsel at court. If the parents' self-interests are not obvious (after all, it could be simply that the parents do not believe their child's case requires or would benefit from an attorney), the judge could accept the waiver and not appoint counsel. Moreover, the requirement in numerous states that parents agree with the youth's decision to waive counsel would be meaningless. Even more suspect is the situation in which the parent, instead of the child, could waive the right to counsel, which is possible in the state of Washington if the youth is younger than 12.

The Nature of Defense Representation in Juvenile Court

Assuming that counsel is either retained or appointed, the next question becomes the type of representation the youth will receive in juvenile court. The American Bar Association began a serious inquiry into this subject in the mid-1990s. Their initial report disclosed disturbing findings about the youth's access to counsel and the quality of representation provided by defense attorneys in juvenile court regards (Puritz et al. 1995). Since then, similar examinations have been conducted in a number of states with similarly disturbing results. Beginning in Texas (Stewart et al. 2000), and followed by inquiries in Louisiana (Celeste and Puritz 2001), Georgia (Puritz and Sun 2001), Kentucky (Puritz and Brooks 2002), Virginia (Puritz et al. 2002), Ohio (Brooks and Kamine 2003), Maine (ABA 2003), Maryland (Cumming et al. 2003), Montana (Albin et al. 2003), North Carolina (Grindall 2003), Pennsylvania (Miller-Wilson 2003), and Washington (Calvin 2003), the ABA discovered certain consistent tendencies regarding defense representation in juvenile court. Generally, defense counsel had little or no training in juvenile matters, and they were not appointed until the detention hearing or later, which was a considerable time after proceedings (and conversations with the youth) had been initiated. Public defenders and even many appointed counsel had extremely high caseloads that rendered their assistance ineffective in many, if not most, cases. Defense attorneys were pressured by judges to move and settle rather than to try cases, and appointed counsel were under pressure to quickly resolve cases or face the threat of not receiving more appointments. Defense attorneys were not paid the same as their counterparts in criminal court and often received the same compensation whether the case was tried or negotiated. Finally, juveniles were frequently encouraged (or pressured) by judges to do without the services of counsel. These findings are significant, because it means that many juveniles are not being given adequate due process in juvenile court. Just how unique most of these findings are to juvenile court would be difficult to establish.

Although many defense attorneys who work in juvenile court are experienced, competent, and committed to providing effective assistance of counsel, we saw in Chapter 8 that defense representation can be problematic in ways that are either unique to or aggravated in juvenile court. Simply put, the representation provided by many juvenile court defense attorneys is compromised by lawyers who may (1) care too much, (2) care for the wrong client, (3) care too little, or (4) know too little.

Lawyers who *care too much* are unique to juvenile court. They are the ones who act like *guardians* and are motivated by the defendant's treatment needs and not in the youth's legal interests. The most obvious invitation to defense counsel to adopt this role occurs when counsel is permitted to serve simultaneously as guardian *ad litem* for the child. Guardians *ad litem* are charged specifically with pursuing the child's treatment interests. Although this joint appointment is prohibited in Minnesota and Wisconsin and is criticized by experts (Geraghty 1998; Green and Dohrn 1996; Ross 1996), Illinois openly and regularly permits the practice (Geraghty 1998), which has been sanctioned by the appellate courts of that state.[11] Other states, such as Wyoming, are less clear in telling defense counsel to act like guardians in juvenile court when counsel are instructed to consider "the best interests of the child."

Even if state law neither commands nor recommends that defense attorneys become guardians, juvenile court judges commonly steer counsel in that direction, and many defense attorneys simply believe in the appropriateness of representing juvenile clients differently than they do supposedly responsible adult clients. Defense counsel could be particularly reluctant to let juveniles think they "beat the rap," or to allow youth to return to an abusive home or neighborhood or to self-destructive criminal activities. Complicating matters is the fact that, for some youth at least, juvenile court intervention would mark an improvement in their living conditions, and counsel could know before trial what will happen if the defendant is adjudicated.

Lawyers who *care for the wrong client* are also unique to juvenile court. These are attorneys who represent the parents' interests instead of the juvenile's. The problem may be more obvious when the parents retain counsel themselves, but it cannot be ruled out when counsel is appointed. Simply put, some parents want their children removed from the home, and adjudication could be the only way to achieve (or at least to guarantee) that result. These parental desires were explored in Chapter 8. Regardless of the motivation, parents can either command retained counsel or pressure assigned counsel to pursue an adjudication in lieu of an acquittal (Sanborn 1995b). Although a number of jurisdictions mandate the presence of counsel, this mandate does not by itself address or resolve this conflict-of-interests situation. Only nine states have demanded separate counsel for the child if this conflict exists with the parents—assuming, of course, that the conflict can be detected. Another "wrong client" situation involves the potential problem that arises when defense counsel represents multiple defendants who have conflicting interests. Representing multiple clients is more likely to occur in juvenile court than in criminal court. Nevertheless, only the District of Columbia and Minnesota have created a special duty for the juvenile court judge to ensure that dual representation does not compromise the defense of any one client.

Lawyers who either *care too little* or *know too little* are not unique to juvenile court. However, it seems their presence is easier to explain and even to justify in juvenile court. The care-too-little lawyer can be either a nonadvocate or a "burnout." Juvenile court can be a particularly good home for both types, for different reasons. The *nonadvocate* regards juvenile court as "kiddie court" where nothing serious happens to offenders, by virtue of adjudication or disposition. This is perhaps not an unreasonable view of juvenile court. Moreover, even juvenile court judges who are not inclined to force defense attorneys to be guardians could certainly prefer or insist that they not become unrestrained advocates. Defense attorneys might even be instructed officially to be somewhat nonadvocates, as in the Family Court Rules of South Carolina:

> Counsel shall not attempt to further argue any matter after he has been heard and the ruling of the court has been pronounced. No argument shall be made on objections to admissibility of evidence or conduct of trial unless specifically requested by the court. (Rule 9(b))

Again, the fact that some youth could witness an improvement in their living conditions via an adjudication could certainly encourage some defense attorneys to modify (if not abandon) their advocacy. The same approach could be adopted by *burnouts* who simply do not care about the representation they provide juvenile defendants. To be sure, burnouts can be found in adult court. Juvenile courts provide them an especially safe haven, however. The relative low visibility of juvenile court allows burnouts generally to hide from public scrutiny, and the relatively low stakes and beneficial outcomes of juvenile court intervention allow them to hide their true lack of concern and effort. Juvenile court burnouts can argue simply that their tendency to not contest the state's case actually stems from their having adopted a guardian-like role. The nonadvocate types can offer the same argument.

The *know-too-little* lawyers also hail from two camps: They may be inexperienced or incompetent. The juvenile court-as-appropriate-training-ground mentality justifies the presence of fresh-out-of-law-school lawyers who are performing in their first job. Whether the defendant receives effective assistance of counsel from these individuals will depend on a number of factors:

- The inherent capabilities of the attorney

- The amount of training the attorney receives

- The extent to which the judge (or maybe the prosecutor or PO) compensates for the attorney's lack of experience

The incompetent attorney is one who, even with adequate experience, still would not get it. Luck is most likely to account for a defendant's receiving effective assistance from this attorney. Nevertheless, juvenile court provides the same safe haven and excuses for the know-too-little group as it does for the care-too-little attorneys.

Overall, the philosophical and structural peculiarities of the juvenile court enable defense representation to be fundamentally different in that court than what is expected and tolerated in criminal court. Although advocate-oriented defense attorneys who fight cases just like they would or do in adult court operate in some juvenile courts, it is unrealistic to expect defense representation to match what is provided adult defendants. In other words, given two sets of 100 cases having the same dimensions (charges, evidence, legal issues, etc.), defense attorneys in juvenile court should be expected to file fewer motions, contest fewer cases, and file fewer appeals than comparably situated defense attorneys in criminal court.

Defense Case Preparation

A defense attorney's preparation for trial in juvenile court involves the same three major stages that occur in criminal court:

1. Assembling and examining the evidence and case against the defendant

2. Preparing a pretrial strategy (what, if any, motions to file), together with gauging the likelihood of adjudication and the results of such

3. Determining what is in the defendant's best interests (both legal and treatment) and estimating the best way to ensure the most favorable results

Defense attorneys engage in many of the same activities as described earlier for the prosecutor, including inquiring into what the other side wants in the case and whether an informal resolution is preferable to trial. There are some serious differences, however. Whereas defense attorneys almost certainly will have access to less evidence than that available to the prosecutor, they alone have access to the defendant and the family. Defense attorneys must also decide whether to file various pretrial motions and ultimately will have to advise the defendant as to whether an informal resolution or a trial is the wiser option. Unlike their counterparts in criminal court, juvenile court defense attorneys need to be familiar with available treatment programs (and which is most appropriate for the youth's situation) and with various social variables affecting the case (e.g., school record, strengths and weaknesses of the family). Again, some or all of this work may not occur until the day the matter is listed for trial.

The Right to a Speedy Trial in Juvenile Court

Potentially critical during this case preparation stage is the amount of time that has elapsed since the charges were filed against the youth. The U.S. Supreme Court has not addressed whether juveniles have a constitutional right to a speedy trial. Most jurisdictions have either ignored the topic completely or have established weak standards that do not put much pressure on juvenile courts to adjudicate matters expeditiously. However, six states have recognized the victim's right to a speedy trial or expedited resolution of the case (AZ, FL, MI, MN, NV, UT).

We saw in Chapter 10 that most jurisdictions (44) require an expedited adjudicatory hearing for detained youth. This is *not* the same as granting a right to a speedy trial (as many as 95 percent of defendants in some juvenile courts are *not detained* prior to trial). Rather, these trial deadlines simply limit the duration of pretrial detention. If the case exceeds the deadline, at best the youth is simply released from detention while the case proceeds (usually without any deadline at that point).

Fewer jurisdictions (27) have created an obligation on the prosecutor to bring the case against a released defendant to trial within so many days.[12] Two of these states (NE, NY) have extended a right to speedy trial to status offenders too. The clock starts running at various points among these 27 states, with the filing or serving of the petition being the most common. Florida alone begins counting time when the youth is taken into custody. Using the petition as the triggering mechanism for the clock provides the state with several days or weeks of additional time following arrest. Similarly, the number of days permitted ranges from a low of 30 to a high of 180. More important, perhaps, many of these states allow extensions of either a considerable number of days (and even up to a year) or an unspecified duration to be granted the prosecution, typically for *good cause*. Frequently, the clock stops (or tolls) for an uncertain length for such events as pretrial hearings, and Wisconsin even includes court congestion and scheduling. Moreover, the time requirement in six states (FL, ID, LA, MN, NM, NY) demands only that the trial actually begins before the deadline. Thus, calling one witness and then granting a continuance of unspecified length would satisfy the requirement.

Finally, only eight states (FL, GA, LA, MS, NH, NM, NY, WA) have declared either in statute or case law that the deadline is *mandatory*. That is, the state's violating the requirement would have to result in the prosecution being permanently dismissed (i.e., the petition would be dismissed *with prejudice*), but four of these states (FL, LA, NM, NY) demand only that the trial commence within the deadline. Another nine states (AZ, IL, IA, MN, NE, NV, ND, SC, WY) have found the requirement to be *directory* only. That is, a violation either would not stop a trial from occurring beyond the deadline or would cause the prosecution to be only temporarily dismissed (i.e., the petition would be dismissed *without prejudice*). Thus, the prosecutor could eventually reinstate the same charges (together with a brand new clock) (Butts and Sanborn 1999).

As is the case with detained status offenders and their eligibility for an expedited trial (see Chapter 10), it is difficult to determine whether the trial deadlines established for released delinquents always apply equally to their status offense counterparts. Many jurisdictions generally suggest that delinquents and status offenders released pending trial are to be given equal consideration in scheduling adjudicatory hearings.[13] States with speedy trial provisions for delinquents (see Appendix J) divide in applying these provisions to status offenders. While some states suggest (CA, GA, MI, NV, TN), other states specify (IL, IA, LA) that the provisions are the same for both sets of defendants. Nevertheless, while three states (NE, NH, NM) call for a shorter time period for status offender trials (including half the number of days in Nebraska), Colorado and Minnesota allow for a longer pretrial delay in status offense cases. In fact, compared to delinquents, status offenders in Colorado can wait one and a half times (90) the days for an adjudicatory hearing, and in Minnesota the delay can be twice (120) as many days.

The behavior of the vast majority of jurisdictions in the speedy trial area has been consistent with traditional juvenile justice philosophy by:

- avoiding setting time restraints on prosecutors altogether;

- establishing standards that are lax or provide numerous exceptions and extensions; and

- providing prosecutors with escape mechanisms if there are violations of time deadlines.

These maneuvers present minimal obstacles to the system in successfully adjudicating delinquent youth.

Although it has been far from perfect in creating and adhering to them, the adult system has been more dedicated to establishing time requirements because the Sixth Amendment right to a speedy trial has been held binding on the criminal court by the Supreme Court (*Klopfer v. North Carolina* 1967) and because of a basic proposition:

$$\text{justice delayed} = \text{justice denied}$$

Historically, juvenile courts' priorities have been geared to dispensing treatment. Nevertheless, failure to hold the juvenile system accountable to deadlines also violates a major tenet of juvenile justice:

$$\text{treatment delayed} = \text{treatment denied}$$

Juvenile court history is replete with urgings that youth be helped quickly, if not immediately, which is the major reason the PO's plan is usually developed prior to trial. Failure to require the state to prosecute juvenile defendants expeditiously has several possible negative consequences:

1. The youth remains in a negative situation, contributing to a deterioration of his or her problems, sometimes including physical injury.

2. The absence of consequences for illegal behavior undercuts whatever deterrent effect juvenile court can have for these arrested youths, and can encourage the commission of more offenses by these juveniles.

3. The absence of consequences for arrested juveniles becomes known to others not yet arrested, further deteriorating any possible deterrent effect throughout the neighborhood.

4. Youths becoming recidivists due to a second arrest before trial on the first offense complicate the court's intervention for these offenders by possibly eliminating diversionary programs and even some initial stages of probation (see Butts and Sanborn 1999).

In short, delay can contribute to the youth's becoming "worse," which could result in the system's response becoming "worse" and in the youth being denied treatment programs that could be both cheaper and more effective (e.g., a youth otherwise headed for diversion or probation could end up incarcerated instead) (see Butts and Sanborn 1999).

Listing the Case for an Adjudicatory Hearing

Despite efforts that prosecutors and defense attorneys put into the case before the trial date, there are no guarantees that, as the matter is called for trial, an adjudicatory hearing will occur. No trial will commence if one of the necessary parties has not appeared (prosecutor, defendant, defense attorney, witness), if necessary evidence has not yet been examined or delivered to either the prosecutor or the defense attorney, or if pretrial issues such as a motion to suppress illegally seized evidence have yet to be resolved. A successful defense motion (remember those from Chapter 11) could mean no trial would occur on that date and possibly not at any future date. Conversely, an unsuccessful defense motion does not mean that a trial will result, since an informal resolution or the defendant's decision unilaterally to plead guilty could still occur.

Assuming that the prosecutor has not worked something out with the defense and believes sufficient evidence exists to adjudicate, only the lack of a witness or piece of evidence should prevent the case from going forward from the state's view. Of course, the defense could not be ready to go to trial as well. If all the necessary elements are not available at this moment:

• the trial could begin with the available evidence and witnesses being introduced, then a continuance could be granted to complete the case;

• the whole matter could be continued to a later date, especially if no time deadlines are threatened thereby;

- the case could be temporarily withdrawn (i.e., without prejudice) by the prosecutor, hoping to get the case together eventually; or

- the case could be permanently withdrawn (i.e., with prejudice) by the prosecutor (realizing prosecution of the case is wrong or hopeless) or dismissed by the judge (punishing the state for failing to prosecute within a reasonable or specified time or simply promoting the interests of justice or the child).

Using Masters or Referees to Conduct the Adjudicatory Hearing

In adult court only a judge or a magistrate can be in charge of trial proceedings. Both are judicial figures legally empowered to deliver verdict (i.e., to acquit or convict) against defendants, although magistrates are authorized to hear only less serious crimes such as misdemeanors. In 24 states, however, juvenile courts let referees or masters, who are not bestowed with verdict power, conduct an adjudicatory hearing. We saw in Chapter 8 how using referees can result in significant financial savings for juvenile courts.

The eight other states that use masters have avoided any controversies or problems by allowing them to conduct only preliminary hearings and not trials (MT, RI, WV, WI, WY) or by equipping them with actual verdict power (AZ, CT, IA).[14]

The 24 states that use nonverdict-empowered referees to conduct trial split evenly as to whether the defendant must consent to this practice.[15] But research has shown that even where consent is required, there are considerable pressures to allow the master to hear the case. Refusal can mean serious inconvenience, as the case would have to be postponed for trial before a judge, who almost definitely will learn that this defendant has been uncooperative with the court (Sanborn 1994b). Some states have restricted the scope of situations in which referees can conduct trials to those involving misdemeanors or nonserious crimes (DE, TX, UT), crimes for which incarceration is not possible (DE, NJ), or nonjury trials (AK, CO, MI).

When masters conduct trial without verdict power, the following transpires. After hearing the case and making all necessary rulings (e.g., admissibility of evidence), the referee forms conclusions as to whether guilt has been proved by the prosecution. He or she then writes or tape records a synopsis of the critical evidence (or lack thereof) that formed the basis of his or her conclusions and submits this abbreviated package to the judge, together with a "guilty" or "not guilty" *recommendation*. The judge reviews the package and recommendation and either agrees (the verdict matches the recommendation) or disagrees (the verdict differs from and reverses the recommendation).

What happens as the judge reviews the recommendation varies from state to state. The defendant is allowed to challenge a guilty recommendation in all states (much like appealing a guilty verdict in adult court). Prosecutors may or may not be allowed to appeal a not guilty recommendation or a guilty recommendation of a charge less serious than what was originally charged. There may or may not be a rehearing, as opposed to the judge's simply reviewing the package without listening to observations from either prosecution or defense. There may or may not be an opportunity for either side to present additional or new evidence at the review stage. These variations are not particularly critical.

Problems arise as long as a judge is allowed to reverse previous findings by the master that were in the defendant's favor, as can occur in all 24 states, with or without a prosecutor's request and with or without new evidence from the state.

The U.S. Supreme Court was asked to examine the legitimacy of trials-by-referees in a little-known case, *Swisher v. Brady*, in 1978. The case came out of Maryland, where prosecutors were allowed to appeal an unsatisfactory recommendation as well as to reargue the matter (including, of course, the master's conclusions) before the judge. No new evidence could be submitted by the state, however. The Court upheld this practice in a 6–3 vote. The Court determined there was no *double jeopardy violation* because the defendant was not forced to undergo a second *trial*. Rather, the referee system involved "a single proceeding which begins with a master's hearing and culminates with an adjudication by the judge" (1978, 215). Although jeopardy attached at the referee hearing, according to the Supreme Court, it merely continued at the judge review level (or was *one continuous* jeopardy, instead of two distinct sets of jeopardy, or double jeopardy). Thus, the Court developed a rather novel interpretation of this two-tier process on which many juvenile courts are seriously financially dependent and that, despite its financial attractiveness, *exists in no comparable context in criminal court*. The obvious question the *Swisher* decision invites is: If this process is constitutionally sound, why don't criminal courts use masters in this capacity? The most likely answer follows in the next few paragraphs, which capture most of the ideas presented in the *Swisher* dissent, authored by Justice Thurgood Marshall.

The trial-by-master scenario creates two constitutional problems. The first involves *double jeopardy* and applies to those defendants for whom the original master recommendation was either not guilty or guilty of a charge less severe than that identified in the petition. For both of these situations the state has a *second opportunity* (made even worse if the prosecutor is permitted to reargue the case or to present new evidence at the judge's review stage) *to convince a (second) factfinder* that the defendant is guilty. That is, having failed to secure a satisfactory outcome from the referee, the prosecutor can passively (if no reargument or no evidence is allowed) or actively (if either reargument or new evidence is allowed) attempt to obtain the desired result from a judge.

To fully appreciate this evolution it is important first to recognize that, although the word does not suggest it, the master's *recommendation* is tantamount to a *verdict*. The master is the only factfinder at the trial and the only person who decides on the evidence, including its weight and credibility (and admissibility). The recommendation issued by the master is thus substantively indistinguishable from conclusions drawn by the trial judge or jury in adult court where the word *verdict* is used instead.

If the master's recommendation is, in truth, a verdict, then the judge's review produces a *second* verdict, which can reverse the first and amount to double jeopardy. If the prosecutor is allowed to introduce additional evidence at the judge's review, nothing short of a second trial has occurred. If all the prosecutor can do is reargue the facts and conclusions (as in *Swisher*), there is nothing to distinguish this two-tier progression from a prosecutor's trying to convince an appellate court, through argument alone, that a previous not guilty verdict should be reversed. Even if the judge's review is limited to the record of the trial (i.e., no argument or new evidence, and technically no state appeal), this is still the same as an appellate court's being able to consider and reverse not guilty verdicts. All of these instances are examples of double jeopardy where the state has two chances to convict (a failure before the master can be turned into a success before the judge).

The second constitutional problem involves *due process*. Simply put, it is *unfair* to be convicted by someone (here, the judge) who was not even present at the trial and saw no evidence or witnesses firsthand. The juvenile's attorney in *Swisher* failed to present this claim to the Supreme Court, which refused to consider it because of that fact. Logically speaking, the trial-by-master system *has to violate either double jeopardy or due process (or both)*. Either the juvenile is truly subjected to two verdicts (in violation of double jeopardy) or is exposed to only one verdict issued by a judge who was nowhere near the trial (in violation of due process). The majority in *Swisher* ducked this logic problem. The Supreme Court has never been asked to revisit this issue.

The Nature of Judicial Decision Makers in Juvenile Court

Whether a master or a regular judge conducts the trial, the next question becomes the type of justice the youth will receive from this individual in juvenile court. Although many judges who work in juvenile courts are experienced, competent, and committed to producing just findings and rulings, we saw in Chapter 8 that, like defense representation, judicial decision making can be problematic in ways that are either unique to or aggravated in juvenile court. Simply put, the decisions tendered by many juvenile court judges are compromised by judges who (1) know too much, (2) care too much, (3) do too much, (4) know too little, or (5) care too little.

Judges who *know too much* are a special problem in juvenile court, since no jury can compensate for or neutralize the judge's prejudicial knowledge. Things judges know about defendants while conducting trial but ideally should *not* know include: (1) the defendant's prior record (and perhaps what the record entails), (2) evidence that is not admissible at trial, and (3) that the defendant or the family have problems.

Statutes in Iowa, New Mexico, and Washington specifically instruct their juvenile court judges to be impartial. Furthermore, the law in 11 states provides for a change of judge when that person's neutrality is questionable.[16] How helpful these provisions are in ensuring an impartial judge in juvenile court is doubtful, however. The simple truth is that judges frequently have to know prejudicial aspects about defendants because of the juvenile court's structural peculiarities.

Many juvenile courts are one-judge operations in which the one person presides at all pretrial stages as well as at the trial. Also possible is that judges are simply allowed or assigned to do both levels even in the absence of personnel limitations. So, for example, although the judge at a detention or bail hearing is privy to all three of the above items of information, this person will routinely conduct trial as well. Similarly, trial judges who have heard motions to suppress are likely to have had access to evidence that is inadmissible at trial. Judges can also secure some of this prejudicial information from having heard previous cases involving this defendant (or perhaps siblings). Even judges without previous contact with a particular defendant can learn prejudicial information from having access to the youth's court record or the PO's plan (which is prohibited by law in most jurisdictions but nevertheless still occurs). Even more plausible and permissible is contamination resulting from:

- the defendant's having multiple issues simultaneously before the judge (such as trial on one matter *and* revocation of probation on another or an open disposition or a review of the youth's probation or institutionalization);

- the presence of a habitual offender prosecutor or defense attorney;

- the presence of the defendant's PO or the institutional representative who transported the youth to court; and/or

- the presence of a particularly thick (but unread) court record or the use of a certain color file folder for juveniles on probation.

These are all subtle ways of telling the judge the defendant has a prior record. Less subtle is the prosecutor's announcement to the judge that the defendant has a case in court today (perhaps before another judge) for disposition or that the youth has just experienced a failed transfer to criminal court (or simply that the youth is a recidivist).

A detained youth at trial screams *problem* to a judge. This is another situation of judges knowing too much. First, it is virtually impossible for the trial judge *not to know* that the youth is being detained, as one or more of the following is usually present:

- The defendant is in cuffs or shackles.

- The defendant is wearing special detention clothing.

- The defendant enters the court via a special door.

- The sheriff accompanies the defendant into court.

- The case is listed for an expedited trial.

- Someone simply announces it as such.

Thus, the Montana statute that prohibits the youth from wearing institutional (i.e., detention) clothing at the adjudicatory hearing is probably of marginal use in eliminating the judge's ability to discover the youth has been held in detention. The trial judge usually knows that it was *not* money that prevented the youth's release but rather some significant problem with the youth or family. Moreover, two previous decision makers (probably the PO and a judge or master) must have reached the same conclusion about the youth's being or having a problem. This situation creates an extra pressure on the trial judge not to acquit the defendant. To acquit this youth could mean an obvious problem will go unaddressed. Released defendants do not enter the courtroom with this type of cloud over their heads. (We revisit the trial of detained defendants later.)

Judges who *care too much* are also unique to juvenile court. These are the *parens patriae judges* who mirror guardian defense attorneys. They are concerned primarily that juveniles receive the treatment they need (Sanborn 1994c, 2001a). They are most likely to be influenced by a youth's being in detention. The *parens patriae* judge would be most inclined to:

- not grant a motion to suppress (even when warranted) or perhaps deny some other defense request that could get in the way of an adjudication;

- bend rules of evidence (e.g., perhaps asking a mother during trial how the defendant is doing at home); and/or

- lower the threshold of proof beyond a reasonable doubt (i.e., to adjudicate close and not-so-close cases simply because the defendant appears to need rehabilitation).

The situation of judges who *do too much* occurs when no prosecutor appears in a case or when an inexperienced or incompetent prosecutor represents the state. The absence of a qualified prosecutor in juvenile court can result in the judge's assuming the role of prosecutor as well as judge. Doing so compromises the judge's obligation to remain neutral and removed from the contest. It also makes the judge an adversary to defense counsel. In this situation a defense objection to a judge's question of a witness, for example, has to be ruled on by the same person who asked the question in the first place. This would be like the football captain of the defensive unit having to ask the referee to find offensive holding or pass interference in a play in which the referee had thrown for a touchdown.

The other side of judges who do too much involves those who become managers. This situation can happen in adult court but should be a less severe problem there since cases are heard in public and are virtually automatically appealed. In juvenile court, where there is comparatively little scrutiny from the public or appellate courts, judges tend to have a freer hand to literally take over a case. In this regard, research has found judges who were reported to have forced cases to trial or a guilty plea when defense attorneys had asked for a continuance instead, and judges preempting or terminating defense and prosecution questioning and cross-examination of witnesses (Sanborn 1994c, 2001a).

Finally, judges who *know too little* and *care too little* parallel defense attorneys with these same attributes. Neither is unique to juvenile court—they are just more at home there because of its training ground and laissez-faire mentalities and its low visibility. Two aspects are different for judges, however. The first is that masters or referees who conduct some or all of the trials in several states (DE, MI, NV, NJ, OH, pre-1995 hires, OR) do not have to be attorneys. Serious competency issues could be involved with these individuals knowing too little law and procedure. The second is that some judges who generally know or care too little may have been assigned to juvenile court as punishment or as a kind of phase retirement.

The Private Versus Public Adjudicatory Hearing

We have already seen that the location of the court, the severity of the offense or record, and the possible disposition determine whether a regular prosecutor (or anyone in that role), a regular judge, and any defense attorney will be found at the adjudicatory hearing. These factors (and sometimes the age of the defendant) also determine whether the general public or the media will be permitted to attend trial in juvenile court. Opening the adjudicatory hearing to the public is a relatively recent development. It severely undermines traditional juvenile justice philosophy (and adds to the criminalization of juvenile court). Historically, juvenile court promoted the idea that the adjudication of youth had to remain a private matter so as not to publicly stigmatize the offender and threaten the rehabilitation effort. This notion played a significant part in the Supreme Court's attempt in *McKeiver* to explain that granting juveniles the right to jury trial would be against their interests.

Despite this rhetoric, 34 jurisdictions currently admit the public to the adjudicatory hearing in various circumstances.[17] Some of these states have restricted public access to situations involving older youth, chronic offenders, and those charged with serious offenses,[18] or in either special extended jurisdictions (IL) or serious juvenile offender prosecutions (OH). Most of 34 jurisdictions have elected, however, to permit public attendance for all felonies or for any criminal offense, even when the defendant is relatively young (14), or when there is no minimum age at all (see Appendix K). Several states have opened to the public the adjudicatory hearings of status offenders,[19] while California has granted these youths a right to a public trial.

Five states also specify that the media are permitted to attend adjudicatory hearings (NJ, NM, NY, WA, WI). Many more states may regularly admit the media to the trial without a statutory provision (since the public is already allowed to attend). Interestingly, the District of Columbia and Illinois allow the media to attend but not the general public. As Appendix K reveals, 19 states specifically give the judge the discretion to close the adjudicatory hearing when it serves the defendant's or the public's best interests or when sensitivity to the victim's plight would suggest such a move.

The decision to admit the public is in the hands of juvenile defendants in 19 states; 16 states grant the youth a right to jury trial in certain situations, and eight states extend juveniles a right to a public trial (AK does both) (see Appendix I). Despite the *McKeiver* ruling, 10 states extend the right to jury trial to the "regular" juvenile defendant.[20] Wisconsin recently eliminated this right for juveniles. Another six states (and MT) provide defendants the jury trial right only in certification cases (RI), extended juvenile jurisdiction proceedings (AR, IL, KS, MN, MT), habitual offender prosecutions (IL), or serious youthful offender disposition cases (OH) (see Chapter 12). Victims have also been guaranteed a right to attend the adjudicatory hearing (as well as other hearings) in juvenile court (see Chapter 8). To be sure, to the extent that real trials have occurred in juvenile court during the last three decades, the victim's presence (as well as that of other witnesses) would have been required to provide testimony to prove that the defendant had committed a crime.

Victims and offenders usually wait for hearings in the same area. Does this affect victims in your opinion?

As part of the recent victims' rights movement in juvenile court (see Chapter 8), legislation in 22 states goes beyond recognizing a mere testifying presence to authorizing observation of the entire trial, unless the victim has been sequestered.[21] Victims in New Jersey can even request an open proceeding. Moreover, several states have permitted the victim to bring along a representative or supportive person[22] or an attorney (CO, CT, FL).

Thus, the recent trend undeniably has been to convert the traditionally private adjudicatory hearing into a public forum like the criminal trial. Nevertheless, most trials in juvenile court still are not subject to general public scrutiny. In most cases judges continue to have the discretion to deny admission to the adjudicatory hearing to anyone except those who are employees of the court, parties to the case itself (witnesses, etc.), and researchers or students of the court process (Sanborn 1993b).

The Nature of the Adjudicatory Hearing

Assuming there is no last-minute informal resolution or withdrawal of prosecution, the case will be continued to another date or will proceed to trial. *Gault* and *Winship* guaranteed delinquent defendants five rights, including notice of charges and four other rights directly related to the trial: counsel, self-incrimination, confrontation and cross-examination, and proof beyond a reasonable doubt. Whereas all jurisdictions refer to the youth's right to counsel in delinquency cases in either a statute or court rule, only 33 jurisdictions mention self-incrimination, 33 identify confrontation and cross-examination, and 44 cite proof beyond a reasonable doubt (see Appendix I). Beyond these four rights and ones we have already mentioned (speedy, public jury trial), 24 jurisdictions guarantee juvenile defendants the right to present evidence, which should also enable them to call witnesses and to use the court's subpoena power to force witnesses, if necessary, to appear at trial (another two states cite a right to call witnesses). Numerous jurisdictions identify the defendant's right to be present (15) and to be heard (18). Finally, most jurisdictions (44) require the court to record the proceedings.

Of course, the failure of a jurisdiction to mention any of the *Gault-Winship* rights in their laws cannot serve to deprive a delinquent defendant of these rights. Moreover, it is difficult to imagine any jurisdiction today denying a youth any of the basic rights, such as compulsory process, presenting evidence, or a transcript, among others.

The rights picture at the adjudicatory hearing for status offenders differs somewhat from that for delinquents (see Appendix I). Although most jurisdictions extend most of the *Gault* provisions to status offenders (we already discussed counsel), Iowa holds that these offenders can be denied confrontation of witnesses, while Alabama grants the right of confrontation provided the judge thinks it is in the child's best interests. More important, while many states are silent about status offenders' right not to incriminate themselves (e.g., IL), several states have actually denied this right to such defendants.[23] Status offenders have been even less likely to be granted the standard of proof for adjudication established in *Winship,* although 22 states have adopted proof beyond a reasonable doubt for status offenders as well as delinquents (see Appendix I).

Most jurisdictions (29) have selected a less demanding level of evidence to adjudicate some or all of their status offenders. Most of these jurisdictions have chosen a *preponderance of evidence* as the burden of proof.[24] The remaining states allow their status offenders to be adjudicated on *clear and convincing* proof.[25] Although numerous jurisdictions allow status offenders to be present and to be heard, a few states allow the judge to exclude such defendants from the adjudicatory hearing (NM, SC, TN, VT). Finally, six states grant status offenders a right to trial by jury.

The basic operation of the adjudicatory hearing should parallel procedure in adult court. That is, the prosecution must present its case first in order to prove the defendant committed a delinquent act or status offense with sufficient intent or mens rea. Witnesses should testify (under oath), and physical evidence may be introduced, the admissibility of which is subject to objections by the defense. The defense is given an opportunity to cross-

The adjudicatory hearing parallels the criminal trial. What obstacles are there to receiving a fair trial in juvenile court?

examine any witnesses. Following the state's case, the defense must decide what, if anything, it will present in answer to the state's claims. The defendant may elect or refuse to take the stand. Either side may end up rebutting what the other side has presented. Both sides may be allowed to offer a brief closing argument. Ultimately the judge (and, on rare occasions, a jury) will render a verdict.

Also paralleling criminal trials is the tendency for juvenile trials to be divided into tiers or levels. In adult court, most states divide criminal trials between courts of limited jurisdiction (often called municipal courts) and general jurisdiction. The latter is the major felony court, where jury trials for serious offenses occur. Many states similarly have divided juvenile courts, although they are not as physically and geographically separate as in the adult system. Instead, adjudicatory hearings are *tiered* within the one juvenile court structure. Moreover, there can be two or three tiers (*not* counting status offense prosecutions) in juvenile court, determined by the offense, record, and potential disposition. An example is the situation we examined in Chapter 12, in which eight states have created a second tier for their juvenile courts to which they transfer some of their worst offenders for trial. These tiers determine a number of things, such as:

- whether a judge or a master will preside;
- whether a "real" criminal prosecutor (or anyone) will appear;
- whether the courtroom will be open or closed;
- whether juvenile or criminal court rules or procedure apply;
- whether certain rights will be provided (such as counsel or jury trial); and
- whether the disposition can involve institutionalization.

For example, New Jersey has informal and formal calendars (which appear to be similar to Michigan's consent and formal calendars). In the former, there is no prosecutor and the defendant is not provided counsel, but incarceration is prohibited if the youth is adjudicated. In New Mexico, prosecutions of delinquents and status offenders are guided by special juvenile court rules of procedure, while rules of criminal procedure apply to youthful offenders. All the states that grant the right to jury and public trial and that link an open adjudicatory hearing with age, offense, or record can be said to have at least two tiers. Colorado and Minnesota have established three tiers. In Colorado, those charged with misdemeanors, petty offenses, and violations of ordinances or court orders are not entitled to jury trial, whereas violent offenders are given a jury of only six members and aggravated juvenile offenders can demand a jury of 12. In Minnesota, while those charged with juvenile petty offenses are not provided counsel, regular delinquency charges are associated with all rights except jury trial, and defendants subject to the state's extended jurisdiction are entitled to jury trial.

The Adjudicatory Hearing for Detained Youth

Juvenile defendants who are detained until the time of and during trial are disadvantaged much like their adult counterparts, but probably even more so. We already discussed how the pretrial structure of juvenile court can lead to less opportunity for detained defendants to plea bargain (see Chapter 11) and how these defendants enter the courtroom with a serious stigma (earlier in this chapter). Making matters worse are two other factors: (1) expedited trials for these defendants can lead to a sloppy defense, and (2) these defendants cannot aid their defense.

In their zeal to limit the length of pretrial custody, some juvenile courts have a very short time frame from detention to trial (see Chapter 10). The good news is the limited custody period; the bad news is that defense counsel may not have adequate time to prepare a case but could nevertheless be forced to proceed because of the client's detention status. Research has found defense attorneys who admit they do not provide the same quality of defense to detained defendants as they do to released defendants (Sanborn 1992a). To the extent that juvenile crime is particularly group-oriented (see Chapter 6), detention can also compromise the defendant's ability to establish an alibi or to corroborate a defense. Some youths merely present at a crime scene (and not actually involved in any crime) are likely to run away with the others if and when police arrive. If arrested and detained, then juveniles are disadvantaged if they do not know the names and addresses of witnesses, or if the defense counsel is not motivated or lacks the time to track down the witnesses. Released defendants have a better opportunity to locate (and, of course, to fabricate a defense via) potential witnesses.

What this all can mean—fewer plea bargains or less favorable plea bargains (e.g., the prosecutor won't reduce charges as much for a detained defendant), stigmatized presence at trial, compromised defense—is precisely what the data show. Holding everything else equal (race, offense, record, age), detained defendants should be adjudicated more often and of higher charges compared to those released before trial. Detention results in similar disadvantages at disposition as well, which we will see in the next chapter.

Some Unique Aspects of the Adjudicatory Hearing

While the framework of the adjudicatory hearing is similar to that of a criminal trial, the meat and substance can be very different. In juvenile courts any of the following can happen:

- Rules of evidence specifically are not the same as in adult court (KS, MO).
- Rules of procedure are not at all or not completely the same as in adult court.[26]
- The proof of some crimes (such as a corroboration requirement) or elements of crimes (such as mens rea) require less in juvenile court than in adult court (AL, CA, GA).

- Not all the defenses available to adult defendants (such as insanity) are available in juvenile court (DC, OH).

Even if these items are supposed to be the same, judges can interpret and enforce them differently in juvenile court. Status offense prosecutions are even more likely to operate under civil rules of evidence or procedure.[27]

Moreover, it is likely for the entire atmosphere of the adjudicatory hearing to differ significantly from that of the criminal trial, if for no other reason than the often-present benevolent intentions of the juvenile system (and the fact that there is a lot less at stake). In fact, a number of states still direct their adjudicatory hearings to be conducted informally, unless a jury trial is involved.[28] The general informality provides parents who are so inclined unique opportunities to actively or passively help convict defendants. Besides derailing diversionary efforts (see Chapters 7 and 9) and favorable plea bargains (see Chapter 11), parents can actively work to convict their children by simply criticizing them at trial (perhaps at the invitation of the judge). The parents' comments may or may not be true, but will likely be treated as such. Parents can passively accomplish the same result by their behavior during trial, such as using body language, which can speak volumes to the judge about problems the defendant must have at home (and maybe about the real source of the child's problem).

Informality also allows the trial to be continued from time to time,[29] for the defendant's presence to be dispensed with,[30] or for petitions to be amended after trial has begun. In adult court prosecutors must be careful in charging defendants because serious discrepancies between the charges and what is actually proved at trial can be fatal to the state's case. Things tend to be much looser in juvenile court, however, although a handful of states seem to have adopted the criminal court rule.[31] Many jurisdictions simply allow the judge to amend the petition or charges to conform to (or to agree with) the evidence, and when doing so amounts to a "substantial" departure from the original charge(s), the trial is continued to let the defense adjust.[32] Some states go so far as to allow the petition to be "freely amended as the interests of justice or the youth requires" (AK, MI, NM, WI). Thus, Wisconsin holds that petitions will not be dismissed or adjudications reversed if there is an error or mistake in the petition, as long as it appears that the defendant committed some delinquent act and the court has amended the petition to cure any defects.

It is unclear whether some rights that are constitutionally or statutorily guaranteed to adult defendants must be given to juveniles as well. For example, an adult defendant's constitutional right to counsel includes the latter's being able to deliver a closing argument in a nonjury trial (*Herring v. New York* 1975). Although a number of states have extended this right to juvenile defendants,[33] the matter has been ignored for the most part. The same applies to other rights available in adult court rarely recognized in juvenile court, including the rights to (1) move for dismissal or acquittal (CA, FL, GA, HI), (2) move to vacate adjudication or conviction,[34] or (3) move for a new trial.[35] Of course, states that observe rules of criminal procedure could be granting juvenile defendants these and other rights without requiring a provision in the juvenile code to do so. Moreover, the ready availability of dismissal of cases at the disposition hearing (Chapter 14), of modifying or even terminating the disposition within a short period (and perhaps setting aside the adjudication as well) (see Chapter 15), and of sealing and expunging juvenile court records (see Chapter 15) compensate to some extent for the lack of formal challenge to an adjudication following trial in juvenile court.

In the end, the adjudication process for juvenile defendants can be markedly different from that provided to adult defendants. Juvenile courts have neither shed traditional *parens patriae* ideas and characteristics nor adopted stringent rules and regulations for adjudicating delinquents or status offenders. Although it is certainly possible (and in some places very likely) to receive a fair trial in juvenile court, this typically occurs *despite* the adjudicatory structure (Sanborn 1994b). In short, many juvenile courts have retained a good deal of the original clinic mentality and procedure, which means there is a considerable momentum to adjudicate or convict. Most juvenile courts provide prosecutors at least a few of the following elements that they could only dream about in criminal court:

- No jury to bring skepticism to the fact-finding process
- No public to provide scrutiny of the court actors (especially the judge)
- Guardian defense attorneys and *parens patriae* judges
- Judges well informed about current offense and prior record
- Less demanding law, rules, and procedures
- Detained defendants who enter trial with serious stigma and disadvantages
- Parents assisting in having their children adjudicated
- Fewer defense maneuvers available to short-circuit the process
- Petitions that can be amended and hearings that can be continued
- Adverse initial verdicts by masters that can be revised by judges
- Relatively few appeals launched by defense attorneys (see Chapter 15)

The last item means that the adjudicatory hearing is usually immune from public scrutiny, not only while it is happening, but also permanently after it is finished.

Finally, one unique traditional aspect of the adjudicatory hearing is advantageous to juvenile defendants in promoting their legal interests. Unlike criminal court judges, who can dismiss charges only because of a lack of evidence or prosecution or some other gross unfairness, juvenile court judges in many jurisdictions can dismiss petitions and throw out cases simply if that decision promotes the interests and welfare of the defendant.[36]

The Numbers at Adjudication

Delinquent Youth

After several years (1994–1997) of a consistent rate of adjudication, in 1998 a significant rise occurred in the percentage of delinquency cases ending in adjudication in juvenile court (see Table 13.1). Juvenile courts have regularly found approximately 60 percent of their defendants guilty in recent times (Butts 1996; Stahl 1998, 1999, 2000, 2001, 2003).

Because of the increase in the number of cases processed and prosecuted, a 28 percent increase occurred in the number of delinquency cases (from 496,016 to 634,920) that resulted in adjudication between 1994 and 1999.

Adjudication rates among the four offense categories have been pretty consistent and equal between the years 1990 and 1999, as shown in Table 13.2. During this period, youths 15 and younger were more likely than those 16 and older to be adjudicated delinquent, usually by a difference of 1 to 4 percent. Also, the overall proportion of cases ending in adjudication increased for younger youth between 1990 and 1999 (from 61 percent to 68 percent), as well as for older youth (from 59 percent to 65 percent).

Table 13.1 Juvenile Cases Processed and Adjudicated, 1994–1999

Year	Total Number of Cases Processed at Intake	Total Number of Cases Prosecuted	Percentage of Cases Adjudicated
1994	1,555,200	855,200	58%
1995	1,700,000	855,200	56
1996	1,800,000	983,100	58
1997	1,755,100	996,000	58
1998	1,757,400	1,000,300	63
1999	1,673,000	962,000	66

Males were more likely than females to be adjudicated delinquent during this period, with the one exception being drug offenses in 1999, with the difference being 2–6 percent. Both males (61 to 67 percent) and females (57 to 64 percent) witnessed a significant increase in the percentage of adjudications between 1990 and 1999, especially for person (9 percent for boys) and drug offenses (12 percent for girls). Males had the greatest probability of being adjudicated for property crimes (68 percent), while for females it was drug offenses (68 percent).

Table 13.2 Adjudication Rates by Category, 1990–1999

Offense Category	1990	1995	1999
All delinquency	60%	58%	66%
Person	55	55	63
Property	62	59	68
Drugs	59	58	67
Public order	62	60	67

Source: Puzzanchera et al. (2003b).

Interestingly, blacks were less likely than whites and those from other races to be adjudicated in all four offense categories in 1999. Between 1990 and 1999, the likelihood of adjudication increased for whites (from 62 percent to 68 percent) and for blacks (from 57 percent to 63 percent) in all four offense categories, while it actually declined slightly (from 70 percent to 69 percent) for youth from other races. While whites (70 percent) and youth of other races (75 percent) were convicted most frequently in drug crimes, blacks were adjudicated most frequently in property and public order offenses (65 percent each) (Puzzanchera et al. 2003b).

Status Offenders

Unlike in delinquency cases, the adjudication rates for status offenses have tended to be decreasing rather than increasing. Between 1988 and 1997, the rates of adjudication for the five major groups of status offenses declined.

Obviously, running away is the status offense least likely to end in an adjudication, regardless of age, gender, and race. Youths 15 and younger were more likely to experience an adjudication than those 16 and older (55 percent versus 49 percent). In 1997, while younger juveniles were most likely to be adjudicated in truancy cases (61 percent), older youths were most likely to be adjudicated in ungovernability cases (55 percent). Between 1988 and 1997, the likelihood of adjudication was higher for the younger population for each of the five categories of offenses, while the likelihood of adjudication decreased for both age groups in all five offense categories (Puzzanchera et al. 2000).

Gender did not make a big difference in adjudication rates. Males (53 percent) were slightly more likely than females (51 percent) to be adjudicated in most offense areas in 1997. Except for liquor violations, in which males had a 7 percent greater chance of adjudication (56 percent versus 49 percent), the differences between the genders in the offenses categories ranged between only 1 and 4 percent. Between 1988 and 1997, the likelihood of adjudication declined in all offense categories for both genders.

Racial differences were also minimal (see Table 13.4). In 1997, whites (53 percent) were slightly more likely than blacks (51 percent) and youth from other races (50 percent) to be adjudicated for a status offense. All races experienced a decline in the adjudication rate between 1988 and 1997. In 1997, while whites (57 percent) and blacks (63 percent) were most likely to be adjudicated in truancy cases, youths from other races (64 percent) were most likely to be adjudicated in liquor violations. All three groups were least likely to be adjudicated in runaway cases (Puz-

Table 13.3 Percentage of Adjudicated Status Offenses, by Offense, 1988–1997

Offense Category	1988	1993	1997
All Offenses	66%	54%	52%
Runaway	58	47	38
Truancy	69	55	59
Ungovernable	69	56	57
Liquor	65	57	54
Miscellaneous	67	57	50

Source: Puzzanchera et al. (2000).

Table 13.4 Percentage of Adjudicated Status Offense Cases by Age, Gender, and Race, 1988–1997

Age/ Gender/Race	1988	1993	1997
15 or younger	68%	56%	55%
16 or older	63	51	49
Male	67	56	53
Female	64	53	51
White	65	55	53
Black	65	52	51
Other Races	74	56	50

Source: Puzzanchera et al. (2000).

zanchera et al. 2000). Most of these numbers and tendencies held true throughout the 1990s. The one interesting statistic is that youths of other races were at least 10 percent more likely than white and black youths to be adjudicated in both liquor violations and ungovernability cases (Puzzanchera et al. 2003b).

Summary: Key Ideas and Concepts

- Not a regular criminal prosecutor in all trials
- PO involved in informal resolution of case
- Unique aspects of prosecutor's analysis of a juvenile case
- Resolving pretrial matters at time of trial
- PO disposition plan prepared and available prior to trial
- Not all youth eligible for defense counsel, which also can be waived
- Mandatory counsel in some cases and jurisdictions
- Self-representation rarely guaranteed in juvenile court
- Variation in judge's requirements when youth waives counsel
- Guardian defense attorneys who care about the youth's treatment interests
- Defense attorneys who represent parents rather than the youth
- Juvenile court a good home for defense attorneys who are nonadvocates
- Juvenile court a good home for defense attorneys who are burnouts
- Juvenile court a good home for defense attorneys who know too little
- No constitutional right to a speedy trial in juvenile court
- Adverse consequences with pretrial delay in juvenile court
- Unique aspects of masters conducting trial in juvenile court
- Constitutional problems when masters conduct trial in juvenile court
- Various ways in which judges learn too much about juvenile defendants
- The special problems when a defendant is detained until trial
- Juvenile court judges who know too much about juvenile defendants
- Juvenile court judges who care too much about juvenile defendants
- Juvenile court judges who do too much in juvenile court
- Juvenile court judges who know too little and care too little in juvenile court
- Public adjudicatory hearing another example of criminalization

Discussion Questions

1. What is likely to occur when a regular criminal prosecutor does not appear at the adjudicatory hearing? Discuss the implications for the defendant.

2. What considerations will prosecutors make in preparing a case that are unique to juvenile court?

3. What are the implications in the presence of the PO's disposition plan prior to the trial?

4. What are the implications in pretrial matters not being resolved until the time of trial?

5. Discuss the situations in which the provision of counsel is mandatory for youth. Has enough been done here to ensure that juveniles are adequately represented?

6. Should youths be allowed to represent themselves in juvenile court? If not, why not? If yes, under what conditions?

7. Should juveniles be allowed to waive counsel? If not, why not? If yes, under what conditions?

8. Discuss the various types of defense attorneys likely to appear in juvenile court and the implications for the justice provided the juvenile defendant.

9. Should juveniles have a constitutional right to a speedy trial? If not, why not? If yes, what should be the standard?

10. Discuss the potentially adverse consequences of pretrial delay in juvenile court. What can be done to reduce this delay?

11. What constitutional problems arguably surface when masters conduct trial in juvenile court? Was the Supreme Court correct in its ruling in *Swisher v. Brady*? Is there a double jeopardy or a due process violation present when a judge can reverse a master's recommendation? If there is no constitutional problem in this procedure, why don't adult courts adopt such a practice?

12. Discuss the various types of judges likely to appear in juvenile court and the implications for the justice provided the juvenile defendant.

13. Should the adjudicatory hearing remain private or be opened to the public? If private, why? If open to the public, why and in what situations? What are the implications of such a move?

14. Is the adjudicatory hearing structured to convict? If no, explain how. If yes, explain how.

15. Identify the ways in which the adjudicatory hearing differs from the criminal trial. Is the juvenile defendant provided adequate justice? If yes, defend that position. If no, what needs to be provided juvenile defendants to ensure adequate justice, and what are the implications of the current situation?

Endnotes

1. Even if there is no command in the state law for the prosecutor to appear at the adjudicatory hearing, nothing should prevent the local prosecutor's office from deciding to litigate cases regularly in juvenile court.
2. North Carolina specifically says that self-representation is not an option in juvenile court.
3. The jurisdictions that mandate counsel's appearance "across the board" are: DC, IL, IA, KS, MS, NM, NC, TX, VT. Minnesota comes close to being added to this list. It does not mandate counsel for petty offenders who will not be committed, however, and also allows defendants to waive counsel if stand-by counsel is provided.
4. The states that insist on counsel when the youth is to be committed are: AL, AZ, AR, CT, MT, NH, NY, TN, WI.
5. The states that require counsel when there is no parent are: GA, HI, LA, MI, ND, OH, TN.
6. The jurisdictions that allow the judge to appoint a guardian *ad litem* are: AL, AZ, CO, FED, MT, NM, TN, UT.
7. The states that require the appointment of a guardian *ad litem* are: HI, MN, MS, NE, NM, ND, OH, TX, WY. Four of these states (MN, MS, NE, OH) also require this appointment when the parents are incompetent.
8. The states that require counsel when youths have a conflict of interests with their parents are: AR, CT, GA, IA, LA, MI, MO, ND, OH.
9. The jurisdictions that allow the judge to appoint a guardian *ad litem* are: AL, AZ, CO, FED, IL, MT, NM, RI, TN, TX.
10. The states that demand the appointment of a guardian *ad litem* are: HI, MN, MS, NE, ND, OH, VT, WY.
11. See, for example, *In re KMB*, 462 NE2d 1271 (Ill App 4 Dist 1984); *In Interest of RD*, 499 NE2d 478 (Ill app 1 Dist 1986).
12. A number of jurisdictions (AK, DE, DC, KY) have stated in statutes or case law that there is a right to a speedy trial in juvenile court but have not established deadlines.
13. The jurisdictions in which the scheduling of trial should be the same for delinquents and status offenders are: DC, ID, IN, KY, MO, ND, OH, OK, PA, RI.
14. California offers that the two parties can stipulate to the verdict power, but does not require it.
15. While consent is required in 12 states (AL, AK, CA, CO, GA, MD, MI, MN, MO, NM, PA, TX), it is not required in another 12 states (DE, IN, MS, NV, NJ, ND, OH, OK, OR, TN, UT, VA).
16. A change of judge is acknowledged in: AK, AZ, FL, GA, IN, IA, MN, MO, MT, NM, WI.
17. Inasmuch as theories of rehabilitation do not advocate public awareness of offenders, these new provisions probably reflect other desires, such as community awareness of crime, accountability of court workers, and possibly humiliation of offenders.
18. The states that have limited public access in this way are: AK, CA, GA, HI, LA, ME, MA, MN, MO, SD, UT, WI.
19. The states that allow the public to attend status offense hearings are: AZ, FL, ID, MI, NV, NC, TX.
20. The states that provide a right to jury trial are: AK, CO, MA, MI, MT, NM, OK, TX, WV, WY.
21. The states that provide for victims' attending the entire trial are: AK, AZ, CA, CO, CT, FL, KS, KY, LA, MI, MN, NH, NJ, OK, OR, PA, SD, TX, UT, VA, WI, WY.
22. The states that permit the victim to bring a representative are: AZ, CA, CT, GA, LA, MI, MN, NH, OK, PA, UT, VA, WI, WY.
23. The states that deny this right to status offenders are: GA, MD, MN, MO, OH, PA, TN, VT, VA.
24. The jurisdictions with this level of proof are: AK, AZ, AR, CA, CO, DC, FL, HI, IL, LA, MD, NE, NV, NJ, OR, VT, WA.
25. The states with this level of proof are: CT, IA, KS, MN, MO, NM, NC, PA, TN, VA, WV, WI.
26. The jurisdictions that have different rules of procedure to some extent are: AZ, CA, CT, DC, FL, ID, KS, MD, MO, NM, OR, PA, SD, TX, WA.
27. The states that follow civil rules for status offense cases are: AR, CA, CO, CT, FL, HI, IL, IA, KS, LA, MD, MN, SD, TX, VT, WA.
28. The states that allow for an informal trial are: AK, AZ, CT, DE, HI, IL, MD, MN, MO, NV, ND, OH, PA, TN, UT, WY. Interestingly, Kentucky and South Carolina demand that the adjudicatory hearing be formal.
29. The states that allow the trial to be continued this way are: FL, GA, MD, NY, NC, OH, OR, TN, UT.
30. The states that permit trial in the defendant's absence are: AZ, HI, ID, IL, IN, MO, SC.
31. The states that follow criminal court rules here are: DE, IL, LA, MN, NY, NC, OH.

32. The jurisdictions that allow serious amending of charges are: AZ, CT, DC, GA, ME, MD, OK, OR, RI, SD.
33. The right to deliver a closing argument exists in: CA, LA, MN, MS, MO, NY, UT.
34. Vacating an adjudication is officially recognized in: GA, LA, MI, MN, MO, MT.
35. Moving for a new trial is officially recognized in: CO, DC, FL, LA, MI, MN, MT, SD, UT, WI.
36. Dismissal of petitions is possible in this context in: CA, DC, GA, HI, ID, IL, LA, MI, MS, MO, NY, NC, OH, OK, OR, RI, SC, UT, WV. ✦

Chapter 14

The Disposition Hearing

Focus of Chapter 14

This chapter focuses on the disposition hearing, which is juvenile court's version of sentencing. In this critical stage in the juvenile court process, the youth's treatment needs are supposed to be addressed and a disposition or treatment plan implemented. In the pre-*Gault* era, the entire inquiry involved the disposition only. Juvenile courts jumped over adjudication (the PO had done all that work before the court hearing) and went right to disposition. Among other things, *Gault* insisted on what has been termed a bifurcation, or separation of the trial and sentencing stages. This chapter discusses both the disposition hearing and the possible sentences awaiting adjudicated delinquents and status offenders.

Key Terms

- bifurcation
- combined discretionary/mandatory minimum sentence
- commitment
- community service
- day treatment program
- deferred adjudication or disposition
- differentiated sentencing

- disposition ladder
- mandatory sentence
- minimum sentence
- predisposition report
- probation
- purely discretionary minimum sentence
- shock probation

The Timing of Disposition

A few states explicitly note in their statutes that disposition must be separate from adjudication (GA, MN, MS, TN, TX). Although separate, it is quite possible that the disposition hearing will immediately follow adjudication. This timing is unlike that in adult court, where, unless a sentence bargain has already identified the sentence, weeks usually fall between conviction and sentencing. Apart from Vermont, which expressly forbids immediate disposition in delinquency cases (but not in status offense cases), nearly half of the jurisdictions specifically note that disposition may immediately follow adjudication (see Appendix L). Often all parties must consent to the immediate hearing. Florida, moreover, insists that a presentence investigation must be completed for the disposition hearing to occur so quickly.

Both the philosophy and standard operation of juvenile court promote immediate disposition. First, the philosophy is that, unlike punishment that can be delayed for months (or years) without undermining its purpose (i.e., the offender understands that the punishment is a consequence of illegal but old behavior, while retribution is still satisfied later rather than sooner), *treatment delayed is treatment denied.* That is, the youth needs help now, not months from now. Operationally, barring some unusual problem, nearly every first adjudication is headed to probation in juvenile court (even more likely than the same tendency in criminal court). Probation can be imposed immediately. Even if adjustments need to be made later on, a delay is not needed. In addition, both first offenders with "unusual problems" and recidivists who are not as likely to be headed to probation usually have treatment plans already designed for them before they are adjudicated.

Beyond authorizing immediate dispositions, 32 jurisdictions have identified a timeline within which sentencing must occur (see Appendix L).[1] Speedy justice requirements in the adult system tend to expire once the defendant has been convicted. It would be rare, then, to see sentencing deadlines spelled out in criminal court. Although most of the jurisdictions that have established deadlines have earmarked them for delinquents, a number hold that the deadline applies equally to status offenders. Other states without deadlines have suggested that delinquents and status offenders should be handled equally in scheduling the disposition hearing.[2] Several states have given the sentencing of status offenders a quicker time frame than that provided delinquents.[3]

Like the adjudicatory hearing, the disposition hearing tends to have a shorter time allowance for juveniles in detention versus those who have been released. Although custody status is not likely to change following adjudication, it can't be ruled out that a youth who had been home before and during trial would be placed in detention upon adjudication. Detained and released youth may be temporarily committed to a hospital or other facility to conduct a litany of examinations, including medical, physical, and psychological tests and testing for drug and alcohol dependency. These examinations can also be conducted on an outpatient basis. If the youth is committed, the diagnosis is supposed to be finished quickly so that the commitment is truly temporary. Time limits are not typically specified in statutes, but most commitments should not exceed a range of one (NM, WV) to three months (UT).

As Appendix L demonstrates, with few exceptions, juvenile courts have not been put under serious pressure to reach the disposition decision quickly. Only 21 jurisdictions have established a deadline for youth in detention, and most of these allow a considerable or undefined extension. Violations of the deadline would, at most, require that the youth be released from detention while the disposition decision is completed. Interestingly, Georgia and New York have constructed separate guidelines specifically for their most serious juvenile offenses, called designated felony violations.

The Participants at Disposition

As with sentences in criminal court, dispositions in juvenile court are delivered by a judicial figure, usually the same judge or master who presided over the trial or accepted the guilty plea. Although statutes may state the preference for this outcome (AL, OH), it is possible for a judicial officer who had not adjudicated the defendant to hand down the disposition. Moreover, masters who preside at the adjudicatory and disposition stages technically only recommend adjudication *and* disposition, which must be reviewed and accepted (or adjusted or rejected) by a judge.

POs are also likely to be present at the disposition hearing. In fact, their presence might be mandatory (see next section). Like their counterparts in the adult system, JPOs prepare the all-important predisposition report (PDR) (called a *presentence investigation* in criminal court) on which the judge relies for information about the youth. (We examine this report later in this chapter.) The treatment orientation of juvenile dispositions arguably makes the JPO a more critical figure at sentencing than a PO at an adult sentencing. Whereas the latter has been relegated mostly to collecting record information on offenders, JPOs are expected to fashion a disposition sensitive not only to the youth's behavior, but also to the problems underlying that behavior. Consequently, it is common for the judge to give considerable deference to the PO's disposition recommendation compared to what normally occurs in criminal court.

The prosecutor might not appear at the disposition hearing, which is unusual in criminal court. Although *Gault* certainly marked the beginning of more regular representation of the state by prosecutors, their work is usually considered finished once an adjudication is secured. Whereas in adult court the prosecutor's view on adequate punishment is regarded as both relevant and necessary, in juvenile court this individual's perspective on the youth's treatment needs might not be equally valued or solicited. Some states have explicitly rejected this thinking and have mandated the prosecutor's appearance at disposition (CO, NY, NC, WA). Nevertheless, even in jurisdictions in which the statute reads that prosecutors shall represent the state in *all proceedings*, they may not be present at disposition (e.g., PA; see Sanborn 1996a). Many prosecutors may have no interest in attending the hearing, as the outcome may be relatively insignificant, the outcome may already be known, or prosecutors may have little impact at sentencing in their particular jurisdictions.

Whether a defense attorney will represent the youth at a disposition hearing depends on a number of factors. First, while adult offenders have been guaranteed that right (*Mempa v. Rhay* 1967), the U.S. Supreme Court has not yet extended juvenile offenders a constitutional right to counsel at sentencing. *Gault* was limited to the adjudicatory hearing. Youths who are not going to be incarcerated may not qualify for defense representation provided by the state, especially at this point when adjudication has already occurred. Moreover, defendants (or parents) who have retained counsel may not want to pay for yet another appearance and may dispense with these services (especially if the ultimate disposition has already been suggested or disclosed). Still, many statutes speak to a youth's right to counsel at *all stages* (see Chapter 13). When disposition immediately follows adjudication, there is a greater chance that defense attorneys (and prosecutors, for that matter) will be present.

One unique aspect of defense representation at disposition in juvenile court is the prospect of the attorney relinquishing the *advocate* role (in securing the sanction that least interferes with the child's life or liberty) and adopting instead the *guardian* stance (in pursuing the disposition "most appropriate" in light of the youth's needs and situation, regardless of the level of interference). Defense attorneys are more likely to act like guardians at disposition than at trial (see Chapter 13). Some will switch from advocate to guardian following adjudication. The reasoning here is that while defense attorneys may owe juvenile clients "their day in court," once advocacy has failed to prevent adjudication, the attorney's obligation becomes finding the "right" disposition rather than merely promoting the defendant's wishes per se. Nevertheless, many defense attorneys remain advocates throughout trial and sentencing in juvenile court. A number of factors can influence the defense attorney's decision in this situation:

- The attorney's legal orientation and view of juvenile court
- The court's track record in rehabilitation
- The nature and severity of the potential disposition
- The defendant's and parents' wishes

The victim is a newcomer to the disposition hearing. For decades, the victim was regarded as irrelevant to the outcome of juvenile court proceedings. At most, the court needed the victim's account of the youth's behavior in order to adjudicate the case. The victim was not consulted, however, as to what the court should do with the offender. Moreover, it was common for the victim to be completely unaware of what, if anything, happened to the juvenile. The likely thinking here was that victims could be obstructionists and would have nothing constructive to offer as to the proper disposition arranged by the court. They could also be quite upset if they learned how lenient juvenile courts could be with young offenders. Times have changed. Prosecutors are being instructed to obtain the victim's views on disposition (AZ, LA, MI, MN, MT, NH, WY), and POs are being told either to disclose the PDR to the victim (AZ) or to inform the victim of possible dispositions (MN). More important, 24 states provide for either a victim impact statement (VIS) or a description of the victim's view of appropriate disposition to be introduced at the hearing.[4] Four of these states (CA, CO, TX, VT) demand that the judge take the victim's view into consideration when determining the disposition. Altogether, 20 states allow the victim to attend the disposition hearing.[5] Between these initiatives are 30 states that have dramatically revised disposition so as to include the victim. Of course, unlike in the adult system, the remaining 22 jurisdictions have yet to officially identify the victim as a participant at disposition in juvenile court.

Another newcomer to the disposition hearing is the public. Much like the adjudicatory hearing, the disposition stage is becoming more open to public scrutiny. Jurisdictions that have opened the trial tend to have opened disposition as well (see Chapter 13). Kansas and Montana specifically provide for the public to have access to the sentencing stage in juvenile court, while Washington talks of the arresting officer's right to attend the proceeding. Juries only rarely sentence adult felons, apart from capital cases. In juvenile court, jury sentencing is even rarer, with only Texas calling for it and only when lengthy determinate sentences are involved.

Finally, the defendant and parent are usually required to attend the disposition hearing, although a couple of states permit the youth to be excused from the proceeding (MI, MO). Statutes have increasingly demanded parental inclusion and attendance at all critical hearings. This inclusion is particularly relevant at disposition, since the parent is nearly as likely as the juvenile offender to be sentenced by the juvenile court (see later sections).

The Youth's Rights at Disposition

A sentence bargain or routine probation sentence can make the disposition hearing a mere formality. Otherwise, the severity of the proposed disposition affects the contentiousness, adversariness, and length of the disposition hearing. Unless the defendant, parent, and defense attorney actually welcome the particular disposition, a sentence involving institutionalization should involve greater resistance than probation sentences. The status of the youth's constitutional rights is mostly uncharted territory here, since no U.S. Supreme Court cases have addressed this stage of the juvenile court process. Moreover, constitutional rights are associated mostly with trial rather than sentencing, apart from the severity of the sentence itself. Similarly, adult offenders have not been provided an abundance of constitutional safeguards at this stage.

State statutes have provided some minimal protections. Most common is the defendant's and defense attorney's right to examine the PDR, which only 9 jurisdictions fail to identify in their statutes or court rules.[6] This omission most likely has resulted from oversight rather than an intention to withhold the PDR from the defense attorney. It is difficult to believe that any jurisdiction would deny the attorney access to the report or would have any reason not to disclose the report. Statutes frequently mention the court's authority to withhold the source of or nature of sensitive information about the child, but this pertains only to limited information not revealed to the child, not to the defense attorney. Any disposition delivered by juvenile court in which counsel was prevented from examining the PDR—especially if incarceration was involved—would be subject to appeal and reversal. Also vulnerable to appeal is the disposition of any youth sentenced to an institution after the right to counsel was denied. This situation should also be relatively rare. Appeal would also seem to apply if defense counsel were not allowed either to present evidence or be heard on the question of disposition or to challenge the PDR. Nevertheless, only 19 jurisdictions mention presenting evidence

Disposition hearings usually take place in the same location as trials, often immediately following adjudication. Do juveniles have adequate rights at sentencing?

by defense,[7] while only 14 jurisdictions officially provide for defense challenge of the PDR.[8] Much less clear with both of these rights is whether presenting evidence must include the ability to call witnesses, which only Minnesota and Utah specifically cite, or whether challenging the PDR must include the ability to cross-examine the author(s) of the report, which is only a discretionary right in the District of Columbia and Utah (meaning the court can deny it) and an identified right in only 17 states.[9] Where exercised, this right would mandate the presence of the PO at the disposition hearing and perhaps even other individuals who provided information to the PO.

The rights of status offenders at the disposition hearing are even less frequently mentioned in the statutes. Like their delinquent counterparts, status offenders have been allowed to see the PDR (IL, NH, TN, WY), to challenge its contents (AL, AR, IL, KY, TN, WY) and cross-examine its author (AL, TN, WY), to present evidence (ID, KS, LA, MN, MS, WI), and to make a disposition recommendation.

The Predisposition Report

The PDR compiled by the PO will largely determine the ultimate disposition the youth receives. It is difficult to overstate the importance of the PDR and of the PO who authors it. Research into the perspectives of these POs has found interesting differences among these officials when they examine black versus white delinquents. In short, some POs are prone to stereotype offenders by race and to attribute more serious problems to and recommend more serious dispositions for black youth. The difference in recommended outcomes apparently stems from the perception of POs that blacks commit crimes because they lack individual responsibility, while whites commit crimes because of impoverished conditions (Bridges and Steen 1998).

The PDR goes by various names, with some states using adult court terms such as *PSI* or *presentence investigation* (CO, DE) or *PSR* or *presentence report* (MI).[10] Although some states do not mention this report at all in their statutes (MS, NE, OR), and others barely refer to it (AZ, SD, TX, WA), it is usually a prominent aspect of juvenile justice legislation.

The country divides as to whether the report is mandatory for all cases,[11] or only for serious crimes or sentences of incarceration (IL, NJ, NY, TN) versus its being discretionary.[12] Because of its potential prejudicial impact at trial (see Chapter 13), a number of states specify that the PDR should not be done until adjudication occurs[13] or that no other court officer is supposed to consult the report until after adjudication.[14] The PDR can be mandatory (AK, FL, NV, NH, NM, WI, WY) or discretionary (AR, IL, LA, MN, WA) in status offense cases also.

Use of Teams for the PDR

One modern development in the preparation of the report is the use of *teams* rather than a single PO (IN, NJ, VT). The team—variously referred to as a *multidisciplinary team* (FL, WV, WY), a *juvenile treatment screening team* (MN), an *evaluation team* (MO), or a *youth placement committee* (MT)—can assemble a variety of people, including the PO; police officer; medical, mental, and psychiatric staff; family members; school representative; guardian *ad litem*; family and social services person; prosecutor; public defender;

and offender. Wyoming's team has two levels of membership. While the team must include the parent, the PO, someone from school, someone from the psychological unit, and the prosecutor, the team *may also* include a substance abuse person, the guardian *ad litem*, and other relevant persons.

In many states,[15] the PO and the team examine a multitude of factors (detailed in the next section) officially and formally gathered by way of a risk or needs assessment. The risk assessment is an instrument used in the PDR process that simply lists myriad factors that can pertain to a youth's problems and dangerousness. By using the assessment, the PO is forced both to remain aware of these various factors (i.e., so the PDR does not omit any supposedly crucial variable) and to give them a score that will be used in determining the severity of the youth's problems and dangerousness, and, of course, the corresponding disposition in light of the final score.

Factors in the PDR

The PDR can contain an incredible amount of information for the judge to consider at disposition. Of course, the judge can receive an abundance of information presented orally or in other written documents as well. In short, there is little in the way of limits on what the judge can consider at the disposition hearing. Most statutes continue to instruct the judge to accept *all relevant and material evidence* (see Appendix M), which pretty much parallels the situation in criminal court sentencing. A good deal of the information will concern the *offense* that brought the youth to the court's attention.

Offense-related factors. Some offenses, especially sex offenses, tend to take on a special character and response from the system. More is involved with the offense variable than merely its severity (e.g., felony or misdemeanor). The broader context the court will consider includes where the crime occurred (the child's neighborhood versus school, downtown, etc.), with whom the crime was committed (alone or with delinquent peers), when the crime took place (during school or curfew hours), who was victimized by the offense (especially if the victim was very young, very old, a stranger, a teacher, a parent, or a police officer) and the impact of the crime on the victim, and the level of the youth's participation and sophistication in the criminal act (Sanborn 1996a). Moreover, the severity of the offense may be less important for youth in juvenile court for the first time than for those with prior records of offending (Fader et al. 2001).

Similarly, the *delinquent record* will be detailed (see Appendix M). This record includes more than a simple counting of previous misdemeanors and felonies. It also indicates the age at which the delinquent behavior began, the interval between offenses, and whether there had been an escalation in or tempering of the severity of crimes in the youth's history (Sanborn 1996a). Youth who have been rearrested (between the initial arrest and trial) or who have escaped from detention can be regarded as having a particularly serious record and could be more likely to receive a placement sentence because of that behavior (Fader et al. 2001).

Historically, juvenile courts were directed to regard the offense more as a symptom of the child's problem than as a gauge for the severity or harshness of the court's response to delinquent behavior. Ideally, relatively little emphasis was placed on such items as the youth's offense and delinquent record, although research has found these items to have an effect on sentencing (Frazier et al. 1992; Kempf et al. 1992). Statutes today are more likely to direct the PO's and the court's attention to these and related matters, however. Still, only 22 states specifically cite the seriousness or nature of the offense (or the use of force, violence, or a firearm), while only 24 jurisdictions mention the delinquent record as a factor for disposition (see Appendix M). Similarly, the youth's *culpability*, measured in terms of leadership and purposefulness or sophistication in committing the crime, is also gaining the attention of statutes. Eleven states currently place this variable officially in their disposition criteria (see Appendix M). Finally, the *victim's* personal attendance at the disposition hearing and view of the appropriate disposition for the youth, a VIS, and/or the PO's description of damage done to the victim's person or property have made the victim an important factor in juvenile court sentencing. Thirty-three states allow for one or more of these measures by which the judge can be made dramatically aware of the seriousness of the youth's crime (see Appendix M). Five states have gone so far as to make the age and physical condition of the victim a critical and aggravating factor in juvenile court dispositions (GA, NJ, NY, OH, WA).

Juvenile courts in many more jurisdictions than the ones identified in Appendix M consider offense-related factors even though they are not officially included within statutes or court rules. In some states these factors are mandatory (AK, CT, NJ, OR, WA, WI) and must be considered by the judge at disposition. Other states identify the offense factors as discretionary (MS, NM). In Oregon, offense-oriented factors are mandatory, while other variables (school, job record) are discretionary. Some states link factors specifically with certain types of institutionalization, such as secure placements or boot camps (GA, LA, ME, MI, NJ, NY).

Extralegal factors. It is possible for criminal court sentencing to be restricted almost entirely to offense and record. Although the adult PSI contains information much like that compiled in the PDR, the sentence in criminal court is supposed to be influenced mostly by just offense and record. In fact, sentencing guidelines used by many states today are limited to those two factors exclusively. Sentencing in juvenile court involves much more than just the offense and prior record, however.

Nearly all jurisdictions authorize *examinations* to be conducted on juvenile defendants before trial or prior to disposition. These examinations include analyses of the youth's medical and physical condition, psychological and psychiatric status, emotional problems or learning disabilities, and substance abuse difficulties. Results of these examinations can influence what the judge believes must be done for the youth to resolve his or her problems. For example, a drug abuse problem could encourage, if not force, a judge to commit some first-time offenders who otherwise probably would have been put on probation (Fader et al. 2001). In addition, the presence of mental illness can disqualify the youth from some commitments (and perhaps from adjudication as well) and require placement instead in a mental health facility. Research has found mental illness to be related to commitment dispositions for youth (Fader et al. 2001; Kempf et al. 1992; Tomkins 1990). Similarly, the presence of some disorders (such as fire starting) may require a particular placement in a facility with an appropriate treatment program addressing that disorder. Thus, a case otherwise headed to probation may end in institutionalization as a result of the problems disclosed via these examinations, especially if the family is unable or unwilling to resolve the matter on its own (Sanborn 1996a). Many other extralegal variables can also be important. For example, for juveniles of school age, their *school record* of attendance, performance, and discipline can affect the outcome of disposition (Scarpitti and Stephenson 1971). School record can also entail an evaluation of the child's mental condition and capabilities (e.g., is there any reason to try to force better performance on the child?). Although only 18 states mention an educational history, needs, and plan, school record no doubt plays some role in the sentencing of juveniles younger than 16 (and perhaps even for those above the age of compulsory education laws) in all jurisdictions (see Appendix M).

Perhaps the most volatile extralegal variable is the youth's *family* (Horowitz and Wasserman 1980a, 1980b; Tomkins 1990). Thirty-seven jurisdictions instruct juvenile courts to consider the family situation or history, or the youth's social environment or condition (including the neighborhood in which the child lives) (see Appendix M). The family may be more important as a factor for youths in juvenile court for the first time than for offenders with previous records (Fader et al. 2001). Whether the family is dysfunctional (i.e., unable or unwilling to work with the court) is likely to be more important than the number of parents present in the household (Sanborn 1996a). Quite frankly, it might be impossible for any juvenile court to ignore the family status when constructing a treatment plan. For example, Colorado has a special family preservation program as a condition of probation and as an alternative to placement. The absence of a family to preserve, then, could be interpreted as meaning there is no alternative to placement.

The information the juvenile court desires regarding parents (and perhaps even siblings) can be extensive. For example, Louisiana wants details on the family's composition and dynamics; stability; economic status; participation in community and religious activity; physical, emotional, and mental handicaps; and substance abuse or criminal history. Many states provide for parents to be subjected to many of the same examinations given to adjudicated juveniles.[16]

Passively or actively, the *parents* can dramatically and adversely affect the juvenile's disposition. Passively, parents may have serious problems of their own, whether physical, mental, medical, emotional, or financial, and thus be unable to produce or even to cooperate in a solution to their child's difficulties. Parental substance abuse may make probation seem implausible. Similarly, families with a history of violence can encourage judges to seek a placement for an offender who otherwise could have returned home on probation (Fader et al. 2001). Actively, parents ensure harsher dispositions for their children in a variety of ways. Some parents want their children put away by the juvenile system and actively campaign for that outcome. Adamantly refusing to cooperate with the PO or declaring to the judge in open court that the child is beyond control might secure the youth's incarceration. Refusing to take the child home can also produce this result. Parents also can "cop an attitude" at the bar of the court, showing defiance or disdain for everything, including the system. This attitude can signal to the judge that the parent is the real source of the youth's problem and suggest that a probation disposition would be futile or even counterproductive. Five states specifically tell the judge to consider the parents' attitude in formulating the disposition (AK, KY, NM, RI, SC).

Parents preoccupied with their own pursuits can also bring about the institutionalization of their children. For example, a youth in Ohio who had committed two rapes received a PO recommendation of probation with out-patient treatment but ended up being incarcerated instead. The reason the judge refused the PO recommendation was that both working parents had done absolutely nothing to arrange for their child's transportation to treatment sessions. Consequently, the judge committed the youth to a facility with a sex offender program.[17]

At the other end of the spectrum, parents who succeed in having their children dress well, appear cooperative, and show remorse to the court and the victim; parents who agree to assist the PO with a particular sentence; parents who arrange for satisfactory living conditions (even if that requires securing the help of relatives); or parents who enroll their children in programs or counseling sessions (especially if the youth has an emotional disorder or substance abuse problem) can succeed in minimizing the court's intervention into their children's lives. The last example of assistance might require that parents have and be willing to spend a good amount of money to purchase the counseling for their children. Interestingly, Illinois, Louisiana, and New Jersey list the parents' financial resources as a disposition factor. The level of the parental resistance or assistance to juvenile court and its impact on the youth's disposition can vary considerably by the location of the court (i.e., urban, suburban, or rural) (Sanborn 1996a).

The youth's treatment history is another factor commonly cited as a consideration for the current disposition decision (see Appendix M) (Frazier et al. 1992; Tomkins 1990). Simply put, there can be a vast difference in appropriate treatment responses geared toward offenders in court for the first time versus those who have been put on probation numerous times versus those with previous commitments in their past. Moreover, even those with the same track records of previous dispositions are not always on an equal footing. The quality of the juvenile's performance and response to previous rehabilitative efforts, together with time intervals between dispositions and any escape history, is also critical (Sanborn 1996a).

A number of statutes mention that a youth's *character, habits, and tendencies,*[18] which indicate a potential for successful rehabilitation (or willingness to change behavior), and *attitude about the crime* or a *sense of remorse* (AK, CT, LA, ME, NJ, NM) should be taken into account in the disposition decision (Sanborn 1996a; Tomkins 1990). Similarly, the child's *treatment needs* and *age*[19] have attracted the attention of some legislatures. Once again, these factors probably don't need to be cited officially to affect the disposition. The youth's not needing treatment could result in a dismissal of the case or at least in a moderate sentence. Age can have a complex effect on the sentence. The very young (i.e., 10 to 12 years old) or very old (i.e., 17 or 18 years old) delinquent could be statutorily or practically prevented from being placed (i.e., resources would not be wasted on older youth); thus, age can influence dispositions in opposite directions (Sanborn 1996a). For example, since commitments tend to be prohibitively expensive and relatively limited in number, they might not be "wasted" on an older offender adjudicated for a trivial offense, even if this youth has a serious delinquent and treatment history (Sanborn 1996a). The age variable is further complicated by admission policies of various institutions. That is, in many states institutions of the same caliber nevertheless have different admission ages that could discourage or prevent commitment in a particular case.

Finally, statutes identify a number of *miscellaneous factors* related primarily to the offender or the offense that could play a role in determining the disposition of a particular defendant. These include the following:

- Peer relationships (CO, MO)

- Member of criminal street gang (FL, IL, NJ, WA)

- Aggravating factors in offense (CT, LA, MN, NJ, WA)
- Mitigating factors in offense (CT, LA, ME, NJ, WA)
- Unadjudicated acts (CA, NC, WA, WI)
- Likely or not to reoffend (LA, ME, MA, NJ, NC)
- Accountability or deterrent effect (AK, LA, ME, NJ, NC)
- Need to protect public (AK, FL, GA, LA, ME, MN, NY, NC)
- Victim precipitation of offense (LA, ME, NJ, WA)
- Job history (CO, OR, TN)
- Defendant paid restitution (NJ, OR, WA)
- Defendant, prosecutor, victim recommendation (NM, OR)
- Ability of state to help defendant (AK, NM)

Welfare of the child and family. Juvenile court's historical commitment to the welfare of the child and the family adds another category of factors to the dispositional process. This category involves three interrelated demands of the juvenile court judge (and the PO) in fashioning the appropriate disposition. First, the disposition is supposed to represent what court officials believe to be the *best interests of the child*. Recently, the public's interests have been added to this formula in most jurisdictions. At least 34 states continue to insist that this traditional tenet of juvenile justice be observed at disposition (see Appendix M). This command can mean directly opposite results for defendants with similar crimes and records.

Second, the juvenile courts in 31 jurisdictions are obliged to implement the least restrictive alternative (LRA) (also called least restrictive placement, setting, or disposition). Alaska defines this measure as "that disposition that is no more restrictive than is, in the judgment of the court, most conducive to the minor's rehabilitation taking into consideration the interests of the public" (AK Statute 47.12.140). This translates into a duty for the juvenile court judge not only to invoke the minimum amount of interference into or control of the youth's liberty that is consistent with protection of the public and the rehabilitation needs of the child, but also to show why less restrictive measures are either unavailable or inappropriate. In Alaska the PO must prove by a preponderance of evidence that the recommended disposition is the least restrictive alternative, while in Minnesota the judge must disclose what other dispositions were considered and why they were determined to be inappropriate.

An even greater number of jurisdictions order the court to pursue the least restrictive alternative when status offenders are involved (see Appendix M). In fact, while Alaskan juvenile courts have been instructed to keep the health and safety of the status offenders as a paramount concern, juvenile judges in Massachusetts have been told to take into account the physical and emotional welfare of the youth.

Finally, 46 jurisdictions instruct their juvenile courts to *preserve the child's ties to the family*—to prefer working with the youth at home—and impose a *special duty* on judges whenever dispositions propose to remove youth from their homes. The commitment must further the best interests of the child, meaning that allowing juveniles to return home would have to be contrary to their best interests.[20] Many states go beyond this threshold and demand that before the court can remove the child from the home, the court must have made *reasonable efforts to prevent placement* or to eliminate the need to remove.[21] Even more demanding are requirements that the judge delineate what was done to prevent removal or what could have been done to prevent this disposition,[22] and that commitment occurs only after the judge considers alternatives to out-of-home placements and explains why commitment is necessary.[23] Similarly, several states require status offenders to be referred to crisis intervention before they can be committed.[24]

The court's special duty also affects the choice of placement in a handful of states that oblige the judge to select an institution that is most family-like, closest to the parents' home, least interfering with family autonomy, and least disruptive of family life (IN, MI, OK). The court's special duty continues well into the placement period in 23 states that require the court to make all reasonable efforts to *return the youth home* as soon as practicable or possible.[25] Many jurisdictions with the special measures back them up by requiring the judge to write findings of fact as to why the disposition selected is appropriate and how it satisfies the special directives.[26]

Only two jurisdictions (FED, HI) fail to mention at least one of these three special disposition provisions. The special provisions have a couple of important implications for sentencing in juvenile court. First, barring some unusual circumstances and unless the offense carries a mandatory sentence (see later sections), the vast majority of first-time offenders in juvenile court should be headed for probation or a community-based program. Even defendants with prior records may not be committed in light of the court's special obligations (and because of limited resources and beds and the expense of commitment). Second, the special criteria emphasize the importance of extralegal variables such as the family within the framework of juvenile court dispositions. The more dysfunctional the family (e.g., the more likely that allowing the child to return home would be contrary to his or her best interests), the more likely for commitment to be seen as constituting the least restrictive alternative, and the more likely for the court's special duties in removing a child from the home to be perceived as having been satisfied.

Situational Factors That Can Affect Disposition

Situational factors, which don't tend to be cited in statutes as dispositional criteria, can have a serious influence on the sentence chosen by the court. One problematic factor, which only the Oregon statute mentions as an item to consider at disposition, is whether the youth was held in detention pending trial and disposition. Just as being in detention can have an adverse effect on adjudication (see Chapter 13), it can do so at disposition as well (Bortner and Reed 1985; Frazier and Bishop 1985). Many (perhaps most) juveniles who have been held in detention will be released to community supervision at the disposition hearing, perhaps because conditions changed since the pretrial period or because the judge believes the youth has been "punished" sufficiently after experiencing detention. For juveniles who are eligible generally for commitment, however, those who have been detained are subject to disadvantages that youth who have been released can possibly avoid.

First, detained youth may not have access to plea bargains that are as lucrative as those offered the released population (see Chapters 11 and 13). Moreover, if sentence bargains are permitted in a juvenile court, detained youth may not be able to secure plea bargains with lenient dispositions attached (especially compared to the released crowd). Second, unlike juveniles who have been sent home pending trial, detained youth have had no opportunity to prove that they can be returned home without committing another offense. To be sure, a released defendant who is rearrested prior to the adjudicatory hearing can face serious consequences for violating the law (again) while under court supervision. But the vast majority of juveniles are not rearrested before the disposition of their case (regardless of whether they have committed new offenses) and thus have "proved" to the court that they don't constitute a threat to society. Detained youth, on the other hand, have demonstrated nothing (unless they get into trouble in detention, which can also have serious consequences) and cannot give the judge any concrete proof that they are safe to release. Finally, it is psychologically easier for a judge to order the commitment of youths who have been detained as opposed to those who have been released. Whereas committing the latter means stripping them from their homes and parents at that moment (and creating emotional scenes), placing detained juveniles does not constitute a change in their custody status. Someone else put them in custody some time ago (at the detention stage), so all the judge is doing at disposition is *continuing* rather than instituting a deprivation of liberty (Sanborn 1992a).

System and community resources (statutorily mentioned only by Colorado, Louisiana, and Vermont) are other situational factors that could help determine what can and cannot be done with an offender (Chein and Hudson 1981a; Sanborn 1996a). Simply put, juvenile courts and their communities differ as to the amount of resources (financial, programmatic) available to them. While some have more community-based programs with which to experiment with offenders, others may have more reimbursement from parents that defray the costs of institutionalizing delinquents. As a result, juvenile courts have to set dispositional priorities according to their resource limits, which will not be uniform among all courts within a jurisdiction (or between jurisdictions) (Sanborn 1996a). Similarly, the lack of a bed at a facility could end in institutionalization not being imposed. Some states prohibit commitments to facilities that have reached maximum capacity (e.g., MD).

Resources also can affect the disposition of boys versus girls. Inasmuch as delinquency historically has been a "male thing," greater resources have been devoted to developing programs and institutions for boys than for girls. This gender disparity can work both ways for girls. Some can receive lenient dispositions (at least for their first and second offenses) because of the relative absence of treatment alternatives, while recidivists (and even some first-timers) can receive dispositions that are harsher and quicker than those given to their male counterparts simply because of the same absence of available programs for girls' treatment (Sanborn 1996a).

Another resource aspect that can be critical is the presence of private institutions within the court's dispositional reach. The mere existence of these facilities can expand the number of beds available for committing offenders. Moreover, private institutions in the juvenile justice network tend to have the ability to reject youth who have been analyzed as not fitting into their programs. Thus, juvenile court sentencing can be at the mercy of decisions made by the staff of these private facilities, perhaps to the legal advantage or disadvantage of the youth (i.e., a less or more serious placement may result from the rejection). Similarly, some facilities, such as boot camps, have certain medical and physical requirements the youth could be found to lack, requiring a different disposition (again, perhaps to the youth's legal benefit or detriment).

Other aspects of the particular juvenile court that can influence dispositional outcomes include the court itself (Feld 1991; McGarrell 1993; Sanborn 1996a) as well as the following:

- The judge rendering the decision (Clarke and Koch 1980; Sanborn 1996a; Thomas and Fitch 1975)

- Whether there was a defense attorney; whether this person was a public defender, appointed or retained; and whether this person acted like a guardian or an advocate, or was incompetent (Clarke and Koch 1980; Feld 1993a, 1991; Sanborn 1996a, 1987b)

- The prosecutor's office policy regarding juvenile crime, the prosecutor involved in the case, and whether the prosecutor was allowed to appear and participate at the disposition hearing (Sanborn 1996a)

- The probation officer assigned to the case (and his or her orientation, experience, thoroughness, etc.) and the extent to which supervisors monitor an individual PO's performance and work (Sanborn 1996b)

- The relationships among these four primary court workers (i.e., cooperative versus combative) and whether prosecutors or POs or judges tend to dominate court procedures (Sanborn 1996a)

- The method of adjudication (trial versus guilty plea), whether a trial penalty exists, whether sentence bargains (as opposed to only charge bargains) are permitted, and whether a PDR was ordered (Sanborn 1996a)

Some of these factors can vary both within a court and between courts (making cross-court comparisons difficult) and do not always have the same impact on disposition. In fact, the same factor can have opposite effects. An example is the presence of private counsel retained by the parents. On the one hand, attorneys can help account for the youth's receiving a lenient disposition (apart from any legal ability) simply because the judge can view the parents (and the youth) as already being punished sufficiently by having to pay legal fees. On the other hand, attorneys can help account for the same youth's receiving a harsh disposition by zealously representing the parents' wishes in having the child removed from the home (Sanborn 1996a).

The Pandora's Box of Dispositional Factors

Juvenile court's myriad dispositional factors, many of which are not quantifiable, and its special obligations and directives provide judges with significant discretion at sentencing. Judges are allowed to base dispositions on rather amorphous and vague standards (e.g., what exactly does "dysfunctional family" mean?). The potential to abuse this discretion is considerable (i.e., will dysfunctional family or other extralegal variables be interpreted equally regardless of the race of the offender?).

As we discussed in Chapter 9 on the intake process, juvenile courts should be expected to discriminate against families that are unwilling (a dysfunction of sorts) or unable (a matter of dysfunction or perhaps poverty) to help the court implement a solution to the child's problem. As with the intake decision, these families can affect the dispositional decision as well, especially in choosing between probation and institutionalization. To the extent that minorities are disproportionately represented in the category of dysfunctional family, especially in terms of financial abilities, it would seem reasonable to expect a higher proportion of minority youth both brought into the system (which we saw in Chapter 9) and subjected to harsher dispositions (which the numbers also appear to bear out; see later sections). Whether this situation translates into the juvenile system's being "racist" is difficult to ascertain.

Research Into Factors Affecting Disposition

The Shortcomings of Research

Dispositional criteria are so broad and overinclusive that it is difficult to pinpoint what actually explains any one disposition in juvenile court, let alone sentencing in general (as with other decision-making points). For example, if parents are willing to pay to have their drug-dependent child receive intensive and expensive private substance abuse counseling, a probationary sentence may be given to a relatively serious offender. Moreover, this parental arrangement may entail a secure (but private) commitment of the youth. This private commitment could rival what the juvenile court could have imposed in secure confinement and could even be the same facility the court would have used. Yet the disposition would be counted as constituting probation. This would make sense since the court did not technically commit the child itself but rather released the child to the parents so that they could have him or her committed. At the other extreme, if parents complain furiously about their child's behavior at home and suggest or state a refusal to let the youth back in the house, a sentence of commitment may be given to a relatively innocuous offender. Chances are, anyone examining the sentencing of these two youths would be completely ignorant of the broader context of the dispositional decisions.

Researchers who examine disposition tend to limit their analysis to court records, which have serious shortcomings (especially in the juvenile system). Records do not reveal the nuances and interactions of the dispositional hearing situations like the examples we've given. They also do not tend to address the information gathered during the PDR process when the youth's and the parents' characters are being assessed by the PO. Mostly immeasurable but critical factors such as a dysfunctional family are omitted. Some factors, such as the *nature* of the offense (as opposed to whether it was simply a misdemeanor or a felony), will often be incomplete and will not address the youth's culpability as well. Other factors, such as the age of the offender or the presence of private counsel, can be misleading. Previous treatment data will not necessarily include the *performance* of the offender in the treatment program.

Some factors, such as school record, can be fairly critical in one case and mostly irrelevant in another, perhaps because of the academic potential of the child, which is not likely to be included in the record data. The parents' having money does *not* mean they are willing to spend it, which may or may not matter depending on the youth's offense *and* problem. The researcher may know the parents' financial status, but is unlikely to know whether the parents were willing to devote resources to the situation *or* whether the youth's problem was even one (such as substance abuse) that made private counseling relevant, affordable, or available within the community's reach.

Thus, it is hardly radical to suggest that no record-oriented study has had or ever can have a complete and accurate picture of what explains juvenile court dispositions. Record shortcomings and the failure to investigate more than a few variables probably help explain why studies have reached confusing and conflicting results regarding the factors affecting disposition. Simply put, research efforts have disclosed that many of the various factors covered in this section *have and have not* appeared to affect the disposition decision. Necessarily lost in these analyses of aggregate data (i.e., studying and reporting *all* the dispositions for one or more juvenile courts for an entire year as one gigantic group) is the ability to account for how and why certain factors can be critical in one case and irrelevant in another, and the extent to which any one factor influenced any one disposition.

Research Findings

With all those caveats in mind, it is no surprise that research studies have produced findings that are all over the map, contradicting each other and offering little confidence that research has found the "key" to juvenile court dispositions. Moreover, studies that have found factors that do or do not seem to influence sentencing have examined *very few* of the variables that *could* affect dispositions.

One recent study of dispositions in a Texas juvenile court has attempted to address the factor interaction that complicates research in this area. This research has found that factors such as gender, age, and type of offense were associated with sentence severity in cases that were eligible for transfer to adult court, but they were not associated with dispositions in nonwaiver-eligible cases. In addition, while plea bargaining was related to less severe dispositions only in more serious cases, race had a significant effect only on the outcome of less serious offenses. Unexpectedly, blacks received less severe sentences than whites in this study (Mears and Field 2000).

The Dilemma of Factors Appropriate in Juvenile Court Dispositions

The factors that are supposed to influence sentencing in criminal court are becoming fewer, especially in jurisdictions with sentencing guidelines. That is, offense and record are being designated as almost exclusively responsible for gauging the severity of adult sentences. Any research that would discover elements other than these two factors determining the sentence would call its legitimacy into question. If the offense and record do not explain the sentence, some sort of nonpermissible, illegitimate material must be influencing sentencing in criminal court.

These matters are not as clear-cut in juvenile justice. In fact, juvenile court has been backed into a corner by current commentators and researchers. On the one hand, if offense and record seem to account for juvenile court dispositions (and they are very important and influential), juvenile court is guilty of having been criminalized in yet another capacity, and the need for its continuation comes into question. On the other hand, if extralegal variables seem to steer dispositions (and they are important and influential), juvenile court is guilty of not treating youth equally (at least in terms of their behavior). This no-win situation for juvenile justice mirrors the same issue at intake (see Chapter 9).

Contemporary juvenile courts cannot be oblivious to the severity of the offense and record (if they ever were). Their legal mandate to further the public's interests as well as the child's forces juvenile courts to be sensitive to the nature of the youth's criminality. The additional obligation to the particular victims of juvenile crimes only increases the court's public responsibilities. It seems reasonable for society and legislatures to direct juvenile courts not to disregard how seriously and how often juveniles are preying on the community and to note that these factors should affect dispositions. However, juvenile courts are equally obliged to promote the child's (and the family's) best interests, which means intervening into the family life only when necessary (or as a last resort).

Extralegal variables such as the child's and the parents' character and the parents' personal and financial resources thus become both relevant and critical. Here is where juveniles, equally situated with respect to offense and record, are not equal and may not be treated as such by juvenile courts. That is, neither their problems nor their potential solutions are identical, opening the possibility for different reactions and dispositions from the juvenile court. This situation reflects juvenile court's continued command to individualize its treatment plans for youth, albeit occurring today with greater emphasis on the potentially more equalizing factors of crime and record.

Arguably, race stands alone as the one completely indefensible factor that could influence juvenile court dispositions. In some studies, race purportedly has been found to affect dispositions (Frazier et al. 1992; Kempf et al. 1992), but the inability to disassociate race from other extralegal variables (such as dysfunctional family, system and community resources, and others) makes the findings suspect. Other studies have not found a race effect (DeJong and Jackson 1998; Fader et al. 2001; Secret and Johnson 1997; Tracy 2002). To the extent that racism does exist in juvenile justice, however, it surely is inexcusable and wrong.

Also controversial are class and gender, which, like race, have been found both to matter (Cohen 1975a; Frazier et al. 1992; Sampson and Laub 1993) and to not matter (Bailey and Peterson 1981; Bortner and Reed 1985; McCarthy and Smith 1986; Tittle and Curran 1988) in disposition research. Again, like race, class may be impossible to isolate as a factor and would be inappropriate as an influence on dispositions, except in one context. As suggested earlier, if the youth has a diagnosable problem that can be treated through the purchase of private counseling, money certainly can become an issue at disposition. This solution is philosophically (i.e., the family resolves the problem rather than the court *and* perhaps secures better and quicker services than those offered through the court) and financially (i.e., the system saves considerable resources) consistent with juvenile justice objectives. It also discriminates against the poor. If this result is inherently wrong, the very foundation of juvenile justice is the culprit. Whether appropriate or not, this sentencing discrimination (like that at intake) suggests minimally that using juvenile court adjudications and dispositions in a punitive fashion in the juvenile or criminal justice systems is problematic (see Chapter 12). Finally, gender can work for or against girls at disposition (as discussed earlier), depending on resource availability. Proving outright sexism would probably be as difficult as demonstrating race or class bias. Until female delinquency matches that of males, it is unlikely (and arguably unreasonable to expect) that juvenile justice will devote equal resources to both genders. Whether this sexist resource allocation is appropriate, it does suggest yet another reason to exercise caution in the punitive use of juvenile adjudications and dispositions.

Beyond the race-class-gender trilogy, other extralegal variables may appear less controversial but can be viewed as equally problematic in a fairness context. Many of these variables are inevitable by-products of traditional juvenile justice philosophy. An example is the youth's being legally disadvantaged by virtue of belonging to a dysfunctional family (or having parents with less than stellar character). Removing the family as a variable would redefine (if not eliminate) the mission of juvenile justice, however. Another example is the geography of justice, or variations in dispositions that culminate from differences in system and community resources and court personnel and policies, among other factors. The lack of standardization, such as that secured through sentencing guidelines, has contributed to this geography of justice in juvenile court. Adopting guidelines may reduce dispositional disparities, but it would be difficult, if not impossible, to factor the family element into guidelines (only offense and record tend to fit easily), and thus standardization threatens, if not eliminates, juvenile court's commitment to individualization (and perhaps to the child and family as well).

Dispositional Options in Juvenile Court

As should be clear by now, sentencing a juvenile status offender or delinquent involves much more than simply choosing between probation and institutionalization. For one thing, in many jurisdictions the judge has the authority to dismiss the case (despite sufficient evidence to adjudicate, which has already been found) merely because this result would be in the child's best interests. This outcome was discussed at the end of Chapter 13. While this decision can occur during or at the completion of the trial, the judge may not agree to this outcome until the disposition hearing (and perhaps not until after a PDR is conducted or thoroughly examined).

Even at the late date of disposition, the juvenile system is still poised to avoid adjudication and to retroactively divert the case, especially if neither the offense nor the record is serious. For example, despite the fact that there initially was an adjudication (such that the case proceeded to the disposition stage), an *unadjudication* can result. At least 17 jurisdictions officially retain the traditional standard that two findings are necessary to officially *adjudicate* a youth.[27] Juvenile courts in other states may require both findings without a statutory endorsement. The first finding is the actual commission of the prohibited act with sufficient intent (which would account for the initial adjudication decision). The second is that the juvenile is in need of treatment, rehabilitation, or care (which some statutes say can be presumed when felonies have been committed). Alabama and Georgia require clear and convincing proof that the child needs rehabilitation, while Texas says the youth must need treatment or the public must need protection. Indiana law spells out this requirement as not only the youth having a need for help but also the intervention amounting to treatment that he or she (a) is not receiving, (b) is unlikely to accept voluntarily, and (c) is unlikely to be provided or accepted without the coercive intervention of the court (IN Statute: 31-37-2-1 (2)(A),(B),(C)). Thus, juveniles who have committed illegal acts but are perceived not to need supervision or care could end up not adjudicated. The defense attorney who offers a *factual* guilty plea (see Chapter 11) hopes to take advantage of this *second finding* requirement.

Deferring the Adjudication or Disposition

Similarly, as we noted in Chapter 11 in our discussion of consent decrees, it is possible for judges to pursue a diversionary agreement even in sentencing. Consequently, despite the presence of sufficient evidence to adjudicate, judges in many states can decide to defer the adjudication (AK, GA, IN, OH, PA) or the disposition (ME, NE, NJ, NC, VA, WA).[28] This terminology refers to placing the adjudication or disposition in suspended animation. In both situations the matter is held over the youth's head for an unspecified length of time (FL, GA, MA, NE, PA, SD) or for a specific range of 6 to 24 months.[29] During this period of deferral or continuance, offenders are liable for performing various types of services in exchange for eventual dismissal of the charges. In other words, these are really just late-in-the-day consent decrees. Unlike with consent decrees, however, youths who do not succeed in performing their services should end up automatically adjudicated (assuming proof of inadequate services), as deferred adjudication or disposition will not occur unless either a guilty plea or trial has already demonstrated guilt on the original charges (consent decrees may or may not require an acknowledgment or proof of guilt). In addition, while consent decrees tend to be limited statutorily to first-time, nonserious offenders, "deferreds" are not necessarily limited to that group. For example, Minnesota excludes only those defendants subject to extended jurisdiction proceedings (their most serious offenders), while other states, such as Pennsylvania and Virginia, have not identified any defendant as ineligible for being deferred. Deferreds may also entail more intensive supervision than that extended to consent decrees. Thus, Minnesota allows deferred defendants to experience up to 30 days in detention, while Virginia provides for committing deferreds to boot camp. Finally, it is not uncommon for judges to take a more personal interest and direct role in the supervision of deferred youth as opposed to those on consent decrees.

Judges in jurisdictions that officially lack deferred adjudication provisions may still be able to grant consent decrees or their equivalent at disposition. This task may be too difficult to accomplish in states that consider consent decrees exclusively as either pretrial diversion efforts or solutions in which the youth's guilt is both unknown and unacknowledged. By the time of disposition neither of these conditions still exists and accordingly a consent decree may not or could not be contemplated. Nevertheless, inasmuch as the primary purpose of a consent decree is to allow the youth to avoid a delinquent label and record, denying one simply because the child insisted on trial and had been shown to be guilty could be viewed as unreasonable by the judge.

No Disposition

Even if the youth's adjudication is neither rescinded nor suspended, a disposition per se still may not occur. Several states statutorily provide (and many others may allow) judges the opportunity simply to counsel the child (and the parents) and to release the youth without a disposition.[30] Some such juveniles may be ones who judges feel do not need treatment but do not warrant having their adjudications revoked either.

The Probation Disposition

The vast majority of adjudicated juveniles remain adjudicated and receive a disposition. Of these juveniles, the large majority are in turn placed on probation. Because of both juvenile court's special obligation to preserve the family and the high costs of institutionalizing youth, probation is virtually guaranteed the first offender unless perhaps the offense is heinous or serious (or one with a mandatory term), the family is especially dysfunctional (or nonexistent), or the youth has a type of problem believed to require placement. The relatively high expense of placement and lack of available beds make probation a likely disposition for many repeat offenders as well.

Probation (further explained in Chapter 16) is a period of conditional freedom during which the offender is returned to the community under the supervision of a PO and subject to a variety of conditions. A few youths will be spared the supervision or the conditions. In earlier decades, defining a sentence of probation in both juvenile and adult courts was much more clear-cut. The offender was sent back to the community *in lieu of* experiencing confinement. As we will see, today it is possible to mandate a short period of incarceration and still refer to the sentence as probation. Clearly differentiating probation from (especially short-term) commitments can thus be a difficult task.

Although community supervision of some kind is available in all 49 jurisdictions with status offenders, many states appear not to refer to this supervision officially as probation.[31] Instead, words such as *protective, community supervision,* or *community control* are commonly used to identify status offense probation.

The Length of Probation

In most jurisdictions the duration of probation is an indeterminate number of years, limited only by the maximum age over which juvenile courts retain control or jurisdiction over youth (typically between ages 18 and 21). Thirty-five jurisdictions have maintained this traditional feature of juvenile court sentencing for delinquents, and 40 jurisdictions use this approach for status offenders (see Appendix N). Unlike the case with adult probation, then, the potential length of probation is not specified (other than by subtracting the youth's current age from the maximum age of retention). Obviously, the older the child means the shorter the maximum term of probation, and vice versa. Some youth will do better than comparable adult offenders while others will be worse off as to the length of probation that can be forced upon them. The federal jurisdiction appears to be the only one that officially prohibits a longer period of probation for juveniles. In Michigan and Minnesota very serious offenders can be given an extra two years of supervision (to 21 instead of 19), while in Montana an extra 4 years is possible (to 25 instead of 21). Four states (DE, IA, KY, MA) raise the limit from 18 to 19 years of age if the youth is 18 at disposition.

The remaining 17 jurisdictions have prescribed various time limits for juvenile probation (the federal jurisdiction and Kentucky have also done so, but only for their oldest youth). Maine uses criminal court probation terms for all but minor substance abuse offenses, which have a maximum supervision period of one year. Otherwise, the specified range varies from a low of six months for some offenses (WY) to a high of five years (IL, NH, OR).[32] Thus far, only eight states and the federal jurisdiction have attached longer duration levels of probationary supervision based on the seriousness of the offense.[33] In addition, a number of states include possible extensions of one (AR, NE, NY, NC, WI) or two years (AK), while the District of Columbia permits extensions but does not indicate either how many can be granted or how long they can last. The extensions allow the PO to seek additional time to work with the youth (e.g., to complete a program or to satisfy conditions). A hearing is required at which the PO must show why the extension is necessary or beneficial (see Chapter 15). Jurisdictions without time limits avoid this extra hearing, and the probation period simply continues until all programs and conditions are completed or the youth has reached the maximum age limit.

Finally, while five of these states (AK, AZ, ID, NE, NJ) use the same maximum probation terms for status offenders, New York provides for a one-year-shorter maximum for these youth (two years), but D.C. allows for a two-year-longer term (three years) of probation in status offense cases.

The Location of Probation

Most juveniles placed on probation return to the home in which they lived prior to the adjudication. Family problems (or neighborhood conflict and problems) may prevent this option, however. Most jurisdictions have allowed for this situation, to some degree by permitting youths to stay with relatives or any other reputable or responsible citizen while on probation (see Appendix N). Only 13 jurisdictions fail to mention this option, but juveniles are most likely being placed on probation outside their home even without an official statutory provision. The youth's change of address may require a change of legal custody as well. That is, the new custodian(s) will be legally recognized and required to act as the child's new parent(s). If this change of legal custody is recorded by the court as an out-of-home placement (because of the youth's change of address), researchers could mistakenly infer that this is not an instance of probationary sentence.

The Conditions of Probation

Like criminal court, juvenile court can attach conditions or penalties to probation, ranging from reporting periodically to the PO to some fairly serious obligations on the part of the youth. Statutes tend not to include an exhaustive list of all possible conditions, stating instead that the conditions must be reasonable. Several legislatures have demanded that the conditions be written and formally included in the court record (see Appendix N). Many more jurisdictions no doubt practice this policy too. This requirement makes the probation agreement a contract, paralleling the informal agreement, and reduces the likelihood that youths will be exploited during the process. Depending on their situations, juveniles can expect to be ordered to go to school or to find employment, to attend counseling sessions, or to abide by a curfew set by the court (perhaps hours earlier than that provided in a local ordinance).

The more costly and intrusive probation conditions and penalties are more likely to be authorized officially in the statutes. In fact, failure to mention some of these conditions would probably prevent juvenile court judges from imposing them. Some of the conditions (such as restitution) can be imposed on youth who are institutionalized as well. Like adult offenders, juvenile delinquents and often even status offenders are subject to *fines* in at least 38 jurisdictions (see Appendix N). Many states have opted either to use the criminal court standard as the potential upper limit or to not specify any limit at all for levying fines for most offenses committed by juveniles.[34] In some states the fines can be substantial. For example, Georgia has made a first gun possession and a first or second DUI subject to a $1,000 fine, and a second gun possession or third DUI subject to a $5,000 fine. A dozen jurisdictions have set a maximum fine, which is not based on the number or severity of offenses. The fines range from $100 to $1,000.[35] Some jurisdictions levy fines based on the number of offenses committed (ID, KS, TN) or the number of adjudications (MD). Finally, four states (CA, KY, MO, OH) have established special juvenile court levels of fines that depend on the severity of the offense but not the number (i.e., the most serious charge adjudicated would control).[36]

All jurisdictions identify restitution as a condition of probation for delinquents and status offenders, although Hawaii specifically prohibits restitution in status offense cases (see Appendix N). Unlike fines, restitution is portrayed as a therapeutic intervention that enables the offender to realize the extent of the damage resulting from his or her criminal behavior and to participate directly in repairing that damage. In addition, the victim's recent inclusion as a major player in juvenile court has served to make restitution even more plausible and sometimes mandatory (AZ, WA), particularly if the disposition is probation (CA, MI). Legislatures are disinclined to commit to a maximum amount for a restitution order. In 45 jurisdictions, the sky theoretically is the limit, provided only that the amount is considered reasonable. In fact, California, Idaho, and Michigan officially announce that the amount to which the youth can be held liable has no necessary ceiling. Thus, *all* expenses the victim incurs as a result of the delinquency can be factored into the restitution disposition. Only five states identify a limit to restitution.[37]

Community service is another potential condition of probation for delinquents or status offenders, officially cited in all but four jurisdictions (see Appendix N). Community service can be an alternative (or a supplement) to restitution. Those without financial resources and incapable of paying restitution can still qualify for community service and can be ordered to "work off" their debt to society in general or to the victim directly. Community service can be viewed as even more therapeutic and rehabilitative than financial compensation inasmuch as the youth must personally perform services rather than perhaps having his or her parents pay the restitution. Like restitution, community service can be mandatory for some offenses[38] or all adjudications (DC) or if probation is the disposition (TX). As with restitution, most jurisdictions (31) put no necessary limit on the amount of time to which youth can be ordered to provide community service. New York (10) and Wisconsin (14) are the only two states that place any age restrictions on community service.

Florida and Oregon use criminal court standards to determine the maximum hours for community service. Several states have imposed maximums that are not determined by either offense or record and that range from a low of 50 hours (AK, NY) to a high of 180 days (CO, ME).[39] Some jurisdictions focus instead on the number of adjudications (GA, MD, NV, NJ, NM, NC, VA), and increase the hour requirement for each adjudication.

Another penalty that has attracted considerable attention in legislation is *suspension of a driver's license* (or delaying eligibility for those without a valid license). Only 18 jurisdictions have failed to adopt this measure as a sanction in juvenile court (see Appendix N). At least 16 states have linked the driver's license penalty with status offense outcomes as well. Almost half (15) of the states that promise to suspend a youth's license do not limit the penalty to any particular crime and do not indicate the potential length of suspension.[40] Another 10 states identify a maximum limit to the suspension but do not require a special offense or a prior record. The suspension length among these states ranges from 90 days (MD, MT) to one year (IA, MS), two years (NV, WV), or four years (DE), while Georgia, Minnesota, and South Carolina permit suspension or delay until the age of 18. Finally, 14 states have concentrated on a few offenses as meriting a mandatory suspension of the youth's driver's license.[41]

Partial or Temporary Confinement

Although a probation disposition may suggest the youth is free to "run about town," that may not be the case. Mandating that the juvenile attend school (or work), combined with an early curfew, could mean few or no hours available for the juvenile to roam the streets. Similarly, requiring the youth to participate in what is known as a day treatment program (CO, KY, MO, NJ, OK, WI) is likely to result in little or no daytime freedom. Beyond these measures, even brief periods of actual commitment could also be considered within the probation disposition.

Surprisingly, house arrest or home detention (complete with electronic monitoring) has been identified as a condition of probation for delinquents or status offenders in only 19 states (see Appendix N). Of course, juvenile court judges in many more states may be imposing this disposition without explicit statutory authorization. Although intrusive itself, home detention can represent an alternative to an even more intrusive potential disposition such as institutionalization, so juveniles may elect not to complain and to accept this condition so as to avoid a harsher sentence. Possible conditions accompanying house arrest (e.g., legitimate reasons to leave the house) have not been spelled out in the statutes. In fact, only three states have identified a time limit to home detention.[42]

More controversial than house arrest is the use of regular detention as a condition of probation. Often referred to as shock probation, detention threatens juvenile courts' supposed antipathy to punishment (and is another example of criminalization). Thirty states currently permit judges to order detention for probation-bound delinquents, while only Florida expressly prohibits the use of detention as a dispositional option in juvenile court, and Alabama and Wisconsin hold the same in status offense cases. Five states have established a minimum age for youth subject to a detention disposition, ranging from 10 (ID, IL, NY) to 12 years (OR, WY) of age. Nine states fail to identify a maximum time limit youth can spend in detention as a sentence.[43] It is likely in these states that no detention disposition could last longer than any comparable adult jail sentence. It is common for states to not associate detention eligibility with any particular offense or record.[44] Fifteen states simply prescribe maximum time limits to detention that are not linked with offense, record, or age (other than a minimum one) and that range from five days (OK) to one year (HI, NY).[45] The relatively short periods allowed detention dispositions in most states serve to highlight how arguably punitive and nontherapeutic they are. Finally, eight states have mandated detention in certain situations, frequently specifying only minimum periods rather than maximum limits.[46]

Another probation disposition that can involve temporary commitments are those efforts directed toward substance abusers and sex offenders that are probably available virtually everywhere and are officially identified in at least 28 jurisdictions (see Appendix N). Thus, youths can be deprived of their liberty, perhaps significantly, while identified as being on probation. Commitments in these cases are probably required to be relatively short in, such as 90 days (CA, WY). As a sign of the times, it is becoming increasingly common for juvenile sex offenders to have to register with local authorities[47] and to submit to HIV tests for AIDS.[48] Even DNA testing is starting to be ordered in a few states.[49]

Finally, with respect to probation, a number of states have begun to formally adopt (while countless others have long practiced without official recognition) a more intensive probationary experience, aptly called intensive probation (further described in Chapter 16).[50] Intensive probation tends to differ from regular probation in two respects: The PO has a lighter caseload so as to be able to better counsel and monitor the youth, and the youth is required to report to the PO more frequently than would be the norm under regular probation. Many chronic offenders, particularly if their offenses are not very serious, experience both regular and intensive probation via multiple adjudications prior to being institutionalized. This situation is particularly likely because of the expense of juvenile institutionalization and the relatively small number of youths who can be incarcerated in many jurisdictions (see Chapter 17).

The Disposition Ladder

Probation can involve various degrees of control over youth. In academic terms, these levels represent what has been called the disposition ladder. Figure 14.1 illustrates these possible levels. This figure is not necessarily a representation of what each jurisdiction provides as probation levels and alternatives. Some juvenile courts (especially in urban areas) may have more levels, while some other courts may have fewer levels. The tendency is for youth who recidivate a number of times to climb the ladder and experience incrementally greater control over their freedom and daily lives. The disposition ladder is consistent with juvenile court's overall goal to rehabilitate the delinquent in the least restrictive setting possible, and with each higher rung of the ladder the juvenile court ups the ante a bit by exercising greater control and interference. Of course, a serious offense or problem with the youth could result in institutionalization as a first or second disposition. Juveniles need not climb the ladder one rung at a time (per adjudication).

Institutionalization also contains various levels (see the next section). Although the progress usually tends to be up the ladder with each successive adjudication (depending on the circumstances of the case), it is possible for youths to climb back down the ladder. The precise operation of the disposition ladder depends on factors such as available resources (financial and physical, such as beds) and the judge's and PO's views as to which responses are appropriate for repeat offenders. That is, inasmuch as the previous disposi-

Figure 14.1 The Disposition Ladder—Probation Levels

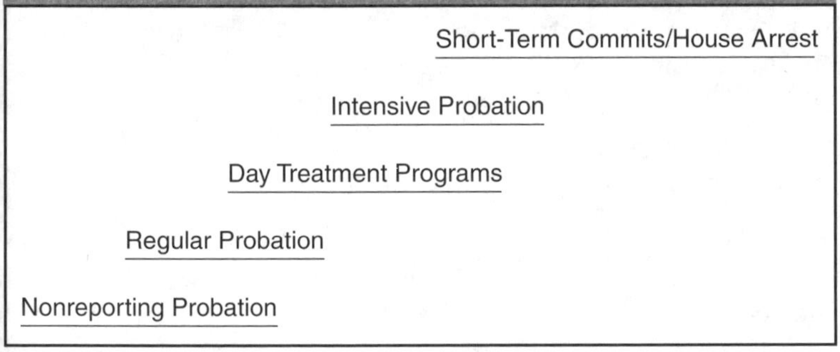

Short-Term Commits/House Arrest

Intensive Probation

Day Treatment Programs

Regular Probation

Nonreporting Probation

tion has failed, as evidenced by the commission of a new offense, the question becomes how much more control and which type of therapeutic intervention are now required to rehabilitate the youth.

The disposition ladder and its hierarchy of sentences make sentence bargaining relevant to juvenile court (see Chapter 11). Simply put, the farther down the ladder the juvenile's disposition, the more chances to recidivate and have still more rungs of the ladder to climb before being threatened with transfer to criminal court.

The Commitment Disposition

Commitment or placement is a period of time during which youth can experience various levels of restraint on their freedom while living outside of their homes. Defining commitment can be every bit as confusing as explaining probation, especially because of the potentially wide parameters of what can be called a placement. For example, should putting youth in foster homes where they live in a "regular" house located in a "regular" residential setting but with families that are not their own immediate ones (but could be relatives) be classified as a commitment (MI) or as probation (CT)? Technically, juveniles have been removed from home (of course, there might not have been a home to begin with), perhaps permanently. This would seem to qualify it as a commitment disposition, *but* the youth may have no more obligations than and no less freedom than regular probationers, which would seem to qualify this as a sentence of probation. In fact, probationers sentenced to even a brief period of detention will experience more confinement than youth committed to foster homes. Nevertheless, any removal from the home would most likely be regarded by the court as a commitment regardless of the amount of restraint or confinement to which the youth is subjected. This definitional quirk has serious implications for research into juvenile court dispositions.

Besides definitional problems, the decision to commit or institutionalize a juvenile offender tends to be much more complex than that surrounding a probation disposition. For one thing, unlike probation, commitments can have a minimum age requirement. States vary considerably with respect to delinquent age requirements (see Table 14.1). While 25 states have identified a minimum commitment age in their juvenile court act, the remaining jurisdictions fail to include an age provision. Although this omission might suggest that the minimum age of juvenile court jurisdiction would then determine the minimum age of commitments, data indicate that many jurisdictions (at least 17) operate with a *de facto* minimum, if not a *de jure* one. Adding to the complexity is the possibility that some commitments (like those to foster and group homes) are not bound by any statutorily identified minimum age, as some of the age restrictions are linked specifically with a particular type of commitment, especially the more serious or harsh facilities. For example, California has a minimum age of 11, but only for commitments to the California Youth Authority, which are the most serious juvenile dispositions in that state.[51]

Most commitments for status offenders do not have a minimum age requirement because of the nature of the homes and facilities in which most of such youth are placed. However, an age requirement would be relevant for status offenders if they were housed in particular delinquent facilities.

Besides age, the nature of the offense or offender can serve to disqualify a youth for certain commit-

Table 14.1 Minimum Age for Commitments	
Age Identified	**Jurisdiction**
8	AZ, NV, NM
10	CO, FL, ID, IN, MS, OK, SD, VA, WI
11	CA, NH, NJ
12	AL, IA, NE, OH, OR, PA, SC, TN, WY
13	IL
Inferred	
7	MA
8	WA
10	DE, GA, KS, LA, MT, NC, TX, VT
11	KY
12	HI, MI, ND, WV
13	AK, DC

ments. For instance, it is common for statutes to forbid committing status offenders with any delinquents;[52] to any secure residence, detention, or jail;[53] to any DOC facility;[54] or to any training school and certain departments or agencies.[55] These statutes reflect the notion of separating status offenders from delinquents, especially in the institutional system.

This separation is not universal, however. While some states suggest status offenders can be committed to facilities housing delinquents (RI, VT), many jurisdictions hold that such commingling of juveniles can occur as a penalty for a violation of probation or a court order for an adjudicated status offender[56] or as a disposition for a second status offense adjudication (AL, DC, ID). Finally, three states (GA, ND, OH) permit status offenders to be committed to a delinquent facility provided it can be demonstrated that these youth are not amenable to probation or any lesser placement.

Another placement-oriented requirement that applies to discretionary commitments (where the judge has a choice) in many states is the judge's special duty to demonstrate that removal from the home is both necessary and represents the least drastic alternative. This duty disappears in mandatory commitment situations, where placement is literally mandated by law. What can be particularly confusing about discretionary commitments is determining exactly whose decision it is to remove the child from the home. Unlike sentencing in criminal court, in most states juvenile court judges share commitment power with the state department that oversees juvenile matters. This sharing of sentencing power can occur in a couple of ways both before and after the disposition hearing. First, it is possible that the failure of the department initially to recommend placement will make it difficult, if not impossible, for the judge to impose a commitment disposition. Statutes frequently instruct judges to defer to the department's recommendation in this regard

(CO, FL, NE, NH, NJ, WY) and, in fact, may demand the judge actually explain and demonstrate the necessity of institutionalizing a youth who has been recommended for community sanctions by the department (CO, FL, WY). Second, in as many as 40 jurisdictions, judges commit youth to the state department rather than to an institution per se, although statutes frequently do not spell this out. The department then determines where to place the youth, which is similar to what the Department of Corrections does in the adult system. However, since commitment dispositions in juvenile court have traditionally carried no specified lengths of time, including minimums, the department can comply with a placement order even when the youth spends no more than a month or so in a diagnostic center and then is released back to the community by the department. In other words, commitment may mean diagnosis and evaluation only rather than treatment via an appreciable amount of institutionalization. In status offense cases, the norm is for the judge to declare that the custody of the youth has been transferred to a department (such as human or children or family services) or to some child welfare licensed agency for placement in a home or a facility.

Another confusing aspect of placements is that across states institutions with the same or similar names may not be very much alike, while places with dissimilar names may be quite comparable. For example, while a facility called a Youth Services Center (YSC) can be a minimum security institution in some states (ME, NV, SC, WV), in other states it is a maximum security facility (MA, MO, NH, NM, WA). Even more confusing are jurisdictions that have various YSCs with different security levels or that have multiple security levels within one YSC.[57] The same variations exist within other major facilities used in the juvenile system: forestry and wilderness camps, treatment centers and facilities, youth or juvenile correctional centers and facilities, training and industrial schools, and youth development centers (see Table 14.2). Moreover, many jurisdictions use such terms as *village* (FL), *school,*[58] *institute* (FL, SC), *house* (DE, FL), *cottage* (DE, FL), and *academy* (FL, MD) that might suggest a minimum security community facility but that actually apply to medium to maximum security "prisons" for juvenile delinquents. It is impossible for outsiders to understand how serious or harsh a commitment disposition is based on only the name of the youth's destination.

Table 14.2 Variations in Titles and Security Levels in Juvenile Facilities

Security Level	Institution				
	Camps	Treatment Centers/Facilities	Correctional Facility	Training School	YDC
Minimum	AL, CA, MN, NM, OR, PA	AL, FL, KY, MD, NJ, NM	CA, IN, KS, MN, SD	NJ, WV	GA, KY, NE, NH
Medium	VA, WA	FL, NJ	IN, KS, MT, OH	IA, MI, SD, WV	FL, GA, KY, NH
Maximum	AZ, OR	AL, MA, MO, PA	AZ, OH, OR, VA	OH, WV	GA, KY, NH, PA, TN
Multiple			ID, KS, LA, ME, MT	NV	

Even facilities with similar programs and security levels may be regarded and used differently from one jurisdiction to another, and even among courts in one state or among judges within one court. For example, boot camps, which tend to be either minimum (IL, IN, NJ) or medium (FL, GA, OR, VA, WA) security facilities, and which apply short-term intensive treatment, can be perceived as appropriate and most useful for first-time, non-serious offenders. In fact, state law may demand that no serious or violent offenders attend a boot camp (FL, VA). It is even possible for juvenile court officials to regard these commitments as probationary sentences. At the same time, however, boot camps can be seen as providing such severely intensive behavior control, albeit briefly, that they should be used only for veteran offenders who have already experienced institutionalization and who deserve just one more effort before being transferred to criminal court. In the juvenile system, besides the security level of the institution, other variables can dramatically influence how various commitment options are used and ranked (in terms of the disposition ladder), including:

- location (i.e., remoteness) of the facility, and distance from the youth's home and family;
- the types of treatment programs available, and perhaps their reputation and success;
- the length of both the treatment programs and the potential stay at a particular institution; and
- the cost of the treatment program (and the parents' ability to pay or to have insurance coverage for the cost).

The ability of some private facilities to reject violent and problematic referrals to their programs should also affect where these institutions are located in the commitment hierarchy.

Despite these ambiguities and lack of uniformity, it is still useful (and hopefully mostly accurate) to construct the commitment half of the disposition ladder as shown in Figure 14.2. Not all jurisdictions have or use all these levels. Some juvenile courts, especially urban ones faced with high recidivism rates, may perceive a need to maximize the number of levels to prevent sending too many juveniles to criminal court (and from spending too much money on commitments). As noted previously, boot camps could be situated at the bottom or top end of the ladder, so they have not been included in the diagram.

What certainly should be true for all jurisdictions is that the various commitment options available to a juvenile court be considered to occupy different levels. That is, committing a youth should involve a choice among facilities, some being more intensive in the control and treatment of delinquents than others (or higher up the ladder). Thus, juveniles who recidivate following a "less intensive" institutional experience can graduate to a "more intensive" facility (unless they are transferred to adult court instead).

The legislatures in 18 states have formally recognized a dispositional hierarchy in the commitment context. Juveniles in these jurisdictions must have been adjudicated of certain serious, violent offenses or must have accumulated certain records before they can be committed to a particular state agency or to a serious or secure facility.[59] These different levels of facilities have been present since the beginning of the juvenile justice system. Be-

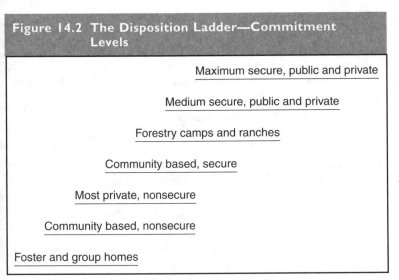

Figure 14.2 The Disposition Ladder—Commitment Levels

Maximum secure, public and private

Medium secure, public and private

Forestry camps and ranches

Community based, secure

Most private, nonsecure

Community based, nonsecure

Foster and group homes

yond these levels, however, juvenile courts have not had levels of sentencing like those of criminal court. In adult court, crime and record have traditionally been related directly to differential sentencing. Whereas a misdemeanor conviction most often means a jail term, different levels of felonies (such as Class A, B, C) typically mean very different amounts of years in prison (or death). Originally and for quite some time, juvenile courts, officially at least, did not establish a direct correlation between crime and record and dispositions.

Differentiated Sentencing

Historically, commitment sentences have paralleled probation sentences in that the length has been indeterminate, not specified in years. Rather, the juveniles have been subject to release when the staff believes rehabilitation has occurred or when the youth has completed the institutional program (especially in private facilities). The outside limit of the commitment has been the maximum retention age of the juvenile court's jurisdiction (or perhaps the maximum sentence available in criminal court, which juvenile court might not be permitted to exceed). This is still the procedure today in large measure. In status offense cases, some states identify maximum terms of institutionalization in terms of months or years, but virtually all are subject to extension.[60] The ready availability of extensions is another reason for the historical absence of maximum sentences. There was simply no need to commit to a particular sentence in juvenile court, since the lack of rehabilitation allowed the system to apply for an extension of time with which to work with the youth and to complete the treatment task.

However, more and more jurisdictions no longer look at juvenile offenders as one amorphous mass but rather see them as belonging to distinguishable categories (or levels). For instance, many states (17) are using labels that plainly separate the more serious and chronic offenders from the general delinquent population for dispositional purposes. Such terms as *designated felons* (GA, NY), *violent offenders*,[61] *serious* or *aggravated offenders*,[62] and *habitual* or *repeat offenders*[63] are appearing officially and frequently in statutes, and perhaps with even greater frequency unofficially in local juvenile courts.

Extended Jurisdiction

Another common method by which to differentiate sentences is simply to allow the state to hold onto one group of offenders for a longer period of time than that commonly allowed in juvenile court. Although juvenile courts do not have jurisdiction over crimes committed by adults (or offenders at least 18 years old at the time of the crime), most juvenile courts can retain jurisdiction over juvenile offenders adjudicated there until after they become adults (as discussed in Chapter 4). Consequently, 17-year-olds who commit offenses can be incarcerated (or given probation) until they are 19 or 21 in most states. If juvenile courts could not retain jurisdiction into the adult years, they would have to lower their maximum jurisdiction age or transfer older defendants en masse to adult court, having had no time to rehabilitate or punish them. Nineteen states have decided to *extend* the juvenile court's jurisdiction over their most serious and chronic juvenile offenders. Eight states refer to this process specifically as extended jurisdiction.[64]

Extended jurisdiction has a number of meanings. We saw in Chapter 12 how several states transfer some of their most serious offenders to the second tier of their juvenile court, thereby subjecting these youths to extended jurisdiction. Adjudication at this level culminates in a combined juvenile/adult sentence. Similarly, four states (MA, NM, OK, VT) that have adopted youthful offender (YO) provisions (which we explored in Chapter 12) also extend the juvenile court's jurisdiction over these offenders.

In sentencing terms, extended jurisdiction works in two ways. Nine states allow sentences to exceed (or to be extended beyond) their "normal" maximum retention age of 17–19 years old and extend jurisdiction one to four years in select cases.[65] Even states with the traditional maximum retention age of 21 allow four (CA, MT) or even 40 years (TX) of extended sentencing in some situations. The second way sentencing via extended jurisdictions occurs is practiced in seven states. These locations sentence their most serious juvenile offenders within their maximum retention age (rather than exceeding it). In five of these states (AR, IL, ME, MN, NM), although the maximum age is 21, sentencing for most youth does not last beyond their 18th or 19th birthdays. Extended jurisdiction sentences permit juvenile courts in these states to control youth until they are 21 years old. The same system is used in Kansas and Wisconsin, although the maximum retention ages are 23 and 25, respectively.

Particular Crimes and Offenders

Sixteen jurisdictions have chosen to focus on one or two particular offenses or have grouped offenses or offenders into one, two, or three categories and allow dispositions to vary by offense or group. In other words, unlike the adult penal code, which tends to link all offenses with a sentence, juvenile statutes in these states isolate only a handful of the most serious crimes or offenders for special sentences. Twelve jurisdictions have concentrated on a few crimes. In eight of these states this has usually meant nothing more than a short mandatory detention or commitment sentence for relatively minor offenses.[66] In the remaining four jurisdictions, however, the focus on particular crimes has more serious potential results. For example, in Illinois a first-degree murder adjudication can result in a commitment to 21 years of age, and in Wisconsin, while Class B felonies can yield a five-year commitment, youths who commit Class A felonies can be institutionalized until they are 25.[67]

Nine states allow longer or harsher sentences for certain labeled offenders, such as serious, repeat, habitual, or violent offenders (AL, AZ, CT, FL, IL, VA), or designated felons (GA, NY). Delaware calls these special youth "in need of mandated institutional treatment." While in some states the potential difference in disposition between these labeled groups and the general delinquent is not dramatic (AL, AZ, DE), the differences between and among groups in some states can be significant, as shown in Table 14.3.

In addition, unlike dispositions for their nonserious or chronic delinquents, Florida provides for designated facility stays of at least 18–36 months for serious or habitual offenders, while Illinois calls for commitment to the age of 21 with no release for five years for its habitual or violent offenders. Finally, in Kentucky, although they are given no special title per se, youths who are adjudicated of three or more offenses must be continued under juvenile court jurisdiction to the age of 18.

Table 14.3 Sentences for Certain Offenders in Select Jurisdictions		
Jurisdiction	**Offender**	**Potential Maximum Sentence**
CT	Nonserious	18 months
	Serious	4 years
	Serious repeat	5½ years
GA	Nonserious	2 years
	Designated felon	5 years
NY	Nonserious	18 months
	Designated felon	5 years
VA	Nonserious	Not specified
	Serious	7 years

Enhanced and Consecutive Sentences

Another criminal court–like provision that has recently been adopted for juvenile courts in several states is the ability to *enhance* the sentence or to impose *consecutive* sentences when the youth is adjudicated for multiple offenses. Eight states currently allow one or both of these provisions when certain aggravating factors are present, such as use of a firearm or an offense committed by a youth while on release or with a bad prior record.[68] Actually, many states may be practicing these measures without formal recognition of their authority to do so in the juvenile court statute. For example, in Arkansas and California, enhanced sentences are identified only in the state penal code—no comparable juvenile provision exists. Nevertheless, appellate courts in both states upheld enhanced sentences issued by juvenile court judges within those jurisdictions.[69] The same situation existed for consecutive sentences in Louisiana and New Jersey, with the same results in their appellate courts.[70]

Multiple Sentence Levels

Ten states have gone farther than establishing only two or three levels of disposition and have come much closer to replicating sentencing in the adult system by having adopted multiple levels or even sentencing guidelines. Four of these states (LA, NJ, OH, OR) focus on the offense alone. Louisiana and Oregon actually allow juvenile courts to impose the potential maximum sentence that is available in criminal court. Whereas Louisiana does not permit the disposition to last beyond the youth's 21st birthday, Oregon has drawn the line at age 25. New Jersey and Ohio have created juvenile court–specific sentences for various crimes. For example, New Jersey has established seven offense levels with corresponding maximum dispositions:

Offense	Maximum Disposition
First/second-degree murder	20 years
Third-degree murder	10 years
First-degree crime	4 years
Second-degree crime	3 years
Third-degree crime	2 years
Fourth-degree crime	1 year
Disorderly persons	6 months

Similarly, Ohio has developed five levels the have both minimum and maximum dispositions:

Offense	Disposition
Third/fourth/fifth-degree felony	6 months to 21
Six sex-related offenses	1–3 years to 21
Attempted murder/aggravated murder	6–7 years to 21
Other first/second-degree felonies	1 year to 21
Murder/aggravated murder	Commit to 21

The remaining six states factor in the prior delinquent record as well as the current offense. The provisions adopted in Colorado, Texas, and Wyoming are almost identical to the sentencing guidelines used by criminal courts in many states. About the only items missing are the grid and perhaps some offenses. For example, Colorado has created six levels of offenders, with names like mandatory, repeat, violent, or aggravated, which call for different sentences for most crimes (some of which are mandatory), depending on the current offense and prior record. Texas has significant determinate sentences for its three most serious levels of felonies:

Offense	Maximum Disposition
Capital/first-degree	40 years
Second-degree	30 years
Third-degree	10 years

Recently, Texas also initiated what it refers to as *progressive sanction guidelines* for juvenile offenders. Seven sanction levels associate current offense with a possible disposition. Moreover, one or two previous adjudications can move offenders up one level unless they are already at the top level. Finally, and similarly, Wyoming recently passed its own progressive sanction format consisting of five levels that link current offense with a disposition. If a second adjudication is equal in severity to an offender's first adjudication, the court can raise the sanction up one level (unless it is already at level five). Unlike Texas, however, Wyoming does not permit any disposition to last beyond the youth's 21st birthday.

In 1999, Kansas and North Carolina joined the state of Washington in adopting full-fledged, adult court–like sentencing guidelines for juvenile offenders. Washington has had such guidelines for more than 20 years. Kansas has identified eight levels of offenders, extensively covering both the severity of offense and prior record, and provides for differential dispositions scaled accordingly. Together with mandatory aftercare (or parole) supervision, Kansas allows sentences to last until the youth is 23. North Carolina assigns points to both the current offense and each prior adjudication. Its grid has three levels for both current offense (violent, serious, minor) and delinquent history (low, medium, high), which together determine whether the youth is eligible for one of three levels of disposition (community, intermediate, commitment). The severity of the current offense determines whether the juvenile court's jurisdiction and power to commit the youth run to the ages of 18, 19, or 21.

Recently, a couple states have adopted sentencing guidelines for juvenile court. Does this development undermine juvenile court objectives?

Washington's guideline formula is not only the oldest, it is also the most developed and criminal court–like. Every conceivable offense is assigned a letter-oriented category, ranging from A to E, and includes positives and negatives. Prior adjudications are given five levels (0, 1, 2, 3, 4, or more). As with criminal court, juvenile courts in Washington factor in the time span between offenses and the possibility of multiple current offenses, and the court can engage in departure sentencing (i.e., beyond the provided range) if there is clear and convincing proof that a manifest injustice would result otherwise. The maximum sentence for the top category of offense (A+), regardless of prior record, is commitment from 180 weeks to the age of 21 (when the juvenile court's jurisdiction expires).

Combined Juvenile/Adult Sentence

Nine states have proceeded beyond sentencing guidelines and allow juvenile court judges to impose a combined juvenile court–criminal court sentence.[71] Massachusetts refers to this specifically as a *combination sentence*, while Alaska calls it *dual sentencing*. In all nine states the judges impose both sentences simultaneously, but the execution of the adult sentence (which can be the same as that which could have been given an adult offender for the same offense in criminal court) is *suspended* or *stayed* on the condition that the youth not violate the juvenile court disposition (or commit a new offense, of course). If the youth either recidivates or violates the terms of the juvenile sentence, the adult sentence can then be implemented (with credit given for the portion of the juvenile disposition that has been served).

Combination sentences represent a kind of merger between juvenile and adult court. They are a transition measure that allows the most serious juvenile offenders to benefit one last time from a juvenile court adjudication, but with the ever-present threat of an adult sentence awaiting failure to successfully complete the juvenile disposition. In Chapter 12, we saw that in seven of the nine states, a transfer hearing (to go to the court's second tier) precedes the trial in which a combination sentence can be imposed. In Alaska and Massachusetts, an indictment is required to make a youth eligible for a combination sentence. Both states offer all juvenile defendants a right to jury trial. When deciding whether to impose a combined sentence in Massachusetts, a judge must consider criteria that are the same as those used in a certification hearing. In Alaska youths who are 16 or older and who commit a certain sex-related offense or a felony-level crime against a person (with a previous adjudication for the same type of offense) are eligible for dual sentencing. The provisions present in the states with combined sentences are listed in Table 14.4.

In Minnesota, Massachusetts, and Montana, these juvenile offenders can receive commitment dispositions that are two, three, and four years longer, respectively, than what regular delinquents can receive in those states. In Alaska, Connecticut, and Kansas, the maximum juvenile disposition available for combined sentences is no more than what other serious juvenile offenders could experience.

Table 14.4 States With Combined Sentences

Jurisdiction	Minimum Age	Title	Maximum Disposition
AK	16	Dual sentencing	To age 19
AR	None	Extended jurisdiction	To age 21
CT	14	Serious repeat	To age 21
IL	13	Extended jurisdiction	To age 21
KS	14	Extended jurisdiction	To age 23
MA	14	Youthful offender	To age 21
MN	14	Extended jurisdiction	To age 21
MT	None	Extended jurisdiction	To age 25
OH	10	Youthful offender	To age 21

Juvenile or Adult Sentence

One final, rather bold example of differentiated sentencing in juvenile court has been adopted by only three states: Massachusetts, New Mexico, and Rhode Island. In these states, the juvenile court judge has authority to select *either* a juvenile *or* an adult sentence for a youth under certain circumstances. To be fair, however, none of these situations involves regular juvenile court. In Massachusetts and New Mexico, this adult sentence possibility is reserved for youths who have been subjected to the delayed judicial transfer procedure that operates in both states (see Chapter 12). If an adult sentence is imposed, the judge has decided to transfer the case to criminal court by imposing an adult conviction and sentence. In Rhode Island, the juvenile or adult sentence can be imposed only from juvenile court's second tier (see Chapter 12), to which the youth had been transferred. Once adjudicated, Rhode Island youths can be given a juvenile disposition of commitment to a training school until the age of 21 or can be given an adult sentence extending beyond the age of 21, with any commitment until that age being served at a training school. Nevertheless, youth given an adult sentence are provided an opportunity to have the balance of that sentenced suspended at a modifying hearing, which precedes the eventual relocation of the youth from the training school to prison. What is important to remember is that in all three states, juveniles had to have been offered a right to jury trial before the judge could select between juvenile and adult sentences.

Finally, and similarly, Michigan's *designated proceeding* allows youth to receive a juvenile or criminal court sentence. However, despite the fact that the designated trial occurs within juvenile court, it is a *criminal* proceeding. Technically, then, it is not juvenile court that is sentencing the youth.

Altogether, 38 jurisdictions have adopted one or more ways in which to level or differentiate dispositions officially in juvenile court. Thus, only 14 jurisdictions have not openly embraced this concept and still maintain the traditional philosophy of approaching the rehabilitation of juvenile offenders as one large undifferentiated mass.[72]

Mandatory and Minimum Sentences

Another important facet of juvenile court dispositions is the availability of mandatory and minimum sentences. Both of these sentences are mainstays of the contemporary criminal court. Their appearance in juvenile court, however, comes off like oil and water. Simply put, while punishment-oriented sentences are perfectly suited to either mandatory or minimum provisions, supposed rehabilitation-focused dispositions are compatible with neither. To some extent, their presence in juvenile court suggests legislatures are in pursuit of punishment and incapacitation more than rehabilitation through dispositions. To some extent, they represent a reaction against the extensive sentencing discretion enjoyed historically by juvenile court judges and state juvenile departments.

Mandatory Sentences

Thus far, mandatory sentences for numerous juvenile crimes have emerged in the statutes of 31 jurisdictions. Although widespread, at least two-thirds of these provisions *do not* involve incarceration and thus do not particularly threaten the sincerity of juvenile court's rehabilitation mission. Adjudications involving drug and alcohol offenses, DUIs, and gun possession or use must result in driver's license revocation or postponement, community service, and/or fines in the juvenile courts of 18 states today.[73] In addition, Arizona, Illinois, and Washington have mandated certain other aspects of a probation disposition. In Arizona, anyone 14 or older who is a repeat felony offender must minimally be given intensive probation. Any youth adjudicated of first-degree murder, a Class X or forcible felony in Illinois, must serve a minimum of five years' probation if not institutionalized. Similarly, sex offenders in Washington are looking at a minimum of two years' probation.

Seventeen states have mandated a period of incarceration when certain adjudications occur. These provisions range from some token time in detention to lengthy terms of institutionalization.[74] For example, at the "lighter" end, Colorado and Washington require a minimum detention stay of 5 or 10 days, respectively, for gun possession. At the middle level, somewhat steeper mandatory commitments are involved in a number of states:

State	Adjudication	Mandatory Commitment
AL	Serious juvenile offender	Min. 1 year, secure
AZ	Aggravated DUI	Min. 4 months
AZ	Aggravated DUI with priors	Min. 8 months
AR	Gun possession	Max. 90 days
CO	Violent juvenile offender	Min. 1 year
DE	Second felony within 1 year	Min. 6 months
FL	Third auto theft	Boot camp
GA	First gun possession	Max. 12 months
GA	Second gun possession	Min. 1 year, max. 3 years
KY	Sex offender	Min. 2 years, max. 3 years
MA	First gun possession	Min. 6 months
MA	Second gun possession	Min. 1 year

Another nine states have adopted rather serious mandatory commitment dispositions for juvenile offenders who have been adjudicated of serious crimes or adjudicated numerous times (AJO = aggravated juvenile offender; DFA = designated felony act; SJO = serious juvenile offender):

State	Adjudication	Mandatory Commitment
CO	AJO + Class 1 felony	Min. 3 years; max. 7 years
CO	AJO + Class 2 felony	Min. 3 years; max. 5 years
GA	DFA + victim = 62/injured	Min. 5 years, secure
IL	13 year old + first degree murder	Min. 5 years (to 21)
IL	Habitual juvenile offender	Min. 5 years (to 21)
IL	Violent juvenile offender	Min. 5 years (to 21)
KY	Three adjudications	To 18
LA	First/second-degree murder	Secure (to 21)
MI	Gun + crime	Adult sentence

NY	DFA + victim = 62/injured	Min. 5 years, secure
WA	Gun + several crimes	Standard range in guidelines
WI	SJO + Class A felony	To 25
WI	SJO + Class B felony	Min. 5 years

Interestingly, Georgia and New York, which have possible serious sentences assigned to their designated felony act violations, mandate placement for an initial period of five years when the victim is 62 years old or older and is seriously injured as a result of the offense.[75]

A final and newly emerging aspect of mandatory sentencing in juvenile court involves requiring a period of aftercare supervision (or parole) when juveniles are released from various facilities. Obviously, this affects only those youths who are incarcerated. Historically, states used to leave this matter completely in the hands of the institution or the local juvenile court. Today, however, 14 states have enacted mandatory aftercare provisions:

State	Commitment	Aftercare Provision
AR	Division Youth Services	Max. 2 years
CO	Department Human Services	Min. 1 year
CO	Boot camp	Unspecified
FL	Boot camp, low risk	Min. 2 months
FL	Boot camp, moderate risk	Min. 4 months
GA	Designated felony, secure	12 months, intensive
KS	Violent/serious/chronic (I, II)	Min. 6 months
KS	Violent/serious/chronic (III)	Min. 3 months
KS	Conditional release violator	Min. 2 months
MI	Boot camp	Unspecified
NJ	All	⅓ of commit time
NY	Designated felony, secure	Unspecified, intensive
NC	Training school	Min. 90 days, max. 1 year
TX	Boot camp	Min. 6 months
WA	Various sex offenses	Min. 24 months
WA	Early release	Unspecified
WV	All	Unspecified
WI	Secure	Unspecified
WY	Noncapital/life crime	Min. 6 months
WY	Boot camp	Min. 6 months
WY	Capital/life crime	Min. 12 months

As the list indicates, most states have earmarked these aftercare provisions for only certain commitments, while some states have not identified a particular duration of the community supervision. New Jersey, alone, prescribes that the length of the aftercare period depends on the length of the commitment disposition. Interestingly, Florida, Kansas, and Wyoming provide for different levels or time periods depending on the type of offender or offense.

Minimum Sentences

Minimum sentences in terms of the length of probation or commitment (and not for items such as community service or fines) have appeared in at least 25 jurisdictions. Thirteen states have minimums that are mandatory and that have already been discussed in the previous section.[76] This section discusses only those minimum sentences that are either purely discretionary (i.e., completely up to the judge) or combined discretionary and mandatory. The latter term means that *if* a certain disposition is imposed (e.g., commitment to a boot camp), *then* a certain minimum sentence *must* apply.

The purely discretionary minimum sentence in some states involves nothing more than the judge's being authorized to set some minimum period of confinement.[77] Five states have specified minimum placement terms of months or years for certain offenses, coming close to replicating criminal court sentences. Kansas, Ohio, and Texas have adopted fairly serious terms in this regard:[78]

State	Offense/Offender	Minimum Commitment
IN	Several felonies	2 years
KS	Violent offender I	60 months
KS	Violent offender II	24 months
KS	Serious offender I	18 months
KS	Serious offender II	9 months
KS	Chronic offender I	6 months
KS	Chronic offender II	6 months
KS	Chronic offender III	3 months
KS	Conditional release violator	3 months
NY	Any felony adjudication	6 months
OH	Third/fourth/fifth-degree felony	6 months
OH	Manslaughter/rape/kidnapping	1–3 years
OH	Attempted murder/aggravated murder	6–7 years
OH	Other first/second-degree felonies	1 year
TX	Capital felony	10 years
TX	First-degree felony	3 years
TX	Second-degree felony	2 years
TX	Third-degree felony	1 year

Not yet widely practiced, the combined discretionary/mandatory minimum sentence requires a specified minimum term once a youth is sentenced to commitment (and occasionally to probation as well). For example, a number of states have mandated a minimum of two to four months stay in a boot camp.[79] Similarly, Kentucky and North Carolina insist that certain commitments must be for a minimum of six months. Georgia and New York have mandated minimum stays for their designated felony adjudications. In Georgia the minimum stay is 12 months unless it is a second such adjudication, which raises the minimum to 18 months. Similarly, in New York, the minimum stay is 12 months unless a Class A felony in involved, which raises the minimum to 24 months. Commitments for Class A felonies in Wisconsin also require a 12-month minimum. Texas and Wyoming both have minimum terms of probation at three and six months for two of the levels of their progressive sanctions format. Texas also has a minimum two-year probation for anyone adjudicated of a felony sexual offense with a child, as well as minimum placement periods of 6, 9, and 12 months, respectively, for three levels of its progressive sanction formula. Finally, although Ohio does not mandate commitment for a juvenile adjudicated of a number of crimes committed with a firearm (such as attempted murder, rape, and aggravated robbery), if this offender is placed, the firearm triggers a mandatory minimum one to three years that must be imposed in addition to *and* consecutively to the base sentence for the adjudicated crime.

Sentencing the Parents

A final major element of dispositions in juvenile court, completely unique to that forum, is the ability of the judge to impose sentence on someone other than the offender, namely, the parent(s). Juvenile courts in most states can command virtually anything short of incarcerating the parent. Juvenile court personnel (especially POs) had complained for some time that the court's lack of authority over parents frustrated their ability to resolve the youth's problems (Sanborn 1995b). Legislatures have responded recently, giving juvenile courts considerable power over parents (see Chapter 8). Chapter 8 identified the dispositions concerning parents in two contexts: financial obligations and performance requirements.

The Numbers at Disposition

Delinquent Youth

Data compiled from the period of 1994 to 1999 demonstrate that juvenile courts have been consistent in their use of delinquent probation vis-à-vis residential placements—which, by the way, were defined as including group homes. Probation has been and continues to be the most common disposition invoked in juvenile court. In fact, during this period the percentage of cases ending in probation rose slightly, while the proportion of cases that resulted in commitments declined slightly (see Table 14.5). Other sanctions, such as restitution, community service, or referral to another agency, also declined during these years (from 15 to 10 percent) (Butts 1996; Stahl 1998, 1999, 2000, 2001, 2003). The remainder of the cases ended in no disposition, at least with respect to the youth being put under the court's jurisdiction. Possible outcomes included in the "no disposition" category are stayed or suspended sentences, simple warnings and release from the court's jurisdiction, and writing essays (Snyder and Sickmund 1999). Between 1990 and 1999, there was an 80 percent increase in the actual number of youth put on probation, while there was a 24 percent increase in the actual number of committed youth.

Between 1990 and 1999, the likelihood that probation would be the court's delinquent disposition was similar in all four offense categories, ranging

Table 14.5	Percentage and Number of Adjudicated Delinquent Cases Resulting in a Disposition		
	Probation	**Residential Placement**	**Other**
1994	53 (275,500 cases)	29 (145,700 cases)	15
1995	54 (298,700 cases)	28 (146,900 cases)	14
1996	54 (306,900 cases)	28 (159,400 cases)	13
1997	55 (318,700 cases)	28 (163,200 cases)	13
1998	58 (366,100 cases)	26 (163,800 cases)	11
1999	62 (398,200 cases)	24 (155,200 cases)	10

Source: Puzzanchera et al. (2003b); Stahl (2003).

from 60 percent of public order offenses to 69 percent of property crimes. In addition, an increase occurred in the use of probation in all offense categories. Drug offenses witnessed the sharpest rise of 9 percent (from 54 to 63 percent) in the type of offenses granted this community sanction. Both person offenses (from 55 to 63 percent) and public order crimes (from 52 to 60 percent) experienced an 8 percent increase, and property offenses that resulted in probation rose 6 percent (from 58 to 64 percent). As to the profile of offenses that resulted in probation during this period, there was an increase in person offenses (from 18 to 23 percent), drug offenses (from 7 to 12 percent), and public order crimes (from 16 to 23 percent), and an interesting decline (from 59 to 41 percent) in the proportion of property offenses that made up the total population of probation cases (Puzzanchera et al. 2003b).

Age and gender were associated with the rise of probation as a disposition. Youth 15 and younger were granted probation more frequently (between 64 and 66 percent) in all four offense categories compared to those 16 and older (between 55 and 60 percent). Similarly, girls were placed on probation more frequently (between 63 and 69 percent) in all four offense categories compared to boys (between 59 and 63 percent). There were no patterns like these in regard to race. However, while whites (66 percent) and youths of other races (73 percent) were sentenced to probation most frequently for drug offenses, probation was the least likely disposition for blacks (55 percent) in this offense area. Instead, blacks were most often (64 percent) put on probation for property crimes (Puzzanchera et al. 2003b).

Interestingly, the age, race, and gender characteristics of offenders were all associated with an increase in the use of probation. Probation among the younger age group (15 and younger) rose more sharply (from 57 to 66 percent) than it did among the 16 and older youth (from 54 to 58 percent). Females witnessed a larger increase in probation dispositions (from 60 to 67 percent) than males (from 55 to 61 percent). Finally, youths from other races experienced a higher increase in the use of probation (from 55 to 63 percent) than did either whites (from 57 to 63 percent) or blacks (from 55 to 61 percent) (Puzzanchera et al. 2003b).

Between 1990 and 1999, the use of delinquent placements declined from 32 percent to 24 percent of all delinquency cases and declined as well in all four categories of offenses. The drop was most pronounced for drug offenses (from 36 to 22 percent) and public order offenses (from 38 to 27 percent). The reduction in the percentage of property crimes (from 28 to 23 percent) and person crimes (from 35 to 26 percent) that resulted in placement were not as marked, but were still substantial during this period (Puzzanchera et al. 2003b). Commitments were most likely in cases of homicide, rape, and robbery and were least likely in cases of vandalism and disorderly conduct (Snyder and Sickmund 1999). One likely explanation for the relatively high rate of placements for public order offenses is that the category contains events such as escapes from confinement, weapons offenses, and violations of probation and parole.

During this time span, the proportion of out-of-home placement cases involving property crime declined (from 50 to 38 percent), while increases were witnessed in the other three categories. So, drug offenses (from 8 to 11 percent), person offenses (from 21 to 25 percent), and public order offenses (from 21 to 27 percent) all rose between 3 and 6 percent in the proportion of placement cases. The commitment profile has changed significantly since 1990, when property offenses constituted half of the cases that resulted in placement (Puzzanchera et al. 2003b).

Although criminal histories were not factored into the analysis, data indicate that as youths grew older they had an increasing likelihood of placement, at least until the age of 17, when commitment rates tended to decline (probably because of a higher rate of prosecution in adult court at this age). For those 15 and younger, there was a 23 percent commitment rate in 1999, while for 16 and older the rate was 26 percent. The older group had a higher rate of commitment (between 22 and 28 percent) than the younger group (between 21 percent and 26 percent) in all four offense categories.

Males were more likely to be committed than females in 1999 (26 percent versus 19 percent), and whites (23 percent) were less likely to be committed than blacks (28 percent) and youths of other races (24 percent) (Puzzanchera et al. 2003b). Age, gender, and race characteristics were associated with declines in the use of commitments for the 1990 to 1999 period, much like the situation with offense categories. For those 15 and younger there was a 9 percent drop (from 32 to 23 percent) in the placement rate, and for those 16 or older there was a 6 percent decline (from 32 to 26 percent). Males witnessed a 7 percent reduction (from 33 to 26 percent) in commitments, as did females (from 26 to 19 percent). Males (between 23 and 28 percent) had a higher commitment rate than females (between 15 and 23 percent) in every offense category. Finally, while whites had a 7 percent reduction (from 30 to 23 percent) in placements, blacks also had a 7 percent decline (from 35 to 28 percent) and youths from other races had an 8 percent decline (from 32 to 24 percent). Although the data do not control for offense seriousness, delinquent record, or previous dispositions, the numbers show that a higher percentage of blacks (between 26 and 33 percent) than whites (between 16 and 26 percent) and youths of other races (between 15 and 28 percent) were committed in each major offense category (Puzzanchera et al. 2003b). In 1999, while whites were most likely to be placed in public order offenses (26 percent), blacks were most likely to be committed in drug cases (33 percent), and youths of other races were more likely to be placed for person offenses (26 percent). Recently compiled data also show a disproportionate number of minority youth committed to secure facilities (see Appendix B).

The average length of stay for committed delinquent youth rose 14 percent from 1993 to 1997—from 96 to 109 days. While the length of commitment for drug offenders actually declined during this time (from 148 to 113 days), an increase was experienced for those who committed person crimes (from 162 to 180 days), property crimes (from 89 to 104 days), and public order offenses (from 22 to 49 days) (Butts and Adams 2001).

One unique and intriguing aspect of juvenile court sentencing is that formally prosecuted but nonadjudicated delinquency cases (which made up roughly 33 percent of prosecuted cases in 1999) can result in dispositions similar to adjudicated cases. Although the vast majority (67 percent) of these cases were granted outright dismissals in 1999, significant numbers of youth were given probation (12 percent) or other sanctions (19 percent), and 2 percent actually resulted in out-of-home placements (Snyder and Sickmund 1999; Puzzanchera et al. 2003b). In 1996, youth voluntarily accepted placement in 16,400 nonadjudicated delinquency cases (Snyder and Sickmund 1999), while in 1999 this number declined to 5,600 (Puzzanchera et al. 2003b).

Status Offenders

As with delinquents, status offenders are most likely to experience probation as a juvenile court disposition. In 1997, most adjudicated status offenders (61 percent) were put on probation, while 14 percent were placed outside the home. Another 23 percent of status offense cases resulted in "other" dispositions, which included fines, restitution, community service, or a nonresidential treatment or counseling program. The other dispositions were prevalent in liquor violations. A small number (3 percent) of status offenders were given no disposition despite their adjudication (Puzzanchera et al. 2000).

As Table 14.6 shows, youth classified as runaways (28 percent) and ungovernable (23 percent) were significantly more likely to be placed than were those adjudicated with miscellaneous offenses (13 percent), truancies (11 percent), and liquor violations (7 percent) in 1997. Probation was the most likely disposition for all five offense categories, but especially for truancy (74 percent), liquor violations (63 percent), and ungovernability (63 percent). Smaller proportions of those charged with running away (58 percent) and miscellaneous offenses (37 percent) were placed on probation. The disposition trend for status offenders mirrored that of delinquents. Between 1988 and 1997, the use of probation expanded (from 59 percent to 61 percent of all cases), while the percentage of placements declined (from 17 percent to 14 percent of all cases). The only offense that bucked this tendency was truancy, which, despite legislative initiatives to resolve the matter in the community, experienced a modest increase (from 10 percent to 11 percent) in commitment sentences and a decline (from 80 percent to 74 percent) in probation. Truancy also experienced the largest increase (90 percent) of the number of cases that resulted in commitments (Puzzanchera et al. 2000).

With the exception of running away, younger offenders (15 and younger) were slightly more likely to be placed for status offenses than were older offenders (16 and older). Again, runaways and ungovernables were most likely to be placed, and truants were most likely to be granted probation regardless of the age group (and race and gender). As Table

Table 14.6 Status Offense Dispositions, by Offense and Percent Change, 1988–1997				
Placement				
Status Offense	**1988**	**1993**	**1997**	**Percent Change**
All offenses	8,700	10,700	11,600	34%
Runaway	2,000	2,700	2,500	26
Truancy	1,400	2,300	2,700	90
Ungovernable	2,700	2,600	2,800	5
Liquor	1,300	1,200	1,500	17
Miscellaneous	1,300	1,900	2,100	63
Probation				
Status Offense	**1988**	**1993**	**1997**	**Percent Change**
All offenses	30,800	36,300	50,200	63%
Runaway	3,900	4,900	5,300	35
Truancy	11,300	14,200	17,600	56
Ungovernable	5,300	5,300	7,700	44
Liquor	8,600	8,500	13,700	60
Miscellaneous	1,700	3,400	5,900	247

14.7 shows, between 1988 and 1997, both age groups witnessed a decline in the use of placements. Although 14 percent of both males and females were committed as a result of status offense adjudications in 1997, males were more likely than females to be committed for each of the major offense categories. Both genders were committed less frequently between 1988 and 1997. With the exception of ungovernability, females were more likely than males to be put on probation. Finally, blacks were more likely to be placed than whites and those from other races in the major offense categories, with the exception of ungovernability, for which whites prevailed. Blacks were also more likely than those from other races and whites to be placed on probation (Puzzanchera et al. 2000).

Like delinquents, status offenders who were not adjudicated were usually granted dismissals (67 percent, or 51,000 cases) at sentencing, but 10 percent (or 7,200) were put on informal probation, less than 1 percent (200) were placed, and 23 percent (17,200) encountered informal sanctions (such as restitution and community service) in 1997 (Puzzanchera et al. 2000).

Although this concludes our discussion on dispositions for the moment, the topic has not yet been exhausted. In Chapter 15, our examination of *review* and *modification hearings* will show how sentences can be modified, adjusted, and even extended long after the conclusion of the disposition hearing.

Table 14.7 Status Offense Dispositions by Age, Gender, and Race, 1988–1997			
Placement			
Age/Gender/Race	**1988**	**1993**	**1997**
15 years or younger	20%	20%	16%
16 years or older	12	14	11
Male	16	17	14
Female	17	18	14
White	16	13	13
Black	19	23	20
Other races	18	20	9
Probation			
Age/Gender/Race	**1988**	**1993**	**1997**
15 years or younger	64%	63%	63%
16 years or older	53	55	57
Male	58	58	59
Female	62	62	64
White	57	58	60
Black	70	66	65
Other races	65	57	61

Summary: Key Ideas and Concepts

- Necessary separation of adjudicatory and disposition hearings
- Disposition immediately following adjudication
- Treatment delayed is treatment denied
- JPO very critical figure at disposition
- Possibly no prosecutor at disposition hearing
- Possible guardian defense attorney at disposition hearing
- Victim a factor today in juvenile sentencing
- Public attendance at the disposition hearing
- Lack of constitutional rights at disposition hearing
- Mandatory or discretionary PDR

- Team development of PDR
- Virtually anything considered at disposition hearing
- Myriad factors that can affect disposition
- Unique obligation that disposition promote the child's best interests
- Importance of family in juvenile court disposition
- Detained youth disadvantaged at disposition
- Situational resource factors potentially critical at disposition
- Factors having opposite effects at disposition
- Contradictions in studies that have examined dispositional factors
- Diversion possible even at postadjudication
- Two findings needed to adjudicate a youth
- Deferring adjudication and disposition to avoid a delinquent record
- Imposing no disposition on an adjudicated youth
- Problem defining what a probation disposition is
- Most dispositions involve probation
- Time period not associated with probation in most jurisdictions
- Juvenile court able to impose fines on delinquents
- Restitution and community service nearly universal dispositions
- Suspending or delaying a driver's license becoming popular penalty
- Increasing availability of house arrest as a disposition
- Controversial use of detention as a probation sentence
- Problem defining what a commitment disposition is
- Minimum age requirement for delinquent commitments
- General prohibition of placing status offenders with delinquents
- Confusion over names given juvenile facilities
- Placing juvenile offenders in categories for sentencing purposes
- Extended jurisdiction to retain control over most serious offenders
- Harsher dispositions for particular crimes and offenders
- Enhanced and consecutive sentences for repeat offenders
- Multiple sentencing levels and guidelines in juvenile court
- Juveniles subject to combined juvenile/adult sentence
- Juveniles subject to juvenile or adult sentence
- Probation the most common juvenile court disposition

- Nonadjudicated delinquents and status offenders receiving dispositions
- Unique aspect of sentencing parents in juvenile court

Discussion Questions

1. Should defense attorneys be advocates or guardians at disposition? What factors should influence the answer?

2. Should the victim play a role at the disposition hearing? If no, why not? If yes, in what capacity and to what extent? What are the implications of allowing victim participation at this hearing?

3. What are the implications of the parents' playing a large potential role at disposition? Is it appropriate for the parents to have such an effect on the proceedings?

4. Discuss the disadvantages experienced by detained youth at disposition. Is it appropriate for these youths to be disadvantaged? What, if anything, can be done about this situation?

5. Can research resolve the question as to the factors that affect dispositions? If yes, what is the answer? If no, what does research need to do in order to answer the matter?

6. Should probationary sentences include periods of confinement? Are such sentences purely punitive, or are they rehabilitative?

7. Should placement in a group or foster home be counted as a commitment or a probation sentence? What are the implications of counting it as a commitment sentence?

8. Should status offenders be committed with delinquents? If no, why not? If yes, in what situations and under what conditions?

9. Should juvenile court sentencing be designed according to the severity of the offense and/or record? If no, why not? If yes, what does this say about juvenile court? What are the implications of juvenile courts having enhanced and consecutive sentences and multiple levels of sentencing? Is the combined sentence idea sound?

10. Should parents be subject to juvenile court sentencing? If no, why not? If yes, in what situations and with what penalties?

Endnotes

1. Four of these 32 states simply mention that disposition should take place without unnecessary or unreasonable delay (AK, DE) or as soon as possible (IA, MT).
2. The states with deadlines that are the same for delinquents and status offenders are: CA, GA, LA, MD, MI, MS, VT, WI, WY. The states without deadlines that have suggested the times should be the same for delinquents and status offenders are: HI, ID, IN, MT, OH, OK, RI.

3. The states that provide priority timing for status offense disposition hearings are: CO, IL, MN, NJ, PA, WA.
4. The states that allow the VIS to be introduced at sentencing are: AK, AZ, CA, CO, CT, FL, GA, IL, IA, LA, MD, MI, MN, MO, MT, NH, NJ, NY, TX, UT, VT, VA, WI, WY.
5. The states that allow the victim to attend the disposition hearing are: AK, AZ, CA, CO, FL, KS, KY, LA, MI, MN, NJ, OK, OR, PA, SD, TX, UT, VA, WI, WY.
6. The right to examine the PDR is not mentioned in: FED, MS, NE, NV, OR, RI, SC, SD, WI.
7. The right to present evidence is identified in: AK, CA, CT, DC, FL, ID, IN, LA, ME, MD, MN, MS, MO, NY, NC, OH, UT, WA, WI.
8. The defense can challenge the PDR in: AL, AR, DC, GA, ID, IL, IN, KY, LA, MD, OH, OK, PA, UT.
9. The right to cross-examine the author of the PDR is recognized in: AL, CO, CT, DE, GA, HI, LA, ME, MI, MN, MO, MT, NY, NC, TN, WA, WY.
10. Otherwise the PDR is called: PD Study (AL, WA), Social Study (GA, PA), Social History (OH, VA), Family Assessment (SC), Individual Treatment and Service Plan (OK), Case Service Plan (MI), and a Social Investigation Report (IL).
11. The PDR is mandatory in: AK, CA, FL, ID, IN, IA, KS, KY, MA, MI, MT, NH, SC, UT, VT, WI, WY.
12. The PDR is discretionary in: AL, AZ, AR, DE, GA, HI, ME, MD, MN, MO, NC, ND, OH, PA, RI, SD, TX, VA, WA, WV.
13. The PDR is not supposed to be conducted until after adjudication in: GA, HI, IN, MN, NJ, NM, OH, PA, SD, UT, VT, VA, WA, WV.
14. The PDR is not supposed to be read until after adjudication in: AK, DE, DC, FL, ID, MO, NH, NC, TN, WY.
15. The team use of a risk and needs assessment measure is endorsed in: AK, AZ, AR, CO, FL, KS, MT, NC, OK, TX.
16. Parents are subjected to the same examinations as their children in: AR, GA, IN, MD, MO, MT, NH, NC, OR, SD, WI, WY.
17. See *State v. Matha*, 669 NE 2d 504 (Oh App 9 Dist. 1995).
18. The youth's character and habits are considered in: DC, FED, KY, LA, MA, MI, MO, PA, RI, SC, TN, VA.
19. The child's treatment needs are identified in: AK, LA, ME, MI, MS, NJ, NY, NC; and the youth's age is mentioned in: AK, IA, NJ, NC, VA.
20. Returning children home would have to be contrary to their interests in: AL, AR, CA, CO, DC, GA, IL, IN, KS, LA, ME, MA, MI, MN, MS, MO, NJ, NY, ND, OK, SC, TN, TX, VA, WV, WI.
21. Reasonable efforts to avoid placement are required in: AL, AR, CA, GA, IL, IA, KS, ME, MA, MI, MS, MO, NE, NY, OH, OK, OR, SC, TN, TX, WV, WI.
22. The actions taken to avoid placement must be identified in: AK, MI, MO, OR, SC, TN, WI.
23. An explanation as to why commitment is necessary is required in: AR, CO, DC, IL, IN, MI, MS, MO, OK, TN, TX, VA, WI.
24. Status offenders must be referred to crisis intervention before commitment in: FL, IL, MI, NV, NJ, NM, TN, UT, VT, WA.
25. Reasonable efforts to return the youth home as soon as possible are required in: AL, AR, CA, GA, IL, IA, KY, ME, MI, MN, MS, MO, NE, NY, NC, ND, OH, OK, OR, SC, TN, TX, WI.
26. Judges are required to write findings of fact in: AK, DC, FL, GA, ID, IL, LA, ME, MN, NJ, NY, NC, OH, OK, TX.
27. Two findings are required to adjudicate a youth in: AL, CA, DC, GA, IL, IN, LA, MD, MS, NH, NY, ND, PA, TN, TX, VT, WV.
28. While Washington insists on defendants' surrendering a right to trial and stipulating to the charges to secure a deferred disposition, most jurisdictions allow this disposition to occur after trial (and, in fact, after a finding of involvement in the offense). Thus, adjudication on the original charges would be unnecessary (and redundant) at this point. Other states have given various names to the same phenomenon, which appear to be dispositional (i.e., postadjudication) options. These names include *place the petition on file* (RI), *adjournment in contemplation of dismissal* (NY), *continuance under supervision or advisement* (IL), *continuance without finding or judgment or declaring the child to be a ward of the court* (CA, MA, MN), and *withholding or suspending adjudication or judgment* (FL, IA, SD).
29. The times identified in the statutes range from 6 months (CA, MN, NY, NC, OH) to 12 months (AK, IN, LA, ME, NJ, RI, VA) to 18 months (IA) to 24 months (IL, WA).
30. The no disposition option is identified in: LA, MI, MN, MS, NH, NJ, WI, WV.
31. The states that do not call community supervision of status offenders probation are: AL, AK, AR, CA, CO, CT, FL, HI, IL, IA, KS, MA, MN, MS, NV, NJ, NM, NC, OH, OR, PA, VT, VA, WA, WI, WY.
32. Illinois (19) and Oregon (23) attach an upper age cutoff that would reduce the maximum five-year probation term available for some defendants. Other jurisdictions have identified upper limits to their proba-

tion sentences of one year (AZ, DC, KY, ME, WY), two years (LA, NE, NC, WA, WI), three years (AR, FED, ID, NJ, NY), and four years (AK).

33. The states that have established a longer term of probation for more serious offenses are: AZ, IL, ME, MI, MN, MT, WI, WY.

34. The states that use the criminal court fine schedule are: GA, ME, MI, MT, NJ, NM, NC, OK, OR, WI, WY. The states that don't specify a limit for fines are: AZ, DE, HI, NV, ND, PA, UT.

35. The maximum fines in these jurisdictions are $100 (WV), $200 (SC, WA), $250 (AL, NH), $300 (CO, DC), $500 (AR, MS, VA), $700 (MN), and $1,000 (SD).

36. In California, a felony ($1,000) can be fined 10 times the amount of a misdemeanor ($100). Kentucky has established three levels of fines: $100 for violations, $250 for misdemeanors, and $500 for felonies. Missouri groups violations with misdemeanors ($25) and doubles the fine for felonies ($50). Finally, the Ohio legislature has devoted the most energy to constructing a table of fines for juvenile delinquents only. Four levels of misdemeanors are fined between $50 and $225, and six levels of felonies (including murder) are fined between $300 and $1,800.

37. In the District of Columbia the maximum is $300, while in New York the limit is $1,500, provided juveniles are 14 and 10 years of age, respectively. Wisconsin caps the restitution amount at $250, but only for youths under 14 years of age. Defendants above that age are exposed to no limit. These three jurisdictions are the only ones that attach any age requirement to restitution liability. While the most serious offenses in North Carolina have no limit, less serious offenses cannot result in an order for more than $500. Finally, Illinois allows restitution up to $2,500, per victim, per act. Thus far, North Carolina and Wisconsin are the only two states that have created multiple levels of restitution liability, depending on age (WI) or offense (NC).

38. Community service is mandatory for some crimes in: AZ, CA, FL, GA, IL, MN, NV, NJ, NM, TX, UT, VA, WI.

39. Within this range are states with maximums of 120 hours (MS, KY), 200 hours (WA), 500 hours (TX), and 90 days (SD).

40. The potential length of suspension is not identified in: AR, FL, ID, IL, IN, KS, LA, MO, NC, OH, OK, OR, RI, SD, VA, WY.

41. Delaware promises a one-year suspension for driving without a license. Otherwise, mandatory suspensions of various lengths have been linked to four types of offenses: alcohol and drug use (IN, MD, MN, NV, UT, VA, WA, WI), DUI (AZ, DE, ME, MS, TX, VA), gun possession (MN, NV, OH, VA, WA), and graffiti (NV, TX).

42. Wisconsin's limit is 30 days, and six months is the longest possible in New Hampshire. Ohio places the maximum length at the age of 18 or that which is possible in criminal court (whichever is less).

43. The states that do not identify a maximum time limit to a detention sentence are: AL, AK, AZ, CA, MA, MI, TX, VT, WA.

44. Nevertheless, North Carolina allows 14 days of detention for more serious offenses but only 5 days for less serious ones. Idaho claims that juveniles are subject to 90 days of detention per misdemeanor and 180 days per felony, while Illinois states simply that the juvenile period of detention cannot be greater than the comparable jail term. Virginia focuses instead on adjudications, limiting a first adjudication to 30 days of detention but permitting a second adjudication to result in 180 days. Similarly, Indiana and Kentucky have established different levels of detention primarily according to age. In Indiana, those younger than 17 can receive the lesser of 90 days or the comparable jail term, while those older than 17 can receive the lesser of 120 days or the comparable adult term. Kentucky has created three age levels of younger than 14, 14–15, and 16 and older who can be sentenced to 35, 45, and 90 days of detention, respectively.

45. New York emphasizes that the detention of one year must occur in a nonsecure setting. Within this range are maximums of 15 days (NM), 30 days (MI, OR, UT, WI), 45 days (CO), 60 days (NJ), 90 days (AR, GA, MS, SD), and 180 days (WY).

46. Arizona is the only state to focus on DUI. A first adjudication for this offense ends in 24 hours of detention, while a second adjudication guarantees 30 days; an aggravated DUI means a minimum detention stay of 4 months, which is doubled for those with a prior record. Alabama and Michigan have responded seriously to offenses committed by youth armed with a firearm. In Alabama, a felony of this nature converts the youth into a serious juvenile offender, triggering a minimum commitment of one year in a secure facility. Thus, although Alabama refers to this disposition as one involving detention, it is perhaps more closely related to a regular commitment to a facility that is not a detention center per se. Michigan allows detention sentences in these cases to be guided by the criminal code (or adult sentence). Finally, possession of a gun has attracted the attention of five states. While Arkansas allows a maximum detention order of 90 days, Colorado and Washington call for *minimum* stays in detention of 5 and 10 days, respectively, for this offense. Similarly, Massachusetts demands a *minimum* of 6 months in detention for a first adjudication and double that minimum time for a second adjudication, while Georgia mandates not

more than one year for a first adjudication and somewhere between one and three years for a second adjudication (as with Alabama, this latter sentence might be a regular commitment rather than a detention sentence).

47. Sex offenders are required to register in: AZ, IN, MA, MI, MN, MT, NC, WA, WI.
48. HIV tests are required in: AZ, DE, GA, IN, KY, MS, NJ, NY, OR, TX, UT.
49. DNA testing can be ordered in: IL, MI, MN, OR, VA, WI.
50. Intensive probation is identified as a sentence in: AZ, CO, CT, GA, NC, VA, WA, WI.
51. Colorado and Indiana typically authorize placements at the age of 12, but certain serious offenses can lower the qualifying age to 10. Similarly, Nebraska had established a minimum age of 12 unless a murder, manslaughter, or violation of probation (VOP) is involved, in which case no minimum age is specified. In New Jersey the minimum age is 11 unless arson or a first- or second-degree crime is involved, for which there is no minimum age.
52. Placement of status offenders with delinquents is prohibited in: AK, AR, DC, HI, IN, MD, NE, NJ, NM, NY, TN.
53. Placement of status offenders in secure facilities or detention is prohibited in: CO, ID, KY, MT, NH, NM, ND, OH, OK, UT, WA, WV, WI.
54. Placement of status offenders in a DOC facility is prohibited in: AZ, IL, IN, LA, OR.
55. Commitment of status offenders to a training school or to certain state agencies is prohibited in: CA, IA, MA, MS, MT, NV, ND, OK, SD, TX, VA, WY.
56. Status offenders can be placed with delinquents for a violation of probation or a court order in: AR, CT, DC, HI, ID, IN, KS, LA, NE, NH, NC, SC, SD, TX, UT, VA, WA, WI.
57. While YSCs with different security levels exist in AL, AK, CO, FL, IL, MD, MI, and OK, YSCs with multiple security levels exist in AK, LA, and OK.
58. Facilities called schools that are at medium or maximum exist in: CT, DE, MD, MA, NM, OH, WA, WI, WY.
59. These prerequisites for serious commitments are required in: AL, AR, CA, ID, IN, IA, KS, KY, ME, NE, NV, NJ, OK, OR, PA, TX, VA, WI.
60. For example, limits for status offense commitments have been identified as 6 months (MA, WA), 1 year (WI, WY), 18 months (KS, NY), 2 years (AK, GA, NM, ND), or 3 years (HI, MD).
61. States that use a violent offender category are: CO, IL, KS, NV, NC, OK, TX.
62. States that use a serious or aggravated offender identity are: AL, AR, CO, CT, FL, KS, NV, NC, OK, PA, VA, WI.
63. States that have adopted a habitual or repeat offender category are: AZ, CO, CT, FL, IL, KS, NV, OK, TX.
64. The eight states are: AR, DE, IL, KS, MN, MT, NH, NC.
65. Sentences can be extended one (KY, NC, OK, VT), two (MI), three (FL), or four years (DE, MA, NH, NC).
66. Short mandatory commitments are possible for gun possession (AR, GA, MA), sex offenses (KY), auto theft (FL), DUI (AZ), or crimes committed with a gun (AL, MI).
67. Similarly, in the federal jurisdiction, crimes less serious than a Class C felony have a potential three-year commitment sentence, and crimes above that level are punishable by five years of commitment. Indiana provides for commitment to the age of 18 for murder and four other serious crimes, and a potential two-year disposition for less serious felonies.
68. The eight states are: AZ, AR, CA, LA, NJ, OH, OK, WA.
69. See, for example, *B.J. v. State*, 937 S.W.2d 675 (AR. App. 2 Div. 1997); *In re Jovan B.*, 25 Cal.Rptr.2d 428 (CA. 1993); *In re Tameka C.*, 91 Cal.Rptr.2d 730 (CA. 2000).
70. See, for example, *State in Interest of T.L.V.*, 643 So.2d 690 (LA. App. 2 Cir. 1994); *State in Interest of J.L.A.*, 643 A.2d 538 (N.J. 1994).
71. The nine states are: AK, AR, CT, IL, KS, MA, MN, MT, OH.
72. The 14 jurisdictions are: DC, HI, ID, IA, MD, MS, MO, NE, ND, SC, SD, UT, VT, WV.
73. For example, drug and alcohol offenses must result in either revocation or postponement of a driver's license (IN, MD, MN, NV, TX, UT, VA, WA, WI) and/or in community service (CA, TX, UT, and WI, which also mandates a fine) in 10 states. Seven states mandate the license loss (AZ, DE, ME, MS, TX, VA), community service (AZ, GA, VA), or a fine (AZ, GA) for DUI adjudications. Similarly, seven states will take a driver's license (MA, MN, NV, OH, VA), impose community service (IL, MN, NV), or levy a fine (GA) for gun possession or use. Otherwise, the driver's license penalty will result from a graffiti (NV, TX) or driving without a license (DE) adjudication, while mandatory community service will be imposed for graffiti (IL, NM), auto theft (FL, NJ), eluding police (NJ), battery at school (CA), a public transit crime (CA), any gang-related crime (IL), or in *all* adjudications (DC, TX) in some locations. Three states have mandated restitution for graffiti (NV) or in *all* adjudications (AZ, WA).
74. New Jersey rewards a second adjudication of auto theft with a mandatory 30 days, which rises to 60 days if anyone is injured as a result of the offense or if there is an adjudication for eluding the police with a similarly serious injury. Arizona responds to a first and second adjudication for DUI with mandatory de-

tention periods of 1 and 30 days, respectively. California recently (1999) mandated commitment when a youth is adjudicated for committing a violent offense with a firearm, but did not specify any length of time.

75. Kentucky and Wisconsin phrase the disposition as the *jurisdiction* over the youth lasting until a certain age, without stating that the entire period must involve commitment. Louisiana's secure commitment to the age of 21 also applies to those who commit aggravated rape, kidnapping, armed robbery, and treason. Michigan commits any youth adjudicated of committing an offense with a firearm to the length of time identified in the state's penal code for adult offenders. Finally, Washington provides that youth adjudicated of having a firearm and committing any crime for which the guidelines call for more than 30 days' confinement will require the juvenile court judge to impose the standard range of the sentencing guidelines. Moreover, being armed will also result in an extended sentence of two, four, or six months (for Class C, B, and A crimes, respectively), which must be served consecutively to the standard range disposition. This can mean several years of institutionalization, depending on the severity or category of the crime.

76. The 13 states are: AL, AZ, CO, DE, GA, IL, KY, LA, MA, MI, NJ, NY, WA.

77. This is the case in Colorado, Connecticut, the District of Columbia, and Missouri. In Colorado this authorization has been limited to repeat and violent offenders, while in Connecticut it is aimed at serious offenders. Nevertheless, Indiana and Montana permit the judge to place the child minimally to the age of 18. In Indiana this sentence is reserved for youth between the ages of 13 and 16 who are adjudicated of murder, rape, kidnapping, criminal deviant conduct, or armed robbery. Similarly, juveniles adjudicated of murder and aggravated murder in Montana can be given a minimum commitment sentence to the age of 21.

78. The several felonies in Indiana include any personal felony, Class A and B drug felonies, and Class A and B burglary felonies; Indiana also require two previous felony adjudications to qualify for this minimum commitment. Indiana is the only state that associates a minimum age (14) with these potential minimum sentences. In Ohio, aggravated robbery and arson also merit the minimum sentence of 1 to 3 years.

79. Minimum stays in boot camps can be for two months (CO, FL if low risk), three months (TX, WY), or four months (FL if moderate risk, WA). ✦

Chapter 15

Postdisposition Hearings and Matters in Juvenile Court

Focus of Chapter 15

As with criminal court, juvenile justice experiences a number of postadjudication hearings that can prove to be critical, such as that involved in the right to an appeal. Unlike criminal court, however, juvenile court relies on a rather elaborate postadjudication process to fine-tune the disposition. Once a sentence is given in adult court, it is considered final. The sentence can be appealed, but that maneuver is usually unsuccessful for the defendant, especially if the sentence is neither a capital nor a lengthy one. In juvenile court, on the other hand, a disposition is supposed to further the child's treatment interests and is not considered final simply because it was handed down by a judge. The juvenile disposition is readily available for adjustment if the original sentence turns out to be inconsistent with the youth's treatment needs. This chapter explores this rather unique and important but typically ignored aspect of juvenile court.

Key Terms

- aftercare
- appeal
- bootstrapping
- early release
- intermediate sanctions
- mandatory public disclosure

- modification hearing
- parole
- review hearing
- sealing and expunging records
- violation of probation (VOP) hearing

The Right to Appeal

Immediately upon adjudication, a few states will allow youth to appeal their adjudication (KS, OK, SD, TX). The more common policy, however, is to require a disposition to be delivered before appeal is possible.[1] Although the right to appeal an adjudication and disposition is certainly respected everywhere, some states have no provision in their juvenile code (MD, ND, PA, VT, WI), while others bury the provision in a section on rights in general or at sentencing (AK, CT, IL, OH, OK). New Jersey simply asserts that juveniles have the same statutory and constitutional rights as adults. The remaining jurisdictions have a separate section dealing with the right to appeal, including Arizona, which has a detailed procedure and policy. Maine even lists three goals of juvenile appeals:

- To correct errors in the application and interpretation of the law

- To insure substantial uniformity of treatment to persons in like situations

- To provide for review of juvenile court decisions so that the legislatively defined purposes of the juvenile justice system as a whole are realized

Obviously, the juvenile can appeal an adverse order. Unique to the juvenile court is the permission for *any aggrieved party* to appeal.[2] This suggests parents would have standing to appeal an adjudication or disposition of their children, particularly (but not only) if they were to lose custody of them. Some states specifically identify parents as having a right to appeal.[3] Although Alabama prohibits the state from appealing rulings of the juvenile court, other jurisdictions have granted the state the same appellate rights as exist in criminal court. Many statutes identify specific situations in which the state can appeal in juvenile court. These situations include a motion to suppress (CA, MO, NY, OR), a modification of disposition (AK, CA, DE), vacating an adjudication (AK, CA, DE, OR), a dismissal of a case before jeopardy attaches (CA, DE, FL, KS, NY, OR), an unlawful disposition (CA, DE, FL, NY), an invalid construction or interpretation of a statute (DE), an order granting a new trial (DE, FL), and a denial of a transfer petition.[4]

Juveniles should be allowed to appeal their adjudications and dispositions, as well as modifications of dispositions and revocations of probation and parole. Transfer to adult court is also an appealable matter. While some states permit youth to challenge the transfer immediately,[5] others force the youth to wait until after conviction in adult court (CA, CO, TN). A judge's decision to transfer a case is usually reversed only if discretion was abused or the decision was clearly erroneous.[6] Moreover, several states hold that a guilty plea by a youth in criminal court in effect erases any previous defects in the transfer process.[7] However other jurisdictions will still

Appeals of juvenile court adjudications are relatively rare. What effect does this have on the juvenile court process?

allow an appeal despite the juvenile's guilty plea in criminal court.[8] Kansas grants appeals concerning *departure sentences* via sentencing guidelines (i.e., the judge selects a sentence beyond that which appears to "fit" the youth's situation), and Washington similarly authorizes appeals when dispositions fall outside the standard range of the guidelines.

Many jurisdictions place a time limit on the youth's ability to file an appeal, the most popular of which is 30 days.[9] Nevertheless, the deadline can be as soon as from 5 to 20 days.[10] Massachusetts simply uses the term *forthwith*. Juveniles' rights at appeal are rarely identified but should include, if anything, a right to counsel (HI, ME, TX), a right to present evidence (HI, KS, MS), and a right to secure a transcript of the proceeding they are appealing.[11]

Most often the appeal is *on the record,* meaning the issues considered are limited to the record compiled in the challenged juvenile court proceeding.[12] A few states call for a *de novo appeal,* indicating that matters can be freshly contested on the appellate level (AL, OR, TN). Most jurisdictions also note that an appeal does not stay or suspend the execution of the juvenile court order, but that the appellate court may allow the appeal to have that effect.[13]

Perhaps the most important aspect of appeals of decisions made in juvenile court is that they are rare when compared to those of adult court. Whereas virtually all criminal court convictions are appealed (especially if there has not been a guilty plea), the opposite is true in the juvenile system. A number of potential factors can contribute to this situation:

- Guardian defense attorneys

- Relatively lenient adjudications and dispositions (or at least the perception of this)

- Disproportionate number of burned-out and incompetent defense attorneys

- Court orders that expire before the appellate process would reach a decision

- Youth and/or parents not aware of or not interested in pursuing (or paying for) an appeal

An important result of this relative dearth of juvenile appeals is that the day-to-day operation of the juvenile court and of the decisions made there receive little appellate court (or outside) scrutiny.

Postdispositional Hearings

Even after juveniles are adjudicated and are serving a sentence, on aftercare, or under parole supervision, they are subject to a variety of hearings in juvenile court. Unique to juvenile court is the review hearing, whose primary purpose is to determine the youth's progress in the disposition. Also possible is a modification hearing in which, like adult offenders, youths (or their families) can request the court to modify, reduce, or even terminate the terms of the disposition order. The person or agency supervising the youth can petition the court seeking to modify or terminate as well. Unlike adult court, however, juvenile court permits the state (i.e., the prosecutor, PO, or juvenile department) to request a modification of the disposition that actually increases its harshness (such as from probation to commitment, or from one level to a higher level of placement) or *extends* its length (such as adding a year or two to the sentence) simply because the youth's rehabilitation (or perhaps the public's protection) needs a change of setting or additional time. Finally, like criminal court, juvenile court provides a violation of probation (VOP) hearing to determine whether a *violation of probation or parole* has occurred and what, if any, penalties should be imposed on the youth as a result of this violation.

How juvenile courts approach these three inquiries (review, modification, and VOP) varies considerably and can be confusing. Although some states clearly demarcate the three areas, devoting a hearing specifically to each (CO, MI, OK), in some jurisdictions it appears possible to combine the inquiries, especially reviews and modifications. Doing so makes sense, inasmuch as a poor review of the youth's disposition could easily call for its modification. Moreover, if a youth is saddled with a VOP charge, it would be logical for a VOP hearing to serve the purposes of all three inquiries (Did the youth violate probation? How is the youth doing on probation, otherwise? Does the probation order need to be modified?). Despite the obvious overlap, we will examine the three inquiries separately.

Review Hearings

The review hearing is a natural complement to the disposition hearing. Whereas the latter determined what the youth needed in terms of rehabilitation, the former determines whether the original assessment was accurate. Specifically, the review process is geared to analyze any or all of the following:

- The continuing necessity for the disposition
- The youth's compliance with the disposition order
- Services offered the youth and family
- The youth's (and parents') progress in treatment
- The parents' efforts to correct any problems
- Efforts made to unify the youth with the parents
- Prognosis for the youth's return home

Considering the potential importance of this inquiry, statutory provisions vary widely regarding the review process in juvenile court. Five jurisdictions have no provision in this area (DE, FED, HI, MT, NJ). Hawaii only mentions a postdisposition review hearing and a right to counsel at that proceeding, and New Jersey has only a detention review hearing (see Chapter 10). Even jurisdictions with review hearings are somewhat prone to limit them to only delinquency cases[14] or to only status offense cases (AZ, MA, NV, NM, TN). In some states (RI, TN, WI) only foster care or permanency review hearings are identified, which might apply to both delinquents and status offenders. Of course, juvenile courts in these locations may not need official statutory authorization per se to demand a review of juveniles under a disposition order in their jurisdiction. In addition to the lack of statutory provisions, many statutes indicate that reviews may be *discretionary* on the court's part, especially if probation is the disposition (CO, FL, ID, VA), but also when the youth has been committed as well (CT, DC, SD). Even when reviews are *mandatory* they can

Review hearings are usually conducted in small rooms. Is it to a juvenile's advantage or disadvantage to have a review hearing?

be seriously limited to apply only to commitments,[15] or only to some commitments,[16] to parole (OH, SC, WV), or to sex offenders (FL, KY, WA). In the end, only nine states require across-the-board reviews for all juvenile court dispositions.[17] Also, in the review context, a number of states require a *permanency placement hearing*, primarily for youths (delinquent and status offenders) who have been placed in foster care.[18]

The time frames within which at least the initial review must occur vary as well, mostly ranging from 3 to 18 months. Some states simply use terms such as *periodically* (CO, FL, MD, ND) or don't specify a time frame at all (ID, UT). Some states have two time frames, depending on whether the disposition is probation or commitment. Although failure to hold the review hearing within the deadline should not lead to the release of the youth (from probation or institutionalization), it could provide the youth with grounds to file a petition challenging continued confinement (ID).

Unique to the juvenile system is that even when youths are sentenced to commitment in a facility, they may be assigned to POs' caseloads in order to monitor their progress in rehabilitation programs (ME, NE, SC). POs in some states operate some commitment facilities as well (CA, KS, NV, SC). Also, JPOs can be obligated to report to the court on all measures taken with youth on probation and how they did in various treatment programs.[19]

The nature of the review process also varies. What should be fairly standard is that the PO or the institutional caseworker is responsible for drafting a report that addresses the relevant topics. A number of states provide that these reports must be made available to the juveniles, who are typically allowed to submit their own reports.[20] These reviews are usually pro forma (i.e., simply reporting what had been done thus far and how well the youth is doing) and do not recommend any changes in the youth's status. The pro forma review could easily require no more process than the mere filing of the report (AK, IL, KY, LA, OH, WY). That is, there is no legal need for a formal court hearing to implement the recommendation contained in a pro forma review.

A hearing of some sort is more likely to be required when the review proposes a *de-escalation* in the court's hold on the youth via recommendations to eliminate some or all conditions of probation, terminate placement, or terminate court supervision or jurisdiction altogether. This hearing gives the state an opportunity to object to any such de-escalation. Nevertheless, many states continue to emphasize that the court can terminate its jurisdiction at any time, usually provided that the rehabilitation mission has been accomplished.[21]

One unique aspect of the juvenile system's parole or early release of a juvenile inmate (or the de-escalation of a commitment sentence) is the extent to which the juvenile court judge serves as *the* decision maker in this situation. Unlike in the adult system, where this decision typically occurs within the confines of the correctional system (i.e., through a parole hearing), juvenile justice frequently vests this authority in the judge or divides it between the correctional agency and the judge. Thus, in some states (AR, CA, FL, OK, SC), juvenile court judges can recommend or even order the release of a youthful inmate. Similarly, some states (AL, FL, MS, NC, SD, WY) require juvenile facilities to notify the court of an impending release or actually to secure the court's approval before releasing at least some juvenile offenders.[22] Consequently, a court review or parole hearing is likely to precede the placing of youth on aftercare status.

A review also definitely ceases to be pro forma when the recommendation involves an *escalation* in the court's hold on the youth, with potential changes such as:

- adding conditions to probation;
- increasing the intensity of probation supervision;
- moving from probation to institutionalization;
- increasing the level of incarceration; and/or
- extending the duration of the court's jurisdiction.

This is a situation in which a review hearing merges with a modification hearing and some of the statutory confusion begins. In some jurisdictions, although it is not clearly stated, changes that would escalate the court's control of the youth may automatically trigger the convening of a modification hearing (rather than a review hearing) with its greater protections. Within the context of the review process, only a handful of states officially provide rights such as notice of review,[23] counsel (MI, OK), or a hearing itself,[24] while Alaska, Michigan, and North Dakota appear to require a hearing only when the review calls for incarceration or for increasing the system's control of the youth.

Modification Hearings

Modification of disposition orders has caught more of the legislatures' attention than the review process has, although a number of jurisdictions (AZ, DE, FED, MA, MT, NV) appear to have no provision in this area. Most statutes list three sources who can seek to modify the sentence: the youth and parent,[25] the prosecutor and supervising agent,[26] and the juvenile court judge.[27]

Provisions for modifying the disposition do not tend to differ for delinquents vis-à-vis status offenders, with the exception of those in California. In that state only POs are authorized to pursue modification on behalf of the state in status offense cases, whereas prosecutors are also permitted to do so in delinquency cases.

Obviously, modification can work to either escalate or de-escalate the original disposition. The youth (or his or her parents) would most likely seek to de-escalate the sentence. Sometimes the supervising agent will seek the same. One reason to de-escalate the disposition order is to claim that the sentence was unduly severe (as in adult court). The North Carolina statute has identified factors for the juvenile court judge to consider when this claim is made:

- Seriousness of the offense

- Culpability of the youth

- Dispositions given to similar offenders (7B-2600)

Otherwise, statutes usually require the party seeking de-escalation to demonstrate that a "significant change of circumstances" has occurred that warrants a reduction or termination of the court's supervision. Serious advances made by the juvenile with respect to attitude change, payment of restitution, and successful completion of school, vocational, or treatment programs would be examples of what could constitute a significant change.

On the other hand, parties seeking to escalate or to extend the disposition order must prove that the conditions or setting of the original sentence were insufficient or inappropriate (and need to be modified) or that the initial time allowance was inadequate to achieve rehabilitation of the youth or protection of society (and needs to be extended). Statutes might use the "substantial change of circumstances" language in this context too. The level of proof required of the party desiring escalation is not usually identified, but Iowa, Minnesota, and Rhode Island specify that *clear and convincing* proof is the burden, while Indiana declares that this party must prove that the objectives of the disposition order have not been accomplished but that continuing the order has a *probability of success.* California requires a *supplemental petition* that alleges *facts sufficient to support the conclusion* that the previous disposition has not been effective in rehabilitating the youth. Many states do provide youths with a right to a modification hearing,[28] especially if a more restrictive disposition or removal from the home will occur. In fact, Mississippi, New Mexico, and Vermont equate this proceeding with an adjudicatory hearing. Beyond the hearing itself, nevertheless, relatively few statutes detail rights such as the right to notice,[29] the right to counsel (AK, MI, OK, TX), the right to be heard or present evidence (GA, MI, NY, ND, OK, WI), or the right to confront and cross-examine witnesses (NY, OK) that must be granted youth at a modification hearing.

A legislature's failure to mention these basic rights does not necessarily mean that juveniles are deprived of these rights when dispositions are indeed modified. Two realities probably contribute to the absence of legislation in this area. The first is juvenile court's historical aversion to defendants' rights. The second is that escalating the disposition order could be regarded by legislatures and appellate courts as simply enabling juvenile courts to do now what they could have done legally in the first place. That is, modifying the disposition so as to *increase* the supervisory aspect of the sentence entails merely placing constraints on the youth that are no more severe than what could have been implemented at the disposition hearing (especially since there are so few restraints on a judge's discretion while sentencing juveniles). Even youth whose modification requires a move from a probationary sentence to a commitment sentence end up no worse off than they could have been from the start. To be sure, an adult offender subject to such a modification would be guaranteed (minimally) counsel and a hearing with the right to both present and refute evidence, but that is because adults have a liberty interest that does not so clearly apply to juveniles (remember *Schall v. Martin* from Chapter 10). Moreover, adults would not experience such adjustments or modifications of sentence in the absence of either a new offense or a violation of probation. Nevertheless, with juveniles "new infractions" have never been a prerequisite for modifying the disposition.

The same logic applies to extending the length of the disposition. A number of states specify that extensions of either probation or commitment can occur in increments usually between 12 and 24 months.[30] However, none of these states (or those that don't mention extension lengths) permit the ultimate sentence to persist beyond either the maximum disposition that could have been imposed from the beginning or the regular or extended maximum age of juvenile court jurisdiction. Arguably, eliminating or hampering the juvenile court's modification process could work to the disadvantage of many youths, since the temptation would exist to sentence more juveniles closer to or at the maximum disposition to guarantee the system's ability to hold onto these offenders for as long as is believed necessary (much like the adult system does in some cases). Nevertheless, it would be interesting to see the U.S. Supreme Court's response to an appeal by a youth whose disposition had been escalated or extended without one or more of the basic due process rights.

Violation of Probation/Parole (VOP) Hearings

Juvenile court proceedings surrounding VOPs have been spelled out in the statutes in greater detail than those for review or modification hearings. This may be because VOPs have a parallel and prominent existence in criminal court and because the U.S. Supreme Court has extended adult offenders certain due process protections in this context (see *Mempa v. Rhay* 1967). Both Maine and Washington announce that juveniles and adults are entitled to the same due process at this stage. Whether the Supreme Court would demand as much is unclear. Nevertheless, many other jurisdictions have identified a number of rights juveniles have at a VOP hearing. These rights include a hearing,[31] counsel,[32] notice of charges,[33] confrontation and cross-examination,[34] to present evidence and to be heard,[35] protection against self-incrimination,[36] speedy hearing,[37] compulsory process,[38] and presenting witnesses.[39]

Moreover, six states have indicated that the VOP proceeding is supposed to be equal to an adjudicatory hearing (KS, MS, NM, TN, VA, WY), while California and Nebraska provide the same if a new offense is the basis of the VOP. Minimally, any juvenile facing a VOP charge is likely to be given a hearing, notice of charges, the protection against self-incrimination, the ability to be heard and present evidence, and, if the result could be (re)institutionalization, counsel as well. While some states indicate that VOP proceedings are the same for delinquents and status offenders,[40] there could be subtle differences, such as giving the status offender a guardian *ad litem* instead of regular defense counsel (KS).

Serious differences can exist between the VOP proceeding and the adjudicatory hearing. There easily could be less in the way of due process in VOP hearings (which is true for the adult system as well), especially if a new offense and adjudication are not the basis of the VOP. For example, the right to confront and cross-examine witnesses may not always be respected at a VOP hearing, as is mentioned in some statutes (MN, SD, UT). Similarly, the defendant's right to compulsory process can be denied during a VOP proceeding, and trial-like rules of evidence are unlikely to be observed there. In fact, Arizona and Nebraska allow the admission of all reliable evidence. Finally, the level of proof required to find a VOP is typically less than that needed to adjudicate, although at least three states insist on proof beyond a reasonable doubt in both situations (CO, GA, NM). It is much more common for jurisdictions to demand less evidence when a VOP is alleged. Thus, either *clear and convincing* (AL, MN, WV) or even a mere *preponderance of evidence*[41] is often cited as the required standard of proof for VOPs. Again, this is similar to adult VOP proceedings. The rationale for less due process at a VOP hearing is twofold: The rights detailed in the Constitution are linked specifically with criminal charges and trials rather than with VOP hearings, and not only have defendants already been provided these rights at trial but the liberty that might be taken from them at this point (i.e., postconviction) is only conditional (because these offenders could have been put away and not given probation in the first place or could have been denied parole or early release).

Juveniles found to have violated probation or parole face a variety of consequences. Comparatively speaking, the consequences are steeper for status offenders found to have violated probation, supervision, or a court order. In some states these individuals are now considered delinquents.[42] Moreover, a VOP adjudication also can result in status offenders experiencing restrictive or delinquent placements and even detention, although usually only for brief periods of time.[43] This conversion of a status offender into a delinquent is referred to as bootstrapping, a topic we address again in Chapter 16. If a new adjudication for a delinquent offense has occurred, all the options regularly available at a disposition hearing for such offenses are within the judge's discretion to impose at this time. When the terms or conditions of probation or parole have been violated, most states simply announce that the original disposition order can be "enlarged, extended, or modified,"[44] while parolees face the prospect of returning to a facility to complete the sentence (ID, WA, WI) or adjustments to the terms of their parole. Louisiana has spelled out the potential consequences for a probation violation in detail:

- Reprimand and warn the child

- Order that the supervision be intensified

- Impose additional conditions to the probation

- Extend the period of probation

- Order the probation be revoked and execute the suspended sentence (LA Childrens' Code, Art. 914)

The last provision, which other states also endorse (CA, ID, WA, WI), underscores just how serious the sanctions attending a violation of probation can be. Revocation of probation means an end to the period of conditional liberty and the beginning of some form of institutionalization. Similarly, other jurisdictions identify various periods of detention that can follow a VOP determination,[45] including jail time (CO, KS, NV). In fact, Louisiana and Washington provide that the illegal possession of a firearm mandates a probation revocation or parole modification, respectively, and a period of incarceration as well. Level-oriented states, such as North Carolina and Wyoming, specify that those who violate probation can climb one sanction level by virtue of that violation. At a minimum, VOP juveniles who remain on probation will likely experience additional conditions or responsibilities to remain in the community. Illinois and Wisconsin have adopted and promoted the idea of structured, intermediate sanctions, which simultaneously increase the penalties for a VOP while avoiding the hardships and costs of institutionalization.

Juvenile-Adult Court Reviews

A new special breed of review/VOP hearings has emerged as a result of the sentencing merger between juvenile and adult courts (see Chapters 12 and 14). In the previous chapter we discussed the combination sentences imposed on youth that have been adjudicated on juvenile court's second tier, typically via an extended jurisdiction proceeding. That is, they are given a juvenile court disposition together with an adult court sentence that is stayed or suspended. Similarly, in Chapter 12 we saw that many states permit the adult court to impose a juvenile court disposition on some of the youths convicted in that forum (often as youthful offenders—YOs) and to suspend the criminal sentence to see how well the youth satisfies the conditions of the disposition. Most of these jurisdictions require a review hearing in juvenile court when the youth turns between 17 and 21 to assess his or her progress and rehabilitation.[46] The juvenile court can also hold a series of the hearings at various stages (MI, MO, VT) or the adult court (FL, IA, WV) may have the authority to review the youth's disposition in this context.

The stakes inherent in this review make it fundamentally different than the traditional pro forma review of the youth's juvenile court disposition. Frequently at issue is whether or not the juvenile will end up with a criminal court conviction or sentence. Thus far, some states (AR, VA) apparently have not developed any policy or procedure to address this question, while some others (KY, RI, MO) have simply identified the judge's options at this review, which include:

- discharge of the defendant from probation or commitment;
- continuation of probation or commitment;
- release on parole or aftercare; and
- refer to the adult system (i.e., to DOC).

A few states (IA, MI, OK, VT), however, have proceeded beyond merely acknowledging these options and have implemented a new and major decision-making stage for juvenile court, complete with transfer to criminal court–like criteria for the judge to use in conducting this review. Michigan provides the most detail in disclosing what the judge should consider or review:

- Youth's participation in education, counseling, and work programs
- Youth's willingness to accept responsibility
- Youth's behavior in placement
- Youth's prior record, character, and physical and mental maturity
- Youth's potential for violent conduct
- Recommendation by the institution
- Other information submitted by the prosecutor or youth

The juvenile commonly has the burden to prove (typically by a preponderance of the evidence) that he or she has indeed been rehabilitated and will not present a serious risk to public safety (MI, RI, VT).

VOP hearings are also significant for youth who have been given a combined juvenile court–criminal court sentence by either court. Simply put, a sustained VOP can result in the imposition of the original, stayed criminal court sentence, together with a criminal court conviction.[47] In fact, Michigan insists on this result if the youth is adjudicated or convicted of either a felony or a misdemeanor that calls for more than one year of incarceration. Moreover, this youth would not be given any credit for time served on probation preceding the adjudication or conviction.

Although juveniles should not experience any more hearings regarding their liability for the offense that brought them to the juvenile court's attention, there are other issues concerning the court record that result from an adjudication, one element of which involves another hearing in juvenile court.

The Nonconfidential Juvenile Court Record

Contrary to the old days when a juvenile court record was discoverable only through somewhat extraordinary means, the situation today is that the youth's adjudication is likely to become well known without much, if any, effort on the part of the curious.

Tell the Public

Historically, juvenile court records were open to public inspection (i.e., by someone other than court workers or parties to the case) only upon court order. Today a court order is still necessary to open these records in some situations, but it is not necessary in many situations. As a general rule, juvenile arrest and court records tend to be open to the public if the adjudicatory hearing itself was open (see Chapter 13)[48] and/or if the youth was transferred to adult court.[49] If public safety is an issue and the police need help apprehending the youth, his or her records are also prone to public exposure.[50] More important, however, juvenile justice policy today has mandated that the juvenile court *shall release* or that the public *shall have access* to youths' court records in several situations. This mandatory disclosure involves arrest,[51] charging,[52] detention (IN), any escapes,[53] diversion of the case (AK, WV), transfer to adult court,[54] adjudication,[55] and any VOP (CO, ID).

Although most states that publicize the youth's records wait until an adjudication has occurred, this is certainly not a universal feature. Similarly, while some states mention a minimum age (such as 12, 13, or 14) for the youth's records to become a public document,[56] many of these states remove the requirement and permit disclosure of the records in serious and chronic cases,[57] and other states have no age requirement whatsoever.[58] Once again, some of these jurisdictions link the mandatory disclosure to only or mostly cases of violence,[59] weapons,[60] murder,[61] drugs (AK, IL, WV), or sexual assault,[62] many also require the record of any offense,[63] any felony,[64] any second arrest or adjudication (AK, GA, HI, MS, OK, WI), any third felony charge (MA), or any gang-related incident (IL) to result in public disclosure.

A few of these jurisdictions have provided escape clauses to the mandatory public disclosure. For example, for some very young defendants, juvenile court judges in some states (KS, ID, UT, VA) are allowed to block disclosure (and perhaps to close the adjudicatory hearing as well) if that would be in the youth's best interests. Similarly, the New Jersey statute permits its juvenile court judges to stop disclosure if the youth can demonstrate a "substantial likelihood that specific and extraordinary harm would result from such disclosure" (2A:4A-60). Alaska allows the same, provided the crime is an isolated incident, the defendant is considered not to pose a danger to the community, or the victim agrees.

Not all public disclosure of juvenile court records is mandatory. Several states permit the juvenile court judge to decide whether to release the youth's name and record (and perhaps prints and photos as well) in certain contexts.[65] Some states have both mandatory and discretionary disclosure, depending on the situation involved.[66] Even the discretionary disclosure can require a minimum age of 12 or 13 in certain situations (DE, NH); for a serious, violent, or weapons-related offense (CT, LA, NH, SC, VA); or for a chronic offender (LA, NV, NH, ND). Statutes rarely address the public nature of status offense records, but at least two states (IN, MO) prohibit public disclosure in this regard.

Tell the School

The public is not the only entity to which youths' court records must be disclosed. The school has also been mandated to receive information concerning the youth's records in various contexts, including arrest,[67] charging,[68] transfer to adult court (NC, OR), dismissal of the petition (NC), adjudication,[69] modification or vacation of adjudication (NC), disposition,[70] probation sentences,[71] and releases from facilities.[72]

Although none of the statutes that mandate record disclosure to the school links the disclosure with an age requirement, many states limit the information to cases involving violence or murder,[73] weapons,[74] drugs,[75] serious felonies,[76] or sex-related offenses.[77] Nevertheless, in some cases, no offense requirement is identified[78] or perhaps only a felony,[79] second adjudication (MT), or any school-related offense (CA, MN, NJ, OH, SC).[80]

The origin of the information can range from the police to the prosecutor to POs and judges. The recipient is usually the superintendent of the school district or the school principal, but it can be a teacher. To ensure that all necessary parties receive this information, a number of states insist that the superintendent and principal share all record information with all teachers or supervisors who will come into contact with the affected youth,[81] along with SROs (AR), other students (VA), and even bus drivers (WV). To ensure follow-through, statutes are beginning to demand that the youth's move to a new school means the school officials must be informed about their new pupil.[82]

Disclosure to the school also can be discretionary on the court's part (ND, TN), often in situations where the offense was less serious than that which mandates disclosure (MN, OR). Statutes may also specify that police (AK, CA, IL, VA, WA, WI), prosecutors (AL, WA), intake (KS), or the PO (MO) may inform the school of events surrounding juvenile offenders. In this regard, Alaska has directed law enforcement to work with *all* schools to develop procedures for the disclosure of information and to ensure that the information arrives there as soon as possible. Finally, some statutes continue to reflect the more traditional position that schools have a right of access to court records regarding any of their pupils,[83] putting the discovery burden on the school.

Disclosure of status offense records to the school has not yet received much attention in the statutes. While Alaska and New Jersey permit such disclosure, Montana prohibits it.

Sealing and Expunging Juvenile Court Records

Like adult court, juvenile court provides for sealing and expunging records of offenders adjudicated there. But, consistent with other developments in the current "get-tough" era, neutralizing juvenile court records is becoming increasingly more difficult. If the prosecution does not result in an adjudication (or some other arrangement where the court has supervision over the child), statutes tend to provide for the immediate destruction of court records.[84] For those who come under the control of the court, sealing the record becomes possible for most youth at a certain age or when a certain amount of time has passed since either the adjudication or the disposition was completed or the jurisdiction over the youth expired. Thus, for a youth to petition the court for sealing or expungement, usually one to ten years must have transpired since the juvenile had to answer to the system.[85] Otherwise, the youth must be between 16 and 38 years of age to petition the court.[86]

A number of states have two,[87] three (CO), or four (WA) levels, which are usually associated with the severity of the record (i.e., offense severity) (e.g., CA, FL) or with the level of court process (i.e., diversion versus adjudication) (e.g., CO, MI). Sometimes the two ages refer to the requirements for sealing and expunging a record, with the older age being necessary to expunge or destroy a record (CA, OK). In addition, a number of states (ID, IL, WV) use both years and age to determine eligibility to seal a record. In these states the statute usually holds that the applicable provision is the one that would be later in time (e.g., ID, IL, WV).

Sealing a record means the adjudication never happened in many states.[88] Nevertheless, as we saw in Chapter 12, the juvenile court record can be used for sentencing in the juvenile or adult system if the youth commits another offense.[89] This use may be prevented by the passage of a certain number of years (OK) or if the individual attains a certain age (NV).

Sealing the juvenile court record is far from automatic today. For one thing, many jurisdictions require that the prosecutor be notified of the youth's petition to seal the records and be given an opportunity to protest or challenge the sealing of the record.[90] Moreover, most statutes insist that there have been no more adjudications or convictions and that none are pending,[91] that the youth cannot have been transferred to adult court (IA, TX, WV), and that the youth does not have a criminal court record.[92] Even more significant is that adjudication in juvenile court for certain offenses can disqualify the youth from sealing a record.[93]

The state may also require that to have their record sealed, youths must demonstrate that they have been rehabilitated[94] or held accountable (ID), that all terms of the dispositional order (e.g., restitution) have been fulfilled (AL, AZ, OK, SC, WA, WI), and/or that it is in their best interests (and not a threat to public safety).[95] North Carolina requires two nonrelated witnesses to testify as character witnesses for the youth, while the Indiana statute has identified several factors for the court to consider in record sealing situations.[96] Finally, if the youth is adjudicated or convicted after the court has sealed the juvenile court records, chances are the records will be unsealed (AL, DC, MT, NJ, NM, WA).

Status offenders are eligible to seal their records at an earlier time than that provided delinquents in some states, and procedures appear to be easier in some states (NC, OH, OK, SC).[97] Obviously, without a delinquent record that could call for disqualification, status offenders are less likely to be prevented from having their records sealed and expunged. Nevertheless, many jurisdictions do not seem to differentiate statutory provisions in the sealing and expunging area for both groups of youth.[98]

Even with sealed records, all is not necessarily forgotten (or forgiven) for juvenile offenders. We saw in Chapter 12 how dramatically a juvenile record can affect criminal court sentencing for youth that commit at least one more offense. Similarly, bail in adult court[99] and parole from prison[100] can be influenced by a juvenile court record. Although most jurisdictions prohibit the use of a juvenile court record to impeach the youth at a later time in criminal court,[101] some states have permitted this practice (AK, CT, IN, NC, OK, SC). Moreover, if the youth testifies to having a good character, some states would allow the juvenile record to act in rebuttal to that claim.[102] It is even more likely to be possible to impeach delinquent youth at a future time if they are witnesses called to testify against someone else.[103] In fact, the U.S. Supreme Court ruled in *Davis v. Alaska* (1974) that a defendant must be allowed to impeach the credibility of a state witness through cross-examination directed at the potential bias of the witness related to being on a probationary status.

Summary: Key Ideas and Concepts

- Very adjustable juvenile disposition
- Perhaps no appeal permitted until after disposition
- Any aggrieved party can appeal juvenile court orders
- State has a right to appeal certain rulings
- Perhaps no appeal of transfer to adult court until after conviction
- Guilty plea in adult court may eliminate right to appeal transfer
- Time limit on ability to appeal
- Uncertain status of defendant's rights at appeal
- Relatively few appeals of juvenile court orders
- Little scrutiny of juvenile court operations
- Unique review hearing to ascertain treatment progress
- Modification hearing that can "increase" juvenile disposition
- Multiple purposes of review hearing
- POs supervising inmates and operating facilities
- Prosecutors and other state officials can seek to enhance dispositions
- Early termination of disposition because of successful rehabilitation
- Juvenile court judge can be person who decides parole or aftercare
- Multiple ways to escalate a juvenile court disposition
- Multiple reasons to de-escalate a juvenile court disposition

- Uncertain status of rights at review and modification hearings
- Possible serious and varied consequences of a VOP finding
- VOPs converting a status offender into a delinquent
- The combined juvenile-adult court review and its significance
- A nonconfidential or public juvenile court record
- Release of juvenile court records to the public and to schools
- Increasing difficulty in sealing and expunging a juvenile court record

Discussion Questions

1. In what situations can the state appeal adverse rulings in juvenile court? Is it appropriate to let the state have a right to appeal? Why or why not?

2. Should parents have a right to appeal rulings concerning their children? Why or why not?

3. Should youth transferred to adult court be allowed immediate appeal or be forced to wait until after conviction in criminal court? Defend your answer.

4. What are the implications of so few appeals of juvenile court adjudications?

5. Are review/modification hearings appropriate? In other words, should the state (POs, prosecutors, correctional administrators) be allowed to keep going back to juvenile court until they get it right?

6. Should VOP hearings differ when the youth could end up having a criminal court conviction as a result?

7. Should status offenders be threatened with delinquent status when they violate probation or a court order?

8. Should juvenile court records be disclosed to the public or the school? If not, why not? If so, why and in what situations?

9. Should juveniles be allowed to seal and expunge their juvenile court records? If not, why not? If so, why and in what situations?

Endnotes

1. The states that require disposition before an appeal are: GA, IA, ME, MS, NY, NC, OR, TN, WY.
2. The states that allow any aggrieved party to appeal are: AL, CT, HI, IA, LA, MD, MA, MN, MT, NM, OR, VA, WA, WY.
3. The states that specify a parent's right to appeal are: AK, DE, FL, ME, MS, MO, NE.
4. The prosecution can appeal a denial of transfer in: AR, CA, FED, FL, HI, ID, IL, IA, KS, LA, ME, MN, ND, OK, SC, VA.
5. Youths can immediately appeal a transfer order in: AL, AR, FED, FL, GA, ID, LA, ME, MD, MI, MN, NM, NC, OK, PA, UT, VA, WV.
6. Abuse of discretion is required to reverse a transfer order in: AL, IL, IN, IA, LA, MD, MO, NC, PA, SD.
7. A guilty plea will have this effect in: AZ, ID, IA, MN, MO, NV, NM, NC, SD, TN.
8. Appeal is permitted despite a guilty plea in: MA, MI, ND, OH, OK, PA, WA.

9. Thirty days is the standard in: DE, IN, MN, MO, NH, OR, RI, TX, UT.
10. Identified limits in days are: 5 (ME), 10 (KS, MS, NC, TN, VA), 14 (AL), 15 (AZ, LA), and 20 (HI).
11. A transcript is guaranteed in: AZ, CA, DC, LA, RI, TX, WV, WY. The rules that apply to appeals of juvenile court orders can be criminal (NC, WA), civil (MN, NV, RI, SD, TX), chancery (AR), equity (OR), or appellate court (NM, SC, WY) rules of procedure.
12. The appeal is on the record in: DE, KS, ME, MT, NE, NM, NC, WA.
13. This policy is followed in: AL, DE, DC, FL, GA, HI, IA, LA, ME, MD, MA, MS, MO, MT, NH, NM, OR, RI, SC, TN, TX, UT, VA, WV.
14. Reviews are limited to delinquency matters in: CT, DC, ID, IN, KY, MD, NY, ND, OH, OR, SC, TX, UT.
15. Mandatory reviews apply to only commitments in: AR, CA, GA, ID, IL, IN, IA, KS, MD, MI, NE, OR, VT, WY.
16. Mandatory reviews apply to only some commitments in: AL, CO, CT, MO, NY, NC, UT.
17. All juvenile court dispositions must be reviewed in: AK, LA, ME, MD, MN, MS, NH, OK, PA.
18. Permanency placement hearings are required in: AL, AK, AR, CA, CO, IA, LA, MD, MI, MN, OK, PA, RI, TN, VT, VA, WI.
19. POs are obligated to do these reports in: AL, IL, IN, KY, ME, MO, NC, OH, TN, VA, WI.
20. Youth can submit their own reports in: AK, AR, CA, IN, ME, MD, MI, OK.
21. Successful rehabilitation can end the disposition in: AL, CA, FL, GA, IN, KY, MI, NV, NM, NY, ND, OK, SC, SD, UT, VT.
22. Judicial approval for release in needed in: FL, KS, NJ, OH, RI, TN, TX, VA.
23. Notice of review is required in: CO, GA, ME, MI, MO, NC, OR.
24. Notice of the hearing is required in: CA, CO, GA, IN, MO, NC, OK.
25. The youth and/or the parent can seek to modify the sentence in: AL, CA, CT, GA, IL, IA, KS, MS, MO, NJ, NM, NY, NC, OH, RI, SC, SD, TN, TX, UT, VT, WA, WV, WI.
26. The prosecutor and/or the supervising agent can seek to modify the sentence in: AL, AZ, CA, GA, IN, IA, KS, LA, MI, MO, MT, NY, NC, ND, OH, OK, OR, PA, RI, SD, TN, TX, UT, VT, VA, WA, WV, WI.
27. The judge can seek to modify the sentence in: IL, IA, KS, ME, MO, NC, ND, OH, OK, OR, PA, SD, TN, TX, VT, VA, WA, WI.
28. The right to a modification hearing is granted in: AL, AK, CA, CO, CT, GA, HI, IA, MI, MN, MS, NM, NY, NC, ND, OK, OR, PA, SD, TX, UT, VT, WV, WI.
29. Notice of the hearing is guaranteed in: AK, CA, CT, GA, IA, MI, MN, MS, NM, NC, ND, OK, OR, WA, WV.
30. The extensions are possible in increments of 12 (AK, GA, NM, NC, WI), 18 (CT), or 24 (AK, CO, GA, MI) months.
31. A hearing is guaranteed in: AK, AZ, CA, CO, DC, FED, FL, ID, IL, KS, KY, ME, MI, MN, MS, NE, NJ, NM, NY, NC, OH, OK, SC, SD, TN, UT, VT, VA, WA, WV, WI, WY.
32. Counsel is guaranteed in: AK, AZ, CO, DC, FED, FL, ID, IL, KS, KY, ME, MI, MN, MS, NE, NM, NY, NC, OH, OK, SC, SD, TN, UT, VT, VA, WA, WI, WY.
33. Notice of charges is guaranteed in: AZ, AR, CA, CO, DC, FED, FL, IL, KS, ME, MI, MN, MS, NE, NJ, NY, NC, OH, OK, SC, SD, TN, UT, VT.
34. Confrontation and cross-examination is guaranteed in: AK, AZ, IL, KS, ME, MI, MN, MS, NE, NY, NC, SD, UT, VT.
35. Presenting evidence and the right to be heard are guaranteed in: AZ, FL, KY, ME, MI, MN, MS, NE, NY, NC, OK, SD, TN, UT, VT, WI.
36. The protection against self-incrimination is guaranteed in: AK, KS, ME, MI, MS, NM, TN, VA, WY.
37. A speedy hearing is guaranteed in: MI, MN, SD.
38. Compulsory process is guaranteed in: AK, CO, MI, MN, SD.
39. Presenting witnesses is guaranteed in: NE, TN.
40. VOP proceedings are the same for delinquents and status offenders in: AL, GA, HI, ID, KY, MD, MS, MT, NE, OK, TN.
41. A preponderance of evidence is the burden of proof in: AK, AZ, AR, DC, ID, IL, ME, MI, NC, SD, TN, TX, VT, WA, WI.
42. These status offenders are considered delinquents in: CO, CT, DC, MS, MT, NJ, NY, OH, OK. It takes two VOPs for the status offender to become a delinquent in Wisconsin.
43. Delinquent or restrictive placement is possible in: AR, CT, DC, HI, ID, IN, KS, LA, NE, NH, NC, SC, SD, TX, UT, VA, WA, WI.
44. The original disposition can be treated this way in: AK, CO, FL, ID, KS, MN, MS, NJ, NM, NY, NC, SD, TN, TX, UT, VA, WY.
45. Periods of detention are possible in: AR, CA, CO, FL, ID, KS, NV, NC, WA.
46. The age requirements are 17 (MO), 18 (IA, KY, OK, RI, VT), 19 (MI), or 21 (MT).
47. The adult sentence can be imposed in: FL, IA, MI, MN, MT, VT, WV.

48. The records are open in this context in: AZ, CA, FL, GA, ID, IA, ME, MI, MN, NV, OK, SD, VA.
49. The records are open following transfer in: AR, CO, GA, IL, MO, OK, RI, SD, VT, WV, WI.
50. The records are open in this context in: AK, CA, LA, ND, TX, WY.
51. Arrest requires disclosure in: FL, ID, IN, OK, OR.
52. Charging requires disclosure in: AK, CO, ID, IN, IA, KS, LA, MA, OK, PA, UT, WA, WV.
53. Escape or unauthorized absence requires disclosure in: AR, CA, CO, CT, OK, TX.
54. Transfer to adult court requires disclosure in: CO, FL, KS, MA, OK, VT, WV.
55. Adjudication requires disclosure in: CA, GA, HI, ID, IL, IN, KS, KY, LA, MA, MI, MS, MO, MT, NV, NJ, ND, OK, PA, UT, TN, VA, WV, WI, WY.
56. The ages identified are 12 (IN), 13 (AK, IL), or 14 (CO, HI, ID, KS, LA, MA, OK, PA, TN, UT, VA, WV).
57. The age requirement does not apply to serious or chronic cases in: CO, ID, IL, IN, KS, LA, OK, PA, WV.
58. There is no age requirement in: AR, CA, CT, FL, GA, IA, KY, MI, MS, MO, MT, NV, NJ, ND, OK, OR, TX, WA, WI, WY.
59. Cases of violence are disclosed in: CO, HI, KY, LA, NJ, OK, PA, TN, VA, WV, WI, WY.
60. Weapons cases are disclosed in: AK, CO, IL, KY, MS, OK, WV.
61. Murder cases are disclosed in: HI, IL, IN, KY, MS, MO, PA, TN, VA, WV.
62. Sexual assault cases are disclosed in: IL, MS, NV, ND, PA, TN, VA, WV.
63. A case involving any offense can be disclosed in: IN, KS, MI, MT, WA, WV.
64. Cases involving any felony can be disclosed in: AK, CA, FL, ID, IL, IN, IA, MO, NC, OK, UT, VA, WY.
65. The release of the youth's records is discretionary in several situations (e.g., arrest and adjudication) in: CA, CT, DE, IA, LA, NV, NH, OK, OR, SC, VA, WI, WY.
66. The release of these records can be both mandatory and discretionary in: CA, LA, ND, OK, OR, WI, WY.
67. Schools are informed of youths' arrests in: AR, FL, LA, MN, MT, NJ, SC, WI.
68. Schools are informed of charges against youth in: FL, NJ, NC, WV, WI.
69. Schools are informed of adjudications in: AL, AR, CA, CT, GA, IL, IA, KY, ME, MN, MT, NV, NH, NJ, ND, OR, PA, SC, UT, VT, VA, WA, WI.
70. Schools are informed of all dispositions in: CA, FL, KY, MN, NJ, NC, OR, WI, WY.
71. Schools are informed of all probation dispositions in: OR, UT, WA, WV.
72. Schools are informed of all releases in: CO, OR, MN, SC, VA, WA.
73. Cases of violence and murder are disclosed in: FL, LA, ME, MN, NJ, SC, UT, VA, WA.
74. Weapons cases are disclosed in: AR, CA, IL, KY, MN, NJ, OR, SC, UT.
75. Drug cases are disclosed in: CA, KY, LA, MN, MT, NJ, OR, SC, VA, WA.
76. Very serious felonies are disclosed in: AL, AR, GA, MN, NJ, OR.
77. Sex-related offenses are disclosed in: CA, FL, ME, MN, NV, ND, VT, VA, WA.
78. No offense requirement is identified for disclosure in: KY, MT, NJ, OR, UT, WA, WV.
79. A felony is all that is required for disclosure in: CT, FL, IA, KY, NC, PA, WI.
80. Any school-related offense is subject to disclosure in: CA, MN, NJ, OH, SC. The New Hampshire statute suggests that the court does not have to inform the school if disclosure would be harmful to the youth and it is not necessary for the school to be aware of the record in order to be able to deal with the youth.
81. Teachers must be informed of the youth's record in: AL, CA, FL, GA, LA, ND, PA, VT, WA, WV, WI.
82. The states demanding this notice are: CA, CO, GA, MT, NV, NC, OR, PA, VT, WA, WV, WI. Florida has developed a statewide information-sharing system involving the Florida Departments of Education, Juvenile Justice, and Law Enforcement, while California has legislation permitting the development of such a system.
83. Schools have a right of access to court records in: AL, AK, AR, CA, CO, GA, MS, ND, OK, SD.
84. Immediate destruction of court records is required in: AL, CO, CT, DE, GA, LA, MS, NE, NY, OH, OK, OR, TX.
85. The requirement in years can be 1 (CO, OR, SD, UT, WV), 2 (AL, DC, GA, IA, KS, KY, LA, NJ, NM, OH, TX, VT), 3 (ME, MT, NV), 4 (CO, CT), 5 (AK, CA, FL, ID, LA, OR, PA, VA, WA), 6 (CA), or even 10 (AR, CO, IL, OK, WA), depending on the severity of offense and record.
86. The requirement in age can be 16 (CT, NC, NY), 17 (IL, MI, MO, WI), 18 (AK, AZ, CA, ID, NC, OR, PA, SC, WA), 19 (VA, WV), 20 (MS), 21 (AZ, AR, MD, NH, NV, OK, TX, WY), 23 (KS, WA), 24 (AL, FL, NV), 25 (AZ, MT), 26 (FL), 28 (MN), 30 (MI, NV), or even 38 (CA), depending on the severity of the offense and record.
87. The states with two levels are: AK, AZ, AR, CA, FL, LA, MT, NV, WA.
88. Sealing a record has this effect in: AL, CA, CT, DC, GA, ID, KS, KY, ME, NV, NM, NC, OH, OK, OR, SC, TX, UT, VT, WA, WV, WY.
89. The record can still be used for sentencing in: CO, LA, ME, MT, NV, OK, SD, TX, WA.
90. Prosecutors must be notified of sealing records in: AZ, CA, CO, DE, DC, GA, ID, IA, MT, NE, NV, NJ, NM, NC, OH, OK, OR, PA, SD, UT, WA.

91. There can be no additional adjudications or convictions in: AL, AZ, CA, CO, CT, DE, DC, GA, ID, IA, KS, KY, LA, ME, MT, NV, NJ, NM, NC, OK, OR, SC, SD, TX, UT, VT, WA, WY.
92. The youth cannot have a criminal court record in: AZ, ID, LA, MN, NV, OK, OR, TX, WV.
93. Sealing can be ruled ineligible when murder (DE, IL, KS, LA, OH, OR, WA), sex-related cases (CO, ID, LA, NV, OR, WA), serious felonies (CO, DE, KS, KY, LA, NV, NY, NC, SC, TX, VA, WA), cases of violence (CO, ID, LA, NV, OH, SC, WY), kidnapping (ID, OR), drug offenses (ID), extended jurisdictions cases (MN), presumptive transfer cases (CA), excluded offenses cases (AZ), direct file cases (CO), all open adjudicatory hearing cases (GA), or any felonies (KY) are involved.
94. Youth must demonstrate that they have been rehabilitated in: AK, AZ, CA, CO, GA, ID, NV, OH, SD, UT, VT, WY.
95. Youth must make this showing in: CO, DE, ID, IN, IA, OK, OR, WI.
96. These factors include the best interests of the child, the age of the person during the person's contact with the juvenile court or law enforcement agency, the nature of any allegations, whether there was an informal adjustment or an adjudication, the disposition of the case, the manner in which the person participated in any court-ordered supervision services, the time during which the person has been without contact with the juvenile court or with any law enforcement agency, whether the person acquired a criminal record, and the person's current status (31-39-8-3).
97. The range here is from 17 (WY) to 18 (FL, NH), 19 (AZ), or 21 (CA) years of age.
98. There does not appear to be any differentiation in: CT, DC, GA, ID, IN, NJ, NM, TX, UT, VT, VA, WV.
99. A juvenile record can affect bail in: CT, ID, MD, NC, PA, WI.
100. A juvenile record can affect parole in: CA, CT, GA, IL, MD, MS, ND, PA, TN, VT, VA, WV, WI.
101. A juvenile record cannot be used to impeach in: AL, AZ, AR, CA, CO, CT, DC, FL, IL, KY, LA, MD, MA, MI, MN, MO, NE, NJ, NM, NY, OH, OR, PA, RI, SD, TN, TX, UT, VA, WA, WV, WI.
102. The juvenile record can be used in rebuttal in: GA, KS, MO, NJ, OH, OK, UT.
103. The juvenile record can be used to impeach a youth who testifies against another person in: AL, AK, AR, DC, FED, IL, KS, LA, ME, MI, MS, NJ, NC, PA, RI, SC, SD, TN, WA. ✦

Community and Institutional Corrections in Juvenile Justice

- Chapter 16: Prevention and Treatment in the Community
- Chapter 17: Juvenile Institutions

Focus of Section VI

In this section we explore the correctional component of juvenile justice. You will see how juvenile justice has developed an extensive system of programs in local communities through which nondelinquent juveniles are given encouragement not to commit offenses, while adjudicated juveniles are provided treatment programs designed to prevent recidivism. This analysis includes an in-depth consideration of probation, the most common sanction in juvenile court. In the institutional context, we examine detention centers and long-term facilities to which youths are committed after adjudication. We also review the dimensions of various treatment approaches. ✦

Prevention and Treatment in the Community

Focus of Chapter 16

Chapter 16 addresses the important community component of the juvenile justice system. Most youths adjudicated in juvenile court are headed to a community sanction. The same applies to the substantial number of youth diverted from the system. In the community we find some of the juvenile system's best treatment programs, which can serve as centers to rehabilitate those found by the court to be delinquents or status offenders (as a disposition), to help those given a chance by the court to avoid an official record as an offender (as a diversion), and to deter those who might be tempted to commit an offense from doing so (as a prevention measure). It is in the community that the *subsystem* of juvenile justice comes to life. The juvenile justice system expands into and engages the community via these programs.

Key Terms

- classification
- community corrections
- comprehensive gang model
- comprehensive strategy
- drug courts
- guided group interaction
- gun court
- intensive aftercare program
- medical model
- prevention programs
- primary prevention

- radical nonintervention
- reintegration model
- restitution
- restorative conferencing models
- restorative justice
- secondary prevention
- standard conditions
- supervision role
- teen courts
- treatment programs

Community Corrections and Juvenile Justice

Community corrections involves a vast array of programs used in the juvenile and criminal justice systems to treat and punish offenders. These programs range from prevention efforts to correctional ones, as in probation. Both the juvenile and adult systems rely heavily on community corrections in dealing with offenders. In fact, most offenders in both systems will be sentenced to community corrections instead of to institutional programs, as in jails or prisons.

The juvenile justice system differs significantly from the adult system in handling individuals who enter it. The overriding difference relates to the proportion of juvenile intake cases handled informally. In 1999, 43 percent (711,100) of cases were not formally petitioned to court, yet 52 percent (432,000) of the nonpetitioned cases ended up with some form of supervision (Puzzanchera et al. 2003b).

Second, of the 962,000 cases (57 percent of intake) formally petitioned to court, 33 percent (315,500) were nonadjudicated (found not guilty). Yet a significant proportion of them (33 percent) came under some form of supervision. Two percent were placed out of home, 12 percent were placed on probation, and 19 percent received some *other sanction* (community service, ordered to pay restitution).

Third, according to the 1999 data three court decisions (not petitioned, not adjudicated, and adjudicated) culminated in youth being "placed." The total number of cases placed was 160,800, a mere 9.6 percent of total intake. Under the guidelines adopted recently by OJJDP, the word *placed* can refer to any residential facility, whether one in the community or an institution for long-term care (to be discussed in Chapter 17).

What this all means is that (1) the juvenile system assigns a vastly disproportionate percentage of its cases to community programs, and (2) probation supervision is required, directly or indirectly, for that disproportionate share. For example, youths assigned to "probation only" are supervised directly by the PO; no other person or agency is involved with them. But for a youth placed in a residential program in the community, the direct supervision of the youth belongs to the facility's staff, and the PO's involvement is indirect.

Juvenile Probation

Probation is the most widely used sanction in the criminal and juvenile justice systems. In the adult system, a press release issued by the U.S. Bureau of Justice Statistics on August 28, 2001, revealed that of 6.5 million adult offenders under correctional supervision, 3.8 million were on probation. These are "static" statistics in that they represent head counts. As we have noted, the proportion of juveniles under probation *supervision* vastly exceeds the proportion in the adult system.

Probation unofficially began in 1841 when John Augustus, a Boston boot maker, bailed a drunkard out of jail. Augustus was permitted to supervise the offender and was told to report the offender's progress to the court. As the years went by he took on more and more offenders. By the time his work ended in 1858, he had supervised over 5,000 men, women, and children.[1]

After Augustus's death, his work with children was carried on by Rufus R. Cook, a representative of Boston's Children's Aid Society. In 1869, a law passed in Massachusetts authorized the state agent for the Board of Charities to investigate cases of children tried in the courts, to attend trials, and to receive children for placement if ordered by the courts. The preferred placement of children was with families. Between 1869 and 1870, 23 percent of juvenile offenders were handled in this fashion (Sutherland and Cressey 1978). Juvenile probation was significantly enhanced and formalized in 1899 with the formation of the first juvenile court, in Chicago, which permitted the suspension of sentence and specifically required the appointment of probation officers (Barnes and Teeters 1959).

The Complexity of Juvenile Probation

An argument can be made that probation for juveniles is far more extensive and complex than that for adults. Take the Juvenile Services Bureau of the Los Angeles County Probation Department, for example. Juvenile probation officers (JPOs) are responsible for providing the juvenile court with investigative reports, the equivalent of the adult presentence investigation. With respect to status offenders, the unit handles incorrigible youth and habitual truants or those with severe school behavior problems. The PO at intake receives referrals from law enforcement, parents, schools, the District Attorney's Truancy Mediation Program, and the Los Angeles County Department of Children and Family Services. The intake officer has a considerable number of alternatives for dealing with wayward children. Among them are the following:

1. Crisis intervention by intake PO

2. Referral of child with parents to a reconciliation and mediation program if the problem is deemed to be one of communication between parent(s) and child

3. Referral to the Gang Alternative and Prevention Program if the child is under 14

4. With the consent of parent and child, informal supervision up to six months

5. Filing a formal petition

6. Community service, counseling, and parenting classes

Juvenile probation in Los Angeles County is also involved in the following:

- Specialized gang suppression programs

- Regular court-ordered supervision of adjudicated delinquents

- The School Crime Suppression Program, in which school-based POs deal with their clients regarding attendance, in-person contacts, referral to services, and academic assistance

- The Gang Alternative and Prevention Program: Specialized caseload of clients who live in high-crime neighborhoods, where gangs are active and drug abuse is present; about 2,500 juveniles are supervised in this program

- Community Education Centers: Nonresidential school programs for clients having difficulty in school and for youths recently released from camps

- Out-of-home placement: Residential treatment center, group home, or foster care placement

- Teen court: A diversion program for first-time, nonserious offenders; the program is administered by a PO, volunteer bench officers, and a jury of six peers (there are eight teen courts in Los Angeles County)

- Camp to Community Transition Program: A 30-day furlough prior to release from camp, which is intensively supervised

- Family Preservation Probation: Can call on service providers to deal with family problems

- Community Law Enforcement and Recovery: A multi-agency mobile team that patrols neighborhoods where there is much gang activity; POs ride along and can identify youth who are violating probation conditions

- Specialized warrant team: POs work with sheriff's deputies to identify and arrest probation absconders

We can easily see that juvenile probation, at least in large urban areas, does considerably more than merely provide direct supervision of juveniles. Not only do POs perform a multitude of other tasks, but they work in partnerships with a considerable number of public and private agencies.[2]

What Is Probation?

As odd as it may seem, some aspects of probation are unclear. For instance, is probation a sentence? Does a judge state from the bench: "I sentence you to two years of probation"? Only a few state laws provide for probation as a sentence in itself. A common definition of probation might be "conditional freedom in lieu of incarceration." Stated in these terms a sentence of incarceration would be *imposed* by a judge, but its *execution* would be suspended for probation. Implied in this statement is that failure to abide by the terms of probation could result in incarceration. The word *conditional* in this definition means the probationer must adhere to certain rules, or conditions, of probation. These conditions are divided into two categories: *standard* (or those rules that all probationers must obey) and *special* (those that are tailored to the individual).

Common examples of standard conditions are as follows:

1. You must obey all laws—federal, state, municipal.

2. You shall not possess a firearm.

3. You shall not use, possess, or sell alcohol or drugs.

4. You must report to your probation officer as directed.

5. You shall not leave the state without the permission of your probation officer.

6. You shall attend school or be employed.

7. You shall permit your probation officer to visit you at home.

Special conditions relate to either extra control or services. Several examples are as follows:

- Counseling/therapy
- Community service
- Paying restitution
- Paying fines and court costs
- Refraining from associating with ____

Supervising Clients

The supervision role of POs is largely twofold: assistance and surveillance. The surveillance role is essentially checking to see that the juvenile client is obeying the conditions of probation. Inevitably, the juvenile will violate one or more rules. The PO's response is significant. It is largely determined by the type and degree of rule violation and the working style of the PO. For instance, research has revealed four major working styles (Glaser 1964; Klockars 1972):

1. Punitive officer. The working style of the punitive officer is to focus on the client's obeying the rules. The underlying assumption is that if juveniles adhere to the conditions of probation they are on the road to rehabilitation.

2. Therapeutic officer. These POs concentrate on counseling the offender. They are inclined either to overlook minor violations of the rules or, better, to use them as fuel for counseling.

3. Synthetic officer. In the real world of supervision, this is the working style most commonly used. It is the combination of punitive and therapeutic styles. In many respects it is akin to parenting.

4. Time server. This is a PO who appears to be in a state of semiretirement, one who goes through the motions and exerts just enough effort to get by. Some believe these POs are either burned out or have become cynical and simply do enough to get by.

The most common form of supervision is reporting to the PO in the office. The genesis of this method was the thinking of reformers early in the twentieth century that casework counseling with a skilled PO is the best method of helping others. This is an outgrowth of the medical model of corrections, in which *communication* between helper and client resolves the client's problems. During the 1960s–1970s, this method of supervision fell into disfavor as the reintegration model of corrections entered the picture and gained many advocates (O'Leary and Duffee 1971).

Underlying the shift from the medical model to reintegration was what had become obvious during this period: Casework/social work–trained probation and parole officers were few and far between. The entry-level education requirement for a PO position was *preferably* in psychology or social work, but in the real world it turned out to be a B.A in anything. So, the reintegrationists reasoned (correctly) that juveniles might be best served by public and private agencies that specialize in helping people who had problems and offer a variety of services. These services include Alcoholics Anonymous, substance abuse programs, family counseling, employment services, children's mental health clinics, and youth recreation centers. In the reintegration model the PO becomes a *broker* and *advocate*. The PO learns the community, refers the youth client to the appropriate service, and monitors progress.

To supervise clients appropriately, to provide counseling, or to refer them to an appropriate service, the PO must know what *risk* the clients present and what *needs* they may have that require assistance. In corrections, the process that provides the answers to these questions is most often referred to as *classification*.

Classifying Clients

In adult and juvenile corrections, classification is the process of categorizing clients into groups and organizing an agency's staff and resources to deliver services to them. Perhaps the earliest, and certainly the most rudimentary, classification was separating males from females in institutional settings. Moreover, in the not-too-recent past, it was common in adult probation and parole for agencies to assign male officers to supervise males and female officers to supervise females. That particular assignment is a thing of the past, as probation and parole agencies have taken on significantly larger numbers of female POs, while client caseloads remain overwhelmingly male. The Bureau of Justice Statistics reported that in the nation the ratio of adult male to female POs was three to two (Maguire and Pastore 1996).

Currently, the two broad classification categories for criminal justice clients are *risk and needs*. Risk instruments estimate the likelihood of an offender's reoffending. They are used in criminal justice much like actuarial methods are used by insurance companies to determine premium rates. We know that certain automobile drivers are high risk because they have characteristics that put them in a group of similarly situated drivers, such as age (young), male, commission of moving violations, and so on. The fact that people are placed in a high-risk driver group does not predict that they will have an accident, but they have a higher probability of causing accidents than those in low-risk groups.

Wisconsin uses the assessment instrument in Figure 16.1 to determine risk for juveniles on probation and therefore the intensity of supervision. Reviewing the instrument reveals that some questions are merely related to historical facts, but some require the judgment or recall of others. For instance, numbers 1, 2, and 4 are a matter of looking into juvenile court records. For number 3, if an assault is not a matter of police or juvenile record, answering the question depends on self-report or reporting from others, such as a parent. It also requires making a distinction between a schoolyard scuffle and an outright assault, which constitutes a crime. Numbers 5 and 6 require a definition and a judgment. A one-night disappearance of a girl may be classified as running away or as something else if she merely stayed with a friend in defiance of parental orders. Similarly, precisely what constitutes a school behavior problem could be troublesome.

Risk (and needs) instruments include manuals to guide the classifier to facilitate judgment calls. For instance, to classify misbehavior in the classroom as a problem, a requirement of "referral to the principal's office" might be the guide found in a manual. Question 7 could be problematic if victimization from such abuse is not part of the official record. If it is not, the answer would depend on self-report or reporting from family members. Ju-

Figure 16.1 Wisconsin Delinquency Risk Assessment Scale

	Score

1. Age at First Referral to Juvenile Court Intake
13 or under 2
14 1
15 or over 0

2. Prior Referrals to Juvenile Court Intake
None 0
One or two 1
Three or more 2

3. Prior Assaults (includes use of a weapon)
Yes 2
No 0

4. Prior Out-of-Home Placements
None or one 0
Two or more 2

5. Prior Runaways (from home or placement)
None or one 0
Two or more 2

6. School Behavior Problems (includes truancy)
None or only minor problems 0
Serious problems noted 2

7. History of Physical or Sexual Abuse as a Victim
Yes 1
No 0

8. History of Neglect as a Victim
Yes 2
No 0

9. History of Alcohol or Other Drug Abuse
Yes 2
No 0

10. History of Serious Emotional Problems
Yes 1
No 0

11. Peer Relationships
Good support and influence 0
Negative influence, most peers involved in delinquent or lack of peer
    relationships 1
Strong negative influence, most peers involved in delinquent behavior such as
    gang involvement 2

Total Risk Score: _____

Risk Classification:	0–5	Low risk
	6–9	Medium risk
	10–13	High risk
	14 or above	Very high risk

venile offenders may claim to have been victimized so as to play the "don't-blame-me game." Family may not be forthcoming if perpetrators are members of the family. The same comments can be made for numbers 8 through 11.

After the classifier has reviewed the record and interviewed the youth, and possibly a parent, the 11 scores are added to give a total risk score, with a maximum possible score of 21. If the youth has already been on probation when the classification process takes place, the PO might find himself or herself returning to the judge who adjudicated the case. Suppose a youth "earned" 21 points and the PO, from the interview, gets the clear impression that the youth is not only a high risk but also poses a threat to others. The PO would likely ask the judge to add special conditions such as a tight curfew, day reporting, and even electronic monitoring.

Risk classification instruments always include overrides based on clinical judgments. For instance, we have pointed to a number of instrument items that depend on self-report or the reporting of others. Suppose, after calculating the scores, a youth's risk classification stands on the border of medium and high risks, say nine. If the classifier has some doubts about the veracity of the reporting of others, the PO can classify the youth under the high-risk category and provide a written statement for the records.

Intensity of Supervision

The 1980s was the decade of *intensive supervision.* Burgeoning jail and prison populations strained municipal and state budgets, and overcrowded institutions resulted in a flood of inmate lawsuits. In an attempt to cope with these mounting problems, policymakers reasoned that some offenders who would likely be sentenced to incarceration terms could be supervised in the community if the supervision was intensive—that is, if there were frequent contacts between POs and client. These principles can be applied to juvenile aftercare (after a youth's release from an institution), as we will see toward the end of the chapter.

The states of Georgia and New Jersey shared the spotlight for such programs in the early 1980s. In Georgia (Erwin 1987), intensive caseloads contained 25 clients with two POs—one a surveillance officer, the other a PO who did the counseling and bureaucratic work of probation. The intensity of the supervision was five face-to-face (F–F) contacts per week. In New Jersey (Pearson 1988), intensive POs made 28 contacts per month (F–F, home visits, employment checks, and telephone contacts). The program was referred to as "prison without walls" by the New Jersey Administrative Office of the Courts, the agency that runs the program. This level of supervision contrasts sharply with regular probation, in which POs in urban areas can have caseloads that run as high as 200 probationers. Caseloads this extreme have been cited as virtually guaranteeing ineffectiveness or as being a slap on the wrist (Kurlychek et al. 1999).

Intensive probation can also include forcing the youth to attend school or counseling in a strictly supervised correctional setting, such as a day treatment center. Here the youth's free time each day is severely limited to nonschool hours, and even that time may be under control via electronic monitoring or house arrest. Day treatment centers can also serve as a reintegration tool for youths working their way back into the community after being released from a facility.

Figure 16.2 Lucas County Juvenile Court Needs Assessment

	Score
1. Family Relationships	_____
Stable/supportive 0	
Some disorganization/stress 3	
Major disorganization/stress. 6	
2. Parental Problems (Check all that apply/Add points)	_____
Inadequate discipline. 1	
Emotional instability 1	
Criminality 1	
Substance abuse 1	
Physical/sexual abuse 1	
Family violence. 1	
Marital discord 1	
3. Support System	_____
Youth has support system or none needed. 0	
No family/external support. 1	
4. School Attendance	_____
No problem 0	
Some truancy. 1	
Major truancy 2	
5. School Behavior	_____
No problem 0	
Some problem 1	
Major problem 3	
6. Substance Abuse	_____
No use. 0	
Experimenter 1	
Former abuse/in recovery 3	
Occasional use. 4	
Abuse 8	
7. Emotional Stability	_____
No problem 0	
Some problem, occasional interference 1	
Major problem, serious interference 2	
8. Peer Relationships	_____
Good support/influence. 0	
Associations with occasional negative results 1	
Associations primarily with negative results. 2	
9. Health	_____
No problem 0	
Some health problems 1	
Major handicap/illness. 2	
10. Sexual Adjustment (Check all that apply/Enter highest)	_____
No problem 0	
Prostitution. 1	
Sex offense 1	
Sexual identity/awareness problems. 1	
Pregnant/has child 3	
11. Structured Activities	_____
Involvement 0	
No involvement. 1	
Total Score:	_____

As state after state opted for intensive supervision (usually designated ISP) and researchers were permitted to examine programs, one conclusion emerged: The meaning of ISP is whatever an agency defines it to be. In some cases, it is one F–F contact a week; in others, it is two F–F contacts per month. Returning to the risk instrument we just discussed, the level of intensity is whatever an agency chooses. Thus, among the numerous juvenile probation departments in Wisconsin, the definition of intensive is likely to vary significantly. In addition, research has not disclosed reductions in recidivism for youth on ISP (Barton and Butts 1990; Land et al. 1990; Weibush 1993).

Needs Assessment

Figure 16.2 is a typical needs instrument. This type of assessment requires far more self-reporting, reporting by others, and judgment calls than what is needed for assessing risk. Consider numbers 1 and 2. While some subitems may be a matter of record (e.g., criminality in number 2), most of them would be recorded as judgments made by others about a youth's family. The answers to some of these items require standard definitions, which would be found in manuals. For instance, with respect to item 4 something must distinguish between *some* truancy and *major* truancy. The same comment applies to number 5. Finding the answers to some items may be difficult for the classifier and could require considerable interviewing with the youth and parents.

When the process is completed, a juvenile on probation is given a needs score. But a score here has much less meaning than a risk score. In the needs assessment, the total score has less value than the individual item scores. The work of the supervising PO really begins at this point. It is not uncommon for juvenile probationers to accumulate points for family disorganization, parental substance abuse or marital discord, school behavior problems, substance abuse, emotional instability, and poor peer relationships. The multi-problem youth presents a major challenge for the PO. Which problem or problems get the attention? Overprogramming the youth is a road to failure. The PO must draw up a treatment plan that the juvenile can handle. Operationalizing a needs assessment is much more difficult than doing so with a risk assessment.

Diversion

We now turn to a practice that was always in effect but in the 1960s seemed to be newly discovered. The practice is *diversion*, the legal aspects of which we discussed in Chapter 9's coverage of intake. Its revival may have been a result of the President's Commission on Law Enforcement (1967), which provided diversion with widespread attention.

Diversion as juvenile justice policy came to the fore in the late 1960s. We noted some controversy in its definition in Chapter 9. It is commonly thought of as a way to keep offenders, especially juveniles, out of the system. Nejelski (1976, 393) offers the following as a definition of diversion: "the channeling of cases to noncourt institutions, in instances where these cases would ordinarily have received an adjudication (or fact-finding) hearing by a court." Note that diversion in this sense means avoiding judicial processing and also means directing the divertee *to* some sort of service. For juveniles, this would mean that diversion is to be practiced by police and intake workers of the juvenile court. Nejelski (1976, 394) also offers a more practical definition: "a diversion is merely the turning or redirection of something from its normal path. In the juvenile justice system, diversion takes place at *each stage*" (emphasis added). In the practical world of juvenile justice, anything short of incarceration, whether temporary detention or commitment to a long-term institution, constitutes diversion. Thus, any juvenile in the adjudicated, nonadjudicated, and nonpetitioned categories, other than those placed, is a diverted case.

Teaching children about the processes of the justice system is a major part of diversion efforts. How much punishment power should be available to juveniles serving on teen court?

And in the *placed* category, those juveniles placed in out-of-home, community residential facilities would be considered diverted. Therefore, it is safe to say, using the "practical" definition of diversion, about 95 percent of juveniles under juvenile justice supervision have been diverted. As suggested in Chapter 9, such a broad definition of diversion strips it of meaning.

History of Diversion

Most writers give credit to the 1967 report of the President's Commission on Law Enforcement and the Administration of Justice with seeding the diversion movement, especially in the case of juveniles. The theoretical foundation for this policy development was labeling theory, which came to the fore in the early 1960s. The major contribution to labeling as a theoretical perspective relative to a commitment to deviance (not original cause) was the work of Howard Becker (1964). In a nutshell, if a person is labeled as deviant, in time his or her self-concept changes and, through a self-fulfilling prophecy, lives up to the deviant label. For instance, if we were to persistently call a group of first graders "stupid," according to labeling, they would turn out to be failing pupils.

While labeling theory is held in less regard by criminologists today, it exerted a powerful influence on the juvenile justice system in the 1960s and 1970s. However, labeling theory alone did not explain the diversion movement. Institutional facilities once thought of as appropriate environments for curing the mentally ill and rehabilitating criminals were coming under fire at about this time. In the mid-1950s the nation was rocked by a number of serious prison riots. As a result, some observers turned their attention to the evils and failures of prisons (Bagdikian and Dash 1972; Mitford 1974; Murton and Hyams 1969).

In the mental health field, revelations of two kinds were prompting change. One was the development of psychoactive drugs, which permitted some mentally ill patients to live and function in the community. The second was the revelation of the brutal conditions that existed in many mental health hospitals, graphically depicted in a Frederick Wiseman documentary *Titticut Follies*. Many hospitals were depopulated as more and more patients were returned to and treated in the community.

Furthermore, the effectiveness of correctional treatment, especially under conditions of confinement, was being called into question. The best-known examination of correctional rehabilitative programs at the time was carried out by Lipton et al. (1975). The most public statement in this regard was made by Martinson (1974), who was attributed with the off-repeated phrase "Nothing works."

Given the events and studies of this period, the obvious policy implication was to avoid incarceration, if at all possible, especially for status offenders. Youth advocates also believed juveniles should not be subject to the stigma of judicial processing.

One of the outgrowths of the President's Crime Commission was the passage of the Omnibus Crime Control and Safe Streets Act of 1968. The bill authorized the formation of the Law Enforcement Assistance Administration (LEAA), whose primary mission was to fight crime by providing grants to law enforcement, prosecutors, and correctional agencies, both public and private. By 1974, LEAA had funded 74 diversion projects operated by police, probation, and private and public social service agencies (Palmer and Lewis 1980). Some advocates went as far as to say that radical nonintervention should be practiced, such that all juvenile offenders, except the serious and dangerous, should simply be left alone. The claim was that the system does more harm than good and that most juveniles mature and do not reoffend (Schur 1973).

Net Widening

It was not long after diversion became widespread official operative policy that critics sprang up, using the term *net widening* as their focus of attention. Blomberg (1983) defined this term as referring to the "actual extension of the reach of the juvenile justice system through diversion programs which increase the overall proportion of the population subject to some form of service or control" (29). The following hypothetical example illustrates Blomberg's definition.

A police officer comes across a boy attempting to steal another youth's bicycle. Among the officer's choices are to (1) arrest the youth or (2) lecture him and take him home to his parents. In the view of some, option 2 is true diversion (Saul and Davidson 1983). Our officer is also aware of a third option: a counseling program for wayward youth, funded by LEAA. The officer escorts the youth to juvenile court intake and makes a strong plea that the intake officer take no formal action but refer the youth (with parental contact and consent) to the counseling program. Under option 3, the net has widened, since there is some control extended over the youth. In the eyes of many critics, this well-intentioned act can result in as much stigmatization as formal processing. Thus, while advocates of diversion point out that being diverted is voluntary, in reality it can be quite coercive and involuntary (Polk 1984). If the youth (and parent) decline the offer of counseling, there is a good likelihood the case will proceed formally. Further, to accept diversion, the youth must admit guilt. To do otherwise would likely result in the intake worker's filing a petition.

Critics also argue that it would be difficult to avoid net widening as time goes on. Programs have been developed to serve diverted youth, and much is at stake in terms of funding, jobs, and organizational survival (Saul and Davidson 1983). Some of this is illustrated in evaluations of diversion programs. Rausch and Logan (1983) pointed out in a study in Connecticut that diversion programs "overdo" their services. While petitioned children were often simply released or placed on informal probation, personnel in diversion programs rarely concluded a case with one or two contacts. Rausch and Logan (1983) speculated that if services were to be brief, authorities might conclude that the programs were not necessary.

Diversion Today

Scholars do not write much today about the concept of diversion itself or about its pros and cons. Nevertheless, in practice it is still the most preferred option for juvenile justice officials. If we return to the 1999 data presented at the beginning of the chapter, we can gain some perspective on the scope of youth diverted. These data do not include diversion that takes place prior to juvenile court intake, such as by police. But of those who entered intake in 1999, 711,100 (43 percent) were not petitioned. This constitutes the proportion of juveniles who fit the first definition of diversion in that they avoided formal court processing. Of this number, the 279,100 cases that were dismissed fit the conceptualization expressed by Saul and Davidson (1983), which is true diversion that has no services. The alternative definition of diversion—that is, at *any stage*, or avoiding incarceration—involves huge numbers of juveniles, both adjudicated and nonadjudicated.

We now discuss two diversion programs that are growing at a significant rate: teen courts and juveniles drug courts.

Teen Courts

Teen courts, a "judicial" process made up largely or solely of teenagers, represent a growing diversion program. It is estimated that in 1991 there were 50 such courts in the nation (Butts et al. 1999) and that by the end of the decade there were 675 (Butts and Buck 2000). While there are variations of the court around the country, its basic purpose is to informally handle status offenders and first-time nonserious delinquent offenders. A national survey, sponsored by OJJDP and carried out by the Urban Institute, revealed that in 1998 teen courts handled 65,000 cases (Butts et al. 1999). Youth referred to teen court tended to be younger than age 15, to have no prior record, and to have committed a nonserious offense, such as vandalism, shoplifting, minor assault, petty theft, alcohol possession, or disorderly conduct. In fact, the vast majority of teen courts reported that they rarely accepted any youth charged with a felony or who had a prior arrest record (Butts et al. 1999). In diverting substantial numbers of juveniles from formal court processing, the process not only lessens the juvenile court's workload but also has some positive effects on participants.

There are four basic teen court models (Butts et al. 1999):

1. Adult judge: An adult serves as judge and conducts the process. Teens play all other roles.

2. Youth judge: Similar to the adult judge model except that a youth serves as judge.

3. Tribunal: A youth attorney presents the case to a panel of three youth judges, who decide the outcome.

4. Peer jury: A youth or an adult presents the case to a youth jury, which in turn questions the defendant and decides the outcome.

Youths who come before teen courts admit guilt in 87 percent of the courts surveyed. The most common sanction handed down is community service, followed by letters of apology to victims, apology essays, serving on a teen court jury, drug and alcohol classes, and restitution (Butts and Buck 2000). The close ties between teen court and the victim make this diversion similar to restorative justice programs (to be discussed later in chapter).

Teen courts are promoted as offering at least four benefits: accountability, timeliness, cost saving, and community cohesion (Butts and Buck 2000).

The juvenile court, law enforcement, the prosecutor's office, the probation department, and private agencies have all been affiliated with running the teen courts across the country. The case volume tends to be small—most courts (59 percent) identified processing fewer than 100 cases annually. The problems acknowledged most often by the teen court programs entail a lack of funding, an inability to retain teen volunteers, and lack of sufficient referrals.

Some programs have been evaluated. Reduction of recidivism is the most desirable outcome measure, but no program can make an unchallenged positive claim in this regard. The major stumbling block in seeking solid evaluations is methodological, specifically in developing comparison groups. Notwithstanding this handicap, some programs have claimed reductions in recidivism (Hissong 1991), while others have not (Seyfrit et al. 1987). Some evaluations have discovered other benefits for participants in teen courts. Most youths express satisfaction with the process, a more positive view of the judicial process, improved self-esteem, positive attitudes toward authority, and greater knowledge of the legal system.

Juvenile Drug Courts

Drug courts are a relatively new and unique way of dealing with substance abusers. In 1989 the Florida Supreme Court provided a one-year leave of absence to a circuit court judge to come up with a solution to the constant flow of drug offenders into Dade County's (Miami) justice system. Judge Herbert M. Klein, after six months of thought and consultation with public and private entities, and with the cooperation of the county attorney, came up with the idea of a drug court. Structured as a diversion program, the message to eligible candidates was "complete the treatment, and your case will be dismissed and your record sealed" (Finn and Newlyn 1993, 14). Since then the number of drug courts has escalated significantly across the nation.

The first juvenile drug court started in early 1995. By 2001, more than 140 juvenile drug courts were in operation and another 125 were in the planning stage (BJA 2003). The primary impetus for the growth of adult drug courts and the start-up of juvenile programs was the Federal Violent Crime Control and Law Enforcement Act of 1994 (Cooper and

Bartlett 1996). Title 5 of the act authorized the United States Attorney General to provide block grants to state and local governments for this purpose.

Juvenile drug court programs run from nine months to one year. Eligibility for program participation is ordinarily restricted to nonviolent drug or drug-related offenders. The court team includes judge, prosecutor, defense attorney, treatment provider, and probation officer. Juveniles and their parents are often required to sign statements accepting the program and following through on all requirements. The goals of the drug court program include the following (BJA 2003):

- Provide immediate intervention, structure, and treatment via judicial monitoring.
- Improve functioning, address problems, and help to resist drugs.
- Improve skills to advance education, self-concept, and positive relationships.
- Strengthen families by helping them provide guidance and structure.
- Promote youth accountability and service providers' accountability.

Juvenile drug courts adopt a comprehensive 16-item strategy that includes the following (BJA 2003):

- Collaborative planning
- Teamwork
- Clearly defined target population and eligibility criteria
- Judicial involvement and supervision
- Monitoring and evaluation
- Community partnerships
- Comprehensive treatment planning
- Developmentally appropriate services
- Gender-appropriate services
- Cultural competence
- Focus on strengths
- Family engagement
- Educational linkages
- Drug testing
- Goal-oriented incentives and sanctions
- Confidentiality

Drug court programs are usually set up in phases, with the intensity of youth participation decreasing as the youth passes from one phase to the next. Most participants agree that the personal attention of and participation by the judge is probably the most important element of the program. Both adult and juvenile drug courts were conceived to be preadjudication diversion programs. That purpose in the juvenile version may be changing. Cooper (2001) believes that most juvenile drug courts are postadjudication. It is "preferred by many because the court has more authority after guilt has been established and more options are available in the event the youth fails to complete the program" (6). This position may not sit well with those who believe in the value of diverting nonserious juvenile offenders from formal handling.

Since the juvenile drug courts are in the beginning stages of development, evaluations are scarce. Those studies that have been done are internal and process-oriented. That is, they are reporting what is going on—number of clients, number of contact, dropouts, and so on. It will take a bit of time to develop methodologically sound evaluations.

We turn our attention now to a sampling of the extensive number of prevention and treatment programs for juveniles in the community. Keep in mind that these two approaches are not mutually exclusive. That is, prevention programs do not deal exclusively with nondelinquents, and treatment programs do not deal exclusively with delinquents. We know from self-report studies that many youths have committed delinquent acts but have never been caught. Thus, a program designed to prevent delinquency may well deal with nondelinquents *and* delinquents.

Juveniles in Community Correctional Programs

In 1999, 398,200 (62 percent) of adjudicated youth were placed on probation. At the beginning of this chapter we also noted that other categories of youth (for example, nonpetitioned and nonadjudicated) were also placed under some form of probation supervision. In 1999, a substantial number of youth were *placed*—a term that means being put in an out-of-home residential facility. Unfortunately, under the rules adopted by OJJDP, placement can mean anything from a training school to a camp, ranch, private placement facility, or group home (Snyder and Sickmund 1999). Juveniles who are placed in the community are under the direct supervision of the facility's staff but are still under the indirect supervision of probation. This situation holds true if the court ordered placement as a condition of probation.

Given the rules used by OJJDP, *placed* could mean any residential setting other than a youth's home. This variation makes a precise tally of the number of youth under probation supervision difficult. An educated guess at this figure could go like this. Earlier in this chapter we noted that about 989,100 juveniles were ordered to be under some form of probation supervision in 1999 (revisit Figure 9.1). This assumption included youth petitioned and nonpetitioned, adjudicated and nonadjudicated, and "other sanctions" such as restitution, community service, and treatment, since we believe probation officers are involved to some degree in the youths' court-ordered sanctions. In 1999, another 163,800 juveniles were *placed*, a good proportion of whom were actually under community supervision because of the location and nature of the placement (e.g., a group home). At bottom, then, in 1999 alone more than 1 million juveniles were sentenced to some form of probation supervision. (We will look at more numbers in this context at the end of the chapter.)

Preventing delinquency and treating the delinquent can be a large and expansive undertaking. Until the 1980s, treating delinquents took center stage. Corrections, as a subsystem of the criminal justice/juvenile justice systems, is designed largely to deal with the convicted/adjudicated (or at least those who are diverted). Reinforcing this view is the fact that the adult system has always received the lion's share of government funds, because of the incarcerated-to-community-supervision ratios and the high costs of operating prisons.

To be sure, delinquency prevention programs existed for decades, but they were few and far between. The emphasis on treatment over prevention is clear if one examines the two postwar presidential commissions: the President's Commission on Law Enforcement and the Administration of Justice, ordered by President Johnson in 1965, and the National Advisory Commission on Criminal Justice Standards and Goals, ordered by President Nixon in 1971. The volumes produced by the commissions placed more emphasis on the adult world and on rehabilitation.

But by the mid-1970s a number of significant changes had occurred:

- A number of studies of the effects of correctional treatment clearly demonstrated limited success.

- One state after another passed mandatory sentences, requiring incarceration for designated crimes. And about 20 states passed determinate sentence laws eliminating discretionary parole.

- The prisoners' rights movement, which began in 1964, essentially ended in 1974. Prisoners have won few lawsuits at the Supreme Court level since that year.

These changes relate to the adult criminal justice system and reflect a generally conservative view of crime and the criminal. Whereas the 1950s–1960s reverberated with welfare reform, civil rights legislation, and reform for the criminal, the last two decades have focused on deterrence, retribution, and incapacitation. A reflection of these views is the dramatic increase in America's jail and prison populations that began in earnest about 1980.

We must also take note of another significant change, one that started in the mid-1980s: escalating juvenile crime. As we noted in Chapter 5, serious juvenile crime began a rapid ascent at that time. Today, we are immersed in hundreds of delinquency prevention programs scattered across the country.

Prevention Programs

Scholars, practitioners, and researchers have made a distinction between prevention programs and treatment programs. This is a somewhat false dichotomy, since all programs attempt to prevent delinquency. We can clarify the matter by inserting an adjective before the word *prevention:* Primary prevention, like an inoculation, attempts to prevent delinquency from ever happening, while secondary prevention (treatment programs) attempts to prevent reoffending.

Delinquency prevention programs can be divided into two more broad categories. The first can be referred to as "one size fits all." As Gibbons and Krohn (1991) put it, at one time society was seen as the patient, and we had to repair "the social and economic fabric of our society" (327). This idea promoted macrolevel, large-scale neighborhood programs such as the Chicago Area Project. These programs produced few positive results in terms of curtailing delinquency. A second-generation delinquency prevention model has evolved over the past 20 years. It is microlevel, more narrowly focused, and based largely on re-search obtained directly from at-risk youth.

Macrolevel Prevention Programs

A truism in the prevention of juvenile delinquency has been that loving parents who hold to prosocial values and are supported by a stable neighborhood will raise children to be upright, good adult citizens. This truism was especially acceptable if parents were also supported by good schools and houses of worship. The focus on the family and its imme-diate environmental conditions was the basis for a number of major delinquency preven-tion programs in the years before and after World War II.

The first such program was inspired by the juvenile delinquency research of Shaw and McKay (1942) in Chicago. Their research over the first three decades of the twentieth cen-tury led them to the conclusion that delinquency was the product of social disorganiza-tion, or the inability of social institutions to control children. The rates of delinquency during the study periods remained highest in the areas characterized by immigrants, ten-ement housing, high poverty levels, and industrialization.

The program that resulted, called the Chicago Area Project, started in 1929, with Clif-ford Shaw as its first director. It focused on several neighborhoods with the highest levels of delinquency. The project leaders used what was available in neighborhoods, including the employment of indigenous citizens who knew the territory well, churches, schools, and settlement houses (Kobrin 1959). Project activities focused on recreation, school im-provement, sanitation, employment assistance, and a concentration of prosocial activi-ties in settlement houses. Over three decades, the Chicago Area Project assisted thou-sands of juveniles and adults, and supporters claimed various degrees of success based on the number of police contacts (Kobrin 1959). In actuality, we cannot make any firm con-clusions about the project, since no research element was built into it (Lundman 1993).

In the early years of the John F. Kennedy administration, a program similar to the Chicago Area Project was formulated and implemented. Supposedly, President Kennedy (or a close adviser) was impressed with a book by Richard Cloward and Lloyd Ohlin, *Delinquency and Opportunity* (1960). The authors believed that lower-class boys had the same aspirations of achievement and success as their middle- and upper-class peers, but were not provided with equal legitimate opportunities. In their view, this situation was the leading cause of lower-class delinquency.

This thinking led to the formulation of a major delinquency prevention program called Mobilization for Youth (MFY) (Lemann 1991). The project began in lower Man-hattan in 1962. Its two basic goals were to open legitimate opportunities for youth and to organize adults so that they could take the necessary steps to improve their neighbor-hoods. As with the Chicago Area Project, staff made significant use of settlement houses, work opportunities for youth, recreation, and school tutoring. Adult civic groups were formed, citizens were apprised of voting rights and procedures, and they were provided with the necessary services to gain welfare assistance. MFY consumed millions of dollars over a half dozen years in its quest to reduce delinquency. It did so to some degree, but nearby nonserved neighborhoods recorded similar trends (Katkin et al. 1976).

After World War II the Department of Agriculture sponsored 4-H clubs in an attempt to involve youth in wholesome activities. Vista Volunteers (the urban version of the Peace

Corps) opened storefront offices in urban areas and worked with youngsters in recreation, counseling, tutoring, and problem solving (Trojanowicz 1978). In 1965, the Department of Labor established the Neighborhood Youth Corps, which worked with students and dropouts in job skills, work experiences, and on-the-job training.

These programs, as well as the Chicago Area Project and the Mobilization for Youth project, are classified as delinquency prevention programs. They are a mixture of primary and secondary programs since, in any neighborhood or group of juveniles, there are likely to be both youth who are not delinquent and those who have been adjudicated.

Prior to World War II one distinct primary prevention program took place in the Cambridge-Somerville communities of Massachusetts. It was simply called the Cambridge-Somerville Youth Study Project. Schoolteachers, police officers, and playground workers were asked to nominate boys, under 10 years of age, who they thought would eventually get in trouble with the law. From several thousand boys, the project staff was able to come up with 325 matched pairs, who were then randomly assigned to experimental (serviced) and control (nonserved) groups. The project hired 19 workers over the course of the program, though only 10 were working at any one time. The project began in 1939 and was designed to run for 10 years. Each worker had a caseload of 30–35 boys. Workers were to assist the youths and their families in any way except to provide them with direct financial aid. Examples of the services provided were (Lundman 1993):

- tutoring;

- educational trips;

- employment assistance for family members;

- development of hobbies; and

- procure psychological treatment for youth and/or family members.

During the first two years of the project, workers averaged 11 direct contacts per youths per year, 12 contacts per year with the family, and 12 contacts per year in the community, such as at schools.

World War II had a profound effect on the project, of course. Some fathers were drafted, and some families moved for wartime employment prospects. The attrition rate was such that by December 31, 1945, only 72 of the original 325 matched pairs were still available (Lundman 1993). Two outcome measures were used to compare experimental boys to the controls: school performance and referrals to the juvenile court. There were no significant differences between the groups. In fact, the experimental boys were referred to court at a slightly higher rate than the controls (Katkin et al. 1976).

With the increasing influence of psychology and psychiatry after World War II, much of the emphasis on dealing with juvenile delinquency turned to treating the delinquent. Corrections saw a dramatic rise in the medical model of treatment and significant increases in the various forms of group therapy. Also, as we will see in Chapter 17, starting in the mid-1960s behavior modification became widely adopted, especially in juvenile correctional institutions. The technique was also used in community corrections (in the form of behavioral contracts) and in group homes.

But in the past decade or so, attention has again turned to prevention programs. This trend may be a result of the recent studies on serious and violent juveniles, which clearly demonstrate that the eventual serious delinquent displays signs of trouble at an early age (see Chapters 5–6). Whatever the reason, OJJDP has provided considerable resources to programs that focus on early prevention, and many of them relate to family and children.

OJJDP and Microlevel Prevention Programs

With the passage of the Juvenile Justice and Delinquency Prevention Act in 1974, the OJJDP began almost three decades of providing funds for the care and treatment of juvenile delinquents. The early efforts of the agency focused on three basic goals: deinstitutionalization of status offenders, separation of juveniles from adults in adult institutions, and removal of juveniles from adult jails and lockups. In 1992, a fourth basic goal was added: addressing the disproportionality of minorities in confinement. But since the mid-1980s the emphasis has shifted to new priorities (most states have achieved the first two goals, and progress is being made with respect to the fourth). Largely motivated by the work around the nation on such projects as the Causes and Correlates of Delinquency and the initial results of the Serious and Violent Juvenile projects in Denver, Pittsburgh, and Rochester, New York, OJJDP has settled on a comprehensive strategy for Serious, Violent, and Chronic Juvenile Offenders (Wasserman et al. 2000). The comprehensive strategy (CS) is OJJDP's plan to prevent serious and violent delinquency. Its ultimate goal is "a continuum of services, including research-based prevention programs that address risk factors in the community and a system of research-based graduated sanctions that provide a range of dispositional alternatives for youth in the juvenile justice system based on their risk of reoffending and need for treatment" (Coolbaugh and Hansel 2000, 3; see Figure 16.3).

The comprehensive strategy effort differs significantly from earlier macrolevel prevention efforts, which assumed that a "one size fits all" approach would get the job done—whether that involved recreation programs or neighborhood civic associations. The CS offers a series of programs from prenatal care to correctional aftercare. Each program is designed to reduce risk factors that contribute to delinquency or build buffers that protect at-risk youth.

Since 1996, OJJDP has provided technical assistance to three pilot sites: in Lee and Duval Counties, Florida, and San Diego County, California. In Duval County the planning committee consists of a wide range of community stakeholders, including the sheriff's office, mayor's office, county attorney, public defender, school and children's agencies, and faith-based organizations. The committee has decided that Duval County's five major risk factors are:

- economic deprivation;
- early academic failure;
- family management problems;
- lack of commitment to school; and
- availability and use of drugs.

The following are examples of programs, still in the early or developmental stages, designed to deal with these risk factors:

Figure 16.3 Overview of the Comprehensive Strategy

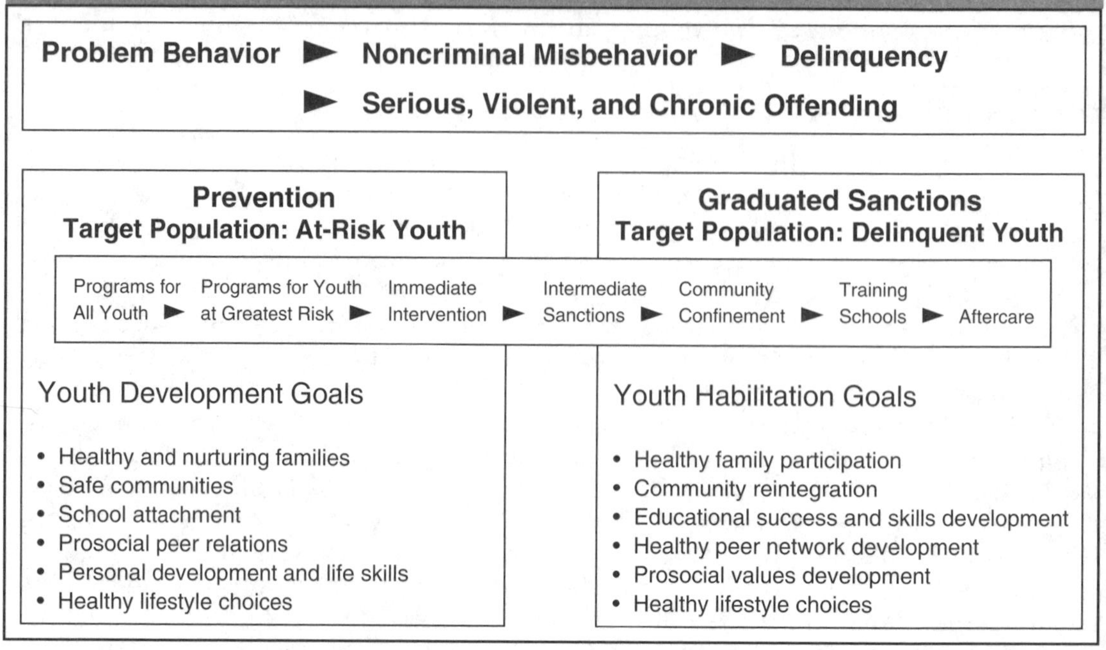

Problem Behavior ▶ Noncriminal Misbehavior ▶ Delinquency
▶ Serious, Violent, and Chronic Offending

Prevention Target Population: At-Risk Youth	Graduated Sanctions Target Population: Delinquent Youth

Programs for   Programs for Youth   Immediate   Intermediate   Community   Training
All Youth ▶ at Greatest Risk ▶ Intervention ▶ Sanctions ▶ Confinement ▶ Schools ▶ Aftercare

Youth Development Goals

- Healthy and nurturing families
- Safe communities
- School attachment
- Prosocial peer relations
- Personal development and life skills
- Healthy lifestyle choices

Youth Habilitation Goals

- Healthy family participation
- Community reintegration
- Educational success and skills development
- Healthy peer network development
- Prosocial values development
- Healthy lifestyle choices

1. Project Abundant Life: This program provides youth and families with after-school activities, weekend tutorial services, family enhancement services, job and career training, computer training, and GED classes.

2. Families and Schools Together (FAST): This program is an eight-week cycle of families involved with a team of counselors who focus on school failure, prevention of youth and family substance abuse, and reduction of family conflict and stress.

3. Together We Will Program (ZIP Code 32209): The ZIP code identification is used for this program because most of the risk factors appear in this geographic territory. Programs address six priority risk factors:

   - Tutoring and mentoring
   - Computer skills classes
   - Recreation programs
   - FAST
   - Family financial counseling
   - Mental health counseling

In the other two pilot counties, CS programs are similarly designed to address specific risk factors. OJJDP is also providing considerable funds directed at specific problems. For instance, beginning in fiscal year (FY) 1995 it provided funds to five jurisdictions to implement its prevention, intervention, and suppression program called comprehensive gang model. The model contains five key strategies:

1. Mobilize communities.

2. Provide youth opportunities.

3. Suppress gang violence.

4. Provide social intervention via social services and street outreach activities.

5. Facilitate organizational change and development among community agencies.

By FY 2000 OJJDP was providing additional funding to several jurisdictions that had been doing well in achieving comprehensive gang model goals. One example is the city of Mesa, Arizona, whose program consists of:

- job skills development;

- counseling;

- drug and alcohol treatment and prevention;

- tattoo removal services; and

- outreach activities.

The Mesa program has developed partnerships with police, adult and juvenile probation, the United Way, local Boys and Girls Clubs and other youth-serving agencies, and private business organizations.

Gang units tend to be proactive in their attempt to reduce the extent of gang-related crime. Why has this prevention effort been so successful lately?

OJJDP is actively involved in and funding several mental health initiatives. Through the staff of Northwestern University's Medical School, juvenile detainees in the Cook County (Chicago) detention center were psychiatrically interviewed between 1995 and 1998. By 2000, the investigators had tracked the original sample of 1,830 juveniles interviewed in detention. The project is in process.

In 1992, the National Institute of Mental Health (NIMH) began a long investigation of the effects of medication and treatment for children with attention deficit/hyperactivity disorder (ADHD). Although ADHD is classified as a childhood disorder, 70 percent of affected children continue to experience symptoms into adolescence. In 1998, OJJDP provided funding to follow those youth in the NIMH sample who eventually had contact with the justice system.[3]

To complete our discussion of prevention programs, we turn to the two specific targets that seem to get the most attention and resources: school and family. Again, OJJDP is actively involved in school and family programs across the country, providing funding and technical assistance.

Schools

It seems there has always been a connection between the schools and juvenile delinquency. According to conventional wisdom, achieving students went into adulthood as good citizens while poor-performing pupils dropped out of school and got into trouble. This view received a significant boost when the President's Commission on Law Enforcement and the Administration of Justice (1967) issued its final report (*The Challenge of Crime in a Free Society*). The report contained such statements as, "the school . . . is a public instrument for training young people" and "it is the principal public institution for the development of a basic commitment by young people to the goals and values of our society" (69). Moreover, the commission held some schools (located in the slums) responsible for delinquency. It said that the school is "one of the last social institutions with an opportunity to rescue the child from other forces, in himself and his environment, which are pushing him toward delinquency," and "there is considerable evidence that some schools may have an indirect effect on delinquency by the use of methods that create the conditions of failure for certain students" (69).

These are strong words and, unfortunately, the commission did not provide the solid research required to back up this claim. But this was the liberal 1960s, and blaming social and government institutions for personal failures was very much in vogue. Whether schools today are truly responsible, to any degree, for causing juvenile delinquency is beyond our discussion. It is enough to say that OJJDP has committed significant resources to school settings as a place to prevent delinquency.

Another interesting twist involving the school is school-based probation. In this version of probation, the PO works directly in the school, keeping tabs on the youth in a variety of contexts, including, of course, school attendance. In the school setting these POs are able to contact youth on a much more frequent basis than they can with traditional probation (Kurlychek et al. 1999). According to OJJDP analysis, the most promising interventions are (Loeber et al. 2003):

- classroom and behavior management programs;
- multicomponent classroom-based programs;
- social competence promotion curriculums;
- conflict resolution and violence prevention curriculums;
- bullying prevention;
- after-school recreation programs;
- mentoring programs;
- school organization programs; and
- comprehensive community interventions.

Truancy

Truancy is a major societal problem. Research clearly shows that truancy is positively correlated with substance abuse, gang activity, and crimes such as burglary, auto theft, and vandalism (Baker et al. 2001). Law enforcement agencies from several cities report that high rates of truancy are related to daytime burglaries and vandalism (Baker et al. 2001).

Over the past decade, truancy has increased significantly. About 10 years ago, 150,000 New York City pupils were absent on any given day and in Los Angeles it was 62,000 (Garry 1996). The September 10, 2001, issue of *U.S. News and World Report* stated that in Fresno, California, 28,000 of its 79,000 school age children were classified as truants in the 1999–2000 period. In the same period, the truancy rate rose from 20 percent to 28 percent in Newport News, Virginia. In 1998 truancy accounted for 26 percent of the status offenses handled formally by the juvenile courts (Baker et al. 2001).

The OJJDP has become actively involved in providing financial grants to local governments in order to reduce truancy. In 1999, it provided grants of $50,000–100,000 to nine sites across the country (Baker et al. 2001). There are some common threads in the truancy prevention programs that have sprung up during the 1990s. Most of them involve the county attorney, a system of sanctions (some of them criminal) aimed at parents, the state's children and youth department, parenting classes and tutorial services. A sampling of these programs can be found in Box 16.1.

Box 16.1   Selected Truancy Prevention Programs

1. In Oklahoma City, THRIVE (Truancy Habits Reduced Increasing Valuable Education) is a direct threat-and-check program that started in 1989. Police refer a truant to a truancy processing center. The youth's parent is called and the youth is either released in an hour or detained in the Youth Services Shelter. The county attorney sends a letter to the parents informing them of the consequences of a toughened state truancy law. Attendance is then monitored. Authorities report improved attendance, a reduction in dropouts, and a reduction on daytime burglaries.

2. In Peoria, Arizona, the Save Kids Partnership program started in 1995. If a student accumulates three unexcused absences, the parents are immediately informed. If unexcused absences reach five, the county prosecutor sends a warning letter to the parents. If a sixth occurs, the prosecutor files criminal charges against the parents and offers them a deferred prosecution diversion program. The program involves a risk assessment of the youth, group counseling for the youth, and parenting skills classes. If all programs are completed and the youth is attending school, charges are dropped. If there is any program failure, criminal proceedings begin.

3. The truancy prevention program in Jacksonville, Florida, begun in 1999, is similar to Save Kids Partnership. In addition, a behavioral contract is negotiated with the youth and his parents, and a case manager makes home visits to check up on family compliance.

Sources: Garry (1996); Baker et al. (2001).

DARE

The best-known and widely used drug abuse prevention program is DARE (Drug Abuse Resistance Education). The program began in the Los Angeles School District in 1983. Originally, the program operated with police officers lecturing children in elementary schools. The results from research studies were not encouraging. Although some youths displayed a changed attitude toward drug use, research had not disclosed any positive impact on the extent of drug use or any difference in the use of substances between DARE youth and nonparticipants (Clayton et al. 1991; Ringwalt et al. 1991; Rosenbaum et al. 1994).

DARE is the major drug prevention program for juveniles. What accounts for its not having a significant impact in reducing drug use?

Recently, the curriculum has been revised (violence is a focus as well as tobacco, alcohol, and drug use), abbreviated from its original 17-lesson format, and extended to lower grades (all the way to kindergarten). The renovation of DARE resulted from a $13.7 million grant awarded in 2001 to the University of Akron by the Robert Wood Johnson Foundation. The University of Akron developed a "state-of-the-art substance abuse prevention curriculum." Currently, DARE police officers are supposed to serve as "coaches" who assist youth in operationalizing "research-based refusal strategies in high-stakes peer pressure environments." Students are shown brain imagery that demonstrates how substance use negatively affects mental activity, emotions, coordination, and movement. Lessons are also learned via mock courtroom exercises that highlight the social and legal consequences of substance use and violence. The curriculum is being tested in six cities that include 80 high schools and their 176 feeder middle schools, involving as many as 50,000 students. The preliminary findings of the Year One (seventh grade) curriculum are encouraging (University of Akron 2003):

- More students had better decision-making skills (6 percent higher scores than the control group).

- More students found drug use socially inappropriate and believed fewer peers used drugs (a 19 percent reduction in normative beliefs about the prevalence of substance use among peers compared to control groups).

- More students learned how to refuse alcohol, tobacco, and marijuana (refusal skills were significantly higher—5 percent—among students with the new curriculum compared to control group students).

- Fewer students reported intent to use inhalants (scores were significantly lower—by 4 percent—among students with the new curriculum).

Table 16.1 DARE Curriculum at Various Levels	
Kindergarten to Second Grade Curriculum	Being Safe
	Drug Safety
	Learning to Say "No"
	About Feelings
Third/Fourth Grade Curriculum	Rules to Keep Safe
	Drugs May Help or Harm
	Saying "No" to Drug Offers
	Feeling Special
	Dare to Say "No"
Fifth/Sixth Grade Curriculum	Purposes and Overviews of DARE Program
	Tobacco and You
	Smoke Screen
	Alcohol and You
	The Real Truth
	Friendship Foundations
	Putting It Together
	Personal Action
	Practice! Practice! Practice!

Similarly, the "Year Two" study results demonstrate that students who had received the seventh-grade curriculum continued in the eighth grade to "have improved scores on decision-making skills and beliefs that drug use is socially inappropriate." Table 16.1 presents the new DARE curriculum for elementary schools (*http://www.dare.com*).

GREAT

A parallel school-based program directed by police, but aimed at gangs, emerged in the early 1990s as the result of a collaborative effort between the Bureau of Alcohol, Tobacco, and Firearms and the Phoenix Police Department. Much like DARE, the GREAT program (Gang Resistance Education and Training) was expanded nationwide by 1993. GREAT is a life-skills competency program taught by local police. Its objectives are identified as to "enable youth to develop positive attitudes toward police officers, avoid conflicts, be responsible, set positive goals, and resist peer pressure." Although the program is aimed at youth in middle schools, GREAT also offers a third- and fourth-grade curriculum. The program runs nine weeks, with a lesson taught each week. There is also a summer follow-up project. In essence, GREAT hopes to encourage kids to resist the pressure to join gangs and to engage in peaceful conflict resolution instead of violence. GREAT relies on the lessons listed in Table 16.2.

ATF reports that national evaluations of its GREAT program have disclosed the following positive results (Esbensen and Osgood 1999; Esbensen et al. 2001):

- Lowers the rate of delinquency

- Lowers the rate of gang affiliation

- Lowers the likelihood of acting compulsively

- Increases positive attitudes toward the police

- Increases the number of friends involved in prosocial activities

- Increases the commitment to peers promoting prosocial behavior

Table 16.2 Lessons of GREAT
Introduction Students become acquainted with the program and the officer.
Crimes/Victims and Your Rights Officers discuss the impact crime has on victims and neighborhoods.
Cultural Sensitivity/Prejudice Students examine their own cultures; learn to appreciate cultural differences and how they impact the community. They also discuss the harmful behaviors resulting from prejudice.
Conflict Resolution (Discussion) Students learn a six-step process enabling them to resolve conflicts without using violence.
Conflict Resolution (Practical Exercises) Students apply the six-step conflict resolution model to real-life situations.
Meeting Basic Needs Students are taught how to become better equipped to meet their basic needs.
Drugs/Neighborhoods Students discover how drugs and gangs interfere with the peaceful coexistence of a neighborhood.
Responsibility Students learn the diverse responsibilities of individuals in their community.
Goal Setting Through role playing and discussion, officers show students the importance of setting goals in life.
Source: Bureau of Alcohol, Tobacco, and Firearms (ATF) (n.d.).

- Increases the commitment to school
- Increases the communications with parents about children's activities

The research did not find any reduction in gang participation, however (Esbensen et al. 2001).

The Family

The family has always held the lead position in socializing children into adolescence and even early adulthood. Of the main social institutions, the family gets the credit when adolescents turn out to be responsible, law-abiding citizens. Over the last 40 years scholars and social critics have pointed to the disintegration of the American family as a cause of many social problems. High divorce rates and single teenage mothers have made major contributions to family disintegration. OJJDP is apparently so convinced of these assertions that "the core principle of OJJDP's prevention strategy is to strengthen the family as a unit and provide resources to families and communities" (Kumpfer and Alvarado 1998, 1). You may have noticed, in the discussion of prevention strategies in this chapter so far, how often the family in involved. Kumpfer and Alvarado (1998) have compiled a number

---

Box 16.2   Family-Based Programs

Kumpfer and Alvarado (1998) provide a useful website that offers more programs than are outlined here, giving two- to three-page descriptions of various family programs that are currently underway: *www.strengtheningfamilies.org.*

Here are some examples:

1. Functional Family Therapy in Salt Lake City, Utah. The primary goal of the program is "to improve family communication and supportiveness while decreasing the intense negativity so often characteristic of these families." The two-page information sheet supplies the age range of juveniles for which this program is appropriate, the required skills of the therapist, program costs, training costs, and evaluations if they have been completed.

2. The Multisystemic Therapy Program in Mt. Pleasant, South Carolina. This program, focused on the youth's environment, deals with family relations, peer relations, and school performance. As with the Salt Lake City program, the information sheet provides the program elements and requirements.

3. The Adolescent Transition Program in Eugene, Oregon. This family intervention program is designed for youths returning to the community from a long-term period of incarceration. The program focuses on family management skills, limit setting and supervision, problem solving, and improved family relationships and communication patterns.

The brief and useful information sheets also provide the program's address, telephone number, and e-mail address.

---

of family-based programs that have demonstrated effectiveness. The most effective programs have been those that deal with behavioral parent training, family skills training, family therapy, and comprehensive family support (see Box 16.2 for a sample of these programs).

Postadjudication Programs

Most juveniles who are processed through the juvenile court, officially or unofficially, and who remain under court supervision are on standard probation. That means they report to their POs on some fixed schedule. Because of large caseloads in urban areas, routine reporting is most likely be monthly and takes place in the PO's office. Increasingly, this form of supervision has been referred to as "fortress probation" (Reinventing Probation Council n.d.; Maloney et al. 2001). This reference is a focal point of attempts to get POs out of their offices and into neighborhoods to do their work.

Under special conditions, some juveniles are assigned to particular programs or particular settings. Some attend 12-step programs fashioned after Alcoholics Anonymous, some receive psychotherapy, and some are assigned to residential settings.

Before discussing some correctional treatment programs and techniques, we need to reiterate a particular point. There have been very few pure primary prevention programs for juveniles. The Cambridge-Somerville Youth Study Project may have been one of the few of this kind, since the upper age for the boys selected for the project was 10. Programs designed to be prevention programs may, in actuality, deal with delinquents as well as nondelinquents. For instance, a program like DARE, which deals with sixth-grade students, may contain nondelinquents, hidden delinquents, and possibly official delinquents. The same probably holds true if families or communities are targets of prevention programs. With this in mind, we will discuss several programs specifically designed to treat adjudicated delinquents.

Behavior Modification

In Chapter 17 we will discuss the correctional application of the principles of behaviorism, with techniques such as token economies. The preferred environment for a token economy is an institution because of the staff's ability to control certain environmental factors. Staff can easily observe behavior, structure activities, and consistently manipulate rewards and punishments. It is difficult for POs to do the same with their clients because of their lack of control over behavior and environmental factors. Under the circumstances of probation (and aftercare) the closest behavioral program that can be implemented is a contract, in which the youth agrees to achieve certain objectives that the PO can verify (school attendance and grades, for example) and the PO can administer rewards (easing curfew) or punishments (increased reporting).

Guided Group Interaction

The small-group residential treatment center has become the preferred residential setting for delinquents, rather than the large training school. The pioneer program of this kind is Highfields, begun in 1950 in Hopewell, New Jersey. The facility holds 20 boys, ages 16 and 17, who are placed there as a condition of probation. The core of the program, and what made Highfields a nationally acclaimed treatment program is the process called guided group interaction (GGI), a unique form of group therapy.

In the traditional form of group therapy, 8 to 12 clients sit in a circle. One member of the circle is the group leader/therapist, who is usually an employee of the agency or is at least a nonclient. The setup in GGI is different: There is no group leader in the circle of clients; the facility's employee (leader) sits *outside* the circle. The 10 teens who make up the group run the process themselves, with the staff member's role restricted to keeping subjects on track and summarizing and drawing conclusions at the end of the session (usually 90 minutes). Interaction among the residents in their living situation and during the day at work provides grist for the therapeutic process. The constant interaction and the requirement that all youths provide their autobiographies to the group form the core of Highfields' GGI. There are no restraints on language in the sessions, which may include shouting and considerable street language.

Highfields was evaluated internally, which, predictably, produced positive results. But it was not any evaluation that made GGI the most copied group treatment process in juvenile corrections; rather, it was the impressive group process witnessed by thousands of visitors.

New Jersey has opened two more residential treatment centers for boys, Warrenfields and Oceanfields. Other jurisdictions have used Highfields as a model for their programs, and some even used the suffix "fields" in their names (e.g., Southfields in Louisville, KY) (Finckenauer 1984). New York State developed a number of centers along the Highfields model called START (Short-Term Adolescent Treatment) (Bartollas 1985). Guided group interaction provided the core foundation for youth programs, residential and nonresidential, around the country for several decades after the original Highfields opened in 1950.

Best Practices for Probation and Community Corrections

Among the many pursuits and initiatives of OJJDP has been the identification and adoption of interventions that are most likely to produce the most success. OJJDP has been engaged in a search, literally, for the best practices that would further two previously unrelated missions, accountability and treatment. In short, the federal agency has encouraged a *balanced approach* that combines the interests of the juveniles and the community. We saw in Chapter 1 that juvenile court's purpose is no longer singular or just for the youth and family. Rather, juvenile courts tend to be under an obligation to promote community safety and the punishment as well as the rehabilitation of the youth. What has emerged from OJJDP's initiative have been such ideas as graduated and intermediate sanctions that impose accountability on the offender, while not forgetting or ignoring the interventions that would most likely achieve the youth's rehabilitation. Effective programs within the accountability sphere have been found to contain the following elements (Beyer 2003, 10):

1. Recognizing where each youth is developmentally and building on each youth's individual strengths

2. Combining restorative restitution (see next section) and community service with victim input and various approaches to bring young offenders face to face with their victims

3. Teaching juvenile offenders how to make positive choices and resolve disputes without aggression, helping them understand how their actions have affected their victims, and discouraging them from viewing other people as potential targets

4. Using flexible, graduated sanctions and recognizing that punishment does not make a young person accountable

5. Empowering families to support youth's positive activities and efforts to succeed in school

6. Connecting youth with prosocial peers

7. Conducting program activities in the communities in which participating youth live (and for youth returning to the community after confinement)

In addition, OJJDP has been dedicated to the support and promulgation of research that would assist the identification of best practices. The findings of several research studies have implications for guiding public policy, especially in developing programs that will help in the prevention of misbehavior and the rehabilitation of offenders in the community (and in facilities). First, research has discovered that the most effective programs (Lipsey 1992):

1. concentrate on changing behavior and improving prosocial skills;

2. focus on problem solving with juveniles and their families;

3. have multiple modes of intervention; and

4. are highly structured.

Second, the general conclusions reached for establishing effective programs include the following:

1. Court intervention should start early in an attempt to interrupt developmental pathways before serious, violent, and chronic delinquency emerges (Huizinga et al. 1994).

2. A juvenile's risks and needs must be identified and matched to the intervention. In considering the most appropriate disposition, public safety must not be confused with appropriate treatment. The youth's offense is not a good indicator of what kind of programming is required to change the individual's behavior (Greenwood 1996).

3. Programs must incorporate a comprehensive array of interventions and services of sufficient duration to address entrenched problem behavior patterns (Huizinga et al. 1994).

Third, the interventions themselves should do the following (Kurlychek et al. 1999, 4):

1. Concentrate on changing negative behaviors by requiring juveniles to recognize and understand thought processes that rationalize negative behaviors (Greenwood and Zimring 1985).

2. Promote healthy bonds with, and respect for, prosocial members within the juvenile's family, peer, school, and community network (Hawkins and Catalano 1992).

3. Have a comprehensible and predictable path for client progression and movement. Each program level should be directed toward and directly related to the next step (Altschuler and Armstrong 1984).

4. Have consistent, clear, and graduated consequences for misbehavior and recognition for positive behavior (Altschuler and Armstrong 1984).

5. Recognize that a reasonable degree of attrition must be expected with a delinquent population (Community Research Associates 1987).

6. Provide an assortment of highly structured programming activities, including education or hands-on vocational training and skill development (Altschuler and Armstrong 1984).

7. Facilitate discussions that promote family problem solving.

8. Integrate delinquent and at-risk youth into generally prosocial groups to prevent the development of delinquent peer groups (Huizinga et al. 1994).

9. Engage the community to create and support prosocial community activities in which youth can succeed, and also schools to provide help to families with problem children (Huizinga et al. 1994).

Restorative Justice

Consistent with the pursuit of balanced approaches is the recent movement for restorative justice, which promises to take juvenile justice (and criminal justice as well) in a different direction from the past. Restorative justice redirects attention from punishing or rehabilitating the offender to the broader aspects of the effects of the offenders' behavior on victims and the community. Rather than ask, "What punishment do offenders deserve?" and "What treatment should they get?" we ask, "What harm have they done to the victim and the community?" The processes involved in restorative justice focus on both repairing the harm done (holding offenders accountable for their behavior) and preventing reoffending (OVC Bulletin October 2000).

The principles and processes of restorative justice include restitution to the victim, service to the community, rebuilding the offender, repairing harm to the community, victim-offender mediation, and the involvement of victim, offender, and various representatives of the community. Restitution, the payment of reparations by the offender to the victim, dates to prebiblical times. It was a significant element of punishment protocols for centuries, but receded into the background by the end of the nineteenth century. Participants at the International Penal and Penitentiary Congress, held in Paris in 1895, bemoaned the fact that restitution was rarely used as an element of the punishment process of many nations (Barnes and Teeters 1951).

Ignoring restitution to victims may have been connected to the rise of Lombrosian criminology and Freudian psychology in the late nineteenth and early twentieth centuries. These two schools of thought promoted the view that behavior (criminal or aberrant) is determined by factors beyond the control of the actor. Thus, the focus of medicine and penology was to cure the patient-offender. But by the 1970s views of crime and criminals had changed dramatically. The notion of the criminal as sick changed to the criminal as bad or evil. This shift provided the advocates of victims a significant opening as players in the criminal justice system. Rather than putting large sums of money toward the rehabilitation of the offender, society would be better off if the offender repaid the victim for the harm done by the crime. By the 1980s, a growing number of states and the federal government were requiring restitution as part of the criminal sanction. Studies that have examined restitution as a sentence have found it to have a positive impact in reducing recidivism (Allen 1994; Butts and Snyder 1992; Schneider 1990; Schneider and Schneider 1985).

Community service, or unpaid service as part of a court sentence, has a shorter history than restitution in the United States. The first known use of community service was in 1966 in Alameda County, California (Beha et al. 1977), as a sanction for motor vehicle offenses. Since then, use of community service has grown considerably, usually as a condition for probation.

There are more than 300 victim-offender mediation (VOM) programs in the United States, most of which are found in the juvenile justice system. VOM is primarily "dialogue driven, with emphasis upon the victim's needs, offender accountability, and some restoration of losses" (OVC July 2000, 3). Research on VOM programs reveals that victims express greater satisfaction with the justice system and are less fearful after meeting offenders, that offenders are more likely to be held accountable for their acts and to complete their responsibilities, and that offenders who met their victims subsequently committed fewer and less serious offenses (OVC July 2000).

Bazemore and Umbreit (2001) explored four restorative conferencing models, programs that bring together victims, offenders, and members of the community in nonadversarial meetings to hold offenders accountable for their actions and repair the harm they did. The four models are as follows:

1. **Victim-offender mediation.** This dialogue includes victim, offender, and mediator and is intended to right the wrongs committed by the offender.

2. **Community reparation boards, also known as youth panels, neighborhood boards, or community diversion boards.** In one form or another they have been in existence in the United States since the 1920s. Vermont currently makes the greatest use of reparation boards. Boards consist of citizens who, under the supervision of the court, meet with adult offenders. In the process, victims and citizens have the opportunity to confront offenders. With approval of the court, boards hand down sanctions and continue to monitor compliance.

3. **Family group conferencing.** In at least four states (MN, MT, PA, VT), these conferences bring together the people most affected by the crime, which can include the victim, offender, and family and friends of both. A facilitator contacts all parties in order to explore their willingness to participate in and abide by the final decision of the conference.

4. **Circle sentencing.** This is an updated version of a common traditional sanctioning process practiced by aboriginals in Canada and among some Native Americans. After an apparently lengthy period of nonuse, the practice was renewed in the Canadian Yukon Territory in 1991. Sentencing circles may include victim and perpetrator, their friends and relatives, the judge, the police, the prosecutor, the defense attorney, and any other interested party. The gathering involves an opportunity for anyone to speak, a healing process for the victim, and a consensus on the sentence for the offender. By 1996, at least one pilot program had begun in Minnesota.

When Bazemore and Umbreit (2001) surveyed the four models in a multisite project they found that participating parties expressed satisfaction with the process, that they held a greater degree of confidence in and respect for the criminal justice/juvenile justice systems, and that the potential for expanded use in the juvenile system far exceeds that for the adult system.

Restorative justice as a process to deal with offenders will grow in the coming years (Smith 2001). Advocates favor a process free of the official adult and juvenile systems. Nevertheless, the highly acclaimed Reparative Boards in Vermont were started by the state's department of corrections in 1995 (Bazemore and Umbreit 2001), Kay Pranis started as the restorative justice planner for Minnesota's Department of Corrections

(Smith 2001), and a juvenile mediation program was started in several West Virginia counties in 1997 by the chief probation officer of the state's First Judicial Circuit Court (Smith and Lombardo 2001). Although it is too early to make any assessment about outcomes, it is obvious that official, government-sanctioned programs are as much part of the restorative justice movement as the nongovernmental type.

Finally, the probability for greater growth of the process for juveniles over adults is likely for several reasons:

1. OJJDP has, for the past six or seven years, addressed the disproportionate incarceration rates of minority youth. The restorative justice process would be one more resource for proponents of diversion.

2. Restorative justice diverts the focus of attention from the offender to the victim and the community. For adults, society may be better served by a punishment model. For juveniles, we may be able to build on accountability and responsibility.

3. The rise of the victims' rights movement (especially in juvenile court) has provided victims a greater say in what happens in a juvenile case (see Chapter 8), giving restorative justice significant opportunity to spread in the juvenile system.

One potential limitation of restorative justice is that, much like teen courts, it is used only when the offense and record of the youth are not very serious (Levrant et al. 1999).

Juvenile Gun Courts

Besides teen and drug courts, another specialty court recently developed for youth is the juvenile gun court. The gun court is not typically used as a diversionary mechanism, however. Rather, it was developed to provide juvenile courts with sanctions that would be stronger than those usually available and that would enhance accountability. They have been used for nonviolent offenders charged with gun offenses (or in possession of other weapons) who merit the quick and special attention of the juvenile system. The principal elements of the program are (Sheppard and Kelly 2002, 3):

• early intervention (prior to end of court proceedings);

• short-term, intensive programming (one 2- to 4-hour session);

• intensive educational focus on the harm of guns; and

• inclusion of a wide range of court personnel working with the community.

The educational component, focusing on the extensive harm perpetrated by guns, is the backbone of the program, together with the encouragement to use nonviolent means to settle disputes. Also attractive is the fact that the gun court's proceedings occur shortly after arrest, so youths do not have long waits for an adjudicatory hearing. Thus far, the program has been designed for nonviolent, nonchronic offenders.

The Jefferson County (Birmingham, Alabama) juvenile gun court has been identified as a model program. The court accepts first-time, nonviolent gun offenders, usually charged with gun possession. More serious gun-related crimes (such as armed robbery) are processed by the regular juvenile court. Youth eligible for the gun court are taken to the detention center, where they are fingerprinted, subjected to intensive intake screening, and drug tested. The vast majority (95 percent) plead guilty (called pleading "true") at the detention hearing, while others have a trial date set within 10 working days. Youths considered to be low risk for violence are placed directly in the program, while those considered high risk for violence are sent to a state detention center. The gun court youths attend boot camp (see Chapter 17) for 28 days while their parents attend a parent education program. Following release from the boot camp, the juveniles are put through decreasing phases of intense supervision, including house arrest for the first 30 days. For the next 6 months to 2 years, the youth will be under a PO's supervision. Those who do not experience an adjudication or conviction within the next 2 years may file a petition to have their records sealed. Once individuals reach age 24, they can have their records destroyed. The sealing and destruction of records provisions make the gun court dangerously close to a true diversion effort. Research on this program has shown a significantly better recidivism rate than control groups (Sheppard and Kelly 2002).

Intensive Aftercare Program

Completing the spectrum of community correctional interventions is the intensive aftercare program (**IAP**) that awaits some youths released from an institution or boot camp. The idea behind IAP is that juveniles require carefully scrutinized follow-up on their release from custody. Even though youths respond well to a treatment program while in a facility, that does not automatically mean they will retain the positive effects of the program when they return to their old neighborhood. The IAP is based on integrated delinquency theories and offers five principles (Altschuler and Armstrong 1994, 4):

1. To prepare youth for progressively increased responsibility and freedom in the community

2. To facilitate youth-community interaction and involvement

3. To work with both the offender and targeted community support systems (e.g., families, peers, schools, employers) to establish constructive interaction and to help youth adjust successfully to the community

4. To develop new resources and supports where needed

5. To monitor and test the youth and the community on their ability to deal with each other productively

As with so many other aspects of community corrections, IAP requires an assessment of the youth's risks and needs (and abilities), now in the community context, together with an analysis of the services available in the community (able to serve the youth's needs), all of which is backed up by intense supervision and accountability or sanctions for violations. IAP has five components related to this assessment (Altschuler and Armstrong 1994):

1. Assessment, classification, and selection criteria

2. Individual case planning

3. Integrating surveillance and services based on risk factors

4. Balanced incentives and graduated sanctions

5. Service brokerage with community resources and linkage to social networks

Although OJJDP has funded IAP development in four states (CO, NV, NJ, VA), and research has shown positive results on recidivism rates (Sontheimer and Goodstein 1993), some obstacles still stand in the way of IAP success. What has been found necessary for IAP to succeed are (Altschuler et al. 1999):

• preceding parallel services in the corrections facility and careful preparation for aftercare;

• adequate funding to provide truly intensive supervision and service delivery;

• formal assessment of offenders to determine which youth need highly intrusive supervision and enhanced treatment-related services; and

• reduction in caseloads and intensification in level of contacts with youth.

The Numbers at Probation

Delinquent Youth

Getting a complete picture of the numbers of juveniles who are "serving" terms of probation or community supervision is nearly impossible, as we have hinted throughout this chapter. The unknown figure should include juveniles in community "placements" who are actually carried on a probation caseload and those subject to some of the "other sanctions" referred to in juvenile court dispositions. Also not officially tabulated in juvenile court statistics are youths on aftercare status, reporting to a PO often for an undetermined length of time.

Deriving a probation number for the delinquent population requires adding three groups of youth: nonpetitioned, nonadjudicated, and adjudicated. Between 1993 and 1999, millions of youth were put on probation for delinquent acts, with or without court processing or adjudication (see Table 16.3).

During the last three years for which data are available (1997–1999), a remarkable consistency can be seen in the characteristics of delinquent-charged youth from the three groups put on probation. The gender breakdown during this period was 76 percent male and 24 percent female. Although the numbers did not change for gender in these three years, as recently as 1988 and 1989 females made up only 18 percent of those put on probation. In terms of age, those between 14 and 16 constituted 62 percent of the juveniles given a probation disposition between 1997 and 1999. Finally, as to race, while whites were 69 percent of the youth put on probation, blacks accounted for 28 percent and youth from other races made up 3 percent of juveniles given probation by juvenile court (Black 2001; Puzzanchera 2003c; Scahill 2000).

Once again it must be emphasized that the figures in Table 16.3 do not include the many thousands from each of these three groups who were given "other sanctions" by the juvenile court that would have involved reporting to and possibly working with a probation officer. These numbers also do not include status offenders, for whom a probation disposition is also very likely.

Status Offenders

For status offenders the numbers are even more questionable or incomplete, inasmuch as those who are not petitioned are not included within the juvenile courts' statistics. Tabulating just adjudicated and nonadjudicated status offenders (and again ignoring the many thousands given "other sanctions"), the numbers put on probation between 1993 and 1997 are given in Table 16.4. Obviously, the total number of juveniles under community supervision is large and ever-expanding.

Table 16.3 Probation Dispositions Involved in Delinquency Cases, 1993–1999

Year	Nonpetitioned	Nonadjudicated	Adjudicated	Total
1993	191,700	74,100	254,800	520,600
1994	196,100	77,800	264,500	538,400
1995	239,900	86,000	283,300	609,200
1996	246,100	81,200	306,900	634,200
1997	242,100	84,800	318,700	645,600
1998	246,800	52,600	366,100	665,500
1999	239,800	39,000	398,200	677,000

Sources: Butts et al. (1996a, 1996b); Sickmund et al. (1998); Stahl et al. (1999); Puzzanchera et al. (2000, 2003a, 2003b).

Table 16.4 Probation Dispositions Involved in Status Offense Cases, 1993–1997

Year	Nonadjudicated	Adjudicated	Total
1993	8,900	36,400	45,300
1994	7,860	38,740	46,600
1995	9,400	41,000	50,400
1996	8,590	49,770	58,360
1997	7,200	50,200	57,400

Source: Butts et al. (1996a, 1996b); Sickmund et al. (1998); Stahl et al. (1999); Puzzanchera et al. (2000).

Summary: Key Ideas and Concepts

- Disproportionate number of youth assigned to community supervision
- Significant breadth of activities that fall within a PO's responsibilities
- Probation may or may not be a sentence
- Probation as conditional freedom
- Standard versus special conditions of probation
- Twofold nature of PO supervision
- Various working styles of POs

- Supervision method as medical or reintegration model
- Classification of offenders for assignment of services
- Classification of offenders according to risks and needs
- Intensive supervision an alternative to incarceration
- Intensive supervision varying in application among jurisdictions
- The intricacies of a needs assessment
- Association between diversion and labeling theory
- Net widening as a consequence of diversion
- Teen and drug courts as diversion programs
- Interchanging populations of prevention and treatment programs
- Different audiences in primary and secondary (treatment) prevention programs
- Different targets and scopes of microlevel and macrolevel prevention programs
- Comprehensive strategy aimed at serious and violent delinquents
- Schools as settings for prevention programs
- DARE and GREAT as school-based prevention programs
- Family preservation and development as prevention strategy
- Guided group interaction as effective and copied treatment intervention
- Restorative justice as expanded victim-offender mediation program

Discussion Questions

1. What characteristics make defining probation difficult? How should the practice be defined?

2. What are the implications of the widespread community network upon which the juvenile justice system relies?

3. Are any conditions attached to probation that should not be permitted? Are there any conditions not currently imposed on youth that should be adopted by juvenile court? Should probation for delinquents differ from that experienced by status offenders? If not, why not? If yes, in what way(s)?

4. How long should probation last? Should youths have the same controls over the length of probation that adults have, or should the duration depend on the youth's response to rehabilitation?

5. How many opportunities, generally, should juveniles have on probation? In other words, how soon (or by how many adjudications) should juvenile courts be looking to institutionalize delinquent youths?

6. Which should be more important in determining the probationary experience for youth, their risks or their needs? Why does one prevail over the other?

7. How much of a problem is net widening? Is it sufficient to prevent diversion?

8. What limits should be placed on cases that are eligible for teen and drug courts? What limits should be placed on the sanctions available to these courts?

9. Is it realistic to separate primary from secondary prevention? Should a different program be used by primary versus secondary prevention programs?

10. What prevention strategies are the most promising? Are there approaches that could be successful but haven't been adopted yet? What might they include?

11. Did your elementary or secondary school have a DARE program? What was it like? Was it successful? If not, why not? If yes, in what way(s)?

12. What prospect does restorative justice have in stemming the tide of delinquency? Are there any cases that would be inappropriate for this treatment strategy?

Endnotes

1. Augustus published a first-person account of his work up to 1851 (APPA 1984). At that time he had assisted 1,102 men and women. Later he included children in his work. A journalist named Ball Jenner claimed he had assisted 5,000 men, women, and children by 1858.

2. The information in this section was obtained from the following website: *http://probation.co.la.ca.us scripts/JFSB.html.*

3. The source of the preceding information on gangs and mental health is OJJDP's 2000 annual report. ✦

Chapter 17

Juvenile Institutions

Focus of Chapter 17

In this chapter we explore the myriad facilities in which juveniles can be institutionalized for treatment or for punishment. These facilities are much more diverse than the jails and prisons that house adult inmates. While some juvenile institutions resemble adult jails and prisons, others look like college campuses and can even be the house next door. This diversity makes it difficult to make any broad statements, positive or negative, about the institutional network of the juvenile justice system. Researching the phenomenon can also be difficult, inasmuch as those investigating the situation may or may not be accurately assessing the type of facility in which the youth is living.

Key Terms

- behavior modification
- boot camps
- CHAPTERS
- corporal punishment
- cottage-style training school
- deinstitutionalization
- detention center
- disproportionate minority confinement
- foster homes
- group homes
- halfway house
- hidden juvenile corrections
- inmate culture
- institutional model
- meta-analysis
- operant conditioning
- privatization
- reception center
- reform school
- right to treatment
- therapeutic community
- token economy
- training school
- wilderness programs

Putting Juvenile Institutions Into Context

The corrections subsystem of the criminal justice system is ordinarily divided into two seemingly distinct components: institutions and community-based programs. The examples that immediately come to mind are the four basic functions of corrections—prisons, jails, probation, and parole. People who are in jail or prison are not able to come and go as they please—walls, bars, concrete, steel, and high-tech equipment assure us that those inmates are kept securely confined. On the other hand, offenders who are under probation or parole supervision are, for the most part, free to come and go.

Nevertheless some inmates leave jails and prisons daily in order to go to work (work release) or to go home on a brief *furlough*. Most inmates, though, are denied these privileges because correctional authorities believe them to be high risks and a potential danger to the community. So, within any penal institution varying degrees of restraint may be placed on inmates. Some institutions themselves are categorized by the degree of restraint exercised over their inmates. Thus, we have *minimum-*, *medium-*, and *maximum-*security prisons. Most jurisdictions divide their facilities into more than three levels of security, operating open camps, farms, and supermax prisons.

The corrections situation we have descended for adults is applicable to juveniles as well. Most juveniles on probation or aftercare (parole) can pretty well come and go as they please, subject to parental controls, while others are under curfew restrictions, and still others are under tighter control through electronic monitoring.

The variations in adult institutions are also present in juvenile institutions. Postadjudication, long-term care has traditionally taken place in large, campus-like institutions. Juveniles live in large, dormitory-style cottages and walk across campus to various activities. One of the trends of the past 20 years has been to construct small, secure facilities that outwardly resemble adult jails. Large states often have two types of facilities, open training schools for low-risk youth and secure facilities for high-risk youth. Many states also operate satellite ranches and forestry camps. While the degree of direct restraint on juveniles in the last two is less than for other forms of incarceration, their geographical isolation is an effective escape deterrent. Finally, large states also have separate intake facilities, variously titled Northern Youth Reception Center and Clinic (California) or Reception and Evaluation Center (South Carolina). Small states have just one institution that must serve as intake evaluation and open and secure long-term care. An example is the Rhode Island Training School, opened in 1900, which holds males and females and includes a 20-bed secure assessment and treatment unit.[1]

Just as the jail serves as the entry point for confining recently charged adult offenders, the detention center serves that purpose for juveniles. Originally conceived as a pretrial holding facility, the detention center has developed into a multipurpose facility.

This chapter is divided into two major sections. In the first we shall discuss short-term facilities and several current issues and trends surrounding this correctional function. In the second portion we will explore the significant aspect of long-term incarceration of juveniles.

Juvenile Detention

Juvenile *detention* is the juvenile version of adult jail in that it is primarily a holding facility at the entry point of the juvenile justice system. The National Juvenile Detention Association (NJDA), after laboring for three years, finally arrived at a definition:

> Juvenile detention is the temporary and safe custody of juveniles who are accused of conduct subject to the jurisdiction of the court who require a restricted environment for their own or the community's protection while pending legal action. (Roush 1996, 33)

This definition is very narrow and would seem to apply solely to youths charged with delinquency or under the court's supervision, such as on probation. In effect, it excludes a number of other categories of youths who usually occupy beds in detention centers.

The complete definition goes beyond the opening statement and includes the provision of services offered, including education, visitation, communication, counseling, continuous supervision, medical and health care, nutrition, recreation, and reading. Including these elements yields a definition of detention that goes far beyond a mere holding facility.

The government structure of juvenile detention centers mirrors that of the adult jail system. The centers are either state-based, operated by a state agency such as the Department of Corrections (DOC) or a youth and family services department, or locally based. In the local system, the administration could be a municipality, a county, or the juvenile court itself. Let's look at two examples of the major governmental structures, Delaware and New Jersey.

Delaware's system is state-based. That is, the DOC, in addition to operating prisons and parole supervision for felons, also provides confinement for pretrial detainees and convicted misdemeanants and supervision for probationers. The state-based system also applies to juveniles. The operating agency, which oversees all juvenile correctional functions, is the Division of Youth Rehabilitative Services, located in the Department of Services for Children, Youth and Their Families. The Division runs the state's two detention centers.

New Jersey, on the other hand, has a more traditional system. The adult pretrial/misdemeanant function is county-based in jails, while the prison system for felons lies in the state's DOC. Juvenile detention is also county-based, although not all of the 21 counties has a facility. Such a local system often results in rather small units. For instance, the populous Camden County has a detention center constructed in 1980, with a rated capacity of 37. The fact that each of Camden's neighboring counties has a detention center was no doubt a contributing factor in determining capacity. Rural Salem County, in the most southerly part of the state, has no detention center; the number of children requiring detention is so few that operating one would be cost prohibitive, so authorities there use Gloucester County's facility. There is somewhat of a tradeoff here, since Salem County has a status offender shelter that Gloucester County uses.

Who Is in Detention?

The NJDA definition of detention makes clear that its function is to temporarily hold juveniles who are accused of conduct subject to the jurisdiction of the juvenile court. That has traditionally pertained to youth in a preadjudicated status. But according to the national survey performed by the American Correctional Association (1997) on March 31 1997, less than 50 percent of the 19,419 youth detained were in that status (see Table 17.1). The numbers compiled by OJJDP later that year are similar. Of the 27,680 juveniles detained on

Table 17.1 Youth in Detention, March 31, 1997			
Preadjudicated	Adjudicated	Committed	Postdisposition
8,304	4,830	3,070	3,215
Source: Adapted from: ACA (1997), Table p. XV.			

October 29, 1997, 13,234 (or 48 percent) were awaiting an adjudicatory hearing in juvenile court (Sickmund 2002a).

Like its adult counterpart, the jail, the detention center serves other categories of children:

- On any given day, there are youths who have already been adjudicated delinquent and are awaiting a disposition hearing. During that waiting period they will be visited by probation officers whose task is to prepare predisposition reports for the court.

- Another type of detained youths are those who have been adjudicated, for whom a disposition has been handed down, and they are awaiting out-of-home placement. If that placement is the state's training school, they are likely to be transferred in a matter of days. But if the placement is a community residential facility, the youth may have to await intake evaluation and, if accepted, may have to await an empty bed. The wait could stretch into weeks if the placement is an out-of-state facility. For instance, the much-heralded Glen Mills School of Pennsylvania takes young men from around the country. Aside from whatever travel arrangements that must be made, Glen Mills, like all private programs, has an intake policy that means a detained youth would have to be evaluated. In Jacobs' (1990) study of a county juvenile court system, he found the longest posthearing detention stays related to children awaiting long-term placement. OJJDP data from 1997 identify this category as the second most prominent (28.5 percent of detainees) type of detention (Sickmund 2002a).

- Other youth in detention are committed juveniles, serving a juvenile court disposition. According to the ACA's (1997) National Juvenile Detention Directory, on March 31, 1997, 39 states held 3,070 youths as commitments. Advocates of this practice argue that a short stay in a nearby detention center is preferable to a commitment to a distant training school. Critics argue that the practice mixes different classifications of youth and that detention centers are not designed for treatment (Schwartz et al. 1987). More telling, the practice raises the specter of net widening. A youth committed to a detention center for 30 days is no doubt on probation upon release. If the commitment option were not available, would not the disposition be probation? Is the purpose to teach the juvenile a lesson? Are juveniles scared straight by short-term incarceration? For juveniles detained prior to adjudication, a short-term commitment does not seem to add to whatever shock effect they may have originally experienced. For the vast majority of juveniles who remain at home prior to adjudication, perhaps a 30–60 day interruption of life (school, for example) may be more harmful to the youth than the benefit it purportedly provides to society.

- A fifth category of youth in detention is youths who may have been arrested moments or hours ago and whose status is in limbo.

- Sixth, youths are held in detention as alleged probation/parole violators, awaiting a revocation hearing.

- Finally, a good number of youths in detention could be awaiting a hearing regarding transfer to adult court, although they could be categorized by some as awaiting trial in juvenile court. On October 29, 1997, OJJDP counted 544 youth waiting for a certification hearing and another 1,058 awaiting a hearing or trial in adult court (Sickmund 2002a).

In 1997, 95 juveniles were in detention for every 100,000 in the population (Snyder and Sickmund 1999). Appendix O portrays the detention and commitment rate for all the jurisdictions in the United States.

Detention Facilities

The American Correctional Association (ACA) annually sponsors the collection of national correctional data that are compiled into useful directories. One of the recent directories is devoted to juvenile detention (ACA 1998). From the ACA directory we culled out 301 facilities that fit our conceptualization of detention centers. We did not consider any facilities that did not record any children in the *preadjudication* status on the day of record, March 31, 1997. The most likely reason for not recording any child present is that the facility is not a detention center. Some facilities listed in the directory are clearly not detention centers. The Minnesota Correctional Facility—Red Wing—is an example. Also, we did not consider facilities designated *staff* secure, since they are unlocked shelters for status offenders.

The 301 facilities are grouped into rated capacity categories (see Table 17.2). It should be noted that 234 (77.7 percent) of the 301 detention facilities have capacities of

Table 17.2 Rated Capacities of Detention Centers

Rated Capacity	Number
10 or Less	34
11–20	87
21–30	51
51–100	42
101–200	17
201–300	4
Over 300	4

Source: ACA (1997).

50 or fewer beds. Respondents to the ACA survey reported daily per capita costs, showing that juvenile detention is very costly. Table 17.3 depicts these costs in collapsed categories. While the largest representation of facilities (128) is in the *under-$100* category, most of those facilities reported daily costs of $75 or more. At $100 the annual cost is $36,500, a figure exceeding what is considered the high end for adult incarceration

Table 17.3 Juvenile Detention Costs	
Per Capita/Per Diem	**Numberof Facilities**
Under $100	128
$100–119	53
$120–129	27
$130–139	17
$140–149	13
$150–199	27
$200–249	3
$250 or more	4
Source: ACA (1997).	

costs. There is a direct relationship between total costs and the number of staff. Table 17.4 highlights several selected detention centers chosen to demonstrate the relationships among rated capacity, population counts on March 31, 1997, staffing, and per capita/per diem costs.

One could argue that if the facilities in Table 17.4 are typical of juvenile detention, then high costs are due to *overstaffing*. In each case, staffing is more than double the rated capacities, and in some cases it is double the actual populations in overcrowded facilities.

On the other hand, Table 17.5 shows what are no doubt cases of *understaffing*. Correctional scholars and practitioners may wonder how one can properly administer a 24-hour-a-day, 365-day-a-year institution with a total staff of 10 or 12. It takes 5.5 people to man a correctional post (as we will see later in this chapter). With rare exceptions, juvenile detention centers are coed, which requires a female on duty even if there are no girls in the center at any one time. There is no way to predict

Table 17.4 Selected Detention Facilities				
State	**Rated Capacity**	**Population 3/31/97**	**Number of Staff**	**Per Capita/ Per Diem**
Alaska	35	63	126	$143
Connecticut	22	35	49	120
Illinois	30	31	70	100
Iowa	40	45	86	165
Kansas	33	40	88	150
Massachusetts	30	47	73	106
Montana	8	8	22	150
New Jersey	20	17	42	120
New Mexico	6	3	17	105
Oregon	8	9	23	150
Pennsylvania	8	8	66	118
Source: ACA (1997).				

Table 17.5 Selected Detention Facilities

State	Rated Capacity	Population 3/31/97	Number of Staff	Per Capita/ Per Diem
Louisiana	13	11	12	$101
Maine	13	13	12	65
Mississippi	12	8	9	75
New Mexico	10	10	12	63
Oklahoma	6	6	8	134
Oregon	10	10	8	100
Tennessee	10	15	10	141
Utah	6	11	6	115

Source: ACA (1997).

Table 17.6 Juveniles in Jail, 1993–2002*

Year	Tried or Awaiting Trial as Adults	Held as Juveniles
1993	3,300	1,000
1994	5,100	1,600
1995	5,900	1,800
1996	5,700	2,400
1997	7,007	2,098
1998	6,542	1,548
1999	8,598	860
2000	6,126	1,489
2001	6,757	856
2002	6,112	1,136

Source: Gilliard (1999); Beck and Karberg (2001); Harrison and Karberg (2003).
*Counts at midyear.

when a girl will be referred to the facility. The presence of a female worker is, of course, only a part of a total staffing pattern.

What is depicted in Table 17.5 may reflect the lack of civil service laws or policies that regulate public service. Civil service usually limits the workday/workweek before overtime compensation must be paid. Only 50 of a total of 544 agencies reported detention run by a state agency. The majority are administered by local government, sheriff's or police departments, and private contractors. A second possible explanation may be that workers in these jurisdictions are not unionized.

A trend that child advocates condemn is the increasing number of juveniles held in adult jails. Table 17.6 shows the increase during the 1990s. This particular practice runs counter to the spirit of the JJDP Act of 1974, the mandates in its reauthorizations and the efforts of the OJJDP.

History of Juvenile Detention

With the birth of the juvenile court in 1899, the need to detain children became apparent. For status offenders and dependent and neglected children, juvenile courts purchased homes that were overseen by house parents. Serious delinquents were detained in jails and training schools.

The secure detention facility emerged primarily after World War II. In 1930, there were 141 facilities, and by 1967 there were 242. The American Correctional Association (1998) reports 547 such institutions on March 31, 1997.

Congress passed the Juvenile Justice and Delinquency Prevention Act of 1974 (JJDPA) after prolonged senate hearings about the horrible conditions and practices in juvenile institutions. A significant aspect of the law is a word synonymous with juvenile justice—deinstitutionalization. The federal government used funding as an incentive for states to refrain from institutionalizing status offenders. Since then, the government has also been working with states to keep juveniles out of adult jails.

The effects of the deinstitutionalization movement were felt everywhere. A number of training schools for girls closed, largely because most incarcerated girls were status offenders. Some states adapted to these circumstances by designating a cottage for girls at the boys training school. Another effect was the development of unlocked shelters (or shelter care) for status offenders, rather than secure detention.

The other significant movement during this period was the *accreditation* of correctional organizations. Begun in the mid-1970s by the ACA with the support of the federal Law Enforcement Assistance Administration (LEAA), accreditation for a prison holds the same meaning as accreditation for a hospital or university—it has conformed to certain standards.

The forerunner in detention standards may have actually occurred in 1946 at the National Conference on the Prevention and Control of Delinquency. The conference produced 13 standards, including the following:

- No child should ever be held in adult jail or lockup.

- Detention intake should be in the hands of the juvenile court.

- Programs should be available—education, social life and recreation, and spiritual guidance.

- There should be a medical examination on entry and a nurse on duty in large institutions.

- There should be clinical child guidance services for first aid treatment for acute emotional disturbances and for more intense study. (Roush 1996)

Among the reasons given for earning accreditation is that it may serve as a buffer to liability. While accreditation may not immunize a facility, it certainly is a mainstay in matters of legal defense. Nevertheless, fewer than 10 percent of juvenile detention centers are accredited (Roush 1996).

Conditions in Detention

Perhaps because so few detention centers are accredited, many have been found to suffer from improper conditions and have been the subjects of lawsuits. The problems that most often plague secure detention centers occur in the following areas (Puritz and Scali 1998; Burrell 1999):

- Overcrowding (where youth may actually be sleeping on floors)

- Safety (threats of violence and physical and sexual assaults)
- Restraints/isolation (use of mechanical restraints and excessive isolation)
- Education (lack of full days of education and special education programs)
- Health care (lack of health screening and medical and dental staff)
- Recreation (inadequate services and outdoor recreation)
- Staffing/training (poor staff-to-inmate ratios and lack of training)
- Environment (fire and safety hazards, poor physical conditions, dirty clothes)
- Treatment (inadequate counseling and programming)
- Fairness (improper restrictions on visitation and correspondence)

The Juvenile Detention Alternative Initiative (JDAI) that we discussed in Chapter 10 has been busy not only in reducing the number of youths held by POs at intake and by judges at detention hearings, but also in improving the conditions in detention centers. The list of improvements registered at the four sites sponsored by JDAI has been impressive (Burrell 1999). The effort to bring about change (in both detention centers and long-term facilities) has been captured in an acronym, CHAPTERS, that addresses most of the cited problems (Burrell 1999):

Classification and separation issues (e.g., protection of suicide prone youth)
Health and mental health care
Access to counsel, the courts, and the family
Programming, education, exercise, and recreation
Training and supervision of institutional staff
Environment, sanitation, overcrowding, and privacy
Restraints, isolation, punishment, and due process
Safety issues for staff and confined children

Rehabilitation in Detention

Treatment programming in preadjudication detention has always been the norm. The commitment to provide programs is strengthened by the fact that most youths who gravitate to detention are from the lower classes, are usually deficient in academics, and come from troubled families (Roush 1996). Standard rehabilitation programs in juvenile detention are schooling and counseling in some form. In addition, programs can include life skills, anger management, or parenting classes.

In the 1960s, the NCCD advocated the initiation of the casework process when a youth entered detention. That view is still favored by child advocates and the National Juvenile Detention Association. But a question still exists: Should there be programming of this kind in a *preadjudication* status?

Civil libertarians are inclined to believe that those charged with crime should not assist their accuser. They object to *some* programs for juveniles. For instance, education programs do not draw fire from civil libertarians but counseling programs do. Counseling, especially in groups, tends to thrive on self-revelation. Whether one calls it group therapy, group counseling, or a "rap" session, the exchange among group members about their experiences provides grist for the therapeutic mill. In pre-*Gault* days, detention staff routinely reported on a detainee's detention behavior during *adjudicatory* hearings. Under these circumstances, some of which still exist today, youths may unwittingly provide information harmful to themselves in the judicial process. Moreover, in the disposition hearing, where hearsay is admissible, self-harm is even more likely to occur.

For the correctional purist, any treatment intervention prior to a finding of guilt is both premature and intrusive. Correctional intervention, by definition, is to correct something that is "broken." The notion of "broken" relates to whatever personal problems the offender has that contributed to the offense. The connection between offender and offense remains questionable, however, until a finding of guilt.

The issue becomes more complex when we recognize the growing number of states that permit an adjudicated youth to be committed to a detention center as part of a disposition. Complications come about from the mixing of preadjudication youth with those serving a disposition. Most detention centers are not large enough, nor are they designed, to completely separate the two classifications of youth. The problem is compounded when we realize that, with rare exception, juvenile detention centers are coed. Providing the kind of programming that civil libertarians and correctional purists object to for adjudicated youth and denying the same to the accused would no doubt crease significant management problems.

The Costs of Detention

Costs for juvenile incarceration are always significantly higher than those for adults. There are two major reasons for this difference: staffing and facility size. Earlier in this chapter we noted that 77.7 percent of detention facilities have capacities of 50 or fewer beds (see Table 17.2). We also noted that staff in detention centers often outnumber the youth in residence.

Approximately two-thirds of the operating costs of institutions, whether prisons, hospitals, or colleges, are the costs of personnel. In large measure these costs are attributed to salaries and fringe benefits. In institutional corrections, staff are usually divided into three categories: administrative, custody, and treatment. In addition, there are always others retained on a contractual basis, such as physicians and psychiatrists, as well as a large number of volunteers and college interns.

Detention centers are responsible for conducting classes for detained juveniles. How much does this responsibility contribute to the costs of the facility?

Administration of Detention

A detention center, at minimum, has an administrator in charge of the facility (the most common title is *superintendent*). Detention facilities with capacities of 100 or more are also likely to be staffed by other classifications of administrative personnel, such as a business manager or personnel officer. In the smaller facilities, workers in any job classification may fill in for others. For instance, when the center's cook is off, it is common for the social workers or custody staff to fill in. Thus, job sharing in most juvenile detention facilities is a necessity.

Custody Staff

Juvenile custody staff go by various titles—*childcare worker, group leader,* and *group supervisor* are probably the most frequently used. The title preferred by the National Juvenile Detention Association is juvenile *careworker* (Roush 1996). Careworkers are the 24-hour-a-day, 365-day-a-year employees responsible for order and security in a locked institution. They are the most numerous of the staff.

It is the custody requirements, coupled with the facility's small size, that make juvenile detention expensive. Because of the routine daily activities, staffing gets to an irreducible minimum. Some of the center's children will be in a classroom, some will be in arts and crafts, and some will have to be transported to court. New arrivals have to be processed, and some will have visitors. Some youth will be scheduled for a clinical evaluation. So even in a facility with a capacity of 25 or 30, it is common to have five custody staff on duty.

Detention centers frequently have the same types of security as adult jails. What psychological impact does detention have on juvenile inmates?

Total custody staff for a detention center can easily outnumber residents. A *correctional post* is a designated assignment, such as the worker who sits inside a sealed-off booth and controls entry and exit. This post must be manned 24 hours a day, 365 days a year. When we factor in the ordinary work week (5 days), vacation time and holidays, and the inevitable days lost to illness, it takes 5.5 people to man a post. If we then include administrative treatment staff, we can understand why detention costs so much. Some organizations cope with this budget challenge by hiring casual workers who are paid an hourly wage and receive no fringe benefits.

Treatment Staff

The minimum treatment staff found in detention centers is one teacher and one caseworker. The number of such workers rises with the capacity of the facility. All juvenile institutions have an education program. Mandatory schooling for those less than 16 years of age requires this program to be in detention, even though the average length of stay is counted in days. Nearly as equally required by circumstances is a *caseworker,* who provides individual counseling, mediates child-parent relationships, and handles the case through the system. The caseworker is the traditional link between the center and the juvenile court.

Finally, we noted earlier that detention staff is augmented by clinicians and physicians on a contractual basis and volunteers and student interns. The ACA (1998) recorded that 1,813 volunteers were active in detention centers in 1997.

Boot Camps

Like detention centers, boot camps are short-term facilities, but, unlike detention, they serve as a dispositional resource for juvenile court (and adult court as well). Boot camps are basic military training operations that promote structure and discipline. The first one emerged in 1983 in Georgia and was designed for adults. The first juvenile version opened in Alabama in 1990 (Cronin 1994) and can be considered a reflection of the get-tough movement in juvenile justice. At one time, boot camp was regarded as the panacea for juvenile crime. Ideally, boot camps were seen as accomplishing a wide variety of important goals, including deterrence, incapacitation, punishment, accountability, rehabilitation (through self-discipline and improved health and fitness), cost saving, and reduction in institutional overcrowding (Cronin 1994; Peters et al. 1997).

There was never any doubt about the military nature of boot camps, especially since the name itself was borrowed from the military. All characteristics of these camps are military-oriented, ranging from the clothes worn by staff and juvenile to the barracks in which the youths live. Titles used to address each other, the protocol, drills, and interaction between staff and youth are military. Youths are grouped into platoons and are rewarded and punished as a group. Verbal confrontations and intimidation are regularly used by staff (Felker and Bourque 1996). The daily operation of a boot camp is regimented, and virtually every minute is dedicated to a particular task, whether drilling, eating, attending class, exercising, or sleeping. Military time is used to detail exactly where youths will be and what they will be doing, with roll calls occurring at least once nearly every waking hour (Cass and Kaltenecker 1996).

Because of its physically demanding regimen, boot camp is limited both in the youths that qualify for admission (no physical, medical, or mental problems) and in duration (the typical length is 90 days but can run to 6 months).

One major controversy is how boot camps fit into the disposition framework. That is, are they enhancements for probation or alternatives to incarceration? Should the youth with a first adjudication be put in boot camp as a supplement to a first probation sentence, or should the youth be one with a significant delinquent record on the verge of being put away? Should boot camps be considered as probation dispositions because of their brevity (like shock probation), or are they examples of institutionalization because of their intensity? In fact, some judges may regard boot camp as an alternative to transfer to adult court, after the youth has experienced several institutional dispositions in juvenile court. As we saw in Chapter 14, some jurisdictions statutorily limit boot camps to nonviolent, nonchronic offenders, eliminating any likelihood of using them as an alternative to transfer.

The one certain thing about boot camps is that they did not turn into the panacea for juvenile crime. In fact, research has tended to find that boot camp has little positive—and sometimes even a negative—effect—on reducing recidivism (Cronin 1994; MacKenzie 1994; Peters et al. 1997). Boot camps also do not operate without incidents, despite the strict regimen. Three boot camps (in Cleveland, Denver, and Mobile) that were supported through funding from OJJDP experienced a significant number of escapes, fights, and instances of insubordination, among other violations. The proportion of inmates involved in these incidents ranged from 69 percent in Denver (1.9 per youth) to 82 percent in Cleveland (2.6 per youth) and 91 percent in Mobile (3.4 per youth) (Bourque et al. 1996). Nevertheless, there have been some positive outcomes from the Cleveland and Mobile boot camps. More than half of the Cleveland youths and more than three-fourths of the Mobile youths improved one or more grades in areas such as reading skills, math, spelling, and language (Peters et al. 1997). Although all the OJJDP-sponsored camps offered a 6- to 9-month community-based aftercare program, one observation on the deficiencies of some programs (and perhaps part of the reason for no reduction in recidivism) is the lack of an intensive aftercare program (Cronin 1994).

We now turn our attention to long-term incarceration—institutions for juveniles most often referred to as reformatories or training schools.

Overview of Juvenile Incarceration

There are two ways to conceptualize incarceration: by the degree of *confinement* and by *system processes*. We will see here that confinement means more than being held behind locked doors. We will also discuss the various processes the system uses to navigate a juvenile from beginning to end.

The first place of confinement for an arrested juvenile is a detention center or perhaps shelter care. Once adjudication has taken place, the disposition most frequently imposed is probation. In today's world, probation can even include incarceration. A condition of probation may be to serve 30 days, more or less, in a detention center. Further, as a condition of probation, juveniles may be assigned to a residential facility in the community (foster or group home, halfway house, or treatment center), perhaps for an extended length of time. While probation conditions like these do not restrain juveniles through locks and fences, control is exercised by program structure and the threat of full incarceration in the event of probation violation. Moreover, since youths are committed to these residential locations, the dispositions are officially tallied as placements or commitments. As we noted in Chapter 14, this situation makes it difficult to comprehend and discuss (or research) the institutional network for juvenile offenders.

Foster homes amount to little more than the people next door agreeing to take one or more youths into their home in return for a subsidy from the state. A group home can be a regular residential house with a good number of youths or a large, orphanage-like facility housing hundreds of youth. Both foster and group homes should operate as options for delinquents and status offenders who require somewhere other than their own home (if there is one) in which to live, but otherwise qualify for a community-based sanction. Halfway houses can look like the smaller version of group homes and house delinquent youths requiring more supervision than the foster and group home youths (or youths reintegrating into the community after release from an institution). Juveniles sentenced to foster and group homes and halfway houses would likely travel there directly from juvenile court without visiting the juvenile correctional network directly. For juveniles facing true, long-term out of the community institutionalization, the first stop will be at a reception center.

Reception Centers

The next dispositional step in our system overview is commitment to the state's youth corrections agency.[2] In large states, committed youth are likely to begin their long-term incarceration in a reception center that could also be known as an *assessment* or *diagnostic center*. A youth's stay in this facility is likely to be several weeks, depending on the extensiveness of the intake/diagnostic process of the agency. Classification of the youth can result in a number of permanent assignments available from the reception center:

- Transfer to a secure institution

- Transfer to an open institution

- Assignment to a boot camp

- Assignment to a forestry camp

- Assignment to an outward bound program

In small states the first three (secure institution, open institution, and boot camp) and the intake/diagnostic process take place in one facility. That institution is likely to be a campus setting with open cottages and a secure unit.

In some jurisdictions juvenile court judges can make a direct commitment to the state youth corrections agency's boot camp, bypassing the state's intake process. Some agencies operate their own community residential facilities to reintegrate youths into the community after earning aftercare release (parole). During the rehabilitation era of the 1960s–1970s, some agencies experimented with immediate parole from reception centers. One of the most watched of these was the California Community Treatment Project. A program like this, granting release to offenders shortly after being incarcerated, was unpopular among law enforcement agencies. Nor did juvenile court judges applaud it. In a judge's mind, when he or she commits a youth, it means the court has exhausted all possible community options and that incarceration is called for.

Reception centers can be used in another controversial manner. In a number of jurisdictions the court is authorized to commit the adjudicated youth to a reception center for the purpose of evaluation *prior* to a final disposition. In such a case the youth is housed in a correctional facility, which often holds a variety of juveniles.

This practice has its supporters. Reception centers are heavily staffed with diagnostic workers, far more than at a detention center. Clinical workups are carried out more conveniently than if the youth lived at home, which would require a number of appointments. Also, the facility's staff are able to report to the judge how well the youth has adjusted to institutional life, a factor that may be critical in the final disposition. Finally, a week or two in a correctional institution may provide the "shock therapy" some believe has rehabilitative effects. Critics argue that correctional staff have never been perfect at physically separating different classes of offenders and some youths are bound to be victimized. Furthermore, disrupting a youth's life (if living at home at the time of adjudication) even for a few weeks, for the sake of administrative convenience, is seen as the needless overreach of the court's authority.

Long-Term Institutions

The institutions in which juvenile offenders live come in a variety of sizes and physical configurations. Furthermore, those institutions and the correctional agencies that operate them go by a variety of names. The American Correctional Association (ACA 1998) produces an annual directory of state adult and juvenile correctional agencies, which provides a state-by-state listing of departments, institutions, and paroling authorities.

Juvenile offenders are committed to the state juvenile *correctional agency,* though only nine states use the word corrections or correctional in their titles, as in Arizona's Department of Juvenile Corrections. In 23 states *services* is used, as in Department of Youth Services (MO), and seven states include the word *family,* as in the Department of Family Services (WY). These two terms may reflect a modern trend not only to separate juvenile corrections from its adult counterpart but also to incorporate it into a larger, comprehensive service agency. For example, in Delaware the Division of Rehabilitative Services (juvenile corrections) is located in the Department of Services for Children, Youth, and their Families. Likewise, whereas the term training school was almost universal in the past, the majority of juvenile institutions prefer names such as *youth center* (AK) and *youth services center* (AR). Titles in other states include *juvenile correctional facility* and *juvenile prison.*

The nature of a training school, which historically was also referred to as an *industrial school* or perhaps a *development center,* ranges from small cottage units to relatively large, prisonlike facilities. Training schools can be open or secure, single-sex or coed, and private or public. Some training schools specialize in rehabilitating certain offenders, such as sex offenders or fire starters. For example, the Ethan Allen School in Wisconsin is for serious sex offenders. A student must progress through six treatment phases in order to earn release. In Tennessee, the Woodland Hills School is a maximum security institution, surrounded by a 15-foot fence, for multiple recidivists. In 1996 the population was made up of 120 males and 24 females. The institution offers academic and vocational classes and a variety of treatment techniques, ranging from anger management to substance abuse treatment, speech/language therapy, and psychiatric care. Students also have one hour of physical education and one hour of free recreation daily. Privileges are earned through a point system. Students who present severe behavioral problems are assigned to a 12-bed segregation unit that has its own academic program. The average stay in segregation is three months (Clayton 1996).

Many training schools in numerous states have earned bad reputations for their lack of education and rehabilitation programs and their prevalence of physical abuse (see "Conditions in Juvenile Corrections," later in this chapter). For many locations, the reputation has been earned and reports of abuse can be pulled up regularly via the Internet. One notable exception to this negative reputation is a private facility known as the Glen Mills School in suburban Philadelphia. The school, situated on a 779-acre campus that could easily pass for a Victorian-style college, is a 600-plus student facility. Visitors to the school are impressed by the orderliness and cleanliness of the facility and the politeness of the students. There are no locks or bars. The entire staff is male. Glen Mills emphasizes academic education. Five distinct academic groups meet for four hours daily. Much time is also devoted to athletics. Glen Mills students regularly win state championships in gymnastics, powerlifting, and track and field; they excel in football as well. Some students have won scholarships to such universities as Temple, Maryland, West Virginia, Syracuse, and Virginia Tech.

As we saw in Chapter 16, the core of the program is the development of a prosocial student culture through guided group interaction (GGI). The school has rejected the traditional clinical, one-to-one model of correctional treatment in favor of the group confrontational model. The program is structured to immerse youth in an environment in which physical safety is assured, and respect and rewards result from prosocial behavior. Every weekday morning at 9:00 students in groups of 10 to 12 are involved in a one-hour GGI session. Most of the daily regimen is divided between academic and athletic endeavors. At 9:30 p.m. students have a cottage townhouse meeting that involves discussing the problems of daily living and disseminating information about activities, athletic achievement, and upcoming events.

The profile of the Glen Mills student is a 16.5-year-old, black gang member from an urban area (mostly Philadelphia). On admission, students test at grade 5.9 verbal and 5.8 math. Nearly half (43 percent) of the students have three to four prior arrests, and 24 percent have five or more. Commitment offenses range from assault (16 percent) to armed robbery (17 percent) and burglary (23 percent). Nevertheless, Glen Mills has achieved a lot academically. By 1983, 200 students had earned a GED and 72 had gone to college (paid for by Glen Mills). By 1990, the school had achieved 1,000 GEDs, and 133 students had gone to college. Despite these accomplishments, by 1985, about 50 percent of discharged students had been arrested and 35 percent had been reincarcerated (Grissom and Dubnov 1989; Ferrainola and Grissom 1990; Bartol and Bartol 1998).

Wilderness Programs/Camps/Ranches

A major part of the juvenile institutional network used in many states are the wilderness or *challenge* programs. Perhaps the largest such program in the country is Vision Quest (VQ), founded in 1973. VQ identifies its approach to delinquents as an "emphasis on staff's role as parents rather than counselors; the use of rigorous outdoor activity, living history, and historical re-enactment that connect youth to their heritage and culture; and the blending of military influences with treatment and education" (*www.vq.com*). VQ is actually a private, multifaceted operation sponsoring a variety of settings that include what are called full circle camps (AZ, FL, NJ, PA), hat corps camps (PA), Madalyn Programs for young women (FL, NJ, PA), homequest programs (AZ, DE, FL, PA), group homes (AZ, CO, NJ), shelter care (CO, PA), and alternative schools (AZ, DE, PA). VQ uses what it calls *guided centering*, a treatment approach that aims to provide youth greater stability and balance in their emotions, perceptions, and behaviors. The program has 10 elements:

- New environments and experiences
- Supportive staff
- Physical challenges
- Treatment

- Customs and ceremonies
- Education
- Community service
- Cultural competency
- Family reunification
- Vocational assessment and planning

One facet of the VQ operation consists of a wagon train trip in which the youth learn how to cook, to tell direction, and to develop basic survival skills. VQ provides an intensive experience in a supportive environment under the direction of active adults who serve as protective role models. Its services are designed specifically to help youth:

- be in a safe environment;
- deal with and overcome the pain and anger they have from their past;
- experience success and positive reinforcement from supportive and caring staff;
- learn to trust people with their feelings and thoughts and accept support;
- learn to work in a team, accept and give support, and exhibit leadership;
- recover from mistakes and get back on track with support from staff;
- be challenged by new experiences and environments to think and act in new and positive ways; and
- work hard to achieve significant accomplishments.

Although a review of research literature finds wilderness and challenge programs to have only weak effectiveness in reducing recidivism (Lipsey and Wilson 1998), VQ claims that 69 percent to 86 percent of its participants have not been reincarcerated in recent years.

Public Versus Private Facilities

OJJDP actively monitors the number of facilities available to the juvenile population and the number of youths committed there. In October 2000, 1,203 facilities were identified as public and another 1,848 were listed as private, for a total of 3,061 facilities in the United States serving juvenile offenders (Sickmund 2002a, 2002b). These numbers highlight one of the controversies surrounding the institutionalization of youth: choosing between a public or private facility in which to house youth. As we noted in Chapter 14, private facilities have had the luxury of accepting and rejecting prospective inhabitants according to whether a youth fits into their program, while public facilities, being run by the state, tend to have to accept most, if not all, youths who land at their doors. Moreover, private facilities also accommodate youths committed by their families in order to receive some sort of (often substance abuse) treatment. These "voluntary" commits can include youth who have neither committed nor been charged with an offense. The differences between private and public facilities with respect to the population of youth, the caliber and traits of the staff, and the atmosphere of the institution can be staggering. Also controversial is that while private facilities have been filled predominantly with white juveniles, public facilities disproportionately experience a minority population.

In its 1997 census of juveniles in residential placement, OJJDP found that more than half (57 percent) of all facilities mix violent offenders with nonviolent ones and that this situation was much more likely to occur in public (79 percent) than in private (43 percent) institutions. Only 29 percent of facilities mixed juveniles younger than 13 with those older than 15. This situation was more common among public (40 percent) than private (21 percent) facilities, while 59 percent of the youths mixed in this way were in public institutions. Juveniles under the age of 12 were most likely to be found in private facilities. Minorities were disproportionately held in public facilities. Whereas 28 percent of public places had a 75–100 percent minority population, only 21 percent of private facilities were constituted in this manner. Moreover, 30 percent of private (and only 19 percent of public) facilities had less than a 25 percent minority population. Not surprisingly, then, while two-thirds of white youth are placed in public facilities, more than three-fourths of minorities are held in public facilities. Most facilities (52 percent) are male only, and a mere 15 percent are female-only. The remaining one-third of the facilities are mixed-gender. More public facilities (51 percent) are mixed-gender than are private ones (22 percent), which in turn are more likely to be female-only (20 percent) than are public facilities (6 percent). Finally, private facilities tend to be smaller than public ones. Whereas 72 percent of the youths in private facilities are held in one with a capacity of *fewer than* 111, 62 percent of youth in public facilities are held in one with a capacity of *more than* 110 people. Thus, although 60 percent of juvenile facilities are private, 70 percent of juveniles are confined in public facilities (Sickmund 2002a).

By far the most controversial aspect of the long-term incarceration of youth is their being held in adult prison, usually through a sentence received after conviction in criminal court. Although we will not explore the dimensions of adult prison here, suffice it to say that the number of youthful offenders subjected to prison is substantial (see the "Numbers at Corrections" section later in this chapter), and that according to a number of reports, penal policy has not yet adapted to the presence of juvenile inmates (Bishop and Frazier 2000).

Juvenile Populations

How many juveniles are incarcerated in long-term facilities? This is a difficult, if not impossible, question to answer for several reasons:

1. From 1974 to 1997 OJJDP gathered data on incarcerated children and reported the information in a document commonly referred to as Children in Custody. This was replaced in October 1997 by the Census of Juveniles in Residential Placement (CJRP), a collection of more comprehensive data than its predecessor (Moone 1998).

2. We usually think of juvenile delinquents as youths under the age of 18, but in three states (CT, NY, NC) a 16-year-old is considered an adult offender, and in ten states the adult age begins at 17. Since an age definition of *juvenile* is essen-

tial, OJJDP decided that in gathering information on incarcerated youth, under 21 would provide the definitional age (Snyder and Sickmund 1999).

3. Gallagher (1999) reported that on October 29, 1997, there were 125,805 young persons *assigned beds* in 1,121 public and 2,310 private residential facilities (holding alleged or adjudicated delinquents or status offenders). Of the 3,431 facilities, 2,844 had at least *one* juvenile who met all the following four criteria:

   • Under 21

   • Charged with or court adjudicated for an offense

   • Placed in the facility because of the offense

   • Assigned to a bed on October 29, 1997

   Of the original 125,805 juveniles, 105,790 met the four criteria.

4. In the last few years the type of facility where juveniles reside is largely lost in the reporting. In 1995, Moone (1997a) reported 69,075 juveniles in public juvenile residential custody, which includes secure and nonsecure facilities for preadjudicated and postadjudicated youths. Also in 1995, Moone (1997b) reported 39,671 juveniles in private residential facilities. The terms used to designate custodial confinement are (1) residential facility, (2) residential placement, and (3) out-of-home placement. Any of the terms can mean (1) training school, (2) foster care, (3) group home, or (4) residential treatment facility.

5. Even the latest and most comprehensive survey across the whole system (Snyder and Sickmund 1999) casts little light on the subject. The survey asked each respondent a question to determine whether youths were confined by *staff* or by *locked doors and/or gates* after school hours. Using this definition of security, they reported that 7 of 10 youths were confined during the afterschool hours by at least one locked door or gate. In a concluding statement the authors of the report make a rather ominous extension of this finding: "The vast majority of juveniles in residential placement in public facilities were confined under locked arrangements. For juveniles in private facilities, the reverse was true" (Snyder and Sickmund 1999, 205). In a cottage-style training school where students move about the campus throughout the day, going from one activity to another, it is common to lock the door to the cottage at night, as much to keep people from entering as from leaving.

The revised method of reporting juveniles in custodial confinement mixes preadjudicated and postadjudicated youth and does not permit separation of institutional confinement from traditional community-based residential placement. Thus, there is no way to separate the juvenile felon in a state training school from either an emotionally disturbed youngster in a psychiatric facility or a status offender in a shelter or foster home. Despite these caveats and limitations, we present estimates of the correctional population at the end of the chapter.

History of Juvenile Institutions

There are several perspectives on the reasons for the development of incarceration. Some give the Quakers of Philadelphia credit for the invention of the penitentiary two centuries ago as a humane alternative to capital punishment (Clear and Cole 1997). Alternatively, some would argue that incarceration is nothing more than a tool for capitalism's need for slave labor (Rushe and Kirchheimer 1939). A third explanation is that incarceration was developed as a means to control the poor (Crompton 1997). A further purpose of the laws was to control the children of the laboring class, as we discussed in Chapter 2.

In January 1825 the House of Refuge opened in New York City. It began as a philanthropic venture, a corporation chartered by New York State (Robinson 1923). The House of Refuge was first located in what today would be midtown Manhattan but was then a rural area. Its first site was a remodeled military barracks. The institution was relocated several times until 1854, when it landed on its permanent location, 30 acres on Randall's Island in the East River (Reeves 1929). The thinking of the facility's founders was that it was to be a combination of school and factory. In its permanent location it looked like a prison—large buildings surrounded by a "formidable wall of enclosure" (Reeves 1929, 34).

As the House of Refuge movement progressed, many of the reformers became concerned over a number of things:

1. Children were committed for an indeterminate term that could last until their 21st birthday.

2. House of Refuge managers had complete control over children. They had the authority to apprentice them, indenture them, or farm them out. Some magistrates were so concerned about this situation and the long period of indeterminacy that they sentenced some children to the local jail as the lesser of two evils (Teeters and Reinemann 1950).

3. The Houses of Refuge looked like prisons.

4. Boys and girls lived under one roof.

By midcentury further reform of the juvenile incarceration movement was imminent. City life among the lower classes was perceived as harmful, especially for children. Charles Loring Brace, author of the book *The Dangerous Classes*, advocated the open spaces of farmland (Mennel 1998). Under Brace's direction trainloads of children from the eastern cities rumbled into the Midwest, dropping off children at farms along the way. Thousands of children were dispatched in this fashion from the 1850s through the remainder of the century. It was a practice, though, that was destined to end. Some argued it was senseless to transport children halfway across the country when there was adequate space in the east. Another argument came from east coast city institutions left short-handed because of *placing out* (Simonsen and Gordon 1982).

Brace's policy had competition from the outset, competition that was to eventually win out. Accepting the contention that the prisonlike houses of refuge may have done more harm than good, and also accepting the notion of family life outside the city, the *cottage plan* was put into operation in 1854 in Massachusetts. Massachusetts gets credit for opening the first state-run reform school at Westborough in 1847 (later called the Lyman

School because of a $60,000 donation by shipping magnate Theodore Lyman) (Kett 1977). But it was the girls' school, opened in 1854, that was the first to use the *family plan,* modeled after the institutions in Mettroy (France) and the Rauke Haus (Germany). This approach satisfied critics, since girls lived in cottages overseen by housemothers rather than the congregate style in the Houses of Refuge. The Ohio State Reform School for Boys, opened in 1857, was the first male school to adopt the cottage plan (Kett 1977).

By midcentury the reform school/training school movement was well under way. Mennel (1998) believes the major reasons for its growth was the development of public education, the decline of apprenticeships, and the growing number of unattached males in the cities. By the 1880s, the emphasis on agriculture was shifting to industrialized shops with children engaged in manufacturing (Mennel 1998).

The turn of the century saw an increased emphasis on opening training schools for girls. One reason was the *progressive movement,* which contributed significantly to the social engineering of the early twentieth century. The emphasis on girls increased with a major infusion of federal funds from April 1, 1918, to July 1, 1920, for the purposes of social hygiene: "to develop quickly a program for the protection of soldiers and sailors against venereal disease by aiding in the development and enlargement of facilities to care for and treat infected women and girls" (Reeves 1929, 44).

Postwar corrections. The manner in which corrections deals with offenders largely depends on the current view of the offender. For instance, two centuries ago the Quakers were responsible for the construction of the Eastern State Penitentiary in Philadelphia. The Quakers viewed criminals as sinners and promoted a system of solitary confinement, solitude, and penitence. At the turn of the twentieth century, the concept of *determinism* was gaining strength as the works of Lombroso (1968) and Freud (1920, 1933) came to the fore. The growth and popularity of psychology, and especially psychiatry, promoted the medical model of treatment for people's ills. While the corrections version of the medical model was put into practice in the 1930s (Clear and Cole 1997), it was in a nascent state during the Great Depression and the World War II years. After the war the medical model of corrections bloomed in every sense of the word. Much of its growth was due to the development of psychiatry. Before World War II there were about 4,000 psychiatrists in the United States, but by 1970 there were over 23,000 (Rappeport 1977). By 1966, at least 26 cities employed psychiatrists in a variety of capacities, and juvenile courts relied heavily on them (Robitscher 1980).

According to Freud, the causes of mental illness are in the patient's subconscious mind. The medical model, as it relates to criminals, "refers to a treatment approach that considers the commission of crime primarily the result of an emotional disturbance in the individual offender" (Lehman 1972, 204). Only through some form of psychotherapy are patients/criminals able to understand the cause of their problem (insight). Once insight occurred, a cure was thought possible.

There is no way to tell how long it will take to effect a cure. Patients committed to state hospitals were sent there for an indefinite period. Similarly, in the criminal justice system the preferred term of confinement was the *indeterminate sentence.* In the decades following the war, legislative bodies and corrections officials cooperated in an attempt to make the medical model work. The program that came closest to the psychiatric version was a prison in Patuxent, Maryland, which opened in 1955. Formulated by a group of psychiatrists under a legislative mandate, any offender committed there, whatever the crime, received a term of zero to life.

At that time, the juvenile system resembled this approach except that the upper limit of the term was the juvenile's age of majority, most often the 21st birthday. Irrespective of the offense—felony, misdemeanor, or status—all juvenile commitments to the youth correctional system were for the same indefinite term.

The medical model is based on a number of assumptions:

1. Deviant behavior is a product of mental abnormality or emotional disturbance. (The correctional version of the medical model is not quite the psychiatric one. The causes of deviant behavior are attributed to social factors as often as to psychological factors.)

2. Correctional authorities through a classification process are able to determine the cause(s) of the deviant behavior and prescribe appropriate treatment.

3. Through periodic evaluations and program adjustments, correctional staff can effect positive change.

4. Correctional authorities have the ability to determine readiness to return to the community on aftercare. The authority to release juveniles lies in the institutional staff, who are in the best position to make this determination since they are the treaters.

These dynamics help set up conflicts between custodial and treatment staffs. The *custody staff* generally view their charges as rotten or bad kids, while *treatment staff* see them as troubled or disturbed youth. As a result, treatment staff generally view custody staff as hard-nosed oafs, while custody staff view treatment staff as milksop softies who find excuses for crime. To be sure, institutions that place greater emphasis on treatment are less likely to have staff conflict than custodially oriented facilities (Zald and Street 1964).

By the late 1960s, the idealism of the 1950s gave way to reality. Research found that few correctional programs and treatment techniques successfully reduced recidivism (Bailey 1966; Lipton et al. 1975), and juvenile correctional authorities and researchers could not empirically support the rehabilitation model. Furthermore, a number of reports and books (discussed in a later section) and the Attica riot of 1971 revealed many of the terrible conditions of confinement. Correctional institutions, both juvenile and adult, had been operated on the basis of administrative convenience (Luger 1973) that often resulted in the violation of inmates' civil rights.

Inevitable change. In the early 1970s, U.S. Senator Birch Bayh conducted hearings on juvenile delinquency and juvenile justice. The major result of these efforts was passage of the Juvenile Justice and Delinquency Prevention Act of 1974 (JJDPA). From the outset, Congress appropriated significant funding in order to accomplish certain goals:

• Divert juveniles from the juvenile justice system.

• Separate status offenders from delinquents in confinement situations.

• Remove status offenders from incarceration settings—deinstitutionalization, commonly referred to as DSO.

• Remove juveniles from adult jails and lockups.

The status offender (SO) mandate has been a particularly annoying aspect of the act. Almost every jurisdiction in the nation passed laws outlawing the incarceration of status offenders, whether in a secure detention facility or training school, or their placement with adjudicated delinquents. By the late 1970s jurisdictions developed open shelters and group homes as alternatives. But the inevitable happened: What does one do with the SO who persistently runs away from open programs?

In 1980, as a response to intense lobbying by juvenile court judges, Congress amended the JJDPA to permit the institutionalization of SOs who violate a valid court order (Bartol and Bartol 1998). In other words, if an alleged SO is remanded to a shelter but runs away, he or she can be detained in a secure detention facility. Also, if adjudicated SOs on probation violate their terms via status behavior (truancy or curfew violation), the juvenile court has the authority to commit the youths to a training school. The juvenile court can thus turn status offenders into delinquents (Bartol and Bartol 1998). Chesney-Lind and Shelden (1998) claim that about twice as many girls as boys are incarcerated as probation and parole violators, a practice they term bootstrapping status offenders into delinquents.

Evaluating DSO programs is difficult. The first problem encountered in any study is to define *status offender*. "Pure" status offenders are rare, which means that programs for SOs are usually "contaminated," since some SOs have delinquent records (Siegel and Senna 1991). Furthermore, the contamination factor is exacerbated to the extent that bootstrapping takes place.

Today, the DSO movement is still viable, as states such as Maryland, Oklahoma and West Virginia have closed some training schools. Yet a question persists: Has the overall incarceration of children declined?

Hidden Juvenile Corrections

Institutionalizing juveniles (especially status offenders) has long been an issue in juvenile justice. One leading reformer in this area, Jerome Miller, years ago carried out a bold program of closing Massachusetts's juvenile training schools, transferring most of their youth into community-based programs. In addition, the JJDPA in 1974 mandated removing SOs from institutions and creating open, community programs for them. The primary intent of all this was to avoid incarcerating children who had not committed crimes. Considerable data indeed support the deinstitutionalization movement, not only for SOs but for incarcerated children in general, and it started before the JJDPA. Between 1970 and 1974 the number of children in public correctional facilities declined from 57,691 to 33,732 (Lerman 1980). One-day counts in training schools in 1971, 1974, and 1979 fell from 35,960 to 25,379, to 23,200 (Krisberg et al. 1986).

The DSO movement also apparently had its intended effect. The number of official SOs in public long-term and short-term institutions declined from 3,376 in 1977 to 2,293 in 1985 to 2,245 in 1989 (Siegel and Senna 1991).

A state can be in compliance with the mandate of the JJDPA if the designated populations in *public correctional institutions* decline (Lerman 1980). And in that sense the DSO movement has fulfilled its promise. Critics argue, though, that taken as a whole, the percentages of children incarcerated have not changed. Things have simply been shifted around so as to form a system of hidden juvenile corrections.

The impetus for this development comes from two sources: the child guidance clinic movement/mental health industry and the privatization of correctional services. The growth of child guidance clinics since the 1920s has made a significant contribution to this conversion. The tendency to define delinquent behavior as "acting out" or as a symptom of emotional disturbance became sufficient grounds to commit a child to a psychiatric facility (Lerman 1980). Other diagnostic categories also sufficient to commit are "troublesome," "sexually promiscuous," and "inability to function" (Chesney-Lind and Shelden 1998). In 1971, juvenile admissions to private hospitals accounted for 37 percent of *all* juvenile admissions; by 1980 this figure had risen to 61 percent (Chesney-Lind and Shelden 1998). Krisberg and Schwartz (1983) support the claim of a shift from traditional juvenile corrections to mental health facilities with data collected from the Minneapolis–St. Paul metropolitan area. Between 1976 and 1980 a significant increase occurred in juvenile psychiatric commitments, from 1,123 to 1,775; patient days increased from 46,718 to 74,201.

The U.S. Supreme Court may have lent a hand in this matter in *Parham v. J.R.* (1979). J. R. was a ward of the state who had cycled through a number of foster homes until he was placed in a hospital because he needed a structured environment. The suit brought on the child's behalf argued that he was deprived of liberty without due process. The Supreme Court disagreed, stating the medical fact-finding procedures were reasonable and consistent with constitutional safeguards. Furthermore, the state, acting as guardian, acted in the child's best interest by committing the child for treatment.

Another helping hand in this matter is the sources of funding for hospitalization of this kind: Medicaid and SSI of Social Security (Lerman 1980). Chesney-Lind and Shelden (1998) note that significant profits can be made by filling hospital beds.

The second aspect of hidden juvenile corrections lies in the privatization of corrections. There is no doubt that over the last several decades the percentage of status offenders in public correctional institutions has declined. Ideally, under the intent of the JJDPA of 1974, they should be handled in open community-based programs. However, that may not be the actuality, especially for girls.

The commitment of girls to the state training school has always been with the best intentions. By and large, it was done to keep the girl from running away or to stop her from becoming sexually promiscuous. This assertion has been supported by the fact that the ratio of girl SOs to boy SOs has traditionally exceeded 3 to 1 in training schools. Chesney-Lind and Shelden (1998) note that prior to 1974, 71 percent of girls in training schools were status offenders, while only 24 percent of boys were. That figure for girls has declined since that year. Instead, these girls have gone to private facilities. It is a relatively easy matter to designate a child *dependent* or *neglected* and commit the child to a private institution. Some data essentially support this assertion. By 1979, the percentage of girl SOs in public institutions had declined 40 percent, but between 1979 and 1991 it increased 27 percent in private institutions (Chesney-Lind and Shelden 1998). Also, between 1974 and 1979 the percentage of girl admissions (36 percent) to private facilities increased more rapidly than that for males (13 percent) (Krisberg and Schwartz 1983).

The total population of juveniles in private facilities rose from 36,190 to 39,671 between 1991 and 1995 (Moone 1997a). Private facilities may hold delinquents, status offenders, dependent or neglected children, or those who require psychiatric care. As we noted earlier, the recent reporting format by OJJDP does not distinguish among the various types of facilities—training school, group home, foster care, or residential treatment center. The data only inform us that of the 39,671 children in private facilities on February 15, 1995, 17,781 were delinquents, 5,700 were status offenders, and 16,177 were non-offenders. The 5,700 SOs are more than double the status offenders (2,245) that Siegel and Senna (1991) reported in public institutions in 1989. Americans have placed an increasing amount of resources into private correctional and psychiatric programs, and children have followed the dollars.

Privatizing Juvenile Corrections

The involvement of private interests in corrections dates back two centuries to the beginning of the penitentiary movement. Private contractors managed the production of goods in the Auburn (NY) prison in the 1820s (Clear and Cole 1997); indentured convicts helped the embryonic economy of the new British colony, Australia (Hughes 1987); and the notorious convict lease system in post-Civil War period enriched many contractors and plantation owners (Ayers 1984). But the actual operation of an adult prison by private business interests is relatively recent and is attributed largely to severe crowding in American prisons over the past two decades.

The private sectors' involvement in juvenile corrections also dates back about two centuries. The House of Refuge, opened in 1825, was a philanthropic endeavor. The George Junior Republics, started in the late 1800s, is an example of private involvement, and perhaps the best-known juvenile facility, Glen Mills School, is also privately operated.

Further, numerous community-based correctional programs, adult and juvenile, are privately operated. Therefore, the growth of the private sector in running juvenile correctional institutions should not arouse much attention. But it has. Private corrections has made it into the print media and has increasingly become a topic on the Internet. One reason for the increased attention arises from significant problems that have surfaced from juvenile facilities. Another reason is that many of the involved private parties are publicly traded, for-profit corporations. The two largest private correctional services are the Corrections Corporation of America and the Wackenhut Corporation.

There are a number of reasons to favor the privatization of public services. First, private organizations are free of politics and bloated bureaucracies. Second, government organizations are insulated from competition and thus do not suffer if they are inefficient. In fact, they are funded year after year irrespective of performance. Third, private firms are not burdened with civil service and government unions, which protect ineffective workers and stand in the way of adapting to changing circumstances (Muhlhausen 1996).

Critics do not disagree with these assertions but do argue that actual practice does not always square with theory. What has come to light recently are a large number of allegations of abuse, horrible living conditions, and lack of programs in juvenile institutions in several states—all run by private enterprise.

In Tallulah, Louisiana, a youth facility came under fire and ended up in federal court. Allegations included boys getting broken noses and perforated eardrums, enduring hours of idleness in stifling heat, being given meager food and clothing, and receiving no treatment for emotional problems. The idea for this youth facility came from a Tallulah businessman who saw it as a partial solution to the economic plight of the town of Tallulah. He formed the Trans-America Company and won a no-bid contract to run the facility.

In 1998 another private institution in Louisiana, the Jena Juvenile Justice Center, had difficulty convincing a federal judge that all was in place to open for business. Six months after it opened, a court-appointed prison expert reported many shortcomings in Jena's operation (now owned and operated by Wackenhut), including poorly trained staff, teachers who did not teach, nonexistent vocational education, and physical abuse of youth. By March 2000, conditions at Jena had not improved. A New Orleans family court judge ordered six juveniles, whom he had sentenced to Jena, removed from the facility after finding they had been brutalized by guards, had been kept in solitary confinement for months, and had been deprived of shoes, blankets, education, and medical care. The U.S. Department of Justice sent experts to Jena to continue an investigation it had begun in 1998. At issue have been inadequate clothing, food, and rehabilitation programs. Low pay and poor management have led to high personnel turnover. Although Jena was originally conceived as a drug rehabilitation institution, the investigators found virtually no such programs.

The same set of circumstances exists in other states as well. Private firms running juvenile facilities in Colorado, Texas, and South Carolina have been successfully sued. The U.S. DOJ has been involved in the Louisiana cases and in suits in Kentucky, Georgia, and Puerto Rico. Yet private entrepreneurs continue to become involved in juvenile institutions. In 1997, Equitable Securities Research released a report titled "At Risk Youth: a Growth Industry." Publicly traded juvenile corrections companies made net profits of $75 million in 1996.[3]

Institutional Program Models

In juvenile corrections the institutional model is likely to be structured around rehabilitative activities. One of the common models after World War II was the *school model*, in which students started off their stay as freshmen and then moved through sophomore, junior, and senior stages to aftercare. The primary vehicle of rehabilitation in this case has been education and social casework. Passages through the stages are based on educational achievement, although social promotion is as prevalent here as it is in the public schools. Too often, this model has become a time-based process—that is, youths are "promoted" based on time in the program. This is especially likely to happen when institutions are crowded.

In the two postwar decades considerable experimentation and innovation occurred in corrections. Two of the approaches that became popular during this period were the behavioral model and the *therapeutic community*.

The Behavioral Model

In the 1960s many juvenile correctional authorities adopted a behavioral model, which eventually became known as behavior modification (BM). Based on the principles laid down by psychologist John Watson in a groundbreaking paper delivered in 1913 and touted as a cure-all for society's ills by psychologist B. F. Skinner (1953, 1972, 1974), BM attempts to mold behavior through the manipulations of rewards and punishments.

Skinner's cutting-edge research, involving rats and pigeons that pushed levers in order to obtain food, provided psychology with the concept of operant conditioning. Animals can *learn* to push a lever for food by way of repeated trials in which they are rewarded for desired behavior. For the animal to "unlearn" or extinguish the learned response (pushing a lever), the reward must be consistently withheld. After a number of futile trials, the animal ceases to push the lever.

For many years Skinner argued that all that was required in raising children was the application of the principles of operant conditioning. He based his ideas on the assumption that human beings are born a blank slate and therefore are completely shaped by their environment. Behaviorists supported this notion by turning to animal experiments that provided or withheld rewards.

Juvenile corrections immediately seized on this approach. Behavior modification programs spread quickly in institutional services after the groundbreaking work by Cohen and Filipczak (1989) done at the federal Training School for Boys in the mid-1960s. BM presumably works well in an institutional setting because of the staff's ability to control environmental factors.

In a BM program, a regimen is developed that sets out behaviors that are to be rewarded. For juveniles in a training school, such behaviors include rising on time, making one's bed, and obeying all rules. The regimen also includes rehabilitative activities such as school attendance, school performance, and participation in counseling sessions. Rewards come in the form of points that can be spent for "hard" and "soft" items. Examples of hard items are candy, ice cream, toiletries, and room decorations. Soft items include being able to stay up late, extra TV time, and even home furloughs. Some programs are structured so as to make release to aftercare contingent on earning and keeping a certain number of points. Misbehavior or the failure to perform the assigned tasks results in the loss of points through fines. This idea of granting and rescinding points based on appropriate and inappropriate behavior is referred to as a token economy.

In the typical BM program, line staff are the primary managers of the operation since they are in immediate contact with the students. Their contacts extend 24 hours a day, seven days a week—a critical aspect of BM, since targeted behaviors occur in evenings, on weekends, and on holidays. Furthermore, the vehicle of rehabilitation (awarding points) is usually placed in a wide variety of staff—youth care workers, social workers, teachers, recreation workers, and so on. Line workers, then, become "treaters" as well as "controllers," a role often demeaned in corrections. Moreover, the day-to-day practices in a BM program require little training and no formal education, enabling it to be installed with little or no staff resistance.

Behavior modification programs began in the 1950s with mentally and emotionally disturbed patients. Researchers soon discovered that gains made in an institution fade away when the patient returns to the home environment. Brown et al. (1989) observed that children in a hospital setting are more likely to retain their gains upon returning home if the parents are trained to continue the program of the hospital. A child soon regresses if that is not the case.

Correctional researchers have come to the same conclusion (Braukman et al. 1975). Recidivism rates of those treated with behavior modification are no better than those for untreated youths (Finckenauer 1984; Lillyquist 1980). During the 1960s–1970s when BM reached its highest degree of popularity, it was even tried in adult prisons. Here, too, there was no solid empirical support for its rehabilitative value. In fact, the use of BM has been subverted to gain and maintain control over inmates and youth in juvenile facilities (Brown et al. 1989). Support for this assertion is seen in the use of BM in juvenile detention facilities where the length of stay is measured in days and weeks, obviating BM as a rehabilitative tool.

Critics further argue that BM cannot achieve its rehabilitative goals for several reasons:

1. Merely getting youth to achieve certain behavioral objectives without getting to the source of their problems is self-defeating. BM should be used as an adjunct of a program of therapy or counseling.

2. The failure of generalizability or the failure of the learned behavior in an institution to transform to delinquency prevention once a youth is released. Getting students to make their beds, finish their homework on time, gain a grade in reading, and so on seems to have little impact on whether they will rejoin their delinquent peer group upon release.

3. The failure to maintain a routinized system of rewards and punishments when a youth is released to the community on aftercare. One cannot depend on even the most conscientious parents to set out prosocial behavioral objectives and stick to a system of rewards and punishments. Accomplishing this in the environment from which most institutionalized youth come is an especially daunting task. Furthermore, aftercare workers are not in contact with their charges often enough to make behavioral contracts meaningful.

Thus BM, once viewed as a corrections panacea, has lost its luster as an effective vehicle of rehabilitation. In short-term detention facilities, it is used as a control mechanism. In long-term institutions it can be used effectively to control a youthful population so that applying some other treatment has a chance to take hold. In this respect it is similar to the use of Thorazine in psychiatric institutions—to calm the patient so therapists can do their work.

The Therapeutic Community

Until the 1960s, the typical training school was compartmentalized—that is, each employee had a job description that outlined his or her duties. In this type of system, cooks cooked, nurses performed nursing duties, and maintenance staff did maintenance work. Incarcerated juveniles marched off to a school building, which was separate from their living quarters across campus. When youths were scheduled to see their social worker, they walked across campus to the administration building for their appointment. The one certain result of this traditional setup was fractured or nonexistent lines of communication between and among staff. So, when Johnny was late for an appointment with his social worker, his excuse was that the cook held him up (Johnny had a job in the kitchen). In reality Johnny had been released on time from his job but he stopped off in the maintenance shop to chat with some friends, then sneaked behind a building to grab a quick smoke. Unless the social worker took the time to call the kitchen to verify Johnny's claim, the blame for his tardiness lay with the cook. Such circumstances (and more serious ones—did Johnny steal Jimmy's pencil in school? Did they have a fight in the kitchen?) are multiplied by the number of students and their activities across the campus. These circumstances regularly plague staff because they are constantly dealing with a youth's version of what occurred or are "ping-ponging" back and forth with other employees about the youth's behavior. The problem goes far beyond daily incidents. In treatment in this traditional setting, the therapist knows little about Johnny's interaction with other youths or about group-living in a cottage.

Among other things, the therapeutic community (TC) is designed to at least cope with these kinds of problems. The TC was pioneered by Dr. Maxwell Jones (1953) in England after World War II. He found that by engaging all hospital staff in the treatment process, greater gains were attained in treating psychologically incapacitated combat veterans of the war.

Another program that developed in the early 1950s would also play a part in the development of TCs in corrections. A group of alcoholics and drug addicts formed Synanon, the private self-help drug rehabilitation program that would become nationally known by the early 1960s. In addition to the core elements of participation by all members of the program, Synanon became known for its confrontational style of "group therapy," which involves a no-holds-barred, street language exchange among group members.

In the early 1960s, TCs were tried in several adult prisons (Bartollas and Conrad 1992). With disenchantment for the rehabilitation model and the early stages of prison crowding, the prison-based TC faded away. The setting that maintained it, however, was the Synanon-type drug programs based in the community. Small, stand-alone living units such as halfway houses lend themselves to the TC model.

The cottage-style training school is close to the ideal setting for the TC. The cottages are separate living units, which minimizes unwanted intermingling among youths. This arrangement also provides significant potential to develop a unit-management organization. Several key elements are involved in this program:

1. A core element of the TC is the cottage team. Rather than having the teacher and social worker in separate buildings and away from the cottage, staff become a team whose base is the cottage. Classes are held in the cottage and custody staff are teacher aides. All group meetings take place in the cottage.

2. Organizational authority becomes "flattened." That is, instead of many decisions moving vertically through a chain of command, they are made at the cottage level. The upper management of the institution must decide what decisions it can live with at the cottage level. Decisions about incarcerated youth are "stacked" from the least consequential (extra TV time) to the most consequential (released to aftercare). A stand-alone, self-help program like Synanon achieves the maximum TC process, since all the residents participate in all decisions. In a juvenile training school one of the TC goals is to maximize the number and gravity of decisions made at the cottage level.

3. A standard in the TC for juveniles is a behavioral contract. The contract ideally is the way a youth proceeds through the institution, from the point of intake to aftercare. With staff, a youth negotiates certain objectives to be achieved in given time periods. Objectives most often found in contracts relate to educa-

tion, treatment, and behavior (rules, infractions). With the achievement of behavioral objectives, the youth is given rewards, the most significant of which are furloughs, work/education release, and release to aftercare. Unlike a BM program where points are issued for daily behavior, rewards in a TC contract are issued for achieving a specific objective. For instance, passing the eighth-grade reading test may earn a day pass to visit family.

4. Grouped work is at the core of treatment. For TCs, there are usually two kinds of groups. The one that focuses on changing the youth is a confrontational type, most often guided group interaction (GGI). GGI sessions are often scheduled four or five times a week. The second group is a general unit or cottage meeting. Whereas GGI sessions are closed to all but the 10 or 12 youths and team members, cottage meetings include team members, all youths and other staff—cooks, clerks, and maintenance staff. Under optimum conditions, unit meetings, over time, do much to avoid one of the most frequent statements by institutional staff: "I don't know what's going on around here."

This model accomplishes a number of essential elements for successful treatment:

• The major decision makers in youths' lives are those closest to them in many ways—the team.

• Placing most program activities within the living unit maximizes the potential for building and maintaining a prosocial culture.

• The maximized staff-youth interaction, plus the cottage meetings, which includes other staff members, does much to minimize the game playing and manipulating that young offenders are prone to do.

Best Practices for Education and Rehabilitation in Juvenile Corrections

Education is one of the key ingredients of any rehabilitation program in a correctional setting. OJJDP has been instrumental in identifying the two key elements of any successful correctional education program: educator training and establishment of an educational culture. As to training educators, the National Juvenile Detention Association's Center for Research and Professional Development (CRPD) has developed a National Training Curriculum for Educators of Youth in Correctional Facilities. OJJDP provided funding to the CRPD to develop and test the curriculum. The nine curriculum components are (Brooks and White 2000):

• current trends and issues in juvenile justice and education of juvenile offenders;
• institutional culture;
• student assessment;
• curriculum;
• teaching and learning;

- behavior management;

- social skills;

- transition (reintegration into the community); and

- program and classroom evaluation.

This comprehensive curriculum helps prepare educators unfamiliar with the realities of juvenile confinement to gauge and engage committed youth in the educational process.

The National Office for Social Responsibility (NOSR) conducted an 18-month study to assemble a guide for establishing an appropriate educational culture in juvenile facilities, one that promotes the development of academic skills as well as social and moral reasoning. According to NOSR, effective educational practices adopt eight components (Gemignani 1994):

- Effective schools (comprehensive program fully supported by administration and staff, taught by a sufficient number of competent educators)

- Administrators (who endorse the value of education, continuously training educators and instilling respect for the program among all staff)

- Academic programs (developing cognitive skills, using cooperative and peer learning, and a variety of instructional strategies)

- Special education (educators and staff trained to help and interact with learning disabled youth, using an educational program geared to that audience)

- Psychoeducational programming (development of problem-solving skills, moral reasoning, and communication and social skills)

- Employment training (providing students with knowledge, skills, and attitudes needed in entry-level jobs; developing basic skills, thinking skills, responsibility, sociability, and honesty)

- Transitional services (helping to move youth home or to independent living)

- Program evaluation and research (rigorous evaluation studies of effective educational programs and practices)

As we will see in the next section on effective treatment programs, educational instruction is a vital part of and complements what therapists attempt to accomplish with juveniles.

Despite earlier observations that with respect to treatment "nothing works," recent reviews of the literature have discovered numerous examples of effective rehabilitation of juvenile offenders (Andrews et al. 1990). Lipsey and Wilson (1998) provided an invaluable service by identifying the most and least effective treatment programs though a meta-analysis, which is a literature review that organizes the results of many studies that have the same focus and uses a statistical technique to compare the results of the studies. Lipsey and Wilson analyzed 83 studies of serious offenders in institutionalized settings. The following discussion represents their analysis of various studies that have identified the most effective treatment approaches.

Effective treatment requires a careful analysis of targeted youths, including their problems and the interventions most likely suited to these problems. The treatment needs to be administered by adequately trained staff (preferably mental health professionals) who use approaches that have a history of success, such as cognitive and behavioral treatment. The treatment needs to last a reasonable length of time and should be matched in intensity to the risk level of the youth (Loeber and Farrington 1998; D. L. MacKenzie 1999).

The two most consistently positive interventions (15 percent to 20 percent reduction in recidivism compared to a control group) were those involving *interpersonal skills training* and *teaching family home programs.* In the first group, the most successful programs involved social skills training (Spence and Marzillier 1981), aggression replacement training (Glick and Goldstein 1987), and social interactional skills programming (Shivrattan 1988), all of which use methods of instruction, discussion, and education, among other techniques. The teaching family home interventions involved both behavior modification–oriented group homes that were community-based, and family-style approaches conducted by teaching parents (Kirigin et al. 1982; Wolf et al. 1974). In part, this intervention succeeded because of a close supportive relationship developed between the teaching parents and the small number of juveniles. Also found to be positive (a 10 percent to 15 percent recidivism reduction) were three behavioral programs involving incarcerated youth. Two programs focused on aggression and anger control. While one used cognitive mediation training through small discussion groups and attempted to develop youths' problem-solving skills and to modify attitudes that supported being aggressive (Guerra and Slaby 1990), the second used stress inoculation and sought to develop coping skills (Schlicter and Horan 1981). The third intervention involved reinforcement therapy for girls who were trained to act as peer counselors for newly arriving inmates (Ross and McKay 1976).

Three community residential programs were the next most successful interventions. While two involved counseling and educational and vocational support (Minnesota Governor's Commission 1973; Auerbach 1978), the third entailed group discussions within a therapeutic community that emphasized youths' developing self-responsibility (Allen-Hagen 1975). Three multiple services interventions also displayed positive effects. Two were in cottage living settings (Kawaguchi 1975; Seckel and Turner 1985), and all three involved educational services, vocational training, and job securing and maintaining strategies (see also Thambidurai 1980). One of the programs also contained a recreation component and instruction on time management, interpersonal relationships, rule conformity, and personal responsibility (Seckel and Turner 1985). Less effective treatments were discovered in individual counseling, guided group, and group counseling programs. Finally, weak differences in recidivism rates were found among employment-related, drug abstinence, and wilderness/challenge interventions, and the weakest effects came from milieu therapy (Lipsey and Wilson 1998).[4]

Disproportionate Minority Confinement

In 1988 the JJDPA was amended to address the overrepresentation of minorities in confinement. The mandate from the amendment requires each participating state to develop a plan to reduce the proportion of minority juveniles detained or confined in secure detention, correctional facilities, jails, or lockups if their proportion exceeds the proportion of those groups in the general population.

The disproportionate minority confinement (DMC) initiative began in 1991 with OJJDP selecting five states as pilot programs: Arizona, Florida, Iowa, North Carolina, and Oregon. The project was to consist of two 18-month phases, the first to determine the extent of the problem, the second to design and implement corrective action.

Florida has focused its attention on intake and law enforcement's use of citations. Iowa has concentrated on community-based problem identification and solutions; it offers cultural competency training programs to those who interact with minorities. North Carolina has developed detailed plans for corrective action within local juvenile justice systems and other juvenile delinquency systems. Oregon has focused DMC programs that affect various aspects of the juvenile justice system, such as advocacy at intake and counseling and mentoring services in minority communities.

None of the five pilot states was able to reach its objectives in the 18-month allotted period. Several requested 12-month extensions (Rhoden 1994; Devine et al. 1998)

The Institutional Subculture

A reasonable question is whether the inmate culture, found in adult male and female prisons (Clemmer 1940; Sykes 1958; Irwin 1970; Giallombardo 1966; Propper 1981), is present in institutions for boys and girls. More or less, the answer is yes.

Polsky (1965) observed the boys of Cottage 6 at "Hollymeade" training school in their living quarters and in the dining room. The most relevant findings that emerged from his observations were certain behavioral themes and their cottages' social structure. The most dominant theme was *aggression,* the ultimate method of expressing authority and the means of abusing the weaker boys. The frequent form of aggressive communication was ranking, or a verbal putdown (Polsky 1965, 62). *Scapegoating* the newcomer and the weaker boys was a frequent occurrence in the cottage and was the funnel through which aggression and ranking flowed. Polsky depicted the social structure of Hollymeade in the form of a diamond (see Figure 17.1). Those at the top of the power structure, together with their associates, devised a *coolie* system whereby Bushboys and Scapegoats washed their clothes, served food to them in the dining room, and handed over snacks and desserts on command. In the day-to-day dynamics of cottage life, everyone but one had someone to peck at.

When the child savers adopted the cottage plan, a "good Christian couple" was deemed to be the ideal staff in the children's living quarters. The couple would be surrogate parents for youths who desperately missed this aspect of growing up in the evil city. Polsky (1965) devotes a chapter specifically to Cottage 6's houseparents. In general, this particular staff grouping was drawn from aging economic failures in life. They quickly learned the nuances of controlling 20 or so teenage boys. They formed unpopular alliances with cottage leaders, providing them with special rewards; in turn, these boys helped control the cottage. Polsky notes that the Cottage 6 parents even joined the leaders in scapegoating the defenseless, low-status boys.

Bartollas and colleagues (1976) studied Ohio's end-of-the-line juvenile training school for hard-core recidivists. Fifty percent of the 15- to 18-year-olds were diagnosed as dangerous, 20 percent as emotionally disturbed. Each cottage of the institution housed 24 juveniles. The racial composition of the facility was 51 percent black and 49 percent white. The line staff was 97 percent black. Bartollas et al. (1976) found a vertical social structure based on aggression, intimidation, and exploitation. The researchers found four levels in the cottage hierarchy:

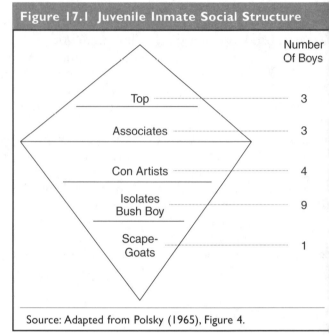

Figure 17.1 Juvenile Inmate Social Structure

Number Of Boys

Top — 3

Associates — 3

Con Artists — 4

Isolates Bush Boy — 9

Scape-Goats — 1

Source: Adapted from Polsky (1965), Figure 4.

1. Heavy—the cottage leader, physically strong, with leadership qualities

2. Lieutenants—four youths who formed the second tier and provided support for the leader

3. The bulk of the cottage population divided into an upper black half and lower white half

4. Scapegoats—as in Polsky's (1965) study, the few who did the bidding of the upper part of the hierarchy

There were a few "independents" in the cottage who were physically strong, stayed to themselves, and did their time in order to get out. Those at the top two levels were aggressive and constantly posturing, exploiting the lower levels for goods, services, and sex. Those who sought sex aggressively were called "booty bandits." Victims of aggressive sex were always white, and most often aggressors were black. Line staff could not recall any instance of white on black aggressive sex.

Only a few studies of the male juvenile inmate culture have been carried out. What seems to be clear, though, is that it resembles the social order of adult prisons. What is obviously inevitable in these settings is the development of a vertical social hierarchy based on physical aggression, which, in turn, is the dominant theme overlaying intimidation and exploitation.

Incarcerated Girls

Just as the male juvenile inmate social system mirrors the adult prison, the girl social system mirrors that of adult female prisons. The basic element of the inmate world of girls is the *make-believe family*. Giallombardo (1974) studied three training schools for girls and found the family to be the foundation social unit of imprisoned girls. Girls proceeded through courtship rituals and a formal marriage ceremony. Giallombardo also found familiar *argot* roles (as she did in an adult female prison [1966])—*butch* (lesbian) and *femme* (straight). The former were further divided into *true butch* (lesbian inside and outside) and *trust-to-be-butch* (homosexuality as an institutional adjustment).

A marriage is always performed by a butch, and if there is marriage, there must also be divorce. The rules for both, as well as for courtship, are clearly spelled out and known by all. The girls develop a number code for certain aspects of life and relationships. If a girl calls out "110," it means "I love you." The number 711 means marriage; 117 means divorce.

The kinship relationships of family form the core of institutional life for the girls. Father and mother have son and daughter. The latter are usually the younger inmates and often are kin (nephews and nieces) to other families. The functions of the family are:

- protection, affection, and mutual aid (goods and services);
- to help maintain social control in the institution; and
- to keep the young in line through the fear of exclusion.

Propper (1982) examined seven training schools, three of which were designated coed. She found the same basic structure that Giallombardo (1974) had found but emphasized a major distinction between homosexual behavior and the presence of make-believe families. She pointed out that there could be confusion in assuming that the former is always present in the latter. In other words, girls did form make-believe families without also becoming involved in homosexual behavior. Her findings include the following:

1. The incidence of make-believe families is as prevalent in coed institutions as in those that house only girls. In the former, boys are involved in families.

2. Homosexual marriages are rare.

3. Most families are sister-sister and mother-daughter combinations. There are very few instances of extended families.

4. Homosexual behavior is unrelated to family membership.

5. Less than 10 percent of the girls adopt the male role.

As with the culture of adult female prisons, girls formed make-believe families, and like their adult counterparts, kinship ties had more to do with life than homosexual behavior. We noted earlier that the culture of boys' institutions largely mirrors that found in adult prisons. Common to female institutions is satisfying affectional needs and the desire to nurture and assist others. Common to male institutions is aggression, which is the conduit for exploitation and intimidation.

The Right to Treatment

No one would argue against the right to humane treatment for incarcerated adult criminals or juvenile delinquents. Over the past three decades the federal judiciary has provided convicted felons with the minimum guarantees of food, clothing, shelter, and medical care. But there have been no successful attempts to argue for the right to rehabilitative treatment for adult offenders. The state has the right to punish convicted felons, without rehabilitation, as long as the punishment is carried out humanely and constitutionally.

The issue may be different for juveniles, however. The juvenile justice system was founded in 1899 on the concept of *parens patriae* (see Chapter 2). It is clear that under this doctrine, a court can supersede the rights of parents and child. When the juvenile court was established, it was easy to accept this doctrine, since the court promised help. As we have seen, the status quo went unchallenged until the turbulent 1960s.

The first peek into the world of juvenile justice came about because of the willingness of the federal judiciary to listen to challenges to the workings of *parens patriae* in practice. The U.S. Supreme Court handed down several decisions, starting in 1966, that provide juveniles with some procedural safeguards in juvenile court proceedings (see Chapter 3). But perhaps the greatest public attention to the problems of the juvenile justice system was derived from several books published during this same period.

Juvenile correctional institutions turned out to be a far cry from the benevolent environments conceived by nineteenth-century child savers. Writers like Howard James (1971) of the *Christian Science Monitor* managed to obtain permission to visit a number of juvenile facilities. For instance, he interviewed Robert P. Heyne, superintendent of the Indiana Training School for Boys, in his office. Mr. Heyne at one point removed a leather strap from a desk drawer, the instrument used to flog misbehaving youth. Mr. Heyne was soon to be a party in the federal case *Nelson v. Heyne* (discussed later in this chapter).

James also visited the Ferris School for Boys outside of Wilmington, Delaware. In this case he had to enlist other state officials to gain access to the school. Contrary to common practice in juvenile training schools, Ferris provided little or no education programming for the 202 boys housed there in the late 1960s. There was a shortage of teachers and education space, there was no remedial reading program, and $3,000 worth of library books remained in unopened cartons. Staff there, too, used corporal punishment. Slapping boys in the face was a common practice, and at times angry staff resorted to punching and kicking the residents. Medical records at Ferris revealed five boys with punctured eardrums.

Another investigator who managed to gain admittance to several juvenile institutions was Kenneth Wooden (1976). His book is replete with examples of abuse, which took various forms. For instance, a common practice in Texas at the Gainesville State School for Girls was to induce pregnant teens to abort. Wooden gathered some of his material by sitting in on the *Morales v. Turman* trial during the summer of 1973. The case was actually instigated by a series of articles published in the *El Paso Times* pointing out that a disproportionate number of juveniles committed to Gainesville State School came from El Paso County, most of whom had not been represented by counsel and were forbidden to communicate with attorneys (Wooden 1976).

During the *Morales* trial testimony, it was clear that institutional staff of the Texas Youth Council (TYC) used beatings, solitary confinement for weeks at a time, and tear gas to control the youth. Further, at the Crockett Unit for Girls, the diet was so nutritionally inadequate that more than 80 percent of the girls had to be treated with the antibiotic tetracycline for nutrition-related skin problems.

In Chicago during the early 1970s, a young attorney with the Legal Assistance Foundation, Patrick Murphy (1977), took up the cause of abused juveniles in the juvenile system in Illinois. The Illinois Industrial School for Boys at Sheridan was described by staff as no more than a jail with the usual prisonlike solid steel or barred cells. A consulting physician testified that he would routinely prescribe the tranquilizer Thorazine based on a telephone call from a nurse, a request that in turn had been relayed to her by guards at the facility. In psychiatric practice, Thorazine was to be used only within a total treatment regimen. In court, a psychiatrist testified that the use of Thorazine in any other way made no sense (Murphy 1977).

Basis for the Right to Treatment

There are a number of sound theoretical, historical, and legal bases for a policy of a right to treatment (RT) for incarcerated juvenile delinquents. No such issue arises for juvenile offenders located in the community. But for incarcerated youths, the need to control large numbers of adolescents, confined to relatively small spaces, is in itself an environmental stressor. Rebellious, obstreperous adolescents can try the patience of the most well-intentioned person. We can therefore see how a system originally intent on saving children transformed itself into one of control. Thus, the issue of the right to rehabilitative treatment for incarcerated juveniles arose alongside other rights issues:

- The historical basis for the right to treatment (RT) is the concept of *parens patriae*, which involves the trade-off of due process rights for the promise of rehabilitation.

- Traditionally, and until the 1970s, juvenile statutes included the phrase *in the best interests of the child* to describe the juvenile court's role in the life of the delinquent or wayward child.

- In 1960, Morton Birbaum argued for the constitutional right to treatment for the incarcerated mentally ill. The basis for his argument was that those patients had been deprived of liberty without due process safeguards provided criminal defendants. The same argument can be made for juvenile delinquents.

Birbaum's argument was soon to be affirmed in the judiciary. A number of relevant adult mental health cases were litigated in the decade of the mid-1960s–1970s. In *Rouse v. Cameron* (1966) the defendant successfully argued "not guilty due to insanity" and was committed to a mental health facility. Four years later a federal court ruled that the only reason to confine the defendant against his will beyond the maximum term for the crime he was charged with (one year) was for the purpose of treatment. In 1971, a federal court in *Wyatt v. Stickney* held that it is a denial of due process if a person is committed involuntarily to a mental institution in a noncriminal case and is not provided with treatment.

The Case for Juveniles

The case for the right to treatment for juveniles would appear to be stronger than for adult mental illness. In 1967, a federal circuit court (*Creek v. Stone*) stated that the juvenile code required the juvenile court to ensure an institutional environment similar to what a child should have gotten at home. *Creek* was a detention case, as was *Martarella v. Kelly* (1972). In that case, a federal district court ruled that the unhealthy and punitive conditions of confinement constituted cruel and unusual punishment. The court specifically outlined what would constitute treatment: education programs, caseworkers, recreation workers, a specific amount of recreation per day, and reasonable access to psychiatric care, and it went as far as to designate the child-to-staff ratios.

The case for RT for juveniles confined in training schools would seem to be stronger than for those in detention situations. In a vein similar to *Rouse,* courts have traditionally approved of longer incarceration for juveniles than for adults for the same crime on the basis of the treatment provided to them.

In 1972, a district court in Rhode Island handed down a wide-ranging decision addressing the conditions of confinement in a boy's training school (*Inmates of Boys Training School v. Affleck*). After reviewing such practices as strip cells and solitary confinement plus poor education programs, the court set minimum standards in a number of areas related to institutional life. They included reading lights in the evening, appropriate clothing, clean bedding, personal hygiene supplies, clothing changes, access to books and periodicals, daily showers, and nursing staff on duty 24 hours a day. The courts concluded that juveniles had a statutory right to treatment and that the very purpose of the juvenile justice system was rehabilitation.

In Texas, the TYC came under fire in 1973 and ended up in federal district court. The court ruled that incarcerated juveniles had a right to treatment, established certain standards that related to education, staffing, and medical care, and ordered the TYC to submit a plan that would implement the court's order. The court noted that TYC's Dr. Turman, in his pretrial deposition, stated that the only purpose of the TYC was rehabilitation.

The last notable RT case for juveniles was *Nelson v. Heyne* (1974). Testimony at trial in the lower court had illuminated such practices as corporal punishment, solitary confinement, and the use of tranquilizing drugs to control behavior at the Indiana Training School for Boys. The circuit court, referencing the *Martarella* case, declared that juveniles had an affirmative right to treatment. The court also addressed punishment at the institution by referring to the standard laid down in *Furman v. Georgia* (1972), a capital punishment case. A punishment is excessive and unnecessary if a less severe punishment would serve the same purpose. Beatings that were commonplace in the school were unnecessary and therefore excessive and violated the Eighth Amendment's prohibition against cruel and unusual punishment. So too was the use of drugs for control purposes rather than as part of a rehabilitation program.

The Status of RT Today

Beyond the mid-1970s, court battles over RT were relatively few and unsuccessful. The Supreme Court ruled in 1981 in *Ralston v. Robinson* that a juvenile incarcerated in an adult prison does not have a right to treatment. In 1986, a federal circuit court (*Santana v. Collazo*) ruled that the government can incarcerate juveniles for public safety reasons without necessarily providing a full range of rehabilitation programs.

Notwithstanding the recent policy changes in toughening both juvenile and adult punishment, the legal challenges to correctional practices that took place over two decades ago did have a positive effect. In the mid-1970s, the American Correctional Association, aided by funding from the Law Enforcement Assistance Administration, began an accreditation process for some aspects of corrections. An accredited prison, juvenile detention center, or probation agency has passed muster on a long list of standards. The accreditation standards for a correctional institution run into the hundreds and cover every operational function. From the outset, many correctional agencies lined up to apply for accreditation, a tedious and lengthy process. But once an institution was accredited, it took on the prestige of an accredited hospital or university in that the institution had achieved an acceptable level of meeting operational standards. Beyond that, accreditation was also viewed by practitioners as a defense to litigation.

Coincident in time with the ACA's accreditation project, the Institute of Judicial Administration of the American Bar Association developed juvenile justice standards, covering the complete spectrum of the system. Taken together, the work of the ACA and the IJA/ABA projects form the foundation and basis for lawful, humane, and rehabilitative environments for juvenile offenders.

Protecting the Rights of Incarcerated Juveniles

In the 1970s, Congress passed several pieces of major legislation protecting the rights of incarcerated people. In 1975, it passed the Individuals with Disabilities Education Act (IDEA), which guarantees educational programming for individuals, ages 5 to 21, who are disabled. Disabilities that come within the purview of the law are mental retardation; hearing, speech, language, or visual impairment; serious emotional disturbance; orthopedic impairment; specific learning disabilities; autism; and traumatic brain injury.

Several studies of juveniles have revealed disabilities ranging from 42 percent in Arizona to 60 percent in Florida and Maine. Since the passage of the law, 25 IDEA class action suits have been filed, 15 of them during the 1990s (Puritz and Scali 1998).

Three other laws, passed in 1975, 1978, and 1986, provide the basis for a right to treatment:

1. Persons with Developmental Disabilities (PADD)

2. Protection and Advocacy System for Individuals with Mental Illness (PAIMI)

3. Protection and Advocacy System for Individual Rights (PAIR)

Collectively, these acts are referred to as *P and As* (protection and advocacy). They provide federal funds to the states, which in turn place the authority to act on behalf of disabled people in agencies independent of public and private services. Each P and A has the authority to investigate neglect, abuse, or the violation of rights, has the right to examine client records, and has the right to pursue legal or administrative remedies.

Further protection of the rights of those incarcerated comes from the Civil Rights of Institutionalized Persons Act (CRIPA) passed by Congress in 1980. The act gives the Department of Justice (DOJ) the authority to bring suit if the rights of incarcerated people are violated. As of November 1997, the DOJ had investigated 300 institutions, 73 (25 percent) of which were juvenile detention or correctional facilities. Before bringing suit the DOJ attempts to negotiate a settlement or consent decree. In 1998 the DOJ was investigating 22 detention and treatment centers and monitoring 34 juvenile facilities through consent decrees (Puritz and Scali 1998).

Conditions in Juvenile Corrections

Despite juveniles' constitutional right to treatment and the protection of congressional statutes, the conditions in many juvenile facilities leave a lot to be desired, as we have seen already in various parts of this chapter. The last major survey of these institutions, sponsored by OJJDP, was conducted in 1991. The survey used three sets of standards, including those established by the American Correctional Association, the National Commission on Correctional Health Care, and the American Bar Association/Institute of Judicial Administration. The survey covered four major categories that contained 12 areas of concern. The most widespread and substantial problems involved living space, security,

Table 17.7 Conformance Rates Among Juvenile Facilities		
Areas of Concern	**Percentage of Confined Youth in Facilities That Conform**	**Percentage of Facilities That Conform**
Basic needs		
Living space	24%	43%
Health care	26	35
Food, clothing, and hygiene	39	35
Living accommodations	52	49
Order and security		
Security	20	27
Controlling suicidal behavior	25	51
Inspections and emergency preparedness	67	55
Programming		
Education	55	57
Recreation	85	85
Treatment services	68	60
Juvenile rights		
Access to community	25	25
Limits on staff discretion	49	76
Source: Parent et al. (1994), Table 2.		

Table 17.8 Annual Estimates of Incidents in Juvenile Facilities	
Type of Incident	**Estimated Incidents per Year**
Injuries	
Juvenile-on-juvenile	24,200
Juvenile-on-staff	6,900
Staff-on-juvenile	106
Escapes	
Completed	9,700
Unsuccessful attempts	9,800
Acts of suicidal behavior	17,600
Incidents requiring emergency health care	18,600
Isolation incidents	
Short term (1 to 24 hours)	435,800
Longer term (more than 24 hours)	88,900
Source: Parent et al. (1994), Table 3.	

health care, and control of suicidal behavior—not unlike the problems that surface in detention centers. These problems emerged in many facilities, as shown in Table 17.7.

One disturbing finding of the survey is that facilities are most in compliance with recreation standards and least in compliance with basic needs and security areas. Also discouraging is the annualized estimate of the variety of institutional incidents, including assaults and escapes (see Table 17.8).

Obviously, to the extent that this survey would discover as bad (or worse) results in current conditions suggests that juvenile corrections has a long way to go to satisfy basic standards for the confinement and protection of youth. Moreover, to the extent that rehabilitation is the desired goal of juvenile corrections, these results work against the prospect of achieving that objective. Ironically, a recent analysis of adult facilities housing youthful offenders disclosed a higher compliance rate with basic program offerings such as special education (90 percent), formal elementary and secondary education (93 percent), and GED preparation and counseling programs (100 percent each) (Austin et al. 2000). What is most puzzling is that, as we will see in the "Costs of Corrections" section shortly, the per capita costs for juveniles far exceed that of adults.

The Numbers at Juvenile Corrections

One of the more interesting findings of the 1997 OJJDP census is that almost half of the youths in confinement were located in facilities with a capacity of fewer than 110, which helps explain the serious costs of juvenile corrections that we explore in the next section. Table 17.9 details the distribution of confined youth by virtue of the capacity of the facility.

Table 17.9 Percentage of Youth Confined in Sized Facility

Number of Residents	Percentage of Youth Confined	Number of Residents	Percentage of Youth Confined
<31	20%	201–350	14
31–110	28	>350	21
111–200	17	*Total*	100%

Source: Sickmund (2002a).

Delinquent Youth

In Chapter 14 we mentioned the juvenile court data showing that during the last several years of the 1990s, 145,000–164,000 delinquent youths were committed each year to a juvenile residential placement. Juveniles do not tend to remain in placements for long, even in long-term facilities, whether they are delinquents or status offenders. For example, juveniles released in 1994 had served an average of 147 days in public facilities and 109 days in private facilities. For 1997 releases the average stay was 192 days in a public facility and 174 days in a private one (L. R. MacKenzie 1999). In 1997 only one-third of committed juveniles remained in placement six months after admission (Snyder and Sickmund 1999). In light of the relatively small standard size of juvenile facilities and the relatively high cost of juvenile institutionalization, coupled with the rehabilitation focus and relative lack of punishment, this relatively quick turnover of committed youths should not come as much of a surprise. According to the OJJDP census, 98,913 youths were in residential placement because of delinquency on October 29, 1997, while that figure was 104,237 on October 27, 1999 (Sickmund et al. 2004). Accompanying the delinquents in the 1997 census were 2,774 inmates who had been sentenced to a juvenile facility after conviction in adult court (Sickmund 2002a). There were also 12,549 youth confined for probation or parole violations (Gallagher 1999). Among the delinquents, most of the offenders had committed a personal crime (33.4 percent) or a property crime (30.2 percent), while few had committed either a drug offense (8.8 percent) or a public order offense (9.2 percent). In terms of gender (but this includes status offenders), 86.5 percent of those institutionalized were males. Again, including status offenders, very few of the inmates were age 13 (4.3 percent) or younger (2 percent). More than one-fourth were 14 (10.9 percent) or 15 years old (20 percent). Half of the

Table 17.10 Inmates Under the Age of 18 in State and Federal Prisons, by Gender, 1998–2002

Year	Male	Female	Total
1998	4668	195	4863
1999	4027	167	4194
2000	3721	175	3896
2001	3010	137	3147
2002	2943	112	3055

Sources: Harrison and Karberg (2003), Table 5; Beck, Karberg, and Harrison (2002); Strom (2000).

Table 17.11 Percentage of Inmates Under 18, by Age, Gender, and Race, 1985, 1990, 1997			
Characteristic	1985	1990	1997
14 and younger	0%	0%	1%
15	2	3	4
16	18	17	21
17	80	80	74
Male	97	98	97
Female	3	2	3
White	32	21	25
Black	53	61	58
Hispanic	14	15	15
Other race	1	1	2
Source: Strom (2000), Tables 6, 7.			

youths were either 16 (26.7 percent) or 17 (23.3 percent), while 12.4 percent were older than 17.

As indicated in Chapter 12, some juveniles charged with crime end up prosecuted in criminal court and sentenced to adult prison. At yearly counts conducted in state and federal prisons, the number of juveniles (defined as younger than 18) confined in prison rose constantly between 1985 (2,300) and 1997 (5,400) and then declined just as constantly (see Table 17.10).

Not surprisingly, perhaps, over the past 20 years the profile of inmates under the age of 18 in prison has been disproportionately older (i.e., 17), male, and black (see Table 17.11).

While the mean minimum sentence given this population increased from 35 months to 44 months between 1985 and 1997, the mean maximum sentence declined from 86 months to 82 months. The mean sentence actually served remained at 37 months in 1985, 1990, and 1997 (Strom 2000).

Status Offenders

The 1997 OJJDP census found 6,877 status offenders in residential placement; by 1999 that figure had dropped to 4,694 (Sickmund et al. 2004). In recent times status offenders have constituted 4–6 percent of the youth in residential placement (Gallagher 1999). In both 1997 and 1999, most status offenders had been committed for incorrigibility (41 percent and 39 percent, respectively) or running away (22 percent and 23 percent). In both surveys truants accounted for 19 percent of those in residential placement. The remaining status offense population in 1997 was divided among curfew violations (3 percent), alcohol offenses (4.6 percent), and "other" offenses (10 percent) (Gallagher 1999).

One final figure of interest is the custody rate (per 100,000 youth) for juveniles, including both delinquents and status offenders. OJJDP compiled the rates for these youth at both detention and residential placement for each jurisdiction across the country. Serious variation can be seen in how some states rely on holding youth in custody to a much greater extent than other states (please see Appendix O).

The Costs of Juvenile Corrections

Previously, we referred to the prohibitive costs of detention. Perhaps the final thought to keep in mind is that juvenile justice is expensive, regardless of whether the resources it

State	Adult	Juvenile	State	Adult	Juvenile	State	Adult	Juvenile
AZ	$ 53.44	$167.84	MS	$ 38.10	$ 70.00	OR	$ 62.42	$139.28
CO	77.31	187.17	MO	35.78	120.74	RI	100.13	225.00
CT	72.91	487.63	NH	68.12	259.50	SC	35.54	135.00
DE	60.39	170.42	NJ	76.13	153.00	SD	31.63	129.92
KS	54.14	170.00	NY	96.73	215.00	TN	47.62	175.67
LA	33.68	146.69	NC	65.29	163.00	TX	43.63	113.46
ME	92.84	299.11	ND	53.83	120.60	VA	57.34	163.00
MD	61.48	138.11	OH	59.93	203.27	WA	71.13	161.72
MI	79.83	318.00	OK	46.14	222.17	WV	47.47	175.98

Table 17.12 Average Daily Cost per Offender, 2002

Source: Adapted from ACA (2003).

receives are adequate or are distributed to the proper places and initiatives. According to the 2003 ACA *Directory* of adult and juvenile correctional budgets, a much higher cost per offender is found with juveniles than with adults, sometimes three or more times as great. Table 17.12 identifies the states that listed the average daily cost per offender for both juveniles and adults.

When we consider the cost per offender together with the relatively limited number of both facilities for

Institutionalization of each youth costs approximately $35,000 per year, mainly because of educational, recreational, and treatment costs. What do these expenditures suggest with regard to prevention and diversion efforts?

youths and beds within these facilities, it is easier to put the juvenile court's dispositional tendencies into context.

Release From Incarceration

During the postwar period, when the medical model was the primary method of delivering rehabilitative services, the institutional staff was presumed to be in the best position to know a youth's readiness for release to aftercare. A committee made up of various staff members routinely reviewed the progress of youth and would, at some point, recommend aftercare to the facility superintendent for final approval.

Today, this staff model exists in only a few states (DE, NE, TX, WA). Changes made over the past few decades reflect the sociopolitical changes our nation has undergone in its perception of and dealing with offenders. The American Correctional Association (1998) provides some examples of what exists today.

Some states have a youth parole board (in at least four, members are gubernatorial appointments) (CA, CO, IN, NM, SC, UT, WI). In three states the parole board for adults is also the release authority for juveniles (IL, ME, NJ). In five states the committing court is also the release authority (IA, KS, MI, PA, WV). In Idaho and Ohio the youth agency must get the committing court's approval for release. Finally, in six states the executive director/commissioner of youth corrections authorizes release (CT, HI, MN, MO, ND, OK).

Summary: Key Ideas and Concepts

- Difficulty in defining detention because of its multiple-purpose nature
- Detention coming under state or local control
- High costs associated with detention, especially because of staffing
- Significant number of youths held in jail
- Incentives to remove status offenders from institutions
- Low level of accreditation of juvenile facilities and myriad problems
- Controversy over rehabilitation of preadjudicated youth in detention
- Controversy over mixing preadjudicated with adjudicated youth in detention
- Military-oriented boot camps for youth as products of the get-tough movement
- Variety of alleged goals to be served by boot camps
- Controversy over use of boot camps as probation or alternative to incarceration
- Merger between probation sentences and residential placement
- Controversial use of immediate parole from a reception center
- Controversial use of reception centers for "shock therapy"
- Wilderness (challenge) programs promoting survival skills but not effective
- Controversy surrounding nature and use of private versus public facilities
- Near impossibility in accurately counting juvenile "inmates"
- Early diverse influences in development of private facilities
- Influence of psychiatry in development of the medical model
- Critical assumptions of the medical model
- Potential conflict between custody staff and treatment staff

- Implications of converting status offenders into delinquents
- Camouflaging incarceration via a mental health or private commitment
- Development and advantages of private interests in juvenile corrections
- Operant conditioning and the manipulation of rewards and punishments
- Reasons that behavior modification approach alone cannot succeed
- Variety of elements involved in a therapeutic community
- Requirements for successful correctional educational programs
- Meta-analysis showing treatment programs that are most and least successful
- Implications of a mandate to reduce disproportionate minority confinement
- Varied nature of the male and female juvenile inmate code
- Development and basis for a juvenile offender's right to treatment
- Extra protections secured via the rights of disabled juvenile inmates
- Disturbing results of the assessment of the conditions in juvenile confinement
- Small number of juveniles in residential placement on any one day
- Decreasing number of juveniles in adult prisons
- Varying detention and commitment rates for juveniles among states
- High per offender costs of incarcerating juveniles versus adults

Discussion Questions

1. Should community residential placements such as foster and group homes be counted as sentences of probation or as commitment? What are the implications of counting them one way or the other?

2. Should juveniles be held in jails? If yes, when and under what conditions? If no, does that include youths who have been transferred to or convicted in criminal court?

3. Should detention centers (and other juvenile facilities) be forced to be accredited? Would that improve the conditions that have been attributed to these centers? What other solutions can you offer for the problems encountered here?

4. Why have boot camps turned out not to be the panacea for juvenile crime? Do they have any value? How should they be used, if at all? For whom are they appropriate, if anyone?

5. When judges sentence a youth to institutionalization, should the facility (e.g., a reception center) be able to return the youth immediately to the community? If not, why not? If yes, when and under what circumstances?

6. Should reception centers be used as shock therapy? What are the advantages and disadvantages of such a usage?

7. Why do wilderness programs generally have ineffective results in reducing recidivism? What type of offender belongs in such a program, and is there any particular type of youth who should not be committed there?

8. What do you make of the controversy in the use of private versus public facilities for juvenile offenders? What should be the policy in the use of these facilities? Is it appropriate that facilities for youth are operated by for-profit, private organizations, such as Wackenhut? Should private facilities be allowed to house both offenders and nonoffenders?

9. How should juvenile inmates be counted? Should states in which an "adult" is 16 or 17 be tallied as a juvenile or as an adult? Does it matter that voluntary commitments are included within the incarcerated population?

10. Is it appropriate for criminal courts to sentence youth convicted there to juvenile facilities even when they are chronological juveniles? Is it appropriate for criminal courts to sentence juveniles convicted there to adult prison despite their age? What are the implications to this cross-fertilization for both inmate populations? Is there an alternative to this situation?

11. What are the implications of hidden juvenile corrections? Does it matter that some committed youth are not tallied among the residential population because of where they are institutionalized? Is this practice dishonest?

12. Is there any one particular treatment approach that should work for most youths? If yes, what? If your answer is no, what are the implications for institutions that might have to provide a variety of treatment modalities in order to rehabilitate its population? Should youth be segregated by virtue of their problems and needed treatment? Is that feasible, efficient, or possible?

13. What does a juvenile offender's constitutional right to treatment mean to you? What would institutions have to provide to satisfy this right? If there is such a right, what are the implications for youths in the community who do not commit offenses but yet do not have access to treatment programs?

14. What are the detention and commitment rates for your state? What do you think is the impact of the fact that some states have a younger maximum juvenile court age than others? What does it say about a state when it has a particularly high (or low) rate of juvenile institutionalization?

Endnotes

1. The information provided here on juvenile institutions is from the American Correctional Association 1998 *Directory*.
2. Because the topic of this chapter is incarceration, we restrict our discussion to that subject. We acknowledge there are many more dispositions available to the juvenile court.

3. Several sources were consulted in developing this section on privatizing corrections. See Muhlhausen (1996); *The New York Times*, July 15, 1998, "Profits at a Juvenile Prison Come With a Chilling Cost"; *The New York Times*, March 16, 2000, "Privately Run Juvenile Prison in Louisiana Is Attacked for Abuse of 6 Inmates"; "Jena Juvenile Center Continues to Have Trouble" June 19, 1999 (*www.cjconsultant.com*); "Juvenile Crime Pays," February 1998 (*www.corpwatch.com*); *Chicago Tribune*, September 27, 1999, "Broken Teens Left in Wake of Private Gain."

4. For an extensive listing of the research studies that were a part of the meta-analysis conducted by Lipsey and Wilson (1998), consult their reference section. ✦

Future Directions in Juvenile Justice

• Chapter 18: The Future of Juvenile Court

Focus of Section VII

In this final section we take a look to the future to contemplate what juvenile court might look like. We have no crystal ball to perform this maneuver, and much of what the future brings will depend on unkown entities, such as the political climate and juvenile crime rate in the next several years. Before we engage in this prognostication, we will look back briefly to consider how juvenile justice has evolved. ✦

The Future of Juvenile Court

Focus of Chapter 18

In this final chapter we take a quick look back at the evolution and current status of the three major themes in juvenile justice. We then attempt to forecast what can be expected of the system in the future. A lot is at stake in this future, both for juvenile offenders and for the society that has to deal with them.

Key Terms

- abolition of juvenile court
- dual processing
- unequal processing
- unique processing

Putting the History of Juvenile Justice Into Context: The Three Major Themes

In the Preface we noted that three interrelated, major themes would be evident throughout most of the text: unique processing in juvenile justice compared to criminal justice, unequal processing within juvenile justice, and dual processing with respect to both rehabilitating and punishing juvenile offenders in the juvenile system. All three themes have been essential characteristics of the juvenile court from the day it opened its doors. Among the three themes, virtually the entire essence of juvenile justice can be explained. Today all three are still present in the juvenile system, albeit none in its original condition. A brief review of each will help put both the past and the future of the juvenile justice system into context.

The first theme concerns the unique way in which juvenile offenders are processed, especially during their tenure in juvenile court. Originally, juvenile court officials (as well as other officials, such as police) had virtually unlimited authority over juveniles charged with an offense. They had no rights to protect them and were forced to rely completely on the integrity of those officials. Whether that authority and integrity were abused depended on the location of the court and on the official(s) involved. This uniqueness was modified, but certainly not erased, via *In re Gault* and *In re Winship*, the only U.S. Supreme Court cases to grant youths (five) trial-related rights.

Defendants processed in juvenile court continue to lack important constitutional safeguards and experience situations that would not be tolerated in criminal court. Thus, what is important for any student or observer of juvenile justice to remember is that, compared to criminal court, officials in juvenile court *still* enjoy more authority over defendants. The foundation of justice in juvenile court is firmer than it was originally, but it is not of the same caliber as that of criminal court. This situation has serious implications when it comes to the severity of the juvenile court's response to juvenile offenses (such as being able to retain control over youths until the age of 25) and to the ability of criminal court to factor a defendant's juvenile court record into its sentencing formula (such as striking out on the first pitch in criminal court).

Also important to realize is that not everything unique to juvenile justice is negative or unfair. Pursuit of the offender's best interests is a positive facet of juvenile court and quite unique as well. Juvenile justice is a lot more ameliorative to its population than criminal justice is, which is the essence of the third theme. To the extent that we do not want to do to juvenile offenders what we do to adult offenders, we have plenty of reason to support the uniqueness of juvenile justice. Therein lies probably the strongest argument for the preservation of juvenile court. We want to respond to most juvenile offenders with unique ameliorative interventions, like juvenile court does. In the end, there is still very much that is unique in the processing of youth in juvenile justice.

The second theme concerns the unequal processing of youth in juvenile court in terms of behavioral history (i.e., offense and record), which, not coincidentally, is another aspect of the unique processing of youth vis-à-vis adults. Originally, juvenile court announced that it was a clinic (also explaining the lack of rights), and, as such, that its focus went well beyond mere manifestations (i.e., the behavior) of youths' problems. It is doubtful that the offense and record were ever truly immaterial, but other major characteristics of the youth's life, such as family, neighborhood, schooling, peer association, and any disorders or limitations (among other things), were always supposed to play a part in what treatment response the court would fashion. The intervention into juvenile justice by the U.S. Supreme Court modified the ability of juvenile court to act like a clinic, but to the extent that this modification has occurred, only the adjudicatory hearing has been implicated. And even the adjudicatory hearing is not immune today from clinic-like influences (such as the guardian defense attorney and the *parens patriae* judge), which, of course, affect the fairness of the proceeding as well.

In short, juvenile justice is *still* largely about who the youth is (in addition to what the youth has done). Youths, comparably situated in terms of behavior, who differ meaningfully in terms of life characteristics are still subject to different or unequal processing in juvenile court. To be sure, some states have attempted to reduce, if not remove, this tendency, and some have even adopted sentencing guidelines, a direct repudiation of juvenile justice philosophy. But only three states have done so to date. The majority position is one still compatible with historical juvenile justice. This situation has serious implications when it comes to the unequal processing of youth of different races, gender, and class.

Again, the severity of sentences from juvenile and adult courts is implicated. Unfortunately, the only way to completely neutralize the disparity is to remove the rehabilitation mandate from juvenile court or to ignore the youth's life characteristics, which is saying the same thing. Moreover, to the extent that the disparity is a result of differences in life circumstances and not race or gender, there is no reason to regard the unequal processing as negative or unfair. To permit juvenile court to compensate for the family that can't or won't assist in resolving the child's problem is logical, while producing some unequal results. Tailoring rehabilitation-oriented responses to the problem situation of the youth is what makes the system unique and worthy of preservation. In the end, there is still very much that can be unequal in the processing of youth within juvenile justice.

The third theme concerns the dual processing nature of juvenile justice. That is, the system both rehabilitates and punishes. Originally, the juvenile court promoted both but officially acknowledged only the rehabilitation component. Although rehabilitation was probably the major focus of the system, and was probably the thrust of the vast majority of dispositions, some youths, especially serious and chronic offenders, were subject to rather Spartan conditions in rather nasty locations. Even if treatment regimens were offered in these institutions, punishment had to play a part. More important, punishment and rehabilitation need not be regarded as mutually exclusive or completely incompatible. Even youths that were placed in fine institutions and received excellent treatment services were forcibly deprived of liberty and thus experienced punishment. Thus, juvenile justice has been about both rehabilitation and punishment from the beginning. To be sure, recent get-tough times have escalated the punitive orientation and capabilities of juvenile court. Enhanced punishment is a major part of the criminalization effect, and the granting of some rights to juvenile defendants has facilitated this growth in punitiveness. Nevertheless, not all aspects of increased punitiveness are negative or unfair. It is appropriate that public safety factors into juvenile court operation and that juveniles are being held more accountable for their behavior.

Nevertheless, some observers have taken this trend too seriously and claim that juvenile court has abandoned its commitment to rehabilitation. They might also note that criminalization and the lust for punishment are all-consuming and come ironically at a time when serious juvenile crime is down, as we have seen. These observations are pure hyperbole. Simply because juvenile justice is more punitive today when it deals with serious/chronic offenders does not mean that it has abandoned its objective in pursuing the betterment and treatment of the vast majority of youthful offenders. This is especially true since so relatively few youth are serious/chronic offenders. Moreover, the expansion of prosecutorial transfer, often portrayed as another example of criminalization, facilitates removal of the most serious and chronic juvenile offenders. Ironically, prosecutorial transfer decreases rather than increases criminalization, since juvenile crime calling for the harshest responses from the state can be removed from juvenile court jurisdiction. The vast majority of juvenile offenders are neither serious nor chronic in delinquent behavior, and the juvenile court is not reacting in a truly punitive capacity with them. The proof can be found in a number of ventures, such as the amount of resources dedicated to rehabilitation programs in juvenile facilities (compare the average daily costs of juvenile and adult inmates), to subsidizing OJJDP's numerous goals (primary of which is identifying the best practices to adopt in both community and institutional interventions), and to investing so significantly in prevention programs. These expenditures represent a commitment to rehabilitation, not a rejection of it. In the end, there is still very much of the dual nature of both rehabilitating and punishing youth in juvenile court.

So, although the contemporary juvenile court differs from the one that emerged in 1899, it has retained a good deal of the characteristics that marked its beginning. Juvenile court has changed, but many of the changes, such as the infusion of due process and accountability, have been enhancements rather than detriments. In other words, despite the passage of more than 100 years, the intervention of the U.S. Supreme Court, the temporary demise in the credibility of rehabilitation, and the expansion of serious juvenile crime (at least between the mid-1980s and mid-1990s), for better or worse, juvenile court has retained much of its original philosophy and practice. This is important to realize because predicting future changes in juvenile justice depends on a careful and accurate description of its current status as well as an appreciation of how relatively little juvenile court has changed and what it has weathered. In other words, juvenile court has, if not a Teflon personality, a remarkable ability to accommodate change and to adapt. This is not to say that juvenile courts won't undergo some transformation in the future, especially depending on some developments that could transpire, but it does suggest that drastic renovations should probably not be expected. Appreciating this fact will help in developing a future forecast and in accepting or rejecting the plausibility of what some observers have indicated lies ahead.

Putting the Future of Juvenile Court Into Context

Gauging the future of the juvenile court is an inexact science at best. Certain predictions are relatively easy, however. Those who have advocated the abolition of juvenile court (Ainsworth 1991; Federle 1990; Feld 1990, 1993b) will continue to do so, unsuccessfully. Predictions of the court's demise rely on false premises, such as its purported abandonment of rehabilitation (Whitehead and Lab 2004). Whether other prominent scholars will join this cause of abolition is more uncertain. But failure seems guaranteed because the basic commitment to preserve juvenile court, particularly for the nonchronic and nonserious offenders (i.e., the majority), seems steadfast.

Another safe bet is that more examples of the criminalization of juvenile court will emerge, although more procedural rights for juvenile defendants will not be among them. It certainly appears that the destiny of juvenile court is to adopt more characteristics of its adult counterpart, especially with regard to greater influence being exerted by prosecutors (and perhaps by victims as well). Nevertheless, the political powerlessness of juveniles should guarantee that the increased punitiveness of the juvenile system will not be matched by increased procedural and substantive safeguards vis-à-vis the state. Finally, despite the juvenile court's movement away from "complete benevolence," nonchronic and nonserious offenders will continue to receive mostly rehabilitative-oriented interventions in the juvenile system. Advances have been made in identifying the most successful treatment interventions, and more research should take this cause even farther. Even chronic, serious offenders prosecuted in juvenile court will fare much better than comparably situated criminals in the adult system. Everything is relative. These realities, coupled with the "relative" expediency of the juvenile court process, should ensure the survival of the juvenile system for the foreseeable future. That does not mean there cannot be serious challenges to the basic tenets of the juvenile system within that timeframe.

Factors Affecting the Future

Of all the possible influences on the future of the juvenile court, perhaps none will be more critical than the juvenile crime rate in the next decade. We have already discussed the infamous juvenile crime wave between 1984 and 1994 (see Chapter 5). This crime wave explains much of the expansion of prosecutorial power in transferring youth to adult court (see Chapter 12) and most of the developments in the area of the juvenile court record, including making it a public record and more difficult to expunge (see Chapter 15) and allowing it to be factored into criminal court sentencing (see Chapter 12). Although it is difficult to imagine juvenile court's "letting up" if the juvenile crime rate remains as depressed as it has been during the last 10 years or so, it is easy to picture the court's becoming even more punitive and harsh should a repeat of the violence of the mid-1980s to the mid-1990s reoccur. That crime wave encouraged some prominent scholars to anticipate a "ticking time bomb" (Fox 1996) and to predict an onslaught of violence by so-called "superpredators" by the end of this decade (DiIulio 1995, 1996).

This prediction was based on demographic projections of the number of youth who will occupy the most crime-prone years (15 to 19 years old) around the year 2010. Recent reversals in the juvenile crime rate have led to both denouncements of this dire prediction and a retraction of the prediction by its authors. Nevertheless, if anything close to a respiking of juvenile violence develops within the next decade, the effect on juvenile court processing of offenders could be substantial. If increased violent crime were to occur, several crime control-oriented objectives could be advanced, such as:

- reducing the maximum juvenile court age;

- expanding the population of youths eligible for transfer to adult court;

- shifting more of the transfer power from the judge to the prosecutor;

- increasing the number of serious offenses and chronic offenders subject to maximum and mandatory sentences in juvenile court and ensuring that more of these involve incarceration; and

- extending the use of the juvenile record in criminal court sentencing to more jurisdictions.

Other factors, more local than the national crime rate, could be influential in any one jurisdiction. Perhaps the most poignant of these is the "bad case." Any state that is rocked by an especially violent episode (such as multiple deaths in a school shooting) can react by enacting serious revisions in the juvenile code, especially if that code was perceived as preventing an "appropriate" result to the youth violence in the first place. For example, shortly after the murders of four middle school students and a teacher in Jonesboro, Arkansas, a few years ago, the legislature in that state drafted a serious revision in juvenile court procedure. Until the shootings, youths had to be 14 or older at the time of the offense to be transferred to adult court. The fact that the murderers in Jonesboro were 11 and 13 at the time guaranteed them the "safe haven" of juvenile court (and a disposition that cannot last beyond their 21st birthdays). The legislature's response was to introduce a transfer to juvenile court's second tier (see Chapter 12) for murder candidates of any age, with a possible life sentence hanging over their heads if they are not rehabilitated by the age of 21. Similarly, Michigan's reaction to a six-year-old killer who had to be prosecuted by juvenile court was to create the designated proceeding (see Chapter 12), in which violent offenders of any age can be channeled into adult court (i.e., the converted juvenile court), where they can receive an adult conviction and sentence. Of course, the code may not prove to be the "villain" in a "bad case." As we noted in Chapter 12, judges have been notorious for not transferring youths to adult court. The failure of one judge to transfer a 15-year-old murderer in Boston largely explains why Massachusetts today has both offense exclusion and the delayed judicial transfer procedure discussed in Chapter 12. Without a doubt, egregious situations like these around the country have contributed to important changes in various facets of the juvenile court's operation (especially at transfer) and could continue to have this effect in the future.

Beyond the bad case scenarios, there is always the prospect that an individual (such as a prosecutor) or a group (such as the state's prosecutor or public defender association, victims' rights advocates, or restorative justice proponents) will lobby the legislature, seeking changes in the juvenile code. A single prosecutor's decision to make fighting juvenile crime a priority (and a political issue) can seriously affect the operation of the local juvenile court (e.g., wresting control of charging away from the PO). Higher political aspirations on this prosecutor's part could lead to taking the crime-fighting campaign to the state capital in pursuit of favorable legislation. If past is prologue, recent statutory revisions suggest that pro-prosecution forces will not be the only ones who successfully pursue the legislature. Groups representing victims and those who believe in reorienting the system toward restorative justice principles can be expected to witness continued success via more legislatures' adopting measures that support those causes. Finally, the jury is still out on whether research will disclose that the recent "get-tough" movement has achieved its objectives and whether any legislatures would modify these measures if indeed the data were negative.

Probable Developments

To the extent that the future will represent "more of the same," several developments can be expected to come about (or, more accurately, to continue):

- More prevention efforts (especially targeted at drugs, gangs, and guns)
- More emphasis on victims' input
- More emphasis on parental liability
- Expansion of graduated sanctions or alternatives to institutionalization via home detention/electronic monitoring, curfew restrictions, and intensive probation
- Expansion of restorative justice measures, but only in less serious/divertable cases
- Expansion of those eligible to be processed by juvenile specialty courts (i.e., teen, drug, gun)

- More development of team approaches to resolving juvenile misbehavior, linking various court personnel, school personnel, parents, and community service providers

- Some increase in transfer to adult court, especially in granting prosecutors more control over the decision, and perhaps in more jurisdictions adopting transfer to a second tier of juvenile court

- More minimum and mandatory sentences, particularly through the use of restitution, community service, and suspension of a driver's license, but also possibly through incarceration in cases of drugs, violence, and gang-related offenses

- More emphasis on deinstitutionalization of both delinquents and status offenders, especially targeting minorities

- More emphasis on holding juvenile court officials accountable for their decisions, especially by subsidizing research into the effectiveness of these decisions

- More use of the juvenile's record in adult court sentencing, especially if more states move to sentencing guidelines in which juvenile records can be "quietly" integrated into the sentencing formula (as opposed to "openly" counting adjudications as "strikes" or including them within habitual offender statutes)

- More development of reverse transfer, juvenile court sentencing following conviction in criminal court, and youthful offender sentencing, all of which can compensate for overzealous prosecutors and inflexible statutes

These "developments" would reflect a continuation of the two-prong renovation of juvenile justice that is nearly two decades old. That is, juvenile justice reform has been concentrated primarily on two fronts: the initial offender and the chronic or violent offender. The front and back ends of juvenile justice have been beefed up in this campaign. At the front end, the system has become more serious about promoting prevention and diversion efforts to keep juveniles from committing offenses, and to deal more seriously with those who commit their first offense (i.e., juveniles are to be held accountable for their behavior). Restorative justice perhaps has its greatest potential here, and can most meaningfully include the victim in the solution of juvenile delinquency. At the back end, recent transfer and sentencing measures (in both juvenile and adult courts) reveal juvenile court's (and society's) reduced tolerance toward serious and chronic juvenile offenders. This, too, has been brought about in order to hold youth accountable, and, this, too, has great potential for victims to affect decisions made in juvenile court. At both ends of the campaign, parents have been held accountable for the offenses committed by their children. There is every reason to believe this two-prong campaign will persist.

Concluding Remarks: Abolish or Retain Juvenile Court?

In the final analysis, whether and in what condition juvenile justice will survive will depend on perceptions of its value and the prospect for alternatives. The juvenile system's claim to fame is offering a concerted effort to develop and implement a remedy for problems that lead juveniles into misbehavior, and juvenile court is its staging area. Unlike criminal court, juvenile court places its emphasis on the best interests of the offender and on the disposition or problem resolution stage instead of on the process of finding guilt. That is, in juvenile court treatment interests are as critical as legal interests. Unlike criminal court, juvenile court is dedicated specifically to not ruining the life chances of offenders by imposing exceptionally harsh dispositions and permanent, debilitating records. To the extent that it is desirable to maintain these approaches to and focuses on juvenile offenders (as opposed to focusing on guilt and punishment), the idea of relocating them en masse to criminal court (via the abolition proposal) should cause concern. Arguably, maintaining juvenile court is the lynchpin necessary to retaining the juvenile justice system and its mostly ameliorative approach to youth.

At the same time, keeping the focus on the youth's best interests and rehabilitation and not on process has implications for juvenile court and juvenile justice. One implication is that there is a limit to how serious and chronic juvenile offending can be while concurrently maintaining a focus on the offender's best interests (i.e., to the exclusion of the public's). Another is that juvenile court should not have the authority to impose harsh or extended sentences that promote incapacitation and punishment (or enhanced criminalization). Limits on the youth's best interests and on punishment capacity, in turn, suggest that not all juvenile offenders should be processed in juvenile court or the juvenile justice system.

In other words, rather than sending all juvenile offenders to criminal court and abolishing juvenile court, the more balanced and logical answer seems to be to preserve juvenile court for the vast majority of, but certainly not all, juvenile offenders.

Summary: Key Ideas and Concepts

- Juvenile court changed but still enjoys unique processing of juveniles

- Unique processing both advantages and disadvantages juveniles

- Juvenile court changed but still uses unequal processing of juveniles

- Juvenile court still both rehabilitates and punishes juveniles

- Rehabilitation not abandoned in juvenile justice

- Abolition of juvenile court is not a part of the future

- Increased criminalization of juvenile court is a possibility

- Prospects for increased due process in juvenile court as remote

- Politics and juvenile crime rate important factors affecting the future

- Individual jurisdictions affected more by local events and "bad cases"

- Vast majority of future developments merely a perpetuation of recent initiatives

- Positive results achieved in juvenile court not achievable in criminal court

Discussion Questions

1. Upon review, what elements of current juvenile justice are still unique? On balance, is juvenile justice's uniqueness more to a youth's advantage or disadvantage? What, if any, of the disadvantages attributable to the uniqueness of juvenile justice could be modified or eliminated?

2. What are the implications of the unequal processing of juvenile offenders in juvenile court? Are these implications acceptable? Is there any alternative to pursuing rehabilitation and responding to offenders unequally (in terms of behavior)? Assuming there is none, what does that say about what should happen to juvenile offenders in juvenile court?

3. What evidence is there that juvenile court has not abandoned its commitment to rehabilitation? Has the juvenile court become too punitive? If so, has that detracted from its mission to rehabilitate? Should there be limits on the punitive capacity of juvenile court? What are they?

4. What factors are most important in gauging the future of juvenile justice? What do they suggest for the future? If they come to pass, what are the implications for juvenile court?

5. Is the abolition of juvenile court desirable or plausible? What would be better or worse if abolition were to occur? What renovations, if any, would you make in criminal court to accommodate the influx of juvenile offenders? What outcomes would you expect in terms of sentencing in criminal court and institutionalizing juvenile offenders? ✦

Appendixes

Appendix A: Disproportionate Arrest Rates for Minority Youth

38 Reporting Jurisdictions: Index Value*

AL	1.2	DC	1.1	MD	2.2	NY	1.9	SC	1.4
AK	1.4	FL	1.7	MA	3.0	NC	1.6	TN	2.0
AZ	1.1	GA	2.1	MN	1.8	ND	2.3	UT	1.0
AR	1.6	ID	2.0	MS	1.3	OH	2.1	VA	2.2
CA	1.1	IL	.5	MO	1.8	OK	1.1	WV	1.8
CO	1.1	IA	2.7	MT	1.1	OR	1.4	WI	1.7
CT	3.0	KS	2.6	NE	1.9	PA	2.1		
DE	1.4	LA	1.5	NJ	2.1	RI	1.6		

* Index value is derived by dividing the percentage of minority juveniles arrested by the percentage of minority juveniles in the total population at risk.

Source: Adapted from Leiber (2002).

Appendix B: Disproportionate Minority Confinement

A. Disproportionate Minority Confinement in Detention
43 Reporting Jurisdictions: Index Value*

AL	1.3	ID	1.5	MO	3.4	RI	2.6
AK	2.0	IL	2.1	MT	1.7	SC	1.7
AZ	1.4	IN	4.1	NE	3.6	SD	3.1
AR	1.3	IA	7.9	NJ	3.3	TN	3.7
CA	1.2	KS	4.5	NM	1.2	TX	1.3
CO	2.3	KY	5.5	NY	2.9	UT	3.3
CT	4.8	LA	1.5	NC	1.7	VA	1.8
DE	2.3	MD	2.8	ND	3.7	WA	2.5
DC	1.1	MA	3.8	OK	3.3	WV	2.6
FL	2.3	MN	6.7	OR	2.1	WI	4.9
GA	1.6	MS	1.4	PA	5.5		

B. Disproportionate Minority Confinement in Adult Jail
22 Reporting States: Index Value*

AL	.8	ID	1.5	MA	4.7	TX	2.0
AR	2.2	IL	.3	MN	2.8	UT	1.7
CO	1.4	IN	2.7	MS	1.2	WA	1.0
CT	6.6	KS	3.0	OK	1.7	WI	1.7
FL	1.9	KY	1.8	SC	1.7		
GA	1.8	LA	1.4	SD	2.7		

C. Disproportionate Minority Confinement in Adult Lockups
9 Reporting States: Index Value*

CT	2.9	KS	1.3	TX	1.3
IL	1.2	MA	2.4	UT	1.2
IN	3.3	OK	1.7	WI	6.8

D. Disproportionate Minority Confinement in Secure Facilities
40 Reporting Jurisdictions: Index Value*

AL	1.3	DC	1.1	LA	2.3	NY	2.4	SD	2.2
AK	2.4	FL	2.8	MD	3.4	NC	2.0	TN	3.0
AZ	1.6	GA	1.9	MA	3.3	ND	4.3	TX	1.6
AR	2.7	ID	1.7	MN	5.2	OH	3.0	UT	4.8
CA	1.3	IL	2.0	MS	1.8	OK	4.8	VA	2.1
CO	2.1	IN	3.2	MT	1.8	OR	2.1	WA	3.7
CT	4.5	IA	6.6	NJ	3.0	PA	6.1	WV	2.0
DE	2.7	KS	3.9	NM	1.2	SC	1.6	WI	5.5

* Index value is derived by dividing the percentage of minority juveniles confined in secure facilities by the percentage of minority juveniles in the jurisdiction's total population at risk.

Source: Adapted from Leiber (2002).

Appendix C: Deadline for Filing Petitions When Youth Is In "Detention"

Jurisdiction	Clock Begins	Hours	Jurisdiction	Clock Begins	Hours
AZ	D	24 (I)	MS	D	By DH
AR	DH/T	24 (I)/96 (I)[a]	MO	D	By DH
CA	T	48 (E)	NE	DH[c]	48 (E)
CO	DH	72 (E)[b]	NJ	D	By IH
CT	D	24 (E)	NM	T	48 (E)
DE	D	Forthwith	NY	DH	96 (I)
DC	D	By DH	NC	D	12 (B)/24 (I)[d]
GA	DH	72 (I)	ND	D	Promptly
HI	D	24 (E)	PA	D	24 (E)
ID	D	24 (E)	SD	T	48 (E)
LA	DH	48 (I)	TN	D	Promptly
ME	D	240 (I)	UT	D	120 (E)
MD	D	Immediately	WA	D	72 (E)
MI	D	By PH	WI	D	By DH
MN	D	By DH	WY	D	Promptly

[a] = Whichever time period is sooner.

[b] = Deadline can be extended an unspecified amount for good cause.

[c] = In Nebraska, a court order replaces the detention hearing.

[d] = The longer time period applies to detentions occurring on weekends or holidays.

D = detention; T = taken into custody; DH = detention hearing; IH = initial hearing; (I) = includes weekends and holidays; (E) = excludes weekends and holidays

Appendix D: Jurisdictions With Time Limits for Detention Hearings

Jurisdiction	Clock Begins	Hours	Extensions
AL	D	72 (I)	
AK	D	48 (I)	
AZ	D	48 (I)	

Jurisdiction	Clock Begins	Hours	Extensions
AR	D	72 (E)	
CA	T[a]	48 (I)	
CO	D	72 (E)	
CT	T	48 (E)	≥ 72 hours total
DE	D	24 (E)	Good cause extension
DC	T	24 (E)[b]	
FED	D	Reasonable time	
FL	T	24 (I)	
GA	D	72 (E)	
HI	P	48 (E)	
ID	D	24 (E)	
IL	T	48 (E)	
IN	T	48 (E)	
IA	D	24 (E)	
KS	D	48 (E)[c]	
KY	D	24 (E)/48 (E)[d]	
LA	D	72 (I)[c]	
ME	D	48 (E)[c]	
MD	P	24 (E)	8-day good cause extension
MA	D	24 (E)	
MN	T	36 (E)[c]	2–24-hour extension
MS	T	72 (E)	
MO	D	72 (E)	
MT	T	24 (E)	
NE	T	24 (E)	Court order only
NV	D	6 (E)/72 (E)[c, e]	
NH	T	24 (E)[f]	
NJ	IH[g]	48 (E)	48-hour extension for no attorney
NM	P	24 (E)	≥ 72 hours total (E)
NY	D	24 (E)	≥ 72 hours total
NC	D	24 (E)	≥ 120 hours secure/≥ 168 hours nonsecure
ND	D	96 (I)	

Jurisdiction	Clock Begins	Hours	Extensions
OH	D	24 (E)	
OK	T	24 (E)	
OR	D	36 (E)	
PA	D	72 (I)	
RI	D	24 (E)	
SC	T	48 (E)	
SD	T	48 (E)	
TN	D	72 (E)	≥ 84 hours total
TX	D	48 (E)	
UT	D	48 (E)	48-hour extension for parent to attend
VT	D	48 (I)	24-hour good cause extension
VA	T	24 (E)	72-hour extension for witness
WA	P	72 (E)	
WV	T	24 (I)	
WI	D	24 (E)	48-hour extension to protect youth
WY	T	72 (I)	

[a] = If youth is transported from another county, the clock begins with detention in the receiving county.

[b] = The exclusion is for Sundays only.

[c] = Jurisdiction provides for a detention hearing within 24 hours for those held in jail.

[d] = The shorter time limit applies for intermittent holding facilities; the longer limit applies to regular holding facilities and secure detention.

[e] = The 6-hour limit applies to counties with more than 100,000 population.

[f] = The exclusion is for Sundays and holidays only.

[g] = The initial hearing has to occur the morning following the taking into custody.

D = beginning of detention; T = taken into custody; P = petition filed; IH = Initial hearing; (I) = includes Saturdays, Sundays, and holidays; (E) = excludes Saturdays, Sundays, and holidays.

Appendix E: Jurisdictions With Expedited Trials in Detention Cases

Jurisdiction	Clock Starts	Number of Days	Extensions
AK	A	30	Good cause[a]
AZ	D	30	
AR	B	14	Good cause[a]

Jurisdiction	Clock Starts	Number of Days	Extensions
CA	B	15[d]	
CO	B	60	
DE	A	30[b]	
DC	B	30[g,j]/45[c]	30 days[j]
FED	A	30	Good cause[a]
FL	B	21[g]	Good cause[a,m]
GA	C	10	
HI	B	7	7 days
ID	D	45[g]	Good cause[a]
IL	B	15/45[c]	30–70 days[c]
IN	C	20[d]	
IA	B	7	
LA	D	30[g]	Good cause[a]
MD	B	30	30 days[o]
MA	C	21/60[e]	
MI	A	63	
MN	D	30[g]	Good cause[a]
MS	A	21	
NE	C	180	
NH	D	21	14 days
NJ	A	30[b]	Good cause
NM	A/C/E[f]	30[g]	
NY	D	14/3[c,g]	3 days
NC	A	5	Upon review hearing
ND	A	14	Good cause[a]
OH	C	10	Good cause[a]
OK	B	10[j]/30	10[j]/60[p] days
OR	C	28[g,h]	28 days
PA	C	10	10 days
RI	B	30	30 days
SC	A	90[j]	Exceptional circumstances[a]
SD	A	90	Under treatment[n]

Jurisdiction	Clock Starts	Number of Days	Extensions
TN	A	30	
TX	C	10°	Good cause[a]
VT	C	15	
VA	A	$21^{i,j}$	
WA	D	30	
WI	D	20	
WV	A	30^k	Good cause[a]
WI	D	20	
WY	B	60^j	

A = taken into custody/detention begins; B = detention hearing or court order; C = petition filed or served; D = initial appearance, arraignment, plea hearing, advisory hearing; E = found competent to stand trial.

[a] = Length of extension not specified.

[b] = If no trial within 30 days, upon motion of defendant, court shall within 72 hours fix date for trial, unless it grants a continuance.

[c] = Severity of offense determines time limit.

[d] = Excludes weekends and holidays.

[e] = Times are for nonjury and jury trial, respectively.

[f] = Whichever of these occurrences is latest.

[g] = Statute emphasizes that trial must *commence* only.

[h] = Statute does not apply to murder, attempted murder, conspiracy to commit murder, and treason.

[i] = Statute specifies detention must be secure.

[j] = Statute specifies trial or transfer hearing must occur.

[k] = Deadline is for nonjury trial only.

[l] = 30-day extension can be repeated additional times, 30 days at a time.

[m] = Must be reviewed every 72 hours.

[n] = Statute says if at the 90th day the youth is in the process of treatment that has a specified duration, temporary custody can be extended to the end of treatment.

[o] = This 30-day extension is allowed after an unsuccessful transfer motion.

[p] = This 60-day extension is allowed in murder cases.

Appendix F: Requirements in the Juvenile Court Guilty Plea Process

Jurisdiction	Intelligence	Accuracy	Voluntariness
Alabama	A, B, C, E	Optional	No
Arizona	A, D, G	Optional	No

Jurisdiction	Intelligence	Accuracy	Voluntariness
California	A, B, C, D, E, F, G	Yes	Yes
Colorado	A, B, C, D, G	Yes	Yes (+)
Connecticut	A, C	Yes	Yes
Delaware	A, B, C, D, E, F	Yes	Yes (+)
District of Columbia	A, B, C, D, F, G	Yes	Yes (+)
Florida	A, B, C, D, F, G	Yes	Yes (+)
Georgia	A, B, C, D, F	Yes	Yes (+)
Hawaii	A	Optional	No
Idaho	A, B, C, G	Yes	Yes (+)
Illinois	A, D, F, G	No	Yes
Indiana	A, B, C, E	No	Yes
Iowa	A, B, C, D, F	Yes	Yes (+)
Kansas	A, B, C	Yes	Yes
Kentucky	A	No	No
Louisiana	A, B, C, E	Yes	Yes
Maryland	B, D, G	No	Yes
Michigan	A, B, C, D, F, G	Yes	Yes (+)
Minnesota	A, B, C, D, F, G	Yes	Yes (+)
Mississippi	A, B, E	Yes	Yes
Missouri	A, C	Yes	No
Nebraska	A, B, E, F	Yes	Yes
Nevada	A, B, C	No	Yes
New Hampshire	A, C	No	No
New Mexico	A, B, C, D, F	Yes	Yes (+)
New York	A, B, C, F, G	Yes	Yes
North Carolina	A, B, C, D, F, G	Yes	Yes (+)
Ohio	A, B, C, D, E, F, G	Optional	Yes
Oregon	A, B, G	No	Yes
Rhode Island	A, B, C	Optional	No
South Dakota	A, C, E	Yes	No
Tennessee	A, B, C, D, F	Yes	Yes (+)

Jurisdiction	Intelligence	Accuracy	Voluntariness
Texas	A, B, C, E, F, G	No	Yes (+)
Utah	A, B, C, D, G	Yes	Yes (+)
Wisconsin	A, B, C, E, F	Yes	Yes (+)
Wyoming	A, C	No	No

A = advice of rights
B = disclosure of penalties
C = discussion of charges
D = disclosure of consequences of guilty plea
E = discussion of nature of proceedings
F = defendant personally warned and pleads
G = transaction on record
(+) = inquiry into threats or plea bargains

Appendix G: Judicial Transfer Provisions

Jurisdiction	Minimum Age	Type	Offenses
AL	14	Regular	Any crime
AK	None	Presumptive	Unclassified/Class A person felony
	None	Regular	Any crime
AZ	None	Regular	Any crime
AR	14	Regular	10 major offenses; handgun
	14	Regular	Any felony + 3 PFADs w/n 2 years
CA	16	Regular	Any crime
	14	Presumptive	5 murder offenses
	14	Regular	22 violent offenses
CO	12/14	Presumptive	Situations below + 2 PFADs or 2 previous probation revocations via felonies
	14	Regular	Any felony
	12	Regular	Class 1/2 felonies crime of violence
DE	16	Regular	Any crime
	16	Regular (M)	7 violent offenses
	14	Regular	Any felony
	None	Regular	Any delinquency + nonamenable

Jurisdiction	Minimum Age	Type	Offenses
DC	15	Regular	Any felony
	None	Regular	Firearm + school
	16	Regular	Any crime while committed
	15	Presumptive	7 violent offenses
FED	15	Presumptive	Lead role in organization
	15	Regular	Violent felony + drugs/firearms
	13	Regular	5 violent crimes
FL	14	Regular (M)	Any felony + 3 PFADs
	14	Regular (M)	7 violent felonies + previous same AD
	14	Regular	Any crime
GA	15	Regular	Any crime
	13	Regular	Life/death crime
HI	16	Regular	Any felony
	14	Regular	Class A felony
	14	Regular	Any felony + 2 PFADs
	None	Regular	Murder + attempt
ID	18	Regular	Any offense before 18
	None	Regular	9 violent felonies
	14	Regular	Any crime
IL	15	Presumptive	Many violent felonies
	13	Regular	Any crime
IN	16	Regular	Any felony
	14	Regular	Heinous/aggravated offense
	10	Regular	Murder
IA	14	Regular	Any crime
	None	Regular	Excluded offense
KS	14	Presumptive	Many serious felonies
	None	Presumptive	Any felony + PFAD
	None	Regular	Any crime
KY	18	Regular	Any offense before 18
	16	Regular	Class C/D felony + PFAD

Jurisdiction	Minimum Age	Type	Offenses
	14	Regular	Class A/B felony; capital
	14	Regular	Any felony + previous YO convictions
LA	14	Regular	7 violent felonies
ME	None	Presumptive	9 violent felonies
	None	Regular	Class B/C crime
MD	15	Regular	Any crime
	None	Regular	Life/death crime
MA	14	Regular	Felony + previous commit
	14	Regular	Crime + injury/weapon
MI	14	Regular	Any felony
	None	Regular	Designated offense
MN	16	Presumptive	Firearm or presumptive prison
	14	Regular	Any felony
MS	13	Regular	Any crime
MO	12	Regular (M)	6 violent felonies
	12	Regular (M)	Any crime + 2 PFADs
	12	Regular	Any felony
NV	14	Presumptive	Several violent felonies
	14	Regular	Any felony
NH	15	Presumptive	11 violent felonies
	15	Presumptive	Any felony + 4 PFADs
	None	Regular	Any felony
NJ	14	Presumptive	20 offenses
	14	Regular	Any offense
NM	14	Regular	13 violent crimes
	14	Regular	Any felony + 3 PFADs w/n 3 years
NC	13	Regular	Any felony
ND	16	Regular	Any crime
	14	Presumptive	5 violent felonies
	14	Presumptive	Any felony + 2 PFADs
	14	Regular	Crime + injury

Jurisdiction	Minimum Age	Type	Offenses
OH	14	Regular	Any felony
OK	None	Regular	Any felony
OR	15	Regular	Murder + class A/B crime
	None	Regular	5 violent crimes
PA	15	Presumptive	9 violent felonies + PFAD
	14	Presumptive	Any offense + deadly weapon
	14	Regular	Any felony
RI	16	Presumptive	Any offense after certification
	16	Regular	Any felony
	None	Regular	Life crime
SC	16	Regular	Class E, F felonies + misdemeanors
	14	Regular	Class A/B/C/D felonies
	None	Regular	Murder + criminal sexual conduct
SD	16	Presumptive	Class A, B, 1, 2 felonies
	None	Regular	Any felony
TN	16	Regular	Any crime
	None	Regular	9 violent felonies
TX	15	Regular	2°, 3°, + state jail felonies
	14	Regular	1° felony
	10	Regular	Capital felony
UT	16	Presumptive	9 violent felonies
	16	Presumptive	Any felony + weapon with same PFAD
	14	Regular	Any felony
VT	10	Regular	11 violent felonies
VA	14	Regular	Any felony
WA	17	Regular (M)	6 violent felonies
	15	Regular (M)	Class A crime
	None	Regular (M)	Escape during commit to 21
	None	Regular	Any crime
WV	14	Regular	Violent person + drug felonies
	None	Presumptive	6 violent felonies

Jurisdiction	Minimum Age	Type	Offenses
	None	Regular	Any felony + 2 PFADs
WI	18	Regular	Any offense before 18
	15	Regular	Any crime
	14	Regular	9 violent felonies
	14	Regular	Any felony + gang
WY	13	Regular	Any crime
(M) = mandatory; PFAD = previous felony adjudication; AD = adjudication.			

Appendix H: Prosecutorial Transfer Provisions

Jurisdiction	Minimum Age	Type	Offenses
AL	16	Excluded	Many violent/drug felonies
AK	16	Excluded	Serious personal felonies
AZ	15	Excluded	Several violent felonies
	15	Excluded	Felony + 2 PFADs
	14	Concurrent	Several violent felonies
	14	Concurrent	Felony + 2 PFADs
AR	16	Concurrent	Any felony
	14	Concurrent	Many violent felonies
CA	16	Concurrent	Many violent offenses
	16	Concurrent	Felony + PFAD after 14
	14	Excluded	Many violent offenses
CO	16	Direct file	Class 3 + PFAD
	14	Direct file	Class 1, 2
CT	14	JC shall send	Capital, Class A, B, C, D
DE	16	Excluded	Several felonies + PFAD
	15	Excluded	Felony + escape
	15	Excluded	Felony + firearm
	None	Excluded	Many violent felonies
DC	16	Excluded	Several violent felonies
FED	16	JC shall send	Many felonies

Jurisdiction	Minimum Age	Type	Offenses
	16	JC shall send	Drug crimes + same PAD
FL	16	Concurrent	Any felony
	16	Concurrent	Misdemeanor + 2 previous ADs (1 felony)
	16	Excluded	Violent personal felonies + same PAD
	14	Concurrent	Life/death crimes
GA	15	JC shall send	Burglary + 3 same PADs
	14	JC shall send	Many violent crimes
	13	Excluded	7 violent crimes
	None	Concurrent	Life/death crime
ID	14	Excluded	9 violent crimes
IL	15	JC shall send	Forcible felony w/gang + PFAD
	15	JC shall send	Any felony w/gang + forcible PFAD
	15	JC shall send	Discharge firearm at school
	15	Excluded	Many violent crimes
	15	Excluded	Drugs at various locations
	13	Excluded	Escape/bail jump after transfer
	13	Excluded	Murder/sex assault
IN	16	Excluded	13 violent/drug crimes
	10	Excluded	Felony + previous felony conviction
IA	16	Excluded	11 violent/drug crimes
	16	Excluded	Felony/aggravated misdemeanor w/AC same convictions
KS	16	Excluded	Felony + PFAD
	16	Excluded	Commitment-related crimes
	16	Excluded	Felony while commit/escape + PAD
KY	14	Excluded	Felony + firearm
LA	15	Excluded	Murder 1°, 2°; aggravated rape/kidnapping
	15	Concurrent	13 violent/drug crimes
MD	16	Excluded	13 violent/drug crimes
	14	Excluded	Life/death crime
MA	14	Excluded	Murder 1°, 2°
MI	14	Direct file	Many violent crimes

Jurisdiction	Minimum Age	Type	Offenses
	14	JC shall send	Any felony + previous transfer
	None	Designated	Specified juvenile violation
MN	16	Excluded	Murder 1°
	14	JC shall send	Felony + previous felony conviction
MS	17	Excluded	Any felony
	13	Excluded	Life/death crime
	13	Excluded	Felony + firearm
	13	Excluded	Felony + previous transfer
MT	17	Excluded	Many serious felonies
	16	Direct file	8 violent offenses
	12	Direct file	Rape + murder
NE	16	Concurrent	Any misdemeanor
	None	Concurrent	Any felony
NV	16	Excluded	Sex/weapon crimes + PFAD
	None	Excluded	Murder/school assault
NJ	16	JC shall send	11 violent felonies
NM	15	Excluded	Murder 1°
NY	14	Excluded	14 violent crimes
	13	Excluded	Murder 2°
NC	13	JC shall send	Class A felony
ND	14	JC shall send	Many violent crimes
OH	16	JC shall send	Category 1 crime
	16	JC shall send	Category 2 + firearm or previous category ½ AD
	14	JC shall send	Category 1 + previous category ½ AD
OK	16	Excluded	Several serious felonies
	15	Excluded	Murder 2° + violent crimes
	13	Excluded	Murder 1°
OR	15	Excluded	17 violent crimes
PA	15	Excluded	8 violent crimes + deadly weapon
	15	Excluded	6 violent crimes + same PAD
	None	Excluded	Murder

Jurisdiction	Minimum Age	Type	Offenses
RI	17	Excluded	4 violent crimes
RI*	16	JC shall send	Any drug felony + drug PFADs after 16
SC	16	Concurrent	Class A–D felony; felony w/maximum of 15 years
	14	JC shall send	Any offense w/maximum of 10 years + 2 PFADs or 2 AC convicts of same
TX	14	JC shall send	Any felony + AC conviction
UT	16	Excluded	Murder + aggravated murder
	16	Excluded	Any felony + previous secure commit
VT	16	Concurrent	Any crime
	14	Excluded	5 violent crimes
VA	14	JC shall send	Various murders
	14	Concurrent	12 violent crimes
WA	16	Excluded	7 serious violent offenses + many violent offenses w/ previous serious violent AD or 2 violent ADs or 3 lesser felony ADs after 13 years old
WV	14	JC shall send	6 violent crimes
	14	JC shall send	Violent personal felony + same PAD
	14	JC shall send	Any felony + 2 PFADs
WI	10	Excluded	5 violent crimes
WY	17	Concurrent	Any crime
	14	Concurrent	11 violent crimes
	14	Concurrent	Any felony + 2 PFADs

AC = adult court; PFAD = previous felony adjudication; AD = adjudication; PAD = previous adjudication.

* = Rhode Island provision states that the youth shall be waived to adult court or certified to the second tier of juvenile court.

Appendix I: Statutorily Recognized Rights at the Adjudicatory Hearing

Jurisdiction	Rights	Jurisdiction	Rights
AL	A^{a*} B* C D* E* F*	AZ	A^{a*} B E F H
AK	A B C D E G H I	AR	A^{a*} E* F* G^b H* I

Jurisdiction	Rights	Jurisdiction	Rights
CA	A^{a}* B* C* D* E F* H* I* K L*	NE	A* B* C* D* E* F* H* J*
CO	A* B E F G	NV	A^{a}* (C) (D) E F H
CT	A^{a}* B* C* D* E (F) H L*	NH	A* D* E* (F) (H) K
DE	A^{a} D E F H K	NJ	A^{a}*
DC	A^{a}* B* C* D* E F* H L*	NM	A^{a}* B* C* D* E F* G H* K
FED	A*	NY	A^{a}* (B) E* F L
FL	A^{a}* B (C) D* E F* J K L*	NC	A^{a}* (B) (C) (D) E F* I
GA	A^{a}* B D* E* F* (H) J* K	ND	A^{a}* B (D) E* F* (H) J* K (L)
HI	A^{a} B E F* H	OH	A^{a}* B D* E* F* G^{b} (H) K
ID	A^{a}* B C D E* F* H* J (O)	OK	A B* D* E* F G
IL	A* B C D* F G^{b} H* (J) K L*	OR	A* D* E F* H J* K L*
IN	A* B* C* D* E* F H* K	PA	A^{a}* D* E F* (H) J* K L
IA	A^{a}* E F*	RI	A* B* C* D* E* F G^{b} H* J*
KS	A^{a} E G^{b} H L	SC	A^{a}* B* D* E*
KY	A* B C D E*	SD	A^{a}* (D) E* F* H*
LA	A^{a}* B* D* E F H* I J K	TN	A^{a}* B (C) D* E F* H* J* K (L)
ME	A^{a} F	TX	A^{a}* B* C* E* F G
MD	A^{a}* B E F	UT	A^{a}* B* C* D E* F* H* J* K L*
MA	A* E* F G* (L)	VT	A^{a}* B F*
MI	A^{a}* B C D E F* G* H J	VA	A* F I L
MN	A^{a}* B* D* E* F* G^{b} H* J* K (L)	WA	A^{a}* B C D E F H* I J
MS	A^{a}* B* D* E* F H* K	WV	A^{a}* B* C D E F* G H* J* K
MO	A^{a}* D E F* J K (L)	WI	A^{a}* (C) (D) E F (H) I
MT	A^{a}* C* D* E* F* G* (H) J* K L*	WY	A^{a}* B C* D* E* F G* H* J* K L*

A = counsel; B = self-incrimination; C = confrontation; D = cross examination; E = proof beyond a reasonable doubt; F = transcript/record; G = jury trial; H = compulsory process (or calling witnesses); I = public trial; J = be heard; K = present evidence; L = be present.

^{a} = right recognized at all proceedings

^{b} = jury trial recognized in only certain special proceedings

* = right associated with status offense cases also

( ) = right mentioned only in status offense cases

Appendix J: Jurisdictions With Speedy Trial Provisions

Jurisdiction	Clock Begins	Deadline in Days	Extensions
AZ	IA	60(D)[a]	
CA	P	30[a]	
CO	IA	60[d]	
FL	T	90(M)[a,c]	Exceptional causes
GA	P	60(M)	
ID	IA	90[c]	Good cause
IL	P	120(D)[a]	
IN	P	60[a]	90 days
IA	P	60(D)	Good cause
LA	IA	90(M)[c]	Good cause
MD	P	60[b]	Extraordinary causes
MA	P	30[b,e]	
MI	P	180[a]	Good cause
MN	IA	60(D)[c,f]	Good cause
MS	P	90(M)[a]	
NE	P	180(D)	
NV	P	60(D)	1 year interest of justice
NH	IA	30(M)	14 days
NM	P	120(M)[b,c]	60 days good cause
NY	IA	60(M)[c]	30 days
ND	P	30(D)	Good cause
SC	P	40(D)	Good cause
TN	P	90	Good cause
VA	P	120	
WA	IA	60(M)[a,b]	
WI	IA	30[a]	
WY	IA	60(D)	Good cause

IA = initial appearance or pretrial hearing; P = filing or service of the petition; T = taken into custody.
(D) = time limit is directory; (M) = time limit is mandatory.

[a] = Clock may stop for case-related events.

[b] = A new clock is possible when transfer to adult court is denied or a competency hearing is held.

[c] = Deadline refers to commencing trial only.

[d] = Jury trials are exempt from deadline.

[e] = 60 days allowed for jury trials.

[f] = 90 days allowed for extended jurisdiction proceeding.

Appendix K: Jurisdictions With Open Adjudicatory Hearing Provisions

Jurisdiction	Minimum Age	Minimum Offense/Record
AK	None	Any if under court supervision
	None	7 serious felonies
	16	Felony and PFAD
	16	Sexual abuse of a minor
AZ	None	All[a,b]
CA	None	28 serious charges[a]
CO	None	All[b]
DE	None	Felony
FL	None	All[b]
GA	None	Designated felony[a]
	None	Any if previous AD[a]
HI	16	Certain murder charges[b]
	16	Class A felony + PFAD[b]
	16	Class B/C felony + 2 PFADs[b]
IL	13	EJJP + HOP
ID	14	Felony[b]
IN	None	Felony or murder[a]
IA	None	All[b]
KS	16	All[b]
LA	None	Crime of violence or felony + PFAD
ME	None	Murder, class A/B/C crime, 2d class D
MD	None	Felony[b]

Jurisdiction	Minimum Age	Minimum Offense/Record
MA	14	Felony + previous DYS commit
	14	Bodily harm offense
	14	Offense + silencer/teargas/firearm
	None	Murder 1°, 2°
MI	None	All on formal calendar[a]
MN	16	Felony[b]
MO	None	Class A/B felony
	None	Class C felony + 2 class A/B/C/ PFADs
MT	None	All
NV	None	All[b]
NJ	None	All[b]
NM	None	All[b]
NY	None	All
OH	10	Serious youthful offender
OK	None	All + previous AD
PA	14	Felony
	12	9 major felonies
SD	16	Violent/drug offense
TX	14	All
UT	14	Felony
	14	Class A/B misdemeanor + previous misdemeanor/felony charge
	16	All[b]
VA	14	Felony[b]
WA	None	All[b]
WI	14	9 major felonies
	10	Homicide offenses
	None	Felony + previous AD

[a] = Judge can close trial in deference to victim.

[b] = Judge can close trial if in defendant's and/or public's best interests.

PFAD = previous felony adjudication; AD = adjudication; EJJP = Extended juvenile jurisdiction proceeding; HOP = habitual offender prosecution.

Appendix L: Jurisdictions With Deadlines for Disposition Hearings in Juvenile Court

Jurisdiction	Deadline (# of Days)	Specials/Extensions
AL[a,e]		
AK[a]	No unnecessary delay	
AZ[a]	30 (D)	30 days
	45 (R)	Good cause[b]
AR	14 (D)	
CA[a,f]	10 (D)[c]	
	30 (R)	15 days
CO[e]	30	SO
	45	Detention priority
CT[a]		
DE[a]	No unreasonable delay	
DC[a]	15 (D)	
FED	20	Good cause[b]
FL[a]	15 (D)	
GA[a,f]	20	Designated felonies
	30 (D)	Good cause[b]
ID[a]		
IL	Expedited (D)	SO
	15 (D)	15 days
IA	ASAP	
LA[a,e,f]	30	Good cause[b]
ME	60	
MD[a,e,f]	14 (D)	14-day periods
	30 (R)	
MI[f]	35 (D)	Good cause[b]
MN[a,e]	15	SO
	15 (D)	15 days
	45 (R)	30 days

Jurisdiction	Deadline (# of Days)	Specials/Extensions
MS[a,f]	14 (D)	Good cause[b]
MO[a]	30 (D)	
MT	ASAP	
NV[a]	60[d]	1 year
NH	21 (D)	
	30 (R)	
	30	SO
NJ	14 (D)	SO
	30 (R)	SO
	30 (D)	Good cause[b] JD
	60 (R)	JD
NM[e]	30 (D)	
	45 (D)	Diagnostic commit
NY	10 (D)	10–30 days
	20	Designated felonies
	50 (R)	10–30 days
ND[a]		
OH[a]		
OK[a]		
PA[a]	Expedited (D)	SO
	20 (D)	JD
SD[a]		
TN[a]	15 (D)	Good cause[b]
	90 (R)	Good cause[b]
UT[a]		
VT[e,f]	15–30	
VA	30 (D)	Good cause[b]
WA[a]	14	SO
	14 (D)	Good cause[b]
	21 (R)	Good cause[b]
WI[f]	10 (D)	

Jurisdiction	Deadline (# of Days)	Specials/Extensions
	30 (R)	
WY[a,f]	60	

(D) = detention; (R) = released

JD = juvenile delinquent; SO = status offender

[a] = Disposition hearing may immediately follow delinquency adjudication.

[b] = A good-cause extension of unspecified length is permitted.

[c] = Excludes weekends and legal holidays.

[d] = Clock starts when petition is filed, rather than at adjudication.

[e] = Disposition hearing may immediately follow a status offense adjudication.

[f] = Deadlines are supposed to apply to delinquents and status offenders.

Appendix M: Jurisdictions Identifying Factors to Be Included in the PDR

Jurisdiction	Factors	Jurisdiction	Factors
AL	A F H K L	KS	B E F G H J K L
AK	B C D E F G H I J K L	KY	A B E G H J K L
AZ	E F J K	LA	A B C D E F G H I J K L
AR	A F H I J K L	ME	A B C D F H J K L
CA	A E G J K L	MD	E F H K* L
CO	B C E F G H J K* L	MA	C F G H K* L
CT	A B C D E F K* L	MI	A C E F H J K* L
DE	A B C E F J K L	MN	A B C D E F H I J K L
DC	A C F H K L	MS	A B C D K L
FED	C F H	MO	A E F H J K L
FL	A B C D E F G I J K L	MT	A E F H J K* L
GA	A B C E F H J K L	NE	A F K* L
HI	A F	NV	B C F J K
ID	A C F G H I K L	NH	E F G H K L
IL	A C E F H J K L	NJ	B C D E F H I J K* L
IN	A F J K L	NM	F H J K* L
IA	A B C D E F K L	NY	A B C E F G H J K L

Jurisdiction	Factors	Jurisdiction	Factors
NC	A B C D F G H J L	TN	A F G H J K L
ND	A F H K* L	TX	A E F K L
OH	A B E F L	UT	A E F H J L
OK	A E F G H J K* L	VT	A E F H L
OR	B C E F G H I J K* L	VA	B C D E F H I J K L
PA	A E F H J K L	WA	A B C E I J
RI	F G H J L	WV	F H J K L
SC	F H K L	WI	B E F G H J K L
SD	A E F J K	WY	A E F G H L

A = all relevant and material evidence; B = offense; C = delinquent record; D = culpability; E = victim impact; F = mental and physical examinations; G = school record; H = family situation; I = treatment history; J = best interests of the child; K = least restrictive alternative; L = special duty before removing youth from home.

* = Least restrictive alternative applies only to status offenders.

Appendix N: Jurisdictions Identifying Characteristics of Probation Dispositions

Jurisdiction	Probation Characteristics	Jurisdiction	Probation Characteristics
AL	A B D E F J K	IL	(A) B C D F* G H J K
AK	F G J	IN	A B C F G H* I J K
AZ	B C E* F* G* H* I J K	IA	A* B C F G H
AR	B C D E* F G* H I* J	KS	A* C E F H I K
CA	A* B C E F G* I* J K	KY	A C E F G I J
CO	A* B C D E F G* J	LA	(A) B C D F G H K
CT	A B C F G*	ME	B C E F G H J
DE	A E F G H I	MD	A B C E F G H* K
DC	B E F G* K	MA	A* F J
FED	A F	MI	A* B E F G J
FL	A B C D F G* H I K	MN	A* B C E F G* H* K
GA	A E* F* G* H* J	MS	A B C E F* G* H J
HI	A* B C E F G* J	MO	A B C E F* G H I
ID	E F* G* H* J* K	MT	A B C E F* G* H* I*

Jurisdiction	Probation Characteristics	Jurisdiction	Probation Characteristics
NE	B C F* G*	RI	A* B C F* G* H* K
NV	A B C E* F* G* H* I* K	SC	A* E* F* G* H*
NH	(A) B C D E* F* G* I	SD	A* C D E* F* G* H* J*
NJ	B C E F G H J K	TN	A* C E* F G*
NM	A* E F G H J K	TX	A* B C D F* G* H* I J K
NY	B C D F* G* J K	UT	A* B C E* F* G* H J
NC	B C D E F G H I J K	VT	A C E F J
ND	A* E F* G H K	VA	A* B C E F G* H* I J K
OH	A* D E* F* G* H* I* J* K	WA	E* F G J K
OK	A* B C E F G H I J K	WV	A C E F G H
OR	(A) B C E F G I K	WI	(A) B C D E* F* G* I* J K
PA	A* E F* G	WY	B C E F G* H* J K

A = no duration specified; B = relative can assume custody of youth; C = reputable citizen can assume custody of youth; D = written conditions; E = fine; F = restitution; G = community service; H = driver's license; I = home detention; J = detention; K = sex and/or drug treatment.

* = applies also to status offenders

( ) = applies only to status offenders

Appendix O: Custody Rates for Juveniles in 1997, for Detention and Residential Placement

State	Detention	Commitment	Total	State	Detention	Commitment	Total
AL	79	262	348	GA*	172	307	480
AK	75	329	418	HI	13	86	106
AZ	99	239	344	ID	43	102	145
AR	27	167	198	IL*	78	205	286
CA	154	386	549	IN	93	269	366
CO	116	242	379	IA	73	222	307
CT**	69	436	508	KS	123	256	386
DE	173	229	402	KY	51	190	243
DC	332	297	662	LA*	115	459	582
FL	130	261	394	ME	56	156	220

State	Detention	Commitment	Total	State	Detention	Commitment	Total
MD	105	166	273	OK	69	126	196
MA*	82	110	194	OR	34	319	389
MI*	108	263	375	PA	62	238	302
MN	54	198	258	RI	57	348	412
MS	34	181	218	SC*	99	328	427
MO*	58	175	248	SD	84	410	556
MT	21	236	266	TN	66	290	358
NE	111	236	353	TX*	72	252	327
NV	183	267	460	UT	74	172	247
NH*	24	127	154	VT	23	44	70
NJ	122	142	266	VA	168	230	399
NM	79	262	336	WA	91	244	335
NY**	53	267	323	WV	101	97	200
NC**	43	152	196	WI*	56	300	359
ND	132	200	336	WY	26	467	511
OH	101	229	332				

* Jurisdiction over youth ends at age 16.

** Jurisdiction over youth ends at age 15.

Source: Snyder and Sickmund (1999, 189).

Glossary

A

Abolition of juvenile court Idea that juvenile court has outlived its purpose or utility or does not provide adequate due process and that all defendants should be prosecuted in criminal court.

Adjudication Term referring to the juvenile court's finding a youth to be involved in the alleged offense. Except for the legal effect, it is the equivalent of a conviction.

Adjudicatory hearing Name give to the juvenile court version of a criminal trial. Historically, and in most situations today, the hearing has been conducted in private. The public and the media have not been admitted. Recently, several states have made the adjudicatory hearing a public experience for older and more serious offenders.

Advocate Defense attorney concerned with securing an acquittal or the best possible legal outcome in the case and not necessarily the best treatment outcome.

Aftercare Juvenile system's version of parole, or that period after one's release from an institution.

Alford plea Situation in which the defendant pleads guilty but claims to be innocent.

Amenability hearing The second stage of a judicial transfer hearing, addressing the ability of the juvenile system to effectively rehabilitate the offender.

Appeal Juvenile's right to challenge an adverse finding or ruling (as with an adjudication).

Appointed or assigned counsel Defense attorney who represents an indigent (poor) defendant because the public defender is either unavailable or representing a co-defendant.

Arraignment Also known as a plea hearing because it is the stage of the court process where the defendant enters a plea of guilty or not guilty to the charges.

At-risk youth Juveniles who are not yet delinquent but who are in danger of becoming so.

B

Balanced approach Idea that juvenile court should balance the interests of the youth with the interests of society, rather than focusing exclusively upon the child's best interests.

Becker hearing A proceeding held in the state of Washington when the prosecutor delays the prosecution of a youth long enough for the accused to chronologically become an adult before trial. If the delay appears to have no justification, the prosecutor loses the authority to pursue the matter in adult court.

Behavior modification Therapeutic intervention that uses reinforcements to encourage desired behavior and disincentives or punitive consequences to discourage undesired behavior.

Beyond a reasonable doubt Standard of proof required in juvenile and adult court in order to adjudicate a juvenile of a delinquency and, in some states, of a status offense too.

Bifurcation The separation that is supposed to occur between the adjudicatory and disposition hearings.

Bill of Rights The first ten amendments to the Constitution in which are located many of the rights associated with the arrest and trial process, as well as other important rights (such as freedom of speech, press, and religion).

blended sentence Disposition given on the second tier of juvenile court (and also by criminal court) that combines a juvenile and an adult court sentence.

boot camp Military-like, intense setting in which youths receive physical training and discipline for a short period of time.

bootstrapping Converting status offenders into delinquents by adjudicating them of status offense probation or court orders.

C

case rates The figures that represent how many youths are affected by or involved in a particular situation (detention, institutionalization) per 100,000 youths in the population.

certification Alternative name given by many states to the transfer of youth to adult court.

CHAPTERS Acronym standing for the eight-component initiative that aims to improve the conditions and operation of juvenile detention centers and other facilities.

charge bargain One of the two types of plea bargaining in juvenile (and adult) court. It usually involves reduction in the severity of the charges and is often linked with a sentence bargain or a no pros bargain.

Chicago women The group of prominent women who were instrumental in the founding of the juvenile court in Cook County in 1899.

child savers Alternate name for the Chicago women based on the title of a book written by Anthony Platt about their activities in Cook County.

children in need of supervision (CHINS) Popular term associated with status offenders. Many other labels borrow the *INS* part of the acronym and precede it with an *m, j,* or *p*.

chivalry hypothesis Theory that suggests police (and perhaps other court officials as well) will ignore certain illegal behavior of young females or react more harshly to them than they would to boys of the same age (and behavior).

classification Analysis of juveniles conducted after adjudication to determine if and where they should be institutionalized and with what treatment programs.

cohort Group of individuals born in the same year(s) whose behavior is tracked over many years to discover their delinquent history and characteristics that are associated with offending.

colloquy Exchange, typically verbal, between the defendant and a court official to ascertain whether the youth is intelligently and voluntarily surrendering the right at issue (such as a guilty plea surrendering the right to trial).

combined discretionary/mandatory minimum sentence A disposition that the judge has the discretion of whether to implement (e.g., the decision to commit a youth) but that, once chosen, comes with a mandatory minimum term.

combined sentence Disposition that literally combines a juvenile and adult sentence. It is issued by either the juvenile court's second tier or adult court. It involves imposing an adult sentence that is stayed while the youth serves a juvenile court sentence. Successful completion of the juvenile sentence means the adult sentence is canceled.

commitment Sentencing a youth to an institution.

community-based shelter Popular name for a facility that detains status offenders pending trial or disposition.

community corrections Term meant to capture the array of programs and services available in the community that are associated with the youth's sentence of probation.

community policing Policing strategy that involves closely linking police with a community to collaboratively define and resolve local problems.

community service Popular disposition that involves a youth's working in the community, without compensation, as payment for offense committed.

community supervision Another way to refer to probation or the process of placing the offender under the watch of a probation officer.

competency hearing Proceeding used to determine whether a youth is capable of understanding the proceedings and assisting in the defense of the case.

complete sentence bargain Plea bargain in which all the details of the sentence agreement are fully understood and presented to the judge as a package for acceptance or rejection.

comprehensive gang model Strategy that attempts to suppress gangs while improving conditions in the community so as to discourage the development of gangs.

comprehensive strategy A broad-based approach to serious and violent juvenile delinquency, including prevention programs and rational, graduated sentencing alternatives.

concurrent jurisdiction One method of prosecutorial transfer to adult court, stemming from the prosecutor's authority to initiate prosecution in either juvenile or criminal court because both courts share (or have concurrent) jurisdiction.

conditional freedom The youth's freedom in the community with conditions attached as a result of being adjudicated and placed on probation or because the youth has just been released from an institution on parole.

confidentiality Term meant to convey how juvenile courts were to operate in secrecy and were dedicated to not identifying youth who committed offenses.

consent decree Diversionary disposition that requires youths to perform certain tasks in exchange for avoiding a delinquent or status offense record. It resembles an informal agreement except that it constitutes a somewhat more negative court record for the youth.

corporal punishment Physical striking of juveniles permitted historically in both schools and treatment facilities. In previous times it amounted to serious beatings of committed delinquent youths and formed the basis of a right to treatment and protection from cruel and unusual punishment.

cottage-style training school Physical facility design for institutionalized youth that was an attempt to replicate "normal" family life.

court of last resort Idea that juvenile court was supposed to be involved in a youth's life only when the family could not resolve the youth's problem.

crime control model Philosophy that supports quick and efficient resolution of charges and dedication of most resources toward policing and punishing offenders rather than toward attorney's fees.

criminalization effect Term meant to capture how juvenile court is becoming similar to criminal court in a number of respects (e.g., prosecutors managing intake).

curfew laws Ordinances that typically demand those under age 18 to be off the streets (unless on lawful mission) by 11 p.m. or midnight.

D

day treatment program Probationary sentence that involves the youth's attending a special program or school during the daytime.

decriminalize When the state removes a behavior from the penal code, or any listing of action that are illegal.

defense attorney Individual responsible for representing the youth accused of an offense.

defense of infancy The common law provision that made it impossible to convict anyone youn ger than 7 years of age, and difficult to convict youth between the ages of 7 and 14.

deferred adjudication or disposition When a youth has been adjudicated but the adjudicatio or disposition is put on hold (as with a diversion) to see if the youth can successfully complete program, in which case the charges will be dismissed.

deinstitutionalization Initiative, especially connected to status offenders, designed to remov youth from adult jails and prisons or delinquent facilities.

delayed judicial transfer Process operating in Massachusetts and New Mexico whereby th judge's decision to transfer a youth to criminal court is delayed until after the trial in juvenile cour and at the time of adjudication/conviction.

delayed reverse transfer Judge's decision to impose a juvenile sentence after conviction in crim nal court.

delinquency Acts committed by juveniles that for adults would be crimes. In some states th boundaries of delinquency are broader than those for crime and can include ordinance violation and behaviors illegal for youth only.

designated proceeding Michigan's conversion of a prosecution in juvenile court into a crimina prosecution. Although the proceeding and the conviction are criminal, the judge can issue a juve nile sentence.

detention Traditionally, the secure custody of a youth pending trial, disposition, or an opening a a facility to which the youth has been committed. Today, the definition includes youths sentence to a detention center much like adults sentenced to short-term stays in jail.

detention center A location where delinquents are held in secure custody prior to trial and wher they serve short-term sentences following adjudication in juvenile court. These centers constitut the juvenile system's version of adult jail.

detention diversion advocacy project Initiative specifically geared to removing youths from se cure detention and, ideally, from any detention experience.

detention hearing Proceeding to which youths in nearly all states are entitled within a short tim after they are held in detention following arrest.

differentiated sentencing Where juvenile court sentences in levels (as with adult court) instead c just giving the offender an indeterminate sentence to the age of 21. So, a first-degree felony woul definitely call for a more serious disposition that a felony of a lesser degree.

direct file Another way to refer to concurrent jurisdiction. It refers to a prosecutor's authority t transfer a case to criminal court by directly filing it there, without the need for a juvenile court c criminal court judge to approve of such a move.

discretionary exclusion Transfer to criminal court. It constitutes the decision made by a judge c prosecutor to choose the adult court over the juvenile court for prosecution of the case.

dismissal bargain A youth's agreement to perform certain tasks or services in exchange for a dis missal of the charges. It can be an informal agreement, a consent decree, or a nol pros bargain.

disposition Juvenile court's term for sentence; used in criminal court as well.

disposition hearing Juvenile court's version of a sentencing hearing that is supposed to be bifur cated or separated from the trial.

disposition ladder Plateaus or levels of sentencing in juvenile court that represent the state's engaging in incrementally greater control over a youth who either does not respond well to a less intrusive or controlling treatment effort or has reoffended.

disproportionate minority confinement The statistical reality that most jurisdictions disproportionately incarcerate minority youth.

diversion Kicking a youth's case out of the formal court process so as to avoid imposing a negative label (e.g., delinquent). Diversion usually occurs at the intake stage but can also be a juvenile court disposition.

domino theory The idea that granting juvenile defendants too many rights (particularly jury trial) would result in the juvenile and adult systems becoming too similar, and that this would encourage legislature to eventually abolish juvenile courts.

double jeopardy Protection against being criminally prosecuted twice for the same crime. It has been interpreted by the U.S. Supreme Court to prohibit being prosecuted in juvenile court *and* adult court for the same offense.

Drug Abuse Resistance Education (DARE) program Police-directed program conducted with elementary-level students in the school setting that aims to enhance children's social skills in an attempt to reduce their drug use.

drug court Diversionary mechanism that seeks to encourage a youth's acceptance of and performance in a treatment program in exchange for an eventual dismissal of the charges.

dual processing The idea that the juvenile justice system engages in both treatment and punishment of youthful offenders, depending upon the severity of the offense and the juvenile's delinquent record.

due process model Philosophy that emphasizes the need to control governmental power and accordingly seeks to maximize the defendant's rights. It is based on the idea that money is appropriately spent on lawyers and trials to check the powers of the state.

E

early release Another way to refer to parole or aftercare. It involves the discretionary decision made by an institutional representative to allow the youth to leave the facility prior to the expiration of the sentence.

electronic monitoring Device that allows the probation officer to keep tabs on the youth via the electronic signals the device attached to the offender emits. It informs the PO if and when the youth leaves home without authorization or enters an area in the community that is off-limits.

exclusionary rule Rule of evidence that prohibits the admission of evidence at trial that has been seized illegally by the police or prosecution.

expunging records Traditionally, destruction of a youth's records when he or she reached adulthood, allowing the youth to report that there had never been an adjudication. It currently means that a youth who never gets in trouble again can declare a clean record, but youths who reoffend may see the reappearance of the juvenile court records in criminal court.

extended juvenile jurisdiction prosecution Measure adopted in several states that singles out the most serious juvenile offenders for an extended length of juvenile court jurisdiction. These youths can be under the court's control for a considerable length of time. In most states they are transferred to a second tier of the juvenile court, where they will be given a jury trial before the imposition of the extended sentence.

F

family court Another name by which juvenile courts are known, especially in states that have jurisdiction over many matters, such as family-related issues.

field investigation A police officer's analysis and investigation of an alleged incident at the scene of the incident.

Fifth Amendment The amendment in the Bill of Rights that affords defendants the right not to incriminate themselves or be subjected to double jeopardy.

fines Financial penalties imposed on youths in many states that may be in addition to other demands such as restitution or community service.

foster home Family-like placement in a residential community that usually involves allowing youths to live with families to which they are not related, typically because of the inadequacies of the natural family (or perhaps the lack of one altogether) or problems in the neighborhood of the natural family.

Fourteenth Amendment due process clause The constitutional standard that controls the operation of juvenile court, whereas the Bill of Rights (the first ten amendments) applies to criminal court. This standard demands basic or fundamental fairness and not necessarily all of the rights associated with a criminal court prosecution.

Fourth Amendment The amendment in the Bill of Rights that controls the state's policing power, particularly the authority to arrest and to search and seize.

G

gang A group that enjoys a sustained relationship, a common purpose, and a special allegiance among its members and that engages, at least occasionally, in illegal activities.

gang migration Idea that gangs relocate to areas other than their origin because of law enforcement pressures or the expansion of drug markets.

Gang Resistance Education and Training (GREAT) program Police-directed program conducted with upper-level elementary students in the school setting that aims to enhance their ability to resist pressures to join in and participate with gangs.

gatekeeper An individual (such as a police officer or intake worker) empowered to decide whether to invoke formal processing against a youth charged with an offense.

get-tough movement Trend among states, especially in the 1990s, to make the outcomes of all juvenile court dispositions (including diversions) more serious and to exclude more serious and chronic offenders from juvenile court.

group home Institution that can be as small as a residential house containing several children to a large building housing several hundred youths (such as an orphanage) who need a home in which to live while under the court's supervision.

guardian Defense attorney who is more concerned with the youth's treatment interests and ensuring that he or she receives rehabilitation than with the youth's legal interests.

guardian ad litem Attorney (but not a defense attorney) appointed to serve specifically to pursue the child's best (i.e., treatment) interests.

guided group interaction Intervention that places youths in a group setting where each is confronted by the others concerning their past behavior.

guilty plea Admission a youth offers to having committed the offense, obviating the need for an adjudicatory hearing.

gun court Special proceeding in which youth charged with certain, nonserious weapons offenses are given an opportunity to earn an eventual dismissal of charges following participation in a diversion/treatment program.

H

halfway house Residential setting that looks like a house. Used in the juvenile system as a location that helps youths reintegrate back into the community after long-term placement.

hidden juvenile corrections Practice whereby youth are institutionalized in private hospitals and mental health facilities rather than in formal delinquent and status offense facilities, seemingly (but not really) resulting in a decrease in the number of institutionalized offenders.

home detention Allowing youths to remain at home during the pretrial stage, usually under strict conditions (including possibly electronic monitoring) to not leave the home.

house arrest An alternative way to refer to home detention, but could also involve a disposition from juvenile court that could force an adjudicated delinquent or status offender to be confined to the house for a considerable amount of time.

House of Refuge Institution created by the Quakers to reform and educate the mostly poverty-stricken youth over whom they exercised *parens patriae* duties.

I

implicit plea bargain Guilty plea that is offered with an expectation of reward but has not been openly negotiated or bargained.

incomplete sentence bargain Plea bargain indicating that the youth has an agreement related to the outcome (such as a prosecutor recommending a disposition) but that no definite sentence has been agreed to between defense and prosecution.

indeterminate sentence Traditional disposition in juvenile court that is open ended, meaning that the system has control over the youth until he or she reaches the upper age limit of the system (usually 21) or is rehabilitated.

index crime The eight major offenses (murder, robbery, etc.) that comprise Part I crimes. The FBI focuses on these crimes in reporting the crime rate in the United States.

individualization Juvenile court's obligation to be responsive to the particular youth's problem(s) rather than merely reacting routinely to the youth based on his or her offense and record.

informal adjustment/probation Term used in most jurisdictions to refer to the diversionary agreement reached between the defendant and the PO at intake. It requires one or more tasks on the part of the youth for the charges to be dismissed.

in loco parentis Concept that applies usually to school personnel who "stand in place of the parents."

inmate culture The culture that develops among inmates in institutions. There is a hierarchy, a division of labor, and perhaps various types of exploitation among the inmate population.

institution Term that applies to facilities in which youth are confined, especially for long terms.

institutional model The treatment orientation (i.e., therapeutic intervention) of the institution housing youth.

intake Initial decision-making stage in juvenile court that determines whether the case will be forwarded for formal processing or diverted from the system.

intake officer Individual who determines the outcome of intake. It could be a person who also serves as a probation officer.

intensive aftercare program (IAP) Intensive community supervision programming for youths who have experienced institutionalization and are reintegrating into the community.

intensive probation Community supervision that is more intensive or subject to much greater scrutiny by the probation officer. It usually involves more frequent contacts between the youth and the PO than that experienced in regular probation and most likely involves a relatively small case load for the PO.

intermediate sanctions Punishments that are graduated and offered as alternatives to institutionalization. The idea is to have consequences short of commitment for those who either violate probation or parole or recidivate after serving a term of probation.

interrogation Process in which police question the accused concerning the alleged charges.

invariant hypothesis Theory that crime peaks during a youth's teen years.

J

judge Individual who presides at trial and is responsible for sentencing adjudicated offenders.

judicial transfer Judge's authority to send a juvenile's case to criminal court, typically based on his or her lack of amenability to juvenile court treatment.

jurisdiction Authority of the juvenile court to hear or try a case. Also used to refer to locations such as states.

juvenile An individual who, because of age, is legally responsible for an offense as a child rather than as an adult. Most jurisdictions require that that age be less than 18 at the time of the offense but others use 17 and 16 instead. Moreover, some jurisdictions deny juvenility to those who have been previously convicted in criminal court or who have committed certain serious offenses as a juvenile.

juvenile assessment center Another way to refer to intake, usually involving an assessment of the youth's risks and needs and suitability for juvenile court processing.

Juvenile Court Act Legislation that enables a juvenile court to enjoy jurisdiction over a variety of situations involving youths and adults. Often connected particularly with the first such legislation in 1899 in Cook County, Illinois.

juvenile delinquent The title given to a youthful offender who commits what would be considered a crime if committed by an adult.

Juvenile Detention Alternative Initiative Movement sponsored by the Annie E. Casey Foundation that supports the active pursuit of alternatives to the secure (or any) detention of youth.

Juvenile Justice and Delinquency Prevention (JJDP) Act of 1974 Critical congressional legislation that promoted the separation of status offenders from delinquents, the deinstitutionalization of status offenders, and the removal of these youths from delinquent facilities and adult prisons and jails. The removal of delinquents from adult facilities or at least their separation from adult inmates was also part of the legislation. The act has been amended to address the disproportionate confinement of minorities.

K

Kent hearing Name given to the judicial transfer hearing (to send a youth to criminal court).

L

labeling theory Concept suggesting that juveniles are prone to internalize labels given to them and that they will become more committed to delinquent values and actions when they are officially designated as delinquents.

law enforcement One of the roles attributed to police that involves their enforcement of the laws and making arrests as opposed to maintaining order or servicing the community. Also an alternative term used to refer to "police" officers.

least restrictive setting Obligation, usually on the judge's part, to ensure that the intervention chosen for the youth is no more restrictive than necessary. In other words, the court must show that it would not be possible to rehabilitate the youth with a less restrictive disposition.

legal factors Those factors affecting decision making that are considered authorized by law. The literature suggests that only these factors are legitimate in influencing outcomes of decisions made in juvenile court. Some might consider these factors to be limited to the offense and the delinquent record.

legal interests Succinctly means that youth are "better off" without any legal finding being made against them. Most obviously, this means it is better not to be adjudicated than to be found guilty of anything, but it also means that any finding short of complete vindication constitutes an adverse result for the youth.

M

macrolevel prevention program Large-scale neighborhood programs geared to prevent a variety of social problems, especially delinquency.

mandatory exclusion The *necessary* prosecution in criminal court of someone most of the country regards as a juvenile. This includes states that identify the beginning age of adult defendants as 16 or 17 years of age (instead of 18), and jurisdictions that hold that a previous transfer to or conviction in adult court converts a juvenile into an adult for purposes of criminal liability.

mandatory initial detention Occurs when arrest for certain serious offenses automatically requires the PO to hold the youth in detention at least until a detention hearing.

mandatory public disclosure Occurs when arrests and adjudications for certain serious offenses, often coupled with an age requirement, mandate that the court inform the public of these developments.

mandatory sentence A particular disposition that must be imposed by the court upon adjudication of certain offenses. This could mean mandatory institutionalization in serious offense cases or mandatory community service in less serious cases.

master Also known as a referee, among other names. A person authorized to function like a judge at various juvenile court stages, including detention/preliminary hearings and even adjudicatory and disposition hearings. Controversy arises when such an official conducts trial because he or she cannot render a verdict and must submit a recommendation of guilty or not guilty to a judge who can uphold or reverse the recommendation.

medical model Perspective holding that delinquency is a result of some maladjustment or illness on the part of the offender rather than a deliberate and rational choice to commit crime. This model forms the basis for the indeterminate sentence and for many rehabilitation programs.

mens rea A necessary element in proving a crime occurred: the offender's awareness of or intent to commit an offense.

meta-analysis Technique of assembling a large number of studies with a similar focus and using a statistical technique to compare the results of the studies.

microlevel prevention program Narrowly focused, research-based prevention programs aimed particularly at at-risk youth.

minimum sentence Often a discretionary, but sometimes a mandatory, decision to impose some minimum requirements, such as an amount of time that must be spent on probation or in a facility.

Miranda warnings Rule associated with the *Miranda v. Arizona* decision, which requires suspects in custody to be warned (typically by the police) that they have the right to remain silent, that anything they say can be used in court, and that they have a right to consult an attorney that will be provided to them if they cannot afford one.

modification hearing Proceeding held while the youth is serving a sentence to determine whether the sentence needs to be adjusted one way or another.

Monitoring the Future (MTF) Survey Annual self-report survey conducted with high school seniors, and some adults, that addresses school crime and drug use.

N

National Crime Victimization Survey (NCVS) Annual survey of households conducted by the U.S. Census Bureau to discover reported and unreported crime.

National Incident-Based Reporting System (NIBRS) Data analysis that reviews index crime and other offenses along a number of dimensions, including the date and time offenses were committed.

National Youth Gang Survey (NYGS) Annual survey conducted by OJJDP that measures the numbers of gangs and gang members as well as certain characteristics of gangs, such as race, age, and gender of the members.

neglected youth A youth who is either neglected or abused by a parent. In many states this youth comes under the jurisdiction of juvenile court.

net widening Term that captures one of the effects of diversion. It refers to both the increase in the number of youths who can be subject to the control of the juvenile system (compared to what would happen if all youths were formally processed) and the expansion of the juvenile system into the community via the extensive programs dealing with diverted juveniles.

nolo contendere plea Plea that is the functional equivalent of a guilty plea but that is officially a plea of "no contest." The defendant stands convicted by virtue of this plea, but if the victim wants to sue the offender the plea cannot be used in civil court to obtain a conviction there. This plea has little relevance in juvenile court because of its limited benefit to the defendant.

nol pros bargain A deal that, in exchange for dropping some or all charges, the defendant will perform tasks, such as those required via informal agreements or consent decrees, or will plead guilty to other charges.

nonnegotiated guilty pleas A variety of guilty pleas that do not involve negotiation between the defendant and the state but that may be offered in the hopes of gaining some tactical advantage or a reward from the judge. Such a plea may also reflect a defendant's desire not to challenge the case without an ulterior motive.

not guilty plea Defendant's choice to contest the charges, meaning that a trial will be necessary if the prosecutor wants to continue to pursue prosecution of the case.

O

ffense exclusion One of the two ways in which prosecutorial transfer to adult court occurs. It involves the legislature's prohibiting juvenile court from adjudicating certain crimes, usually because of the severity of the offense or record.

ffice of Juvenile Justice and Delinquency Prevention (OJJDP) Agency created by the JJDP ct of 1974 that serves a critically important role in monitoring events in juvenile justice across the ountry, sponsoring research in the field, and developing model programs for the prevention of denquency and the treatment of offenders.

pen facility Juvenile institution that could literally be in the open fields, such as wilderness amps, or that have walls but do not have secure barriers like barbed wire and gun turrets.

perant conditioning Promoting learning through the use or withholding of rewards.

rder maintenance Role of police that involves keeping the peace and clearing the streets more han pursuing and arresting criminals.

rder of protection Court order that commands an individual, perhaps a defendant or a parent, ɔ perform a task, to stop doing a certain activity, or to stay away from someone (especially a ictim).

ɔ

arens patriae doctrine Legal principle misinterpreted or misapplied by the Pennsylvania Supreme Court. Originally, it was used in England by the king to appoint a guardian to manage the esate of a child of nobility who became an orphan. It was defined by the Pennsylvania court to mean hat the state has the license and duty to raise children it believes are not being raised properly.

arens patriae figure A juvenile court judge who is more concerned with ensuring that juveniles eceive the treatment they need rather than justice per se.

arental liability Laws, most of which are of recent origin, that impose financial and behavioral esponsibilities on parents because of their children's behavior. It ranges from requiring parents to ay for virtually all the costs of prosecuting and rehabilitating their children to having them particɔate in the child's treatment program.

arents Individuals responsible for rearing the youth and who wield influential power in the juvenile system. They can seriously advantage or disadvantage a child by the way in which they interact vith system officials, especially the judge and the PO.

arole Criminal justice term for juvenile aftercare or release from an institution before the expiation of the sentence and with conditions imposed upon release.

art I offenses Another way to refer to index crimes. They include the eight major crimes: murer and nonnegligent manslaughter, forcible rape, robbery, aggravated assault, burglary, larceny/ heft, auto theft, and arson.

art II offenses The 21 less serious offenses than those tracked as Part I, including many misdeneanors and drug abuse violations.

atterns The environmental contexts within which delinquency occurs, including schools, drugs, nd gangs.

etition The official charging document of the juvenile court. It is the functional equivalent of an nformation in criminal court.

lacement Term used by juvenile court, like commitment, to refer to the institutionalization of a outh.

plea bargaining The defendant's trade of a guilty plea for a charge and/or sentence consideratio from the state, much as in criminal court.

policing authorities The various sources of individuals who enjoy policing authority over juve niles, including police, parents, and school officials.

predisposition report (PDR) Juvenile court's version of a presentence investigation. It involve the PO's gathering of a considerable amount of information about the offender, ranging from fam ily dimensions to neighborhood characteristics to his or her offense and treatment/delinquen history.

preliminary inquiry The investigation conducted by the PO at intake.

preponderance of evidence Level of evidence initially required to adjudicate youth in juvenil court (until 1970); still the level of proof used in some states for status offenders.

presumption of release The juvenile system's directive to police and intake workers that youth are presumably going to be released to the parents in lieu of a prolonged stay at the police statio or in detention.

presumptive detention Because of the severity of the offense, detaining youths unless they ca demonstrate they can be released without a problem.

presumptive judicial transfer Version of judicial transfer in which the amenability burden i placed on the youth instead of the state. That is, transfer to adult court is presumed unless th youth can demonstrate that he or she is amenable to juvenile court treatment. It is usually limite to more serious, more chronic, or older offenders.

pretrial stage Important time period during which preliminary matters in the case (motions o pleadings) will be heard and possibly the charges can be resolved without proceeding to trial.

prevention programs Community-based interventions offered to delinquents and nondelin quents with the objective of encouraging youth to desist from committing offenses (or joinin gangs or using drugs).

preventive detention The pretrial secure custody of juveniles to prevent "another" offense. It i openly and permissibly practiced in all jurisdictions.

primary prevention An attempt to prevent delinquency from happening or to keep the youth nonoffender.

private facility A historically prevalent institution in the juvenile system run by a private grou (frequently religiously oriented) instead of by the state. Most can reject prospective inmates wh do not fit into the facility's treatment regimen.

privatization Movement to expand the extent of private entrepreneurial control in the juvenile fa cility network. Recent additions to the private groups in the juvenile system are for-profit agencie such as Wackenhut and Corrections Corporation of America as opposed to religious orders or phil anthropic organizations.

probable cause Standard of evidence required to arrest delinquents (and perhaps status offend ers in some states) and to sustain charges against them at a detention, preliminary, or transfe hearing.

probable cause hearing A hearing which can occur in a number of different ways, such as at detention or transfer hearing, but always involves forcing the state to demonstrate that there i probable cause to believe the youth committed the alleged offense.

probation Sentence of youth to a community-based sanction rather than to an institution.

probation officer (PO) Historically, the person who was probably the most powerful member o juvenile court and today is the individual responsible for many activities in juvenile court (an many more than in criminal court), including deciding whether and how a youth should be di verted, transferred, and sentenced.

prosecutor Individual responsible for determining what charges to file against a youth and, in many situations, in what court. The prosecutor is also expected to either negotiate an outcome with the defense or try the case.

prosecutorial transfer The prosecutor's authority to decide to bring charges against a youth in adult court. Transfer is usually limited to older offenders or to those with serious charges or chronic offending histories.

public defender A defense attorney who usually works on a full-time basis representing poor or indigent defendants.

punishment gap The idea that a youth with a record of chronic offending in juvenile court would still be regarded as a first offender his or her first time in criminal court. The term might also be used to refer to the fact that some youths can receive a harsher sentence in juvenile court than they would in adult court.

purely discretionary minimum sentence Situation in which the juvenile judge is authorized but not compelled to set a minimum sentence as a disposition.

purpose clauses Philosophical messages located in the statutes of nearly every jurisdiction that identify the purposes the legislature has in mind for juvenile court.

Q

Quakers Socially prominent and influential group responsible for introducing the prison and the House of Refuge for juveniles.

quid pro quo exchange The notion that juveniles must surrender or trade their rights (such as counsel and jury trial) in order to receive the state's rehabilitation.

R

radical nonintervention Philosophy that embraced labeling theory in the extreme and advocated the diversion of nearly all juvenile offenders in order to avoid branding them delinquent.

reasonable suspicion Level of evidence less demanding than probable cause that is associated with police activities such as stop and frisk.

reception center Facility to which youths are temporarily committed in order to diagnose their problems and to determine which, if any, institution is the proper location for rehabilitation.

recidivism Term that applies to youths committing second or subsequent offenses.

recidivist impact Allowing the criminal court to use the juvenile court record against a defendant such that the offender would be considered a repeat offender even though this is his or her first time in criminal court.

referee Another term for master or lower judicial figure in juvenile court.

reformatory Facility that first housed juvenile criminals apart from the rank-and-file adult prison population. It emerged after Houses of Refuge and added to the movement to separate juveniles from adults. Some reformatories were former Houses of Refuge. They could include some juvenile criminals and less serious adult offenders. There are few remaining today.

reform school Long-term facility in which juveniles are institutionalized. It is typically associated with more serious offenders who are relatively high up the disposition ladder or at the juvenile prison level, but the name can be applied to a lower, midlevel facility as well. Some reform schools were previously Houses of Refuge. They may or may not have serious educational and rehabilitation programs.

regular judicial transfer A form of juridical transfer to adult court in which the amenability burden is on the state to prove that the youth cannot be rehabilitated by the juvenile system.

rehabilitation The reason for the initiation of the juvenile system, dealing with offering young offenders therapeutic interventions in the hope of stopping their offense behavior.

rehabilitation model Philosophy suggesting that money and resources are better spent on rehabilitation programs than on lawyers and court processes.

reintegration model An approach in which the PO becomes a broker and links the youth with agencies and programs in the community to reinforce law-abiding behavior.

released on own recognizance (ROR) Method by which the court releases the accused pending trial without having to post any money or bond.

residential placement Technically means any commitment that involves a change in the youth's residence and thus can range from a foster home to a juvenile prison.

restitution Offenders' paying part or all of the damages and losses incurred by the victim.

restorative conferencing models Ways in which the offender, the victim, and the community are brought together in order to operationalize the restorative justice philosophy.

restorative justice Modern-day version of victim-offender mediation that seeks to repair the harm done to the victim. It entails a voluntary confrontation between the offender and the victim and perhaps others, in an attempt to educate the offender about the harm created by the offense and to encourage acceptance of responsibility by and a showing of remorse from the offender.

retained counsel Defense attorney hired personally by the defendant (or by the parents).

retention age The age to which the juvenile system can maintain control over the offender, or how long one can remain on juvenile probation or in an institution.

reverse transfer An adult court judge's authority to send a case placed in adult court (usually by prosecutor) back in juvenile court for trial.

review hearing Proceeding held periodically that addresses the youth's progress (or lack thereof) with the disposition. It can result in modifying (or even terminating) the sentence and implementing new strategies to help the youth and/or the parents.

revocation A court's or institution's decision to revoke or cancel the youth's probation or parole status because of a violation of the terms of the conditional freedom or a new arrest.

right to treatment The idea that because juveniles surrender so many of their rights in the juvenile system it is incumbent upon the system to offer real rehabilitation programs and not engage simply in incapacitating or warehousing youths.

risk (or needs) assessment Criteria used in analyzing the risk presented by a youth and the intervention required to address that risk.

S

school rule violation Student violation of rules that apply only to the school setting (and do not include crimes), for which the student is liable to be searched by school personnel.

school searches Searches for rule violations or crimes (such as drugs and weapons) conducted in the school setting, ranging from locker searches (for which there are no constitutional controls) to searches of students' private property (such as school bags), for which there are only minimal constitutional controls over school personnel.

sealing records Process whereby the youth's juvenile court record is sealed. It is supposed to prevent any outsider from finding out about the youth's offense history, but it has not always worked.

at way. Today it is harder to seal records in cases of serious offenses, and it is more likely that re-
ords will be referred to state agencies for permanent storing.

arch and seizure Activity in which authorities look for evidence of crime but also perhaps evi-
ence involving status offenses and school rule violations.

condary prevention Treatment program aimed to convince delinquents not to reoffend.

cond tier of juvenile court Special adoption in several states of a more serious level of juvenile
urt intervention to which the youth usually must be transferred. On this level, youths tend to be
titled to jury trial and to a combined juvenile court–adult court sentence.

cure facility Any facility from which youth can not simply walk out, including detention cen-
rs and long-term institutions. It can range from minimum locked doors security to maximum
med guards security.

lf-report surveys Questionnaires that ask youths to report on themselves as to their recent de-
nquent and status offending history.

lf-representation Defendants' choice to represent themselves rather than to rely on a defense
torney. It is permitted in only a few states for juveniles.

lf-transfer Youths' decision to send their own cases to adult court. It tends to be limited to youth
ove a certain age.

ntence bargain A guilty plea offered in the hope of reducing or influencing the sentence se-
cted by the judge.

ntencing guidelines Standardization adopted in only a few states for juveniles. The disposition
sentence is based on a matrix that factors in the current offense and the delinquent record.

rious Violent Juveniles (SVJ) The research project sponsored by OJJDP to study factors asso-
ated with the development of violent juvenile offenders.

rvice A police role that probably dominates the officer's typical workday. It involves taking care
people and crises rather than looking for offenders or keeping the peace.

elter care The status offender's version of detention, involving nonsecure custody pending trial.

ock probation A probationary sentence that includes at least some time in confinement, typi-
lly to be served in a detention center.

cial factors The variables that influence outcomes in juvenile court that are not linked with the
fense and prior record, they include such items as the school record, the nature of the family
nit, the neighborhood, the youth's amenability to treatment, and his or her treatment history. The
ctors tend to be portrayed in the literature as illegitimate influences because of their ability to be
anipulated to discriminate against certain populations, but they have been critical in the sys-
m's approach to youth.

cioeconomic status (SES) The economic condition of the family that is related to income,
roperty value, and other indicators of wealth, which is reported as lower, middle, and upper
asses.

ecial conditions Conditions of probation that are imposed on a particular offender (e.g., sub-
ance abuse counseling) and not to the general probation population (e.g., reporting to one's PO).

eedy trial A right guaranteed to juveniles in only a minority of jurisdictions that involves initi-
ing a prosecution against a juvenile within a limited amount of time.

andard conditions Conditions that apply to all probationers alike, such as reporting to the PO
not leaving the jurisdiction without authorization.

ation adjustment Police discretion to divert the case at the police station and not refer the mat-
r to juvenile court. It could involve personal monitoring of the youth by the officer.

status offense Behavior that is illegal for juveniles only, including truancy, tobacco use, and cu few violations.

stop and frisk Police authority, on reasonable suspicion, to temporarily detain youth, questic them, and, if there is a reason to fear they are armed, conduct a pat down or frisk for weapons.

superpredators The identity given to the "next generation" of especially violent juveniles th have been predicted to emerge by the end of the early twenty-first century.

supervision role The probation officer's job to provide youth both assistance and supervision monitoring.

T

taking into custody Juvenile system term for arrest. It is not just a matter of semantics, sin youths who have been taken into custody can report they have never been arrested.

teen court Diversionary effort through which minor offenses committed by youths without a d linquent record can be brought before a panel of juveniles who will litigate the matter and har down a disposition (of very limited import).

therapeutic community The idea that all staff of a facility (and not just treatment personnel) a responsible for the rehabilitation of the youth as a collective effort.

three strikes law Criminal court provision that offenders convicted a third time for certain c fenses "strike out" and receive a life sentence in prison.

token economy Behavior modification tactic in which participants are given points for appropi ate behavior and surrender points for inappropriate behavior. It can also involve dollars instead points, and, although it is used most effectively in an institutional setting, it can also be used in community program.

totality of circumstances Test that usually applies to examining the voluntariness of a juvenile waiver of a right (such as silence or counsel) and includes all the circumstances surrounding th waiver (such as being warned of rights).

training school Juvenile system term for what is usually a prisonlike facility for delinquents. A though the facility can range from a group of cottages with minimal security to adult prisonli buildings and fences, this institution is always near the top of the dispositional ladder.

transfer to adult court An always discretionary decision made by a judge or a prosecutor to sen the youth's case to criminal court for trial rather than to prosecute the case in juvenile court would be allowed by law.

treatment history A record of how the youth has fared with previous efforts at rehabilitation. also includes a listing of the previous dispositions. The treatment history is instrumental in dete mining sentence on subsequent adjudications in juvenile court and in gauging the desirability transfer to criminal court.

treatment interests A youth's interests in receiving the rehabilitative services of the juvenile sy tem. These interests often conflict with the youth's legal interests (not to be adjudicated) becau the only way to receive rehabilitation in many situations is for the court to adjudicate the offende

treatment programs Myriad interventions offered by the juvenile system and its satellites in tl community, ranging from diversion efforts to probation conditions to institutional regimens.

trial dockets Times allotted for the prosecution of offenders. Juveniles were given separate tri dockets or times for their trials before they received a separate court system.

trial penalty The idea that youths who choose to exercise their right to trial (in lieu of pleadir guilty) will be punished for doing so. It is much more likely to prevail in criminal court than in j venile court, which should be much less inconvenienced by defendants' exercising their right to trial.

truancy Youth's violation of compulsory education laws by skipping school.

U

unequal processing The idea that the juvenile justice system does not respond equally to offenders in terms of their behavior. Thus, two youths with identical records could be processed differently, especially if their problems are not the same or if the families' abilities to resolve the problems are not equal.

Uniform Crime Reports (UCR) Official source of crime data kept by the FBI that classifies crimes according to index criteria and characteristics of the offender, such as age, race, and gender.

unique processing The idea that the juvenile justice system processes youthful offenders differently than the criminal justice system processes adult criminals. Much of this uniqueness involves juvenile defendants not having the same rights as adults accused of crime.

use of force The amount of force police use in effecting an arrest. Police may use reasonable force that does not exceed what is necessary to bring about the arrest. Deadly force or the use of lethal means by the police is permissible only when the police or the community encounter a deadly threat from the offender.

V

venue The location in which a case may be prosecuted. While for adults it is limited to the area in which the incident occurred, for youth it includes where they live.

vertical prosecution Situation in which one prosecutor is responsible for handling the case from beginning to end, possibly including transfer to adult court and conducting the prosecution in that forum.

victim impact statement Controversial announcement, either verbal or written, that identifies, often in serious detail, the extent of the victim's loss and suffering brought about by the offender's acts.

victimization survey Data collection method that attempts to discover the "dark figure" of crime, which is crime that is not reported to the police. These surveys are valuable in demonstrating that the UCR covers only the tip of the iceberg in terms of the extent of crime.

victim-offender mediation (VOM) Strategy that places (an agreeable) victim in direct contact with the offender to benefit both parties. While the victim can receive satisfaction at letting the offender know the impact of the crime, the offender can realize that impact and show remorse. It is called restorative justice in many places today.

victims' rights Notion that victims should be allocated rights in court. Although the movement started only recently in juvenile court, victims' rights in that forum exceed what has been granted in criminal court. They can include granting the victim a right to a speedy trial or to insist on prosecuting a case and even to negating a plea bargain reached with the defendant.

violation of probation/parole (VOP) hearing Proceeding that examines whether the probationer or parolee has violated a condition of his or her conditional freedom or has committed a new offense (also a violation). It tends to afford the accused fewer rights than granted the defendant at trial.

W

waiver Another term used by many locations to refer to transferring a youth to criminal court.

waiver of counsel A youth's right to dispense with the services of a lawyer. Waiver here means surrender and can apply to a variety of rights (such as to silence).

Warren Court The title given to the Supreme Court during the time in which Earl Warren served as chief justice. This court was known for its liberal, prodefendant rulings.

wilderness programs Challenge programs that place youth in outdoor settings to help them develop survival skills, as well as receive vocational education.

working style Categorization of the variety of ways in which POs (and police or other personnel) conduct their business.

writ of habeas corpus The right to petition the court that requires the state to justify its holding someone in custody.

Y

youthful offender (YO) Term given by many states to a young offender being processed typically for the first time in adult court. The youthful offender is often given a lenient sentence and the opportunity to have the adult conviction erased upon the successful completion of that sentence.

Z

zero-tolerance laws Measures adopted by schools that prohibit *all* forms of drugs and weapons (including, perhaps, aspirin and hatpins) and demand harsh reactions from the school administration, including possibly expulsion.

Informative Websites

American Bar Association Juvenile Justice Center
  www.abanet.org/crimjust/juvjus/
American Correctional Association
  www.aca.org
Annie E. Casey Foundation's Juvenile Detention
  Alternatives Imitative
  www.aecf.org/initiatives/juvenile/foreward.htm
ATF School Safety Resources
  www.aft.treas.gov/schoolsafety.htm
Be a Mentor
  www.beamentor.org
Big Brothers Big Sisters of America
  www.bbbsa.org
Boot Camps
  www.boot-camps-info.com
Building Blocks for Youth
  www.buildingblocksforyouth.org
Bullying.com
  www.bullying.org/public/frameset.cfm?w=s
Center for Safe Schools and Communities
  www.center-school.org/
Center for the Prevention of School Violence
  www.juvjus.state.nc.us/cpsv
Center on Children and the Law
  www.abanet.org/child/
Center on Juvenile and Criminal Justice
  www.cjcj.org/
Children's Defense Fund
  www.childrensdefense.org
Coalition for Juvenile Justice
  www.juvjustice.org/
Common Sense About Kids and Guns
  www.kidsandguns.org/
Community Oriented Policing Services
  www.usdoj.gov/cops/
Council of Juvenile Correctional Administrators
  www.cjca.net
Criminal Justice Policy Foundation
  www.cjpf.org
Department of Health and Human Services
  www.hhs.gov
Department of Homeland Security
  www.dhs.gov
Department of Justice
  www.usdoj.gov/
Department of Treasury
  www.ustreas.gov
Disproportionate Minority Confinement
  www.ojjdp.ncjrs.org/dmc/index.html
Drug Abuse Resistance Education (D.A.R.E.)
  www.dare-america.com/
Federal Job Listings
  www.fedwork.gov

  www.usajobs.com
  www.jobs4police.com
Fight Crime: Invest in Kids
  www.fightcrime.org/
International Association of Chiefs of Police
  www.theiacp.org/
Justice for Kids and Youth
  www.usdoj.gov/kidspage/
Juvenile Boot Camps
  www.juvenile-boot-camps.com
Juvenile Info Network
  www.juvenilenet.org/
Juvenile Justice Evaluation Center
  www.jrsa.org/jjec/
Juvenile Justice FYI
  www.juvenilejusticefyi.com/index.html
Juvenile Justice—World Wide Web Sites
  www.ncjrs.org/jjwww.html
Juvenile Law Center
  www.jlc.org/
Juvenile Sex Offender Research Bibliography
  www.ojjdp.ncjrs.org/juvsexoff/sexbibtopic.html
Lawyers for Children
  www.lawyersforchildren.com/
Mentor Girls
  www.mentorgirls.org
Mothers Against Drunk Driving
  www.madd.org/home
National Alliance for Safe Schools
  www.safeschools.org/
National Center for Institutional Alternatives
  www.ncia.net/ncia
National Center for Juvenile Justice
  www.ncjj.org/
National Center for Juvenile Justice State Profiles
  Database
  www.ncjj.org/stateprofiles
National Center for Mental Health and Juvenile
  Justice
  www.ncmhjj.com
National Center for Missing and Exploited
  Children
  www.missingkids.com/
National Center for Sex Offender Management
  www.csom.org
National Center for Youth Law
  www.youthlaw.org
National Center on Education, Disability, and
  Juvenile Justice
  www.edjj.org/
National Council of Juvenile and Family Court
  Judges
  www.ncjfcj.org/

National Council on Crime and Delinquency
www.nccd-crc.org/
National Crime Prevention Council
www.weprevent.org/
National Criminal Justice Reference Service
www.ncjrs.org/
National Gang Crime Research Center
www.ngcrc.com/
National Institute of Corrections
www.bop/nicpg/nicmain
National Institute of Justice
www.ojp.usdoj.gov/nij/
National Juvenile Detention Association
www.njda.com
National Mentoring Center
www.nwrel.org/mentoring
National Mentoring Partnership
www.mentoring.org
National Organization for Youth Safety
www.noys.com/
National Police Athletic League
www.nationalpal.org/
National School Safety Center
www.nssc1.org/
National Youth Court Center
www.youthcourt.net/
National Youth Development Information Center
www.nydic.org/
National Youth Gang Center
www.iir.com/nygc
National Youth Violence Prevention Resource
Center
www.safeyouth.org/
Office of Community Oriented Policing Services
www.cops.usdoj.gov/

Office of Justice Programs
www.ojp.usdoj.gov/
Office of Juvenile Justice and Delinquency
Prevention
www.ojjdp.ncjrs.org/
Police Foundation
www.policefoundation.org/
Resources for Youth
www.preventviolence.org
Résumé Development Sites
www.myfuture.com
www.resume-place.com
www.monster.com
Safe Schools Coalition
www.safeschools-wa.org/
School Violence Resource Center
www.svrc.net/
The School Zone
*www.whitehousedrugpolicy.gov/schoolzone/
index. html*
Take a Bite Out of Crime
www.mcgruff-safe-kids.com/
Teen Boot Camp
www.teen-bootcamp.com/index.html
Teens, Crime, and the Community
www.nationaltcc.org
Urban Institute—Publications on Corrections and
Offenders
*www.urban.org/content/PolicyCenters/Justice/
Publications/Publications.html*
Youth Crime Watch of America
www.ycwa.org/
Youth Link
www.youthlink.org/

References

Ainsworth, J. 1991. Re-imaging childhood and reconstructing the legal order: The case for abolishing the juvenile court. *North Carolina Law Review,* 69:1083–1133.

Albin, B., Albin, M., Gladden, E., Ropelato, S., and Stoll, G. 2003. *Montana: An assessment of access to counsel and quality of representation in delinquency proceedings.* Washington, DC: American Bar Association, Criminal Justice Section, Juvenile Justice Center.

Allen, F. A. 1964. *The borderland of criminal justice: Essays in law and criminology.* Chicago: University of Chicago Press.

Allen, F. A. 2000. Forward. In J. Fagan and F. E. Zimring's (Eds.), *The changing borders of juvenile justice: Transfer of adolescents to the criminal court.* (pp. ix–xvi). Chicago: University of Chicago Press.

Allen, P. 1994. *OJJPD model programs 1993.* Washington, DC: U.S. Department of Justice.

Allen-Hagen, B. 1975. *Youth crime control project: A final report on an experimental alternative to incarceration of young adult offenders.* Washington, DC: U.S. Department of Justice.

———. 1993. *Conditions of confinement in juvenile detention and correctional facilities.* Washington, DC: U.S. Department of Justice.

Altschuler, D. M., and Armstrong, T. L. 1984. Intervening with serious juvenile offenders: A summary of a study on community based programs. In R. Mathias, P. DeMuro, and R. J. Allison's (Eds.), *Violent juvenile offenders: An anthology.* San Francisco, CA: National Council on Crime and Delinquency.

———. 1994. *Intensive aftercare for high-risk juveniles: Policies and procedures.* Washington, DC: U.S. Department of Justice.

Altschuler, D. M., Armstrong, T. L., and MacKenzie, D. L. 1999. *Reintegration, supervised release, and intensive aftercare.* Washington, DC: OJJDP.

Altschuler, D. M., and Brounstein, P. J. 1991. Patterns of drug use, drug trafficking, and other delinquency among inner-city adolescent males in Washington, DC. *Criminology,* 29:589–622.

American Bar Association and the National Bar Association (ABA/NBA). 2001. *Justice by gender: The lack of appropriate prevention, diversion, and treatment alternatives for girls in the justice system.* Washington, DC: ABA/NBA.

American Bar Association, Juvenile Justice Center and New England Juvenile Defender Center (ABA). 2003. *Maine: An assessment of access to counsel and quality of representation in delinquency proceedings.* Washington, DC: American Bar Association, Criminal Justice Section, Juvenile Justice Center.

American Correctional Association (ACA). 1997. *National juvenile detention directory.* Lanham, MD: ACA.

———. 1998. *Juvenile and adult correctional departments, institutions, agencies, and paroling authorities.* Lanham, MD: ACA.

———. 2003. *2003 directory: Adult and juvenile correctional departments, institutions, agencies, and probation and parole authorities.* (64th ed.). Lanham, MD: ACA.

American Probation and Parole Association (APPA). 1984. *A report on the labors of John Augustus.* Lexington, KY: APPA.

Anderson, E. 1994. The code of the streets. *Atlantic Monthly,* 273(5):81–94.

Andrews, D. A., Zinger, I., Hoge, R. D., Bonta, J., Gendreau, P., and Cullen, F. T. 1990. Does correctional treatment work? A clinically-relevant and psychologically-informed meta-analysis. *Criminology,* 28(3):369–404.

Arnette, J. L., and M. C. Walsleben. 1998. *Combating fear and restoring safety in schools.* Washington, DC: U.S. Department of Justice.

Arrestee Drug Abuse Monitoring (ADAM) Program. 2000. *1999 annual report on drug use among adult and juvenile arrestees.* Washington, DC: National Institute of Justice.

———. 2001. *2000 annual report on drug use among adult and juvenile arrestees.* Washington, DC: National Institute of Justice.

———. 2003a. *2001 annual report on drug use among adult and juvenile arrestees.* Washington, DC: National Institute of Justice.

———. 2003b. *2002 annual report on drug use among adult and juvenile arrestees.* Washington, DC: National Institute of Justice.

Asbury, H. 1928. *The gangs of New York.* New York: Alfred A. Knopf.

Associated Press. "Guns are no. 2 cause of death among the young, data show." *New York Times,* April 9, 1996, A16.

Auerbach, A. W. 1978. The role of the therapeutic community 'street prison' in the rehabilitation of youthful offenders. *Dissertation Abstracts International,* 38(09):4532B. University Microfilms No. 78–01086. Ann Arbor: University of Michigan.

Austin, J., Johnson, K. D., and Gregoriou, M. 2000. *Juveniles in adult prisons and jails: A national assessment.* Washington, DC: U.S. Department of Justice.

Ayers, E. L. 1984. *Vengeance and justice: Crime and punishment in the 19th century American South.* New York: Oxford University Press.

Bagdikian, B. H., and Dash, L. 1972. *The shame of prisons.* New York: Pocket Books.

Bahlmann, D. W., and Johnson, S. J. 1978. At long last credibility: The role of the attorney for the state under Indiana's new juvenile code. *Indiana Law Journal,* 51:593–619.

Bailey, W. C. 1966. Correctional outcome: An evaluation of 100 reports. *Journal of Criminal Law, Criminology, and Police Science,* 57:153–160.

———. 1981. Preadjudicatory detention in a large metropolitan juvenile court. *Law and Human Behavior,* 5:19–43.

Bailey, W. C., and Peterson, R. D. 1981. Legal vs. extra-legal determinants of juvenile court dispositions. *Juvenile and Family Court Journal,* 32:41–59.

Baker, M. L., Sigmon, J. N., Nugent, M. E. 2001. *Truancy reduction: Keeping students in school.* Washington, DC: U.S. Department of Justice.

Bannister, A. J., Carter, D. L., and Schafer, J. 2001. A national police survey on juvenile curfews. *Journal of Criminal Justice,* 29:233–240.

Barnes, C. W., and Franz, R. 1989. Questionably adult: Determinants and effects of the juvenile waiver decision. *Justice Quarterly,* 6:117–135.

Barnes, H. E., and Teeters, N. K. 1951. *New horizons in criminology,* 2nd ed. New York: Prentice-Hall.

———. 1959. *New horizons in criminology,* 3rd ed. New York: Prentice-Hall.

Bartol, C. R., and Bartol, A. M. 1998. *Delinquency and justice: A psychosocial approach,* 2nd ed. Upper Saddle River, NJ: Prentice Hall.

Bartollas, C. 1985. *Correctional treatment: Theory and practice.* Englewood Cliffs, NJ: Prentice Hall.

Bartollas, C., and Conrad, J. P. 1992. *Introduction to corrections,* 2nd ed. New York: Harper Collins Publishers.

Bartollas, C., Miller, S. J., and Dinitz, S. 1976. The exploitation matrix in a juvenile institution. *International Journal of the Sociology of Law,* 4:257–270.

Barton, W. H., and Butts, J. A. 1990. Viable options: Intensive supervision programs for juvenile delinquents *Crime and Delinquency,* 36(2):238–256.

Bastion, L. D. 1993. *Criminal victimization.* Washington, DC: U.S. Department of Justice.

Bazemore, G., and Umbreit, M. 2001. *A comparison of four restorative conferencing models.* Washington, DC U.S. Department of Justice.

Beck, A. J. 2000. *Prison and jail inmates at midyear 1999.* Washington, DC: U.S. Department of Justice.

Beck, A. J., and Karberg, J. C. 2001. *Prison and jail inmates at midyear 2000.* Washington, DC: U.S. Department of Justice.

Beck, A. J., Karberg, J. C., and Harrison, P. M. 2002. *Prison and jail inmates at midyear 2001.* Washington, DC U.S. Department of Justice.

Becker, H. S. 1964. *The other side: Perspectives on deviance.* New York: Free Press of Glencoe.

Beha, J., Carlson, K., and Rosenblum, R. H. 1977. *Sentencing to community service.* Washington, DC: Department of Justice.

Bell, D., and Lang, K. 1985. The intake dispositions of juvenile offenders. *Journal of Research in Crime and Delinquency,* 22:309–328.

Bernard, T. J. 1992. *The cycle of juvenile justice.* New York: Oxford University Press.

Beyer, M. 2003. *Best practices in juvenile accountability: Overview.* Washington, DC: U.S. Department of Justice.

Bishop, D. M., and Frazier, C. E. 1991. Transfer of juveniles to criminal court: A case study and analysis of prosecutorial waiver. *Notre Dame Journal of Law, Ethics and Public Policy,* 5:281–302.

———. 1992. Gender bias in juvenile justice processing: Implications of the JJDP Act. *Journal of Criminal Law and Criminology,* 82:1162–1186.

———. 1996. Race effects in juvenile justice decision-making: Findings of a statewide analysis. *The Journal of Criminal Law and Criminology,* 86:392–414.

———. 2000. Consequences of transfer. In J. Fagan and F. E. Zimring (Eds.), *The changing borders of juvenile justice: Transfer of adolescents to criminal court.* (pp. 227–276). Chicago: University of Chicago Press.

Bishop, D. M., Frazier, C. E., Lanza-Kaduce, L., and Winner, L. 1996. The transfer of juveniles to criminal court: Does it make a difference? *Crime and Delinquency,* 42:171–191.

Bjerregaard, B., and Lizotte, A. J. 1995. Gun ownership and gang membership. *Journal of Criminal Law and Criminology,* 86:37–58.

Bjerregaard, B., and Smith, C. 1993. Gender differences in gang participation, delinquency, and substance use. *Journal of Quantitative Criminology,* 4:329–355.

Black, D., and Reiss Jr., A. 1970. Police control of juveniles. *American Sociological Review,* 35:63–77.

Black, M. C. 2001. *Juvenile delinquency probation caseload, 1989–1998.* OJJPD Fact Sheet #34. Washington, DC: U.S. Department of Justice.

Block, C. R., and Block, R. 1993. *Street gang crime in Chicago.* Washington, DC: U.S. Department of Justice.

Block, C. R., Christakos, A., Jacob, A., and Przyblyski, R. 1996. *Street gangs and crime: Patterns and trends in Chicago.* Chicago: Illinois Criminal Justice Information Authority.

Blomberg, T. G. 1983. Diversion's disparate results and unresolved questions: An integrated evaluation perspective. *Journal of Research in Crime and Delinquency,* 20:24–38.

Blumstein, A. 1995. Violence by young people: Why the deadly nexus? *National Institute of Justice Journal.* No. 229:2–9. Washington, DC: U.S. Department of Justice.

Bogen, D. 1980. Beating the rap in juvenile court. *Juvenile and Family Court Journal,* 31(3):19–22.

Bonnie, R. J., and Grisso, T. 2000. Adjudicative competence and youthful offenders. In T. Grisso and R. G. Schwartz (Eds.), *Youth on trial: A developmental perspective on juvenile justice.* (pp. 73–103). Chicago: University of Chicago Press.

Bookin-Weiner, H. 1984. Assuming responsibility: Legalizing preadjudicatory juvenile detention. *Crime and Delinquency,* 30:39–67.

Bortner, M. A. 1982. *Inside a juvenile court: The tarnished ideal of individualized justice.* New York: New York University Press.

———. 1986. Traditional rhetoric, organizational realities: Remand of juveniles to adult court. *Crime and Delinquency,* 32:53–73.

Bortner, M. A., and Reed, W. L. 1985. The preeminence of process: An example of refocused justice research. *Social Science Quarterly,* 66:413–425.

Bourque, B. B., Cronin, R. C., and Pearson, F. R. 1996. Boot camps for juvenile offenders: An implementation evaluation of three demonstration programs. Washington, DC: NIJ.

Braga, A. A., Kennedy, D. M., Piehl, A. M., and Waring, E. J. 2001. *The Boston gun project: Impact evaluation findings.* Washington, DC: National Institute of Justice.

Braukman, C. J., Fixsen, D. L., Phillips, E. L., and Wolf, M. M. 1975. Behavioral approaches to treatment in the crime and delinquency field. *Criminology,* 13:299–331.

Bridges, B. S., and Steen, S. 1998. Racial disparities in official assessments of juvenile offenders: Attributional stereotypes as mediating mechanisms. *American Sociological Review,* 63:554–570.

Brooks, C. C., and White, C. 2000. *Curriculum for training educators of youth in confinement.* Washington, DC: U.S. Department of Justice.

Brooks, K., and Kamine, D. 2003. *Justice cut short: An assessment of access to counsel and quality of representation in delinquency proceedings in Ohio.* Washington, DC: American Bar Association, Criminal Justice Section, Juvenile Justice Center.

Brown, B. S., Wienckowski, L. A., and Stolz, S. B. 1989. Behavior modification: Perspective on a current issue. In Kratcoski, P. C., (Ed.), *Correctional counseling and treatment.* 2nd ed. Prospect Heights, IL: Waveland Press.

Browning, S. L., Cullen, F. T., Cao, L., Kopache, R., and Stevenson, T. J. 1994. Race and getting hassled by the police: A research note. *Police Studies,* 17(1):1–11.

Bureau of Alcohol, Tobacco, and Firearms. 1999. *Youth crime gun interdiction initiative for 27 communities 1998.* Washington, DC: Bureau of Alcohol, Tobacco, and Firearms.

———. 2000. *Youth crime gun interdiction-crime gun trace reports 1999.* Washington, DC: Bureau of Alcohol, Tobacco, and Firearms.

———. 2002. *Youth crime gun interdiction-crime gun trace reports 2000.* Washington, DC: Bureau of Alcohol, Tobacco, and Firearms.

———. n.d. *Gang resistance education and training. www.atf.gov/great/atf.htm.*

Bureau of Justice Assistance (BJA). 2003. *Juvenile drug courts: Strategies in practice.* Washington, DC: U.S. Department of Justice.

Bureau of Justice Statistics (BJS) 1999. *Criminal victimization in the United States, 1996.* Washington, DC: U.S. Department of Justice.

———. 2000a. *Homicide trends in the United States.* Washington, DC: U.S. Department of Justice.

———. 2000b. *Criminal victimization in the United States, 1997.* Washington, DC: U.S. Department of Justice.

———. 2000c. *Criminal victimization in the United States, 1998.* Washington, DC: U.S. Department of Justice.

———. 2001. *Criminal victimization in the United States, 1999.* Washington, DC: U.S. Department of Justice.

———. 2002. *Criminal victimization in the United States, 2000.* Washington, DC: U.S. Department of Justice.

———. 2003a. *Criminal victimization in the United States, 2001.* Washington, DC: U.S. Department of Justice.

———. 2003b. *Criminal victimization in the United States, 2002.* Washington, DC: U.S. Department of Justice.

———. 2004. *Sourcebook of criminal justice statistics 2002.* Washington, DC: U.S. Department of Justice. *www.albany.edu/sourcebook.*

Burrell, S. 1999. *Improving conditions of confinement in secure juvenile detention centers.* Baltimore, MD: Annie E. Casey Foundation. *www.aecf.org.*

Butts, J. A. 1994. *Delinquency cases in juvenile courts, 1992.* Washington, DC: OJJDP.

———. 1996. *Delinquency cases in juvenile courts, 1994.* Washington, DC: OJJDP.

Butts, J. A., and Adams, W. 2001. *Anticipating space needs in juvenile detention and correctional facilities.* Washington, DC: OJJDP.

Butts, J. A., and Buck, J. 2000. *Teen courts: A focus on research.* Washington, DC: U.S. Department of Justice.

Butts, J., Hoffman, D., and Buck, J. 1999. *Teen courts in the United States: A profile of current programs.* OJJPD Fact Sheet #118. Washington, DC: U.S. Department of Justice.

Butts, J. A., and Sanborn Jr., J. B. 1999. Is juvenile justice just too slow? *Judicature,* 83:16–24.

Butts, J. A., and Snyder, H. N. 1992. *Restitution and juvenile recidivism.* Washington, DC: U.S. Department of Justice.

Butts, J. A., Snyder, H. N., Finnegan, T. A., Aughenbaugh, A. L., and Poole, R. S. 1996a. *Juvenile court statistics 1993.* Washington, DC: OJJPD.

———. 1996b. *Juvenile court statistics 1994.* Washington, DC: OJJPD.

Calvin, E. M. 2003. *Washington: An assessment of access to counsel and quality of representation in delinquency proceedings.* Washington, DC: American Bar Association, Criminal Justice Section, Juvenile Justice Center.

Campbell, A. 1984. *The girls in the gang.* New York: Basil Blackwell.

———. 1990. Female participation in gangs. In C. R. Huff (Ed.), *Gangs in America.* (pp. 163–182). Newbury Park, CA: Sage Publications.

Campbell, J. S., and Retzlaff, P. D. 2000. Juvenile diversion interventions: Participant description and outcomes. *Journal of Offender Rehabilitation,* 32:57–74.

Cass, E. S., and Kaltenecker, N. 1996. The development and operation of juvenile boot camps in Florida. In D. L. MacKenzie and E. E. Hebert (Eds.), *Correctional boot camps: A tough intermediate sanction.* (pp. 179–190). Washington, DC: National Institute of Justice.

Celeste, G., and Puritz, P. 2001. *The children left behind: An assessment of access to counsel and quality of representation in delinquency proceedings in Louisiana.* Washington, DC: American Bar Association, Criminal Justice Section, Juvenile Justice Center.

Cemkovich, S., Giordano, P., and Pugh, M. 1985. The missing cases in self-report delinquency research. *Journal of Criminal Law and Criminology,* 76:705–732.

Chaiken, M. R. 1998. *Kids, cops, and communities.* Washington, DC: U.S. Department of Justice.

Chambliss, W. J., and Nagasawa, R. I. 1969. On the validity of official statistics. *Journal of Research on Crime and Delinquency* 6:71–77.

Champion, D. J. 1989. Teenage felons and waiver hearings: Some recent trends 1980–1988. *Crime and Delinquency,* 35:577–585.

Champion, D. J., and Mays, G. L. 1991. *Transferring juveniles to criminal courts: Trends and implications for criminal justice.* New York: Praeger.

Chandler, K. A., Chapman, C., Rand, M. R., and Taylor, B. M. 1998. *Students' reports of school crime: 1989 and 1995.* Washington, DC: Bureau of Justice Statistics.

Chein, D. B., and Hudson, J. 1981. Discretion in juvenile justice. In D. Fogel, J. Hudson (Eds.), *Justice as fairness: Perspectives on the justice model.* (pp. 160–192). Cincinnati: Anderson.

Chesney-Lind, M. 1973. Judicial enforcement of the female sex role: The family court and the female delinquent. *Issues in Criminology,* 8:51–59.

———. 1977. Judicial paternalism and the female status offender: Training women to know their place. *Crime and Delinquency,* 23:121–130.

———. 1988. Girls in jails. *Crime and Delinquency,* 34:150–168.

———. 1998. Women in prison: From partial justice to vengeful equity. *Corrections Today,* 60:66–73.

Chesney-Lind, M., and Shelden, R. G. 1992. *Girls, delinquency, and juvenile justice.* Pacific Grove, CA: Brooks/Cole Publishing Co.

———. 1998. *Girls, delinquency, and juvenile justice.* 2nd ed. Belmont, CA: West/Wadsworth.

Clarke, E. E. 1996. *A case for reinventing juvenile transfer: The record of transfer of juvenile offenders to criminal court in Cook County Illinois.* Chicago: Children and Family Justice Center, Northwestern University.

Clarke, S. H., and Koch, G. G. 1980. Juvenile court: Therapy or crime control, and do lawyers make a difference? *Law and Society Review,* 14:263–308.

Clayton, R. R., Cattarello, A., and Walden, K. P. 1991. Sensation seeking as a potential mediating variable for school-based prevention interventions: A two year follow-up of DARE. *Journal of Health Communications,* 3:229–239.

Clayton, S. L. 1996. Tennessee youth development center instills values. *Corrections Today*, 58:108–110, 154.

Clear, T. R., and Cole, G. F. 1997. *American corrections*. 4th ed. Belmont, CA: Wadsworth Publishing Co.

Clement, M. J. 1997. A five-year study of juvenile waiver and adult sentences: Implications for policy. *Criminal Justice Policy Review*, 8:201–219.

Clemmer, D. 1940. *The prison community*. Boston: The Christopher Publishing House.

Cloward. R. A., and Ohlin, L. E. 1960. *Delinquency and opportunity*. New York: Free Press.

Cogan, N. H. 1970. Juvenile law, before and after the entrance of *"Parens Patriae." South Carolina Law Review*, 22:147–163.

Cohen, A. K. 1955. *Delinquent boys: The culture of the gang*. Glencoe, IL: Free Press.

Cohen, B. 1981. Reporting crime: The limits of statistical and field data. In A. S. Blumberg (Ed.), *Current perspectives on criminal behavior*. 2nd ed. New York: Alfred A. Knopf.

Cohen, H. R., and Filipczak, J. 1989. *A new learning environment*. Boston: Authors Cooperative Inc.

Cohen, L. E. 1975a. *Delinquency dispositions: An empirical analysis of processing decisions in three juvenile courts*. Washington, DC: Law Enforcement Alliance of America.

———. 1975b. *Pre-adjudicatory detention in three juvenile courts: An empirical analysis of the factors related to detention decision outcomes*. Washington, DC: Law Enforcement Alliance of America.

———. 1975c. *Who gets detained? An empirical analysis of the pre-adjudicatory detention juveniles in Denver*. Washington, DC: Law Enforcement Alliance of America.

Cohen, L. E., and Kluegel, J. R. 1978. Determinants of juvenile court dispositions: Ascriptive and achieved factors in two metropolitan courts. *American Sociological Review*, 43:162–176.

———. 1979. The detention decision: A study of the impact of social characteristics and legal factors in two metropolitan juvenile courts. *Social Forces*, 58:146–161.

Cohen, R. "Poor youths swarming to Las Vegas are blamed for rise in gang violence." *New York Times*, October 15, 1991, A16.

Comment. 1966. Criminal offenders in the juvenile court: More brickbats and another proposal. *University of Pennsylvania Law Review*, 114:1171–1228.

Community Research Associates. 1987. *Assessment of model programs for chronic status offenders and their families*. Washington, DC: U.S. Department of Justice.

Conley, D. J. 1994. Adding color to a black and white picture: Using qualitative data to explain racial disproportionality in the juvenile justice system. *Journal of Research in Crime and Delinquency*, 31:135–148.

Cook, P. 1998. The epidemic of youth gun violence. In *Perspectives on Crime and Justice: 1997–1998 Lecture Series*. Washington, DC: U.S. Department of Justice.

Coolbaugh, K., and Hansel, C. J. 2000. *The comprehensive strategy: Lessons learned from the pilot sites*. Washington, DC: U.S. Department of Justice.

Cooper, C. S. 2001. *Juvenile drug court programs*. Washington, DC: U.S. Department of Justice.

Cooper, C. S., and Bartlett, S. R. 1996. *Juvenile drug courts: Operational characteristics and implementation issues*. Washington, DC: American University.

Costello, J. C. 1980. Ethical issues in representing juvenile clients: A review of the IJA-ABA standards in representing private parties. *New Mexico Law Review*, 10:255–278.

Cox, T. C., and Falkenberg, S. D. 1987. Adolescents attitudes toward police: An emphasis on interaction between the delinquency measures of alcohol and marijuana, police contacts and attitudes. *American Journal of Police*, 6:45–62.

Coxe, S. 1967. Lawyers in juvenile court. *Crime and Delinquency*, 13:488–493.

Crews, G. A., and Tipton, J. A. 2000. *A comparison of public school and prison security measures: Too much of a good thing?* Koch Crime Institute. *www.kci.org*.

Crompton, F. 1997. *Workhouse children*. Phoenix Mill, UK: Sutton Publishing Ltd.

Cronin, R. C. 1994. *Boot camps for adult and juvenile offenders: Overview and update*. Washington, DC: National Institute of Justice.

Crowe, A. H. 2000. *Jurisdictional technical assistance package for juvenile corrections*. Washington, DC: OJJDP.

Crowe, T. D. 1991. *Habitual juvenile offenders: Guidelines for citizen action and public responses*. Washington, DC: OJJPD.

Cumming, E., Finley, M., Hall, S., Humphrey, A., and Picou, I. P. 2003. *Maryland: An assessment of access to counsel and quality of representation in delinquency proceedings*. Washington, DC: American Bar Association, Criminal Justice Section, Juvenile Justice Center.

Curley, T. 1997. Easing teens into the driver's seat. *USA Today* (April 21, 1997):3A.

Curry, G. D., Ball, R. A., and Decker, S. H. 1996. Estimating the national scope of gang crimes from law enforcement data. *National Assessment of Law Enforcement Anti-Gang Information Resources*. Washington, DC: National Institute of Justice.

Curry, G. D., and Decker, S. H. 1998. *Confronting gangs: Crime and community*. Los Angeles: Roxbury Publishing.

———. 2002. *Confronting gangs: Crime and community.* 2nd ed. Los Angeles: Roxbury Publishing.

Curry, G. D., Fox, R. J., Ball, R. A., and Stone, D. 1993. *National assessment of law enforcement anti-gang information resources: Final report.* Washington, DC: National Institute of Justice.

Curry, G. D., Maxson, C. L., and Howell, J. C. 2001. *Youth gang homicides in the 1990s.* OJJPD Fact Sheet #03. Washington, DC: U.S. Department of Justice.

Davidson II, W. S., Redner, R., Admur, R., and Mitchell, C. 1990. *Alternative treatments for troubled youth: The case of diversion from the justice system.* New York: Plenum Press.

Dawson, R. O. 1992. An empirical study of kent style juvenile transfers to criminal court. *St. Mary's Law Journal,* 23:975–1054.

———. 2000. Judicial waiver in theory and practice. In J. Fagan and F. E. Zimring (Eds.), *The changing borders of juvenile justice: Transfer of adolescents to the criminal court.* (pp. 45–81). Chicago: University of Chicago Press.

Dean, C. W., Hirschel, J. D., and Brame, R. 1996. Minorities and juvenile case dispositions. *Justice System Journal,* 18:267–285.

Decker, S. and VanWinkle, B. 1996. *Life in the gang: Family, friends, and violence.* New York: Cambridge University Press.

Decker, S. H., Pennell, S., and Caldwell, A. 1997. *Illegal firearms: Access and use by arrestees.* Washington, DC: U.S. Department of Justice.

Dedel, K. 1998. National profile of the organization of state juvenile corrections systems. *Crime and Delinquency,* 44:507–525.

DeJong, C., and Jackson, K. C. 1998. Putting race into context: Race, juvenile justice processing, and urbanization. *Justice Quarterly,* 15:487–504.

Devine, P., Coolbaugh, K., and Jenkins, S. 1998. *Disproportionate minority confinement: Lessons learned from five states.* Washington, DC: U.S. Department of Justice.

DeVoe, J. F., Peter, K., Kaufman, P., Ruddy, S. A., Miller, A. K., Planty, M., Snyder, T. D., and Rand, M. R. 2003. *Indicators of school crime and safety: 2003.* Washington, DC: U.S. Department of Justice.

DiIulio, J. D. 1995. The coming of the super-predators. *The Weekly Standard,* November 23, 1995.

———. 1996. How to stop the coming crime wave. *Manhattan Institute Civil Bulletin,* 2:1–4.

Dorne, C., and Gewerth, K. 1995. *American juvenile justice: Cases, legislation, and comments.* San Francisco Austin and Winfield.

Dungworth, T. 1977. Discretion in the juvenile justice system: The impact of case characteristics on prehearing detention. In T. Ferdinard (Ed.), *Juvenile delinquency: Little brother grows up.* (pp. 19–44). Beverly Hills, CA: Sage Publications.

Dunham, H. W. 1958. The juvenile court: Contradictory orientations in processing offenders. *Law and Contemporary Problems,* 23:508–527.

Dunworth, T. 2000. *National evaluation of the youth firearms initiative.* Washington, DC: U.S. Department of Justice.

Egley Jr., A. 2000. *Highlights of the 1999 national youth gang survey.* Washington, DC: OJJPD.

Egley Jr., A., and Major, A. K. 2003. *Highlights of the 2001 national youth gang survey.* OJJPD Fact Sheet #01 Washington, DC: U.S. Department of Justice.

Elliott, D. S., and Ageton, S. S. 1980. Recognizing differences in self-reported and official estimates of delinquency. *American Sociological Review,* 45:95–110.

Elliott, D. S., Dunford, F. W., and Knowles, B. 1978. *Diversion: A study of alternative processing practices: An overview of initial study findings.* Boulder, CO: Behavioral Research Institute.

Elliott, D. S., and Voss, H. 1974. *Delinquency and dropout.* Lexington, MA: Lexington Books.

Erickson, M. L. 1971. The group context of delinquent behavior. *Social Problems,* 19:114–129.

———. 1973. Group violations and official delinquency: The group hazard hypothesis. *Criminology,* 11:127–160.

Erickson, M. L., and Jensen, G. 1977. Delinquency is still group behavior: Toward revitalizing the group premise in the sociology of deviance. *Journal of Criminal Law and Criminology,* 68:262–273.

Erwin, B. S. 1987. Evaluation of intensive probation in Georgia: Final report. Atlanta, GA: Department of Corrections.

Esbensen, F., and Huizinga, D. 1993. Gangs, drugs, and delinquency in a survey of urban youth. *Criminology,* 31:565–590.

Esbensen, F., and Osgood, D. W. 1997. National evaluation of G.R.E.A.T. *NIJ Research in Brief.* Washington DC: National Institute of Justice.

———. 1999. Gang resistance education and training (G.R.E.A.T.): Results from the national evaluation. *Journal of Research in Crime and Delinquency,* 36:194–225.

Esbensen, F., Osgood, D. W., Taylor, T. J., Peterson, D., and Freng, A. 2001. How great is G.R.E.A.T.? Results from a longitudinal quasi-experimental design. *Criminology and Public Policy,* 1:87–118.

Fader, J. J., Harris, P. W., Jones, P. R., and Poulin, M. E. 2001. Factors involved in decisions on commitment to delinquency programs for first-time juvenile offenders. *Justice Quarterly*, 18:323–341.

Fagan, J. 1991. *The comparative impacts of juvenile court and criminal court sanctions on adolescent felony offenders.* National Institute of Justice. Washington, DC: U.S. Department of Justice.

———. 1995. Separating the men from the boys: The comparative advantage of juvenile versus criminal court sanctions on recidivism among adolescent felony offenders. In J. C. Howell, B. Krisberg, J. D. Hawkins, and J. J. Wilson (Eds.), *Serious, violent, and chronic juvenile offenders: A sourcebook.* (pp. 238–260). Thousand Oaks, CA: Sage Publications.

Fagan, J., and Deschenes, E. P. 1990. Determinants of juvenile waiver decisions for violent juvenile offenders. *Journal of Criminal Law and Criminology*, 81:314–347.

Fagan, J., Deschenes, E., Piper, E., and Forst, E. 1986. *The juvenile court and violent youth: Determinates of the transfer decision.* San Francisco: Center for Law and Social Policy.

Fagan, J., Forst, M., and Vivona, T. S. 1987. Racial determinants of the judicial transfer decision: Prosecuting violent youth in criminal court. *Crime and Delinquency*, 33:259–286.

Fagan, J., and Pabon, E. 1990. Contributions of delinquency and substance use to school dropout among inner-city youths. *Youth and Society*, 21:306–354.

Fagan, J., Piper, E., and Forst, M. 1986. *The juvenile court and violent youth: Determinants of the transfer decision.* San Francisco: Center for Law and Social Policy.

Federle, K. H. 1990. The abolition of the juvenile court: A proposal for the preservation of children's legal rights. *Journal of Contemporary Law*, 16:23–51.

Feld, B. C. 1978. Reference of juvenile offenders for adult prosecution: The legislative alternative to asking unanswerable questions. *Minnesota Law Review*, 62:515–618.

———. 1981. Legislative policies toward the serious juvenile offender: On the virtues of automatic adulthood. *Crime and Delinquency*, 27:497–521.

———. 1983. Delinquent careers and criminal policy: Just desserts and the waiver decision. *Criminology*, 21:195–212.

———. 1984. The decision to seek criminal charges: Just desserts and the waiver decision. *Criminal Justice Ethics*, 3:27–41.

———. 1987. The juvenile court meets the principle of offense: Punishment, treatment, and the difference it makes. *Boston University Law*, 68:821–915.

———. 1988a. *In re Gault* revisited: A cross-state comparison of the right to counsel in juvenile court. *Crime and Delinquency*, 34:393–424.

———. 1988b. Juvenile court meets the principle of offense: Punishment, treatment, and the difference it makes. *Boston University Law Review*, 68:821–915.

———. 1989a. Bad law makes hard cases: Reflections of teen-aged axe-murderers, judicial activism, and legislative default. *Law and Inequality: A Journal of Theory and Practice*, 8:1–101.

———. 1989b. Right to counsel in the juvenile court: An empirical study of when lawyers appear and the difference they make. *Journal of Criminal Law and Criminology*, 79:1185–1346.

———. 1990. The punitive juvenile court and the quality of procedural justice: Disjunctions between rhetoric and reality. *Crime and Delinquency*, 36(4):443–466.

———. 1991. Justice by geography: Urban, suburban, and rural variations in the juvenile justice administration. *Journal of Criminal Law and Criminology*, 82:156–210.

———. 1993a. *Justice for children: The right to counsel and the juvenile courts.* Boston: Northeastern University Press.

———. 1993b. Juvenile (in)justice and the criminal court alternative. *Crime and Delinquency*, 39(4):403–424.

———. 1997. Abolish the juvenile court: Youthfulness, criminal responsibility, and sentencing policy. *Journal of Criminal Law and Criminology*, 88:68–136.

———. 1999. *Bad kids: Race and the transformation of the juvenile court.* New York: Oxford.

———. 2000. Legislative exclusion of offenses from juvenile court jurisdiction: A history and critique. In J. Fagan and F. E. Zimring (Eds.), *The changing borders of juvenile justice: Transfer of adolescents to the criminal court.* (pp. 83–144). Chicago: University of Chicago Press.

Felker, D. B., and Bourque, B. B. 1996. The development of boot camps in the juvenile justice system: Implementation of three demonstration programs. In D. L. MacKenzie and E. E. Hebert (Eds.), *Correctional boot camps: A tough intermediate sanction.* (pp. 143–158). Washington, DC: National Institute of Justice.

Fenwick, C. R. 1982. Juvenile court intake decision making: The importance of family affiliation. *Journal of Criminal Justice*, 10:443–453.

Ferguson, A. B., and Douglas, A. C. 1970. Study of juvenile waiver of rights. *Juvenile Court Judges Journal San Diego Law Review*, 21:12–36.

Ferrainola, S., and Grissom, G. 1990. Great expectations. *Corrections Today*, 52:118–126.

Finckenauer, J. O. 1984. *Juvenile delinquency and corrections.* Orlando, FL: Academic Press.

Finkelstein, M. M., Weiss, E., Cohen, S., and Fisher, S. Z. 1973. *Prosecution in the juvenile courts: Guidelines for the future.* Washington, DC: U.S. Department of Justice.

Finn, P., and Newlyn, A. K. 1993. Miami drug court gives drug defendants a second chance. *National Institute of Justice Journal,* 227:13–26.

Fogelson, R. M. 1977. *Big-city police.* Cambridge, MA: Harvard University Press.

Forst, M. L., and Blomquist, M. E. 1991. Cracking down on juveniles: The changing ideology of youth corrections. *Notre Dame Journal of Law, Ethics, and Public Policy,* 5:323–375.

Fox, J. A. 1996. *Trends in juvenile violence: A report to the United States Attorney General on current and future rates of juvenile offending.* Washington, DC: Bureau of Justice Statistics.

Fox, S. J. 1970a. Juvenile justice reform: An historical perspective. *Stanford Law Review,* 22:1187–1239.

———. 1970b. Prosecutors in the juvenile court: A statutory proposal. *Harvard Journal on Legislation,* 8:33–53.

Frazier, C. E., and Bishop, D. M. 1985. The pretrial detention of juveniles and its impact on case dispositions. *Journal of Criminal Law and Criminology,* 76:1132–1152.

Frazier, C. E., Bishop, D. M., and Henretta, J. C. 1992. The social context of race differentials in the juvenile justice dispositions. *Sociological Quarterly,* 33:447–458.

Frazier, C. E., and Cochran, J. K. 1986a. Detention of juveniles: Its effects on subsequent juvenile court processing decisions. *Youth and Society,* 17:286–305.

———. 1986b. Official intervention, diversion from the juvenile justice system, and the dynamics of human services work: Effects of a reform goal based on labeling theory. *Crime and Delinquency,* 32:157–176.

Freud, S. 1920. *A general introduction to psychoanalysis,* translated by Joan Riviere. New York: Liveright.

———. 1933. *New introductory lectures on psychoanalysis.* New York: Norton.

Fritsch, E. J., Caeti, T. J., and Taylor, R. W. 1999. Gang suppression through saturation patrol, aggressive curfew, and truancy enforcement: A quasi-experiment test of the Dallas anti-gang initiative. *Crime and Delinquency,* 45:122–139.

Fritsch, E. J., and Hemmens, C. 1995. Juvenile waiver in the United States 1979–1995: A comparison and analysis of state waiver statutes. *Juvenile and Family Court Journal,* 46(3):17–35.

Fritsch, E. J., Hemmens, C., and Caeti, T. J. 1996. Violent youth in juvenile and adult court: An assessment of sentencing strategies in Texas. *Law and Policy,* 18:115–136.

Gallagher, C. A. 1999. *Juvenile offenders in residential placement, 1997.* OJJDP Fact Sheet #96. Washington, DC: U.S. Department of Justice.

Garry, E. M. 1996. *Truancy: First step to a lifetime of problems.* Washington, DC: U.S. Department of Justice.

Gemignani, R. J. 1994. *Juvenile correctional education: A time for change.* Washington, DC: U.S. Department of Justice.

Geraghty, D. 1998. Ethical issues in the legal representation of children in Illinois: Roles, rules, and reforms. *Loyola University of Chicago Law Journal,* 29:289–298.

Giallombardo, R. 1966. *Society of women.* New York: John Wiley and Sons.

———. 1974. *The social world of imprisoned girls.* New York: John Wiley and Sons.

Gibbons, D. C., and Krohn, M. D. 1991. *Delinquent behavior.* 5th ed. Englewood Cliffs, NJ: Prentice Hall.

Giblin, M. J. 2002. Using police officers to enhance the supervision of juvenile probationers: An evaluation of the Anchorage CAN program. *Crime and Delinquency,* 48:116–137.

Gilbert, G. R. 1977. Alternative routes: A diversion project in the juvenile justice system. *Evaluation Quarterly,* 1:301–318.

Gilliard, D. K. 1999. *Prison and jail inmates at midyear 1998.* Washington, DC: U.S. Department of Justice.

Glaser, D. 1964. *The effectiveness of a prison and parole system.* Indianapolis, IN: Bobbs-Merril.

Glick, B., and Goldstein, A. P. 1987. Aggression replacement training. *Journal of Counseling and Development,* 65:356–362.

Gold, M. 1966. Undetected delinquent behavior. *Journal of Research on Crime and Delinquency,* 3:27–46.

Gottfredson, D. C., and Barton, W. H. 1993. Deinstitutionalization of juvenile offenders. *Criminology,* 31:591–611.

Gottfredson, M. R., and Hirschi, T. 1990. *A general theory of crime.* Stanford, CA: Stanford University Press.

Gould, L. 1969. Who defines delinquency?: A comparison of self-report and officially reported indices of delinquency for three racial groups. *Social Problems,* 16:325–336.

Graff, R. W. 1973. *Handbook for juvenile court judges.* Reno, NV: National Council of Juvenile Court Judges.

Green, B. A., and Dohrn, B. 1996. Children and the ethical practice of law. *Fordham Law Review,* 64:1281–1298.

Greenfeld, L. A., and Snell, T. L. 1999. *Women offenders.* Washington, DC: U.S. Department of Justice.

Greenfeld, L. A., and Zawitz, M. W. 1995. *Weapons offenses and offenders.* Washington, DC: U.S. Department of Justice.

Greenwood, P. W. 1996. Responding to juvenile crime: Lessons learned. *The Future of Children,* 6(3):75–85.

Greenwood, P. W., and Zimring, F. E. 1985. *One more chance: The pursuit of promising intervention strategies for chronic juvenile offenders.* Santa Monica, CA: Rand.

Griffin, P., Torbet, P., and Szymanski, L. 1998. *Trying juveniles in adult court: An analysis of state transfer provisions.* Washington, DC: Office of Juvenile Justice and Delinquency Prevention, Office of Justice Programs, U.S. Department of Justice.

Griffiths, C. T., and Winfree, L. T. 1982. Attitudes toward police: A comparison of Canadian and American adolescents. *International Journal of Comparative and Applied Criminal Justice,* 6:127–141.

Grindall, L. 2003. *North Carolina: An assessment of access to counsel and quality of representation in delinquency proceedings.* Washington, DC: American Bar Association, Criminal Justice Section, Juvenile Justice Center.

Grisso, T. 1980. Juveniles' capacities to waive their *Miranda* rights: An empirical analysis. *California Law Review,* 68:1134–1165.

———. 1981. *Juveniles' waiver of rights: Legal and psychological competence.* New York: Plenum Press.

Grisso, T., Tomkins, A., and Casey, P. 1988. Psychosocial concepts in juvenile law. *Law and Human Behavior,* 12:403–438.

Grissom, G. R., and Dubnov, W. L. 1989. *Without locks and bars: Reforming our reform schools.* New York: Praeger.

Guerra, N. G., and Slaby, R. G. 1990. Cognitive mediators of aggression in adolescent offenders: 2. intervention. *Developmental Psychology,* 26:269–277.

Guggenheim, M. 1996. A paradigm for determining the role of counsel for children. *Fordham Law Review,* 64:1399–1433.

Hamparian, D. M., Davis, J. M., Jacobson, J. M., and McGraw, R. E. 1985. *The young criminal: Careers of the violent few.* Washington, DC: U.S. Department of Justice.

Hamparian, D. M., Estep, L. K., Muntean, S. M., Priestino, R. R., Swisher, R. G., Wallace, P. L., and White, J. L. 1982. *Youth in adult courts: Between two worlds: Major issues in juvenile justice information and training.* Columbus, OH: Academy for Contemporary Problems.

Hamparian, D. M., Schuster, R., Dinitz, S., and Conrad, J. P. 1978. *The violent few: A study of violent juvenile offenders.* Lexington, MA: Lexington Books.

Handler, J. F. 1965. The juvenile court and the adversary system: Problems of function and form. *Wisconsin Law Review,* 1965:7–51.

Harms, P. 2003. *Detention in delinquency cases, 1990–1999.* OJJPD Fact Sheet #07. Washington, DC: U.S. Department of Justice.

Harrison, P. M., and Karberg, J. C. 2003. *Prison and jail inmates at midyear 2002.* Washington, DC: U.S. Department of Justice.

Hart, N. C. 1832. *Documents relative to the house of refuge, instituted by the society for the reformation of juvenile delinquents in the city of New York.* New York: N. C. Hart.

Hawkins, J. D., and Catalano, Jr., R. F. 1992. *Communities that care: Action for drug abuse prevention.* Seattle, WA: Developmental Research and Programs.

Hicks, D. 1978. Here's looking at you, kid: Prosecutors in the juvenile court process. *Pepperdine Law Review,* 5:741–768.

Hill, K. G., Howell, J. C., Hawkins, J. D., and Battin-Pearson, S. R. 1999. Childhood risk factors for adolescent gang membership: Results from the Seattle social development project. *Journal of Research in Crime and Delinquency,* 36:300–322.

Hindelang, M. J. 1971. The social versus solitary nature of delinquent involvement. *British Journal of Criminology,* 11:167–175.

Hirschel, J. D., Dean, C. W., and Dumond, D. 2001. Juvenile curfews and race: A cautionary note. *Criminal Justice Policy Review,* 12:197–214.

Hirschi, T. 1969. *Causes of delinquency.* Berkeley: University of California Press.

Hirschi, T., and Gottfredson, M. 1983. Age and the explanation of crime. *American Journal of Sociology,* 89:552–584.

Hissong, R. 1991. Teen court—Is it an effective alternative to traditional sanctions? *Journal for Juvenile Justice and Detention Services,* 6:14–23.

Holtz, L. E. 1987. *Miranda* in a juvenile setting: A child's right to silence. *The Journal of Criminal Law and Criminology,* 78:534–556.

Horowitz, A., and Wasserman, M. 1980a. Formal rationality, substantive justice and discrimination. *Law and Human Behavior,* 4:103–115.

———. 1980b. Some misleading conceptions in sentencing research: An example and a reformulation in the juvenile court. *Criminology,* 18: 411–424.

Houghtalin, M., and Mays, G. L. 1991. Criminal dispositions of New Mexico juveniles transferred to adult court. *Crime and Delinquency,* 37:393–407.

Howell, J. C. 1997. Youth gang drug trafficking and homicide: Policy and program implications. *Juvenile Justice*, 4:9–20.

———. 1998. *Youth gangs: An overview.* Washington, DC: U.S. Department of Justice.

———. 2000. *Youth gang programs and strategies: Summary.* Washington, DC: Office of Juvenile Justice and Delinquency Prevention.

Howell, J. C., and Decker, S. H. 1999. *The youth gangs, drugs, and violence connection.* Washington, DC: U.S. Department of Justice.

Howell. J. C., and Lynch, J. P. 2000. *Youth gangs in schools.* Washington, DC: U.S. Department of Justice.

Huff, R. C. 1998. *Comparing the criminal behavior of youth gangs and at-risk youths.* Washington, DC: U.S. Department of Justice.

Hughes, R. 1987. *The fatal shore.* New York: Alfred A. Knopf.

Huizinga, D. 1997. The volume of crime by gang and nongang members. Paper presented at the Annual Meeting of the American Society of Criminology. San Diego, CA.

Huizinga, D., Loeber, R., and Thornberry, T. 1994. *Urban delinquency and substance abuse: Initial findings.* Washington, DC: U.S. Department of Justice.

Hurst, Y. G., and Frank, J. 2000. How kids view cops: The nature of juvenile attitudes toward police. *Journal of Criminal Justice,* 28:189–202.

Hutson, H. R., Anglin, D., Kyriacou, D. N., and Spears, K. 1995. The epidemic of gang-related homicides in Los Angeles County from 1979 through 1994. *The Journal of the American Medical Association,* 274:1031–1036.

Inciardi, J. A. 1987. *Criminal justice.* 2nd ed. San Diego, CA: Harcourt Brace Jovanovich Publishers.

Institute of Judicial Administration/American Bar Association (IJA/ABA). 1980. *Standards relating to prosecution.* Cambridge, MA: Ballinger Publishing.

Irwin, J. 1970. *The felon.* Englewood Cliffs, NJ: Prentice Hall.

Jacobs, M. D. 1990. *Screwing the system and making it work.* Chicago: University of Chicago Press.

James, H. 1971. *Children in trouble.* New York: Pocket Books.

Jensen, E. L. 1994. The waiver of juveniles to criminal court: Policy goals, empirical realities, and suggestions for change. *Idaho Law Review,* 31:173–204.

Jensen, E. L., and Metsger, L. K. 1994. A test of the deterrent effect of legislative waiver on violent juvenile crime. *Crime and Delinquency,* 40:96–104.

Johnston, L. D., O'Malley, P. M., and Bachman, J. G. 2002. *Monitoring the future: National results on adolescent drug use, volume 1: Secondary school results.* Bethesda, MD: National Institute of Drug Abuse.

———. 2003. *Monitoring the future: National results on adolescent drug use, volume 1: Secondary school results, 1975–2002.* Bethesda, MD: National Institute on Drug Abuse.

Jones, M. 1953. *The therapeutic community.* New York: Basic Books.

Juvenile Justice Bulletin. 1998. *Serious and violent juvenile offenders.* Washington, DC: U.S. Department of Justice.

———. 1999. *Violence after school.* Washington, DC: U.S. Department of Justice.

———. 2000. *Kids and guns.* Washington, DC: U.S. Department of Justice.

Katkin, D., Hyman, D., and Kramer, J. 1976. *Juvenile delinquency and the juvenile justice system.* North Scituate, MA: Duxbury Press.

Kaufman, P., Xianglei, C., Choy, S. P., Chandler, K. A., Chapman, C. D., Rand, M. R., and Ringel, C. 1998. *Indicators of school crime and safety 1998.* Washington, DC: U.S. Department of Education and Bureau of Justice Statistics.

Kawaguchi, R. M. 1975. *Camp Fenner Canyon evaluation: Final report.* Los Angeles: Los Angeles County Probation Department.

Kelly, B. T., Huizinga, D., Thornberry, T. P., and Loeber, R. 1997. *Epidemiology of serious violence.* Washington, DC: U.S. Department of Justice.

Kempf, K. L., Decker, S. H. and Bing, R. L. 1992. An analysis of apparent disparities in the handling of black youth within Missouri's juvenile justice systems. *Justice Professional,* 6:109–134.

Ketcham, O. W. 1965. Legal renaissance in the juvenile court. *Northwestern Law Review,* 60:585–635.

———. 1967. Guidelines from *Gault:* Revolutionary requirements and reappraisal. *Virginia Law Review,* 53:1700–1718.

Kett, J. F. 1977. *Rites of passage.* New York: Basic Books.

Kinder, K., Veneziano, C., and Fichter, M. 1995. A comparison of the dispositions of juvenile offenders certified as adults with juvenile offenders not certified. *Juvenile and Family Court Journal,* 46(3):37–42.

Kirigin, K. A., Braukmann, C. J., Atwater, J. D., and Worl, M. M. 1982. An evaluation of teaching-family (achievement place) group homes for juvenile offenders. *Journal of Applied Behavior Analysis,* 15(1):1–16.

Klein, M. W. 1993. Attempting gang control by suppression: The misuse of deterrence principles. In M. W. Klein, C. L. Maxson, and J. Miller (Eds.), *The modern gang reader.* (pp. 304–313). Los Angeles: Roxbury Publishing.

———. 1995. *The American street gang: Its nature, prevalence, and control.* New York: Oxford University Press.

Klein, M. W., Maxson, C., and Cunningham, L. 1991. Crack, street gangs, and violence. *Criminology,* 29:623–650.

Klockars Jr., C. B. 1972. A theory of probation supervision. *Journal of Criminal Law, Criminology, and Police Science,* 63:550–557.

Kobrin, S. 1959. The Chicago area project: A 25-year assessment. *The Annals of the American Academy of Political and Social Sciences,* 322:20–29.

Kravitz, M. 1973. Due process in Ohio for the delinquent and unruly child. *Capitol University Law Review,* 2:53–85.

Krisberg, B., Litsky, P., and Schwartz, I. 1984. Youth in confinement: Justice by geography. *Journal of Research in Crime and Delinquency,* 21:153–181.

Krisberg, B., and Schwartz, I. 1983. Rethinking juvenile justice. *Crime and Delinquency,* 29:333–364.

Krisberg, B., Schwartz, I., Litsky, P., and Austin, J. 1986. The watershed of juvenile justice reform. *Crime and Delinquency,* 32:5–38.

Kumpfer, K. L., and Alvarado R. 1998. *Effective family strengthening interventions.* Washington, DC: U.S. Department of Justice.

Kurlychek, M., Torbet, P., and Bozynski, M. 1999. *Focus on accountability: Best practices for juvenile court and probation.* Washington, DC: U.S. Department of Justice.

Kurtz, D. P., Giddings, M. M., and Sutphen, R. 1993. A prospective investigation of racial disparity in the juvenile justice system. *Juvenile and Family Court Journal,* 44:43–59.

Land, K. C., McCall, P. L., and Williams, J. R. 1990. Something that works in juvenile justice: An evaluation of the North Carolina court counselors' intensive protective supervision randomized experimental project, 1987–1989. *Evaluation Review,* 14(6):574–606.

Lanza-Kaduce, L., Bishop, D. M., Frazier, C. E., and Winner, L. 1996. Changes in juvenile waiver and transfer provisions: Projecting the impact in Florida. *Law and Policy,* 18:137–150.

Laub, J. H., and MacMurray, B. K. 1987. Increasing the prosecutor's role in juvenile court: Expectations and realties. *Justice System Journal,* 12:196–209.

Lee, L. 1994. Factors determining waiver in a juvenile court. *Journal of Criminal Justice,* 22:329–339.

Lehman, P. E. 1972. The medical model of treatment-historical development of an archaic standard. *Crime and Delinquency,* 18:204–212.

Leiber, M. J. 1995. Toward clarification of the concept of "minority" status and decision making in juvenile court proceedings. *Journal of Crime and Justice,* 18:79–108.

———. 2002. Disproportionate minority confinement (DMC) of youth: An analysis of state and federal efforts to address the issue. *Crime and Delinquency,* 48:3–45.

Leiber, M. J., and Mack, K. Y. 2002. Race, age, and juvenile justice decision making. *Journal of Crime and Justice,* 25:23–47.

———. 2003. The individual and joint effects of race, gender, and family status on juvenile justice decision making. *Journal of Research in Crime and Delinquency,* 40:34–70.

Leiber, M. J., Nalla-Mahesh, K., and Farnworth, M. 1998. Explaining juveniles' attitudes toward the police. *Justice Quarterly,* 15:151–174.

Leiber, M. J., and Stairs, J. 1999. Race, contexts, and the use of intake diversion. *Journal of Research in Crime and Delinquency,* 36:56–86.

Lemann, N. 1991. *The promised land.* New York: Alfred A. Knopf.

Lerman, P. 1977. Discussion of differential selection of juveniles for detention. *Journal of Research in Crime and Delinquency,* 14:166–172.

———. 1980. Trends and issues in the deinstitutionalization of youths in trouble. *Crime and Delinquency,* 26:281–298.

Levin, D. J., Langan, P. A., and Brown, J. M. 2000. *State court sentencing of convicted felons, 1996.* Washington, DC: U.S. Department of Justice.

Levin, N. L. 1968. The role of the lawyer in juvenile proceedings. *Pennsylvania Law Association Quarterly,* 39:427–435.

Levrant, S., Cullen, F. T., and Wozniak, J. F. 1999. Reconsidering restorative justice: The corruption of benevolence revisited? *Crime and Delinquency,* 45:3–27.

Lilliquist, M. J. 1980. *Understanding and changing criminal behavior.* Englewood Cliffs, NJ: Prentice Hall.

Lincoln, S. B. 1976. Juvenile referral and recidivism. In R. M. Carter and M. W. Klein (Eds.), *Back on the street: Diversion of juvenile offenders.* (pp. 321–328). Englewood Cliffs, NJ: Prentice-Hall.

Lipsey, M. W. 1992. Juvenile delinquency treatment: A meta-analytic inquiry into the variability of effects. In T. Cook, H. Cooper, and D. S. Cordray (Eds.), *Meta-analysis for explanation.* (pp. 83–127). New York: Russell.

Lipsey, M. W., Cordray, D. S., and Berger, D. E. 1981. Evaluation of a juvenile diversion program. *Evaluation Review,* 5:283–306.

Lipsey, M. W., and Wilson, D. B. 1998. Effective intervention for serious juvenile offenders: A synthesis of research. In R. Loeber and D. P. Farrington (Eds.), *Serious and violent juvenile offenders: Risk factors and successful interventions.* (pp. 313–345). Thousand Oaks, CA: Sage Publications.

Lipton, D. R., Martinson, R., and Wilks, J. 1975. *The effectiveness of correctional treatment: A survey of treatment evaluation studies.* New York: Praeger Publishers.

Liska, A. E., and Tausig, M. 1979. Theoretical interpretations of social class and racial differentials in legal decision-making for juveniles. *Sociological Quarterly,* 20:197–207.

Lizotte, A., and Sheppard, D. 2001. Gun use by male juveniles: Research and prevention. *Juvenile Justice Bulletin.* Washington, DC: U.S. Department of Justice.

Loeber, R., and Farrington, D. P. 1998. Never too early, never too late: Risk factors and successful interventions for serious and violent juvenile offenders. *Studies on Crime and Crime Prevention,* 7:7–30.

Loeber, R., Farrington, D. P., and Petechuk, D. 2003. *Child delinquency: Early intervention and prevention.* Washington, DC: U.S. Department of Justice.

Lombroso, C. 1968. *Crime, its causes and remedies.* Monclair, NJ: Patterson Smith.

Lou, H. 1927. *Juvenile courts in the United States.* Chapel Hill: University of North Carolina Press.

Lubow, B. 1997. *The juvenile detention alternatives initiative: A progress report.* Baltimore: The Annie E. Casey Foundation.

Lubow, B., and Barron, D. 2000. *Resources for juvenile detention reform.* OJJPD Fact Sheet #18. Washington, DC: U.S. Department of Justice.

Luger, M. 1973. Tomorrow's training schools. *Crime and Delinquency,* 19:545–550.

Lundman, R. J. 1993. *Prevention and control of juvenile delinquency.* 2nd ed. New York: Oxford University Press.

———. 1994. Demeanor or crime? The Midwest City police-citizen encounters study. *Criminology,* 32:631–653.

———. 1996a. Demeanor and arrest: Additional evidence from previously unpublished data. *Journal of Research in Crime and Delinquency,* 33:306–323.

———. 1996b. Extralegal variables and arrest. *Journal of Research in Crime and Delinquency,* 33:349–353.

Lundman, R. J., Sykes, R. E., and Clark, J. P. 1978. Police control of juveniles: A replication. *Journal of Research in Crime and Delinquency,* 15:74–91.

Mack, J. W. 1909. The juvenile court. *Harvard Law Review,* 23:104–122.

MacKenzie, D. L. 1994. Results of a multisite study of boot camp prisons. *Federal Probation,* 58(2):60–66.

———. 1999. *Commentary: The effectiveness of aftercare programs—Examining the evidence.* Washington, DC: U.S. Department of Justice.

MacKenzie, L. R. 1999. *Residential placement of adjudicated youth, 1987–1996.* OJJPD Fact Sheet #117. Washington, DC: U.S. Department of Justice.

Maguire, K., and Pastore, A. L. 1996. *Sourcebook of criminal justice statistics 1995.* Washington, DC: U.S. Department of Justice.

———. 2004. *Sourcebook of criminal justice statistics 2001.* [Online]. *http://www.albany.edu/sourcebook/.*

Males, M. A. 2000. Vernon, Connecticut's juvenile curfew: The circumstances of youths cited and effects on crime. *Criminal Justice Policy Review,* 11:254–267.

Maloney, D., Bazemore, G., and Hudson, J. 2001. The end of probation and the beginning of community justice. *Perspectives,* 25:22–30.

Martinson, R. 1974. What works? Questions and answers about prison reform. *The Public Interest,* 35:22–52.

Maxson, C. L. 1995. *Street gangs and drug sales in two suburban cities.* Washington, DC: U.S. Department of Justice.

———. 1998. Gang members on the move. *Bulletin.* Washington, DC: U.S. Department of Justice.

Mays, G. L., Fuller, K., and Winfree, L. T. 1994. Gangs and gang activity in southern New Mexico: A descriptive look at a growing rural problem. *Journal of Crime and Justice,* 17:25–44.

McCarthy, B. R. 1987. Preventive detention and pretrial custody in the juvenile court. *Journal of Criminal Justice,* 5:185–198.

———. 1989. A preliminary research model for the juvenile and family court. *Juvenile and Family Court Journal,* 40:43–48.

McCarthy, B. R., and Smith, B. L. 1986. The conceptualization of discrimination in the juvenile justice process: The impact of administrative factors and screening decisions on juvenile court dispositions. *Criminology,* 24:41–64.

McCarthy, F. B. 1994. The serious offender and juvenile court reform: The case for prosecutorial waiver of juvenile court jurisdiction. *Saint Louis University Law Journal*, 38:629–671.

McDowall, D., Loftin, C., and Wiersema, B. 2000. The impact of youth curfew laws on juvenile crime rates. *Crime and Delinquency*, 46:76–91.

McGarrell, E. F. 1993. Trends in racial disproportionality in juvenile court processing: 1985–1989. *Crime and Delinquency*, 39:29–48.

McGarrell, E. F., Olivares, K., Crawford, K., and Kroovand, N. 2000. *Returning justice to the community: The Indianapolis juvenile restorative justice experiment.* Indianapolis: Hudson Institute.

Mears, D. P., and Kelly, W. R. 1999. Assessments and intake processes in juvenile justice processing: Emerging policy considerations. *Crime and Delinquency*, 45:508–529.

Mears, D. P., and Field, S. H. 2000. Theorizing sanctioning in a criminalized juvenile court. *Criminology*, 38:983–1019.

Meehan, P. J., and O'Carroll, P. W. 1992. Gangs, drugs, and homicide in Los Angeles. *American Journal of Diseases of Children*, 146:683–687.

Mennel, R. M. 1973. *Thorns and thistles: Juvenile delinquents in the United States, 1825–1940.* Hanover, NH: University Press of New England.

———. 1998. Attitudes and policies toward juvenile delinquency in the United States. In P. M. Sharp and B. W. Hancock (Eds.), *Juvenile delinquency.* 2nd ed. (pp. 19–40). Upper Saddle River, NJ: Prentice Hall.

Miller, W. B. 1975. *Violence by youth groups as a crime problem in major American cities.* Washington, DC: National Institute for Juvenile Justice and Delinquency Prevention. U.S. Government Printing Office.

Miller, W. B. 1977. The rumble this time. *Psychology Today,* May, pp. 52-59, 88.

Miller, W. B. 2001. *The growth of youth gang problems in the United States, 1970–1998.* OJJPD. Washington, DC: U.S. Department of Justice.

Miller-Wilson L. S. 2003. *Pennsylvania: An assessment of access to counsel and quality of representation in delinquency proceedings.* Washington, DC: American Bar Association, Criminal Justice Section, Juvenile Justice Center.

Minnesota Governor's Commission on Crime Prevention and Control. 1973. *An evaluation of the group residence program for juvenile girls, June 1972–April 1973.* St. Paul: Minnesota Department of Corrections.

Minor, K. I., Hartmann, D. J., and Terry, S. 1997. Predictor of juvenile court actions and recidivism. *Crime and Delinquency*, 43:328–344.

Mitford, J. 1974. *Kind and unusual punishment: The prison business.* New York: Vintage Books.

Moone, J. 1997a. *Juveniles in private facilities, 1991–1995.* OJJDP Fact Sheet #64. Washington, DC: U.S. Department of Justice.

———. 1997b. *States at a glance: Juveniles in public facilities, 1995.* OJJPD Fact Sheet #69. Washington, DC: U.S. Department of Justice.

———. 1998. *Counting what counts: The census of juveniles in residential placement.* OJJPD Fact Sheet #74. Washington, DC: U.S. Department of Justice.

Moore, J., and Hagedorn, J. 2001. *Female gangs: A focus on research.* OJJPD. Washington, DC: U.S. Department of Justice.

Morgan, T. "6 indicted in 9 murders linked to a drug gang." *New York Times,* March 3, 1989, B2.

Muhlhausen, D. B. 1996. *Reform schools reformed: How competitive tendering saves your money.* The Calvert News Series, Summer Vol. 1 #3.

Murphy, P. T. 1977. *Our kindly parent . . . the state.* New York: Penguin Books.

Murton, T. O., and Hyams, J. 1969. *Accomplices to the crime.* New York: Grove Press.

Myers, D. L. 2001. *Excluding violent youths from juvenile court: The effectiveness of legislative waiver.* New York: LFB Scholarly Pub.

Myers, S. M. 2002. Police encounters with juvenile suspects: Explaining the use of authority and provision of support. Ph.D. Dissertation. SUNY Albany.

National Advisory Commission on Criminal Justice Standards and Goals (NAC). 1973. *Police.* Washington, DC: U.S. Government Printing Office.

———. 1976. *Report of the task force on juvenile justice and delinquency prevention.* Washington, DC: U.S. Government Printing Office.

National Advisory Committee for Juvenile Justice and Delinquency Prevention (NAC). 1980. *Standards for the administration of juvenile justice.* Washington, DC: U.S. Government Printing Office.

National Youth Gang Center. 1999. *1996 national youth gang survey.* Washington, DC: U.S. Department of Justice.

———. 2000. *1998 national youth gang survey.* Washington, DC: U.S. Department of Justice.

Nejelski, P. 1976. Diversion: The promise and the danger. *Crime and Delinquency*, 22:393–410.

Newman, D. J. 1966. *Conviction: The determination of guilt or innocence without trial.* Boston: Little, Brown and Company.

Nimick, E., Szymanski, L., and Snyder, H. 1986. *Juvenile court waiver: A study of juvenile court cases transferred to criminal court.* Pittsburgh: National Center for Juvenile Justice.

Notes. 1966. Juvenile delinquents: The police, state courts, and individualized justice. *Harvard Law Review,* 79:775–810.

———. 1967. Rights and rehabilitation in the juvenile courts. *Columbia Law Review,* 67:281–341.

Notes and Comments. 1979. *Swisher vs. Brady:* Does a juvenile court rehearing on the record after a master has made proposed findings violate double jeopardy or due process? *Maryland Law Review,* 39:395–425.

Noyes, A. D. 1970. Has *Gault* changed the juvenile court concept? *Crime and Delinquency,* 16:158-162.

Office of Juvenile Justice and Delinquency Prevention (OJJDP). 1999. *Report to the congress on juvenile violence research.* Washington, DC: U.S. Department of Justice.

———. 2001.*OJJDP Annual Report, 2000.* Washington, DC: DOJ.

O'Leary, V., and Duffee, D. 1971. Correctional policy: A classification of goals designed for change. *Crime and Delinquency,* 17:373–386.

Osbun, L. A., and Rode, P. A. 1984. Prosecuting juveniles as adults: The quest for "objective" decisions. *Criminology,* 22:187–202.

Osgood, D. W., O'Malley, P. M., Bachman, J. G., and Johnston, L. D. 1989. Time trends and age trends in arrests and self-reported illegal behavior. *Criminology,* 27:389–417.

OVC Bulletin, July 2000. *The restorative justice and mediation collection: Executive summary.* Washington, DC: U.S. Department of Justice.

OVC Bulletin, October 2000. *Victims, judges, and juvenile court reform through restorative justice.* Washington, DC: U.S. Department of Justice.

Owens, R. P., and Wells, D. K. 1993. One city's response to gangs. *Police Chief,* 58:25–27.

Packer, H. 1968. *The limits of the criminal sanction.* Stanford, CA: Stanford University Press.

Palmer, T. B., and Lewis, R. V. 1980. A differentiated approach to juvenile diversion. *Journal of Research in Crime and Delinquency,* 17:209–229.

Parent, D. G., Leiter, V., Kennedy, S., Livens, L., Wentworth, D., and Wilcox, S. 1994. *Conditions of confinement: Juvenile detention and corrections facilities.* Washington, DC: U.S. Department of Justice.

Paulsen, M. G. 1957. Fairness to the juvenile offender. *Minnesota Law Review,* 41:547–598.

Pearson, F. S. 1988. Evaluation of New Jersey's intensive supervision program. *Crime and Delinquency,* 34:437–448.

Peters, M., Thomas, D., Zamberlan, C., and Associates. 1997. *Boot camps for juvenile offenders.* Washington, DC: U.S. Department of Justice.

Petersilia, J., Greenwood, P. W., and Lavin, M. 1978. *Criminal careers of habitual felons.* Washington, DC: U.S. Department of Justice.

Pickett, R. S. 1969. *House of Refuge: Origins of juvenile reform in New York state, 1815–1857.* Syracuse, NY: Syracuse University Press.

Pisciotta, A. W. 1982. Saving the children: The promise and practice of *parens patriae,* 1838–1898. *Crime and Delinquency,* 28:410–425.

Platt, A. M. 1972. *The child savers: The invention of delinquency.* Chicago: University of Chicago Press.

Podkopacz, M. R., and Feld, B. C. 1995. Judicial waiver policy and practice: Persistence, seriousness, and race. *Law and Inequality: A Journal of Theory and Practice,* 14:73–178.

———. 1996. The end of the line: An empirical study of judicial waiver. *Journal of Criminal Law and Criminology,* 86(2):449–492.

Pogrebin, M. R., Poole, E. D., and Regoli, R. M. 1984. Constructing and implementing a model juvenile diversion program. *Youth and Society,* 15:305–324.

Polk, K. 1986. Juvenile diversion: A look at the record. *Crime and Delinquency,* 30:648–659.

Polsky, H. W. 1965. *Cottage six.* New York: John Wiley and Sons.

Pope, C. E., and Snyder, H. N. 2003. *Race as a factor in juvenile arrests.* Washington, DC: OJJPD.

Portune, R. 1971. *Changing adolescent attitudes toward the police.* Cincinnati, OH: Anderson.

Poulos, T. M., and Orchowsky, S. 1994. Serious juvenile offenders: Predicting the probability of transfer to criminal court. *Crime and Delinquency,* 40:3–17.

President's Commission on Law Enforcement and the Administration of Justice. 1967. *The challenge of crime in a free society.* Washington, DC: U.S. Government Printing Office.

Propper, A. M. 1981. *Prison homosexuality.* Lexington, MA: Lexington Books.

———. 1982. Make-believe families and homosexuality among imprisoned girls. *Criminology,* 20:127–138.

Purdom, T. J. 1970. Juvenile court proceedings from the standpoint of the attorney for the state. *Texas Tech Law Review,* 1:269–322.

Puritz, P., and Brooks, K. 2002. *Kentucky-advancing justice: An assessment of access to counsel and quality of representation in delinquency proceedings.* Washington, DC: American Bar Association, Criminal Justice Section, Juvenile Justice Center.

Puritz, P., Burrell, S., Schwartz, R., Soler, M., and Warboys, L. 1995. *A call for justice: An assessment of access to counsel and quality of representation in delinquency proceedings.* Washington, DC: American Bar Association, Juvenile Justice Center.

Puritz, P., and Scali, M.A. 1998. *Beyond the walls: Improving conditions of confinement for youth in custody.* Washington, DC: U.S. Department of Justice.

Puritz, P., Scali, M. A., and Picou, I. 2002. *Virginia: An assessment of access to counsel and quality of representation in delinquency proceedings.* Washington, DC: American Bar Association, Criminal Justice Section, Juvenile Justice Center.

Puritz, P., and Sun, T. 2001. *Georgia: An assessment of access to counsel and quality of representation in delinquency proceedings.* Washington, DC: American Bar Association, Criminal Justice Section, Juvenile Justice Center.

Puzzanchera, C. M. 2000. *Juvenile court placement of adjudicated youth, 1988–1997.* OJJPD Fact Sheet #15. Washington, DC: U.S. Department of Justice.

———. 2002. *Juvenile court placement of adjudicated youth, 1989–1998.* OJJPD Fact Sheet #02. Washington, DC: U.S. Department of Justice.

———. 2003a. *Delinquency cases waived to criminal court, 1990–1999.* OJJPD Fact Sheet #04. Washington, DC: U.S. Department of Justice.

———. 2003b. *Juvenile court placement of adjudicated youth, 1990–1999.* OJJPD Fact Sheet #05. Washington, DC: U.S. Department of Justice.

———. 2003c. *Juvenile delinquency probation caseload, 1990–1999.* OJJPD Fact Sheet #06. Washington, DC: U.S. Department of Justice.

Puzzanchera, C. M., Stahl, A. L., Finnegan, T. A., Snyder, H. N., Poole, R. S., and Tierney, N. 2000. *Juvenile court statistics 1997.* Washington, DC: OJJPD.

Puzzanchera, C. M., Stahl, A. L., Finnegan, T. A., Tierney, N., and Snyder, H. N. 2003a. *Juvenile court statistics 1998.* Washington, DC: OJJPD.

———. 2003b. *Juvenile court statistics 1999.* Washington, DC: OJJPD.

Rand, M. R. 1994. *Guns and crime.* Washington, DC: U.S. Department of Justice.

———. 1998. *Criminal victimization 1997: Changes 1996–1997 with trends 1993–1997.* Washington, DC: U.S. Department of Justice.

Rantala, R. R. 2000. *Effects of NIBRIS on crime statistics.* Washington, DC: U.S. Department of Justice.

Rappeport, J. R. 1977. Patuxent experiment [editorial]. *The Bulletin of the American Academy of Psychiatry and the Law.* 5(2):v-vii.

Rausch, S. P., and Logan, C. H. 1983. Diversion from juvenile court: Panacea or pandora's box. In J. R. Klugel (Ed.), *Evaluating juvenile justice.* Beverly Hills, CA: Sage Publications.

Reeves, M. 1929. *Training schools for delinquent girls.* New York: Russell Sage Foundation.

Reinventing Probation Council. n.d. *Transforming probation through leadership: The 'broken window' model.* New York: Manhattan Institute for Policy Research.

Rendleman, O. R. 1971. *Parens patriae:* From chancery to the juvenile court. *South Carolina Law Review,* 23:205–229.

Reynolds, K. M., Seydlitz, R., and Jenkins, P. 2000. Do juvenile curfew laws work?: A time-series analysis of the New Orleans law. *Justice Quarterly,* 17:205–230.

Rhoden, E. 1994. Disproportionate minority representation: First steps to a solution. *Juvenile Justice,* 2(1):9–14. Washington, DC: U.S. Department of Justice.

Rich, T., Finn, P., and Ward, S. 2001. *Guide to using school cop to address student discipline and crime problems.* Washington, DC: Office of Community Oriented Policing Services.

Ringwalt, C. L., Ennett, S. T., and Holt, K. D. 1991. An outcome evaluation of project D.A.R.E. *Health Education Research: Theory and Practice,* 6:327–337.

Rivers, J. E., and Anwyl, R. S. 2000. Juvenile assessment centers: Strengths, weaknesses, and potential. *The Prison Journal,* 80:96–113.

Robin, G. D. 1982. Juvenile interrogations and confessions. *Journal of Police Science and Administration,* 10:224–228.

Robinson, L. N. 1923. *Penology in the United States.* Philadelphia: John C. Winston

Robitscher, J. 1980. *The powers of psychiatry.* Boston: Houghton Mifflin Company.

Rojek, D. G., and Erickson, M. L. 1982. Reforming the juvenile justice system: The diversion of status offenders. *Law and Society Review,* 16:241–264.

Rosenbaum, D. P., Flewelling, R. L., Bailey, S. L., Ringwalt, C. L., and Wilkinson, D. L. 1994. Cops in the classroom: A longitudinal evaluation of drug abuse resistance education (DARE). *Journal of Research in Crime and Delinquency,* 31:3–31.

Rosenberg, I. M. 1980. The constitutional rights of children charged with crime: Proposal for the return to the not so distant past. *UCLA Law Review,* 27:656–721.

Ross, C. J. 1996. From vulnerability to voice: Appointing counsel for children in civil litigation. *Fordham Law Review,* 64:1571–1620.

Ross, R. R., and McKay, B. 1976. A study of institutional treatment programs. *International Journal of Offender Therapy and Comparative Criminology: An Interdisciplinary Journal,* 20(2):167–173.

Roush, D. W. 1996. *Desktop guide to good juvenile detention practice.* National Juvenile Detention Association. East Lansing: Michigan State University.

Rowe, D. C., Vazsonyi, A. T., and Flannery, D. J. 1995. Sex differences in crime? Do means and within-sex variation have similar causes? *Journal of Research in Crime and Delinquency,* 32:84–100.

Rubel, R. J., and Ames, N. L. 1986. *Reducing school crime and student misbehavior: A problem solving strategy.* Washington, DC: U.S. National Institute of Justice.

Rubin, T. H. 1980. The emerging prosecutor dominance of the juvenile court intake process. *Crime and Delinquency,* 26:299–318.

———. 1985a. *Behind the black robes: Juvenile court judges and the court.* Beverly Hills, CA: Sage Publications.

———. 1985b. *Juvenile justice: Policy practice, and law.* 2nd ed. New York: Random House.

———. 1989. The juvenile court landscape. In A. R. Roberts (Ed.), *Juvenile justice: Policies, practice and law.* (pp. 110–142). Chicago: The Dorsey Press.

———. 1998. The juvenile court landscape. In A. R. Roberts (Ed.), *Juvenile justice: Policies, practice and law.* 2nd ed. (pp. 205–230). Chicago: Nelson-Hall.

Rushe, G., and Kirchheimer, O. 1939. *Punishment and social structure.* New York: Columbia University Press.

Ryerson, E. 1978. *The best-laid plans: America's juvenile court experiment.* New York: Hill and Wang.

Sampson, R. J. 1986. Effects of socioeconomic context on official reaction to juvenile delinquency. *American Sociological Review,* 51:876–885.

Sampson, R. J., and Laub, J. H. 1995. Structural variations in juvenile court processing: Inequality, the underclass, and social control. *Law and Society Review,* 27:285–311.

Sanborn Jr., J. B. 1984. Plea negotiation in juvenile court. Ph.D. dissertation. SUNY Albany.

———. 1986. A historical sketch of plea bargaining. *Justice Quarterly,* 3:111–138.

———. 1987a. *In re Gault* and the juvenile court: What twenty years of constitutional domestication have wrought. Paper presented at the American Society of Criminology. Montreal, Canada.

———. 1987b. The defense attorney's role in juvenile court: Must justice or treatment (or both) be compromised? Paper presented at the Academy of Criminal Justice Sciences. St. Louis, Missouri.

———. 1992a. Detention in the juvenile court: Adequate protection or arbitrary decision making? Paper presented at the Academy of Criminal Justice Sciences. Pittsburg, Pennsylvania.

———. 1992b. Pleading guilty in juvenile court: Minimal ado about something very important to young defendants. *Justice Quarterly,* 9:127–150.

———. 1993a. Philosophical, legal, and systemic aspects of juvenile court plea bargaining. *Crime and Delinquency,* 39:509–527.

———. 1993b. The right to a public jury trial: A need for today's juvenile court. *Judicature,* 76:230–238.

———. 1994a. Certification to criminal court: The important policy questions of how, when, and why. *Crime and Delinquency,* 40(2):262–281.

———. 1994b. Constitutional problems of juvenile delinquency trials. *Judicature,* 78:81–88.

———. 1994c. Remnants of *parens patriae* in the adjudicatory hearing: Is a fair trial possible in juvenile court? *Crime and Delinquency,* 40(4):599–615.

———. 1994d. The juvenile, the court, or the community: Whose best interests are currently being promoted in juvenile court? *Justice System Journal,* 17:249–266.

———. 1995a. Guardian of the public and/or the child: Policy questions and conflicts for the juvenile court prosecutor. *Justice System Journal,* 18:141–156.

———. 1995b. How parents can affect the processing of delinquents in the juvenile court. *Criminal Justice Policy Review,* 7:1–26.

———. 1996a. Factors perceived to affect dispositions in juvenile court: Putting the sentencing decision into context. *Crime and Delinquency,* 42:99–113.

———. 1996b. Policies regarding the prosecution of juvenile murderers: Which system and who should decide? *Law and Policy,* 18(1, 2):151–178.

———. 1998. Second-class justice, first-class punishment: The use of juvenile records in sentencing adults. *Judicature,* 81(5):206–213.

———. 2000. Striking out on the first pitch in criminal court. *Barry Law Review,* 1(1):7–61.

———. 2001a. A *parens patriae* figure or impartial fact finder: Policy questions and conflicts for the juvenile court judge. *Criminal Justice Policy Review,* 12(4):311–332.

———. 2001b. Victims' rights in juvenile court: Has the pendulum swung too far? *Judicature,* 85(3):140–146.

———. 2003. Hard choices or obvious ones: Developing policy for excluding youth from juvenile court. *Youth Violence and Juvenile Justice,* 1:198–214.

———. 2004. The adultification of youth. In P. J. Benekos and A. V. Merlo (Eds.), *Controversies in juvenile justice and delinquency.* (pp. 143–164). Lexis-Nexis: Matthew Bender and Company.

Sanders, W. 1994. *Drive-bys and gang bangs.* New York: Aldine.

Saul, J. A., and Davidson II, W. S. 1983. Implementation of juvenile diversion programs: Cast your net on the other side of the boat. In J. R. Kluegel (Ed.), *Evaluating juvenile justice.* Beverly Hills, CA: Sage Publications.

Scahill, M. C. 2000. *Juvenile delinquency probation caseload, 1988–1997.* OJJPD Fact Sheet #19. Washington, DC: U.S. Department of Justice.

Scarpitti, F. R., and Stephenson, R. M. 1971. Juvenile court dispositions: Factors in the decision-making process. *Crime and Delinquency,* 17:142–151.

Schlicter, K. J., and Horan, J. J. 1981. Effects of stress inoculation on the anger and aggression management skills of institutionalized juvenile delinquents. *Cognitive Therapy and Research,* 5:359–365.

Schneider, A. L. 1990. *Deterrence and juvenile crime: Results from a national policy experiment.* New York: Springer-Verlag.

Schneider, A. L., and Schneider, P. R. 1984. A comparison of programmatic and ad hoc restitution in juvenile courts. *Justice Quarterly,* 1:529–547.

———. 1985. The impact of restitution on recidivism of juvenile offenders: An experiment in Clayton County, Georgia. *Criminal Justice Review,* 10:1–10.

Schultz, J. L., and Cohen, F. 1976. Isolationism in juvenile court jurisprudence. In M. K. Rosenheim (Ed.), *Pursuing justice for the child.* (pp. 20–42). Chicago: University of Chicago Press.

Schur, E. M. 1973. *Radical nonintervention: Rethinking the delinquency problem.* Englewood Cliffs, NJ: Prentice Hall.

Schutt, R. K., and Dannefer, D. 1988. Detention decisions in juvenile cases: JINS, JDs, and gender. *Law and Society Review,* 22(3):509–520.

Schwartz, I. A., Fishman, G., Hatfield, R. R., Krisberg, B. A., and Eisikovits, Z. 1987. Juvenile detention: The hidden closets revisited. *Justice Quarterly,* 4:219–235.

Schwartz, I. M., and Barton, W. H. 1994. *Reforming juvenile detention: No more hidden closets.* Columbus: Ohio State University Press.

Sealock, M., and Simpson, S. 1998. Unraveling bias in arrest decisions: The role of juvenile offender typescripts. *Justice Quarterly,* 15:427–457.

Seckel, J. P., and Turner, J. K. 1985. *Assessment of planned re-entry programs (PREP).* Sacramento: California Youth Authority.

Secret, P. E., and Johnson, J. B. 1997. The effect of race on juvenile justice decision making in Nebraska: Detention, adjudication, and disposition, 1988–1993. *Justice Quarterly,* 14:445–478.

Seidman, D., and Couzens, M. 1974. Getting the crime rate down: Political pressure and crime reporting. *Law and Society Review,* 8:457–493.

Sellin, T., and Wolfgang, M. E. 1964. *The measurement of delinquency.* New York: John Wiley and Sons.

Seyfrit, C. L., Reichel, P., and Stutts, B. 1987. Peer juries as a juvenile justice diversion technique. *Youth and Society,* 18:302–316.

Shannon, L. 1982. *Assessing the relationship of adult criminal careers to juvenile careers: A summary.* Washington, DC: OJJDP.

Shaw, C. R., and McKay, H. D. 1942. *Juvenile delinquency and urban areas.* Chicago: University of Chicago Press.

Shelden, R. G., and Horvath, J. A. 1987. Intake processing in juvenile court: A comparison of legal and nonlegal variables. *Juvenile and Family Court Journal,* 38:13–19.

Shelden, R. G. 1999. Detention diversion advocacy: An evaluation. *Juvenile Justice Bulletin.* Washington, DC: OJJPD.

Sheppard, D., and Kelly, P. 2002. *Juvenile gun courts: Promoting accountability and providing treatment.* Washington, DC: U.S. Department of Justice.

Shine, J., and Price, D. 1992. Prosecutors and juvenile justice: New roles and perspectives. In I. M. Schwartz (Ed.), *Juvenile justice and public policy: Toward a national agenda.* (pp. 101–133). New York: Lexington Books.

Shivrattan, J. L. 1988. Social interactional training and incarcerated juvenile delinquents. *Canadian Journal of Criminology,* 30:145–163.

Short Jr., J. F., and Nye, I. F. 1958. Extent of unrecorded juvenile delinquency. *Journal of Criminal Law, Criminology, and Police Science,* 49:296–302.

Sickmund, M. 2002a. *Juvenile offenders in residential placement: 1997–1999.* Washington, DC: U.S. Department of Justice.

———. 2002b. *Juvenile residential facility census, 2000: Selected findings.* Washington, DC: U.S. Department of Justice.

Sickmund, M., Sladky, T. J., and Kang, W. 2004. Census of juveniles in residential placement databook. [Online]: *www.ojjdp.ncjrs.org/ojstatbb/cjrp/*.

Sickmund, M., Snyder, H. N., and Poe-Yamagata, E. 1997. *Juvenile offenders and victims: 1997 update on violence.* Washington, DC: U.S. Department of Justice.

Sickmund, M., Stahl, A. L., Finnegan, T. A., Snyder, H. N., Poole, R. S., and Butts, J. A. 1998. *Juvenile court statistics 1995.* Washington, DC: OJJPD.

Siegel, L. J., and Senna, J. J. 1991. *Juvenile delinquency: Theory, practice, and law.* 4th ed. St. Paul, MN: West Publishing Co.

Simonsen, C. E., and Gordon III, M. S. 1982. *Juvenile justice in America.* 2nd ed. New York: Macmillan Publishing Co.

Singer, S. I. 1993. The automatic waiver of juveniles and substantive justice. *Crime and Delinquency,* 39:253–261.

Singer, S. I., and McDowall, D. 1988. Criminology delinquency: The deterrent effects of the juvenile offender law. *Law and Society Review,* 22:521–535.

Skinner, B. F. 1953. *Science and human behavior.* New York: Macmillan.

———. 1972. *Beyond freedom and dignity.* New York: Bantam Books.

———. 1974. *About behaviorism.* New York: Knopf.

Skoler, D. L. 1968. Counsel in juvenile court proceedings: A total criminal justice perspective. *Journal of Family Law,* 8:243–277.

Skoler, D. L., and Tenney, C. W. 1964. Attorney representation in juvenile court. *Journal of Family Law,* 4:77–98.

Smith, D. A. 1984. The organizational context of legal control. *Criminology,* 22:19–38.

Smith, D., and Visher, C. 1981. Street-level justice: Situational determinants of police arrest decisions. *Social Problems,* 29:167–178.

Smith, M. E. 2001. *What future for "public safety" and "restorative justice" in community corrections?* Washington, DC: U.S. Department of Justice.

Smith, R. R., and Lombardo, V. S. 2001. Evaluation report of the juvenile mediation program. *Corrections Compendium,* 26:1–2, 22–25.

Snyder, H. N. 1997. *Juvenile arrests 1996.* Juvenile Justice Bulletin, OJJDP. Washington DC.

———. 1998. *Juvenile arrests 1997.* Washington, DC: OJJDP, U.S. Department of Justice.

———. 1999. *Juvenile arrests 1998.* Washington, DC: OJJDP, U.S. Department of Justice.

———. 2000. *Juvenile arrests 1999.* Washington, DC: OJJDP, U.S. Department of Justice.

———. 2002. *Juvenile arrests 2000.* Washington, DC: OJJDP, U.S. Department of Justice.

———. 2003. *Juvenile arrests 2001.* Washington, DC: OJJDP, U.S. Department of Justice.

Snyder, H. N., and Sickmund, M. 1995. *Juvenile offenders and victims: A focus on violence.* Washington, DC: OJJDP, U.S. Department of Justice.

———. 1999. *Juvenile offenders and victims: 1999 national report.* Washington, DC: OJJDP, U.S. Department of Justice.

Sontheimer, H., and Goodstein, L. 1993. Evaluation of juvenile intensive aftercare probation: Aftercare versus system response effects. *Justice Quarterly,* 10(2):197–227.

Sorrentino, J. N., and Olsen, G. K. 1977. Certification of juveniles to adult court. *Pepperdine Law Review,* 4:497–522.

Spence, S. H., and Marzillier, J. S. 1981. Social skills training with adolescent male offenders: 2. short-term, long-term, and generalized effects. *Behavior Research and Therapy,* 19:349–368.

Stahl, A. L. 1998. *Delinquency cases in juvenile courts, 1995.* Washington, DC: OJJDP.

———. 1999. *Delinquency cases in juvenile courts, 1996.* Washington, DC: OJJDP.

———. 2000. *Delinquency cases in juvenile courts, 1997.* Washington, DC: OJJDP.

———. 2001. *Delinquency cases in juvenile courts, 1998.* Washington, DC: OJJDP.

———. 2003. *Delinquency cases in juvenile courts, 1999.* Washington, DC: OJJDP.

Stahl, A., Sickmund, M., Finnegan, T., Snyder, H., Poole, R., and Tierney, N. 1999. *Juvenile court statistics 1996.* Washington, DC: OJJDP.

Stanfield, R. 1999. *The JDAI story: Building a better juvenile detention system.* Baltimore: Annie E. Casey Foundation.

Steinberg, L., and Schwartz, R. G. 2000. Developmental psychology goes to court. In T. Grisso and R. G. Schwartz (Eds.), *Youth on trial: A developmental perspective on juvenile justice.* (pp. 7–31). Chicago: University of Chicago Press.

Stewart, C. E., Celeste, G., Marrus, E., Picou, I., Puritz, P., and Utter, D. 2000. *Selling justice short: Juvenile indigent defense in Texas.* Washington, DC: American Bar Association, Criminal Justice Section, Juvenile Justice Center.

Strom, K. 2000. *Profile of state prisoners under age 18, 1985–1997.* Washington, DC: U.S. Department of Justice.

Stuphen, R. D., and Ford, J. 2001. The effectiveness and enforcement of a teen curfew law. *Journal of Sociology and Social Welfare,* 28:55–78.

Sullivan, R. "Violent drug gang smashed, police say." *New York Times,* October 24, 1991, B6.

Sumner, H. 1971. Locking them up. *Crime and Delinquency,* 17:168–179.

Sutherland, E. H., and Cressey, D. R. 1978. *Criminology.* 10th ed. Philadelphia: Lippincott.

Sykes, G. 1958. *Society of captives.* Princeton, NJ: Princeton University Press.

Tannenhaus, D. S. 2000. The evolution of transfer out of the juvenile court. In J. Fagan and F. E. Zimring (Eds.), *The changing borders of juvenile justice: Transfer of adolescents to the criminal court.* (pp. 13–43). Chicago: University of Chicago Press.

Teeters, N. K., and Reinemann, J. V. 1950. *The challenge of delinquency.* New York: Prentice Hall.

Teilmann, K., and Landry, P. H. 1981. Gender bias in juvenile justice. *Journal of Research in Crime and Delinquency,* 18:47–80.

Thambidurai, G. A. 1980. A comparative outcome study of a contract parole program for individuals committed to the youth correctional complex in the state of New Jersey. *Dissertation Abstracts International,* 41(01):371B. University Microfilms No. 80–16503.

Thomas, C. W., and Bilchik, S. 1985. Prosecuting juveniles in criminal courts: A legal and empirical analysis. *Journal of Criminal Law and Criminology,* 76:439–479.

Thomas, C. W., and Fitch, W. A. 1975. An inquiry into the association between respondents' personal characteristics and juvenile court dispositions. *William and Mary Law Review,* 17:61–83.

Thornberry, T. P. 1973. Race, socioeconomic status, and sentencing in the juvenile justice system. *Journal of Criminal Law and Criminology,* 64:90–98.

Thornberry, T. P., and Burch, J. H. 1997. *Gang members and delinquent behavior.* Washington, DC: Office of Juvenile Justice and Delinquency Prevention.

Thornberry, T. P., Krohn, M. D., Lizotte, A. J., and Chard-Wierschem, D. 1993. The role of juvenile gangs in facilitating delinquent behavior. *Journal of Research in Crime and Delinquency,* 30:55–87.

Thrasher, F. M. 1927. *The gang: A study of 1,313 gangs in Chicago.* Chicago: University of Chicago Press.

Tittle, C., and Meier, R. 1990. Specifying the SES/delinquency relationship. *Criminology,* 28:271–299.

Tittle, C. R., and Curran, D. A. 1988. Contingencies for dispositional disparities in juvenile justice. *Social Forces,* 67:23–58.

Tomkins, A. J. 1990. Dispositional decisionmaking in the juvenile justice system: An empirical study of the use of offense and offender information. *Nebraska Law Review,* 69:298–345.

Torbet, P., Gable, R., Hurst IV, H., Montgomery, I., Szymanski, L., and Thomas, D. 1996. *State responses to serious and violent juvenile crime.* Washington, DC: OJJDP.

Tracy, P. E. 2002. *Decision making and juvenile justice: An analysis of bias in case processing.* Westport, CT: Praeger.

Tracy, P. E., Wolfgang, M. E., and Figlio, R. M. 1985. *Delinquency in two birth cohorts.* Washington, DC: OJJDP, U.S. Department of Justice.

Triplett, R., and Myers, L. B. 1995. Evaluating contextual patterns of delinquency: Gender-based differences. *Justice Quarterly,* 12:59–84.

Trojanowicz, R. C. 1978. *Juvenile delinquency: Concepts and controls.* Englewood Cliffs, NJ: Prentice Hall.

University of Akron. 2003. *Adolescent substance abuse prevention study: A longitudinal evaluation of the new curricula for the D.A.R.E middle (8th Grade) and high school (9th Grade) programs.* http://www.Dare.com.

U.S. Department of Health and Human Services. 2003. Administration on children, youth, and families. *Child Maltreatment, 2001.* Washington, DC: U.S. Government Printing Office.

U.S. Department of Justice, Federal Bureau of Investigation. 1993. *Age-specific arrest rates and race-specific arrest rates for selected offenses, 1965–1992.* Washington, DC: U.S. Government Printing Office.

———. 1999. *Uniform crime reports 1998.* Washington, DC: U.S. Government Printing Office.

———. 2003. *Uniform crime reports 2002.* Washington, DC: U.S. Government Printing Office.

Varano, R., and Bezdikian, V. 2001. *Addressing school-related crime and disorder: Interim lessons from school-based problem-solving projects.* Washington, DC: U.S. Department of Justice.

Vigil, J. D. 1988. *Barrio gangs.* Austin, TX: University of Texas Press.

Wasserman, G. A., Miller, L. S., and Cothern, L. 2000. *Prevention of serious and violent juvenile offending.* Washington, DC: OJJDP, U.S. Department of Justice.

Weibush, R. G. 1993. Juvenile intensive supervision: The impact on felony offenders diverted from institutional placement. *Crime and Delinquency,* 39(1):68–69.

West, D. J., and Farrington, D. P. 1977. *The delinquent way of life.* London: Heinemann.

Whitaker, C., and Bastian, L. 1991. *Teenage victims: A national crime survey report.* Washington, DC: U.S. Department of Justice.

Whitebread, C. H., and Batey, R. 1981. The role of waiver in the juvenile court: Questions of philosophy and functions. In J. C. Hall, D. M. Hamparian, J. M. Pettibone, and J. L. White (Eds.), *Readings in public policy: Major issues in juvenile justice information and training.* Columbus, OH: Academy for Contemporary Problems.

Whitehead, J. T., and Lab, S. P. 2004. *Juvenile justice: An introduction.* 4th ed. Cincinnati: Anderson.

Williams, J. R., and Gold, M. 1972. From delinquent behavior to official delinquency. *Social Problems,* 20:209–229.

Wilson, J. Q. 1968. *Varieties of police behavior.* New York: Harvard University Press.

Winfree, L. T., and Griffiths, C. T. 1977. Adolescent attitudes toward the police: A survey of high school students. In T. N. Ferdinand (Ed.), *Juvenile delinquency: Little brother grows up.* (pp. 79–99). Beverly Hills, CA: Sage Publications.

Winner, L., Lanza-Kaduce, L., Bishop, D. M., and Frazier, C. 1997. The transfer of juveniles to criminal court: Reexamining recidivism over the long term. *Crime and Delinquency,* 43(4):548–563.

Wizner, S. 1984. Discretionary waiver of juvenile court jurisdiction: An invitation to procedural arbitrariness. *Criminal Justice Ethics,* 3(2):41–50.

Wolf, M. M., Phillips, E. L., and Fixson, D. L. 1974. *Achievement place: Phase II (vol. 1).* Rockville, MD: National Institute of Mental Health, Center for Studies of Crime and Delinquency.

Wolfgang, M. E., Figlio, R., and Sellin, T. 1972. *Delinquency in a birth cohort.* Chicago: University of Chicago Press.

Wolfgang, M. E., Thornberry, T. P., and Figlio, R. M. 1987. *From boy to man, from delinquency to crime.* Chicago: University of Chicago Press.

Wooden, K. 1976. *Weeping in the playtime of others.* New York: McGraw-Hill Book Co.

Worden, R. E., and Myers, S. M. 1999. *Police encounters with juvenile suspects.* Washington, DC: National Institute of Justice.

Wordes, M., Bynum, T. S., and Corley, C. J. 1994. Locking up youth: The impact of race on detention decisions. *Journal of Research in Crime and Delinquency,* 31:149–165.

Wordes, M., and Jones, S. M. 1998. Trends in juvenile detention and steps toward reform. *Crime and Delinquency,* 44:544–560.

Wright, B. R. E., Caspi, A., Moffitt, T. E., Meich, R. A., and Silva, P. A. 1999. Reconsidering the relationship between SES and delinquency: Causation but not correlation. *Criminology,* 37:175–194.

Wyrick, P. A. 2000. *Law enforcement referral of at-risk youth: The shield program.* Washington, DC: U.S. Department of Justice.

Zald, M. N., and Street, D. 1964. Custody and treatment in juvenile institutions. *Crime and Delinquency,* 10:249–256.

Zimring, F. E. 1981. Notes toward a jurisprudence of waiver. In J. C. Hall, D. M. Hamparian, J. M. Pettibone, and J. L. White (Eds.), *Readings in public policy: Major issues in juvenile justice information and training.* Columbus, OH: Academy for Contemporary Problems.

———. 1991. The treatment of hard cases in American juvenile justice: In defense of discretionary waiver. *Notre Dame Journal of Law, Ethics and Public Policy,* 5:267–280.

———. 1998. *American youth violence.* New York: Oxford University Press.

———. 2000. Penal proportionality for the young offender: Notes on immaturity, capacity, and diminished responsibility. In T. Grisso, and R. G. Schwartz (Eds.), *Youth on trial: A developmental perspective on juvenile justice.* (pp. 27–89). Chicago: University of Chicago Press.

Subject Index

A

abolition of juvenile court, 505
adjournment in contemplation of dismissal, 252
adjudicatory hearing, 41, 43–44, 271, 316–342
    provisions, 529–530
advocate, 6, 165–167, 348
aftercare status, 400
age
    arrest data, 70–73, 87
    commitment data, 370
    court jurisdiction, 52–55, 63
    delinquency, 85–88
    detention, 241
    disposition data, 388
    gangs, 108
    probation, 384–385
    status offenders, 205
    transfer to adult court, 289–291
    violent crimes, 118–119
Age-Specific Arrest Rates and Race-Specific Arrest Rates for Selected Offenses 1965–1992, 87
alcohol, 117, 203–204
Alford plea, 248, 270
alibi defense, 250
ameliorated intervention, 9–10
amenability hearing, 280, 282–285
American Bar Association, 322
American Correctional Association (ACA), 467
appeals, 396–397
appointed or assigned counsel, 164–165
arraignment, 247
arrest
    data, 68–76, 86–87, 89–90
    decision to arrest, 130–143
    and race, 140, 511–512
    resisting, 136
    warrants for, 133
assessment center, 466

assessment officer. See probation officer (PO)
at-risk youth, 60
attention deficit/hyperactivity disorder (ADHD), 435

B

bail, 219–220
Becker hearing, 53
behavior modification (BM), 442, 478–480
bifurcation, 345
Bill of Rights, 37, 41, 44, 58
    See also constitutional rights
bindover, 276
blended sentence, 296
blood samples, 151
boot camps, 464–465
bootstrapping, 403
burden of proof, 40–42
Bureau of Alcohol, Tobacco, and Firearms (ATF), 114, 439
Bureau of Justice Statistics (BJS), 99

C

Cambridge-Somerville Youth Study Project, 432
camps, 468–469
capital sentencing, 305
certification, 276
CHAPTERS, 461
charge bargains, 256
Chicago Area Project, 431
Chicago Reform School, 20
Chicago women's group, 21–23
Child Maltreatment 2001, 95
child savers group, 21–23
chins, 59
chivalry hypothesis, 136
cigarette smoking, 117, 203
cins, 59–60
classification of correctional clients, 419–421
cocaine, 116

cohort study, 68, 80–85
colloquy, 267–271
Columbine High School, 67, 98
Columbus, Ohio cohort study, 83–84, 92
combination sentence, 296, 301
community corrections, 415, 443–445
    reparation boards, 446
community-oriented policing, 127–128
community programs for prevention and treatment, 414–52
community service, 366
competency hearing, 248
complete sentence bargains, 257
comprehensive gang model, 435
comprehensive strategy, 433
concurrent jurisdiction, 286
confinement, 367–368
consecutive sentences, 375
consent decrees, 252–254
constitutional controls, 146–149
    See also rights of juveniles
constitutional rights, 24–25, 33–38, 232–234
    See also Bill of Rights
continuance under supervision, 252
continuance without finding delinquency, 252
contrition guilty plea, 265
correctional programs, 429–430
    behavior modification (BM), 478–480
    conditions of, 492–493
    facilities data, 493–495
    facilities for juveniles, 495–496
    institutional models, 478–480
    See also facilities; institutions

cottage-style training school, 481
court, 24–25
    court of last resort, 185
    criminal court data, 306–308
    criminal court vs. juvenile court, 162–163
    history of juvenile court, 21–25
    jurisdiction, 50–65
    juvenile-adult reviews, 404–405
    mandatory exclusion of crimes, 62–64
    personnel, 159–181
    reverse transfer to juvenile court, 294–295
    transfer to adult court, 275–311
crime, 55–57
    crime control model, 4–6
    data, 68–76
    gang involvement, 110–111
    measuring, 67–96
    Part I crimes, 68–69, 89
    Part II crimes, 68–69
    patterns of, 97–120
    reported, 68–70
    violent crime, 113–114, 118–119, 141
criminal justice system
    juvenile justice system differences, 2–4
    language of, 10–11
criminalization effect, 8
criminalization of juvenile court, 51
curfew laws, 56, 128, 203

D

day treatment program, 367
death penalty, 305
decline, 276
defense attorney, 7, 164–167, 250–251, 259–262, 322–325, 347–348
defense of infancy, 27
deferred adjudication, 363
deferred disposition, 252
deferred prosecution, 252
delayed judicial transfer, 280
delayed reverse transfer, 299

delinquency, 22, 53, 56–57, 62, 256
    adjudication data, 338–339
    and age, 85–88
    chronic, 81
    detention, 237–239
    detention data, 494–495
    disposition data, 383–386
    and gender, 89–91
    measuring, 85
    number of cases, 201–203
    parental liability provisions, 173–175
    probation data, 449–450
    and race, 91–92, 238
    risk assessment scale, 420
    and social class, 92
    status offense differences, 57–59
    transfer to adult court, 293
Department of Juvenile Justice, 184
designated felon, 295
designated transfer, 276
detention, 211–243, 336, 455–464
    age, 241
    criteria for, 221–227
    custody rates, 535–536
    deadline for filing petitions, 513
    expedited trials, 515–517
    gender, 240
    hearing, 230–234
    history of, 459–460
    numbers of, 237–239
    presumptive, 222
    preventive, 223
    race, 240
    status offenders, 239–241
    See also facilities; institutions
Detention Diversion Advocacy Project (DDAP), 214–215
diagnostic center, 466
differentiated sentencing, 373, 378–379
direct file, 286
discretionary exclusion, 276
dismissal bargain, 254
disposition
    commitment, 369–373
    criteria, 356–363

delinquency data, 383–386
hearing, 345–390
hearing deadline, 247, 281, 531–533
ladder, 368–369, 373
nonjudicial, 252
options, 362–383
status offenders, 386–388
disproportionate minority confinement (DMC), 485
diversion, 185–187, 190–199, 423–426
    history of, 424–425
DNA analysis, 151
domino theory, 34
double jeopardy, 43, 329
Drug Abuse Resistance Education (DARE), 126, 438–439
drug courts, 427–429
drugs, 98–99, 112–113, 115–117, 438–439
dual processing, 502–505
due process, 5, 37, 41, 330

E

early release, 399
education, 482–484
enhanced sentences, 375
equal justice, 185–186
evaluation team, 350
examinations of juveniles, 352
exclusionary rule, 133–134
expunging records, 407–408
extended jurisdiction, 295, 374

F

facilities for juveniles, 371–372
    See also detention; institutions
factual guilty plea, 266
family, 94–95, 131–132, 173–176, 225–226, 353–356, 440–441, 446
    court, 56
    intervention, 9–10
    See also parents
Federal Bureau of Investigation (FBI), 68–69
felonies, 56, 134
female juveniles. See gender
Ferris School for Boys, 488
field investigation, 129

Fifth Amendment, 37, 42–43, 58, 146, 152
fingerprinting, 150–151
fins, 59
fitness, 276
foster homes, 465
Fourteenth Amendment, 37, 41–42
Fourth Amendment, 58, 143, 152
frisking, 129
fundamental fairness, 34

G

Gainesville State School for Girls, 488
Gang Resistance Education and Training (GREAT), 126, 439–440
gangs, 98–99, 102–113
gatekeeper, 123, 131, 183
gender
    adjudication data, 339–341
    arrest data, 72–74, 87, 89–90
    arrest decision, 136, 139
    and delinquency, 89–91, 238
    detention, 239, 240
    disposition data, 388
    dispositional criteria, 361–362
    gangs, 108, 113
    incarceration, 486–488
    probation, 384–385
    state training schools, 476
    status offenders, 205
    violent crimes, 118–119
geography, 51–52
Gerstein hearing, 231
get-tough movement, 10–11
Glen Mills School, 17
grand jury indictment, 249
group home, 465
guardian, 7, 165–167, 348
guardian ad litem, 174, 322
guided group interaction (GGI), 442–443
guilty pleas, 248, 265–267
    contrition, 265
    factual, 266
    mercy, 265
    nonnegotiated, 265–267

    quick, 266
    requirements, 517–519
    slow, 266
    straight, 265
    trade-seeking, 266
gun courts, 447–448
guns, 98, 114–117, 119

H

halfway house, 465
hearings
    adjudicatory hearing, 41, 43–44, 271, 316–342
    amenability hearing, 280, 282–285
    Becker hearing, 53
    compentency, 248
    detention, 513–515
    disposition, 531–533
    modification, 397, 400–402
    omnibus, 248
    plea, 247
    postdispositional, 395–409
    preliminary, 247–248
    pretrial, 251–252
    probable cause, 280–281
    review, 397–400
    violation of parole (VOP), 402–403
    violation of probation (VOP), 398, 402–405
hidden juvenile corrections, 475–477
Hollymeade training school, 484
homicides, 119
Houses of Refuge, 17–20, 22, 472

I

identification methods, 150–152
improvement period, 252
in loco parentis, 145
incarceration of juveniles, 465–471
    release from, 496–497
incomplete sentence bargains, 257
incorrigibility, 61
index crimes, 68
Indiana Training School, 488

Indicators of School Crime and Safety: 2003, 99
individualization, 185–186
industrial schools, 20
inferior judicial officer, 169–170
informal adjustment, 191
informal agreement, 252
informal processing vs. court referal, 152–153
inmate culture, 485–486
insanity defense, 250
institutional models, 478
institutions, 453–499
    See also detention; facilities
intake conference, 187
intake officer (IO), 143
    See also probation officer (PO)
intake process, 183–207
intensive after care program (IAP), 448–449
intermediate sanctions, 403
interrogation, 129, 143, 146–150
intervention, 9–10
invariant hypothesis, 85–86, 88

J

jail, 216–219
jina, 60
jins, 59
jinss, 60
judge, 167–169, 263, 330–332
judicial transfer, 278–286, 289–291
    provisions, 519–523
jurisdiction, 50–65
    act, 55–56
    age, 52–55, 63
    concurrent, 286
    extended, 295, 374
Juvenile Assessment Center (JAC), 228
Juvenile Court Act, 22
Juvenile Court Statistics 1999, 88
juvenile delinquents. See delinquency
Juvenile Detention Alternative Initiative (JDAI), 215, 461

Juvenile Justice and Delinquency Prevention Act of 1974, 58, 118, 216
Juvenile Justice Bulletin 1999, 101
juvenile justice system
    criminal justice system differences, 2–4
    future of, 501–509
    history of, 3, 14–30, 424–425, 459–460, 472–475
    language of, 10–11
    models of, 4–6
    purpose of, 7–10
juvenile treatment screening team, 350

K

Kent hearing, 280

L

labeling theory, 186
legal interests, 7
legislative transfer, 287
lesser-included offenses, 299
long-term institution, 467–68

M

mandatory direct file, 286
mandatory exclusion of crimes, 62–64
mandatory initial detention, 222
mandatory public disclosure, 405–406
marijuana, 116
master, 160, 169–170, 328–330
medical model of corrections, 418
mens rea, 14–15, 27–28
mercy guilty plea, 265
meta-analysis, 483
microlevel prevention programs, 430–436
minimized intervention, 9–10
minority. See race
Miranda warning, 5–6, 130, 146–149
misdemeanor, 56–57, 134
Mobilization for Youth (MFY), 431
modification hearing, 397, 400–402

Monitoring the Future, 115
multidisciplinary team, 350

N

National Center for Educational Statistics (NCES), 97
National Center for Juvenile Justice, 88, 91
National Crime Victimization Survey (NCVS), 77, 97
National Incident-Based Reporting System (NIBRIS), 97, 101
National Institute of Drug Abuse (NIDA), 115
National Institute of Justice (NIJ) Gang Survey, 109
National Institute of Mental Health (NIMH), 435
National Juvenile Detention Association (NJDA), 455
needs assessment, 422–423
neighborhood courts, 193
net widening, 187, 425–426
no action, 186, 192
nol pros bargain, 254–256
nolo contendere plea, 248
nonjudicial disposition, 252
nonnegotiated guilty plea, 265–267
not guilty plea, 248

O

offense exclusion, 286
Office of Community-Oriented Policing Services (COPS), 127–128
Office of Juvenile Justice and Delinquency Prevention (OJJDP), 102, 433–437, 440, 443
omnibus hearing, 248
operant conditioning, 479
order maintenance, 125
order of protection, 175

P

parens patriae, 19–21, 23–24, 36, 168, 258, 488
parents, 131–132, 225–226, 264, 319, 353–356, 396
    liability, 173–176

parental responsibility
    laws, 173
    sentencing, 383
    See also family
parole, 399
pattern, 97–98
Philadelphia cohort studies, 80–84, 86, 89–92
photographing, 150–151
pins, 59
placing the petition on file, 252
plea bargaining, 256–271
plea hearing, 247
pleading, 247–248
police, 124–155
Police Athletic League (PAL), 126
policing authorities, 125
postadjudication programs, 441–443
postdisposition hearing, 395–409
predisposition report (PDR), 347, 350–356, 533–534
preliminary hearing, 247–248
preliminary inquiry, 187
presentence investigation (PSI), 347, 350
presentence report (PSR), 350
presumption of release, 143
presumptive detention, 222
presumptive judicial transfer, 284–285
pretrial conference, 248
pretrial hearing, 251–252
pretrial stage, 211–273
prevention programs, 414–452
preventive detention, 223
prima facie case, 281
primary prevention, 430
privatization of public services, 477–478
probable cause, 132
probable cause hearing, 247, 280–281
probation, 415–423, 443–445
    data, 449–450
    disposition, 364–367, 534–535
    sentence, 298
    supervision, 421
probation officer (PO), 26, 133, 170–173, 184, 418–419

prosecution option, 199–201
prosecutive merit, 281
prosecutor, 160–164, 250, 260–261
prosecutorial case preparation, 316–318
prosecutorial transfer, 278–280, 286–291
   provisions, 523–526
prospective longitudinal surveys, 86
protection and advocacy (P and As), 491
psychology, 21, 473
public defender, 164–165
public disclosure of records, 405–406
punishment, 223–224
   corporal, 488
   gap, 303
   model, 4–5
purpose clauses, 8

Q

Quakers, 14–20, 22–23, 473
quick guilty plea, 266
quid pro quo, 20, 23, 35, 42

R

race, 108–109, 117
   adjudication data, 339–341
   arrest data, 75–76, 140
   confinement, 484–485
   delinquency, 91–92, 238
   detention, 239–240
   disposition data, 388
   dispositional criteria, 361–362
   drugs, 115–117
   gangs, 108–109
   guns, 115–117
   probation, 384–385
   status offenders, 205–206
Racine, Wisconsin cohort study, 84
ranches, 468–469
reasonable grounds, 132, 281
reception center, 466
recidivist impact, 303, 305
records of juveniles, 302–306, 351
   expunging records, 407–408

nonconfidential juvenile court record, 405–406
   sealing records, 407–408
referee, 160, 169–170, 328–330
referral, 276
reform school, 20, 472
regular judicial transfer, 284–285
rehabilitation, 461–462, 482–484
rehabilitation model, 4–7
reintegration model of corrections, 418
relinquishment, 276
residential placement, 535–536
restitution, 445
restorative conferencing models, 446
restorative justice, 445–447
retained counsel, 164–165
retention age, 54–55
retrospective longitudinal studies, 86
reverse transfer, 294–295
review hearing, 397–400
rights of juveniles, 281
   at adjudicatory hearing, 526–527
   constitutional controls, 146–150
   at disposition, 349–350
   of incarcerated juveniles, 491–492
   right against self-incrimination, 281
   right to appeal, 396–397
   right to counsel, 319–320
   right to speedy trial, 325–327, 528–529
   right to treatment (RT), 487–491
   right to trial by jury, 42–43
   See also constitutional rights
risk (or needs) assessment instrument (RAI), 228
runaway cases, 61, 153, 204–205, 240, 340

S

school, 406, 436
   crime, 98–101
   See also truancy

School Crime Supplement (SCS), 98
school resource officers (SROs), 125
sealing records, 407–408
search and seizure, 143–146
second tier of juvenile court, 295–297
secondary prevention, 430
self-incrimination, 281
self-report survey (SRS), 68, 78–80, 85, 86
self-representation, 320
self-transfer, 276
sentencing
   bargains, 256–257
   blended, 296
   capital, 305
   circle, 446
   combination, 296, 301, 377–383
   complete, 257
   consecutive, 375
   differentiated, 373, 378–379
   enhanced, 375
   guidelines, 304
   incomplete, 257
   mandatory, 379–382
   minimum, 379, 382–383
   multiple levels, 375–377
   with parents, 383
   probation, 298
   youthful offender (YO), 300–302
serious violent juvenile (SVJ), 98, 118–119
shelter care, 212
shock probation, 367
Short-Term Adolescent Treatment (START), 443
Sixth Amendment, 37, 42, 58, 152
slow guilty plea, 266
socioeconomic status (SES), 78
station adjustments, 131
status conference, 248
status offense, 3, 52–53, 55, 57–62, 256
   adjudication data, 340–341
   age, 205
   decriminalization of, 58

delinquency differences, 57–59
detention, 239–241
detention data, 495
disposition, 386–388
gender, 205
number of cases, 203–206
parental liability provisions, 174–175
probation data, 450
race, 205–206
sealing records, 407–408
special titles, 59–60
statutory controls, 149–150
statutory exclusion, 287
straight guilty plea, 265
superpredators, 114, 506

T

teen courts, 193, 426–427
Texas Youth Council (TYC), 488
The Challenge of Crime in a Free Society, 436
The Dangerous Clases, 472
therapeutic community (TC), 480–482
token economy, 479
totality of circumstances, 148
trade-seeking guilty plea, 266
training school, 467–468
transfers

delayed judicial, 280
delayed reverse, 299
designated, 276
judicial, 278–286, 289–291
legislative, 287
presumptive judicial, 284–285
prosecutorial, 278–280, 286–291
regular judicial, 284–285
reverse, 294–295
treatment interests, 7
treatment model, 4–5
treatment programs, 414–452
trial dockets, 21
trial penalty, 264
truancy, 61, 203–205, 437
See also school

U

unequal processing, 502–505
Uniform Crime Reports (UCR), 68–76, 85, 98
unique processing, 502–505
U.S. Supreme Court, 31–46

V

venue, 50
vertical prosecution, 161
victims, 176–179, 263, 348, 445–447
juvenile, 92–96

rights of, 8
victim impact statements (VIS), 178
victim management, 172
victim-offender mediation (VOM), 177, 445–447
victimization survey, 68, 77, 85, 98
violation of probation (VOP) hearing, 398, 402–405
Violent Crime Control and Law Enforcement Act of 1994, 127
Vision Quest (VQ), 468–469
Vista Voluteers, 431–432

W

waiver, 276
waiver of counsel, 320–322
Warren Court, 33–35
Wilderness Programs, 468–469
writ of habeas corpus, 18–19

Y

youth courts, 193
youth placement committee, 350
youthful offender (YO), 295
sentencing, 300–302

Z

zero-tolerance laws, 100

Name Index

A

Adams, W., 386
Ageton, S. S., 79
Ainsworth, J., 277, 505
Albin, B., 321–322
Allen, F. A., 32, 287
Allen, P., 445
Allen-Hagen, B., 214, 484
Altschuler, D. M., 117, 444, 448–449
Alvarado, R., 440
Ames, N. L., 100
Anderson, E., 127
Andrews, D. A., 483
Anwyl, R. S., 228
Armstrong, T. L., 444, 448
Arnette, J. L., 100–101
Asbury, H., 104
Auerbach, A. W., 484
Augustus, John, 415–416
Austin, J., 493
Ayers, E. L., 477

B

Bagdikian, B. H., 424
Bahlmann, D. W., 162
Bailey, W. C., 227, 361, 474
Baker, M. L., 126, 437
Bannister, A. J., 128
Barnes, C. W., 293, 306
Barnes, H. E., 416, 445
Barron, D., 214
Bartlett, S. R., 427–428
Bartol, A. M., 77, 468, 475
Bartol, C. R., 77, 468, 475
Bartollas, C., 443, 481, 486
Barton, W. H., 196, 199, 423
Bastian, L., 94
Bastion, L. D., 77
Batey, R., 277, 287
Bayh, Birch, 474
Bazemore, G., 446
Beck, A. J., 219, 494
Becker, Howard S., 424
Beha, J., 445
Bell, D., 196, 198–199
Berger, D. E., 196

Bernard, T. J., 17–18
Beyer, M., 443
Bezdikian, V., 127
Bilchik, S., 306
Birbaum, Morton, 489
Bishop, D. M., 136, 198, 227, 277–278, 287–288, 306, 356, 470
Bjerregaard, B., 108
Black, D., 129–130, 137, 140
Black, M. C., 449
Block, C. R., 103, 112–114
Block, R., 103, 112, 114
Blomberg, T. G., 425
Blumstein, Alfred, 115
Bogen, D., 165
Bonnie, R. J., 277
Bookin-Weiner, H., 227
Bortner, M. A., 227, 277–278, 285, 292–293, 306, 356, 361
Bourque, B. B., 464–465
Brace, Charles Loring, 472
Braga, A. A., 126
Braukman, C. J., 479
Bridges, B. S., 350
Brooks, C. C., 482
Brooks, K., 321–322
Brounstein, P. J., 117
Brown, B. S., 479–480
Browning, S. L., 127
Buck, J., 426–427
Burch, J. H., 107
Burrell, S., 460–461
Butts, J. A., 201, 291, 293, 326–327, 338, 383, 386, 423, 426–427, 445, 450

C

Calvin, E. M., 321–322
Campbell, A., 108, 113
Campbell, J. S., 196
Cass, E. S., 464
Catalano Jr., R. F., 444
Celeste, G., 321–322
Cemkovich, S., 78
Chaiken, M. R., 128
Chamblis, W. J., 78

Champion, D. J., 278, 287–288, 292, 306
Chandler, K. A., 98–99, 114
Chein, D. B., 357
Chesney-Lind, M., 69, 136, 227, 475–476
Clarke, E. E., 293
Clarke, S. H., 358
Clayton, R. R., 438
Clayton, S. L., 467
Clear, T. R., 472–473, 477
Clement, M. J., 294, 306
Clemmer, D., 485
Cloward, Richard, 431
Cochran, J. K., 196, 227
Cogan, N. H., 19
Cohen, A. K., 78
Cohen, B., 69
Cohen, F., 20
Cohen, H. R., 479
Cohen, L. E., 196, 199, 227, 361
Cole, G. F., 472–473, 477
Conley, D. J., 135
Conrad, J. P., 481
Cook, P., 112, 114
Cook, Rufus R., 416
Coolbaugh, K., 433
Cooper, C. S., 427–429
Cordray, D. S., 196
Costello, J. C., 165
Couzens, M., 69
Cox, T. C., 127
Coxe, S., 164–165
Cressey, D. R., 416
Crews, G. A., 100–101
Crompton, F., 472
Cronin, R. C., 464–465
Crouse, Mary, 18–19
Crowe, T. D., 130
Cumming, E., 321–322
Curran, D. A., 361
Curry, G. D., 103, 111

D

Dannefer, D., 227
Dash, L., 424

Davidson II, W. S., 196, 425–426
Dawson, R. O., 287, 306
Dean, C. W., 198
Decker, S. H., 103, 112–113
Dedel, K., 213
DeJong, C., 361
Deschenes, E. P., 277, 288, 294
Devine, P., 485
Devoe, J. F., 99–100
DiIulio, J. D., 506
Dohrn, B., 323
Dorne, C., 20
Douglas, A. C., 148
Dubnov, W. L., 468
Duffee, D., 418
Dungworth, T., 227
Dunham, H. W., 168
Dunworth, T., 128

E

Egley Jr., A., 106, 108, 112
Elliott, D. S., 78–79, 196
Erickson, M. L., 98, 196
Erwin, B. S., 421
Esbensen, F., 107–108, 439–440

F

Fader, J. J., 351–353, 361
Fagan, J., 117, 277–278, 285, 288, 293–294, 306
Falkenberg, S. D., 127
Farrington, D. P., 81, 484
Federle, K. H., 165, 277, 505
Feld, Barry C., 8, 267, 277–278, 285, 287–288, 292–294, 306, 320, 358, 505
Felker, D. B., 464
Fenwick, C. R., 196, 199
Ferguson, A. B., 148
Ferrainola, S., 468
Field, S. H., 360
Filipczak, J., 479
Finckenauer, J. O., 442, 479
Finkelstein, M. M., 162
Finn, P., 427
Fitch, W. A., 358
Fogelson, R. M., 126
Ford, J., 128
Fox, J. A., 506
Fox, S. J., 15, 18, 21–22, 160, 162
Frank, J., 127

Franz, R., 293
Frazier, C. E., 136, 196, 198, 227, 277, 287–288, 351, 354, 356, 361, 470
Freud, S., 473
Fritsch, E. J., 126, 287, 306

G

Gallagher, C. A., 471, 494–495
Garry, E. M., 437
Gault, Gerald, 36–37
Gemignani, R. J., 483
Geraghty, D., 323
Gewirth, K., 20
Giallombardo, R., 485–487
Gibbons, D. C., 430
Giblin, M. J., 126
Gilbert, G. R., 196
Gilliard, D. K., 219
Glaser, D., 418
Glick, B., 484
Gold, M., 78, 128
Goldstein, A. P., 484
Goodstein, L., 449
Gordon III, M. S., 472
Gottfredson, Michael R., 85–88
Gould, L., 78
Graff, R. W., 168
Green, B. A., 323
Greenfeld, L. A., 89, 114
Greenwood, P. W., 444
Griffin, P., 280, 287, 295
Griffiths, C. T., 127
Grindall, L., 321–322
Grisso, T., 148, 196, 277, 294
Grissom, G. R., 468
Guerra, N. G., 484
Guggenheim, M., 165

H

Hagedorn, J., 113
Hamparian, Donna M., 81, 83–84, 92, 285, 306
Handler, J. F., 32
Hansel, C. J., 433
Harms, P., 237, 239
Harrison, P. M., 494
Hawkins, J. D., 444
Hemmens, C., 287
Heyne, Robert P., 488
Hicks, D., 162
Hill, K. G., 112
Hindelang, M. J., 98

Hirschel, J. D., 128
Hirschi, Travis, 80, 85–88
Hissong, R., 427
Holtz, L. E., 148
Horan, J. J., 484
Horowitz, A., 353
Horvath, J. A., 196, 199
Houghtalin, M., 293, 306
Howell, J. C., 98–99, 103–104, 112–113, 126
Hudson, J., 357
Huff, R. C., 113
Hughes, R., 477
Huizinga, D., 107–108, 112, 444–445
Hurst, Y. G., 127
Hutson, H. R., 112, 114
Hyams, J., 424

I

Inciardi, J. A., 68
Irwin, J., 485

J

Jackson, K. C., 361
Jacobs, M. D., 456
James, Howard, 488
Jensen, E. L., 288
Johnson, J. B., 361
Johnson, L. B., 430
Johnson, S. J., 162
Johnston, L. D., 115–117, 127
Jones, Maxwell, 481
Jones, S. M., 214

K

Kaltenecker, N., 464
Kamine, D., 321–322
Karberg, J. C., 219, 494
Katkin, D., 431–432
Kaufman, P., 99, 101
Kawaguchi, R. M., 484
Kelly, B. T., 118
Kelly, P., 447–448
Kelly, W. R., 183–184
Kempf, K. L., 351–352, 361
Kennedy, J. F., 431
Ketcham, O. W., 32, 165
Kett, J. F., 473
Kinder, K., 293
Kirchheimer, O., 472
Kirigin, K. A., 484
Klein, M. W., 103, 112, 129

Klockars Jr., C. B., 418
Kluegel, J. R., 196, 199
Kobrin, S., 431
Koch, G. G., 358
Kravitz, M., 165
Krisberg, B., 227, 475–476
Krohn, M. D., 430
Kumpfer, K. L., 440–441
Kurlychek, M., 421, 436, 444

L

Lab, S. P., 505
Land, K. C., 423
Landry, P. H., 227
Lang, K., 196, 198–199
Laub, J. H., 85, 160, 162, 361
Lee, L., 288, 294
Lehman, P. E., 473
Leiber, M. J., 127, 198–199,
    227, 511–512
Lemann, N., 431
Lerman, P., 227, 475–476
Levin, D. J., 307–308
Levin, N. L., 165
Levrant, S., 447
Lewis, R. V., 425
Lillyquist, M. J., 479
Lincoln, S. B., 196
Lipsey, M. W., 196, 443–444,
    469, 483–484
Lipton, D. R., 425, 474
Liska, A. E., 198
Lizotte, A., 126
Loeber, R., 436, 484
Logan, C. H., 426
Lombardo, V. S., 447
Lombroso, C., 473
Lou, H., 21, 168, 277
Lubow, B., 214–215
Luger, M., 474
Lundman, R. J., 129–130, 136,
    140, 431–432
Lyman, Theodore, 473
Lynch, J. P., 98–99, 103

M

Mack, J. W., 168, 198–199, 277
MacKenzie, D. L., 464, 484
MacKenzie, L. R., 494
MacMurray, B. K., 160, 162
Maguire, K., 419
Major, A. K., 106, 112
Males, M. A., 128

Maloney, D., 441
Martinson, R., 425
Marzillier, J. S., 484
Maxson, C. L., 103, 105, 112
Mays, G. L., 107, 278, 288,
    292–293, 306
McCarthy, B. R., 196, 199, 227,
    361
McCarthy, F. B., 285, 288
McDowall, D., 128, 288
McGarrell, E. F., 126, 227, 358
McKay, B., 484
McKay, H. D., 431
Mears, D. P., 183–184, 360
Meehan, P. J., 112
Meier, R., 78–79
Mennel, R. M., 15, 17–18, 472–
    473
Metsger, L. K., 288
Miller, W. B., 103, 105, 106,
    112
Miller-Wilson, L., 321–322
Minor, K. I., 196
Mitford, J., 424
Moone, J., 470–471, 476
Moore, J., 113
Muhlhausen, D. B., 477
Murphy, Patrick T., 489
Murton, T. O., 424
Myers, D. L., 278
Myers, L. B., 199
Myers, S. M., 126, 129–131,
    135–137, 139–140, 143

N

Nagasawa, R. I., 78
Nejelski, P., 423–424
Newlyn, A. K., 427
Newman, D. J., 266
Nimick, E., 294
Nixon, R. M., 430
Noyes, A. D., 165
Nye, I. F., 79

O

O'Carroll, P. W., 112
O'Leary, V., 418
Ohlin, 431
Olsen, G. K., 287
Orchowsky, S., 294
Osbun, L. A., 287
Osgood, D. W., 86, 107–108,
    439

Owens, R. P., 129

P

Pabon, E., 117
Palmer, T. B., 425
Parent, D. G., 492–493
Pastore, A. L., 419
Paulsen, M. G., 32
Pearson, F. S., 421
Peters, M., 464–465
Petersilia, J., 78
Peterson, R. D., 361
Peterson, Scott, 51
Pickett, R. S., 15
Pisciotta, A. W., 18
Platt, A. M., 15, 18, 21–22
Podkopacz, M. R., 278, 285,
    293–294, 306
Pogrebin, M. R., 196
Polk, K., 425
Polsky, H. W., 485–486
Pope, C. E., 140–141
Portune, R., 127
Poulos, T. M., 294
Pranis, Kay, 446
Price, D., 162
Propper, A. M., 485, 487
Purdom, T. J., 160
Puritz, P., 232, 321–322, 460,
    491–492
Puzzanchera, C. M., 88, 153,
    201–206, 237, 239, 240–241,
    292–293, 339–341, 384–387,
    415, 449–450

R

Rand, M. R., 77, 114
Rantala, R. R., 101
Rappeport, J. R., 473
Rausch, S. P., 426
Reed, W. L., 356, 361
Reeves, M., 472–473
Reinemann, J. V., 472
Reiss Jr., A., 129–130, 137, 140
Rendleman, O. R., 19
Retzlaff, P. D., 196
Reynolds, K. M., 128
Rhoden, E., 485
Rich, T., 127
Ringwalt, C. L., 438
Rivers, J. E., 228
Robin, G. D., 148
Robinson, L. N., 472

Robitscher, J., 473
Rode, P. A., 287
Rojek, D. G., 196
Rosenbaum, D. P., 438
Rosenberg, I. M., 165
Ross, C. J., 323
Ross, R. R., 484
Roush, D. W., 455, 460–461, 463
Rowe, D. C., 199
Rubel, R. J., 100
Rubin, T. H., 160, 162, 169, 235
Rushe, G., 472
Ryerson, E., 21

S

Sampson, R. J., 85, 136, 138, 361
Sanborn Jr., J. B., 163–164, 166–169, 172, 177, 179, 220, 235, 258–259, 261, 264, 266–268, 277, 280, 285, 288, 291, 303, 305, 323, 326–327, 331–332, 336, 338, 351–354, 357–358, 383
Saul, J. A., 425–426
Scahill, M. C., 449
Scali, M. A., 460, 491–492
Scarpitti, F. R., 352–353
Schlicter, K. J., 484
Schneider, A. L., 445
Schneider, P. R., 445
Schultz, J. L., 20
Schur, E. M., 425
Schutt, R. K., 227
Schwartz, I. A., 456
Schwartz, I. M., 196, 199
Schwartz, I., 476
Schwartz, R. G., 277
Sealock, M., 134, 136
Seckel, J. P., 484
Secret, P. E., 361
Seidman, D., 69
Sellin, T., 82
Senna, J. J., 79, 475, 477
Seyfrit, C. L., 427
Shannon, Lyle, 81, 84
Shaw, Clifford R., 431
Shelden, R. G., 196, 199, 215–216, 475–476
Sheppard, D., 126, 447–448

Shine, J., 162
Shivrattan, J. L., 484
Short Jr., J. F., 78
Sickmund, M., 86, 237, 287, 298, 384–386, 429, 450, 456–457, 469–471, 494–495, 536
Siegel, L. J., 79, 475, 477
Simonsen, C. E., 472
Simpson, S., 134, 136
Singer, S. I., 288, 293
Skinner, B. F., 478–479
Skoler, D. L., 160, 162, 164
Slaby, R. G., 484
Smith, B. L., 196, 199, 361
Smith, C., 108
Smith, D. A., 139
Smith, M. E., 446–447
Smith, R. R., 447
Snell, T. L., 89
Snyder, H. N., 76, 86, 140–141, 152, 237, 287, 384–386, 429, 445, 457, 471, 494, 536
Sontheimer, H., 449
Sorrentino, J. N., 287
Spence, S. H., 484
Stahl, A. L., 114, 201, 291–292, 383, 450
Stairs, J., 198–199
Stanfield, R., 215
Steen, S., 350
Steinberg, L., 277
Stephenson, R. M., 353
Stewart, C. E., 321–322
Street, D., 474
Strom, K., 494–495
Stuphen, R. D., 128
Sumner, H., 227
Sun, T., 321–322
Sutherland, E. H., 416
Sykes, G., 485

T

Tannenhaus, D. S., 277
Tausig, M., 198
Teeters, N. K., 416, 445, 472
Teilmann, K., 227
Tenney, C. W., 164
Thambidurai, G. A., 484
Thomas, C. W., 306, 358
Thornberry, T. P., 107, 112, 196
Thrasher, F. M., 103, 113

Tipton, J. A., 100–101
Tittle, C., 78–79
Tittle, C. R., 361
Tomkins, A. J., 352–354
Torbet, P., 287
Tracy, P. E., 80, 82, 86–87, 89, 92, 135, 227, 361
Triplett, R., 199
Trojanowicz, R. C., 432
Turner, J. K., 484

U

Umbreit, M., 446

V

VanWinkle, B., 113
Varano, R., 127
Vigil, J. D., 104
Voss, H., 78

W

Walsleben, M. C., 100–101
Wasserman, M., 353, 433
Watson, John, 478
Weibush, R. G., 423
Wells, D. K., 129
West, D. J., 81
Whitaker, C., 94
White, C., 482
Whitebread, C. H., 277, 287
Whitehead, J. T., 505
Williams, J. R., 78, 128
Wilson, D. B., 469, 483–484
Wilson, J. Q., 125
Winfree, L. T., 127
Winner, L., 293
Wiseman, Frederick, 424–425
Wizner, S., 277, 287
Wolf, M. M., 484
Wolfgang, Marvin E., 80–82, 86
Wooden, Kenneth, 488
Worden, R. E., 129–130, 135–137, 139–140, 143
Wordes, M., 135, 214, 227
Wright, B. R. E., 78
Wyrick, P. A., 126

Z

Zald, M. N., 474
Zawitz, M. W., 114
Zimring, F. E., 277–278, 292, 444

Case Index

B

Boykin v. Alabama, 395 U.S. 238 (1969), 267–269
Brady v. Maryland, 373 U.S. 83 (1963), 249
Breed v. Jones, 421 U.S. 421 U.S. 519 (1975), 43–46, 251

C

Commonwealth v. Fisher, 62 A. 198 (Pa. 1905), 23–24
Creek v. Stone, 379 F.2d 106 (D.C. Cir. 1967), 489–490

D

Davis v. Alaska, 415 U.S. 308 (1974), 408
Duncan v. Louisiana, 391 U.S. 145 (1968), 42–43

E

Ex parte Crouse, 4 Wharton 9 (Pa. 1839), 18–20, 23, 29, 36, 42

F

Fare v. Michael C., 442 U.S. 707 (1979), 147
Faretta v. California, 422 U.S. 806 (1975), 319
Furman v. Georgia, 408 U.S. 238 (1972), 490

G

Gerstein v. Pugh, 420 U.S. 103 (1975), 230–231

H

Herring v. New York, 422 U.S. 853 (1975), 337

I

Inmates of Boys' Training School v. Affleck, 346 F. Supp. 1354 (R.I. 1972), 490

In re Gault, 387 U.S. 1 (1967), 32, 35–43, 58, 132, 160, 164, 168, 176, 258, 319, 345, 347, 503
In re Winship, 397 U.S. 358 (1970), 40–46, 58, 334, 503

J

J.F.B. v. State, 729 So.2d 355 (Ala. Crim. App. 1998), 300

K

Kent v. United States, 383 U.S. 541 (1966), 32–36, 40, 280, 282, 285–286, 288
Klopfer v. North Carolina, 386 U.S. 213 (1967), 326

M

Mapp v. Ohio, 367 U.S. 643 (1961), 133, 250
Martarella v. Kelly, 349 F. Supp. 575 (SDNY 1972), 490
McKeiver v. Pennsylvania, 403 U.S. 528 (1971), 42–46, 259, 332–333
Mempa v. Rhay, 389 U.S. 128 (1967), 347, 402
Miranda v. Arizona, 384 U.S. 436 (1966), 130, 146

N

Nelson v. Heyne, 491 F.2d 352 (7th Cir. 1974), 488, 490
New Jersey v. T.L.O., 469 U.S. 325 (1985), 144–146, 149, 155
North Carolina v. Alford, 400 U.S. 25 (1970), 268

P

Payton v. New York, 445 U.S. 573 (1980), 133

O

People ex rel. O'Connell v. Turner, 55 Ill. 280 (1870), 20, 22

R

Ralston v. Robinson, 454 U.S. 201 (1981), 490
Riverside v. McLaughlin, 500 U.S. 44 (1991), 230
Rouse v. Cameron, 373 F.2d 451 (D.C. Cir. 1966), 489–490

S

Santana v. Collazo, 714 F.2d 1172 (1st Cir. 1982), 490
Santobello v. New York, 404 U.S. 257 (1971), 271
Schall v. Martin, 467 U.S. 253 (1984), 223, 225, 231–232, 401
Scott v. Illinois, 440 U.S. 367 (1979), 319
Stanford v. Kentucky, 492 U.S. 361 (1989), 297
State v. Collins, 699 So.2d 45 (La. 1997), 284
Swisher v. Brady, 438 U.S. 204 (1978), 329–330, 342

T

Tennessee v. Garner, 471 U.S. 1 (1985), 137
Terry v. Ohio, 392 U.S. 1 (1968), 130
Thompson v. Oklahoma, 487 U.S. 815 (1988), 298

W

West v. United States, 399 F.2d 467 (5th Cir. 1968), 148
Wilkins v. Missouri, 492 U.S. 361 (1989), 297
Wyatt v. Stickney, 325 F. Supp. 781 (M.D. Ala. 1971), 489